CAMP SONGS,
FOLK SONGS

CAMP SONGS, FOLK SONGS

PATRICIA AVERILL

To order additional copies of this book, contact:
Xlibris LLC
1-888-795-4274
www.Xlibris.com
Orders@Xlibris.com
551878

CONTENTS

Dedication
to
Kitanniwa

The "K" is for the kindness shown by friends and counselors here.
The "I" is for the interest in each camper keeping cheer.
The "T" is for the thanks we have for the counselors, everyone.
The "A" is the activities, all of which are fun.
The "N" is for new friends in hope our friendships will stay strong.
The "N" is for the nicest time we'll have all summer long.
The "I" is for the individual happy times we've had.
The "W" is for the wonder of how camp can make girls glad.
The "A" is for the agony that comes when we must part.
KITANNIWA is for every girl with happiness in her heart.

Ginger Hastings, 1961 or 1962

Introduction

The book you are considering treats summer camps as folk communities inhabited by children, adolescents, and young adults. Its focus is music as a body of folklore maintained by individuals in camps. People continually learn songs, but alter the composite repertoire by adding new ones and forgetting others. I describe what is, and has been, sung since the 1920s to show which songs have become folk or folklike.

The research was done in the middle 1970s. I had completed my thesis at the University of Pennsylvania, but had not received my degree yet. My dissertation, *Can the Circle Be Unbroken* (1975), used lyrics of country music recordings to examine changes that occurred when World War II exposed Southern-born whites to a wider world.

I was essentially an historian. The nature of my graduate research took me into classrooms of the folklore department. The more I heard there, the more convinced I became what I had learned as a child in girls' summer resident camps was as much folklore as anything we were studying.

Whenever I broached the subject, my classmates would recall the importance of Eastern, Jewish, progressive coed camps to the incubation of the Folk Revival. I realized the songs I knew not only were part of a folk tradition, but a separate, regional one shared more by women than by men.

The manuscript was finished in the late 1970s, but was lost when sent for review. Those were the days before personal computers. I had carbons, but no longer the time to retype. I had abandoned the peripatetic academic life for work as a computer programmer.

For thirty-odd years, the carbons lay in boxes in the garage. The manuscript slowly turned into an artifact of a middle and upper-middle class culture that since has all but disappeared. Children stopped joining youth groups. Organizations consolidated. Community funding dwindled at the very time capital improvements were needed. Camps, especially those with desirable real estate, were sold.

The reasons it was written, when it was written, were a matter of personal circumstances. Quite by chance, the book captured a tradition in its final flowering.

The Songs

Camp songs are explored at three levels: traditions shared everywhere at the time, traditions unique to women, and those specific to a particular camp.

I sent enquiries to Camp Fire Girls' councils in 1974, and received song books from many. I identified the most popular songs, then sent a questionnaire to other camp directors in 1976. In total, I heard from 175 people who were in camps in 44 states and Canada. I have copies of song books or songbook indexes from 127.

Songsters defined the contours of a folk repertoire. Questionnaires demarcated it as one centered in Ohio and Michigan, but a local variant. The general repertoire diffused from New England to Iowa, Minnesota and Ontario, with exclaves in Texas, Colorado, and along the West Coast.

More than 800 songs reported by at least five people are named in the text. I mention more than 500 others. Less common songs include those from the early years, and from other traditions. The only omitted songs are ceremonial ones, like the "Star-Spangled Banner" (20). Some organizational lyrics, like Camp Fire's "My Blue Horizons" (7) and the Boy Scouts' "On My Honor" (5), primarily serve such official functions.

Nearly 250 independent tunes are mentioned. These include every one identified for a general camp song, and many employed for locally written verses. Whenever possible with a commercial song, I give the name of the songwriter or person responsible for its diffusion. Obscure record numbers are given in parenthesis.

The book divides into five sections. One defines folklore and folk song. Four describe factors that influence traditions. These are the ages of campers, the philosophies of camp directors, the genders of campers, and the locations of camps. I was surprised the most important influences in the Midwest were New England singing schools, German immigrants, and Methodists.

Each chapter examines one song in greater depth. At least two sets of lyrics are given, as collected from an individual or camp, along with the history, distribution, variations, and publishing history. The first variant is always from the camp I attended.

Statistics used for the case studies are based on solicited responses to my questionnaire. Detailed results are summarized by song in Appendix E. Numbers in parenthesis after song titles () represent the numbers of people or camps who voluntarily mentioned them.

The phrase "survey Midwest" refers to the five states I initially grouped together, Ohio, Michigan, Indiana, Illinois, and Wisconsin. The word Midwest encompasses a larger, but more amorphous area.

The Camps

Whenever a camp or individual is named in the text, a code follows in parenthesis (Mich agency coed). This identifies the state where it is located, the sponsor, and, if necessary, the gender composition. The most common codes and their assumed genders are:

BSA	Boy Scouts of America	boys
CFG	Camp Fire Girls	girls
4-H	Four-H	coed
GS	Girl Scouts of the U. S. A.	girls
YMCA	Young Men's Christian Association	boys or coed
YWCA	Young Women's Christian Association	girls

"Sep" is used with camps that have separate programs for boys and girls.

Church camps are identified with the letters P for Protestant, C for Roman Catholic, or J for Jewish. The term Jewish usually refers to a camp sponsored by an organization like B'nai Brith or Habonim. The word also may apply to a private camp organized in the years when anti-Semitism barred Jewish children from many Eastern camps. Appendix C is a list of camps who participated.

Camp Fire Girls

The specific camp used as the example of an individual voice within a tradition is Camp Kitanniwa, sponsored by the Battle Creek, Michigan, Camp Fire Girls. Luther Halsey Gulick (1865-1918) and his wife, Charlotte Vetter Gulick (1865-1938), developed the Camp Fire program in 1910 as a counterpart to the Boy Scouts. He was a former YMCA leader. She had been experimenting at Camp Wohelo in Maine. It was renamed Sebago-Wohelo, then the Luther Gulick Camps and, most recently, the Wohelo Camps. Wohelo is an acronym for work, health, and love.

Camp Fire, for much of its time before the 1970s, had three age divisions. Blue Birds existed for young girls between the ages of seven and nine. They corresponded to the Girl Scouts' Brownies and the BSA Cub Scouts. Horizon Club was equivalent to Senior Scouts, the organization for girls in high school. Camp Fire Girls was the term used for those between, the ones in grades five through eight.

After Dr. Gulick died in 1918, the most important person in the organization was Edith Marion Kempthorne (1881-1976). She visited camps and local councils, promoting the flow of ideas between local and national groups. In those years, Camp Fire was as much a program for adult leaders as it was for youth. In 1920, Sinclair Lewis mentioned the organization in *Main Street* to place his main character, Carol Milford Kennicott.

After Kempthorne left the organization in the middle 1940s, links between the national office and local councils shriveled. Dues went one way. Manuals and annual birthday celebration requirements traveled the other. Local leaders and camps were autonomous.

Camp Kitanniwa

The Gulicks introduced Camp Fire to Battle Creek in January of 1914. John Harvey Kellogg had included them in the first meeting of the National Conference on Race Betterment. The two men probably had met in 1886 when the sickly Gulick was working for the YMCA in Jackson, Michigan, about 45 miles east of Battle Creek.

At the conference, Gulick[*] asked, "what provision do you make in Battle Creek whereby groups of girls [. . .] can go off on a tramp of five miles and find a good place to make a fire and a place to bake some potatoes and have a good time together." Soon after, a woman associated with the Congregational church organized the first Camp Fire group. The next year, the local Seventh Day Adventist press published Ethel Rogers'* book-length description of Sebago-Wohelo (Me girls).

Beatrice Palmer initiated the first camping experiment in 1924 when she rented a cottage at Sherman Lake. The next year, several groups rented the Salvation Army camp located on the interurban line at Saint Mary's Lake for two weeks.

In 1926, Helen Bagley headed the newly organized council. The Kiwanis Club helped buy a site at Clear Lake. "Ki" in the camp name honors that organization. The other parts refer to camp names of people like Palmer and Bagley.[151, 153]

An undated brochure from the years at Clear Lake indicates the program had three divisions, one for girls aged six to ten, one for girls ten to fourteen, and one for girls fourteen to eighteen. In addition, it sponsored a National Summer Training Course for local leaders. Frieda Olsen was the director.

One woman active in Camp Fire in my home town, Lucille Parker Munk, attended some of those training sessions, and remembered Bagley and Olsen. She was born in 1902 and would have been in her twenties when Kitanniwa was established. When she attended Western State Normal School in Kalamazoo, Michigan, she was a Girl Scout. She led the Lakeview Camp Fire group shown "In Town." Lakeview was the wealthy suburb of Battle Creek located on Goguac Lake. It now is part of the city.

Olsen's brochure used the language of business to describe its progressive program. She told parents a girl:

> wants an opportunity to develop her talents, to learn
> new skills, find new friends, and have a chance to be the
> person she wants to be instead of the one her family and
> friends expect her to be

The brochure promised parents, "She will discover as she lives with girls that cooperation, fair play, sound judgment and a sense of humor make living more fun for everyone" and that "she will be 'learning how to live'." It admonished them to: "Invest Your Daughter's Summer for Her, Don't Let Her Spend It."

Kitanniwa's appeal waned during the depression. In 1933, the Kellogg Foundation paid the mortgage debts and assumed ownership. The council received three-month summer leases. Facilities were used in winter to teach healthier living to children.

The Kellogs were members of a church that did not accept the Greek separation of body and soul. The Seventh Day Adventist calling is preparing people for God by helping them purify their bodies.

In 1937, the foundation wanted the camp all year. It bought the Camp Fire Girls a new site near Hastings, Michigan, on Stryker Lake, later called Morris, Morrice, or Middle Lake.[151, 153]

Singing Contexts

Dorothy West (1917-2002) directed Kitanniwa from 1950 to 1964, when it evolved from a progressive camp into a traditional one. A swimming program, which met requirements of the American Red Cross, became the primary activity. First aid, drama, and dance, mentioned in the early brochure, were dropped. Canoeing, camp craft, nature lore, handcraft, and archery were maintained. Games and rowing were added.

Singing was utilitarian. The primary purpose of morning sing was filling an hour as inexpensively as possible. One counselor amused most of the camp while the waterfront staff worked with Blue Birds. She filled the time by teaching an occasional new song, and otherwise started whatever campers requested.

Graces were sung before meals, not from any strong religious impulse, but because it was the proper thing to do. They also imposed discipline by defining when girls could begin eating. In the early 1950s, the only graces were "Morning Has Come" (134), "If We Have Earned the Right" (61), and "For Health and Strength" (87). Others were introduced later by former Girl Scouts.

After-meal singing served similar tactical purposes. It kept girls from getting restless between the time their table was cleared, and all the tables were cleared and they could be dismissed. The music counselor started songs she selected.

On rare evenings, perhaps because of the mood, perhaps because of program needs, the singing period expanded to include general camp and community songs known primarily by staff members.

Those times gave campers their only awareness music could be something more than they already knew.

Recent History

After Miss Dode left in 1964, the camp returned to a normal, but no longer familiar, tenure pattern. Directors, many of whom had come of age in camp, stayed a few seasons. They included Sally Heath, Barbara Call, Roberta Thompson, Diane Haig, Karen Hansen, and Mary Tinsley Unrue.

These happened to be years of social turbulence. Changes in funding rules by United Way forced the camp, whose primary support had come from the upper-middle class, to include girls who previously would not have attended. The destruction of the main lodge, in the spring of 1974, reduced the program to day camping and small-group activities. I was able to visit during the closing session of 1974.

Subsequently, the property was sold to people who refurbished the administrative building and craft cabin for vacation rentals. Most recently, the state has listed it as abandoned by an insurance company.

The land, which probably was cleared when the Grand Rapids Bookcase Company opened a factory in Hastings in the early twentieth century, has continued reverting to second growth hardwood. The presence of hundreds of girls every summer did not slow the natural process much.

Acknowledgments

This book has been a communal effort. Besides Kitanniwa, I visited two camps in Ohio in 1974 and more in Maryland in 1976. I interviewed as many former Kitanniwa campers from my years as I could locate, and listened to whomever, anywhere, who would talk. Many who responded to my questionnaire added personal observations.

Whenever a woman is named in the text, I use both her maiden and married name, if known. The comments often are those of an adult looking back on a younger self. Appendix A lists the young men and women who helped me.

Quotations are given, exactly as I have them, from tapes, letters, or published sources. The way people talk or write about camp is as important as what they say. Comments should not be altered to fit standards of literary English any more than songs should be modified.

Whenever I use material from an undergraduate folklore collection, I follow the student's name with an interlocked double S.[§] Appendix B contains a complete list of papers. Graduate research is treated like any professional work. When possible, I mention camp sources, but not students' friends. Camps and individuals who volunteered information that might embarrass them have been kept anonymous.

I have kept citations to a minimum. As much as possible, information is incorporated into the text. I use an asterisk[*] to indicate an obvious reference exists in Appendix D. When an author has more than one entry, a number is used in raised square brackets.[123] When appropriate, page numbers follow a colon.[123:23] Publication histories for the case studies appear separately in Appendix E. References to those entries are signaled by a dagger.[†]

I have been lucky to live near libraries with special collections, including the archives of the Boy Scouts, once located in New Brunswick, New Jersey. The Library of Congress housed the Archives of American Folk Song in the 1970s. Its music room had a large collection of college songbooks.

The Music Educator's National Conference archive in the University of Maryland library, and the University of Michigan music library both had good collections of public-school music books. The Moody Bible Institute library in Chicago had a large collection of hymnals, Sunday-school, and singing-school books. A used bookshop in Milwaukee, Wisconsin, and a music store in Findlay, Ohio, had surprising caches of useful material.

I was given help by the Girl Scout archives, Albion College's Stockwell-Mudd library, and Battle Creek's Willard Library. Public libraries in Montgomery County, Maryland; New Brunswick and Old Bridge, New Jersey, and Ann Arbor, Michigan, also were consulted.

I am especially thankful for individuals who recently provided information about case study songs and their composers. These include Susan Brooks and Deborah Hooker of Heart of New Jersey Girl Scout Council, Sara Giacalone of The University of Wisconsin Foundation, Maida Goodwin of the Sophia Smith Collection at Smith College, Yevgeniya Gribov of the Girl Scout archives, and Bonnie Kisselstein of the Baldwinsville, New York, public library.

Kevin McGee of Music Sales Corporation and Bruce Greene of World Around Songs helped with copyright permissions. The second assumed ownership of Cooperative Recreation Service. Greene provides similar services.

People I had not seen in more than thirty years were willing to send me copies of their camp photographs. I am extremely grateful to Gene Clough, Gary Flegal, Patricia Ann Hall, June Rushing Leibfarth, Ira Sheldon Posen, Rebecca Quinlan, and Madeline Gail Trichel for taking time to look through their scrapbooks and photo albums. Diane Owen Jordan, Cindy Joyner, Kathleen Munk Sawchuck, Harry Smaller, and Gene Wichmann sent me pictures of friends or relatives.

Others who helped me locate photographs were Frances Bristol of the Methodist Church General Conference archives, Vicki Catozza of the Western Reserve Historical Society, Helen Hargrove and Gayle Haywood of Brentwood Baptist Church in Tennessee, Elizabeth Koroh of the Girl Scouts, Catherine Christ Lucas of the Willard Library, Chris Read of the State Library of South Australia, Margaret Smith of the Kent Historical Society, and Mark Van Winkle of the Wohelo Camps.

College and university archives were also helpful, especially Cindy Brightenburg of Brigham Young University, Becky Jordan of Iowa State University's archives, Heather Lytle of the Denison University library, and Nicole Garrett Smeltekop of the Albion College library. John Kovach, the South Bend, Indiana, County Historian provided information on Dorothy West.

I only wish I knew the names of individuals who helped me in libraries and archives in the 1970s so I could thank them personally. The institutions that support these collections and the libraries, which house them, deserve special praise.

Addendum

The manuscript essentially remains unchanged. I have verified facts and made corrections. Where possible, I have updated information about specific songs, but I did not update case-study bibliographies. New details constantly appear on the internet. It probably is impossible to be as definitive today as it was in the 1970s.

Socially accepted labels for cultural groups have changed. Native American is now the preferred term. I only use Indian when it refers to an out-group stereotype.

Disagreement persists about the vocabulary of race. Only three fundamental legal statuses have existed: slave, freedman, and citizen. Language before the Fourteenth Amendment was clear. Terminology since has varied. Black is the most widely accepted word today.

Terms for the disabled or developmentally challenged are in flux. This is partly because medical understanding is improving. Clear translations between modern and earlier views rarely exist. Some words, like retarded, have multiple synonyms today. Others have been transformed into bland, inoffensive generalities. I have kept period language.

Words in songs and quotations, as mentioned above, have not been altered.

Attitudes toward homosexuality are the most volatile today. The discussion in GENDER INFLUENCES was based on people's understandings of their experiences at that time. Those views could be different today. However, those historic perceptions are the ones that formed traditions through the 1970s.

I have not inserted information about songwriters and performers who have made public statements about their orientation. Some, like Ray Repp, are clear. Many others are more ambiguous.

I understand some controversy exists over the use of "gay" in "Kookaburra" (85). With increased public awareness of what had been a private use of the word, young adolescent snickering is predictable. This is one of the easiest words to change. It was artificial when I was in camp in the 1950s. Common adjectives like "fun," or current slang, or even put downs like "dumb" would fit, without altering the underlying humor of the song.

If you have been in camps since 1980, you know what has changed. If not, this is an imperfect transcription of your memories.

SECTION I

Folklore

The Mermaid: Folklore

Folklore is easier to find than define. Sensitive individuals, like yourself, notice aspects of culture constrained by rules of form you instinctively realize have intrinsic value. After you and others record your memories, scholars identify unifying features.

Francis James Child

Francis James Child (1825-1896) was one of the first taxonomists. In the late nineteenth century, the Harvard English professor combed existing collections. He gleaned what he believed to be the definitive collation of *The English and Scottish Popular Ballads*. He felt confident he had seen "every valuable copy of every known ballad."[287]

Enthusiasts converted his ten volumes into checklists, then rummaged isolated areas for folk music. They soon realized traditional singers made little distinction between old ballads and other songs they learned in their communities. Each collector published his or her versions of Child's ballads, along with what other material each deemed important.

These diverse sets of non-Child materials, along with variations found within the Child corpus, led others to extract new characteristics to separate folklore from dross. Louise Pound* (1872-1958) isolated the traits in *American Ballads and Songs* I use to identify which specific camp songs have become folk or folklike. She did her original work in Nebraska.

Exists in Several Places

Pound's first criterion was a folk song must be found in more than one location. As mentioned in the INTRODUCTION, I sent a song list to camps in all parts of the country in 1976. The responses confirmed some texts inhabited physically delimited areas. Further, knowledge of lyrics was neither random (reflecting no shared cultural values) nor universal (reflecting mass media, public school, or other institutional influences).

Instead, survey responses, personal lists, and formal songsters revealed most new songs entered traditional camps' repertoires through new staff members, and from trips by older campers and CITs, the counselors-in-training. Kitty Smith remembers a chance exchange at Kitanniwa in the early 1970s:

> Another one we used to do was "Itta Bitta Porcupine" (4). Have you ever heard of that? Oh, that was a scream. It was one of those that was a few years ago, and the kids went on a canoe trip down the Au Sauble [river], and that's when we really had a good senior unit, and they met another group of kids. I don't remember . . . they were from another camp and they were going down, and it just so happened that where they camped that night, on the next camping site, was this other group and they taught 'em a "Fishie Song," "Did you ever see a fishie on a hot summer's day" (24).

Camp Fire Girls Networks

Movements of staff and habits of CIT visits conspire to create permanent communication networks between traditional camps, usually those with the same sponsoring organization. These are revealed by small variations shared within distinct geographic locations. Carl Wilhelm von Sydow* called them oicotypes.

Melacoma and Wakoma, both Camp Fire camps in Washington state, substitute "alligator on a fence" in the second verse of "Did You Ever See a Fishie" (24). The limited popularity of other songs suggests the two camps are part of a Camp Fire exchange web located along the Pacific Coast.

One song mentioned only by people in these camps is "I'm Going Fishing" (2) at Wolahi (Calif CFG) and Kilowan (Ore CFG). "Firs of Namanu" (Ore CFG) was cloned from "Firs of Sealth" (Wash CFG, 2). Bing Crosby popularized the underlying tune, "Bells of Saint Mary's" (4), in 1945.

Texas is another state where Camp Fire camps have traded among themselves. Mikie Snell has sung "We Are Hungry" (2) and "Wish Boats" (2) at Waluta (Tex CFG). Leah Jean Ramsey knows the two from other Texas CFG camps. Fewer camps exist in the South, but within the Camp Fire world, counselors move between Texas and Louisiana.

A third important CFG communication network lies in Iowa. Hitaga (Iowa CFG) knows "Good night, slumber sound in peace profound" (2), "Is There a Place" (2), and "Canada" (2). They are sung at Towanyak (Kans CFG), Cimarron (Okla CFG), and Trelipe (Minn CFG), respectively. Freddy Grant's chorus for the last compares the country with a cathedral.

Texas and Central Prairie camps are linked. Some transfer occurs between them and the West Coast, usually through councils in Colorado. Montana has maintained communication with the more Northern Prairie CFG camps. Evidence exists for some interaction between Idaho and the Coast. In 1975, Carl Pfaff observed:

> I have learned that many of Neewahlu's (Ida CFG) songs are identical, or contain minor variations to many of the songs we used at Camp Wintaka (which I directed for the two years prior to my coming north to Idaho).

Wintaka is the California Camp Fire camp shown in "Outdoors."

Within the regions, connections exist between Camp Fire groups and other networks. In Minnesota, a private girls' camp, Kamaji (Minn girls), has adopted "Wohelo Your Maidens Have Gathered" (4), according to Judy Miller. The organizational song is known at Hitaga (Iowa CFG), Towanyak (Kans CFG), and by Vivian Sexton at Shawondasee (Tex CFG).

In California, songs cross between Girl Scout and Camp Fire groups. Skylark Ranch (Calif GS) shares "I Wuv a Wabbit" (5) with Kirby (Wash CFG), Niwana (Wash CFG), and Wasewagan (Calif CFG). "We Don't Live in Castles" (6) is sung at Skylark, as well as at Kilowan (Ore CFG), Namanu (Ore CFG), and Onahlee (Ore CFG).

Northeast Networks

Two aesthetic pools exist in the Northeast. One is found throughout the area dominated by progressive camps. Among the songs known in all girls' camps are "Wee Cooper of Fife" (2) and "It's All Right To Cry" (2). Marilyn Butler knows the Scots ballad from Kehonka (NH girls). Cheryl Robinson learned it at Mawavi (DC CFG). She and Aloha Hive (Vt girls) mentioned the second. Burl Ives recorded Child 277 in 1941. Marlo Thomas introduced the other in *Free to Be . . . You and Me*, a 1974 children's song book that eschewed sexist stereotypes.

Eleanor Crow says, Aloha Hive (Vt girls) favors "folk tunes with some contemporary tunes from Broadway shows." That preference is shared across gender lines. Boys at Loyaltown (NY J boys) in the 1960s were singing "Getting To Know You" (2), "Days of Vacation" (2), and "Go Where I Send Thee" (2). Phyllis Bonnie Newman knows the first from Truda (Me girls). Joann Brisler remembers the second from Marycrest (Vt C girls). The last has been sung at Goodwill/ Pleasant (DC agency sep).

Richard Rodgers and Oscar Hammerstein II introduced "Know You" in *The King and I*. "Vacation" uses the "We won't go home until morning" section of "Malbrouck." The Weavers recorded the last.

Another network in the East is anchored in the more traditional girls' camps in Pennsylvania. Wilma Lawrence (Penna GS), Joan Leight (Penna GS), and Mariana Palmer (Penna) all know "Caravan" (3). Adahi (Penn CFG), Anne Lutz (NY-NJ), and Theresa Mary Rooney (NJ GS) recognize "Sun Is Rising out of Bed" (3).

Ann, Theresa, and Fleur de Lis (NH P girls) have sung "Gray Shadows" (3). Someone at Mount Holyoke wrote the original in 1905 to "Flow Gently Sweet Afton." In 1955, Fleur de Lis used the melody from "Away in a Manger," published in 1887 by the Evangelical Lutheran Church in Philadelphia.

Girl Scouts

Girl Scouts rotate administrative personnel, so songs can move rapidly between their camps. Exchange networks are more discernible in camping histories of individuals, than in songs named by a few locations. This internal fluidity has created a repertoire so distinctive, individuals can be identified as Scouts from the songs they know.

Despite the general movement, a local exchange area has developed in Michigan and Ohio. Marsha Lynn Barker (Mich GS) sings "Born Free, a Heart Must Wander" (2), "I Said I Would Take Heed" (2), and "Poor Man Who Can't See Beauty" (3). Angela Lapham (Mich GS) knows the first. Diana Prickett (Mich GS) remembers the second. The last is recognized by Ann Beardsley (Mich GS), and was collected by Kathleen Solsbury[S] from The Timbers (Mich GS) in 1970.

The Michigan-Ohio Girl Scout music ecotype connects to the one centered in Pennsylvania girls' camps, through staff migration between locations in Pennsylvania, Ohio, and West Virginia. Camps also maintain contacts with local Michigan and Ohio Camp Fire groups, who, in turn have some communication with the Central Prairie group.

Magnet Camps

Movement of individuals, songs, and ideas within communication networks is not fortuitous. Magnet camps generate tremendous loyalty. They become repositories for many traditions while remaining open to new material. Reputations of ascendant camps encourage others to send their counselors-in-training on the visitations required by the American Camping Association for certified CIT programs. Former campers make attractive employees. This becomes important when camps cannot absorb all their own people into their staffs.

Hinterland camps are more folklike. They often preserve traditions forgotten elsewhere. Some maintain contacts with centers of innovation, and only accept new songs after they have been tested elsewhere.

Others, especially private ones, exist in greater isolation. New material enters sporadically, because so many staff members and campers return. They develop idiosyncratic ways. When people do change camps, few of their distinctive songs are general enough to follow.

Kitanniwa, for most of its history, has been a hinterland camp. Its long-standing visitation network includes Detroit's Wathana (Mich CFG) and nearby Holly (Mich GS), Grand Rapids' Keewano (Mich CFG) and nearby Newaygo (Mich YWCA), and Kalamazoo's Merrie Woode (Mich GS).

In the 1950s, some staff members had been to Tannadoonah (Ind CFG) or Eberhart (Ind YMCA coed), both located in southwestern Michigan. Other counselors had gone to church camps influenced by Methodist music traditions or by Seth Clay, a Congregational minister in Otsego. The camp director is those years was a Methodist from Mishawaka in northern Indiana.

Exists through Time

Pound's second imperative was folk songs bore witness to prior lives. At one time, this expectation of age merged with the belief folklore was a relic from a past or dying era. It fostered the view folk songs were survivals from pre-industrial times.

Scholars now realize folklore is universal. No culture's standard public arts, values, and technologies can handle all contingencies. While purists concede folklike material continually is being created, they still believe songs must endure to become folk.

A generation, normally, is measured in the time it takes infants to reproduce themselves, or about twenty-five years. By analogy, a camp generation is about ten, the time needed for people who come to camp as youngsters to return as counselors. This small cohort, who comes of age within a particular camp, nurtures its tradition bearers. Steven Diner says, at Loyaltown (NY J boys) in the 1960s, they sang "Loyaltown Line" (1) because "one bunk learned it from a counselor who claimed he had learned it in camp years ago."

To discover if songs have pedigrees, I showed a late 1940s Kitanniwa song book to three women who had been to the camp. Lucille Parker Munk went in the late 1920s and early 1930s. Carol Parsons Sievert attended from 1934 to 1942. Kathleen Huggett Nye was on staff from 1954 to 1960. I was there from 1951 to 1960, and in Mrs. Munk's Camp Fire council. Their photographs appear in "Rituals," in "Kitanniwa, 1974," and on the front cover, respectively.

Of the 94 songs in the book, 71 were remembered by at least one of us. Four were known only by Lucille. Carol, whose time in camp was most contemporary with the songster, recognized fourteen. The four I alone named were ceremonial ones, like "Holy, Holy, Holy" (15), which also were sung outside camp.

Others were part of the more enduring repertoire. Nine were known by all of us, and fifteen by three. These included endogamous ones, like "Swimming" (42), and public domain songs, like "Down in the Valley" (33).

The twelve known only by Carol and Lucille were CFG standards by W. H. Neidlinger, and camp-specific songs. The five known by Carol and Kathleen included camp-specific ones fading from tradition in the early 1950s. A staff member (Kathleen) remembered them, but not a young camper (me).

Oral Tradition

Pound believed folk songs were learned by being heard. Some scholars reject camp songs as folklore on these grounds. They believe adults impose them on youngsters. This assumes, because camps serve and socialize children, the only legitimate lore is that created by the young beyond the purview of their handlers.

Camps come in many guises. Some match this hierarchical perception. They often measure their success by the numbers of children who attend each season with no expectation any will return. In the past, many were run by men whose formative group-living experiences had been basic training in the military or fraternity initiation weeks. Many have horror stories from such places that make it difficult to understand other possibilities exist.

Camps that foster singing traditions encompass several age groups. Children, usually ranging from late-elementary through early-high school, share activities with college-aged staff, and spend time with their peer groups. Many counselors, who work as song leaders, learned their repertoires in camps. They pass on material in much the same way lore is transferred from older to younger people in any folk group.

Acceptance of songs into a camp repertoire, or even of singing itself, depends on both shared and age-group-specific interactions. A former Texas Girl Scout counselor told Naomi Feldman[§] and Mary Rogers that teaching songs in camp is helped:

> if you've got returning campers who've been to camp
> and they teach their tent mates. And that shows you
> that they're enjoying being there and they're happy by
> themselves. And that's a good sign. It makes you feel the
> best. And also, if you hear a song that you haven't taught,

it gives you an idea of how many years the kids have been
to camp and if you've got some seasoned campers.

In some places, songs are taught formally, using devices like slides
and flip charts. A few use song sheets, but most camp song books
are opened more with new staff during pre-camp training, than with
campers. In most places, a few songs, especially graces, ones used
for ceremonial occasions and those unknown by returning campers,
deliberately are reviewed.

The usual technique combines lining out with rote learning. A
counselor or older camper sings a line, the kids repeat it, then the verse
is sung. Emphasis is on lyrics. Melodies and gestures are absorbed.
Carol Parsons Sievert remembers at Kitanniwa in the 1930s, "those
things you kinda got by singing along and you wouldn't be caught dead
not singing . . . you learn by soaking them up."

Variation

Oral tradition introduces change. The resulting variations are
the most important characteristic of folklore. They also become
something that fascinates some older campers and counselors. Anne
Lutz, who was a natural history specialist for camps located in the
New Jersey-New York Palisades Interstate Park, says:

> I was interested in the ways songs were changed in
> melody and text because of faulty memories. Music
> counselors from six camps had a hard time choosing
> songs all campers could sing at a big get-together because
> they found they were teaching different versions of many
> things.

Variant texts became the source of a counselors' in-group game at
Sherwood (WV GS) in 1976. Angela Lapham recalls:

> This summer we had a staff from several places:
> Michigan, Minnesota, Ohio, Illinois and Wisconsin. I
> think we had at least one variation on most of the songs
> we sang. It got to be a staff joke that if you wanted to
> sing a song your way, you had to teach it first. Sometimes

we learned several versions of a song, and sang whichever
we felt like at that particular moment.

Tristram Potter Coffin* suggested change occurred at two levels
in traditional folk communities. Modifications in words and phrases
produced variants. Alterations in central themes or narratives created
versions.

Much textual variation is caused by individuals who misunderstand
words. Sometimes, this leads to deliberately heightened absurdity,
especially in camps where the preposterous is expected. The
confusion introduced by accidental error is kept, sometimes even
exaggerated. This can be seen clearly in camps where "An Austrian
Went Yodeling" (34) has become an "ostrich."

Localization occurs when camp names are inserted into general
songs, like "Lollypop" (43). In a more elaborate form, a California
Camp Fire camp substitutes Girl Scouts for Watusies in a second verse
to "We're from Nairobi" (14):

> We're from Wolahi, our team is a good one
> We play the Girl Scouts they're seven feet tall
> The Girl Scouts may eat us but they'll never beat us
> Cuz we're from Wolahi and we're on the ball

Situations within camps often define the sorts of corrective
changes that appear. In "Castle on the River Nile" (9), Fleur de Lis
(NH P girls) sang marry "Princess Sallaboo" in 1955. Wanakiwin
(Minn YWCA) sings "Prince Alaboo." N. Cunningham§ collected
"Prince from Kalamazoo" from Ak-O-Mak (Ont girls) in 1949.

The first two have been altered through some form of
rationalization, perhaps combined with a preference for nonsense.
The Ontario girls' camp localized the last to Michigan. Another line
in the Canadian version replaced "elegant style" with "Allegan style,"
after a Michigan city some 25 miles from Kalamazoo.

Total song alteration takes two forms. In one, different outcomes
exist for a tale. "Suitors" (25) is a recent song in which a girl says,
there are suitors at my door. She adds, she will marry only "when
rivers run uphill." Namanu (Ore CFG) and Kotomi (Colo CFG)
have a third verse in which she finds her own true love. Shawnee
(Mo CFG) has a final verse, "And I went against my will [. . .] And

tomorrow I must die." Wakoma (Wash CFG) has a third verse in which the father asks if she will marry, and a fourth, "rivers now run uphill."

In the second form of total song alteration, one or two verse texts, like the original "Suitors," unfurl into longer ones, often through the introduction of narrative elements. This follows what Kaarle Krohn called the "impulse to expansion" found in folk tales.[396:71-77] This development is contrary to the usual folk pattern, which compresses longer texts, sometimes losing narratives altogether.

Augustus Zanzig and Katherine Cartwright published the two stanzas of "Suitors" known in this country. Charles W. Dubs and his wife, the former Clea Machado (1925-2005), made the original translation. A Brazilian radio and television conductor, Giuseppe Mastroianni (born 1935), adapted the music. Dubs, who died in 2010, was an Air Force physicist.

Anonymity

Pound noted, folk songs "have lost all sense of authorship and provenance."[476:xiii] At one time, folklorists posited ballads were completely anonymous group creations. Scholars now accept Phillips Barry's suggestion songs have individual creators. Later, others may alter or re-create them.[254:120]

Although most camp songs have no recognized authors, a few do have known ones, usually those introduced in songsters. Occasionally, one is remembered as being "by someone" at a camp. Mary Lang says campers and staff at Newaygo (Mich YWCA) wrote the "living in tents and cabins" verse of "Boomdeada" (48).

When a desire surfaces to understand a song's origins, a tale may be created. "Blue Walking" (3) has been credited to several camps through explanatory stories called etiological legends. Julie Sherwood[§] was told, someone at Wakatomika (Ohio GS) wrote it after the caretaker died and his dog, Bounce, headed for the woods.

Wilma Lawrence (Penna GS) was told the song "was given to the Girl Scouts to sing at camp by the townspeople where Blue and his master lived." But, she notes, "the Boy Scouts also claim the song is theirs." At Ken-Jockety (Ohio GS), a camp in the same Girl Scout council as Wakatomika, Ann Beardsley reports:

KJ people say it, the legend, started there, but so do people from every other camp that sings it. He's a faithful dog killed somehow protecting his owner. Still wanders around as a ghost occasionally leading back lost campers at KJ, or wherever, and such.

Exists outside Mass Media

In the past, many believed genuine folklore never had been contaminated by the mass media. Some early folklorists sorted their collections into the acceptable and unacceptable. Others found such exercises futile. Cicely Fox Smith* noted, "Patsy Orry Aye" (29) was rejected as a sea chantey because it originated "on shore," perhaps on the stage. She went on:

> The likelihood is that nearly every shanty under the sun, if the truth were known, comes under the same category, and since, moreover, "Poor Paddy" has certainly been long forgotten *except* as a shanty, and has been for years a universal favorite afloat, I take leave to accord a place here to his Odyssey. [emphasis in original]

Some took an anthropological view and reported everything a traditional singer knew, or everything they heard in a community. Such studies were useful ethnographies. They ignored that original insight: there was something distinctive about folk music.

Today, people like Mary and Herbert Knapp look at ways lore is perpetuated, rather than at its origins. They argue, it does not matter if a song or rhyme known by children has been published, recorded, televised, or filmed. To them, "it's still folklore as long as it is learned orally somewhere and exists in different versions."[393:10]

Definition

In other words, the more specifications a camp song meets, the more folklike it is. "Blue Walking" became a local tradition when it survived several summers at Wakatomika (Ohio GS). It became a camp folk song when it was taken to other locations, where the authorship was lost or shrouded in legend, and changes were introduced through oral transmission.

When Ella Jenkins recorded the song (FC 7656), her version ceased to be folklore anywhere it was sung, until individuals and camps altered it through informal learning. The exception would be Juniper Knoll (Ill GS), where Jenkins learned the song, and in camps where it was learned directly from Chicago Girl Scouts. In those cases, the version never ceased to have a folk or folklike status, despite the coincidence of being like a recorded version.

Case Study: The Mermaid

"The Mermaid" (23) is the best example of a certified folk song that migrated through published collections to Kitanniwa where it reemerged as a piece of folklore. Child discovered ballad 289 in *The Glasgow Lasses Garland*.[†] The 1765 song book was published in Newcastle, a Northumberland port in northeastern England (version C at the end of the chapter).

Its first part seems closely related to an older ballad, "Sir Patrick Spens" (Child 58), which shares its verse structure (see version D-A). William Motherwell[*] (1797-1835), a Scots antiquarian poet, believed the latter described a late-thirteenth-century event. The crew, who delivered the Scots princess, Margaret, to her new husband in Norway, drowned on the return voyage in 1281.

"Spens" has not been widely recovered in this country. That scarcity suggests its popularity may have been ebbing in England toward the end of the eighteenth century, when immigrants were importing British traditions into the colonies. The disfavor may have prompted someone to rework the basic shipwreck narrative into a thematically unified tale of defiance and punishment in Old Testament tradition.

Similarities between the two ballads facilitated changes in both, evident by 1825 when Motherwell[†] and George Ritchie Kinloch[†] each collected the two in Scotland. By then, both narratives had sharpened the allusion to the captain's willfulness. Sailing on Easter (C-2) was replaced by sailing on Friday (A-1).

Among the weather proverbs Alan Cheales[*] reported were common upstream from the port of Bristol in 1876 are "Friday's sail / Always fail" and:

> Monday for wealth
> Tuesday for health
> Wednesday the best day of all
> Thursday for crosses
> Friday for losses
> Saturday no luck at all

These rhymes reflected the European belief that beginning any project on the day Christ died brought bad luck.[402:425]

Omens in the two ballads differed. In the one, "the faint outline of the full disk of the moon"[402:743] behind the new moon signified a coming storm (D-I). In the other, a mermaid was seen near rocks (C-2) that would destroy the ship in a tempest (C-5, C-14). Much of the older ballad fatalistically narrated events. The newer dramatized reactions of men confronting impending death (C-8:12).

Singers transformed the final verse of *The Glasgow Lasses'* "Mermaid" (C-14) into a chorus. This has taken on such prominence, it is the one feature that unites and identifies the many variants in this country. Charlotte Duff (Mich girls) titles the song, "The Ocean Waves May Roll." Watervliet (Mich girls) calls it, "Ocean Waves."

When the final verse disappeared, the ballad ended with an anticlimactic suggestion the men died because there was no lifeboat (C-13). A second dereliction of duty by the captain or ship's owners changed the tenor from one of men facing a hubris-inflicted catastrophe to a bureaucratic lessons-learned report.

"The Gallant Ship," which described the shipwreck (A-4), supplanted the lifeboat. William Chappell[†] documented the first known version from a Jewish entertainer in 1840. Charles Sloman (1808-1870) specialized in improvising songs at Evans, a song and supper room in London's Covent Garden. Chappell (1809-1888) was a music publisher and founding member of the first English group to rescue old texts, the (Thomas) Percy Society.

Some thirty-five years later, in 1876, the son of a Hawaiian missionary, Samuel Chester Andrews[†] (1851-1914), included "The Mermaid" in *The American College Songster*. At the time, he was a student at the University of Michigan. The ballad also appeared that year in *Songs of Columbia*,[†] marketed by New York textbook publishers, Joseph Lord Taintor and his brother, Charles Newhall Taintor. They attended Yale, not Columbia.

The verse and tune became standardized in this country, although differences lingered in the order, number and identity of the crew members, and in the widow's location. Delta Upsilon's[†] song book from 1884 seems to be the earliest to include only the four verses sung in camps today.

Explication

Most contemporary campers do not know the significance of sailing on Friday. Jan Smyth says, at Kitanniwa in 1974:

> songs like "Friday Morn" you can only sing on Friday morn. And we were always bummed out if we woke up Saturday morning and we'd forgot to sing it the day before. That was it 'til the next week.

This interpretation involves rationalizing the opening line to the familiar camp schedule. Such an elimination of the supernatural found in European folklore is common in American tradition.

Mermaid

Even the youngest camper knows from canned-tuna commercials that a mermaid is a golden-haired woman with a fish's tail. English poet Robert Graves[*] believed she represented the continuation of the Mycenaean belief that winter occurred when Persephone returned each year to the underworld of her husband, Hades. Her reappearance in spring heralded a new agricultural cycle. Greeks called their underworld sea goddess Aphrodite, and named her the beauty who lured mariners to their deaths.

Mediterranean beliefs returned with the Crusaders to England. Lyre-playing troubadours for Richard I (1157-1199) attached scallop shells to their hats. Eventually, the figure melded with the Saxons' May Bride, who became Marion in the Robin Hood stories.

Graves suggested the comb (C-2) once was the plectrum for strumming lyre strings. The mirror had no clear antecedent. Because it often was round, Graves hypothesized it came from the quince Marion once held. Alternatively, he suggested it might have been part of the Eleusinian mysteries associated with Persephone. Possibly, it was a modernization of the scallop shells associated with Aphrodite and Marion.

The looking glass (C-2) also may be allied with the belief that a reflection is the projection of a soul. If a mirror breaks, the captured essence dies. When the mermaid holds the mirror, especially if it is turned outward, she is luring men's spirits as her beauty arouses their baser selves. The association of the irreducible self with its reflection is older than the invention of glass. It originally was connected with water.

For those with no awareness of European superstitions, the mirror simply may represent the application of conventions. Once the comb was established, the glass followed as another accouterment of a vain woman. The comb was the more stable part. Version A-1 from Kitanniwa had a comb and a brush. Girls mimed the mirror when the mermaid brushed her hair. Version B-1 from Long Lake had the comb and glass.

The Speeches

The number of speeches has varied. Many early singers felt the need to have three, but dramatizing three views of death was difficult. In some, the captain (C-8) and first mate (C-9) each thought about the consequences of his demise for his widow. They were contrasted with a cabin boy (C-11), who thought of his mother. In 1938, Surprise Lake (NY J boys) was singing:

> Oh, the moon shines bright and the stars give light
> Oh, my mammy'll be looking for me
> She may look, she may weep, she may look to the deep
> She may look to the bottom of the sea

They may have learned their version from *Bixby's Home Songs*,[†] published in New York City in 1909.

The cabin boy became such a sentimental icon that, in one version published in 1896 by Joseph Woodfall Ebsworth,[†] the boy spoke a second time:

> "There is One, if he pleases, can bring us ashore, and save
>   us from a watery grave.
> "Our hearts should be light, our ship is water-tight, and
>   sea-room we need not fear;

They were saved. Ebsworth not only was an editor for the Ballad Society, but also an Anglican vicar in Molash, Kent.

Such sentimentality can invoke strong reactions. In 1929, Brooklyn, New York, Boy Scouts described the boy as "a dirty little brat" with no friends. The cook replaced him as comic relief. Child gave priority to the version collected by Motherwell. Its last verse was:

> Out and spoke the cook of our ship,
>   And a rusty old dog was he;
> Says, I am as sorry for my pats and pans
>   As you are for your wives all three.

George Newell introduced the version with "potties" and "kets" in the 1929 *Girl Scout Song Book.*[†]

Land Lubbers

One way the speeches were differentiated was by the ports where the seamen lived. Such cues would have been clearer at the time, when they may have signaled social status and character to the audience. Version C had the captain from Plymouth, the mate from Portsmouth, and the boatswain from Exeter. Another Child source, Thomas Bayne,[†] had the captain from Bristol, the mate from Portsmouth, and the cook from Plymouth. In the 1950s, Kitanniwa used the center of the whaling trade in this country, Salem (A-2).

Ebsworth suggested the use of Bristol was a possible comment on the slave trade. First, he recounted anecdotes about ships forced to jettison their cargo. Then, he inferred the regret the crew felt in verse six of version C came from sacrificing personal wealth to save more valuable freight. Verse seven had 564 people die on a ship we had no reason to believe was a passenger liner. Salem, Massachusetts, also was used by slavers and opium merchants.

This forgotten reality of cargo ships may explain the lines in the common chorus:

> We poor sailors go skipping to the top
> And the land lubbers die down below, below, below

In Spens, there were no passengers. Mrs. Notman[†] sang (D-C):

> And there lay good Sir Patrick Spens,
> And the Scots lords at his feet.

Textual Variation

A comparison of the 1950s versions from Kitanniwa (A) and Long Lake (B) suggests the ballad's form had been set in camps. The differences were those that came from oral transmission. Some camps may retain an older line, perhaps learned from a relative or other tradition. Charlotte Duff (Mich girls) substitutes "For lack of life boats down she went" for the third line in the fourth verse. Zanika Lache (Wash CFG) sings, "For lack of a sail we all went down."

Music

Bertrand Bronson[†] sorted the 42 tunes used with the ballad into three broad melodic groups. The one used in camps is like that reproduced by many American songsters, and like his group B. Kitanniwa's is closest to the variant Mrs. Charles A. Rich[†] of Charlottesville, Virginia, sang for Marie and Winston Wilkinson[†] in 1935.

Some, including Hidden Valley[†] (Md CFG), Tejas (Tex GS), and Tanglewood, use more melisma. The last two allocate only a single note for "blow" and "roll" in the chorus, the one place where many others use several notes for a single word. June Rushing Leibfarth[§] collected the one from Tejas. William Daniel Doebler[§] recorded the last.

Kitanniwa in the 1950s made two changes. Repetition of the final line in a chorus is a familiar device in tradition, but unusual in camp songs. Girls treated it as a two-part echo ending. One group held the last note of the fourth line, while the other sang the fifth. This simple harmonic effect reinforced the song's popularity.

Gestures

Kitanniwa altered the tempo to match simple, mime, hand gestures. They sang the final verse very slowly, tracing a circle parallel with the floor on the first three lines. They sang the final line very quickly. Other camps have their own gestures. This aspect of the song is not transcribed, and varies from place to place.

Popularity

Presumably, the ballad was more popular in the past when it was part of an active college singing tradition. It lingers in girls' camps, especially those of Girl Scouts, who have been influenced by the 1929 song book.

Version A

Text and gestures from Patricia Averill, Camp Kitanniwa (Mich CFG), middle 1950s.

1. 'Twas Friday morn when we set sail,
    And we were not far from shore,[1]
    When the captain spied a pretty mermaid
    With a comb and a brush in her hand.[2]

C. Oh, the ocean waves may roll[3]
    And stormy winds may blow[4]
    But, we poor sailors go skipping to the top[5]
    And the land lovers die down below, below, below[6]
    And the land lovers die down below.[7]

2. Then up spoke the captain of our gallant, gallant ship[8]
    And a well-spoken man was he[9]
    I had me a wife in Salem town[10]
    And tonight a widow she'll be.

Chorus

3. Then up spoke the cookie of our gallant, gallant ship
    And a red-hot cookie was he[11] s-s-s[12]
    I care much more for my pots and my pans
    Than I do for the bottom of the sea.

Chorus

4. Then three times around went our gallant, gallant ship[13]
    And three time round went she[14]
    And three times round went our gallant, gallant ship[15]
    And she sank to the bottom of the sea, kerplunk![16]

Chorus

Gestures
1. Sung faster
2. Brush hair with one hand, looking at palm of other hand as a mirror
3. Move hands forward on top of waves
4. Last word louder, hands cupped to mouth
5. Hands climb rope
6. Hands make diving gesture, thumbs locked, palms down; one group holds the last note
7. Continue motion; other group sings the line
8. Hands across chest
9. Bring index finger across front to make a point
10. Hands folded across chest
11. Lick index finger
12. Hold finger up to imaginary hot pan
13. Sung slowly, finger makes circle as if stirring
14. Sung slower still, same hand motion
15. Sung slower still, same hand motion
16. Sung fast

Version B

Text from camp located at Long Lake, Michigan; collected by Marjorie Morrice, Indiana University, 1950; variations from A emphasized. Gestures from a former Camp Tanglewood camper; collected by William Daniel Doebler, Wayne State University, 1965; variations from A emphasized.

1. Twas Friday morn when we set sail
   And we were not far from **land**
   When the captain spied a **lovely** mermaid
   With a comb and a **glass** in her hand.

C. **O' the stormy winds they blow-o**[1]
   And the stormy winds they roll-ll[2]
   While we poor sailors[3] go skipping **through** the **tops**[4]
   And the land-**lubbers lie** down below, below, below[5]
   And the land-**lubbers lie** down below.[6]

2. Then up **spake** the captain of our gallant gallant ship
   And a well spoken man was he.[7]
   We'll sail and sail till we git home
   Or we'll sink to the bottom of the sea

Chorus

3. Then up **spake** the **cook** of our gallant, gallant ship
   And a red hot **cook** was he, PSST[8]
   Oh I care much more for my **potties** and my **kets**
   Than I do for the bottom of the sea.

Chorus

4. Then three times around went our gallant gallant ship
   And three times **around** went she
   And three times around went our gallant gallant ship
   And she sank to the bottom of sea _____

Chorus

Gestures

1. Cup your hands around your mouth and shout blow
2. Put the palms of your hands, side by side, in front of you, undulating
3. **Point with thumbs to yourself**
4. **Roll hands over each other toward ceiling**
5. Palms of hands like you're pushing someone into the ground
6. **Point to floor with both thumbs; begin with fist and thumb pointing away from body, then roll thumb over fist to point down**
7. **Thumbs in suspenders, stick out chest**
8. Lick index finger on something that looks hot

Version C

First published text, *The Glasgow Lasses Garland*, 1765; reprinted by Francis James Child, *The English and Scottish Popular Ballads* (1882-1898), #289, version A.

1. As we lay musing in our beds,
   So well and so warm at ease,
   I thought upon those lodging-beds
   Poor seamen have at seas.

2. Last Easter day, in the morning fair,
   We were not far from land,
   When we spied a mermaid on the rock,
   With comb and glass in hand.

3. The first came up the mate of our ship,
   With lead and line in hand,
   To sound and see how deep we was
   From any rock or sand.

4. The next came up the boatswain of our ship,
   With courage stout and bold:
   'Stand fast, stand fast, my brave lively lads,
   Stand fast, my brave hearts of gold!'

5. Our gallant ship is gone to wreck
    Which was so lately trimmed;
   The raging seas has sprung a leak,
    And the salt water does run in.

6. Our gold and silver, and all our clothes,
    And all that ever we had,
   We forced was to heave them overboard,
    Thinking our lives to save.

7. In all, the number that was on board
    Was five hundred and sixty-four
   And all that ever came alive on shore
    There was but poor ninety-five.

8. The first bespoke the captain of our ship,
    And a well-spoke man was he;
   'I had a wife in fair Plymouth town,
    And a widow I fear she must be.'

9. The next bespoke the mate of our ship,
    And a well-bespoke man was he;
   'I have a wife in fair Portsmouth,
    And a widow I fear she must be.'

10. The next bespoke the boatswain of our ship
    And a well-bespoke man was he;
   'I have a wife in fair Exeter,
    And a widow I fear she must be.'

11. The next bespoke the little cabbin-boy,
    And a well-bespoke boy was he;
   'I am as sorry for my mother dear
    As you are for your wives all three.

12. 'Last night, when the moon shin'd bright,
    My mother had sons five,
   But now she may look in the salt seas
    And find but one alive.'

13. 'Call a boat, call a boat, you little Plymouth boys,
     Don't you hear how the trumpet[s] sound?
   [For] the want of our boat our gallant ship is lost
     And the most of our merry men is drowned.'

14. Whilst the ranging seas do roar,
     And the lofty winds do blow,
   And we poor seamen do lie on the top,
     Whilst the landmen lies below.

Version D

Selected verses from "Sir Patrick Spens"; version and verse identifications from Francis James Child, *The English and Scottish Popular Ballads* (1882-1898), #58.

Version A, verse 6, shows common verse form and the first sign of foreboding, from a dialogue between Spens and a sailor; Thomas Percy, *Reliques of Ancient English Poetry* (1765), from Scots manuscript; and David Herd, *Ancient and Modern Scots Songs* (1769). Translation follows.

'Mak haste, mak haste, my mirry men all,
   Our guid schip sails the morne:'
'O say na sae, my master deir,
   For I fear a deadlie storm.'

"Make haste, make haste, my merry men all,
   Our good ship sails the morn:"
"O say not so, my master dear,
   For I fear a deadly storm."

Version I, verses 7-8, shows form of the speeches and more overt omen; Peter Buchan, *Ancient Ballads and Songs of the North of Scotland* (1828); and William Motherwell manuscript. Translation follows.

Then out it speaks a guild auld man,
   A guid death mat he dee!
'Whatever ye di, my guid master,'
   Tak God your guide to bee.'

'For late yestereen I saw the new moon
    The auld moon in her arm:'
'Ohon, alas!' says Patrick Spens,
    'That bodes a deadly storm.'

Then out it speaks a good old man
    A good death may he die
"Whatever you do, my good master
    Take God your guide to be

"For late yesterday eve I saw the new moon
    The old moon in her arm:"
"Oh no, alas!" says Patrick Spens
    "That bodes a deadly storm."

Version C, verses 17-18, showing epic style and death of sailors; Motherwell's manuscript, "from the recitation of — Buchanan, alias Mrs. Notman, 9 September, 1826."

The first step that the captain stept,
    It took him to the knee,
And the next step that the captain stepped
    They were a' drowned in the sea.

Half owre, half owre to Aberdour
    It's fifty fathoms deep,
And there lay good Sir Patrick Spens,
    And the Scots lords at his feet.

Kumbaya: Folk Songs

The terms folk, folklore, folk song, and folk music have many meanings. Some overlap, some are contradictory. A few magnify aspects of folklore identified in the last chapter. Others have only the most oblique relation to modern ideas. This chapter reviews the music people in camps, at one time or another, have considered folk.

Vestiges of the Past

Historians of medieval Europe used folk and popular as interchangeable labels for the arts of commoners in a two-tiered, agrarian society dominated by courts, manors, and churches. Child* saw his domain as *Popular Ballads*. When urban areas emerged, the word popular was reallocated to merchants and skilled tradesmen. Folklore remained the property of rural peoples.

Cities mushroomed with the industrial revolution in the early nineteenth century. Some Victorians reacted by hypothesizing an idyllic past when the arts evolved organically from communal life.

Some of these academic views influenced Grace Hodsdon Boutelle* (1897-1945). In 1923, she told Girl Scouts, modal folk melodies had the "rhythmic buoyancy" of morris dances "because in the early days, the dances were sung, and the songs were danced." They originally were sung "with the fine serene impersonality so characteristic of the ancient English villagers."

Morris dances are documented from the middle 1400s, but their iconography suggests older customs. Men performed double-file figures on Whitsunday, the Jewish holiday midway between the spring equinox and the summer solstice, when the new agricultural cycle began. Traditional costumes included bells and faces darkened by earth. The accompaniment came from wooden pipes and small drums, or from bagpipes, not from singing.[497]

Music Education

One institution that separated settled communities in this country from those isolated from trends in metropolitan Europe was the singing school. After the American Revolution, itinerant musicians, like William Billings, held week-long meetings to replace unison psalms with part singing that incorporated musical elements from oratorios.

Georg Friedrich Händel provided the model for the unaccompanied music. His "Hallelujah Chorus" from the 1741 *Messiah* was included in a 1786 singing-school collection edited by Isaiah Thomas.* Händel had become music master to George I in 1710 when the prince was still Elector of Hanover in the Holy Roman Empire.

Eighty years later, Franz Josef Haydn's Hungarian patron, Nikolaus Esterházy, died. Forced to recruit new supporters from the growing middle classes, Haydn began incorporating folk and folklike elements into his orchestral music. He twice visited the center of the Hanoverian court in London between 1792 and 1795. His London symphonies (numbers 93-104), composed in his new style, may have sanctioned nostalgic memories for his audience.

His success stimulated William Gardiner to produce *Sacred Melodies* in 1808. The English hymnal set psalms against passages drawn from the new instrumental music.

Lowell Mason (1792-1872) moved from Medfield, Massachusetts, to Savannah, Georgia, in 1812. He established himself as a traditional singing-school teacher, then choir director for a Presbyterian church. Friedrich Leopold Abel (1794-1820) migrated there in 1817. His uncle, Carl Friedrich Abel, had left Saxony for London in 1759 where he introduced early works of Haydn.

Abel helped Mason create his own version of a Gardiner hymnal. Boston's oratorio society sponsored the work's publication in 1822 as *The Handel and Haydn Society's Collection of Church Music.* Abel had died in the yellow fever epidemic of 1820.

Mason returned to Massachusetts, where he produced the first collection intended for Sunday schools in 1829, *The Juvenile Lyre*. In 1836, he called his first convention to train teachers in the rudiments of European music. Two years later, in 1838, Mason established the first public-school music program in Boston.

Among his students was Luther Whiting Mason (1818-1896). He worked in Louisville, Kentucky, in the 1850s; Cincinnati, Ohio, during the Civil War, and in Boston's public schools. He developed *The National Music Course* while he was in Germany in 1870.

His *Second Music Reader* of 1872 used German songs or songs with German airs ("Song of the Woods"), and works by Franz Josef Greith (1799-1869). The Swiss composer's "Alpine Shepherd" described "hills with snow-peaks [. . .] lit up by rosy dawn." "The Swiss Boy," with his "merry comrades," came "from pine-clad hills and mountains" with "verdant valleys."

Although none of Whiting Mason's songs entered camp repertoires, the idea of setting poems to folk tunes persisted with the *Concord Series*. These public-school books were the outcome of the 1915 Summer School of Music, directed by Thomas Whitney Surette in Concord, Massachusetts, outside Boston.

Concord #14 published "Cloud Ships" (13) in 1924. Homer Howells Harbour wrote the text to a Tyrolese folk tune. Madeline Gail Trichel (La GS) says, she learned it in "Established camp, 1954. I learned this in Scouts, but my mother had sung it as a lullaby when I was a baby." She now sings it to her children. Harbour earned high honors in English from Harvard in 1906. Madeline's photograph appears in "Tradition Bearers."

National Music

Another perception of folk music in camps can be traced to the nineteenth-century formation of nation states. Academics generally did not consider national songs to be folk, because they were used in quasi-ceremonial functions. Stylistic characteristics, like scales, meters, and rhyme schemes, were borrowed from western classical music and poetry.

Nevertheless, the term folk was applied to such tunes in paper-bound songsters sold to schools, and community groups in the years around World War I. The 1923 revision of *The Golden Book of Favorite Songs*[259] introduced a folksong section. "All through the Night" (20) was identified as, an "old Welsh air." It attributed the lyrics to an Oxford-educated industrialist, Harold Edwin Boulton

(1859-1935). Editors described Stephen Foster as "a truly American writer of what may be called the folk-songs of America."

Art and politics had been joined more than a century before in the opening scene of Johann Wolfgang von Goethe's *Egmont*.* The 1788 play contrasted an ideal leader with one who relied upon tyranny for control. Goethe converted the French revolution into the 1568 rebellion by the Protestant Netherlands against the Counter Reformation imposed by the Roman Catholic Philip II of Spain.

A tailor complained, they were forbidden from singing the "new psalms" with tunes that "couldn't be more uplifting." A common soldier in Egmont's entourage answered, his people could "sing what we like." After Napoléon Bonaparte destroyed the Holy Roman Empire of inherited privileges in 1806, but before he invaded Russia, Ludwig van Beethoven wrote an overture and other music for a new production of Goethe's drama in 1810.

After the defeat of the French leader, Vienna's Austro-Hungarian Empire and Saint Petersburg's Russian Empire subsumed cultural enclaves into supranational states. An interest in group traditions spread from politics to music. Some intellectuals believed that, to resurrect their lost arts, they should listen to people who had been preserving ethnic heritages, the folk.

Among those who used folk tunes for deliberate, semi-political reasons is Mily Alexeyevich Balakirev.* In 1866, he published the "Volga Boatmen" (2). Basso Feodor Chaliapin elevated the barge haulers' chantey into a national song in 1913. Balakirev is known better for promoting Tchaikovsky, Borodin, Mussorgsky, and Rimsky-Korsakov as uniquely Russian composers.

In the next generation, Bohemian Antonín Dvořák produced *Three Slavonic Rhapsodies* in 1878, and a *Polanaise* in 1879. While he was in the United States, he heard a Black baritone, Harry Thacker Burleigh (1866-1949), sing "Swing Low, Sweet Chariot" (31). The flute theme in the adagio first movement of his ninth symphony of 1893, *From the New World*, alluded to it.

Still later, in 1899, Nicolas II asserted Russian claims to Finland. Jean Sibelius responded with "Finlandia" (3). After Presbyterians printed an arrangement in *The Hymnal* of 1933, Methodists included the music with "Song of Peace" (9) in their 1935 hymn book. Lloyd Stone (1912-1993) wrote the verses sung in camps. The Hawaiian teacher and poet was 22-years-old at the time.

United States

In the United States, the movement to collect folk tunes, which could be arranged as art songs, led to an interest in Native Americans. Thurlow Lieurance composed "By the Waters of Minnetonka" in 1913. A Minnesota Camp Fire camp later adapted it for a local song that began, "Shining waters, friendly fir trees." It continued, "Tanadoona spirit guide us / To our hearts give of your wisdom."

In 1909, Charles Wakefield Cadman composed "From the Land of the Sky-Blue Water" as the first of his *Four American Indian Songs.* Mrs. Paul Appell (Ill CFG) used the melody for "A Camp Fire Maid" (3) in 1921. Hitaga (Iowa CFG) and Tanadoona (Minn CFG) included it in their song books. Vivian Sexton remembers singing the lyrics in a Texas CFG camp.

The incorporation of Indian symbols into camp and organizational programs drove some individuals to seek better sources. For years, Camp Fire Girls recommended Carlos Troyer's arrangements of Pueblo songs. His "Zuñi Sunrise Song" (7) began "Arise." Despite his name, which he assumed in the 1880s, Charles Troyer was a Frankfurt-born composer who settled in San Francisco. The camp version was simplified by Harvey Worthington Loomis, who had studied with Dvořák in New York.

Ironically, the most successful "Indian" song used in camps was the one adapted for "Across the Stillness of the Lake" (30) from "Pale Moon." The 1920 original did more than use sympathetic, though stereotypic, images of the noble savage in the lyrics by Jesse G. M. Glick. Frederic Knight Logan exploited musical motifs Melissa Parkhurst[*] said were associated with Native music by outsiders.

By the time I learned the camp version in the 1950s, these included changes in rhythm, which had the feel of tom-toms ("across the stillness OF THE lake"). Sustained high notes sounded like ceremonial cries ("oh YE who bear the lofty torch"). These were followed by a drop to the normal, low range with another tom-tom section ("think thoughts of evil NE-E-ver"). Towanyak (Kans CFG) treats the high passage as a solo.

Cecil J. Sharp

Cecil James Sharp (1859-1924) fused diverse interests in folk music in 1906. He challenged the English Board of Education's list of recommended folk songs on the grounds most, in fact, were national songs. The English-born, temporary immigrant to Australia felt children ought to be exposed to their true folk heritage. He began peddling piano-accompanied arrangements of authenticated material for general use.

One way Sharp's influence reached America was through people like Boutelle, who studied with him in England. When she moved to Minneapolis, Minnesota, she introduced legitimated folk songs, like "Wraggle Taggle Gipsies O" (Child 200), to local Girl Scouts. The troop leader was Marjorie Edgar* (1899-1960). She published *Old Songs and Balladry for Girl Scouts* in 1930.

Scout song books maintained a strong bias toward Sharp's perceptions until the 1970s. In 1973, Constance Lavino Bell (born 1929),* of the Chesapeake Bay Council in Wilmington, Delaware, chaired a group who produced a songster more in touch with then current conceptions of folk.

Another subtle way Sharp's influence reached American camps was through the Russell Sage Foundation. While he was visiting Boston in 1915, the wife of the Southern Highland Division director asked him to visit the mountains. Ensuing conversations at the foundation well may have reached the founder of the Camp Fire Girls. Gulick had headed their Department of Child Hygiene in 1913.

In July of the following year, 1916, the CFG magazine, *Wohelo*,* recommended Sharp's *Folksongs from Somerset*, the Troyer collection, and Theresa Armitage's *Junior Laurel Songs*. The just-released public-school music book contained national tunes, and a song dedicated to Camp Fire Girls.

A more obvious way Sharp's influence was felt was his 1917 *English Folk Songs from the Southern Appalachians*. His trip south for Olive Dame Campbell led to the discovery Child ballads were still in active tradition.

Folk Artists

Outlanders began scouring the Southern mountains for antique songs. Local tradition keepers intimated they should be the ones publishing anthologies, and receiving credit for sharing their family and community music. John Jacob Niles was born in Louisville in 1892. He began collecting when Burroughs Adding Machine Company sent him to eastern Kentucky during World War I to sell and service equipment in local stores. He moved to New York in 1925, where he introduced "Poor Wayfaring Stranger" (5). Burl Ives' rendition is the one that entered camp tradition.

Perhaps the most important artists presenting traditional material were Marion Anderson and Paul Robeson. Neither Black should have been considered a folk singer. Both had trained voices, one a contralto, the other a bass baritone. In the era of strict segregation, their performances were as close as many came to hearing genuine Southern music. Robeson recorded "Jacob's Ladder" (46), "Swing Low, Sweet Chariot" (31), and "Steal Away" (6). Anderson performed "Go Down Moses" (5) and "I Got a Robe," sometimes called "Heaven, Heaven" (6).

"Swing Low" and "Steal Away" are credited to Wallace Willis, a slave loaned to the Spencer Academy for Choctaw Boys near Hugo, Oklahoma. The Presbyterian school closed during the Civil War. Its superintendent returned to Princeton, New Jersey. When the Fisk Jubilee Singers were performing in Newark, New Jersey, Alexander Reid shared the songs with their director, George Leonard White.[328]

Copyright Law of 1909

Developments in commercial music contributed to the interest in music called folk in camps in the 1920s, 1930s, and 1940s. The copyright law of 1909 gave publishers the power to refuse reprint rights without payment. In 1923, *The Golden Book of Favorite Songs*[259] only included lyrics to the chorus for "There's a Long, Long Trail" (22). A note promised, the "complete words and music may be had from the publishers named." As a consequence of restricted exposure, only one camp has been reported singing the first verse. The rest know only the chorus. Carol Domoney[S] collected the longer version from Rotary (Mich BSA) in 1955.

More recently, the editors of the Camp Farthest Out (Minn P coed) song book, Eva and Russell Shull, reported, among the "songs which could not be included for reasons of copyright" were "Oh What a Beautiful Morning" (9) and the "Johnny Appleseed Grace" (70).

The law delimited the concept of public domain. Some editors of community songsters and public-school music series avoided paying royalties by using material that never had been copyrighted or whose protection had expired.

Cowboy Songs

One public domain song that entered the camp repertoire was "Home on the Range" (27). John Avery Lomax publicized it in *Cowboy Songs and Other Frontier Ballads* in 1910. Vernon Dahlhart recorded a version in 1927. Kirke Mechem* later discovered Brewster Martin Higley (1823-1911) published the words in a Smith County, Kansas, newspaper in 1873. A local fiddler, Daniel E. Kelley (1845-1905), added the music. Higley was born in southeastern Ohio in Meigs County on the Ohio River. He studied medicine in northern Indiana. Kelley was raised as a carpenter in Rhode Island.

Lomax's book coincided with the glorification of the cattle frontier. In 1908, Anna Morris Clark sent a poem by her stepson to the *Pacific Monthly*, which began "Desert silver blue." Clark, himself, sent more work to the Portland, Oregon, publication. Southern Pacific bought the magazine in 1911, and merged it with *Sunset* to promote Western tourism. Spas for tuberculosis patients were especially popular destinations.

William S. Hart made the first movie western in 1914. Charles B. Clark, Junior (1883-1957), consumption sufferer, became Badger Clark, cowboy poet. He included "Roundup Lullaby" (32) in his 1915 collection, *Sun and Saddle Leather*. Clifton Wellesley Barnes wrote the camp melody. The composer was a member of the class of 1914 at Pomona College, about 33 miles from Hollywood.

Red River Valley

Another public domain scavenger hunt occurred in 1941. Radio stations stopped playing music controlled by ASCAP. The American Society for Composers, Authors and Publishers set and policed copyright payments for members. For ten months, from January to October, stations programmed only public-domain songs, like "Red River Valley" (14), and ones by writers excluded from ASCAP, like "You Are My Sunshine" (10).

Edith Fulton Fowke believed the text for the first referred to the 1870 resistance by descendants of French and Indians, the Métis of present-day Manitoba. Hudson's Bay Company had transferred its, and their, land to the newly created, British-controlled federation of Canada in 1869. Ottawa's government sent troops to affirm its authority. Early versions suggested a lament by a Native or part-Indian girl for a soldier returning east.[330]

The lyric spread quickly on the wheat frontier. In 1897, Edwin Ford Piper earned a degree in English from the University of Iowa. Perhaps inspired by people like Child, he began transcribing songs he remembered from his boyhood. Included in his manuscript were five verses of "Valley" he heard in Nemaha, Nebraska, in 1879, when he was eight years old. He heard it again in Harlan, Nebraska, in 1885, when he was fourteen.[470]

The year before Piper graduated, James J. Kerrigan published the melody in New York City in 1896 as "In the Bright Mohawk Valley." In 1923, poet Carl Sandburg* published *The American Songbag*. His version of "River" had been collected in the Pine Mountain area of southeastern Kentucky by Gilbert Reynolds Combs, a Methodist minister in Lexington.

Texan Carl Tyler Sprague recorded the "Cowboy Love Song" in 1925. Jules Verne Allen* followed in 1929. The Texas-born Allen believed the song came "from Pennsylvania, possibly brought there by early settlers and has been made over to suit the locale."

You Are My Sunshine

Country singer Jimmie Davis and his band director, Charles Mitchell, took credit for "Sunshine." After the copyright law created a new way to earn money, some artists added their names to the lists of composers. They believed songs were more than texts and tunes. The way they were sung and their arrangements created styles that became incorporated into them.

Before the copyright law, composers did not see music as private property. They did believe they should be paid to perform. Theodore

Pappas says his grandfather, Oliver Hood* of LaGrange, Georgia, wrote the text for "Sunshine" on a paper sack in 1933. He performed it with Riley Puckett and with Paul Rice. Rice* later recorded a version with the Rice Brothers Gang. The musicians moved from Georgia to Shreveport, Louisiana, where they worked on radio station KWKH. Davis, who then was local police commissioner, bought the rights from Rice. In 1944, he used it during his successful campaign for governor.

Consensus Folk Music

Publication of mass-market books by Lomax and Sandburg buttressed the emerging interest in folklore by intellectuals and educators. Some began introducing songs called folk into camps. Little distinction existed between those in the public domain, commercial music written in imitation of folk work, and genuine traditional art.

An Augusta (Calif CFG) song book from the 1930s included the Appalachian "Down in the Valley" (33) and "She'll Be Coming 'round the Mountain" (41). Sandburg disseminated both. He collected the first from Frances Ries of Batavia, Ohio. Like several of his sources, she seems to have been connected with his research for the biography of Abraham Lincoln he published in 1926. Batavia was the closest town to Ulysses S. Grant's birthplace.

Will Croft Barnes had published Augusta's "Cowboy's Sweet Bye and Bye" (8) in 1920 in *Tales from the X-bar Horse Camp*. He owned land that once had been part of the Maxwell land grant in Colfax County, New Mexico. The Boy Scouts' Philmont Ranch occupies another part of the grant in the same county.

In 1944, Cecily Raysor Hancock transcribed the songs they were singing at Wilaha (Colo CFG), including "Cielito Lindo" (9). Sandburg had included the 1882 Mexican ranchera by Quirino Mendoza y Cortés. The late 1940s Kitanniwa song book included Lomax's "Get along Little Dogies" (12).

During the 1930s and 1940s, editors of community song books, public-school music books, and general commercial collections groped for ways to present these newly found songs. Their usual format was a classification by regions and occupational groups. Sandburg used the organization. Lomax and his son, Alan, followed with their 1934 *American Ballads and Folk Songs.*

This codification of American folk music persists in Eastern camps. The 1960 song book of the University Settlement Work Camp at Beacon, New York (NY agency coed), integrated songs recorded by artists like Pete Seeger, the Weavers, and the Kingston Trio into the older outline of folk music. It grouped some by origins in "Songs from Other Lands." It classed others, like "Rounds," "Ballads," "Blues," and "Lullabies," by genre.

The section of work songs combined origin and subject. It included "Fillimeeooreay" (29), Leadbelly's "Pick a Bale of Cotton" (17), and the Kingston Trio's "The M.T.A. Song" (19). Lomax's daughter, Bess Lomax Hawes, and Jacqueline Steiner crafted the last in 1949. They modified the first successful country music recording, "Wreck of the Old 97," made by Vernon Dahlhart (1883-1948) in 1924.

Beacon's genre section of sea chanteys included "Sloop John B." (12), composed by Sandburg and Lee Hays. Other camps have sung "Blow the Man Down" (5), a halyard chantey, and "Shenandoah" (33), a river chantey taken to sea as a capstan. Another capstan, "Cape Cod Girls" (6) often is sung "Australia Girls." Halyards were used for continuous work like hoisting sails, capstans for coordinated efforts like raising anchors.

Joseph McCarthy

Several trends converged after World War II. School-music books edited by Marie Teresa Armitage that set poems to traditional tunes were kept in print. Lilla Belle Pitts (1884-1970) used a few camp songs in the *Our Singing World* series beginning in 1950. One song, which seems to have entered camps from these primers, is "Gray Squirrel" (14). Lowell Bond used a Czech tune.[245]

Ruth Crawford Seeger acknowledged a deeper patriotic mood stirred by the depression and second world war. When she published *American Folk Songs for Children* in 1948, she noted all the songs had "partaken of the making of America. Our children have a right to be brought up with it."[504:21]

Their common interest faded during the cold war search for traitors led by Senator Joseph McCarthy. In 1949, J. Edgar Hoover's Federal Bureau of Investigation pressured promoters to cancel Paul Robeson's concerts, because he criticized Southerners who lynched

Blacks. The same year it encouraged the Ku Klux Klan to drive him away from Wo-Chi-Ca, an integrated New Jersey summer camp where he performed every summer.[409]

That year, 1949, happened to see the Weavers release their first successful recordings of folk songs, "On Top of Old Smoky" (18) and "Tzena, Tzena" (11). Later, an FBI informer, Harvey Matusow, denounced two members, Pete Seeger and Lee Hays, as Communists. The quartet lost its Decca recording contract in 1953. In 1955, Matusow* admitted he lied to avoid prosecution for his own activities.

Seeger had joined Communist groups in the 1940s, but had drifted away. In 1955, he refused, on principle, to answer questions from the House of Representatives about his friends or beliefs. Hays had not joined any organizations, but had worked for a school in Arkansas that trained labor organizers and had had friends who were party members.

Professors turned their attention to preserving their academic positions. They devoted themselves to developing more sophisticated forms of analysis, rather than to producing singable anthologies with potentially dangerous lyrics. Their silence left others to provide serviceable folk song collections, unaided by scholarly direction or musical example.

Florence Hudson Botsford

Recreation music professionals in the 1950s retreated to the safety of international folk music, especially that of pre-World War II Germany and Central Europe. Two important precursors were Florence Hudson Botsford and Augustus Delafield Zanzig. She edited the *Botsford Collection of Folk-Songs** for the YWCA in 1922. He compiled *Singing America** for the National Recreation Association in 1940.

Botsford's anthology coincided with the organization's interest, in the years immediately following World War I, with fusing immigrants into the American melting pot. Foreign-born members of the Y, and its supporters, contributed favorite songs.

At the same time, the Y was reaching into areas recently freed from the Austro-Hungarian, Russian, and Ottoman empires. In the early 1920s, Lilian Jackson went to Rumania. Nebraska-born Fjeril Hess (1892-1975) was sports director in Prague and Bratislava. They returned with the four verses of "Above a Plain" (22) that Imogen Ireland* published in 1927.

Katharine Blunt Parker (1867-1953) of Houston, Texas, provided the funding. She was a trained musician. Her husband's position with Baker, Botts law firm limited her activities to patronage, playing piano for an occasional wedding, and directing the local Woman's Choral Club.

Hess later worked for the Girl Scouts. She published histories, memoirs, and novels for adolescents. Two were about the Scouts, *Shanty Brook Lodge* (1937) and *Toplofty* (1939).

Botsford, born Florence Topping around 1867, graduated from Shimer College of Chicago in 1888. The Camp Fire Girls recommended her collection,[150] as did Girl Scout[196] and 4-H[163] leaders. Some public libraries purchased it.

More important, her anthology was used in recreation-training seminars, like those sponsored by the Methodist church for adult leaders at Waldenwoods (Mich). Lucille Parker Munk (Mich CFG) attended one in 1934. Kempthorne used the collection at some CFG National Training Courses in 1933.

Botsford's primary role was spreading an appreciation for international music. Mexico's "Little Owlet" (23) was the only song from her collection in the 1950s Kitanniwa repertoire.

Augustus Delafield Zanzig

Zanzig (1891-1977) was the son of a New York City water department employee. His anthology included songs collected directly, or indirectly, from ethnic groups in this country. He heard "Over the Meadows" (11) "in Los Angeles after a club of sturdy young Czech men and women of that city, through with their gymnasium activities, joined another group of Americans in an exchange of songs and in general singing."[562]

Kitanniwa included his "Walking at Night" (17) and "At the Gates of Heaven" (14) in its 1940s song book. Zanzig learned the first from Stella Marek Cushing (died 1938), the daughter of Czech immigrants. She sang, played violin, and gave dance demonstrations in New Jersey and New York. Aurelio Armendáriz collected the second for the Federal Music Project in New Mexico in 1939.

Cooperative Recreation Service (CRS)

Elmore Lynch Rohrbough (1900-1980) followed Zanzig. His father was a West Virginia-born Methodist teacher, who moved to Colorado. He became a rancher near Aspen.[489] Lynn's wife, Katherine Ferris (1896-1971), graduated from Wellesley in 1917 where she had joined Agora. Of the school's five societies, it was the one that attracted women interested in public affairs.

In the 1920s, the two began preparing materials for friends involved with recreation for church youth-groups. This evolved into the Cooperative Recreation Service. They ran the co-op with other recreation leaders from their home in Delaware, Ohio, some 35 miles north of Columbus.

In the 1940s, the Rohrboughs began publishing custom song books. Their paper-covered, stapled songsters, which measured about 3 5/8" by 5 5/8", provided tunes for all the texts. Some reached a hundred pages. Any group could order a book, and choose songs from those in CRS's file. If it wanted new material, plates were made, and became available to others.

According to Larry Nial Holcomb,* they printed the first in 1940 for the Michigan Methodist church. In 1941, the Danish American Young People's League of Des Moines, Iowa; the Eastern Maine Senior Institute, and The Cooperative League followed. Alta May Calkins (1904-1984) edited *Co-op Song Book*. She gave them their version of "Down in the Valley" (33).[133] Her husband, Gilman Calkins, worked for the Ohio Farm Bureau. She was active in the Epworth League in central Ohio in the late 1930s.

Azalea Trails (Calif GS) is the first camp known by Holcomb to have them publish its songs. Others who have used the service include Adahi (Penna CFG), Elko Lake (NY P coed), Highroad (Va P coed), Indian Trails (Mich coed), Mar-Lu Ridge (Md P coed), Sealth (Wash CFG), and Wildwood (Mass boys).

Music Makers,* issued by the Camp Fire Girls in the 1950s, was typical. Of its 142 songs, nearly half were called "folk songs," most from Europe and the United States. Another 29 were "rounds and canons," while seven were classed as "rhythms, games, dances" and 22 served ceremonial purposes. The remaining 16 "general songs" included nine from CFG or camp tradition like "Green Trees" (56) and "Sing Your Way Home" (26).

Seventy percent of the songs were known by at least five people or camps who cooperated with me in this project. Another 16% were recognized by at least one person or camp. That only 14% of the songs were not reported in tradition somewhere represents an extraordinarily high recognition factor for a collection. It also testifies to the role the Rohrboughs played as active agents in a tradition whose aesthetic taste they shared and helped spread. Their photograph appears in "Collectors."

Leadership Transition

One reason the Rohrboughs became so important was many youth-group central offices abandoned music after World War II. I already mentioned, in the INTRODUCTION, the significance to Camp Fire of Kempthorne's move to England.

The YWCA became more important for perpetuating immigrant, than camp traditions. Mildred Roe's *Girl Reserve Song-Book*[*] from 1923 contained many songs that entered the camp repertoire, including "Father Time" (18), "Mister Moon" (20), and "Skinnamarink" (28).

In 1940, Zilphia Johnson Horton (1910-1956) joined the organization's music committee. Soon after, Marie Oliver (1901-2000) became the group's secretary.[233] Horton directed music at the Methodist-affiliated Highlander Folk School in Grundy County, Tennessee. Oliver had gone to the Methodist's Boston University after she earned her baccalaureate in 1922. Rohrbough had matriculated the same year, but I know no more.

Oliver did use Rohrbough in 1943,[*] but mixed labor songs with the hymns, international tunes borrowed from Zanzig, and camp songs. An early edition of the Y's *Sing Along the Way* included "Shuttles of Commerce," "Solidarity Forever," and "We Shall Not Be Moved" (2). The 1951[*] edition added Caroline Kohlsaat's (1875-1950) setting for "Bread and Roses." James Oppenheim's 1911 poem had become associated with a strike by female workers against the Lawrence, Massachusetts, textile mills in 1912.

Matusow claimed, in 1952, "the Boy Scouts, the Girl Scouts, the YWCA" were "all Communist infiltrated."[424:168] Conservatives criticized Oliver's use of "Joe Hill," a song associated with labor organizers in the Pacific Northwest, the International Workers of the World (IWW). Earl Robinson had written the ballad when he was music director at the Communist Party's Camp Unity (NY coed) near Wingdale, New York, in the 1930s. Robeson had performed there.

Soon after, Oliver* retired to Pacific Grove, California, where she taught music in the public schools, and later piano. In 1957, Mary Wheeler* changed the songster's title to *Sing Along*. More traditional camp songs dislodged the labor ones. Still, she included "Joe Hill" and "Solidarity."

No one followed Janet Tobitt with the Girl Scouts. The Rohrboughs published *Chansons de Notre Chalet* in 1957 for Marion Ross, a former director of the Girl Guides' Swiss compound.

Elvin Oscar Harbin* (1885-1955) published *Paradology* for the Epworth League in 1927. During World War I, he had worked for the YMCA with the army near Memphis, Tennessee. He returned to his home in Louisville, where the Southern Methodist church hired him as director of the Department of Recreation and Culture. He joined the central office of the Methodist's Epworth youth group in 1919. His retirement photograph appears in "Collectors."

John Lawrence Eisenberg* (1914-1997) began working for him, then met Rohrbough at a National Conference of Methodist Youth in Berea, Kentucky, in 1936. From that time, he followed Rohrbough's lead. The Tennessee-born Northern Methodist resigned from the church's General Board of Education in 1952, but remained active as a minister. He and his wife, the former Helen Park (1921-2011), wrote recreation manuals for the YMCA. They went to Rhodesia as missionaries in 1960.

Four-H clubs, which are part of state agricultural college extension services, became interested in camp programs to support rural schools that could not afford music, art, or nature studies. Many had recreation specialists. Arden M. Peterson (1918-1995) was serving that role when I was in 4-H in Michigan in the 1950s. Max Vernon Exner (1910-2004) became the most important in Iowa. Both states used CRS to produce their songsters.

International Songs

Scholars would not accord CRS's international songs the status of folk. *Grove's Dictionary* said the folk music of Germany, the volkslieder, arose in the middle ages and declined in the seventeenth century. Volkstümliches lied, a music of the new middle class, took its place. In the late nineteenth century, university students, touched by the Romantic Movement, revived the earlier songs. Since they were more idealistic than scholarly, their collections mingled volkslieder with volkstümliches lied.

Early twentieth-century youth groups were the source of the Rohrbough's German songs. Zanzig noted in *Singing America*, the "Walking Song" (31), which began "From Lucerne to Weggis fair," had been "a prime favorite among the 'Wandervogel' and other hiking youth of Germany as well as among the Swiss." *Music Makers* reprinted the Zanzig version, with a note it was Swiss.

The association of 1950s international music with the Wandervogel may have limited its appeal in Jewish camps in the East. Many were uneasy with anything promulgated by Adolf Hitler's youth organizations. Instead, they perpetuated the European view of the folk as the lowliest of the lowly, and continued to sing music publicized by the Lomaxes.

At Woodland (NY coed), Norman Studer hired men blacklisted by the anti-Communists to teach American folk music. Norman Cazden and Herbert Haufrecht had campers collect songs and other lore from their neighbors in the Catskills near Phoenicia, New York.[431]

Pete Seeger supported himself by running workshops there, and places like the University Settlement House camp (NY agency coed), Webatuck (NY J coed), and Killooleet (Vt coed). The second, run by Janis Ian's parents, Victor Martin Fink and the former Pearl Yadoff, reused the Camp Unity site. John Seeger, a brother, owned the last.

Folk Revival

All the individuals mentioned, who were involved with using folk songs or tunes in camps, were folk revivalists. They wanted people to sing material that had vanished from, or never been part of, their heritage. All contributed to developments in commercial music in the 1960s called the Folk Revival.

As a genre, it went back to the 1930s. Josef Marais performed his translations of Afrikaans songs for BBC radio in London. He moved to New York in 1939 for NBC radio, and later worked with Rosa de Miranda. They introduced "Pretoria" (23) and "Zulu Warrior" (25).

Burl Ives began a Mutual Broadcasting radio network program in 1946. In the early 1940s, he sometimes worked with the Almanac

Singers. Millard Lempell, Lee Hays, and Pete Seeger formed the group in 1940 to play union and political rallies. Woody Guthrie joined them in 1941. When his health began failing, Fred Hellerman and Ronnie Gilbert joined the group. They then called themselves the Weavers.

Folk Revival Repertoire

After the Weavers disbanded, an occasional commercial artist would make a successful recording of a folk or folklike song. Harry Belafonte produced the "Banana Boat Song" in 1956. The next year, Washington-born Jimmie Rodgers recorded "Honeycomb." The Everly Brothers released the first of their recordings featuring parallel harmony.

Laurie London introduced "He's Got the Whole World in His Hands" (35) in 1958. The same year Dave Guard, Bob Shane, and Nick Reynolds performed in San Francisco as the Kingston Trio. Joan Baez made her first recordings in 1960. Then, in 1962, Bob Dylan, and Peter, Paul and Mary emerged in New York. Albert Grossman, the enterprising manager of Dylan, had brought Peter Yarrow, Noel Paul Stookey, and Mary Travers together the year before.

The new artists recorded both traditional music and new songs written in a traditional style with simple guitar accompaniments. Dynamics of success forced them to seek new material to keep fans buying records and returning to concerts.

Dylan absorbed elements of rock. Baez became more associated with protests against the war in Vietnam. The Kingston Trio and Peter, Paul and Mary recorded more conventional material, like "Scotch and Soda" and "Puff the Magic Dragon" (29).

Some, who had been attracted by their early work, began looking for more substantive music. First, they listened to Folkways reissues of recordings by artists like Guthrie and Leadbelly. Eventually, the Rohrboughs made Guthrie's 1941 "Roll on Columbia" (5) available.

Next, people began searching for 78 rpm records made by Southern Black and Appalachian performers. Thus, a song like "Lonesome Valley" (15), recorded by Kentucky's Bill and Charlie Monroe in 1936, entered the repertoire.

Case Study: Kumbaya

Finally, some went into libraries and started looking through those dusty collections of folk songs made when Child and Sharp first inspired investigators. Eventually, someone found what became "Kumbaya" (90). It had been transcribed as "Come by Yuh" in the sea islands off the southern Atlantic coast, where Gullah was spoken. The African-based dialect dates back to slavery times. According to the Society for the Preservation of Spirituals,[†] who first published the song, "yuh" means here.

Descendants of South Carolina rice planters had organized themselves in 1922 to preserve a language they thought endangered by the emigration of Blacks, and the adoption of standardized hymns. Membership initially was limited to those, colored or white, who were "plantation bred or plantation broken" who met to sing familiar songs. It came to be one of the most exclusive clubs in Charleston, according to novelist Josephine Pinckney.[*]

In the late 1920s, one member suggested they publish a collection to raise money for the medical care and relief of "old time negroes."[469] They were the ones most harmed by the post-World War I collapse of the rice market. Plantations were sold to Northerners for lumber and hunting retreats.

The current version of "Kumbaya" entered camp and commercial music repertoires through Rohrbough. He gave it to Eisenberg, who was spreading it in North Carolina, when Pete Seeger saw him in 1956. Rohrbough also gave it to Anthony Saletan,[†] who shared it with Joe Hickerson[*] (born 1935). With the Folksmiths, Hickerson taught it in New England camps in 1957. They were Oberlin students.

The plates soon were available for CRS song books. In 1957, the YWCA,[†] Girl Guides,[†] and Iowa 4-H[†] included it in song books edited by Wheeler, Ross, and Exner. Rohrbough's source is not known.

Legends

"Kumbaya's" likely origins and diffusion route into the camp repertoire are important because it has become encrusted with etiological legends. The most common view, circulated in headnotes, is the spiritual was brought to this country by a missionary who had served in Angola, then a Portuguese colony. A few songsters

63

suggested that, like Joan Baez's "All My Trials" (12), it moved from the Southern United States to the West Indies. From there, it diffused either to the United States, where it had been forgotten, or to Africa.

Edward Peter Dowdall (Me girls) heard it was Korean. Marilyn Butler (NH P girls) was told, it came from India. John Richard Fort (Vt boys) believes it is Brazilian. High/Scope's (Mich agency coed) song book instructs campers, it is from Nigeria. Sharon Richman (Penna J girls) heard it originally was an American Indian song.

In addition to simple tales ascribing a foreign origin, more elaborate legends developed. Larry Ralston (Ohio 4-H) remembers:

> The thing I've been told, and we passed it on, sounds good, is that it was an old African song and that is was first developed during a storm - or earthquake - earthquake, I guess it was - what was passed on to me. I can't say what it was really. That's really what I think I heard first. That is, I think, it was an earthquake, the he . . . one person, was walking through a village and this is what he saw.

Wilma Lawrence (Penna GS) heard it was about a little child who was ill, whose mother cried, prayed the child would get well, and then sang. Jan Smyth (Ohio P coed) has said:

> First off, this song, the way I learned it, is supposed to be telling a story. Somebody coming into the life of Christ, or having Christ come into his life, whatever. And we learned kumbaya as the first verse, someone's praying, someone's singing, laughing, and so it's supposed to be a jubilant type ending. It starts with the sad verses first and then go on to praying as "Lord, please come to me," and then going into laughing and the singing. And I learned it essentially with just three verses of crying, praying and singing.

Explication

Plantation society was not monolithic. Our common image derives from Harriet Beecher Stowe's *Uncle Tom's Cabin* (1852) and

Margaret Mitchell's *Gone with the Wind* (1936). They described life on cotton plantations, where labor gangs worked the crops.

Rice only would grow on a narrow strip of land along the South Carolina and Georgia coasts where salty ocean and fresh river waters met. The work - planting, picking, damming - demanded special skills. In the early years, rice planters preferred slaves from Sénégal and Gorée, who had some knowledge of rice cultivation. They shunned those imported from Angola and Kongo.[314]

Rice plantations were comparatively small. The wealthiest compensated by owning more land. When the biggest slaveholder, Nathaniel Heyward, died in 1851, he owned 2,340 slaves and 17 plantations. When the next largest, Joshua John Ward, died in 1860, he had 1,139 slaves on 9 plantations. Heyward's averaged 140 people, Ward's 126. Not all worked the crops. Some were infants. Some were domestics. Some were elderly.

James Hamilton failed as a rice grower in the sea islands. In the 1840s, he tried to recoup his losses with a cotton plantation in Georgia run by an overseer. His 6,000-acre venture in Alabama was a business partnership that owned 300 slaves.[534:214-5] Later, he organized a syndicate to grow sugar cane in Texas on 2,375 acres.[534:217] The 130 slaves he transferred from Georgia[534:217] were from "at least six different groups owned by or mortgaged to various individuals or banks."[534:232]

The lives of Wallace Willis and his wife, Minerva, were very different. Their last owner was Raleigh Britton Willis. His grandfather, Britton Willis, lived on the frontier fringes of the slave-owning aristocracy. He was born in North Carolina, fought on the Cherokee frontier in the Revolution, and lived for a time on newly open Cherokee land near Pendleton, South Carolina. When the West opened, he moved to former Chickasaw lands in western Kentucky where tobacco would grow. His family believes he freed three male slaves and their mother when he died in 1844.

Raleigh's father James followed the Chickasaw frontier into northern Mississippi where he owed 320 acres when he died in 1855. In 1852, Raleigh married a woman born in Mississippi who was officially half-Choctaw. She may have been Chickasaw. Government records had merged the two groups in 1837. The couple must have moved soon after to Choctaw-Chickasaw land in Indian Territory, now Oklahoma.

Slaves associated with small land holders like the Willises often lived as apprentices or indentured servants. Wallace and Minerva would have had to speak English to work for a Presbyterian missionary and his family. They probably also learned enough Muskogean to communicate. Ones in Louisiana learned French. Only slaves on the large plantations of Stowe and Mitchell could mix some common African words with English. Those in the humid lowlands of South Carolina were free to develop their own lingua franca because malaria turned people like Hamilton into absentees.

These differences in language and social relations mean very few people could have given "Kumbaya" to the Rohrboughs. He or she may have found it in the book. The go-between might have learned it from a society member, perhaps at one of their concerts.[513] Alternatively, the liaison descended from a subset of the Black population, or had contact with a descendant.

Tobitt and Mary Alison Sanders (1886-1949) are examples of the first. Tobitt included the Society's "Tell John Doin' Call Duh Roll" in the 1939 edition of *Yours for a Song.** "Primus Lan" was reprinted in the 1941 *Sing Me Your Song O!* Both were dropped from the 1960 combined edition,[182] after "Kumbaya" became popular. Sanders cited the collection as her source for "Come en Go wid Me" in *Sing High Sing Low** in 1946. Both Camp Fire Girls and Girl Scouts sold her blue-covered songster in the 1950s.

Marvin Frey (1918-1992) is an example of an individual who could well have learned the song from someone who fled the Southeast. He remembered, his grandparents had migrated from Germany to the Portland, Oregon, area. While his mother, Anna, remained a German Baptist, his father, Charles, "participated in the ministry of a Pentecostal Mission in Portland."[337:9]

William Joseph Seymour, a Black preacher from Centerville, Louisiana, had publicized Pentecostalism in Los Angeles in 1906. His Azusa Street Revival, which lasted until 1915, was noted for speaking in tongues, faith healing, and racially mixed services.

Frey was 17-years-old when he worked three weeks as the pianist and band conductor for a camp meeting in Turner, Oregon, led by a white Pentecostal revivalist, Charles Sydney Price. By then, Eudorus Neander Bell had formalized the movement as Assemblies of God. He established a temporary headquarters in Findlay, Ohio, in 1914.

The next year, the group moved to Saint Louis, Missouri. Findlay's current Pentecostal mission was not established until 1930.

Young Frey next went to Los Angeles to find a Holy Ghost rally, and played a revival where Aimee Simple McPherson was the featured speaker. On the way, he stopped to preach in Oakland, California, at a church where there was a "white pastor, but half the congregation was black."[337:44]

Frey said that, while most churches at the time "want their pianists simply to play four-part harmony as songs were written, but my improvisational playing included elements of rag time, blues and popular music of the day."[337:38]

It was the middle of the depression. He was 18-years-old. After these experiences, he says he wrote "Kumbaya" at a camp meeting in Centralia, Washington. The logging and mining town is more famous for a violent confrontation with the IWW in 1919.

He spent the next decades preaching to Pentecostal camp meetings, where he claimed he sang "Kumbaya." Any believer could have taken the song to a Pentecostal church in Ohio. From there, someone could have shared it with the Rohrboughs.

Pete Seeger[†] instigated the legend about Angola. In the linear notes to his album with Sonny Terry, he implied it might have come from Sam Coles, who "spent his life as a teacher in a mission near Angola."

In fact, Samuel Coles[*] (1888-1957) was a Black from Tilden, Alabama, who spent his early years in the cotton lands of Alabama and Florida. When he was at Talladega College, a teacher suggested he go to Africa for the Congregational Church. In his autobiography, he described his work improving the agricultural and material culture of villagers. He did not mention any interest in music.

The attribution to Angola ricocheted back to Rohrbough. In 1957, the Girl Guides' *Chansons*[†] said, it was "African (Angolan)." The 1959 edition[†] simply claimed, it was a "Spiritual." Rohrbough's notes changed whenever he received new information. He rarely dated revisions.

Sonny Terry was a blind, Black musician from the tobacco Piedmont of North Carolina.

Textual Variation

"Kumbaya" exists in two, similar versions. The A alternative, sung at Kitanniwa in 1974, is like CRS's published text. The song is treated as a defined entity, with a first and last verse, kumbaya, and middle verses with verbs that vary from camp to camp. Most common are singing, praying, laughing, and crying. Sometimes, "come by here" is substituted for one of the kumbaya verses.

The B alternative from Trelipe (Minn CFG) is in the same family as the version recorded by Joan Baez.[†] Although the verses can be set and limited, as in A, it usually is an open-ended alternation of verses with the kumbaya burden. Verb stanzas often are improvised as long as people feel like singing.

Music

At Kitanniwa in 1974, members of the staff sang the chorus and two or three verses through twice to experiment with different sets of guitar chords. In the first of seven repetitions, they began singing in timbraic harmony, that is, in unison with harmonic effects caused by the interaction between overtones of individual voices. On the second repetition, one person tried singing a lower, parallel part. In the third, another person tried a soprano parallel part. Harmonic effects resulting from overtones increased.

Beginning the chorus the second time, timbraic effects with an added part changed into fully balanced two-part parallel harmony. In the fifth repetition, a third parallel part emerged. Tonal richness resulting from the overtones increased in the final two iterations.

Tradition has altered the tune. Judy Taylor (Mich CFG) has heard both 2/4 and 3/4 meters. Many groups, including Kitanniwa,[†] sustain some notes, so the transition between tones is modulated into a form of sostenuto. At Yallani[†] (Calif CFG), the tones are separated more distinctly, as are the lines. Their version has a staccato feel.

Gestures

Recently, gestures have been added. Mary Tinsley Unrue (Mich CFG) heard, they were Indian sign language. Eleanor Crow (Vt girls) was told, they were either deaf language, or Indian, or African. Nancy

Horner (Md CFG) has resolved the conflicting stories. Following one pattern of variation in folklore, she found minute differences that could be rationalized. According to her, if one rolled one's hands outward on "kumbaya," it was Indian. If the hands were rolled inward, it was deaf sign language. Her photograph appears in "Singing."

Popularity

"Kumbaya" spread slowly in tradition. By the late 1950s, it had reached the avant-garde of the Folk Revival. Pete Seeger[†] recorded a version in a Carnegie Hall concert in 1958. The reunited Weavers[†] released the song on a 1959 album. Meanwhile, the German-influenced American Evangelical Lutheran Youth Fellowship[†] used it in a CRS song book in 1958. Baptists[†] and the German-descended Disciples of Christ[†] published it the next year.

In the early 1960s, the song moved into mainstream churches. Methodists,[†] Episcopalians,[†] and Quakers[†] printed it. Joan Baez[†] recorded a live performance in 1962. The spiritual also began seeping into public-school music books published by CRS, and was promoted by Boy Scouts.[†] Commercial song books, which included it, often contained the word "hootenanny" in their titles.

In these years, when a boundary still existed between church and Camp Fire camp repertoires, "Kumbaya" tended to be sung in the first more than in the other. I know I never sang it in camp. I remember learning the B version on the band bus in the early 1960s where it was started by members of the Methodist Youth Fellowship or the local Salem Evangelical Lutheran church. Lucille Parker Munk, whose husband was on the local Methodist college faculty, said, "I loved that." She added, "I don't think I ever sang it at our day camp," Tanawida (Mich CFG).

In the last half of the decade, establishment editors included the spiritual in public-school music books for third, fourth and sixth graders, and sheet music marketed to secondary schools. Presbyterians[†] discovered it. Christian-music companies, like Word of Waco, Texas, began issuing records that included the song.

In the 1970s, more conservative religious groups championed the song. They probably are the ones responsible for redefining it as a ballad of salvation. Cliff Barrows[†] worked with Billy Graham. Bill

Gaither[†] led one of the last traditional Southern gospel vocal trios. Groups like Campus Crusade for Christ[†] published it. In those years, Tom Glazer documented its associations with the civil rights movement in *Songs of Peace, Freedom and Protest.*[†]

Girl Scout[†] and Camp Fire Girl[†] leaders finally included "Kumbaya" in their song books. Most people who answered my questionnaire knew it. The lowest recognition level was among Camp Fire camps in the survey Midwest, where 75% said they had sung it in camp. Other types of Midwestern camps had recognition scores above 90%. About 80% of people in the rest of the country recognized it as a camp song.

A lyric, first sung in Midwestern church camps, spread nationwide. At last, it returned to the Old Northwest Territory to infiltrate singing traditions in girls' camps. There the young women traditionally had attended both a church camp and an organizational one, but kept the two repertoires separate.

Kumbaya Moment

Since this was written, the song has become an eponym for a set of values associated with communal goals, rather than individualistic ones. "Kumbaya" carries a negative connotation of coerced comradery traceable to those attempts by religious groups to coopt the voluntary folk process for evangelistic purposes.

That association increased in the 1980s when corporate managers, threatened by the success of Japanese manufacturing companies, adopted team-building programs based on Outward Bound. The ambitious knew they had to do well. They doubted a week in the wilderness transformed their lupine peers into cooperative sheep.

Most recently, groups, which once might have tried to standardize the song, have been using it as a pejorative term for people who resisted their efforts.

Version A

Text from staff, Camp Kitanniwa (Mich CFG), 1974. Gestures from young girls, aged 10 to 12 years, Wyandot County 4-H Day Camp (Ohio), held at Camp Trinity (Ohio P coed), 1974.

Gestures identified below are repeated for key words.

1. Kumba[1] ya,[2] my Lord,[3] kumba[1] ya[2]
    Kumbaya, my Lord, kumbaya
    Kumbaya, my Lord, kumbaya
    Oh[4] Lord,[3] kumba[1] ya[2]

2. Someone's[5] crying,[6] Lord,[3] kumba[1] ya[2]
    Someone's crying, Lord, kumbaya
    Someone's crying, Lord, kumbaya
    Oh Lord, kumbaya

3. Someone's[5] praying,[7] Lord,[3] kumba[1] ya[2]
    Someone's praying, Lord, kumbaya
    Someone's praying, Lord, kumbaya
    Oh Lord, kumbaya

4. Someone's[5] singing,[8] Lord,[3] kumba[1] ya[2]
    Someone's singing, Lord, kumbaya
    Someone's singing, Lord, kumbaya
    Oh Lord, kumbaya

Gestures
1. Roll hands around each other in outward direction
2. Hands out flat, palms upward
3. Cross self diagonally, with hand, from right shoulder to left wrist
4. Make circle with right thumb and forefinger
5. Point to sky
6. Trace tear down cheek with finger
7. Hands in prayer
8. Move hand outward from mouth following the tune

Version B

Text from Camp Trelipe (Minn CFG), 1970. Guitar chords for first chorus from Ann Beardsley, Camp o' the Hills (Mich GS), 1963-1970; Camp Ken-Jockety (Ohio GS), 1976. Guitar chords for first verse from Clarena Snyder, Great Trails Camp (Ohio GS), 1963, 1965, 1967-1968. Guitar chords for second verse from Shirley Ieraci (Ohio

GS), 1970s. Guitar chords for third verse from University Settlement Work Camp (NY agency coed).

C. Kum (G) baya, my Lord, Kum (C) baya (G)
Kumbaya, my Lord, Kum (C) baya (D)
Kum (G) baya, my Lord (G7), Kum (C) baya (B7)
Oh (C), Lord, Kumba (D) ya (G)

1. Some (D) one's prayin' Lord, Kum (G) baya (D)
Some (F#m) one's praying Lord, Kum (G) baya (A)
Some (D) one's praying Lord, Kum (G) baya (D)
Oh (A), Lord (D), Kum (A) baya (D)

C. Kumbaya, etc.

2. Someone's (A) cryin' Lord, Kum (D7) baya (A)
Someone's cryin' Lord, Kum (D7) baya (E)
Someone's cryin' Lord, Kumbaya
Oh (A), Lord (D7), Kum (E) baya (A)

C. Kumbaya, etc.

3. Someone's sing (D) in' Lord, Kum (G) baya (D)
Someone's singin' Lord, Kumbaya (A7)
Someone's sing (D) in' Lord, Kum (G) baya (D)
Oh (G) Lord (D), Kum (A7) baya (D)

C. Kumbaya, etc.

PHOTOGRAPHS

Camping through Time

Camping through Time

In the early years, large tents were used. When cabins were built, tents were elevated to prestige locations for older campers.

Albert Brown (above) with boys from Jewish Orphan Home at Cleveland, Ohio's Wise, 1924. He published an early version of "Lollypop."

Kitanniwa at Clear Lake site. Girls are wearing middies and bloomers, with long hair.

In Town

Above: Friendly Acres ceremonial fire, 1920s, probably a regional meeting in Battle Creek; group behind the fire has banner for Detroit YWCA. They are wearing middies, some with knee socks, and most with long hair.

Below: Lucille Parker Munk with her Lakeview, Michigan, Camp Fire Girls group, 1929. They are wearing middies with bobbed hair.

In Lodges

Above: Kitanniwa in the original lodge at Clear Lake, 1920s. Girls are wearing middies with long hair. Wooden walls amplified sound.

Below: Kitanniwa in lodge built by Kellogg Foundation, Clear Lake, middle 1930s. Only a few are wearing middies with narrower ties. Many are in slacks or shorts with cropped hair.

CAMP
KITANNIWA
CAMP FIRE GIRLS

Outdoors

Above: Leona Holbrook, Utah, early 1930s. She introduced "Lemmi Sticks."

Top right: Kitanniwa overnight at High Banks Creek, 1956.

Gene Clough at Wintaka, California Camp Fire Girls camp in the San Bernardino mountains, 1969.

Above second left: Marie Gaudette with Girl Scout leaders at Edith Macy, the GS conference center in New York, early 1960s. She wrote "God Has Created a New Day."

Below third left: Patricia Ann Hall, Celio overnight at Redwood Park, 1959. The California Camp Fire Girls are wearing pedal pushers without socks.

Rituals

Right: Lucille Parker Munk wearing the ceremonial gown used in early years, 1950s.

Top: Camp Fire Girls grand council fire at Victory Park band shell, Albion, Michigan, 1958. She is standing in center. Smoke from log cabin fire. Most are wearing navy felt boleros and red scarves.

Bottom: Flag ceremony, Tanawida, the Michigan Camp Fire Girls day camp she directed, 1959.

Routines

Above: Folk dancing at Sebago-Wohelo, Maine private girls' camp, long hair, middies and bloomers, circa 1915.

Below: Rebecca Quinlan at Glen, Ohio Camp Fire Girls camp, short hair and pedal pushers, 1962.

Singing

He Bani Gani Camp Fire group at Maryland Folklife Festival, 1976.
At left, Leah Culp and Nancy Horner. One picture, divided in half,
with some girls doing one gesture and the others a different one.
They are wearing navy shorts, white tops, CFG ties, and knee socks;
a few at right have navy boleros.

SECTION II

Age Group Influences on Repertoire

Age Group Influences on Repertoire

Repertoires exist for both individuals and communities. Each singer, each camper has a body of material he or she believes apropos for a given situation. Even young children make distinctions between songs they know from school, church, and summer camp. A camp's repertoire is a shared agreement among campers, counselors, and administrators that certain ones belong and others do not.

Linda Johnson says, at Hitaga (Iowa CFG) from the middle 1950s through the late 1960s, "if they teach it at unit sing, the kids have to learn it, but doesn't mean they have to sing it in the dining room, and so if the song never gets sung" it disappears. Sally Ann Brockley Parr remembers, at Teedy-Usk-Ung (Penna girls) in the 1950s:

> Part of it was we had a counselor who was in charge of leading songs, like in the dining hall, at camp fires, at family council in the morning, and I think a lot of depended on the songs she liked. If she didn't happen to like the songs, or if she wasn't an old camper, which happened once or twice, then the songs kinda faded out.

Song Types

Most camps recognize the three general groups I call fun, pretty, and other. The last includes all those genres required by camp programs that are not necessarily unique, like graces, patriotic songs for flag ceremonies, and hymns sung in worship services.

Mariana Palmer (Penna YMCA girls) divides the others into quiet and active. Marilyn Dulmatch has an old song list from Tannadoonah (Ind CFG) that used peppy and lively songs, and quiet songs. Kirby

(Wash CFG), Kushtaka (Alaska CFG), Mawavi (DC CF), and Wakoma (Wash CFG) all have used the phrase quiet songs. Vivian Sexton (Tex CFG) calls them lovely.

Shawnee (Mo CFG) has two song books, one labeled Fun Songs, the other Songs. Fun songs is used by Kushtaka (Alaska CFG), Mawavi (DC CFG), and Watervliet (Mich girls). Kirby (Wash CFG) and Watanopa (Mont CFG) prefer pep songs. General is the designation used by Merrowvista (NH P sep) and Ohiyesa (Mich YMCA coed). Kent Burdair Hartung (Iowa YMCA boys) calls his songs fun and cheer or serious. Ones Seth Clay (Mich P coed) labels fun were identified as jolly in the early 1950s by Manhattan's Troop 582 (NY BSA).

Some use terms that identify when songs are sung. Jolene Robinson Johnson (Wash CFG) uses the labels corny songs and evening songs. Zanika Lache (Wash CFG) names them day and evening. Linda Johnson (Iowa CFG) marks songs in her personal collection with an "S" for serenade. Watanopa (Minn CFG) called the latter twilight songs in its booklet from the 1940s.

Others classify songs by the places where they are sung. Vicki Owens says, at King's Lake (Wash GS), "We have two types of songs - 'dining hall songs' (usually rowdy, gestures at times) and 'camp fire songs' - usually mellower with guitar - more modern folk sophisticated." Skylark Ranch (Calif GS) uses those same terms.

Naomi Feldman[§] and Mary Rogers were told, in some Texas Girl Scout camps, the term singing log referred to organized sings held with people sitting on large logs, and to the songs used at the time. Carol Ann Engle says Cherith (NY P girls) calls one group, bridge songs.

Childhood Developmental Changes

Differences in function, time and location, implicit in repertoire labels, suggest things a young camper remembers differ from those an older camper recalls. Even more, the ones an individual appreciates may change every summer.

When children first entered elementary school, several years before they went to camp, Jean Piaget observed much of their conversation was not directed at exchanging information or obtaining a result. It was verbalization, done "for the pleasure of talking, with no thought of talking to anyone."[467:31] When six-year-old boys were working on tasks, they would each be chattering in what he termed a collective monologue. Such habits persisted among slightly older children who already were deploying socialized language.

In the next year, that is by second grade, Robert Petzold found 85% of children he studied could carry a tune. An ability "to maintain a steady beat does not change significantly once the child has completed the second grade."[464:526-527]

Until this time, children saw reality as extensions of themselves. The transition to socialized speech involved developing an awareness of materiality. This began to occur, according to Piaget, around the age of seven or eight, the age of young Blue Birds. He related this to what he called the recognition of the conservation of matter. Such reversibility involved the realization a box remained the same box when it was tipped or moved. This intellectual development took time, as seen in the ways children grasped different aspects of arithmetic.

Marilyn Pflederer* believed this mental development was essential for children to move from experiments with rhythm and tone to a recognition of rhythmic patterns of tones called melodies. Third-grade students, normally eight-years-old, usually could recognize a tune when it underwent some variations in form, like changing tempos. They could not perceive others, like changes in key.

Both she and Petzold found second graders would pay more attention to rhythm than to melody, in situations where the two were tested together. The concept of harmony was difficult to grasp.

Later Childhood Development

In the 1930s, Arnold Gesell began a longitudinal study of children's growth through annual physical examinations, and interviews with them and their parents. He and his colleague, Francis Ilg, found children reached a developmental plateau around age ten. The rate of physical change stabilized. They consolidated advances they had made since the last plateau at age five.[343:212] At this time, just after Blue Birds had flown up to become Camp Fire Girls, they loved to memorize.[343:39, 61] Campers mastered the fun song repertoire.

When eleven-year-old children returned to camp, they were bored if everything was familiar. At Kitanniwa, which offered the same elective programs every year, girls already had participated in their first choice. Now, they either repeated it, or settled for second. In school in the 1950s, before the movement to convert junior highs into middle schools, they were the biggest kids, the natural leaders. Kitanniwa submerged them into the general group, expected them to remain happy with repetition.

They did not return. Kitanniwa had four cabins for young Blue Birds, four for ten-year-olds, four for eleven-year-olds, and three for twelve- and thirteen-year-olds combined. Some drop in participation, between the second and third years in Camp Fire, could be attributed to the movement of girls to junior high schools. My home town certainly provided less organizational support. However, if children were interested, they did not let mere administrative inertia prevent them from doing something. The population decline reflected an institutional failure to appreciate fine gradations of maturation in campers.

The developmental plateau preceded a movement toward more abstract cognitive patterns around the age of eleven or twelve. Among other things, this brought an improved ability to listen. Many music educators considered this fundamental to the ability to sing well.[341:89-90] Until this time, sing periods essentially functioned as collective monologues that allowed each child to sing for his or her own reasons. Around age twelve, the Gesell Institute found, he or she "especially enjoys singing in harmony."[344:133]

Several times when I visited camps, youngsters asked to hear themselves on my tape recorder. Elementary-school-aged children wanted to sing along. If others in the group wanted to listen, they lost interest, began talking, or wandered away. Girls around age eleven or twelve and older were the ones who listened critically.

Adolescent Vocal Changes

During adolescence, girls' vocal cords become thicker and their voices fuller and richer in tone. Boys' vocal cords lengthen. Their voices become deeper.[438:31] During the period when muscles associated with the larynx membranes are acclimating, they cannot always control their voices. This change makes some self-conscious, and less likely to follow the transition to a pretty song repertoire and harmony singing.

A possible disillusion with singing in adolescence has led some music educators to stress the needs of boys over those of girls in picking school repertoire. In 1963, Robert Nye was recommending teachers begin favoring boys' preferences in fourth grade.[448:29]

Experimentation

Differences between fun and pretty songs are not simply ones of age-group related content. One allows children to assess their developing linguistic skills at both mental and physical levels. The other allows adolescents to test their developing listening and sound production abilities.

Experimentation never occurs in a vacuum. Within a society, peers and adults respond to individuals' essays with encouragement, if a skill is desired, or criticism, when it is not. This creates conflicts for people caught between demands of the body and those of the culture. They do not yet have sufficient skill to meet external demands. Activities they enjoy or need to practice may be prohibited.

The young require opportunities to express frustration and structured occasions to do the forbidden. Children's folklore often serves as a medium through which they can ameliorate these conflicts.

The fact older campers and staff sing harmony does not mean such singing should be restricted to times they sing by themselves. Younger campers need exposure to accrue an aesthetic kinship for sounds. In the shared singing periods, junior high or middle school-aged campers absorb the mechanics necessary to gain what Carl Seashore* called cognitive musical maturity.

In Texas, a former Girl Scout counselor told Naomi Feldman[S] and Mary Rogers:

> At Robinwood (Tex GS), since we only had the little kids, we had to stick straight with nonsense and happy fast songs cause slow songs they never could sing well enough that they thought they were pretty and wanted to sing 'em. But at Arnold (Tex GS), the little kids got to hear the older kids so they liked some of the songs that were beyond the Robinwood kids even though they were the same age.

In Michigan, Gary Flegal recalls, at the Van Buren Youth Camp (Mich agency coed), "The harmony singing that I remember the most would be at camp fire when the staff would be standing together and you'd hear the staff doing harmony and that was always, almost an aweing kind of thing on like 'Kumbaya' (90) and 'Thinta' (1), to make you almost not want to sing, just to stand and listen to the staff sing. And now that I'm on the staff, I kinda appreciate that because I like to sing the harmony parts."

His photograph appears in "Staff."

Commercial Music

Camp song repertoires become middens for commercial music. Songs introduced by older campers are absorbed by younger ones who may remember them differently. The sifting of the repertoire by each group reflects their age-defined interests. Over time, bits that have become meaningless are lost and others are burnished.

Mason's singing schools coincided with society shaking off the fetters of Puritan theology. Even though he published sacred texts, he secularized their tunes. His first collection appeared in 1822 during the administration of James Monroe, the last of the presidents who wrote the constitution. Andrew Jackson's rise in the 1820s marked the transfer of power from Virginia and Boston to growing population centers in Ohio, Kentucky, and Tennessee.

Congress's 1820 Missouri Compromise redefined territorial limits for slavery. In 1828, the year Jackson was elected president, New York state abolished slavery. The next year, George Washington Dixon (1801-1860) darkened his face with burnt cork to sing "Coal Black Rose." His working-class audience in southern Manhattan competed with freedmen for low-paying jobs. In 1830, a dancer, Thomas Dartmouth Rice (1808-1860), created Jim Crow. Dixon began singing "Zip Coon" in 1834. His stereotype of the urban dandy was based on the freedman. Dixon's rural rube was based on the plantation slave.[439]

Neither was flattering to Blacks. Although dancing or singing with a darkened face may have had roots in the dancing fools of the morris dances and other English mumming traditions, the meaning changed when Rice made a virtue of impersonating Black accents and gestures. The new personas provided theatrical subterfuges for members of the audience who had been raised in the country, perhaps in New England or New York, the British Isles or some German-speaking state. Many had made the mistakes of both characters in becoming urban working men. They needed ways to laugh at themselves without retribution.

Formal minstrel shows began in 1843 when four men, who previously had worked in teams, joined in a thematic variety program. The Virginia Minstrels sat in a semicircle that dramatized Jacksonian egalitarianism. Imitators followed with a dominant ringmaster or interlocutor, who called upon men to dance or sing. They swapped jokes with the men playing rhythm instruments on the ends, Bones and Tambo (short for tambourine).

Edwin Pearce Christy and Dan Bryant led the most famous companies. In 1850, Christy hired Stephen Foster as his songwriter. Bryant employed the creative force behind the Virginia Minstrels, Daniel Emmett, as an entertainer and songwriter in 1857.

The Civil War curtailed movements of large entertainment groups. Postbellum revulsion against the carnage consigned many familiar tunes to oblivion. College song books preserved the most popular. During this period, Chicago emerged as a second center for music publishing. Some songs that survived in the camp repertoire were written by men when they were the age of students.

When Reconstruction ended in 1877, continental European immigrants were flooding New York. Vaudeville developed. In the South, Jim Crow became the code word for new segregation laws. Blackface humor no longer was broad, but aggressive and focused on its victims. Songs were filled with derogatory references to chicken-stealing, watermelon-loving coons.

Individual blackface acts appeared on urban stages. Elsewhere, minstrel troupes toured smaller cities and frontier boom towns. Individual performers, who were not hired by touring groups, often worked for circuses. Musicians, who before had been soloists doing comic material, were demoted to clowns. Men like Grandpa Jones inherited this expectation. One of the most famous songs from the period, "Oh, Them Golden Slippers" (3), was written in 1879 by a Black composer, James Alan Bland.

World War I coincided with major social changes amplified by the new cinema. Radio broadcast ragtime and other forms of Black-inflected music. Dance bands dominated the airwaves. Musical revues continued on Broadway, but narrative musicals began evolving from European operettas. Overt sentimentality became an embarrassment, which only could be maintained by donning blackface. Al Jolson was the most famous performer who channeled emotions through a distant other. He was born Asa Yoelson in modern-day Lithuania, the son of a rabbi and cantor.

Mechanical reproduction technologies initially created a national audience. Then, in the middle 1920s, recording companies discovered small markets for specialized forms of music they sold to Southern whites as hillbilly and to Blacks as race records. Some companies began marketing "coon" songs made by artists who exaggerated negative stereotypes.

A few performers, like Arthur Collins* (1864-1933), treated themselves and their material with dignity. The baritone was raised a Quaker in Philadelphia. He spent his youth in the clamming town of Barnegat, New Jersey.

Older traditions never died. Minstrel skits were a staple for camp evening programs until World War II. Then, material based on Broadway and television shows became more important. Songs persisted in camp repertoires, stripped of their racial connotations, at least in the North, until people became more conscious of words in the 1960s.

Major cultural changes leave people puzzled by their pasts. They discover songs they enjoyed as children were not as innocent as they seemed. After World War II, some who remembered the songs of the Wandervogel attempted to extricate their musical memories from the Nazis. Since the Civil Rights struggles, others have been reworking minstrel and coon material to salvage the entertaining parts without the racist trappings.

Folklore, like any art that survives the bounds of culture, undergoes this process. If some textual motif or melody persists, it may reflect more about what it is to be human than what it is to be a part of history.

Précis

KOOKABURRA looks at the humor that occurs when individuals test the limits of their bodies and their culture. It borrows ideas developed by Sigmund Freud* in *Wit and Its Relation to the Unconscious*. PEP and the ESKIMO HUNT look at fun songs as corroborations of language acquisition. PEP focuses on formal training from schools.

ESKIMO examines the underlying elements of speech analyzed by Roman Jakobson.* AN AUSTRIAN looks at the sources for fun song tunes. ASH GROVE (harmony) begins a discussion of musical skills that is continued in ROSE (melody) and BOATMEN (rhythm).

Each chapter contains a description of Kitanniwa's repertoire, as distinct from the general one. In some cases, the discussion concentrates on the songs selected for case studies. Others focus primarily on music of the 1950s. Still others compare the 1950s with 1974 and with what went before.

Kookaburra: Humor

Fun song topics are as varied as camp life, limited only by the experiences and imagination of children. However, lyric content does not always explain their popularity. Some are enjoyed for their gestures. Others are preferred because they treat language or music playfully, utilize favored forms of repetition, or tell stories. A few are remembered because they have been banned or deal with taboo topics.

Nonsense

Children favor some for no reason other than they are amusing. Kitty Smith, who has worked with Blue Birds at Kitanniwa, says, "The more nonsensical they are, the better they like them."

Humor in these little songs, often just one or two verses, employs a variety of comic devices. "When Sammy put the paper on the wall" (12), the paste flew, so "like birds of a feather we all stick together," relies on exaggeration in the tall-tale tradition. Cohila (Calif CFG) and Leah Jean Ramsey (Tex CFG) substitute "father" as the subject. Niwana (Wash CFG) has a second verse.

This sort of humor has a special appeal to the eleven-year-old who "likes slapstick humor, especially when things are so impossible they couldn't be true."[344:87] The improbable occurs in "Autumn to May" (8). In "Tangaleo" (5), a donkey "eats with a knife and fork."

Non sequiturs, seemingly irrelevant details, drive "I've Got the Left Hind Foot of a Rabbit" (8), "Oyster Stew" (12), and "Sarah the Whale" (19). Series of non sequiturs dominate the "Horses Run Around" (10), "The Billboard Song" (17), and the "Lunatic's Lullaby" (8). The last three vary from camp to camp, and from season to season, no doubt, because no internal logic freezes sequences.

"Horses" is sung as "A Boy's Best Friend Is His Mother" in some camps. "Lunatic" sometimes is known as "Jeep" or the "Crazy Song."

"A Jogging Along" (14) contrasts statements with their negation, like "a coach and six horses drawn by an old mare." Similar oppositions occur in the Brush Ranch (NM coed) version of "Billy Boy" (11), according to Mary Barnes. Folklorists Iona and Peter Opie cataloged these comic devices, which rely on the "juxtaposition of incongruities," as forms of "tangle talk."[451:24]

Puns

Humor in some fun songs comes from treating the familiar from a new or unexpected angle. Puns are the most common source in camps. They involve the "humorous use of a word involving two interpretations of the meaning."[241] The Opies noted, the "pun is a common ingredient of juvenile jokelore."[451:29] The Gesell Institute found it to be especially popular with ten-, eleven-, and twelve-year-olds.[344:52, 87, 123]

In a way, these are verbal variations on the mathematical realization of the conservation of matter. Children test how far they can extend words before they metamorphose.

Puns are found in "Dewy was the grass on the morn in May / Dewey was the admiral at Manila Bay" (13). "To Ope Their Trunks" (15) exploits two meanings for trunk. Shawnee's (Mo CFG) songbook editor transcribed "they leaf them out" for "leave." Herman's Hermits recorded "I'm Henry the Eighth" (6).

Riddles

Some fun songs use riddling phrases to present the familiar in an unexpected way. In a true riddle, an "enigmatic question in the form of a description whose referent must be guessed"[236] is posed by one person to another. In camp songs, where no dichotomy exists between the examiner and the diviner, the solution may be incorporated into the text.

One song describes "a little pussy / Whose coat was silver gray" with the contradiction, "She'll always be a pussy / She'll never be a cat." This could fit Archer Taylor's* second category of riddles, the ones that describe the concealed object through a comparison with an animal. Instead, the last line reveals, "she's a pussy willow" (8).

Riddling questions, whose solutions cannot be inferred from the questions themselves,[279:52] are found in "I Gave My Love a Cherry" (24). It uses puzzles in the verses, which, in turn, are a riddle about the order of courtship.

Conundrums usually take the form of a question whose answer involves "a play on words, or a pun (some of them quite terrible!), and the combination of far-fetched and unrelated ideas."[319:245] In the Wampatuck (Mass P girls) version of "I Had a Little Chicken Who Wouldn't Lay an Egg" (12), a rooster mates with a fruit tree to produce an eggplant. If it were a conundrum, it would be "what happens if you cross a chicken with a fruit tree?" Other verses have the rooster mate with a cow for eggnog, a hound dog for poached eggs, a gum machine for Chiclets, and a woman for an egghead. In a similar vein, the question, "what happens if a 'Queer Cow' (4) drinks from a frozen stream?" is answered, "it gives ice cream."

A riddling impulse is found in the "Thousand Legged Worm" (6), which emphasizes the defining characteristic one would use to construct a riddle: the missing leg. The "Doughnut" (12) and the "Prune Song" (27) concentrate on defining traits of foods, holes and wrinkles.

Ritualized Problem Handling

Some fun songs provide ritualized ways of dealing with unpleasant aspects of camp life. Arthur Koestler calls them situations "which have become redundant, which cannot be consummated in any purposeful manner."[394:51] Insects, snakes and other "slimy" animals illustrate a redundant situation. People may dislike them, even fear them, but only the worst can be eliminated from the outdoors.

Insects were the central joke in two songs combined in the 1920s by the Brooklyn Scout camps (NY BSA). Their verse, "There Was a Little Skeeter" (7), also is known as "little chigger." They sang their chorus, "The Bugs They Go Wild over Me" (4), to "They Go Wild, Simply Wild over Me." Marion Harris recorded the original in 1917.

Bugs are itemized with flies, chiggers, and ticks in "There Ain't No Flies on Us" (4), and with spiders in "These Buggy Regions Are Absurd" (4). In the second, a camper claims, "I'd rather be an Eskimo" than "find long spiders in my sheet." Sally Ann Brockley Parr (Penna girls) learned "These Polar Regions Are Absurd."

Mosquitos are mentioned in Seabow's (Calif CFG) third and final verse to "Monkeys Have No Tails," and in a 1920s Brooklyn Scout camps (NY BSA) version of "It Ain't Gonna Rain No More" (4). Insects also have been introduced into the Kiloqua (Ohio CFG) version of "Camp Days" (8).

In a Minnesota girls' camp, "Good Morning All You Kamaji Girls" (9) has three lines:

> Ashes to ashes and dust to dust
> If the flies don't get you
> The skeeters must

Duncan Emrich collected it as an independent rhyme with mosquitoes and bedbugs.[319:150] *Paradology*[367] published the textual model in 1927. Its underlying melody is "Good Morning, Mr. Zip Zip Zip" (1). Loyaltown (NY J boys) sings the lyrics written in 1918 by an army song leader, Robert Lloyd.

Carol Shuster[S] collected a parody of the "Girl Scout Pep Song" (7) with the lines, "I is for insects" and "L is for letting mice into the house." In the late 1950s, Kitanniwa's senior unit still was singing "Little Brown Tents" (3). Girl Scouts had published the words in *The American Girl* in 1923. Sally Heath (Mich CFG) thinks the verses were:

> We love ants and we love sun
> Gee but we have lots of fun
>   . . .
> We love bugs and mice a few
> Mosquitoes and daddy long legs too
> Just pack our bags and have them sent
> COD to the little brown tents

She is not sure "if I have 'ants,' 'bugs,' and 'mice' in the right places - the ants in the first verse may be switched with the bugs in the second - but I'm pretty sure this is the way it was." Joseph Eastburn Winner wrote the tune, "Little Brown Jug" (3), in 1869. Sally's photograph appears in "Kitanniwa Staff, 1950s."

A paucity of songs dealing exclusively with insects should not obscure the widespread use of humor to deal with this redundancy. More important than insect songs are casual jokes among campers, along with fleeting references in camp skits, parodies, and local songs. It is the motif, the traditional way of treating the topic, that is folklore.

At Kitanniwa in 1974, young campers referred to one mosquito-infested, willow-lined path as "Bug Alley." Many campers call the powered soft drink "Bug Juice," especially when it is lime flavored. In the 1950s, even folk medicine existed. Returning campers let newcomers know calamine lotion relieved mosquito bites, but nail polish was required for chiggers.

Food

Food is another aspect of camp life over which people exercise little control. Young campers may struggle with eating something that was not cooked or served by a family member. Others may confront casseroles and other deracinated foods like rice pudding for the first time.

In the early years, when the idea of camping was diffusing from its first pioneers, a serviceable body of food lore already existed. After the Civil War, before fraternities built their houses and colleges countered with dormitories, many students lived in boarding houses. In the same years, single, male, urban workers, the ones who frequented vaudeville halls, often lived in rented housing where landlords kept costs as low as possible. Army rations were notorious through World War I. After that, they simply became monotonous and, possibly, poorly cooked.

The most enduring alimentary song begins, "At the boardinghouse where I lived / Everything was growing old / Long gray hairs were in the butter" (10). The most popular army songs are the "Quartermaster's Store" (11), with vermin in the flour, and "Today Is Monday" (15), with its recital of peculiar dishes.

A realization foods can be contaminated informs "Granny's in the Cellar" (5) and "Neath the Crust of the Old Apple Pie" (8). Rimrock (Wash YWCA) sang the second with, "It may be an old rusty nail / Or a piece of our pussy cat's tail."

Despite ritual criticisms of camp menus and a general awareness the cooks' day off means leftovers or cook outs, most camps treat their kitchen staffs with respect. Once a session, many sing "Cookie, Cookie" (30), followed by "We Want a Cook's Parade." Robyn Arthur Kerr (Calif CFG) remembers one camp would tease them by singing, "Monday we have fruit and Jell-O / Tuesday we have Jell-O and fruit."

On weekends, they celebrated with "Jell-O without fruit." The melody was "Reuben and Rachel" (4).

Roberta Tupper Latvala[S] was told, some Presbyterian camps in the 1940s would sing "The Boy Stood on the Burning Deck" with its "Hot Dog!" ending, or "rather it was howled for the benefit of the poor overworked cooks." The verse satirizes an 1826 poem by Felicia Dorothea Hemans about a boy who perished in the 1798 Battle of the Nile. Instead of jumping into the river, he died obediently waiting permission from his father to move.

Beyond concerns about food storage and preparation, which persist among adults in urban legends that plague fast-food restaurants, camp food songs suggest curiosity about origins leads to dismay. "Johnny Verbeck" (26), about a German sausage grinder who falls into his machine, is the most common. He has been called Johnny Rebeck, Danny LuBeck, Johnny Ribeck, Johnny Dobeck, Johnny Ruebeck, Dunderbeck, and Mr. John Rebeck. Reconnaissance remains unchanged.

Hints of cannibalism narrowly escaped in "Boarding House," "Burning Deck," and "Verbeck" betray a certain queasiness about anything one puts in one's mouth. For years, campers have been singing about getting sick after eating a "Baby Bumblebee" (19) and asking "Won't my mommy be proud of me?" Theresa Mary Rooney says, it was banned at a Girl Scout camp she attended. Katie Hickey[S] was told, in a neighboring camp in New Jersey, it was "one of the most popular songs at the camp, and the one most asked for during meal-time sing-a-longs. It was done with appropriate hand motions."

More recently, people have been singing "Nobody Likes Me" (7), so I'll eat worms. Peggy Hays[S] was told, at an Ohio coed camp, "This was the theme song of the younger campers reflecting the undesirability of being the youngest. Sung usually in the dining hall and often led by several campers. Often accompanied by hand gestures indicating the various activities described in the verses." Two women reported its banishment.

Mocking Songs

Not all songs dealing with unpleasant aspects of camp life spring from the need to deal directly, albeit symbolically, with persistent, insoluble problems. In some instances, the source of difficulty may be vague to campers themselves. This produces humor at least once removed from the source of tension.

Jan Williky Boss calls them "mocking songs." She says, they were "the tradition" at Cedar Lake (NJ J coed). They would sing when anything went wrong, like a bad meal, because they liked the camp. It was a form of teasing to express an affection that, in other camps, would have infused the sentimental, pretty songs scorned by Jan's group.

Affectionate criticism permeates a 1957 Hitaga (Iowa CFG) song written by three counselors, Skip Johnson, Patt Kennan, and Freckles Workman:

> I never cared much for little gray mice
> I never thought bugs were very nice
>
> . . .
> I never went out for overnights
> With all those mosquito bites

While the words sound much like other insect lyrics, this one dissects complex emotions provoked by leaving camp after a summer together. The original song, "I'm Beginning To See the Light," was composed in 1944 by Duke Ellington, Harry James, Johnny Hodges, and Don George.

Tawakani (Ida CFG) has a teasing song to Bob Hope's 1938 theme that begins, "Thanks for the memories of cocoa on the table, of oatmeal on the floor." The best-known mocking song in the general repertoire is "Friends, Friends, We Will Always Be" (13).

Naughtiness

Another form of humorous mocking exaggerates one's own naughtiness. This was a more common motif in the early years of camping when physical activities for girls were restricted to a progressive minority. Tans and freckles were used in local camp songs as symbols of a new freedom. Middies, bloomers, even pockets were considered daring innovations, stressed in novels like Jane L. Stewart's *The Camp Fire Girls at the Seashore* of 1914. In a Tanadoona (Minn CFG) song, written to Charles Carryl's "A Capital Ship" (9), the girls "put the bloomers on and middies don / And live in a flapping tent."

Girls, dressed in bloomers and middies, posed in front of their tents in the Kitanniwa photograph reproduced in "Camping through Time."

Jeans and camp uniforms, especially knee socks, still are ridiculed. Vicki Owens learned "Black socks they never grow dirty" (8) in elementary school. The parody of "White Wings" (36) acquires special meaning when Adahi (Penna CFG) sings "Blue Jeans." In Girl Scout camps, Becky Colwell Deatherage (NY GS) has sung "Green Socks." Betsy Wolverton (Ohio GS) knows "Greenies." In a North Carolina camp, the girls sing, "You can tell a Skyland camper if her socks are hanging down."

This mocking, affectionate attitude toward clothing and one's own daring in circumventing rules of proper dress persists in humorous memorats. "Narratives of actual personal happenings"[308:220] ossify when people reminisce. Joyce Gregg Stoppenhagen remembers in 1959, "The last summer I was at Kitanniwa, I took a pair of Levis, you know. I wore them for cookouts and overnights and hikes. I wouldn't wash them. I took them home and my mother looked at me like this."

Some songs insinuate a contrarian familiarity with underwear and nudity. In "I Wear My Pink Pajamas" (20), the narrator celebrates the times when "I hop right in between the sheets with nothing on at all." "I've lost my underwear / I don't care / I'll go bare" (16) is treated autonomously and as the chorus to "Once I Went in Swimming" (7).

Unmentionables are the sole subject of "Underwear, under-wear / How I itch in my woolly underwear" (1), collected by Sally Briggs[§] from another Cedar Lake (NJ J coed) camper. Lyrics like "Skinny dipping time in the river" (1) covet nudity. Ann Beardsley remembers singing it to "Hog Calling Time in Nebraska." In counselors' lounges, one hears talk, often rueful, about swimming bare on weekends between sessions.

Socks

Kitanniwa, like most camps, had a rule girls must wear socks everywhere, unless they were going to and from the swim area. Young campers never questioned such orders, probably took them as part of the etiquette of the exotic. Many still believed the place with the strange night sounds was an alien environment, where the dangers were not yet sussed.

Warnings vary by climate. Young women in California said, they always were told to turn their shoes upside down on overnights, so scorpions would not nest. We were given the same instructions, but the reason was to prevent dew from soaking them. I always assumed we wore socks to prevent scratches from buried twigs. Patricia Ann Hall thinks at Celio (Calif CFG) it was to "prevent blisters and foot infections."

Eleven-year-old girls at Kitanniwa felt confident they understood the dangers of their environment. They had been there several summers, and never seen a wild animal. They knew the paths were safe, and unexplored areas were not. They believed they had learned enough to judge when they should or should not protect their ankles. Whenever they asserted their rights by rejecting their socks, they were sent to their cabins to change, even when it meant they would be late for a meal. Another camp has banned the chant, "Karen ain't wearing no socks, a ding dong!"

Counselors are more cavalier about danger. They have left their high school wombs for college campuses where only the adaptable do well. It is not that dangers do not exist, but they know they cannot let fear inhibit them. In the photographs in "Outdoors" and "Coming of Age," they are the ones who are not wearing socks on out-of-camp overnights.

Counselors, of course, can be wrong. Paul Chitwood remembers when a young man at a Texas Presbyterian camp wore flip-flops to the wash house, and something brushed against his ankle. The director warned, he had startled a coral snake. The shy, but poisonous, animals like wet places.

Male Variations

Naughtiness is not the word boys use to describe the pride they take in their own daring, but the impulse is the same. While girls in the early years of camping considered their clothing to be remarkable, boys felt the same about voluntarily rising in the morning. The secret pride was subverted into its opposite when they sang Irving Berlin's "Someday I'm Going To Murder the Bugler" (8). Boy Scouts still were endorsing the World War I sentiment in their 1970 songster.[*] "Yawning in the Morning" (13) is sung to "Roaming in the Gloaming," introduced in 1911 by Harry Lauder.

Some "aren't I awful/wonderful" songs use the imagery of madness, like the lines "I'm a nut, I'm a pest" from "I'm Wild about Horns" (9). "I'm a nut" from "I'm a Little Acorn Brown" sometimes is known as "I'm a Prairie Flower." The first was introduced in a 1929 film, *A Ziegfeld Midnight Frolic*, as "Eddy Cantor's Automobile Horn Song."

Some camps banned "They're Coming To Take Me Away" (2) for crossing an invisible line. Jerry Samuels recorded the spoof in 1966, using the name Napoleon XIV. Wohelo (RI CFG) has changed "Boom, boom ain't it great to be crazy" (33) to "camping." "I'm a Juvenile Delinquent" (4) is sung to "Yankee Doodle" (6).

Private Repertoire

A camp's repertoire is defined as much by what is excluded, as by what is included. Almost everywhere, young campers sing gross-out songs and older campers or staff members tell dirty jokes, even though they do so knowing they are off limits. Indeed, that is often the reason they are indulged.

Young campers' repertoire of songs, like "Great big gobs of greasy grimy gopher guts" (4) and "The Hearse Song" (4), seems to be horizontal. That is, campers believe the lyrics are known, or potentially knowable, by any member of their peer group. Therefore, they are portable between similar contexts in camp and town.

Children usually commandeer them from one another. Monica Mahe Foster heard the second, which begins "The worms crawl in, the worms crawl out," at elementary school. Margaret Fox learned it from her Girl Scout troop. Gene Clough says, it was "popular among rowdy classmates about 5th grade or earlier." Although it may stretch back to the Crimean war, it probably entered the naughty repertoire when men returned from the European battlefields of World War I.[338] Fowke, who was born in 1919, heard it in Saskatchewan summer camps in the 1930s.[331]

Older campers' sub rosa repertoire diffuses vertically. First, adolescents must see staff members as role models, rather than mere authority figures. This changed perception allows counselor traditions to filter through the age strata. A friend told Richard Fazenbaker,[§] one of the more shocking songs he learned at an Ohio Boy Scout camp was "educational to younger people."

Bawdy Songs

People's memories of camp bawdy songs differ by gender. Young men recollect lyrics that describe loose women, like "Bang Bang Lulu" (2), "Charlotte the Harlot" (1), and "Diamond Lil" (1). There are swagger songs like "Barnacle Bill" (3), but two young men told me their camps banned Chuck Berry's "My Ding-a-Ling," released in 1972. One said the Fugs were verboten. Among the songs on their 1966 album were "Dirty Old Man" and "Group Grope."

Women, before the sexual revolution, lived in a gray area in which the dangers of "yes" and "no" were understood clearly, but "maybe" was negotiable. In 1940, Perianne Stewart[S] was told, people in a northern Michigan Bible camp were exploring the dangers of "No" with "I Must Always Be Respected" (1). The narrator died an old maid.

Later in the decade, women were told, combining the "legs from some old table" (4) with "the arms from a chair" and the "neck from a bottle" would create something more affectionate than they. Both Phyllis Southman[S] and Heather MacPhail[S] collected versions.

Envy of "Yes," the fast woman, was the theme of "I Want To Be a Bad Girl" (1), collected in Illinois by Karin Lindquist[S] in 1950. Leah Culp and Jolene Robinson Johnson knew "I Wish I Was a Fascinating Lady" (2) in the 1970s.

Among the songs known by both young men and young women are "Coming down from Bangor" (4), "Oh, Sir Jasper" (2), "Roll Me over in the Clover" (8), and "Walking down Canal Street" (2). Several did mention the last two had been stopped, at least from dining halls. While both groups have made obvious parodies of "Do Your Ears Hang Low" (61), only women were specific to a female questioner when asked about banned songs in 1976.

Younger adolescents more often discover naughtiness in existing camp songs than learn, or even understand, truly risqué ones. Several have mentioned lewd versions of "Give Me Oil for My Lamp" (10). Carol Shuster[S] was told, young teens in an Ohio Girl Scout camp wanted to sing "Rocka My Soul" (31), because they were bemused by the "bosom of Abraham."

"Mandy was a little Bahama girl" (22) has been banned in at least nine Girl Scout camps. The ballad, related by a man, laments a woman who dies soon after the birth of their child. One woman told me the reason was, some "kids skipped the verse about getting married and sang it to their parents." They blamed the camp for the mischievousness of their daughters.

In Ohio, three young women told Carol Shuster[§] they were not allowed to sing it until evening. One said:

> They (counselors or leaders) told us not to sing it before six pm, or it would rain. She didn't really believe that, though; she said they made that story up because we always wanted to sing it and that they got sick of hearing it. [She] thought the song's popularity was due to its sentimental tone and the fact that our troop liked to harmonize on it.

Another said, she "wasn't sure before what time we weren't supposed to sing it; she thought maybe six pm. She thought that the reason we didn't sing it before six pm was that Mandy was Indian and it was sacrilegious or 'something like that'."

Rain

Threats of rain have been used as excuses to limit other songs. Catherine Mullikin remembers, at Ko-Ha-Me (Mo CFG), "Rise and Shine" was believed to bring rain, and "so we sang it only when we needed such rain." Jo Ann Coco attended a Girl Scout camp where it was banned "because of rain."

Julie Sherwood[§] talked to a former Girl Scout who told her, the "Johnny Appleseed Grace" (70):

> is not sung anymore because it always brings rain. She and all my other informants said that they don't really believe this, but they won't sing the grace. [She] tried to not justify using the grace by saying that someone at National (GSA) said it didn't really qualify as a grace and it wasn't supposed to be sung. She said she had never seen it written down, but someone from the council office had told her that it was to be phased out as a grace. This is why the jinx was attached to it, to help phase it out.

Elizabeth Mills Bachman (Ore girls) and Jo Ann Coco (GS) mentioned the same hexing powers of the song. Several others simply said it was discouraged, because it was not thought appropriate, or was being overused at the expense of other graces.

Rain is, of course, about the most disruptive event that can occur in a camp session. It is so bad, few fun songs dealing with the subject have entered tradition. Sally Briggs[5] was told Cedar Lake Camp (NJ J coed) has a mocking song:

> Camp, what's the matter with camp today
> La da ti da
> Camp, why must it rain every single day
> La da ti da

Most camps use the most recent commercial song, when the need arises to comment on conditions. In the 1940s, Tanadoona (Minn CFG) still was singing "April Showers." Al Jolson introduced it on Broadway in *Bombo* in 1921.

Counselors at Kitanniwa began singing "Raindrops Keep Falling on my Head" (7) when it rained during an overnight in 1974. Glen (Ohio CFG) started the 1969 lyrics when it sprinkled during a serenade. Ann Black remembers, the B. J. Thomas song had been used the previous week in a Glen council fire on the elements.

Bad weather more often figures in genuine superstitions and frequently repeated recollections or memorats, than in songs. At Kitanniwa, Kathleen Huggett Nye says, it "always rains every day the first week" of the season. Kitty Smith recalls the year:

> it rained, oh I think it must have rained most of the summer in '65. It was just terrible . . . In fact it got so bad, we even made a sun and hung it in the counselors' lounge.

Her photograph appears in "Kitanniwa, 1974."

Banned Songs

Many camp directors, who tolerated staff singing off-color material among themselves, faced greater problems in the late 1960s.

They always had been concerned about the use of alcohol. Among songs people remember were discouraged were "Little Gray Mouse" (5), sometimes brown mouse or green frog, and "What Do We Do with a Drunken Sailor" (8).

The chorus to the banned "Salvation Army Song" begins "Away with rum" (9). Vance Randolph[477] collected a fragment in 1941 from Rose O'Neill (1874-1944), a New York-based commercial artist known best for creating the Kewpie figure. Barbara Dane recorded the camp version in 1958. The title also has been used for "Nickel on the Drum" (1) and "Temperance Union" (2). The last begins, "We're coming our brave little band."

"Mountain Dew" (17), on the other hand, is accepted. Lisa Drumm[§] was told in one Ohio Camp Fire camp:

> Often an impromptu square dance starts in the center of the dining hall, and nearly everyone is stomping, clapping or shouting. It is usually sung with a heavy hillbilly accent, and slurred words which gives those singing it a chance to let loose and enjoy fractured English and a different style of music.

Marijuana became a greater threat than cigarettes, because people using matches in dry woodlands could be incapacitated. One undergraduate folklorist heard about an incident when a fire did start.

Two women told me Girl Scout camps banned "Puff the Magic Dragon" (29). One young man said, it "was taboo at Boy Scout camp for a while." One woman remembers when "Rocky Mountain High" (5) was not allowed. In the same years, Ira Sheldon Posen[*] heard "Marijuana Marijuana, LSD LSD" (1) sung to "Three Blind Mice" (14) in a Canadian coed camp. His photograph appears in "Singers."

Stereotypes

More recently, directors have been pressured to remove songs deemed disrespectful by other groups from their camps' repertoires. Songs containing racist and ethnic slurs were identified easily, as were songs that treated disabilities humorously. In the late 1940s, Phyllis Southman[§] collected a version of "On the Dummy Line" with the verse:

> Three little girls all dressed in brown
> Got on the train at Hillsdale town
> Said one to the other there are no seats
> [John Doe] got up and they all sat down

Hillsdale is a town in southern Michigan.

In the 1970s, one camp frowned on "Tall Girls, Short Girls, Fat and Thin" (9). Another stopped singing "My Hat Silk Hat" (39), because several staff members were "heavy set." One banned "Silk Hat" because girls knew "from friends" it was "offensive to Italians."

Theora Trapp[§] collected "Darkey Sunday School" (15) in 1953 from someone who had learned it at the Boy Scout Jamboree held on the Irvine Ranch in California. She also collected "Baptist Sunday School" from Kimball (Mich YMCA coed) in 1955. Vicki Owens now sings "Bible Sunday School." Seth Clay (Mich P coed) follows *Paradology*[367] to call it "Adam and the Gardener."

Editors of Seattle, Washington's Boy Scout song book let campers know the line in the chorus, "Please check your chewing gum and raisins at the door," once had been "shotguns and razors." Those who re-substitute the original words into "Camp Parsons' Sunday School" probably are thinking about life on the frontier, not stereotypes of ruffians common in the first part of the twentieth century.

Native Americans

Pejorative Native American content has been more difficult to eradicate. Many camps with team competitions divide into tribes, which are expected to create group songs and cheers. Most default to material they know from high school or college. These, in turn, borrowed traditions fabricated by groups like Manhattan Democrat's Tammany Society, and the Redman's Lodge, this country's oldest fraternal organization.

Some camps have replaced Indian names for their groups with less-value-laden terms. Kamaji (Minn girls) now has six tribes of the rainbow. Wyandot County, Ohio's 4-H Day Camp may not have improved matters in 1974 when it gave the young girls' groups the names of flowers and those of boys' the names of insects.

Many nonsense songs once were described as Native American. Irondale (Mo BSA) claimed "Kille Kille Wash Wash" (17) was Indian.

In 1929, Brooklyn Scout camps (NY BSA) titled it "Indian Medicine Man." Treasure Island (Penna BSA) called it the "Indian Love Song" in 1920.

As late as 1973, Sally Briggs[§] collected "Qui Quay Quonnie" (6) from a former Boy Scout who liked the song, "partly because the words were reputed to be secret, but also because of the strangeness of the syllables. He mentioned something about an Indian origin of the song, but could not translate it."

Authentic material rarely enters tradition. Sometimes, with songs like "Seeyahnah" (2), the music is too different from our African-spiced European style to be imitated easily. In other cases, like Evelyn Thompson Towle's arrangement of "God of the Mountains" (6), it has been altered too much to make it familiar.

Pow Wow

"Pow Wow" (32) represents the tortuous middle. Stereotypes, like "feathers and war paint" and "long nosed squaw," dominate. Wolahi (Calif CFG) has local verses about "red squaws, small and quaint / In our lipstick and face paint" who can fight with "pots and pans / Bobbie pins and rubber bands." Long Beach, California, Camp Fire Girls have five verses, instead of the usual three.

"Down among the dead men" is the most questionable phrase. Dead men is a slang term for bottles emptied of spirits. In 1898 it meant, "let me get so intoxicated as to slip from my chair, and lie under the table with the empty bottles."[272] It might once have been a deliberate reference to Natives' problems with alcohol. As a naive camper, I thought it referred to survivors of the nineteenth-century campaigns of removal and extermination.

The worst line occurs in the chorus where some word has become garbled. "Old dun cow" is substituted. In 1976, I asked if anyone knew what it should be. Most guessed some version of the bovine. Oweki (Mich CFG) did venture, "old know how." Kirby (Wash CFG) sings, "we are the men of the old dug out." I do not know whether that is a rationalization or the original, but it is something we never would have heard properly in the Midwest. The only Natives we knew used birchbark canoes.

It was not the only such song. "Come, Let's Play We're Indians" (5), with its pun "I will be chief because I'm braver than the rest," was sung in the past. Still, this is the one with the greatest appeal. It even was published by English Scouts.[118] Through the Rover Scouts, a program for young adults, it spread to Italy where it was used for an Indian-style dance in 1947.[122]

There was something about the phrase "we are the Red men tall and straight." It allowed young campers, maybe ten-year-olds, the chance to imagine, for a few seconds, another form of existence, before descending into the nonsense of "old dun cow." The attraction was so strong, the song would not wither away. Six told me camps they attended had to ban it as, to quote one, "OBJECTIONABLE." The camps were sponsored by Camp Fire, Girl Scouts, and public agencies.

Death

Some directors ban or discourage songs that focus on disagreeable aspects of death, like the "Hearse" (4), "Anne Boleyn" (3), and "Blood on the Saddle" (6). At the same time, they accept others that treat death with comic devices mentioned above like exaggeration, which make it seem impossible. The focus of "Alice" (14), "Andy Brown" (16), and "Plug 'ol" (2) is drowning. In "Georgie" (14) and "Belinda" (3), an individual is beheaded. In one version of "Mrs. O'Leary" (31), she jumps to her death. "Belinda" is sung to "Clementine" (23), who also drowned.

In "The Lady Who Swallowed a Fly" (12), a woman dies after eating things too big. An inversion of the inadvertent ingestion of unpleasant animal parts is found in "I'm Being Eaten by a Boa Constrictor" (17) and the "Lady and the Crocodile" (51). Burl Ives recorded the "Lady and the Fly," which was written in 1952 by Rose Bonne and Alan Mills. Shel Silverstein wrote and recorded "Boa Constrictor" in 1962. It soon was released by artists as diverse as the Brothers Four in 1963, Johnny Cash in 1964, and, in 1969, Peter, Paul and Mary.

Richard Fazenbaker[S] was told, a staff member at Butler (Ohio BSA) wrote, "I'm looking over my dead dog Rover" (4). It describes an animal dismembered by a lawn mower. He said, "The song is almost always sung at campfires, and is picked up rapidly by campers, who are often heard singing it throughout the week." It is known in other camps, but, obviously, the personalization added to its appeal. Its tune, "Four Leaf Clover" (7), was written in 1927 by Henry MacGregor Woods and Mort Dixon.

A concern with the disagreeable consequences of eating exists in songs that allude to the anal, rather than oral, needs of individuals. The English sparrow verse for "I Wish I Were" (17) has been barred in one camp, but embraced in others. A reduction of things to their least pleasant aspect, the remains, is found in songs like the sometimes-banned "Garbage Man" (1) and the "Sewer Song" (3). In California, some Camp Fire camps sing,

> Dry bones slippin' in the canyon
> Some of them bones are mine
> Dry bones in the canyon
> Some of them are mine
> Some of them are (name of unit to be dismissed)
> Some of them are mine

as a way to dismiss units from a meal in an orderly fashion.

"Fish and Chips" (40) may originally have been "don't put your dust in my dust pan." It now is sung dirt, junk or muck, and trash can or backyard. Dana Dawn Olmstead (Tex CFG) has sung "trash in my cabin," suggesting the kinds of threatened pranks that exist. Charles Richards says, Covenant Cove (Mich P coed) sings "muck in Elbow Lake." Carol Shuster[§] collected "don't barf in my barf pan." The variant developed when a group began to sing "in a rowdy style" and as the "group got more rowdy, acting like a bunch of drunks."

These themes recur in mocking songs where complaints camouflage affection. In "What Wampatuck Means to Me" (Mass P girls), the girls there the summer of 1974 were singing, "The King's Daughters, slop on the lawn / Dirty brown water, cleaning the john."

Violence

Other songs, which have made some directors uneasy, are those that superficially condone lawlessness. Some have rejected "Waltzing Matilda" (23) and "Desperado" (44) because they mention outlaws. Several have banned "Copenhagen will be taken in the morning" (3).

Such songs may provide the thrill of danger, without committing singers to action. Lawrence Becker[§] had a friend, who relished a song about an unrepentant murderer. The friend believed "Sammy Hall"

(1) had "been made up in this camp from an event that had happened thereabouts."

"Little Bunny Foo Foo" (22) has attracted the most negative attention in recent years, although the hunter in "Little Cabin in the Woods" (49) is not always welcomed. In the first a rabbit goes "hopping through the forest scooping up field mice and bashing them on the head." In a spoken interlude, a fairy godmother materializes, and warns the bunny to cease and desist. After the third time, she punishes him with the pun, "hare today, goon tomorrow." Ka-esta (Ore CFG) ends, "down came the fairy god mother and poof!"

Joann Brisler (Vt C girls) remembers it has been used for skits. Ann Beardsley knows "Fru Fru." In Louisiana, Debra Nails says Girl Scouts sing, "Little Clovis crayfish, backing through the bayou, picking up mosquitoes." He meets Big Mama LaFouche who threatens to "turn you into a bisque."

The household tales, or märchen, collected and edited by Jacob and Wilhelm Grimm between 1812 and 1857, dramatized a moral universe. The world might be murky, filled with unexpected challenges, but after three occurrences, evil was rebuked.

Children suspect the first, and hope for the second. The existence of a fairy godmother, who promises immediate retribution for disobedience, provides cover. A child can test cultural limits and experiment with the aggression of both the rabbit, who breaks rules, and the power of those who enforce them. Within the cloak of nonsense, knowingly assembled from shards of earlier childhood, the song is a rational exploration of probabilities.

A few camps have banned it, perhaps ones that sing only the verse and do not include the entire set of monologues. One has changed the offensive word to "kissing." The tune is often "Puffer Billies" (33).

Male Rebellion

In *Wit and Its Relation to the Unconscious*, Freud suggested young children enjoyed connecting "words without regard for their meaning in order to obtain pleasure from the rhyme and rhythm."[335:717] As children matured and absorbed rational thought patterns, he argued, "the child indulges in them fully conscious that they are nonsensical and derives pleasure from this stimulus [. . .] He now makes use of play in order to withdraw from the pressure of critical reason."[335:717]

Pressures for rationality become so much stronger for adolescents and college students, "the pleasure in 'freed nonsense' rarely dares manifest itself."[335:718] Thus, boys, who cannot admit they like the nonsense sounds of "Kille, Kille," could sing it because it was an Indian song. It was acceptable to sing such lyrics in a Boy Scout camp where Native Americans were esteemed for their bravery and wilderness survival skills.

When pressures for lucid thinking by the adult culture become so severe children cannot distance themselves from the more nonsensical songs, they may reject singing. The Gesell Institute observed rebellion by boys against "sissy songs" begins about age ten.[344:62] Freud suggested the inclination of "boys to act in a contradictory and inexpedient manner is a direct outcome of this pleasure in nonsense" that has been thwarted by "fears to utter nonsense."[335:718]

One director wrote me that, at her private coed camp, "our young boys love to sing for the most part and join in enthusiastically with the girls. Some of the older boys, however, feel that singing is 'beneath' them. They are quite a challenge."

Another, the director of a Camp Fire camp that was experimenting with a coed session, said boys initially resisted singing at meals. After counselors refused food if they did not participate, they slowly joined in. By the end of the session, she said, the boys were enjoying the sing periods.

When Kitanniwa experimented with a coed session in 1974, boys only grudgingly joined after meal sings the first two days. When the staff and other campers, who went on singing, ignored them, they began participating more willingly.

In the two cases, camp structure and staff attitudes provided recalcitrant boys with a distancing excuse: they made me do it! At the same time, they provided singing situations others, demonstrably, were enjoying.

Female Rebellion

In the same way boys' mocking songs take a double twist from those of girls by feigning a dislike for what they admire about themselves, the reaction of girls to the fun-song repertoire is parallax. One former Girl Scout counselor told Naomi Feldman[S] and Mary Rogers, at Robinwood (Tex GS), "Most of the songs we sang were

113

not adult, but children's songs. We only sang them in the role of song leaders."

The role of song leader can become a mechanism for preadolescent girls to maintain some ties with childhood while navigating their way into adulthood. A photograph of the He Bani Gani Camp Fire group (Md CFG) singing at the Maryland Folklife Festival in 1976 shows the oldest member standing next to the young assistant leader and apart from the rest of the group. From that position, she could both sing the gesture songs of the younger girls and establish her maturity.

When I was visiting Valley Mill (Md coed) in 1976, girls around age eleven wanted to lead a song during assembly. They were discouraged. Singing was led by counselors. Two weeks later, the camp owners sent them to the Maryland Folklife Festival. They conducted a spontaneous sing with nine- and ten-year-olds with no adult help. They had no program and floundered a little during the first song. They saw the problem, had a conference among themselves, and asserted control.

Kitanniwa Repertoire

Kitanniwa in the 1950s was too polite to sing exuberant songs that explored anxieties unique to children. Instead of a fantasy children's world perpetuated by older girls, the camp offered entrée into an idealized adult one. From the first evening, when they formally dressed for supper, girls were made aware they had entered an enchanted world of princesses only glimpsed in movies where everything was orderly, and everyone had good manners.

Negro spirituals were acceptable in the all-white camp. Songs of farmers and lower-class whites were not. In those years, that meant anything like "Johnny Verbeck" (26), with its allusions to German customs. "Mountain Dew" (17) carried too many associations with people who had moved north from Kentucky and Tennessee during World War II.

The only songs we sang we knew were Southern were "She'll Be Coming 'round the Mountain" (41) and "Down in the Valley" (33). They also were the only ones with titillating undertones. The first mentioned the food chain. The second used the word "jail."

Lady in the Wilderness was a fun game for the young, but stifling for girls reaching junior high-age who wanted something more than a cabin on a high hill overlooking the wash house. They were the ones who refused to wear socks. When morning sing became monotonous, some stopped attending.

While their reactions resembled those of boys the same age, I always suspected their boycotts were less rejections of childish music, as they were protests against being treated like youngsters. Girls in the senior unit and CITs were exempt from sitting on the hard, wooden floor waiting for others to learn what they already knew. Like the girls at Valley Mill and He Bani Gani, they wanted to be rewarded for having learned the repertoire, and be treated like veteran campers.

Case Study: Kookaburra

"Kookaburra" (85) is a round whose evolution illustrates the dynamics of fun song humor. It began as a single verse written in 1932 by a Melbourne, Australia, boarding-school music teacher. Two years later, Marion Sinclair submitted it to a local Girl Guides contest. Soon after, it was sung at a Jamboree. Sinclair was astonished by:

> the way in which it has gone round the world; but that is because of the international character of the Scout and Guide movements, for whom it was written - the Australian Girl Guides, to begin with, and then it got taken up at a Jamboree, and so "flew away" from its home country.[199]

Boy Scouts[†] published it in England in 1938. Tobitt[†] included the single verse in *Yours for a Song* in 1939.

The round was accepted immediately. Helen Merriam,[§] who lived in the area served by the Kitanniwa CFG council, collected it from a local summer camp in 1940. Phyllis Southman[§] heard it in Wisconsin the same year.

Sinclair (1896-1988) was educated at home where she took refuge in fairy tales and music. After training at Toorak College, she returned to teach and run its Girl Guide program. During World War II, she went to the YWCA where she worked with women in the military. In the middle 1950s, Sinclair worked for a women's rest home in Adelaide, and taught music in a local school.[202]

Explication

The original quatrain is a quasi-scientific description of an unknown animal in its natural habitat being provoked by the narrator to make a characteristic noise. Such actions are no different from those of people who try to make parrots talk or animals in the zoo acknowledge them.

While the verse is simple, it is filled with words that either are alien or used in strange ways. Children are forced to make sense of the familiar turned unfamiliar. The animal in question is a large carnivorous bird called a kookaburra or *Dacelo novaeguineae*. In the eastern third of Australia, it nests in trees or termite mounds.

Helen Merriam[S] called it a "Kuka **Bear**," suggesting it was a type of mammal. Phyllis Southman[S] learned it as "**Cuckoo**berry," making it a songbird. Marjorie Codd[S] collected a beast of burden called a "kucka**burro**" in 1952. In 1976, two Ohio camps recalled television characters drawn from *Yogi Bear* and *Kukla, Fran and Ollie*: Yakewi (Ohio CFG) called it "Cuckoo-**berra**" and Christopher (Ohio C coed) "**Kuka**berry." Seattle Boy Scouts (Wash BSA) sing about something more ferocious, a "Cooka **Bear**a."

Kookaburras originally preferred eucalyptus woodlands. The social animals have adapted to suburban life, and become familiar to most Australians. Eucalyptuses, commonly, are called gum trees. Sap, which collects on the bark, is referred to as gum drops. In this country, we generally associate eucalyptuses with the koala bear and New Zealand. We think of the gum tree as the sweet gum (*Liquidambar styraciflua*) found in the southeastern United States. The animal in the song neither is the expected koala nor is it lurking, in a Southern swamp, like Br'er Rabbit.

In Australia, the bush is a term for any area outside the center of settlement. In the early 1950s at Kitanniwa, some were singing "king of the bushes" instead of "king of the bush is." This transformed the unknown gum trees from empires into shrubs.

Textual Variation

Soon after the song was introduced in this country, new verses were added. June Walters[S] and Martha Jackson Stocker[S] collected the second verse about eating gumdrops in Michigan in 1945. One was from Metamora, the Pontiac Girl Scout camp; the other from Bay City. The verse used a pun on "gum tree" to assimilate foreign images into the familiar adult and older-camper stereotype that all children loved candy. It also changed a factual statement into the slapstick impossible-is-possible contradiction that appealed to eleven-year-olds.

Martha heard the third verse about counting monkeys in Bay City the same summer. The introduction of a simian converted the specifics of eastern Australia into the familiar, but exotic, milieu of jungle movies. On early 1950s Saturday morning television, *The Buster Brown Show* featured the adventures of "Gunga, the East India Boy."

On the surface, this was simply an opposition to the second verse. One made the unknown more familiar. The other made the alien even stranger. The association of monkeys and cuckoos with abnormal behavior introduced a different element. It queried the singer's rationality.

At Kitanniwa in the 1950s, some campers around age ten pointed to friends on the last line of the third verse and shouted "you," instead of "me." Altering pronouns afforded protection from the label. At the same time, when a girl pointed a finger at a friend, she expressed mocking affection, with no overt emotion. The variation also represented a newly acquired intellectual ability to reverse order, and allowed girls to violate societal strictures against finger pointing.

As suggested earlier, when the demands for rationality are greater than the capabilities of humor to cushion them, more extreme actions occur. Kotomi (Colo CFG) substitutes "pinching" (C-3). Muskegon, Michigan's public school camp (Mich agency coed) song book has "killing," a variant found in Oregon by the Knapps.[†] Neewahlu (Ida CFG) simply does not sing the verse.

Differences in responses to this verse are pronounced by gender. Of the 119 women who listed the verses they knew in 1976, nearly two-thirds mentioned this one. Less than a third of the 14 men recognized it.

More recently, some camps have added rhymes familiar from other songs or the playground. Neewahlu (Ida CFG) has one about Kookaburra breaking his knee (B-3). Kotomi (Colo CFG) has one about splinters in his tail (C-4). Another, about the bird sitting on a railroad track, includes an explicit reference to the messy origins of food:

around the bend came the five-fifteen
(Spoken) beep beep - peanut butter

This is a variant of the "peanut sat on a railroad track" verse. Manhattan's Troop 582 (NY BSA) has sung it with "Boom, Boom" (33), Loyaltown (NY J boys) with "It Ain't Gonna Rain No More" (4), and Killoqua (Wash CFG) with "Polly Wolly Doodle" (11). Fowke collected it from Vancouver, British Columbia, children in 1964,[331] and Brian Sutton-Smith[*] in New Zealand. All three added verses have an element of sublimated cruelty like that found in the "killing" verse.

Namanu (Ore CFG) and Becky Colwell Deatherage (NY GS) report the existence of another song, "Kookaburra Has No Work" (2). It has obvious affinities with this text, but a different form. Linda Forrest (born 1947), a music teacher in Putnam City, Oklahoma, released it through Lorenz Corporation. The company specialized in community songsters in the early twentieth century.

Music

Minor interval changes have been introduced into the tune, but the basic melodic pattern has remained constant. Susan Dunn[§] collected a version from the Franklin Settlement House camp (Mich agency) with a slightly altered end for the second tune line. One round group at the Wyandot County 4-H Day Camp[†] (Ohio 4-H) used a variant first line. Many treat the word "Kookaburra" with more emphatic enunciation than is found in the original.

With the addition of new verses, the singing style has been altered. It originally was a four-part round, but young girls at the Wyandot County 4-H Day Camp (Ohio 4-H) used three. Most use two.

More than 70% of those who responded to my questionnaire indicated they have sung it as a round. However, only 40% claim they sing it only as a round. The remaining 30% know it as a straight song.

Popularity

"Kookaburra" is known widely in camps. More than 80% of the people in all girls' camps knew the song. In the survey Midwestern states, more than 71% of the people in boys' camps recognized it and 68% in coed camps. For some reason, it is less known in coed and boys' camps elsewhere in the country. While it has a wide appeal to young campers, who like the sound of the word "kookaburra" and the puns, public-school use may influence its standing with older children.

Sinclair has had reports of its success in Europe, Africa, India, and Southeast Asia. The Australian delegation to a 1985 United Nations conference on women in Nairobi, Kenya, told her, they started the song when asked to contribute something Australian. "To their surprise the singing was taken up by scores of women." She mused, "dear Kookaburra. Nothing else I have written has the magic of those twenty-four small words."[201]

Version A

Text from Martha Jackson Stocker, learned in Bay City, Michigan, 1945; collected by Martha Jackson Stocker, Indiana University. Sung the same, except where indicated, in 1958 when she was a counselor at Camp Kitanniwa (Mich CFG); round. Her photograph appears in "Kitanniwa Staff, 1950s." Sinclair's appears in "Composers."

1. Kookaburra sits on the old gum tree,
   Merry, merry king of the bush is he;
   Laugh, Kookaburra, laugh, Kookaburra,
   Gay your life must be.

2. Kookaburra sits on the old gum tree,
   Eating all the gum drops he can see;
   Stop, Kookaburra, stop, Kookaburra,
   Leave some there for me.

3. Kookaburra sits on the old gum tree,
   Counting all the monkeys he can see;
   Stop, Kookaburra, stop, Kookaburra,
   That's not a monkey that's me.

Version B

Text from Camp Neewahlu (Ida CFG), 1970; variations from A in shared verses emphasized; not a round. Guitar chords from Shirley Ieraci (Ohio GS), 1970s.

1. Kook (A) aburra sits (D7) **in an** old (A) gum tree,
   Merry, merry king (D7) of the bush (A) is he.
   Laugh, kook (D7) aburra, laugh, (A) kookaburra,
   Gay your life (D7) must be (A).

2. Kookaburra sits **in an** old gum tree,
   Eating all the gumdrops he can see.
   Stop, kookaburra!   Stop, kookaburra!
   Leave some there for me!

3. Kookaburra sits in an old gum tree,
   He fell out and broke his knee.
   Poor kookaburra.   Poor kookaburra.
   Glad it wasn't me!

Version C

Text from Camp Kotomi (Colo CFG), 1971; variations from A in shared verses emphasized; round.

1. Kookaburra sits on **an** old gum tree.
   Merry, merry king of the bush is he.
   Laugh, Kookaburra, Laugh, Kookaburra.
   Gay your life must be. **Ha   Ha.**

2. Kookaburra sits on **an** old gum tree.
   Eating all the gum drops he can see.
   Stop, Kookaburra, Stop, Kookaburra.
   Please save some for me. **Yum, Yum**.

3. Kookaburra sits on **an** old gum tree
   Pinching all the monkeys he can see.
   Stop, Kookaburra, Stop, Kookaburra.
   That's not a monkey.   That's me. **Ouch!**

4. Kookaburra sits on an old wooden rail
   He got splinters in his tail
   Cry, Kookaburra, Cry, Kookaburra
   Sore your tail must be.

5. Kookaburra sits on a railroad track
   Along came a train and smashed him flat.
   Poor Kookaburra.   Poor Kookaburra.
   That's the end of that.

Pep: Language

Perfecting language continues after individuals have grasped the rudiments of speech. Each developmental stage brings anxieties about one's skills and hidden, often residual, desires to try culturally excluded alternatives. Lyrics manipulating language are varied. The youngest in camps are mastering pronunciation. Schools are introducing older campers to the complexities of poetic versification.

Onomatopoeia

Onomatopoeia, which occurs "when the sound of a word echoes or suggests the meaning of the word,"[253] grows from early attempts by infants and toddlers to speak. According to Gesell and Ilg, five-year-olds still enjoy identifying the "sounds that animals make" on the pages of "familiar books" when stories are read to them.[343:395] Its importance in fun songs is clear with "The Bee-i-e-i-e" (14). Impersonations are especially frequent in rounds and part songs, as well as in cumulative ones like "An Austrian" (34).

Although daily use of onomatopoeia for communication is restricted to the very young, its treatment becomes more sophisticated in fun songs enjoyed by successively older groups. "Gack goon went the little green frog" (21) becomes "gallump" at Cielo (Calif CFG), "gulk gulk" at Nathan Hale (Conn P coed), "yuk gooh" with Terri Lynn Hicks (Ohio CFG), "erah uh" with Dana Dawn Olmstead (Tex CFG), "blam-um" with Nancy Nelson (Iowa CFG), "barump" with Wesley Cox (NM P coed), and "ah hing" with Suzanne Beaudet (NH GS).

The quatrain repeats the first line three times, with variations from camp to camp in the frog's description. Anne Lutz heard a New

Jersey-New York version with the second line, "Gunk gunk said the Lady Froggie too." June Rushing Leibfarth[S] collected a second verse from Peach Creek (Tex GS), "Now you've heard folks go fidodiodio / But you never heard them go glink, glank, glunk."

Imitated Sounds

Machine guns are imitated in the version of "Swiss Navy" (16) collected by Katie Hickey[S] from Matollionequay (NJ YWCA), and in Kitanniwa's 1974 variant of "Junior Birdsmen" (30). Horns are mimicked in "I'm Wild about Horns" (9) and "Ding Ding Ding Here Comes My Wagon" (12). Carol Parsons Sievert remembers "Puffer Billies" (33) was:

> the first round every camper at Kitanniwa must learn and soon the "chug chug" and "toot toot" is heard all over camp. And why not? They are good sounds to make. It takes a lot of practice to get a good "chug" - it really a very breathy, slusky "chug." The "Toot" sound is accompanied by the action of pulling the cord that makes the whistle blow!

Other onomatopoetic sounds used in fun songs include sniffs, hums, and ohs. "Cocaine Bill" (3) was sung "have a (sniff) on me" in versions collected by Marcia Guilbert[S] from a 1941 Miniwanca (Mich P sep) camper, and by Neola Rae Anderson[S] from a former Black Hawk (Mich BSA) camper. A similar sound was used in a Kilowan (Ore CFG) version of "Camp Fire Girls Are (sniff) High Minded" (12) collected by Alexandra Prentiss.[S] Girls in a Texas Camp Fire camp have sung, "Come to Val Verde where the breezes blow, whoo!"

Eating sounds are popular, perhaps because they are something for which children are censured. "Plant a Watermelon" (24) has the second line, "And let the juice (sssup, sssup - sounds of slurping) run through." Frances Rigoni heard, "Put a watermelon rind upon my grave" at Cielo (Calif CFG). Phyllis Bonnie Newman knows "your grave" from Truda (Me girls). Frank Dumont and Richard P. Lilly wrote the original in 1910.

Charla Calderhead[S] was told, an Ohio church camp sang only one verse to "One Bottle of Pop" (40), "with a popping noise at the end."

This created a pun on a Midwestern term for carbonated soft drinks. People in the South say "coke." The East uses "soda." British Boy Scouts sing "one bottle of beer,"[118] which could refer, with deliberate ambiguity, to ginger beer. The three-part song more commonly is called "Fish and Chips and Vinegar."

"I Wuv a Wabbit" (5) indulges forms of baby talk for people who have long outgrown such speech. Cohila's (Calif CFG) nasal version of "Home on the Range" (27), sung "O gummeir hum warden boffer-lure ram," satisfies the same desire to distort everyday speech. Kissing sounds are added in many versions of "Cannibal King" (32) and "What's your name little boy? / My name is Lemme" (21).

Stuttering

Imitations of stuttering, unlike those of baby talk, are seen as potentially troublesome by camps that have banned "K-K-K-Katy" (4). While stuttering no longer is a common problem for children by the time they reach camp age, children may revert in times of stress.[343:143, 380] Directors know nothing may ever again be as stressful as the first time away from family.

Even so, older campers still like such songs, probably for the repetition of certain hard consonants. Kamaji (Minn girls) sings "K-K-K-Kami." N. Cunningham[S] collected a version of "Ca-ca-ca-castle on the river Nile" from Ak-O-Mak (Ont girls) in 1949 that ended "Ra-doot-ra-doot-da-doo-eh." Fleur de Lis (NH P girls) sang the last line as "rump da du da du da la-a" in 1955.

Black vaudeville comic Bert Williams introduced the 1901 song by John Rosamund Johnson, James Weldon Johnson, and Bob Cole. Cole was the first Black to produce a Broadway show in 1898. The brothers became leaders of the Harlem Renaissance in the 1920s. Geoffrey O'Hara published "Katy" (4) in 1918.

Socialized Language

Before children reach camp age, usually seven, language is "primarily assimilated through ears, rather than eyes."[343:382] Camp coincides with both the transition from egocentric to socialized communication, and the pedagogic transition to written materials. Since "good pronunciation and good grammar have usually been achieved" by third grade,[343:384] this means corrections for small errors that betray breeding or interfere with precise communication. "Ain't She Neat Ha Ha" (13) allows the first word many children are warned not to use.

Spelling

Spelling is the aspect of written language that can be most troublesome in its arbitrariness. A version of "Alleywetter, jaunty alleywetter" (29) in a Cohila (Calif CFG) song book is a visual joke on the differences between spoken and written French.

Since spelling has been an enigma from the first attempts to regularize it, general American folk tradition developed ways of marginalizing consequences of failure. Emrich found repetition of a word, like "If you'll be m-i-n-e, mine" (4) in the chorus to "Under the Bamboo Tree," goes back to nineteenth-century spelling bees.[318:184] The Johnsons and Cole published "Bamboo" in 1902.

Elementary school children uniformly do not consider spelling a chore. Seven-year-olds often like spelling games.[343:154, 396-397] However, by sixth grade, boys may begin to dislike them.[343:459] "Bingo" (50) is the most popular spelling song in camp. Second is "Lollypop" (43), with its verse spelling the camp name.

Adahi (Penna CFG) has a local song spelling its name to the tune for "Skinnamarink" (28). Fleur de Lis (NH P girls) and Skyland (NC girls) also have songs spelling their camp names. El Deseo (NM CFG) chants "a-n-g-e-l-s" after each verse of "All Night, All Day" (33). "It Isn't Any Trouble Just To S-m-i-l-e" (25) substitutes letters for its subject.

Acrostics, like the dedication to "Kitanniwa" (1) written by Ginger Hastings, associate letters with phrases or words that describe aspects of the subject. When transcribed, the letters spell the key word vertically. The "Girl Scout Pep Song" (7) and a 1965 Hitaga (Iowa CFG) lyric, "A - that's ability" follow the pattern. Debby Corey, Mary Ellen Gray, Barb Myers, and Sue Sandy wrote the second for the Agatih unit. Ginger's photograph appears in "Coming of Age."

"Chicken" (11), with its "C, that's the way to begin," pokes fun at both acrostics and spelling bees. Tanadoona (Minn CFG) used the model for "Camp Fire" in the 1940s. Shawnee (Mo CFG) sings "B, that's the way to begin" simultaneously with "I Like Being a Blue Bird"

(8). Acrostics originated as a form of Hebrew poetry now preserved in the books of Lamentations, Proverbs, and Psalms.

Word Formation

Syllabication, a device used in spelling bees, is one technique used by eight-year-olds to "master new words." Others include context, "initial consonants, prefixes and suffixes."[343:396] Dividing words into syllables still is enjoyed by sixth graders.[344:99] Wasewagan (Calif CFG) sings "stew-ed," the unpronounced syllable ending the "Prune Song" (27).

Word formation becomes another mystery as children become more sophisticated. Plural suffixes are spoofed in "Rise and Shine" (67), with its "kangaroosies" who come by "twosies." "Oh in the Moonlight" (12) has "beesies" and "bearsies." A 1940s Tanadoona (Minn CFG) song, "We Are the Camp Fire Girls" (1), mentions campers who "botanize, astronomize, mineralize, geologize." An understanding of superlative formation helps the enjoyment of "Bravo, Bravissimo" (15). The Minnesota camp melody was "Bye Bye Blackbird" (3).

Songs dealing with prefixes often utilize oppositions that poke fun at logic. A Namanu (Ore CFG) lyric, sung to "I've Been Working on the Railroad" (31), has the line, "Their bloomers bagged behind before." A similar opposition is found in "Mules" (10):

> On Mules we find two legs behind
> And two we find before
> We stand behind, before we find
> What the two behind be for

The use of "two," "four," and "be" is reminiscent of autograph verses. Although the song was more common in the past, Mike Olsen (Iowa YMCA coed) still sings it with "horses."

Grammar

The need to learn composition introduces exercises in grammar, the aspect of English classes most disliked by eighth-grade students.[344:459] Subject-verb agreement is violated in "The Froggie He Am a Queer Bird" (3). Sometimes, the verse is combined with "I Know

How Ugly I Are" (2). Lucille Parker Munk remembers the last from the early years of Kitanniwa.

Rules governing objective pronouns are broken in a Kamaji (Minn girls) counselors' song that ends, "Better be good to we!" Verb conjugation is central to a Namanu (Ore CFG) song, "When the Skies above Are Gray," with phrases like "raindrops splishing, splashing, sploshing" and "galish, galash, galoshing." In the past, Boy Scouts sang "Speaky, Spikey, Spookey" (3) or, in Brooklyn (NY BSA), "Speaky, Spikey, Spoke."

Logic

In junior high or middle school, as well as in senior high and college, composition requirements become more exacting. One problem is developing logical arguments for essay tests. Some songs, like "We're here because we're here because we're here" (2), reduce it to the child's game of "Why? Because!" Frederick Thomas Nettleingham[*] called it "The Reason Why," when he published the British military version in 1917. His singing instructions were, "and so on, until exhausted." When Rotary sang "We're here for fun," it kept the circularity, but changed the logic. Carol Domoney[§] collected the Michigan Boy Scouts' version.

Others songs like,

> Old man thought he knew a thing or two
> Because he knew a thing or two he thought he knew it all
> Old man thought he knew a thing or two
> He made them all play ball

use non sequiturs to puncture adult pretensions. Elizabeth Curtiss[§] collected the verse from Talahi (Mich YWCA) in 1944. Brooklyn Boy Scouts (NY BSA) were singing "Old Man Noah" in the 1920s.

Puns develop the logic of:

> Let's go bowling on bowling green
> We can't go bowling on bowling green
> Why can't we go bowling on bowling green
> Because of the king
> What king

June Rushing Leibfarth[S] collected this version from Arnold (Tex GS) in 1962. In 1974, Lisa Drumm[S] was told, the song (2) had been known at Wyandot (Ohio CFG) "for many years, although no one really knows how it originated or what it is about."

Bowling Green, Ohio, a city of some 30,000, is about 125 miles from Wyandot's home base in Columbus. The first major petroleum reserves in Ohio were found in the area in the 1880s. Sometime between 1910 and 1920, the father of Beatrice Leola Lytle[*] (1900-1992) moved from the area to the Oklahoma oil fields. She organized the Houston, Texas, high-school drill team in 1937 that June joined in the early 1960s.

Vocabulary

Selecting the appropriate word becomes a problem when students are criticized for overusing some. Such abuse is sanctioned in "I know a wienie man" (13) and "Long-Legged Sailor" (4). "Wienie" and "hot dog" or "long legged" are used in every possible context.

Emelyn Elizabeth Gardner[*] heard Grace Young of Perry in Shiawassee County, Michigan, treat "did you ever, ever, ever, in your life, life, life" as a counting-out rhyme during World War I. The racial taunt that followed has been replaced by the long-legged / short-legged / bow-legged sailor. In England, the Opies collected it as a handclap rhyme.[453]

Dangers of the thesaurus and pompous alternatives to the familiar are ridiculed in the "Propel Your Craft" (3) alternative to "Row Your Boat" (26). In 1959, some older campers and staff members at Kitanniwa sang "Indicate the Way to My Abode" (2) for "Show Me the Way To Go Home" (3). Terry Wilbur Bolton (Ore P coed) remembers "Three Blind Mice" (14) as "Three Visionless Rodents" (1).

Profanity

Questions of correct vocabulary are satirized in songs eliding profanity. In "Three Fishermen" (51), the group divides on the chorus. One part sings one syllable or word, and the other follows. "The first one's name was Jacob" becomes "Jay Jay," answered by "Cob Cob Cob." When they sail to Amsterdam, many groups sing "Amster Amster" and "shh shh shh." Some add two more verses,

"You shouldn't say that naughty word" and "I'm gonna sing it anyway." Kotomi (Colo CFG) sings the critical verse "Amster" and "girls don't cuss." Some camps have banned the song.

The same pun on a Dutch town named for its river location is found in the "Souse Family" (2). Elizabeth Curtiss[S] collected the "Rotterdam Dutch" from Talahi (Mich YWCA) in 1944. Treasure Island (Penna BSA) and Brooklyn Scouts (NY BSA) cloned it as "The Scout Company" (2) in the 1920s.

Some people fondly reminisce about alternating between profane and public words. Dean Wakefield[S] talked to a former Kiwanis (Mich BSA) camper who told him, "I can remember substituting 'darn' for 'damn' and 'heck' for 'hell' when my father was anywhere near" the group singing "Johnny Verbeck" (26). Similarly, an Ohio Girl Scout told Carol Shuster,[S] when they sang "Three Little Angels" (17), "If adults weren't around the ending was changed slightly to rhyme with the first several stanzas. Supposedly Girl Scouts are good and pure and sons say words like Hell."

Syntax

Demands for clarity in writing are implicit in songs featuring syntactical confusion. Problems with antecedents of pronouns figure in "Mistress Shady" (5) with "I go to court her / I mean the daughter." Zanzig found the song to be widely known in camps in the early 1930s, but to be more popular among boys than girls.[561:525]

Songs playing with grammar seem to have been better known in the early years of camps. One reason, no doubt, is changes in teaching methods following World War II. Certainly, children who come from schools that fail to produce basic literacy may not appreciate all the lyrics in the second verse of "Boris" (1). Steven Diner learned it at Loyaltown (NY J boys) in 1963 as:

> Now Boris came upon a horse, sagging in the middle,
> Boris came upon a horse, playing on a fiddle
> It was Boris not the horse, sagging in the middle
> It was the horse not Boris, playing on the fiddle

A more intriguing explanation for changes in girls' camp repertoires has been the increased acceptance of at least a high school diploma for young women. In the early years of camping, educational aspirations set girls apart from their peers. Songs like Tanadoona's (Minn CFG) "botanize" and a 1938 Kalamazoo Girl Reserve (Mich YWCA) song that substituted "pepability" and "lovability" into "Sociability" (2) did more than poke fun at school. They expressed pride in being part of a special group, privy to arcane secrets the girls had so subjugated, they could treat them humorously.

Alliteration

In later elementary school grades or early middle school years, a concern with reading broadens into the study of literature. Children are introduced to versification techniques. Some already are familiar. They know alliteration, or the use of words beginning with the same sound, from "Faith of Our Fathers" (16) and "God Is Great" (8). "John Jacob Jingleheimer Schmidt" (62), "My Baby Bumble Bee" (19), "Whether the Weather" (10), and the "ticky tacky" in "Little Boxes" (6) are more secular.

Alliteration occurs in two long dances, "Bow Bow Belinda" (6) and "Picking up Paw Paws" (6). Repetition within words, like "Kookaburra" (85), "Sarasponda" (59) and "Tiritomba" (12), may explain the appeal of these international songs in American camps. A Rokilio (Wisc BSA) songbook editor transcribed the last as "Tira Tomba."

Tongue Twisters

Alliteration and onomatopoeia are combined in a song about a puppy named "Rags" (9), who goes "flip-flop, wig-wag, zig-zag." Alliteration and tricky pronunciation are joined in songs involving tongue twisters, like those currently being sung to "John Brown's Body" (6). Carol Parsons Sievert (Mich CFG) intones "blue beetle was bleeding blood" and "one sick seal slipped through the sieve." "One black bear backed up the hill" and "one slick snake slipped on the hill" are sung at Wolahi (Calif CFG). Kotomi (Colo CFG) knows "one mad moose merrily." The "Tongue Twister Song" (10), with its "Glory, glory how peculiar" chorus, evolved from "The Grasshopper Song," with its "They were only playing leapfrog" chorus.

Emrich[319:247] believed tongue twisters harked back to nineteenth-century concerns with elocution as a marker of education. They provided an excuse for adults to indulge the joys of alliteration, to say naughty words by mistake, and to parade their memories with short, virtuoso demonstrations. They could not be mistaken for non-rational or immature behavior. They were a means of self-improvement.

End Rhyme

Alliteration is a special form of rhyme, the repetition of a single sound in systematically varied contexts. With end or masculine rhyme, repeated sounds terminate poetic lines. In a simple example, from an organization song known by eleven women or camps, Dorothy Neece Martin wrote:

> Oh, step along in the Camp Fire **way**
> And make your work merely seem like **play**

"Sweet Violets" (8) mocks this rhyme pattern with its substitution of a pause and glide into the next line, instead of an anticipated naughty word that would rhyme. The same humor is found in "Three Little Angels" (17) and in:

> Lucy had a steamship
> The steamship had a bell
> Lucy went to heaven
> But the steamship went to
> Hello operator

Sally Briggs[§] collected the last (1) from a former Cedar Lake (NJ J coed) camper. Fowke heard "Helen had a steamboat" from Toronto, Ontario, third graders in 1962.[332] "Violets" first appeared in Joseph Kline Emmet's *Fritz among the Gypsies*, an 1882 play that featured comic German characters. Mitch Miller recorded a version in 1958.

An Old King Cole verse for "Boom, boom, ain't it great to be crazy" (33), known at Christopher (Ohio C coed), has a soul/pole rhyme followed by fell/oops! "My Aunt Greek, veedy veedy veep," with her "puss viddy viddy vus" (2) uses internal rhyme within the line to satirize masculine ending. Sally Briggs[§] collected a version of "Aunt Greet" with "cat" and "vat."

Feminine rhyme, in which the last two syllables sound similar, is found in the cheer "Ai Ai **Aikus** Nobody **Like Us**" (8). In North Carolina, girls chant, "Boost for Skyland, be a **booster**, yell and holler like you **useta**." Triple rhyme, a special form of feminine verse, is found in "Michael Finnigin" (14) with his whiskers on his "chinigin" that one sings "aginagin."

The most elaborate manipulation of words to fit the demands of feminine rhyme is found in "Hi Ho Jarum" (7). Lines end with "wreckium," "neckium," "insteadium," "wellium," and "hellium." The 1929 Brooklyn Scouts (NY BSA) song book transcribed it as "Hu-raz-u-ram." Saint Vincent de Paul Ranch (Calif C boys) sings "Old Roger Rum."

Consonance

Consonance repeats similar consonant sounds with different vowels. Larry Ralston (Ohio 4-H) knows the sometimes discouraged "O'Riley is dead and O'Reilly don't know it" (4). Near consonance is maintained when different names are used, like "McGinty and McCarty," as remembered by Rosella Majerczak (Ohio coed).

The names "O'Leary and O'Riley," sung by Susan Conard (Calif CFG), involve a different linguistic phenomenon, metathesis, or the exchange of two sounds. When the names are simply "McCarty and me," as sung by Mary Hoyes (Ohio GS) and Loretta Krebs (Ohio GS), only the Irishness and black humor remains. "In the Vintertime" (5), with the "vind in the westibule," also exploits metathesis.

Assonance

Assonance, the repetition of similar vowel sounds with different consonants, is more likely to be incorporated into a song than made its topic. The long "o" and long "e" are repeated in the organizational "**O**h w**e** cheer for w**o**hel**o**" (10). An appreciation for echoing nuclei may come before children learn fun songs. Gladys Evelyn Moorhead and Donald Pond found children aged two to six took "great delight in rhythmically emphatic speech phrases." These included "experiments with rhyming and assonant syllables and repeated refrains."[433:12]

Rhyming vowels occurred in a canoeing trip song Karen Lindquist[§] collected in 1950:

> Sleep on rocks, eat burned toast, cows come crashing through
> And yet we canoe, canoe, canoe
> Might get sunburn, might get typhoid, impetigo too
> And yet we canoe, can you, canoe

Fowke[331] collected the round, "My dame had a lame tame crane" (3), from Jarvis McCurdy in Toronto. He learned it around 1920.

Case Study Repertoire

Many modern poets have abandoned end rhyme, though they remain sensitive to sound flows within their lines. Camps are more conservative. The only case-study lyric that uses no obvious form of rhyme, "Eskimo Hunt," is attributed to a non-western tradition. "Kumbaya" repeats entire lines that end in gerunds. "Rose" repeats key words within lines.

"Lollypop," "Peppiest Camp," "I Wish I Were," and "Rise and Shine" utilize feminine end rhyme. The other twelve use masculine. "I Wish" and "Rise" apply word-distortion formulas. "Kookaburra," "Rose," and "Eskimo Hunt" employ assonance. Some consonance is deployed in "Pep," "The Cuckoo," and "Eskimo Hunt."

Meter

Perhaps the last subject students broach in high school is poetic rhythm patterns. By that time, if they still are going to camp, they have become more interested in pretty songs than fun ones. No songs satirize meter. Instead, usage reveals what older campers have absorbed.

In our language, alternating a strong sound with a weak one is more common than using one strong syllable and two weak ones. The case-study songs show a preference for beginning with an unstressed syllable. Iambs (xX) dominate "The Mermaid," "Pep," "Skyball Paint," "A Bear," and "Grand Old Duke of York."

While trochees (Xx) are sung as often, most are with songs influenced by other linguistic patterns. An Australian wrote

"Kookaburra." "Kumbaya" and "Rise and Shine" are derived from African-American precursors. "Rose" and the tune for "Swimming" are from England.

Three syllable anapests, with the last part stressed (xxX), are used with "Ash Grove," "A Canoe May Be Drifting," and "Flicker." The same strong metric ending appears in a song cluster from Germany, "The Cuckoo" and "An Austrian." "I Wish I Were" and "The Boatmen" use iambs and anapests.

No song relies solely on dactyls (Xxx). "Witchcraft" and "Eskimo Hunt" use trochees with them. "Lollypop," a parody of a Tin Pan Alley song, uses trochees with many missing unstressed syllables and some anapests.

Case Study: The Peppiest Camp

"The Peppiest Camp" (39) is an alliterative /p/ tongue twister sung at Kitanniwa since the 1930s. It has a spelled section, obscure and obsolete words, masculine end rhyme in the last quatrain (doubt/ about) and feminine end rhyme in the first two quatrains (pokin'/ jokin' and popper/stopper). The pleasure comes from the tricky pronunciation, the shouted "P E P," the speed in the middle part, and the identification with an exuberant camp. Almost all violate rules governing form or correct behavior.

History

"Pep" probably developed in the south in the 1920s. Harbin,[†] who worked for the Southern Methodist Church, published three verses in 1927. Evelyn Hopson Wood[†] (1908-1989) included the last two in the *Camp and Picnic Warbler* in 1929. At the time, she was living in Birmingham, Alabama.

Her version (C) persists at Kamaji (Minn girls) and Skyland Camp (NC girls). Helen Bagley, who was remembered to have been from Georgia, may have brought three verses to Kitanniwa, or they may have arrived through Methodists.

The first quatrain, which begins "The peppiest camp I ever saw," may be derived from, or have a common ancestor with, "The Thinnest Man" (2). Rokilio's (Wisc BSA) first two lines suggest the model for "Pep's" opening verse:

> The thinnest man I ever saw was a man from old
> Hoboken
> And when I tell you how thin he was you'll think that I was
> jokin'

The next lines are close enough to the verses published by Harbin and Wood for someone to see possibilities for merging the two:

> He was as thin as the glue on a postage stamp, or the skin
> of a new potater;
> For exercise he used to dive through the holes of a nutmeg
> grater

The Wisconsin Boy Scout camp used the tune for "Polly Wolly Doodle" (11).

Explication

Words in the middle section date the text. Pepper pot is a thick, Philadelphia soup made with tripe, peppercorns, and vegetables. Legend asserts it first was prepared during the winter of 1777, when provisions were scarce at Valley Forge.

One would need a specialty butcher to buy tripe today. Rubbery linings from cows' stomachs were diced to add flavor. The inexpensive stew would have been a mainstay in boarding houses. Nancy Bryant (Ohio CFG), Ka-esta (Ore CFG), and Wolahi (Calif CFG) now sing "pepper pod." This makes more sense where Mexican foods featuring chilis are eaten. Campbell's stopped selling the soup in this country in 2010, but continues to offer it in Canada.

Skyland (NC girls) sings "vinegar cruet," rather than "stopper" in the last line of the second verse. The one is the container that holds vinegar when it is set on the table, while the stopper fits into the narrow neck of the flat-bottomed glass bottle. At one time, vinegar was served like mustard and ketchup as a condiment.

This practice, still common in parts of Canada, is behind "Fish and Chips and Vinegar" (40). Jolene Robinson Johnson's (Wash CFG) version, which ends the first part "pepper, pepper, pepper pot," perpetuates this historic dietary combination.

"Mustard box," "mustard can" and "mustard bowl," found in early-published versions of "Pep," were used when powdered mustard seed was reconstituted. It has become "mustard jar." When campers only see yellow paste in squeezable, unbreakable plastic containers, even "jar" is obsolete. This and other substitutions probably were unconscious folk rationalizations done by campers, who had problems learning the fast section, and so used the word that made the most sense.

Textual Variation

San Juan Ranch (Conn girls) has adapted "Pep" as the "peppiest horse," according to Elaine Sullivan. Kamaji (Minn girls) in the 1950s and Rosella Majerczak (Ohio coed) use "bunch," while others know "peppiest girls." "You" is sung in place of "I" at Adahi (Penna CFG), Tannadoonah (Ind CFG) and Yakewi (Ohio CFG), reflecting a Mid-Atlantic and Midwestern preference for that pronoun.

Music

In the same way the text may have been synthesized from several existing components, the melody seems to have been derived from several sources. Janet Grady Leckrone[*] and Harbin identified the tune as "It Ain't Gonna Rain" (4). Vivian Sexton (Tex CFG) remembers using "Yankee Doodle" (6).

Kitanniwa's version from the 1950s alluded to "Yankee Doodle" in the first quatrain, only at a faster tempo and with a 3/4, rather than a 4/4 meter. The tongue-twisting second part hinted at the melody for "Polly Wolly Doodle" (11). The tune for the last four lines sounded like "It Ain't Gonna Rain No More."

"Pep" never was perceived to be a medley, despite its melodic contour, but as a lyric with the verse form ABA. Thus, the tunes for the first and third quatrains have drawn closer to each other, as people have tried to sing them alike. This especially is clear with the second line of the first section, which now is close to the second line of "Rain."

The speed valued in the second part, no doubt, has been responsible for modifications in that section. People often treat it as a chant when learning it, or when singing the section very quickly. Then, once the text has been dispatched, individuals try to recover the proper tune. If they perceive the song has a ternary form (ABA), the melody for the second quatrain returns to a flattened form of its original self. If the song is seen to be strophic (AAA), then the tune from the first verse is adapted.

Skyland (NC girls) and Shawnee (Mo CFG) accompany themselves with hand claps. Namanu (Ore CFG) sings it twice, the second time with increased speed.

Sources

"Yankee Doodle" dates to the mid-eighteenth century, according to James Jeffrey Fuld.* He did not find "Polly Wolly Doodle" in print until an 1880 Harvard song book. "Rain" was recorded in 1922 by Wendell Woods Hall. All arose from older, traditional sources. All probably were performed by minstrel acts.

"Chester" (6) is sung to the colonial melody. "Scout Laws in Song" (2) was included in early Treasure Island (Penna BSA) and Brooklyn Boy Scout (NY BSA) song books.

Anne Beardsley (Ohio GS) has six verses for "Polly" (11) in her song book: way down south, my gal Sal, grasshopper sitting on a railroad track, I went to bed, and two about a sneezing chicken. Hitaga (Iowa CFG) sings the first and third. Debbie Saint Pierre§ collected Anne's first verse from the Storer camps (Ohio YMCA coed) in 1973.

The melody is used with "Little Skeeter" (7), "I Eat Worms" (7), "Thousand Legged Worm" (6), "Queer Cow" (4), and, in some camps, "Three Blue Pigeons" (12) and "Second Story Window" (15). In the past, "Polly" was used for "Three Little Pigs" (3) and "Three Good Deeds" (2) at Irondale (Mo BSA) and Brooklyn Scout camps (NY BSA).

Piper believed "Rain" was taken to Iowa from Kentucky,[471] perhaps because Hall's grandfather was born in Todd County, Kentucky, and died in Iowa. Hall's father performed on the lyceum circuit before he moved to Chicago around 1902 to pastor an independent congregation at the Bush Temple of Music. It soon attracted additional verses.

Popularity

Despite the archaic language, obsolete tune and passé emphasis on pep, "The Peppiest Camp" has remained popular in Camp Fire camps. The middle passage is difficult to learn. It may take campers several summers to perfect, a challenge that leads to frequent requests. Carol Parsons Sievert says, "I remember that I was young enough" when I learned it at Kitanniwa "that I had trouble with all the /p/ sounds in it."

Larry Ralston discovered the emotions it evoked when the Wyandot County, Ohio, 4-H resident camping site was moved from Pittenger (Ohio YMCA) to Conger (Ohio 4-H). Older campers refused to substitute the new name into the song. They finally compromised with "4-H pep," in place of the alliterative, tongue twisting "Pittenger Pep."

Version A

Text from Camp Kitanniwa (Mich CFG) song book, late 1940s or early 1950s.

> The peppiest girls I ever knew
> They never come a pokin'
> If I was to tell the pep they've got
> You'd think I was a jokin'
>
> It's not the pep of the pepper pot
> Nor the pep of the popcorn popper
> It's not the pep of the mustard can
> Nor the pep of the vinegar stopper
>
> It's good old fashioned P E P
> The pep you cannot down
> Kitanniwa pep, Kitanniwa pep,
> The peppiest camp around.

Version B

Text from Patricia Averill, Camp Kitanniwa (Mich CFG), 1951-1960; variations from A emphasized.

> The peppiest **camp** I ever **saw**
> **It** never **was** a pokin'
> If I **were** to tell **you** the pep **it had**
> You'd think I was a jokin'

(Quatrain song so fast, almost indistinct)
It's not the pep **in** the pepper pot
The pep **in** the popcorn popper
It's not the pep **in** the mustard **bowl**
The pep **in** the vinegar stopper

It's good old fashioned P-E-P
    (shout letters)
The pep you cannot **doubt**
Camp Kitanniwa, Camp Kitanniwa
    (double time to fit all the syllables into the beats)
The peppiest camp **about**.

Version C

Text from Skyland Camp for Girls (NC girls), possibly 1976; variations from A emphasized.

> **Oh**, it's not the pep of the **popper** pot **or** the pep of the
>   popcorn popper,
> It's not the pep of the **vinegar cruet or** the pep of the
>   **bottle** stopper,
> **It's** good old fashioned p-e-p, the **kind** you cannot down
> It's Skyland, Skyland, Skyland camp, **the best old** camp
>   around.

Eskimo Hunt: Foreign Language and Nonsense Songs

Speech is a physical capacity governed by culture. Its smallest component, a phoneme, is simply a sound. They combine into our basic linguistic units, syllables. Syllables, by themselves or combined with others, create morphemes, which carry set, but incomplete meanings. Thus, **er** can suggest a sound (flick**er**), or imply a comparison (nic**er**), or identify what is doing something (comput**er**). Similarly, **ed** can suggest an action has been completed (look**ed**), or refer to someone's state of being (scar**ed**).

Morphemes combine to create words like camp, camper, and camped, but communicate no information until joined in structured ways. A camper camped at camp is informative, but ambiguous without context. Does it refer to youngsters sleeping outside and cooking over an open fire, or to adults doing comic skits at a rustic retreat?

Folk Etymologies

Infants are bombarded by aural stimuli. Their brains slowly realize noises represent recurring meanings. When individuals later are confronted with a sound they do not quite comprehend, they rifle their memory banks. They seek previous experiences with similar characteristics of vocal tone, facial expression, and context to suggest reasonable facsimiles for missing words or phrases.

In the process, people may create folk etymologies, "plausible but usually incorrect analysis [. . .] of a word whose meaning or spelling or sound is not clear, resulting in the transformation of one word into one more intelligible."[401:398]

Julie Sherwood[S] was told the staff at Molly Luman (Ohio GS) was singing "Frozen Raccoon" one year, rather than "Rosen fra Fuhn" (13), after a counselor overheard a small camper. The accidental parody is not very different from the consciously conceived "Raisin Fried Prunes" Jolene Robinson Johnson (Mich CFG) heard in a camp she visited the summer of 1974. However, the exchange of letters in "raccoon" represents metathesis.

Unfamiliar Words

Variations, introduced by trying to comprehend unexpected sounds, exist in "Tongo" (20). At Kitanniwa in the late 1950s, we believed it was a Korean war-chant, with the second line, "Chim da molly molly aye." In 1962, the Rohrboughs published a Polynesian paddling song with the second line, "Jim nee bye bye oh." As it spread in tradition, the text came to be seen as nonsense. June Rushing Leibfarth[S] collected the second line at Arnold (Tex GS) in 1958 as, "Jim bide boy oh my oh." The next year, they were parodying it as, "Bongo / Jimmy fell in the bayou."

A rationalizing substitution was made in the version of the German "Lachen" (8) collected by Alexandra Prentiss[S] as "Lookin" from Kilowan (Ore CFG). Shawnee (Mo CFG) has altered the German-language grace, "Gelobet Sei" (14), to "Gay lo bed zi." Angela Lapham (Mich GS) sings "Gay-lo-bit." "Lachen" means laugh. "Gelobet sei" means blessed be. Ann Marie Filocco[S] was told, counselors at Lachenwald wrote the first. The Girl Guides camp is near Marburg, Germany, where the Grimm brothers were active. Tobitt[*] introduced the second in 1955.

Transforming songs through correcting apparent errors is not restricted to foreign-language material. Alexandra Prentiss[S] collected the onomatopoeic "Ah-do-ray boom-day ret set set" part of "Sarasponda" (59) from Kilowan (Ore CFG) as "An Oreo." The song the Rohrboughs introduced as a "Dutch spinning song"[133] has been altered to "Sara spunda" at Tanadoona (Minn CFG), with "Oh glory boom day rat tat tat."

Treasure Island (Penna BSA) was singing a nonsense-language passage in the chorus to "Hi Ho Jarum" (7) as "Hali hali hollian, who has the ram" in 1946. Saint Vincent de Paul Ranch (Calif C boys) has altered the line to "skin of a yankee doodlium." Kushtaka (Alaska

CFG) sings "skinny-ma-rinky doodalium." It is clear which other song, "Yankee Doodle" (6) or "Skinnamarink" (28), is known in each camp.

Obsolete Words

Obsolete words may be replaced with very similar, but contemporary ones. In the 1940s, Watanopa (Mont CFG) substituted "hula hula dance" for "hootchie kootchie dance" in the second verse of "Did You Ever See a Fishie?" (24). The first just was becoming known from Hawaii. Philadelphia's 1876 Centennial Exhibition featured the other. Susan Dunn[S] collected a Franklin Settlement House camp (Mich agency) version of "Patsy Orry Aye" (29) that used "second boss" for "section boss."

Kirby (Wash CFG) and MeWaHi (Calif CFG) sing "Are you a flopper," rather than "flapper," in "Are You a Camel" (13). Their change restores logic to the posture song for young campers who no longer understand an allusion to the relaxed style of women in the 1920s.

Distinctions between good camp ladies and frivolous town women continued into the 1930s. Joy Camps (Wisc girls) was singing, "So when you come to camp / Don't try to be a vamp" in 1937. "Vamp" was a label applied to early seductive film actresses like Theda Bara. The tune, "The Merry-Go-Round Broke Down," was recorded by Shep Fields in June of that year. Soon after, Looney Tunes adopted it.

Sometimes anachronistic references are retained for their nonsense value. In "The Billboard Song" (17), a passerby reads peeling layers as if they were concurrent:

> Smoke Coca Cola cigarettes
> Chew Wrigley's spearmint beer
> Ken'L Ration dog food makes your wife's complexion clear
> Simonize your baby with a Hershey candy bar
> Texaco's the beauty cream that's used by every star

Carol Shuster[S] collected this version from an Ohio Girl Scout in 1973.

Both forces are at work in "Chewing Gum," which has become "Bubblegum" (13). Most camps still sing, "My mother gave me a penny, to see Jack Benny," even though the comedian's weekly television show ended in 1965. Ticket prices had risen years before. However, the verse about using a quarter to buy some porter, usually, is altered. Few know porter to be a form of dark beer. At Wampatuck (Mass P girls), they "pay the porter." An Ohio undergraduate heard a bawdy takeoff.

Grammar

Incorrect grammar or unusual syntactic constructions may be corrected or simplified, often unconsciously. Verb structure in "Carry mi' ackee goa Linstead Market" (24) has been corrected to "Carry me aki to Linstead Market" at Cielo (Calif CFG), according to Frances Rigoni.

This song is particularly open to nonsensification. Its patois developed in Jamaica in the seventeenth century, when English and Scots plantation owners imported slaves speaking Niger-Congo languages from areas bordering the Gulf of Guinea. A red-skinned fruit brought from Africa kept the name used by the Akan of Ghana and the Ivory Coast. Ackees were a member of a tropical genus indigenous to semi-deciduous forests with no British equivalent.

American campers, who do not recognize creole grammatical constructions, reassemble what they hear. The editor of the Wolahi (Calif CFG) song book believed they were singing "Kare meaki go," while the Neewahlu (Ida CFG) compiler perceived it as "Carmiacki go." Ka-esta (Ore CFG) sings "Kerry me Yakki, come." Tannadoonah (Ind CFG) knows it as "Karimiachi - Goldenstead Market."

Perceived Origins

Campers' perceptions of songs' origins can contribute to blurred distinctions between foreign-language and nonsense lyrics. Patricia Ann Hall (Calif CFG) says, she always thought "Than a Shay Allee" (8) was Finnish, because its words and phrases sounded like some language, though one she did not recognize. Neewahlu (Ida CFG) believes it is a Swedish ski song. Kotomi (Colo CFG) notes it as a Swiss ski song. Larry Ralston (Ohio 4-H) was assured it was a Norwegian skiing song.

June Rushing Leibfarth[§] was informed, it had been "written at the Chalet in Switzerland, the Girl Scout home, and it's a combination of practically all the languages of girls that come to visit this place. It's no language in particular; it has just got a lot of different words in it."

When a song is seen to use some kind of language, it is believed to have a standard version. Many would trade "Rosen fra Fuhn" for "Rosen fra Fyn," if told Fyn was the correct Danish name for the island birthplace of Hans Christian Andersen. English spell it Funen.

The legitimacy of nonsense comes from an "it's the way it's done" sense of tradition. Watchung Area Scouts (NJ BSA) sing the tag ending to "Bravo, Bravissimo" (15) as "omska lay vu." They would have little reason to conform to boys from Denver (Colo BSA), who use "enskelevo."

Foreign Language Songs

Interest in international language songs is greater among songbook editors than it is among campers. Camp Fire's current edition of *Music Makers** contains 31 songs not in the 1950s version. Four, like "Kumbaya" (90), were already in tradition in the 1970s. The remaining all have some folk attribution, most to non-European culture groups. Only three are sung widely: the Moroccan "A Ram Sam Sam" (28), the Brazilian "Suitors" (25), and the Polynesian "Tongo" (20). A few more have been mentioned, including the Native American "Seeyahnah" (2), the Israeli "Toembai" (2), and Exner's transcription of the German "Abenlied" (3).

Repetition

Campers exercise discrimination when confronted by the wide variety of proffered foreign-language or foreign-originated material. Songs with repeated passages may be accepted because they are easier to learn. The American "Railroad Corral" (12) has "Whoop-ti-i-o, whoop-ti-i-o." A Philippine song alternates a similar "Eppo, ee tye-tye-ay" (20) with "eppo, ee tukey-tukey-ay" in the version known at Neewahlu (Ida CFG).

When near repetition exists, campers convert unfamiliar words to rhymes. In the "Omaha Tribal Prayer" (12), "Wakonda thae-thu" has become "Wokonda dhu-dhu." According to its original collector, Alice Cunningham Fletcher, the song was taught to adolescent boys before they embarked on four-day vision quests that initiated them into the tribe. A boy sang to let the spirits (Wakonda) know he was ready.[325]

Ernest Thompson Seton (1860-1946) introduced her version in *The Book of Woodcraft and Indian Lore*.* He had begun suggesting outdoor activities for a club he called the Woodcraft Indians in the *Ladies' Home Journal* in 1902. He collected his articles as *The Birch Bark Roll* in 1906. He constantly updated it. In 1912, he recommended the Omaha song for opening his Woodcraft League councils.

"Wakonda" alternates with "wohelo" in the Camp Fire Girls' "Processional," which begins "We come, we come to our council fire" (49). Some know it as "Kahinto Kamyo." A change to "wokonda" in one line increases the assonant alliteration.

Reduplicatives

Reduplicative phrases that repeat syllables by varying a phoneme are the most common type of nonsense repetition. The "Rig-a-jig-jig" section of "We Were Starved" (19) alters the **ig** core with different introductory sounds. "Sing-a-ling-a-ling" (10) recombines **ing**. The second has been adapted for local songs by the Kalamazoo Girl Reserves (Mich YWCA) and Skyland Camp (NC girls).

"Itsy Bitsy Spider" (33) repeats the vowel sound in a form of assonance. In the Northeast, the Herald Tribune Fresh Air Camp (NY agency) and Wilma Lawrence (Penna GS) have sung "eency weency." In the Midwest, Tawakani (Ida CFG) and Tanadoona (Minn CFG) sing "eensie beensie."

Ablaut Reduplicatives

A second sort of reduplicative phrase found in fun songs is an extended form of consonance termed ablaut reduplication. Phrases are repeated with vowel variations in the last syllables, like "val di ri, val di ra" in the "Happy Wanderer" (48). "The Cuckoo" (33) employs the scheme for its chorus. In the German "Holla Hi, Holla Ho" (14), the phrases are used as a refrain.

A small modification of extended ablaut reduplication exists in songs that drop syllables from the last words, usually to enhance a sense of melodic termination. In the Czech "Came a Riding" (17), as translated by Martha C. Ramsay, "Zhum ta di ya di da" ends "Zhum ta di ya da." The American "A Jogging Along" (14) has "Hi come along jim along Josie, hi come along jim along Joe." Others alternate /d/ and /l/ phonemes, including "Hey liddy liddy liddy, Hey liddy liddy lo" (10) and "Wadaleache, wadaleo" (34).

Ablaut reduplication patterning persists when oral transmission introduces changes. Rimrock (Wash YWCA) sings "kamasima sima zayo, Kama zimba zimba zee" for the chorus of "Zulu Warrior" (25). Ann Beardsley (Mich GS) learned a version with greater internal rhyme, "Ay cuma zuma zuma zaya, Ay cuma zuma zuma zee." Merrowvista (NH P coed) knows, "Ai k'simba simba simba, Ai k'simba simba zu."

Sometimes choruses end by repeating the last syllable or word like the "huya huya ya" in the Moravian "Castles in Toviska" (8). The Czech "Above a Plain" (22) ends "a huya huya huya ya." A thrice repeated "boom ti airy airy" concludes "boom zip zip" in the Eastern European "Out in the Forest" (16). Similar repetition patterns are found in "Walking at Night" (27) and in "Vive l'Amour" (30).

/H/:/T/ Reduplicatives

The important part of a reduplicative phrase is not the repeated phoneme, but the one that varies. When Henry Wheatley[*] compiled a list of English-language reduplicatives in 1865, he noticed almost half used an /h/ as one member of the pair. Its most common pairing is with /p/, as in "Hokey Pokey" (16). It also may occur with a /b/, /t/, or /d/.[307]

"Down on the Banks of the Hanky Tank" (22) shows the greatest variation in camp fun songs. Merrowvista (NH P coed) and Mawavi (DC CFG) sing "hanky pank." Nancy Simmons (Colo GS) knows "hanky panky." Both restore the more common /h/:/p/ pattern.

Others, like Nancy, have expanded the second word to two syllables to rhyme with the first. June Rushing Leibfarth[§] collected "hanky tanky" from Robinwood (Tex GS) in 1967. Wintaka (Calif CFG) has altered the next line to "bank to bankie" to maintain the new feminine end rhyme. Melacoma (Wash CFG) sings "honky tonky."

Many changes, especially "honky tonky" and "hanky panky," are folk etymologies that arose when people did not know "tank" referred to a reservoir or pond. When "tank" is unfamiliar, then "hanky tank" becomes nonsense. Once the phrase is recognized as a reduplicative, then more familiar reduplicative phrases can be substituted without altering the meaning, even though pond hopping ("hanky tank") becomes bar hopping ("honky tonk").

The camp round is a relic of an older "Frog Song" composed by Charles E. Trevathan. He was known better for frequenting stables on the thoroughbred racing circuit where entertainers passed time and tips. May Irwin introduced his "Way down yonder in the yakety yank" to vaudeville in 1896. Pete Seeger recorded a different alternative as "The Foolish Frog" (FC 7611). Carl Withers* collected a variant jest.

The /h/:/d/ pairing is found in foreign-language nonsense passages sung in American camps where the /h/ sound begins an open syllable. It predominates in "Heide Hey, Heidi Ho" (2), known by Angela Lapham (Mich GS) and Theresa Mary Rooney (NJ GS). An initial /h/ also is used in the chorus for the Swiss "Weggis Song" (31), and in the variously spelled "Hyda" (5).

/ /:/L/ Combinations

Pairing an initial /t/ with an /l/ is more common in international songs, like the nineteenth-century "Marianina tra la la" (11). The Swiss "Vrenalie" (30) has a "tra la la, yo ho ho" chorus. David Kilburn Stevens (1860-1946) kept the "too ra lee, too ra lay" refrain of "Sweet Betsy from Pike" for the "Polar Bear and Crocodile." Camps know it as "Climates" (8).

"Betsy" refashioned "Vilikens and His Dinah," which had "too ral lal." Frederick Robson introduced "Vilikens" to the London stage in 1853. It spread to this country where it was used by political campaigns in 1856. John A. Stone created "Betsy" during the California gold rush. He included it in *Put's Golden Songster* of 1858.[338]

Many nonsense-language passages in foreign songs use an /l/ to begin open syllables that end in vowel sounds, rather than with consonants. This fluidity is pronounced in the Norwegian "Ole Oleanna" (7). Shawnee (Mo CFG) sings the refrain and chorus for "Suitors" (25) as "ah le o bahia." A strong /k/ sound has been introduced into versions sung in the Northwest where Wakoma (Wash CFG) sings "Oh ala ya **bakia**." Namanu (Ore CFG) knows "O alay a **pakea**." A different consonant was introduced to interrupt the vowel flow in "Ole o lo olea **podia**" collected from The Timbers (Mich GS) by Kathleen Solsbury§ in 1970.

/ /:/W/ Combinations

Many nonsense songs alternate two beginning consonant sounds. According to Stuart Berg Flexner, /w/ is the most common phoneme used to begin the second part of a reduplicative.[327:606] A hard /g/ seems to be the sound most commonly associated with /w/ in fun songs. "Ging gang gooley gooley wash wash" (19) has been altered to "Ging gan gu, gerie gerie getsya" by Rimrock (Wash YWCA). Yakewi (Ohio CFG) sings "Shing gan goo, gore gore gacthy."

A similar /k/ to /w/ pairing is used in "Kille Kille Wash Wash" (17), sung "kelly kelly" at Shawnee (Mo CFG). The /k/ to /w/ order is reversed in "A Wooney Cooney Cha a Wooney" (27), as sung at Kitanniwa in the late 1950s. Ohiyesa (Mich YMCA coed) has sung "wuni wuni chow." /W/ has been softened to /u/ at Wawbansee (La CFG), where Debra Nails has heard a hard /k/ in "Aye ooney ooney chi aye ooney."

The /w/ sound or phoneme also has been used in alliterative series in fun songs, often in combination with the syllable "atch" and the phoneme /d/. Kitanniwa was singing "Wadaleache" (34) in 1974. In Ohio camps, the first word may be shortened. Glen (Ohio CFG) knows "waddly ache," according to Nancy Bryant. In the West, the second word more likely is varied, as in the "waddalie achia" sung at Skylark Ranch (Calif GS).

/W/ combinations also are found in the "wachou wachou wachou" phrase of "Tinga Singu" (7), as sung at Ka-esta (Ore CFG). This is Sesotho, a Bantu language spoken in South Africa from Pretoria and Johannesburg south to Lesotho. Girl Guides introduced a version in 1957* from Wycliffe Nkuma and Kathleen F. Hill.* She wrote a history of the Guides in South Africa in 1951.

/ /:/M/ Combinations

/M/ is the second most commonly used sound in camp songs to begin the second part of an alternating, alliterative series. The phoneme is a member of the first class of consonant sounds children learn to articulate, the labials: /b/, /p/, /m/, and /w/.[384:47] Roman Jakobson argued all children acquired categories of language in the same order, although culture and individual biology might alter the timing. Labials were succeeded by dentals, /d/ and /t/, by age three, and then velars, /g/, /k/ and /q/.[385:11] The first vowel was a broad "a," generally with a labial. One of the first consonant oppositions was a labial like /m/ and a dental.[385:10]

When Seattle Boy Scouts (Wash BSA) sing "Quee quo motty-motty-motty-motty dashnik" (6), they are doing more than embellishing a velar velar labial-dental (4x) dental-labial combination. They are drawing on layers of association from their earliest experiences. Blue Haven (NM P coed) sings "Qui qua quonnie monnie donnie monnie dasnic." Neewahlu (Ida CFG) knows "Kee ki money money money money dusty."

/S/:/M/:/D/ Combinations

Children do not fully conquer the sibilant /s/ until they are about seven.[412] Jakobson suggested correct pronunciation depended on the ability to pronounce /d/ and /t/.[384] Some rhyming fun songs combine /s/ with the dental /d/ and the easier labial /m/. Melacoma (Wash CFG) sings "Skidamirink a dink a dink" (28). Towanyak (Kans CFG) has substituted an /m/ for the /d/ in the first part, "Skimmers rinky dink." Namanu (Ore CFG) sings "Skimera rink a dink."

In another song using the /s/:/m/:/d/ combination, which was more common in the past, Tannadoonah (Ind CFG) was using "Shani-mani-dani-mani" (7) in the 1940s. Anne Lutz (NJ-NY) remembers "Shine-a-might-a-Dynamite-a." Kalamazoo Girl Reserves (Mich YWCA) were singing "Shonny monny donny monny" in 1938.

/S/ is combined with /m/ and another bilabial, /p/, in the "stodola pumpa" chorus for "Walking at Night" (17). Fleur di Lis (NH P girls) was singing "stodilly poompa" in the 1950s. Treasure Island (Penna BSA) knew it as "stodola boompa" in 1946. When the chorus is sung faster than the verse, it becomes a tongue twister.

Cultural Differences

Despite the commonalities of biology, American nonsense songs treat reduplicatives differently than do foreign language ones. They rely strongly on the velar (g, k, q) and bilabial (b, p, m, w) phonemes, which are emphasized by alliteration or assonant series. Some are identical rhyme reduplicatives. International lyrics favor open syllables, often in consonant series, and ablaut or rhyme reduplicative phrases.

Anglo-American Nonsense

Some nonsense-language choruses and refrains from British and American folk traditions combine English words with nonsense. Janet White (Md P coed) uses "rink tam body mitchi kamboo" in her version of "Frog Went a-Courtin'" (5). Ann Beardsley (Mich GS) sings "Dickie Bird" (8) with "Dim salla bim ba, Salla du salla chim." Patricia Ann Hall (Calif CFG) has "Bim solla doo solla dim." Nancy Bryant (Ohio CFG) knows "Bim sola bim bam ba, Sola do sola bam."

Scholars believe such nonsense passages may have begun as Celtic or Latin, but were transformed by oral transmission.[289:21] John Thurman and Rex Hazelwood suggested "Qui Quay Quonnie" (6) might be debased Latin.[118]

Descended nonsense words may be rationalized back into English, like the "parsley, sage, rosemary, and thyme" in "Scarborough Fair" (7). The Opies say Joseph Ritson published the phrase with "Can you make me a cambric shirt" in the 1784 edition of *Gammer Gurton's Garland*.[452] Frank Kidson (1855-1926) published "Scarborough Fair" in *Traditional Tunes* in 1891. The founding member of the English Folk Dance and Song Society associated the ballad with "The Elfin Knight" (Child 2).

Another group in Anglo-American tradition manipulates favored sounds, with a preference for "iddle" or "oodle," often prefaced by a /d/ or /f/. This probably was more widespread in camps in the past. In 1938, the Kalamazoo Girl Reserves' (Mich YWCA) song book included "It's a Fine Thing To Sing" (5), with a chorus beginning "Fi-di-dil, doodle-da."

Some draw upon a pool of commonly known phrases. In the middle 1960s, Tawakani (Ida CFG) sang the chorus of "Cannibal King" (32) with:

> Oh, Jason Lee sacola buya!
> Oh, poppa wawa, shinny inny inny
> Oompah, oompah horses horses
> Giddyup giddyup, whoa buck!

The last half of the second line should be familiar from other songs. "Oompah oompah" is used in "Ging Gang Goolie" (19), "Kille Kille

Wash Wash" (17), and "Shinny Minny" (7). Horse-handling language like that in the last line is found in "A Jogging Along" (14).

Flea

"Flea" (39) encompasses the most complicated set of nonsense devices, recombinations, and conventions. It begins with a consonant series "Flea fli flo." In the version used by the Muskegon, Michigan, public schools' camp (Mich agency coed), it incorporates a long assonant series based on a counting-out rhyme, "eeny meeny hexemeeny solameeny dexameeny." Its twelve-part version subsequently has a phrase using common phonemes, "bee bidleoten doten bobo skadeeten dotten wadash shhh." Craig Kneeland (YMCA) knows the last as a cheer, "Bo bo skedetten dotten eh eh eh eh." Monica Mahe Foster learned it with gestures at a church retreat. The Opies noted it was a fad in England in the 1970s.[453]

Scat

While some of this sounds like scat singing, much of it probably was borrowed from college football yells. Ragtime pianist Jelly Roll Morton* told Alan Lomax, scat originally was a vocal technique used by New Orleans musicians to "flavor a song." He says, Louis Armstrong exposed the sound to the general public in 1926. Ella Fitzgerald and Mel Tormé used it as a technique to strip their voices of distracting words so they could interact with musicians as instruments. Cab Calloway turned it into a comic device in the 1930s.

Scat reached the camp repertoire through a different route. "Doodle Doo," which now is sung "Wadaleache" (34), was written in 1924. One composer, Art Kassel, had a band in Chicago, which once employed Benny Goodman. The other, Mel Stitzel was born in Germany, and worked with Morton. Eddie Cantor recorded the song two years before Louis Armstrong's famous "Heebie Jeebies."

Kitanniwa Repertoire

Kitanniwa's song book from the 1940s contained no Anglo-American songs with nonsense passages. Frivolity did creep into choruses of songs known to have European origins but sung in English, like "Marianina" (11) and "In Gorensko" (2).

The same general pattern persisted into the 1950s, when most nonsense passages were found in international songs like "The Cuckoo" (33). Still, there was one American folk song in tradition, "A Jogging Along" (14), and some homophonic two-part songs with one or both parts using onomatopoeia, like "Sarasponda" (59). Toward the end of the decade, a few were assumed to use foreign languages, like "Tongo" (20) and "Ah Wooney Cooney" (27).

At the same time the general camp repertoire treated absurd phrases as something found only in foreign sources, two nonsense items were known by small groups and done privately. The chorus of one,

> Catalina Matalina
> Hoopenbaker Hopenbaker

used a consonant reduplicative followed by an ablaut one. At the phoneme level, it used the /t/:/l/ and /h/:/p/:/b/ pairings with some velar /k/ sounds.

Fourteen individuals or camps recognized the song in 1976, none of whom transcribed it the same. Some agreement existed for the first line. Joyce Gregg Stoppenhagen remembers the second and third as, "Hoopen Steina Wallen Dinah / Hogan Bogan Logan was her name." Mawavi (DC CFG) knows, "Lubinsteina Wobbeleina / Hogan Logan Bogan." Shirley Ieraci (Ohio GS) has, "Ruffacina Ronna Donna / Hooka Pooka Mooka." While Joyce was in camp when I was, she probably learned her version in a church camp where Seth Clay provided the song books.

It is one of several fun songs that convert people's names into rhyming strings. In Mariana Palmer's Pennsylvania version of "Andy Brown" (16), a boy dies in a well because it takes too long to pronounce his name, "Andy choche atha cama to sinara to sinova sammy cammy waky Brown." A few, like John Jacob Jingleheimer Schmidt (62) and "Ivan Skizavitzky Skivar" (10), carry undercurrents of earlier ethnic antipathies.

The second nonsense item from Kitanniwa in the 1950s was a call and response used exclusively by the senior unit in the late 1930s and

1940s. The hollers functioned as legacy totems for older campers who learned them from family members, perhaps mothers, who had been to camp earlier. At the phrase level, the call,

> Hi lo inny minny ki ki un cha cha pee wah wah

used a logical opposition followed by a reduplicative followed by repeated syllables. At a lower level, it used the velar /k/ sound. Its response,

> Hepta minika hepta septa boom de ally ally oo hoo

began with a reduplicative phrase with an internal /h/:/p/ alternation, followed by commonplaces with open vowel endings.

One possible reason for the quarantine in the 1950s was the aesthetic sense that anything suggesting big-band commercial music, like scat, did not belong in camp. Marsha Lynn Barker (Mich GS) says "Flea" (39) was not considered a dining hall song in Girl Scout camps she attended.

There also may have been the feeling that, because many aspired to attend college like the counselors, they must eschew nonsense for rationality. Thus, while the daily schedule was suffused with customs like formal evening meals borrowed from small, liberal arts colleges, some types of Greek traditions were confined to the private repertoires of older campers and staff. Doris Rae Wolf learned "Flea" in her sorority. "Skinnamarink" (28) was included in Montevallo and Rockford College songsters in the 1920s. Carol Flack learned "Cannibal King" in college in the 1950s.

Kitanniwa's purpose changed in the late 1960s. Much of the formality was eliminated. Counselors no longer were called Miss. Girls no longer dressed for dinner. There no longer were flag ceremonies twice a day, like the one shown in "Rituals."

External social upheavals, which forced the transformations, removed restraints on nonsense. During the after meal sings I observed in 1974, no international songs were used as ruses. Lyrics were either all in English, or American songs with nonsense sections like "Skinnamarink" (28), or totally non-English, like "Eskimo Hunt" (21).

Case Study: Eskimo Hunt

"Eskimo Hunt" (21) is one of the few camp songs assumed by some to be entirely in another language. Others, of course, treat it as nonsense. It apparently first was published in a 1962 American Camping Association song book edited by Exner.[†] CRS introduced it as an Eskimo song that dramatized a polar-bear hunt.

Explication

An Eskimo attribution must be treated cautiously. Many songs identified as folk, in fact, are local popular or national songs, easily heard by travelers. They resemble the first wild flowers introduced from some new land that later are discovered to be common weeds, rather than unique endogenous species. Musical transcriptions tend to be standardized to fit American conventions. Lyrics often are completely new, or translations with little fidelity to the spirit of the original.

Exner[*] was born in Shanghai about a year before his missionary father, Sudentenland-born immigrant Max Joseph Exner[*] of the YMCA, returned to this country. If he was the one responsible for the song, that early exposure to Chinese may have conditioned his ear to comprehend non-western tonalities. However, his training in composition in Vienna could have been a strong counter force. His photograph appears in "Collectors."

The Eskimo of northern Alaska depend on whale and caribou for their meat. Other Native groups in the Far North rely on seal, walrus, or polar bear. According to Robert Spencer, hunters bought, traded, inherited or otherwise owned songs, which gave them power over their prey.[519:149] They sang "magic songs as they paddled [. . .] to come as close as possible to the point where it could be estimated that a whale would rise."[519:128] These songs tended to be measured and slow.[519:149]

It is doubtful the CRS song was a hunting song like those noted by Spencer in Point Barrow between 1952 and 1953. More likely, it was something like the faster-paced public song James Murdoch reported in the 1880s from Point Barrow. He was told, men from another village had introduced it when they joined a hunt a few years before. A similar song was reputed to exist in the Yukon.[437:399] Point Barrow is an Alaskan headland jutting into the Arctic Ocean.

The song Murdoch heard children sing, as they danced during particularly bright displays of the northern lights, has the same general form as the Kitanniwa version on the right:

Kióya ke, kióya ke	Hepsi cola misha walka
A, yana, yane, ya,	Oshkosh nuga, oshkosh nuga
Hwi, hwi, hwi, hwi!	Hey missa day missa doe missa day

The second and third lines of both constitute a repeated refrain. Murdoch's first line is a verse, one among many. CRS repeats the first line as a verse.

Textual Variation

Despite the existence of CRS song books, no standard version of "Eskimo Hunt" exists in camps. Since the sounds are alien, individuals rely on familiar sound patterns to reproduce them. The chorus's second line, sung "missa day" at Kitanniwa, has the common /s/:/m/:/d/ combination while "day" includes a broad vowel.

While this line generally is stable in camps, some have substituted the more familiar "iddle" from British folklore: "oh **diddle** ai" (B-C3) at Tannadoonah (Ind CFG) and "ho **diddle** hey" (B-C5) at Big Lake Youth Camp (Ore P coed). Killooleet (Vt coed) has turned it into a permutation exercise, "**hey** little **hi** little **ho** little **hum**" (A-C2), like the familiar "fee fi fo fum, I smell the blood of an Englishman" from "Jack and the Beanstalk."

Widjiwagan's (Hawaii CFG) open assonant series, "at ta ka ta nu va" (A-C2) in the chorus's first line at has been interrupted in some camps with velar consonants. "**A**k**i** a**ki** u am" (B-C4) at Wa-May-Ka (Iowa CFG) resembles a reduplicative. Some have converted the syllables into town names. Kitanniwa sings "**oshkosh** nuga" (A-C1). Big Lake Youth Camp (Ore P coed) knows "ah kee talkee **yuma**" (B-C5).

The verse has an even less recognizable pattern, probably because verses usually entail content while choruses may be all talismanic sounds. Many simply parse contiguous syllables into rememberable combinations. Thus, Widjiwagan's (Hawaii CFG) "hex a cola" (A-V2) becomes "Hey, **takoma**" (B-V2) at Killooleet (Vt coed). Widjiwagan's "mis a wa ta" (A-V2) becomes "mee-sa **water**" (A-V4) at Ticochee (Fla GS).

Music

The CRS tune shares many characteristics with Eskimo music. According to Bruno Nettl, such music is "characterized by the use of complex rhythmic organization and the use of recitative-like singing."[440:8] Melodies range between five and six notes, with an undulating melodic movement that may involve "the use of a series of tones with the same pitch."[440:9] Murdoch noted, individuals had no concept of pitch or tune, but held strict tempos. He thought most songs were "monotonous chants."[437:398]

"Eskimo Hunt" uses five tones. Its verse repeats one tone, with variations for the terminal "a walka." "Oshkosh nuga" repeats a single note, with a rise on the last syllable. "Hey missa day" is sung on one note, repeated on another, then varied with a three-tone arc.

Rhythmic complexity follows from the use of two poetic meters. The verse and first line of the chorus employ trochees (Xx). The chorus's second line uses dactyls (Xxx). When two six-syllable phrases are sung against the same number of musical measures as two four-syllable ones, it feels like part of the chorus is sung faster.

Gestures

"Eskimo Hunt" is an incremental verse repetition song, which functions as a kinesic ballad. That is, with each repetition, a new gesture is used to signal the narrative's progression. Peggy Hays[§] collected a cante fable. These are spoken tales that include pieces of music in the narrative, or musical pieces with spoken sections. She was told, at camp fires at the Storer Camps (Ohio YMCA coed), "just the verse and chorus are used with motions; in the dining hall the story is told."

Despite their standardization in print, the gestures are, perhaps, the most folklike aspect of the song. Rubbing noses, paddling a kayak, and the method for killing an animal are stereotypes, lifted from Eskimo life, and translated into familiar nonnative movements. Similar out-group or exoteric images occur in an Oweki (Mich CFG) verse for "Oh in the Moonlight" (16),

> Why all the little Eskimos put on their warm clothes
> Never rub toesies, always rub nosies

and in "Buggy Regions" (4) at Mawavi (DC CFG):

> I'd rather be an Eskimo
> With fur upon my head

Popularity

"Eskimo Hunt" is not known well outside Camp Fire camps. Rohrbough and Exner may have spread it in the survey Midwest.

The general difficulty in learning enough words to be comfortable may explain why so few mention the song. People recognize it. They have sung it. They do not want to be asked to repeat it. After a summer on Kitanniwa's staff, one woman admitted:

> I still can't get it. I still can't get the idea of, you know, cause it's in my mind as "ak taknova" and here, you know, they go "osh kosh nuga." And so I get up there and so I just go sort of half-heartedly and sorta lip the words, so the leaders don't think I don't know the song. And it's just that I don't know.

Version A

Text a composite of verses and choruses, altered to fit the verse form of Camp Kitanniwa (Mich CFG); the song form, the number and order of verses and choruses follow the pattern of gestures used at Camp Kitanniwa (Mich CFG), after supper sing, 1974.

Chorus 1 and verse 1 from Camp Kitanniwa (Mich CFG), after supper sing, 1974. Chorus 2 and verse 2 are close to the CRS original, from Widjiwagan Camp (Hawaii CFG), early 1970s. Chorus 3 and verse 3 from Linda Regan Knoblauch, Camp Lou Henry Hoover (NJ GS), 1976. Chorus 4 and verse 4 from Judith Bittmann, Camp Ticochee (Fla GS), 1976. Chorus 5 from Carol Ann Engle, Camp Cherith of Western New York (NY P girls), 1960-1975.

Gestures and sounds for verse repeated at the end of each line; gestures for the chorus done throughout the singing of the chorus.

C1 Oshkosh nuga, oshkosh nuga
Hey missa day missa doe missa day
Oshkosh nuga, oshkosh nuga
Hey missa day missa doe missa day
(Hands on opposite elbows; rock arms up and down to
paddle kayak)

V1 Hepsi cola misha walka
Hepsi cola misha walka
(Hands to eyes to scan horizon for seal, say "Ugh")

C2 At ta ka ta nu va, at ta ka ta nu va,
Ay mis a day mis a do a mis a day.
At ta ka ta nu va, ah ta ka ta nu va,
Ay mis a day mis a do a mis a day.
(Paddle kayak)

V2 Hex a col a mis a wa ta,
Hex a col a mis a wa ta.
(Fling harpoon forward with arm, say "Oooo")

C3 A-da-kat-a-know a, a-dat-kat-a-know a
A-mes-a day-mes-a dowa-mes a day
A-da-kat-a-know a, a-da-kat-a-know a
A-mes-a day-mes-a dowa-mes a day
(Paddle kayak)

V3 X-a-cola-mes-a wanna
X-a-cola-mes-a wanna
(Pull seal from hole, arms together at right hip; pull up
diagonally across body; say "Ugh")

C4 Ah-dee kah-dee noo-va, ah-dee kah-dee noo-va
Eh mee-sa day mee-sa doh-la meesa day
Ah-dee kah-dee noo-va, ah-dee kah-dee noo-va
Eh mee-sa day mee-sa doh-la meesa day
(Paddle kayak, sing slowly, heavy weight in kayak)

V4 Ex-a coh-la mee-sa water
   Ex-a coh-la mee-sa water
   (Wave, coming to shore, sing slowly, say "Ummm")

C5 Anta kanta nooga, anta kanta nooga
   Amos adamos, adomis, a day-o
   Anta kanta nooga, anta kanta nooga
   Amos adamos, adomis, a day-o
   (Paddle kayak fast, sing fast, glad to be home)

Version B

Text a composite of verses and choruses, altered to fit verse form of the Storer Camps (Ohio YMCA coed); the song form, the number of verses and order of verses and choruses follow the pattern of gestures and spoken parts used at the Storer camps (Ohio YMCA coed) as collected by Sally Hays, Ohio State University, 1973.

Verse 1 and chorus 1 from Camp Wampatuck (Mass P girls), 1974. Verse 2 and chorus 2 from John Calvi, Camp Killooleet (Vt coed), 1976. Verse 3 and chorus 3 from Camp Tannadoonah (Ind CFG), 1971. Verse 4 and chorus 4 from Mary Ann Wilkens, Camp Wa-May-Ka (Iowa CFG), 1976. Verse 5 and chorus 5 from Terry Wilbur Bolton, Big Lake Youth Camp (Ore P coed), 1976; original included diacritical marks on vowels. Verse 6 from Debra Nails, Camp Marydale (La GS), 1975-1976. Spoken interludes from the Storer Camps (Ohio YMCA coed); collected by Peggy Hays, Ohio State University, 1973.

Gestures for verses done at end of each line; gestures for chorus done throughout line.

> Speaker: Way up north where the Eskimoes live, they don't have supermarkets. So instead of going shopping for their food, they have to go hunting for it. The seal is one of the most important animals they hunt for, because the seal is used for all sorts of things: the meat is used for food,

the skins for clothing, and the fat is used for burning in their lamps. This song is about a man who is leaving home and going out to hunt for a seal for the winter. O. K. He's ready, so let's go. First he has to kiss his wife good-bye. Does anybody know how Eskimoes . . . (someone usually does). Eskimoes kiss by rubbing noses.

V1 Hexa kola missa wada
    Hexa kola missa wada
    Hexa kola missa wada
    (Kiss sound)

Speaker: Now he's getting into his boat

C1 Okka nokka nu way, okka nokka nu way
    Hey mizza day mizza do mizza day.
    (Arms are folded and move up and down in paddle motion)

Speaker: He's looking for a seal

V2 Hey, takoma mitchuaki
    Hey, takoma mitchuaki
    Hey, takoma mitchuaki
    (Hand on forehead in searching motion)

Speaker: Don't see any seals, have to paddle over here

C2 Ati taki umba, ati taki umba
    Hey little hi little ho little hum
    (Same as Chorus 1)

Speaker: He sees one

V3 Ex a cola Mishawaky,
    Ex a cola Mishawaky,
    Ex a cola Mishawaky,
    (Arm like rifle, shout bang after line)

C3 Aki toki nimbo, aki toki nimbo,
    Ay diddle, ai diddle, oh diddle ai,
    (Same as Chorus 1)

Speaker: Let's pick it up

V4 Es si col i mis si wana
    Es si col i mis si wana
    Es si col i mis si wana
    (Bend down and pretend to pick up heavy animal; say ugh!)

Speaker: Oh, it's a big one

C4 Aki aki u Ma, aki aki u Ma
    Hey diddle I diddle O diddle A
    (Same as Chorus 1)

Speaker: Hold it up for everyone to see

V5 Hey ti ko lah mi sho wah kee a
    Hey ti ko lah mi sho wah kee a
    Hey ti ko lah mi sho wah kee a
    (Hold up to show off; say see)

C5 Ah kee talkee yuma, ah kee talkee yuma
    Hey diddle, hi diddle, ho diddle hey!
    (Same as Chorus 1)

Speaker: Now he's going home to his wife

V6 I eks-a-koma-me-sa-wa-ah-saw
    I eks-a-koma-me-sa-wa-ah-saw
    I eks-a-koma-me-sa-wa-ah-saw
    (Rub nose with index finger)

Speaker: Now he's home and they're so happy because they have plenty of food for the winter.

An Austrian Went Yodeling: Melody

The doctrine that text and tune irrevocably are bound into an impregnable composition was unimaginable until the development of lithography in the late 1790s. Alois Senefelder's method of using grease pencils on limestone required less skill than etching copper plates. Printing music and text together became cheaper.

Illiteracy limited its use in England. Archibald Davison[*] suggested, the consequence was hymns were lined out. By 1725, most congregations only used about ten tunes. When Charles Wesley (1707-1788) began writing for the Methodist movement in 1738, he often paraphrased existing songs. Familiarity made it easier to introduce new ideas.

Mason only was interested in improving the quality of congregation singing. He began with familiar verses or hymns. His contribution was refurbishing them with existing or original melodies that fit a new musical aesthetic. Recombination was an extension of existing practice.

"Rock of Ages" (5) began as a 1775 poem by Augustus Montague Toplady. In 1831, Thomas Hastings wrote a new setting called "Toplady" for Mason's *Spiritual Songs for Social Worship*.

Eliza Flower composed the melody for her sister Sarah's "Nearer My God to Thee" (3) in 1841 for William Johnson Fox's *Hymns and Anthems*. When he was preparing *The Sabbath Hymn and Tune Book* in 1856 for congregations, Mason created a new arrangement. Although conceived for dedicated use, it still was given a separate name, "Bethany."

Conventions of serial creativity survived into the early twentieth century. New York Methodist Joseph Yates Peek set Howard Arnold

Walter's poem, "I Would Be True" (13), to music in 1911. His tune was called "Peek."

Garrett Horder adapted John Greenleaf Whittier's "The Brewing of Soma" for his 1884 *Congregational Hymns*. Independently, Hubert Perry composed an oratorio, *Judith*, in 1888. George Gilbert Stocks merged the two in 1924, when he needed a hymn for chapel at the Repton School, Derbyshire. "Dear Lord and Father of Mankind" (8) now is sung to "Repton."

Those leading religious revivals in the South were the ones who saw their works as individual inspirations. Charles Brenton Widmeyer, of Berkeley Springs, West Virginia, wrote "Come and Dine" (5) in 1906 to accompany a sermon for a Nazarene congregation near Hutchinson, Kansas. Daniel Iverson of Lumberton, North Carolina, wrote "Spirit of the Living God" (6) for a Presbyterian revival in 1916 in Florida being led by George Thealby Stephens. Nazarene are a Methodist offshoot.

The new religious creeds stressed individuals and their tangible experiences of salvation. Their articulation coincided with efforts in 1914 by professional songwriters to assert the rights of ownership by forming ASCAP, an organization mentioned in KUMBAYA. In 1917, Supreme Court justice Oliver Wendell Holmes enshrined their argument songs were indivisible objects produced to generate profits. The older view that text and tune were independent entities became a folk aesthetic when it was perpetuated in summer camps.

Tune Survival

The disjunction of text from tune means each can survive the dated or culture-bound qualities of the other. "Ach du Lieber Augustin" (2) surfaced in seventeenth-century Vienna, where it was associated with an itinerant musician who survived the bubonic plague of 1675. No one knew fleas were the bacteria's carriers. People believed being thrown onto a heap of diseased corpses, as Max Augustine had been, meant certain death.

Its tune has been used with "More We Get Together" (32), the "Calliope" (12), and Seth Clay's (Mich P coed) version of "In the Vintertime" (5). The open-ended pun song "Did You Ever See a Kitchen Sink" (6), the "Fish and Chips" part of "One Bottle of Pop" (40), and "If I Had a Windmill" (2) also utilize the melody.

Bryant's Minstrels introduced "Down in Alabam" in 1858. New words were substituted during the Civil War, according to Fuld.* "Old Gray Mare" (2) emerged as a parody around 1915. The melody since has been used for "Here we sit like birds in the wilderness" (14), "Swiss Navy" (16), and "Great Big Gobs" (4). June Rushing Leibfarth§ collected a second verse to "Glink, Glonk" (21) that utilized the tune.

The melody for "Bear Went over the Mountain" (8) and "He's a Jolly Good Fellow" (5) emerged in France after Marie Antoinette heard her son's wet nurse sing it in 1781. Fuld* found evidence the tune for "Malbrouck has gone to battle" existed in the 1760s when it was included in a collection of streets songs. He found nothing to indicate it was any older. Little is known about the servant, Geneviève Poitrine. Even her surname, which translates as "chest," may be ascriptive.

These few facts were obscured by one nineteenth-century Romantic's belief genuine folklore was created in the remote past rather than by living peasants and urban workers. In 1806, François-René de Chateaubriand* heard the melody in Palestine. The Roman Catholic novelist assumed his experience showed it must date from the Crusades. Musically, that was impossible. *Grove's Dictionary** argued its phrasing, scale, and use of the dominant chord were more recent.

Clementine

Similar fanciful tales surround "Clementine" (23). Lester Stern Levy* discovered the lyrics originated in 1863 as a crude song, "Down by the River Lived a Maiden." The 1880s parody of Henry S. Thompson's text usually is attributed to Percy Montross. By the end of the century, even more satiric passages had been added.

Edward FitzGerald Brenan heard young girls sing the tune in the 1920s in a remote Spanish village with "Dónde vas, buen caballero." The fifteenth-century ballad described the meeting of a noble with his dead wife. A rhyme game based on the ghost story was popular in Madrid in 1878, after Maria de las Mercedes died. She was seventeen when she caught typhoid fever on her honeymoon. She died within six months of her marriage to the king.

Brenan liked to think his village was isolated. He never considered how children's lore moved before electronic media, when the village was part of a regional economy. Instead, he suggested, "American and English miners" in the California gold fields "grew so tired of hearing their Mexican comrades sing this ballad day in and day out that they parodied it."[270:109]

Socially, his interpretation was impossible. Americans treated Mexican women as conveniences[421] and drove out non-English speaking miners. If the tune had Iberian origins, Basques were a more likely link between California and Spanish tradition. They had been fleeing wars and famine in northern Spain since Napoléon. Many went to Chile where they became successful merchants. Some moved from there to San Francisco as commission agents.[492] Others went directly to the west coast to work on sheep ranches raising meat.

"Clementine" has been used for "Found a Peanut" (17). A 1942 Joy Camps (Wisc girls) dialogue ballad, "In the City," described a mother who sent her "pampered daughter" to camp and asked if they "tuck you in at nine?"

> Writes the daughter to her mother
> Where the deuce do you think I am?
> Here they toss me out at seven
> More a lion than a lamb

Tune Families

The fact tunes survive more than a few years, spread beyond their geographic origin, and are learned orally implies they undergo changes to exist in variants. June Rushing Leibfarth[§] collected a slightly different melody for "Plant a Watermelon" (24) from Robinwood (Tex GS) in 1966. Hidden Valley (Md CFG) has a variant tune for "Glick Goon" (21). Susan Dunn[§] collected a modified air for "Patsy Orry Aye" (29) from the Franklin Settlement House camp (Mich agency) in 1967.

When variants of a tune become sufficiently individualized to be considered separate songs, a tune family may result. Clusters also may develop when songs with separate origins vary to become like one another.

"Miller's Wedding," a Scot strathspey (dance), was published by Robert Bremner in *A Collection of Scot's Reels and Dances* in 1759. Both "Auld Lang Syne" (9) and "Coming through the Rye" (2) descend from it. While most camps sing "There Was a Girl Who Came to Camp" (7) with "Rye," Namanu (Ore CFG) uses the other. "Rye" has been used for a Hanoum (Vt girls) birthday song.[345] Other lyrics using "Auld Lang Syne" include "Advertise" (2), "Bohunkus" (3), "Mules" (10), "We're Here for Fun" (6), and a Les Chalets Francais (Me girls) "Farewell Song."

Tune Sources

The theme for the *Lone Ranger* radio and television programs has been reused for a Christopher (Ohio C coed) unit song, and for "Harry Has a Head like a Ping Pong Ball" (6). Hidden Valley (Md CFG) sings "Johnny." Sue Ann Thompson Kraus (Ohio CFG) learned "Joey." Sue Hahn and Susan Loftus know "Joe" at Kamaji (Minn girls). Gioachino Rossini composed the melody as part of the overture to his 1829 opera, *William Tell*.

Bob Russell wrote the Boy Scout's words to the "Stars and Stripes Forever" that begin, "There above in the breeze" (5). The tune also has been used for the CFG "Onward We Go with a Song" (13), and "Be Kind to Your Web-Footed Friends" (16). Marilyn Nelson (Calif CFG) knows the last as "fine-feathered friends." John Philip Sousa introduced the march in 1897. Mitch Miller recorded "Friends" in 1958, then used it on his weekly television program, *Sing Along with Mitch*, in the early 1960s.

Operettas have been a resource, especially in the early years when some camps mounted such productions. "I'm Called Little Buttercup" has been used at Patiya (Colo CFG) with "They Call Us the Blue Birds" (3). William Schwenck Gilbert and Arthur Sullivan introduced the original in *H. M. S. Pinafore* in 1878. "Hail, Hail the Gang's All Here" (3), by Theodora Strandberg Morse, used "Come, Friends, Who Plough the Sea" from their *Pirates of Pinzance* of 1879.

"Hail, Hail Scouting Spirit" (11) is sung to "My Hero" from *The Chocolate Soldier*. Oscar Straus produced the operetta in 1908. "Inn of the Starry Sky" (3) uses the overture to *The Light Calvary*, composed by Franz von Suppé in 1866. David Kilburn Stevens wrote the words as "The Boy Scouts" to an arrangement by J. Remington. They first appeared in Marie Therese Armitage's *Junior Laurel Songs* in 1917.

National songs also have been readapted. Luigi Denza's "Funiculi" (7), written in 1880, is the source for "My High Silk Hat" (39) and a local Tanadoona (Minn CFG) song. "The Camp Fire Law" (35) and a Blue Haven (NM P coed) lyric use Jonathan Edwards Spilman's 1837 setting for Robert Burns' "Flow Gently, Sweet Afton."

The "Wayfarer's Grace" (26), which begins "Some hae meat," often is attributed to Burns. He reconfigured an existing work when he visited the family of the Earl of Selkirk, William Douglas-Hamilton, in 1794. Julie Sherwood[S] was told, Juliette Gordon Low introduced it to American Girl Scouts from the Scots Girl Guides.

Pre-World War I Tunes

By far the largest source for fun-song tunes is commercial music. Many come from the nineteenth century. Stephen Foster's "Oh! Susanna" (16) of 1848 has been sung with "Come, Let's Play We're Indians" (5), and an Aloha Hive (Vt girls) "Guest Song." His "Camptown Races" (4), published in 1850, has been used for songs at Hitaga (Iowa CFG), Les Chalets Francais (Me girls), and Brooklyn Scout camps (NY BSA).

"The Yellow Rose of Texas," published in 1853 by Christy's Minstrels, has been used for the "Wohelo March" (3) at Kotomi (Colo CFG), Tayanita (Ohio CFG), and Yakewi (Ohio CFG). It begins, "Wohelo is our watchword / Wohelo is our call." Mitch Miller recorded the original in 1955.

Our Civil War contributed "When Johnny Comes Marching Home Again" (4). It has been sung with Hitaga (Iowa CFG) and Irondale (Mo BSA) lyrics, as well as with "Ants Go Marching" (26). While it was written in 1863 by Patrick Gilmore, some claim it was based on an earlier Irish antiwar song, "Johnny I Hardly Knew Ye." Gilmore was from County Galway on Ireland's western coast. A friend told Debbie Saint Pierre,[S] they sang it during hikes in one camp she attended.

"John Brown's Body" (6) of 1862 has been connected to a camp meeting song formalized as "Say, Brothers, Will You Meet Us." Shortly thereafter, it was used for Julia Ward Howe's "Battle Hymn of the Republic" (11), and later associated with Methodists.[338] Some of its immediate parodies survive in "John Brown's Baby" (20), "John Brown's Flivver" (9), and the Brooklyn Boy Scouts' (NY BSA) "Hang Camp ____ on a Sour Apple Tree." The "glory hallelujah" chorus is used with "Pink Pajamas" (20) and the "Tongue Twister Song" (10).

Other lyrics sung to the tune include "It Isn't Any Trouble Just To S-m-i-l-e" (25), "Little Peter Rabbit" (19), "Mary Ann McCarthy" (5), "Oh, Sir Jasper" (2), and "She Waded in the Water" (8). Brooklyn Scout camps (NY BSA), El Deseo (NM CFG), Irondale (Mo BSA), Namanu (Ore CFG), Sacut (NY BSA), and Watanopa (Mont CFG) have local songs that use it.

"Silver Threads among the Gold" (2) was written by Lawrence College student Eben Eugene Rexford.* He sold it, with other poems, to a would-be composer searching for likely lyrics. Bass singer Hart Pease Danks added music, then sold it to Charles W. Harris in 1873. He, in turn, hawked it to traveling minstrel troupes who wintered in New York or to their agents. Richard Jose recorded it in 1903. The Cornwall-born countertenor had migrated to Nevada, then worked for minstrel troupes in San Francisco.

"At the Boardinghouse" (10) uses the melody. "While the Organ Peeled Potatoes" (5) was sung as a single verse by Joyce Gregg Stoppenhagen at a Michigan church camp. "Organ" was sung with a second verse, "Darling I Am Growing Whiskers," at Gifford (Neb BSA). Katie Hickey§ collected the latter as the second verse to "Boarding House." Gifford (Neb BSA) used Danks' tune for "You're a Wonder" (5), but Vivian Sexton (Tex CFG) sings that with "Reuben and Rachel" (4).

Stage Tunes

A pre-World War I show, *The Girl Behind the Counter*, introduced "The Glow-Worm." The amorous "I Wish I Was a Fascinating Lady" (2), "Roam, Joyous Gypsies" (7), and a Dixie Camps' (Ga sep) song[345] use the melody Paul Lincke composed for his 1902 Berlin operetta, *Lysistrata*. Lilla Cayley Robinson replaced the original lyrics of "Glühwürmchen-idyll" for New York audiences in 1907.

"Heidelberg" first was heard in the 1903 *Prince of Pilsen*. In the 1930s, Red Wing (Penna girls) used it for a local song. The composer, Gustav Luders, migrated to Milwaukee in 1888 from Bremen, in the newly organized German Empire. Frank Pixley produced the lyrics. He came from the Connecticut Reserve part of Ohio.

"Pack up Your Troubles" (5) has been sung in camps in the original form and with clones like "Pack up Your Wieners" (2) and "Pack up Your Duffle" (3). Felix Powell composed it with his brother for a 1915 London production, *Her Soldier Boy*. George Henry Powell used the professional name George Asaf.

Helen Carrington introduced "I'm Forever Blowing Bubbles" in *The Passing Show of 1918*. Leland Stanford Roberts and J. Will Callahan wrote "Smiles" (15) for the same production. The first has been used by Brooklyn Scout camps (NY BSA), and by Texas Camp Fire Girls, according to Vivian Sexton. The second has been used for "There Are Eats" (3). Fleur de Lis (NH P girls) and Tawakani (Ida CFG) adopted it for local songs.

Blanche Ring introduced "Rings on My Fingers" in 1909 in *The Midnight Sons*. An Iowa Camp Fire camp used it for "We're up at Hantesa" (19), then sent the lyrics to the CFG monthly magazine, *Every Girls*,* in 1922.

"Take Me out to the Ball Game" (4) was introduced in vaudeville by Nora Bayes in 1908. Albert von Tilzer and Jack Norworth's song has been used by Glen (Ohio CFG) and Onway (NH BSA). Jody Myers and Beth Strait wrote a local song with it for Hitaga (Iowa CFG) in 1963. David Stanfield Sinclair learned it with Indianapolis Boys' Club words in the 1970s.

Percy Weinrich composed "When You Wore a Tulip" for his wife, vaudeville performer Dolly Connolly. Jack Mahoney's 1914 text has been sung "Are You a Camel" (13), and used at Tanadoona (Minn CFG). *Paradology*[367] included "When You Drove a Buick" (3) and "When You Wore a Sunburn" (3).

Arthur Collins recorded "What You Gonna Do when the Rent Comes Round" in 1905. Mississippi Possum Hunters recorded Harry von Tilzer and Andrew B. Sterling's song as "Rufus Rastus Johnson Brown" (3) in 1930. Collins' version was used for "Tall Girls, Short Girls" (9). The second is known by some camps.

Inter-War Tunes

Commercially written tunes became more idiosyncratic after Holmes upheld the copyright law. Composers favored professional musicians who paid continuing royalties over amateurs who purchased and exchanged sheet music. Camps responded by using songs performed by artists who selected simpler melodies average people could sing.

Al Jolson introduced "Mammy" in 1921. Rebecca Quinlan remembers hearing it with a Lenore-Owaissa (Mass girls) song.

William Daniel Doebler[5] collected a local version from Runels (Mass GS). Skyland Camp (NC girls) also has adapted the melody.

A second critical development in commercial music in the inter-war period was the rise of big bands. They diverted attention away from singers and their words until Frank Sinatra emerged in 1941. Even so, many bands still needed wide-ranging repertoires to provide a full evening's entertainment. Some performed instrumental arrangements of songs already used in camps. A 1939 Victor catalog lists Tommy Dorsey recordings of "Comin' through the Rye" (2) and "Shine on Harvest Moon" (5).

Given these two changes, it is not surprising few commercial songs from the 1920s and 1930s were adopted for enduring, general, fun songs. Among those accepted was "Leave Me with a Smile" for "Once I Went in Swimming" (7) and a local Shawondasee (Tex CFG) song remembered by Vivian Sexton. "Bye Bye Blackbird" (3) has been sung with "Lost Underwear" (16) and local songs at Irondale (Mo BSA), Tanadoona (Minn CFG), and Tonawedan (NY BSA). Charles Koehler and Earl Burtnett wrote the first in 1921. Ray Henderson and Mort Dixon composed the other in 1926.

Anti-Commercialism

Another factor, which contributed to the decreased use of commercial tunes in camps, was the feeling amongst recreation-music and camping professionals that borrowed tunes somehow were inappropriate. In a 1932 book copyrighted by the National Recreation Association, Zanzig complained, "a very large proportion of the tunes used" for camp-specific songs:

> are from popular songs or college ones. In many cases only a word here and there is changed in a college song to make it fit the camp [. . .] it seems strange that young campers out under summer skies produce so little that is good or even merely clever. Some fine folk tunes have also been used for camp-made verses, but even a musician eager for better music in camps must wonder whether poor, trivial tunes with inferior words would not be better than fine tunes with such words.[561:522]

In a similar vein, Kempthorne[*] told CFG leaders in 1934, "Many of our camps have their own books of songs. This is fine, but do encourage learning some new songs each summer. Discourage parodies, and encourage the creative in music as well as words."

College Songs

Criticisms of college music, and the grouping of such songs with commercial ones, may have been a reaction to Rudy Vallée. He sang college and drinking (varsity) songs on his radio programs. These included the University of Maine "Stein Song," which was concocted by Adelbert Sprague and Lincoln Colcord in 1910. They adapted "Opie," a two-step by Norwegian immigrant Emil Andreas Jensen Fenstad. Vallée's revised rendition has been used at Man (NY BSA), Treasure Island (Penna BSA), and the first national Boy Scout Jamboree. The BSA gathering was held near Washington Monument on the mall in Washington, D.C., in 1937.

Vallée's 1934 recording of the "Drunkard Song," better known as "There Is a Tavern in the Town" (7), is the melody for "Head, Shoulders, Knees and Toes" (33). The song, first published in 1883, was sung with local lyrics at Watanopa (Mont CFG) in the late 1940s, and at Fleur de Lis (NY P girls) in the mid-1950s. Patricia Kline[§] collected a local version from Camp-in-the-Woods (NY YMCA coed) in 1954.

"Betty Co-ed," which Vallée recorded in 1930, is used for "Every Kitanniwa Girl is Quite Complete" (21) according to Tawakani (Ida CFG). Patiya (Colo CFG) believes the tune is the closely related "Washington and Lee Swing," written in 1910 by Mark Wentworth Sheafe, Thornton Whitney Allen, and Clarence Aaron Robbins. Some think they, in turn, borrowed from Genaro Codino's "Marcha de Zacatecas" of 1892. "Complete" was included in an Alpha Xi Delta song book in 1935. Some sing "discrete."

Others associated with college drinking songs included Vincent Lopez, who performed "Bell Bottom Trousers" on radio. Lauritz Melchoir had audiences sing along with "Vive l'Amour" (30). "Trousers," derived from a bawdy shanty in 1944 by Moe Jaffe, is used for "Six Little Ducks" (27) at Seabow (Calif CFG). The other, which evolved in Germany before 1818,[338] has been used for Seabow (Calif CFG) and Saint Vincent de Paul Ranch (Calif C boys) songs.

Guidelines promoted for progressive camps by Zanzig and for Camp Fire by Kempthorne may have helped lead to the substitution of international music for fun songs written to commercial melodies in many camps. They did not eradicate college tunes.

Notre Dame's "Victory March" has been used at Les Chalets Francais (Me girls), Christopher (Ohio C coed), James E. West (Ill BSA) and Kamaji (Minn girls), as well as by Pittsburgh Boy Scouts (Penna BSA) and a Michigan CYO camp (Mich C girls), according to Smith.[§] Frank Clark[§] collected a version of "I Was a Virgin" sung to the tune in a New Hampshire coed camp. Michael J. Shea and his brother, John Francis Shea, wrote the fight song for their alma mater.

In the mid-1950s, Fleur de Lis (NH P girls) had a song to "Maybe We Do but I Doubt It" with lines like, "When reveille blows, we hop out of bed / Maybe we do but I doubt it!" Another to "Glory to Dartmouth" had the lines:

> Our camp's a winner
> We've got the stuff
> We've got the colors three
> And that's enough

A 1902 Bryn Mawr song book included the first. It still was a catch phrase in their 1921 yearbook. Origins of the second seem lost.

In the Midwest, Joy Camps (Wisc girls) were using "On Wisconsin" in 1942 for:

> On to Joy Camps, on to Joy Camps
> For the summer days
> More of swimming, riding, hiking
> Through the woodland way

William Thomas Purdy and Carl Beck's song has been used at the Luther Gulick Camps (Me girls). Donald Monroe (1888-1972) wrote the Boy Scouts' "Trail the Eagle" (13). He and his son Keith wrote the Time Machines series of Scout adventures for *Boys' Life* between 1959 and 1989. They used the name Donald Keith. Purdy and Beck were roommates in a Chicago boardinghouse.

Color War Songs

Prohibitions against commercial tunes never penetrated private camps that sponsor local-song writing activities. These often are part of elaborate team competitions called color wars. In some, like Loyaltown (NY J boys), Steven Diner remembers each team or tribe writes a group of clan songs like a pep song, a comic song, and an alma mater. In others, like Lenore-Owaissa (Mass girls), Rebecca Quinlan remembers the songs are incorporated into elaborate routines or performances.

At Miniwanca (Mich P girls) in 1961, each class (age group or unit equivalent) wrote its own alma mater and each mounted an original revue. Marianne Culligan says, in one Oregon Camp Fire camp she attended, "At the end of each week each unit would write a song about their week. These were called 'Forest Echoes'."

Among the 1920s and 1930s songs used for local lyrics are "Five Foot Two" (2) at Hitaga (Iowa CFG) and "Hawaiian War Chant" at Wasewagan (Calif CFG). The first was written in 1925 by Ray Henderson, Joseph Widow Young, and Sam M. Lewis, born Samuel Levine. "War Chant," produced in 1936 by Leleiohoku, Johnny Nobel and Ralph Freed, was recorded by the Dorsey Orchestra.

Patricia Ann Hall remembers a Celio (Calif CFG) song to "California, Here I Come." Namanu (Ore CFG) and Surprise Lake (NY J boys) have local lyrics to the "Ranger Song." Kamaji (Minn girls) has one to "Show Me the Way To Go Home" (3). "Munchkin Land" was used for a 1971 Kamaji (Minn girls) unit song, "We represent the hatchery kids," according to Judy Miller.

Al Jolson introduced the first on Broadway in 1921 in *Bombo*. "Ranger," also known as "We're All Pals Together," is from a 1927 New York revue, *Rio Rita*. "Show Me" was derived in 1925 from "Oh, Mister Won't You Show Me the Right Way Home" by James Campbell and Reginald Connelly. The team used the pseudonym Irving King. *Wizard of Oz* introduced "Munchkin" in a 1939 film.

Recent Commercial Tunes

Post-World War II commercial songs modified for camp or color-war uses include some that enjoyed tremendous popularity. "Tom Dooley" (12), recorded in 1958, has been used at Loyaltown

(NY J boys). Les Chalets Francais (Me girls) modified "Ballad of Davy Crockett" from a 1954 Walt Disney television series. Bubbles Hyland adopted "Zip-a-Dee-Doh-Dah" (11) from Disney's 1946 film, *Song of the South*, for an Hitaga (Iowa CFG) unit song in 1948.

"Wonderful Copenhagen," from *Hans Christen Andersen*, was used by Miniwanca (Mich P sep) in 1971. "Wonderful, Wonderful Camp Hitaga" (Iowa CFG) was written by Susan Dunker, Nancy Files, Clary Lou Illian, Linda Nye, and Karen Wilson in 1953. Danny Kaye starred in the 1953 film.

Others were introduced by performers working in the older tradition of smooth vocal styles that enhanced simple melodies. Perry Como's recording of "Catch a Falling Star" has been used at Wintaka (Calif CFG). His rendition of "Round and Round" has been used at the Franklin Settlement House camp (Mich agency), according to Susan Dunn.⁵ The latter is the tune for "Take a Camp" (2) at Wolahi (Calif CFG) and Wintaka (Calif CFG). He introduced both in 1957 on his weekly television program.

Some novelty songs have been selected for their catchy tunes. "Little Red Rented Rowboat," recorded by Joe Dowell in 1961, has been used at Neewahlu (Ida CFG). "Sugartime" has been adopted at Shawondasee (Tex CFG), according to Vivian Sexton, and by the Cedar Rapids, Iowa, Ki-Tan-Da Camp Fire group (Iowa CFG). The McGuire Sisters introduced it in 1957.

Tawakani (Ida CFG) sings "Tani's Our Love" to Debbie Reynolds' 1957 recording of "Tammy." Hitaga (Iowa CFG) has unit songs set to Don Robertson's "The Happy Whistler" and to Patience and Prudence's "Gonna Get Along without You Now." Sue Willey wrote "Friendly Agatih" in 1958. Clary Lou Illian and Janet Knapp collaborated on "I got along without you / Before I joined you / But I now I can't see how!" for the same unit. Both records were released in 1956.

Camp Songs as Tunes

Camp fun songs, themselves, may become sources for other fun or camp-specific songs. These include a Brush Ranch (NM coed) text to "Bingo" (50), according to Mary Barnes. Blanche Walker wrote an Hitaga (Iowa CFG) Blue Bird unit song to "Itsy Bitsy Spider" (33) in 1952. "Oyster Stew" (12) has been adapted at Kowana (Tenn

CFG). Neewahlu (Ida CFG) has modified "Vrenalie" (30). "We're from Nairobi" (14) has been used at Kamaji (Minn girls), while "Zulu Warrior" (25) has been altered for a Loyaltown (NY J boys) tribal song.

"John Jacob Jingleheimer Schmidt" (62) has been used by Brooklyn Scout camps (NY BSA) and at Christopher (Ohio C coed). Irondale (Mo BSA) has an organizational song to "We're on the Upward Trail" (25). "Skinnamarink" (28) has been adapted at Adahi (Penna CFG) and Watervliet (Mich girls). Homelani (Hawaii P coed) sings, "I love you in the morning when I'm making up my bed / I love you in the evening when I'm snoring off my head."

Case Study Repertoire

The nineteen songs selected for the case studies use both borrowed and original tunes. "Grand Old Duke of York," "Pep" and "I Wish I Were" have melodies derived from older sources. "Duke" evolved from "A-Hunting We Will Go" and "The Farmer in the Dell." The second represents some combination of "Yankee Doodle" (6), "Polly Wolly Doodle" (11), and "It Ain't Gonna Rain No More" (4). Cecily Raysor Hancock has connected the last to the "Sam Hall"-"Captain Kidd" cluster.

Two have direct connections with African-American tradition. "Rise and Shine" descends from "Jacob's Ladder" (46). "Kumbaya" came from a South Carolina sea island spiritual collected in the 1920s. Another, the "Boatmen," was written for the minstrel-show stage in 1843 by Daniel Emmett.

"The Mermaid's" camp tune was standardized by college song books and mass-market songsters, like one published by Samuel Merrill Bixby[†] (1883-1912). His *Home Songs* began as an advertisement for his shoe polish company. It became a separate product in 1909.

Three others borrowed their tunes from commercially successful songs. "Swimming" used "Sailing, Sailing" from 1880. "Lollypop" adapted "Harrigan" from 1907. "A Bear" used "Sippin' Cider" (35) from 1919.

Folk revivals introduced two. "Ash Grove" was published by Edward Jones in an 1802 collection of Welsh songs. "Eskimo Hunt" was promoted by the Rohrboughs as a Native song.

Two commonly are associated with the romanticized west. "Skyball Paint" is presumed to have been written by a still unknown

PATRICIA AVERILL

professional author. The melody for "A Canoe May Be Drifting" shares musical phrases with "Red River Valley" (14).

Other songs were written in camps or by people associated with their sponsoring organizations. A Girl Guide leader, Marion Sinclair, wrote "Kookaburra." Margarett Snyder, a YWCA employee, composed "Witchcraft." "Rose" was published by Janet Tobitt for the Girl Scouts. Judith Czerwinski wrote "Flicker" in a New York Camp Fire camp, then took it to New Jersey Girl Scout camps.

The Cuckoo

The melody for "The Cuckoo" (33) exists in several, very different contexts. Walter Rein[†] and Hans Lang believed it originally was a Tyrolese folk song published in Vienna in 1887. Hans Baumann[†] thought the tune came from Styria, another mountainous region in Austria.

According to Rolf Wilhelm Brednich,[*] Baumann published the words in a 1939 soldier's songster. It reemerged in 1951, the same year CRS released its version through the YWCA.[†]

Katherine Ferris Rohrbough's translation was less earthy than "Und jetzt gang I ans Peterbrünnele." William Graffam translated the first verse for the International Youth Hostel[†] as:

> Oh, now I go to "Peter's Fountain"
> And I drink a glass o' wine
> And I hear there the cuckoo
> In the woods singing fine.

She had "Peter's flowing spring" and "the water's so good." His version focused on a man too poor to marry, and ended with references to Adam and Eve. Her second verse described a man looking forward to matrimony.

Sources for her text may be older than the postwar song. She was raised in the Catskill mountains,[375:23] where she may have heard some variant of another German song. Her third verse (C-3) has no thematic ties with the first three used by Graffam. It does have affinities with ones translated in 1938 by Thomas Royce Brendle[*] and William Stahley Troxell as:

176

The Cuckoo is an able man
Who supports fourteen wives
Guckgu Guckerdigu

The first wife carried wood into the house;
The second builds a fire with it.
Guckgu Guckerdigu

According to Brendle and Troxell, "D'r Guckgu" was "known throughout Germany. In the Pennsylvania Dutch region it has been sung for many generations and probably was brought over in the eighteenth century. We have heard it sung in Lehigh, Dauphin, Schuylkill, and Northumberland counties."

Explication

Connotations of the cuckoo in the three songs are very different. The most common meaning for the bird is the one suggested by the jilted bachelor in "Und jetzt gang I ans Peterbrünnele." The polygamous "D'r Guckgu" inverted that symbol. Rohrbough's song drew upon the bird's associations with spring and role as an oracle.

In England in the 1740s, individuals were instructed to halt in spring when they heard a cuckoo and pluck a hair from between their toes. If the hairs remained unchanged for ten days, their lovers would be true.[447:118] In the nineteenth century, children repeated the rhyme:

Cuckoo, cherry tree
Good bird, tell me
How many years I shall be
Before I get married

The number of calls they heard after the verse was the number of years. In Yorkshire and Lancashire, children asked "how many years afore I die."[447:118] Maria Leach* said, in Germany, similar rituals associated with the bird's return were done to guarantee money and good luck in the future.

The most important symbolic meaning for the cuckoo comes from our culture, which equates the bird with a wall clock. Such clocks are associated with the Black Forest, a mountain range in southwestern

German. European mountains, erroneously, are assumed to all be part of the Alps, which are associated with Austria and Switzerland. The last are identified with skiing and yodeling. The non-cuckoo part of the chorus shares the syllables used with yodeling, oh-lee-ah.

Traditional Gestures

Rohrbough's bowdlerized lyrics probably were never the reason the song was accepted. Rhythmic gestures used with the chorus include beating the thighs on the first phrase. The practice is reminiscent of noises Germans make when they watch skiing and other sports events. This is followed by simple rhythmic gestures, which are incremented with each verse. Thus, the final verse has three cuckoos and three finger snaps at the end of each line, in a manner that imitates those clocks where the birds count out the hour.

A German exchange student told some high-school-aged girls returning from Tanawida (Mich CFG), my local day camp, the song had many more verses. They immediately began to fantasize singing twenty cuckoos in a row. Her visit coincided with the period when the song was enjoying its greatest popularity in Germany, the late 1950s.

Case Study: An Austrian Went Yodeling

The inherent qualities of the chorus and the connotations of the cuckoo could be what led some person or small group to create a new cumulative gesture song. It retains the chorus of the original, along with the idea it is Alpine.

"An Austrian Went Yodeling" (34) probably developed in the late 1960s. It spread so quickly through camp communication networks, it left no traces of its diffusion pattern. By 1976, two-thirds of the young women in traditional camps recognized the song.

Textual Variation

It originally may have been no more than the first three verses: the skier (represented by the sound "swish, swish"), the avalanche ("rumble, rumble"), and the grizzly bear ("grr, grr"). The presence of the last suggests the lyrics originated in the Pacific Northwest. If one were to ask people from Michigan which animal was most likely to harm them if it darted across the road, they would answer whitetail deer. In New Mexico, they would say elk. Among the few places grizzly bears still roam this country are the northern Cascades of central Washington, and the Selkirk mountains in the northeastern part of the state bordering British Columbia and Idaho. Their other refuge is Yellowstone.

Washington's mountains support both downhill and cross-country skiing. It also happens to be one place where Germans fled in the late nineteenth century, when they were forced from the Volga. Russia's Catherine I had invited them to settle in the late 1700s. In Seattle, German singing societies survived the xenophobia of World War I.[554]

Once the bear was introduced, other animals associated with the Alps followed. Mormons[†] published a version in 1970 with a cuckoo, an avalanche, a grizzly bear, a mountain goat ("ba ba"), and a Saint Bernard ("pant, pant"). The dog was bred in the early 1700s to rescue people buried by avalanches.

Others added the dairy cow ("squirt, squirt"). Melodic meter dictated the breed, not logic, not familiarity: Jersey and Guernsey fit, Brown Swiss and Holstein did not.

It could have developed into another animal list like "Old MacDonald" (20). Ann Beardsley (Mich GS) has a version with a road runner ("beep beep zoom"), a dinosaur ("ugh!"), a bunny rabbit ("rrrrr"), and a blood sucker ("sssss"). Ka-esta (Ore CFG) has a mosquito ("buzz"), a bull frog ("ribit"), and a dinosaur ("gong").

Instead, someone decided the cow, which always seems to be a milk cow rather than the grazing one of "Old MacDonald" ("moo moo"), needed a milkmaid ("kiss, kiss"). Melacoma (Wash CFG), drawing upon advertising, makes it a "Swiss Miss."

As soon as a romantic interest existed, someone, maybe the same person, introduced conventions of a courtship ballad. Laura Clare Zahn (Mich CFG), Kotomi (Colo CFG), and Tawanka (Mich CFG) add her father, who shoots the Austrian ("bang, bang"), and Saint Peter ("flutter, flutter"). Elsewhere, the romantic tale has led to a love triangle. Another man "pow pow's" the hero, who then needs an ambulance ("rrrrrr"), at Glen (Ohio CFG), according to Nancy Bryant, and Watervliet (Mich girls).

Converting the list of animals into a ballad led to explicit termination verses. Katie Hickey[§] collected a version with a pigeon that goes "splat." Tawanka (Mich CFG) and Val Verde (Tex CFG) say "amen." Watervliet (Mich girls) has a tree in the skier's path. Adahi (Penna CFG) has an abbreviated verse ending, "and along came the dismal end."

Two camps invoke injunctions from authority. At Niwana (Wash CFG), a counselor says "walk" in the penultimate verse, and a policeman says "stop" in the final. The first is a mocking reference to a common camp rule to walk, not run. The other turns it into an opposition reminiscent of the children's game Red Light, Green Light. At Yukita (Ohio CFG), the last verse becomes a chant when the maiden's dad says, "Bang, bang, you're dead, brush your teeth and go to bed."

The most common textual variation in the new song is the substitution of "ostrich" for "Austrian." Some 20% of the people who know the song use the rationalization for humorous effect. June Rushing Leibfarth[§] heard the opening line of the chorus as "oh dearie."

New Gestures

Most gestures associated with the verses' subjects are conventional, and easily learned. When Laura Clare Zahn at Kitanniwa and the staff at Hidden Valley (Md CFG) were trying to reconstruct the song, each remembered the gestures first. They recalled the lyrics through their embedded associations with movement conventions, like games of Charades.

Debbie Saint Pierre[§] reported a similar use of kinesic memory in a Dayton, Ohio, Methodist Sunday school. Five-year-olds were taught gestures for "This Little Light of Mine" (24), because "they could remember the words by the actions." This may be the reason that, while the verses differ from camp to camp in "An Austrian," movements are less varied.

Music

Expanding the list from a repetition of cuckoos created a requirement for additional music. Marie Winn[†] changed the tempo from 3/4 to 2/4 for this section. In a version collected in New Jersey by Katie Hickey,[§] the introductory notes of the chorus were descending, rather than ascending. The rest was treated as an undulating chant.

Hidden Valley[†] (Md CFG) sustains the opening notes of each verse. Jolene Robinson Johnson[†] (Wash CFG) holds the verse's third line the way Kitanniwa did a generation ago with "The Cuckoo." Susan Orlowski has sung the new song with harmony at Lawrence (Ind C coed).

One conservative force still limits the development of variations in the new song's tune. The 51 people who knew both songs in 1976 represented more than 70% of those who knew "The Cuckoo." They were only 40% of those who sang "An Austrian." Since those who recognized the shared melody were more likely to be older, the sense of the published tune will die when current staff leaves and young campers take their places. Then, one can expect variations will increase until a new tune emerges in some camps, creating a musical family.

Popularity

Not everyone is pleased with the new song. Marsha Lynn Barker (Mich GS) finds it "obnoxious." Judith Bittmann (Fla GS) thinks it "offensive." Jolene Robinson Johnson (Wash CFG) calls it "totally asinine." Marsha and Carol Ann Engle (NY P girls) say it has been banned in camps they attended.

One reason for the critical attitude is, "it goes on for verse upon verse," to quote Kitty Smith (Mich CFG). Counselors, in camp all summer, tire of it quickly. Campers want to sing it repeatedly to learn the chorus. For those at Kitanniwa who like it, "it's a riot" according to Kitty.

"The Cuckoo" always had a ribald or joking quality in Germany, which the new song revived. The reversion may be another reason some people do not like "An Austrian." It offends against a feeling that "in the union of words and music the *basic emotion* of both shall be *identical* or at least in harmony." [emphasis in original]

Seeming inconsistencies between joking texts and lilting tunes in European folk music always created problems for some interested in international songs. Mary Stevens Dickie[*] made the quoted observation in 1929. Her *Singing Pathways* was one of the first collections to adapt folk tunes for youth groups as an alternative to the "'music for revenue' type" tunes. She went on:

> Through the centuries the original words of some of
> the Folk songs have been lost, and occasionally melodies
> of dignity and beauty have been found associated with
> words quite inadequate or unworthy. In these instances
> musical taste and judgment have had to be relied upon to
> determine the real message of the melody.

Conflicts between folk tradition and middle-class values are
constant. Attempts by the better classes to reform immigrants,
especially beer-drinking Germans, have been an undercurrent in
American life. When children are given a choice between the two, only
the one is vital enough to produce a serial creation like "An Austrian."

Version A

Verse pattern from Jolene Robinson Johnson, Camp Sealth (Wash CFG),
1960s; Camp Niwana (Wash CFG), 1969; Camp Kirby (Wash CFG),
1970-1972; Camp Kitanniwa (Mich CFG), 1973-1974. Verse order from
Laura Clare Zahn, Camp Natsihi (Mich CFG) c. 1966; Camp Missaukee
(Mich P girls) late 1960s through early 1970s; Camp-in-the-Woods (Mich
YWCA) early 1970s; Camp Kitanniwa (Mich CFG) 1972, 1974. Gestures
from Jolene Robinson Johnson and Laura Clare Zahn, Camp Kitanniwa
(Mich CFG), 1974. Their pictures appear in "Kitanniwa, 1974."

All verses follow the cumulative pattern of the first, second and final
stanzas. Asterisks (*) indicate the gesture associated with the starred
word earlier in the song is repeated.

1. Oh an Austrian went yodeling
   On a mountain top high
   When along came a skier
   Interrupting his cry

C. Oh lay ah (slap hands on thighs quickly)
   Oh (pause, slap hands on thighs)
       lay ah (clap hands)
       ki ki (snap fingers)
       oh* lay ah* cuckoo (snap fingers)
       swish (sweep hands across front of body in an arc)

Oh* lay ah* ki ki*, oh* lay ah* cuckoo* swish*
Oh* lay ah* ki ki*, oh* lay ah* cuckoo* swish*
Oh* lay ah* ki ki*, a lo (slap hands on thighs)

2. Oh an Austrian went yodeling
   On a mountain top high
   When along came an avalanche
   Interrupting his cry

C. Oh lay ah*
   Oh* lay ah* ki ki*, oh* lay ah* cuckoo* swish* rumble,
       rumble (roll hands around each other in front of chest)
   Oh* lay ah* ki ki*, oh* lay ah* cuckoo* swish* rumble, rumble*
   Oh* lay ah* ki ki*, oh* lay ah* cuckoo* swish* rumble, rumble*
   Oh* lay ay* ki ki*, a lo*

3. a grizzly bear - grr

4. a Saint Bernard - paws in front of chest, two panting sounds

5. a Jersey cow - milk a cow with hands, make sound of milk
   squishing out

6. a pretty maid - kiss kiss

7. her father - bang, bang with gun motions

8. Saint Peter - flutter, flutter

9. Oh an Austrian went yodeling
   On a mountain top high
   When along came a road runner
   Interrupting his cry

C. Oh lay ah*
   Oh* lay ah* ki ki*, oh* lay ah* cuckoo* swish* rumble,
       rumble* grr* pant, pant* squirt, squirt* kiss, kiss,
       bang, bang*, flutter, flutter* beep beep errrr

Oh* lay ah* ki ki*, oh* lay ah* cuckoo* swish* rumble,
    rumble* grr* pant, pant* squirt, squirt* kiss, kiss,
    bang, bang*, flutter, flutter* beep beep errrr
Oh* lay ah* ki ki*, oh* lay ah* cuckoo* swish* rumble,
    rumble* grr* pant, pant* squirt, squirt* kiss, kiss,
    bang, bang*, flutter, flutter* beep beep errrr
Oh* lay ay* ki ki*, a lo*

Version B

Text and gestures from Camp Ka-esta (Ore CFG), 1975; variations from A emphasized.

V. Oh a **Swiss boy** went yodeling
    On a mountain **so** high.
    When along came a (verse)
    Interrupting his cry.

C. **Oh** lay, O; OH a **rock a** ki, **(no gestures)**
    Oh lay, O; OH a **rock a** ki, **(no gestures)**
    Oh lay, O; OH a **rock a** ki, **(no gestures)**
    Oh a rock a ko (motion)

Verse	Motion
1. Avalanche	**Swish**
2. Grizzly Bear	Grrr Grrr
3. St. Bernard	Pant-Pant
4. Jersey Cow	Squirt-Squirt
5. Pretty Girl	**Smack-Smack**
6. **Dinosaur**	Gong
7. **Mosquito**	Buzz
8. **Bull Frog**	Ribet
9. Sheriff	**Bang-Bang**
10. Father	**Clap-Clap**

(Note) You add another **thing** to each verse and then go back down to the first thing.

Version C

Text to "The Cuckoo" from Camp MeWaHi (Calif CFG), 1972; variations from Katherine Ferris Rohrbough's text emphasized. Gestures from Patricia Averill, Camp Kitanniwa (Mich CFG), 1951-1960. Guitar chords from Buck's Rock Work Camp (Conn J coed), 1959.

Asterisks (*) indicate the gesture associated with the word or phrase earlier in the song is repeated.

1. Oh I went to **Saint Petersburg**
   Where the water's so good
   And I heard **there's a** coo-coo **bird**
   As **he sang** from the wood

C. Oh-lee-ah (slap hands on thighs, quickly)
   Oh-lee-**ah** (slap hands on thighs once, clap hands once)
      Coo-ke-ya (snap fingers)
     Oh-lee-**ah*** Co-coo (snap fingers)
   Oh-lee-**ah*** **Coo-ke-**ya* Oh-le-**ah*** coo-coo*
   Oh-lee-**ah*** **Coo-ke-**ya* Oh-le-**ah*** coo-coo*
   Oh-lee-**ah*** **Coo-ke-**ya* Oh (slap hands on thighs)

2. After (D) **winter** comes sun (G) ny days
   That will melt (A) all the snow (D)
   Then (D) I'll marry my maid (G) en fair
   We'll be hap (A) py I know (D)

C. Oh-lee-ah*
   Oh-(D)-lee-ah* Coo-ke-ya* Oh-le-ah* Coo-coo* Co-coo*
   Oh-(A)-lee-ah* Coo-ke-ya* Oh-le-ah* Coo-coo* Co-coo*
   Oh-lee-ah* Coo-ke-ya* Oh-le-ah* Coo-coo* Co-coo*
   Oh-(D)-lee-ah* Coo-ke-ya* Oh*

3. When **I marry** my maiden fair
   She'll have all she desires
   A home for her tending
   And some wood for **her** fire

185

C. Oh-lee-ah*
    Oh-lee-ah* Coo-ke-ya* Oh-le-ah* Coo-coo* Coo-coo*
        Coo-coo*
    Oh-lee-ah* Coo-ke-ya* Oh-le-ah* Coo-coo* Coo-coo*
        Coo-coo*
    Oh-lee-ah* Coo-ke-ya* Oh-le-ah* Coo-coo* Coo-coo*
        Coo-coo*
    Oh-lee-ah* Coo-ke-ya* Oh*

Ash Grove: Pretty Songs and Harmony

Pretty song repertoires include both indigenous and general songs. The first normally are heard only in camp. The others may be sung anywhere. In recreation and progressive camps, they are used whenever slower songs are needed. In more traditional ones, they may be reserved for times when new people are brought into the group who might not know the local songs, like inter-camp visitations. Such songs are recalled when the usual repertoire is exhausted or inappropriate, say during an unusually long camp fire or overnight camping trip.

General songs often are selected because they have pleasant sounds, while indigenous ones are preferred for their meaningful lyrics. One can hear seeming non sequiturs, like elementary-school-aged girls singing the world-weary "Both Sides Now" (13) because the music is nice. Likewise, difficult tunes, like that for "A Bed Is Too Small" (30), continue to be learned because the imagery and themes are important.

At Glen (Ohio CFG), Nancy Bryant has noticed, "fast songs change more often than the slow ones" in the repertoire. Unlike fun songs, which exist in cycles, slower ones remain popular for a long time, then simply disappear. Variations in their use often follow changes in camps' demographic profiles.

Sources

General pretty songs draw on many traditions. Early, campers sang material found in commercial and community songsters. Their choices usually were filtered through college aesthetics. Relatives told Philip LaRonge,§ "we used to sing a lot of 'Bye Bye Blackbird' (3)" at Mooseheart (Ill CFG) in the late 1920s.

Like fun songs discussed in the last chapter, the commercial ones known before and during the depression, generally, came from the years between our Civil War and World War I. "Tenting Tonight" (2) was known at Treasure Island (Penna BSA) in 1920, and in Brooklyn Scout camps (NY BSA) in 1929. "It's a Long Way to Tipperary" (2) was sung by Brooklyn Scouts, and is remembered by Joseph Carleton Borden from Rotherwood (Me boys) in the 1930s. Walter Kittredge wrote the first in 1863.

Among nineteenth-century lyrics known by Treasure Island (Penna BSA) and Irondale (Mo BSA) in the 1920s was "Old Oaken Bucket" (2). Still being sung is "Church in the Wildwood" (8), which William Savage Pitts[*] wrote in 1865. The physician studied music in the early 1850s with a former member of Boston's Handel and Haydn Society. He was nineteen at the time.

Stephen Foster's songs remained familiar until the Civil Rights movement of the 1960s. "Old Black Joe" (11), from 1860, was known by Kitanniwa in the 1950s. Joseph Carleton Borden recalls "My Old Kentucky Home" (9) from Rotherwood (Me boys) in the 1930s. Jean Mayo MacLaughlin (Fla GS) remembers singing "Swanee River" (6) over a century after it was composed in 1851, because "we were in Florida, after all!" Kentucky's state song, written in 1853, has been used for a local song at Les Chalets Francais (Me girls).

The partiality toward Foster reflected a general preference for national music. "Londonderry Air" is used at Seabow (Calif CFG) and the Hart Reservation (Penna BSA). George Petrie published the melody in *The Ancient Music of Ireland* in 1855. Jane Ross had collected it in Ulster. Frederick Edward Weatherly made it "Danny Boy" (2) in 1910.

"Camp Fire Prayer" (38) begins "For nights with stars." Ka-esta believes its tune is "The Tender Apple Blossoms." That is the version of "Londonderry" recorded by John McCormack (1884-1945) in 1923. The concert tenor's voice complemented the strengths of early recording technology.

In the early 1920s, Brooklyn Boy Scout camps (NY BSA) had a marked taste for songs recorded by him. Their songster included his "Killarney" (1), "Minstrel Boy" (1), "Mother Machree" (1), "My Wild Irish Rose" (5), and "That's Peggy O'Neill" (1). Their parodies included "Mother Machree's Old Man" (1), "My Wild Irish Nose" (1), and "A Pretty Spot in Ireland" (1). The last, which featured clothes lost while swimming, was sung to "Where the River Shannon Flows."

Philadelphia, which had been the port of entry for many Scots-Irish immigrants, was more inclined to Scots songs. Treasure Island's (Penna BSA) song book from 1920 included "Annie Laurie" (3), "Blue Bells of Scotland" (1), and "Coming through the Rye" (2). All were recorded by Harry Lauder (1870-1950), a baritone who adopted a comic stage persona. Their one sentimental Irish song, "Believe Me If All Those Endearing Young Charms" (4), was recorded by McCormack.

"Santa Lucia" (4) has been sung in English and with the Boy Scouts' "Footsteps on Distant Trail" (5). Teodoro Cottrau's 1849 transcription has been used with local songs at Les Chalets Francais (Me girls) and Adahi (Penna CFG). The Pennsylvania song begins, "Well do I love the trail," and ends, "But in my window shines the gypsy star." Tenor Enrico Caruso made the Neopolitan melody famous.

Commercial Composers

Commercial songs accepted into the general camp repertoire have not been simply those that enjoyed the greatest notoriety. In the same way some performers were more popular than others, some composers enjoyed a greater gift for creating material that coincided with traditional camp aesthetics.

Among those who have had three or more songs enter camp tradition, some were from German-speaking states or trained there. In 1832, the parents of Henry Kleber* (1816-1896) moved to Pittsburgh, Pennsylvania, from Darmstadt in the duchy of Hessen-Darmstadt. The composer taught singing, then opened a music store. His most famous student, Stephen Collins Foster (1826-1864), was raised in Lawrenceburg, up the Allegheny from Pittsburgh.

Other important composers were from the Midwest. Egbert Van Alstyne was born in Marengo, Illinois, northwest of Chicago. Tanadoona (Minn CFG) adapted his "Drifting and Dreaming" for "Another Day Dawning" (1). "Memories" was used with an early Luther Gulick Camps (Me girls) parting song remembered by Augusta (Calif CFG) in the 1930s. Gus Kahn wrote the lyrics for "Memories" in 1915. Others who contributed to "Drifting" in 1925 were Erwin Roeder Schmidt, Loyal Curtis, and Haven Gillespie.

Richard Whiting, who was raised in Peoria, Illinois, composed "I Want To Wake up in the Morning" (19) and "Til We Meet Again" (4). "Meet" has been used with "Round the Blazing Council Fire" (5). Kahn, who migrated to Chicago from Koblenz in the Palatinate, collaborated with Raymond Egan on the words to "Wake Up" in 1917. Ontario's Egan also wrote the words for "Meet" in 1918. He had met Whiting in Detroit where he was a bank clerk and Whiting a publisher's agent.

Percy Weinrich, born in the mining town of Joplin, Missouri, wrote "Moonlight Bay" (1) in 1912. It has been sung at Fitch (Ohio YMCA), and used for camp-specific songs at Les Chalets Francais (Me girls) and Tawakani (Ida CFG).

Other composers include Ethelbert Nevin, whose "Mighty Lak a Rose" has been used at Tanadoona (Minn girls). He was born in western Pennsylvania, trained in Saxony's Dresden, probably by Heinrich-Wilhelm Böhme, and in Prussia's Berlin by Karl Klindworth and Hans von Bülow. Frank Lebby Stanton wrote the lyrics in 1901.

Theodore Morse composed "I've Got a Feeling for You" in 1904. Mount Holyoke employed it for "Way Down in Our Hearts." The college version since has been adapted at Skyland (NC girls), and in sister camps Miniwanca (Mich P sep) and Merrowvista (NH P coed).

Edward Madden wrote the lyrics. The New Yorker also produced the original words for Weinrich's "Moonlight Bay." Morse was born in Washington, D.C. and sent to the Maryland Military Academy on Chesapeake Bay when he was a young teenager. Somewhere he took piano and violin lessons.

Repertoire Formation

From the depression to the Folk Revival, few commercial songs entered the pretty music repertoire. Part of this can be ascribed to changes in taste described in the last chapter. Part can be attributed to the fact many camps had existed long enough to foster their own traditions. They no longer relied so heavily on exogenous sources. There were both counselors, who had grown up in the camps, and enough returning campers to provide models for newcomers.

However, if a camp ever fails to have that critical mass of tradition bearers, it is forced to replicate the early years of camp singing. In 1976, Hidden Valley (Md CFG) planned a hayride for young Blue Birds. Their goal was to create the positive association between singing and having a good time that precedes aesthetics.

Unfortunately, the staff invited no older, enthusiastic girls to abet their plans. They were in a situation where they could not effectively teach new material. Leaders were forced to forage for songs the girls already knew, like "Row, Row, Row Your Boat" (26) and "Old MacDonald Had a Farm" (20).

Counselors tried the few commercial lyrics they thought the girls might know, like "Swinging on a Star" (2) and "High Hopes" (4). Bing Crosby introduced the first in a 1944 film, *Going My Way*. Frank Sinatra sang the second in the 1959 film, *A Hole in the Head*.

Learning Technique

Pretty songs utilize fewer forms of textual repetition than do fun ones, so the learning process is different. Songs are absorbed, through either conscious memorization or continued exposure. They are remembered in their entirety, or else forgotten. In trying to recall a song, of which she could only remember the first line, Joyce Gregg Stoppenhagen (Mich GS) recapitulated the learning process:

> And I could remember "Baby's boat's a silver moon"
> (19) and then I just dredged it up a few words at a time,
> or I could fit a few words and then skip a few. But I
> remembered the music.

In other words, the tune was learned first, then words were learned in phrases filled by humming. The difficulty came with insignificant words like "the," which begin lines and may serve as triggers to recollecting whole sections.

Medleys

In the 1950s, immediate knowledge of the general slow-song repertoire was receding, as audiences learned from films to become observers rather than participants. As a child, I attended only one program that began with someone leading the assembly in songs like "Three Fishermen" (51). The 4-H awards program in the fall of 1956 was also the only one followed by a square dance in the high-school gymnasium. The much-respected county extension agent soon retired. His successors did not continue his practices.

Processes of oral tradition, which break down and simplify texts, accelerated. Often, only a verse or chorus was remembered from an older song, along with a melody. Medleys became important mechanisms for combining shrunken units into singable pieces.

Paul Nettle[*] believed the first student medley was published in 1733 in the *Augsburger Tafelkonfekt*. A Benedictine monk, Johann Valentin Rathgeber, assembled the collection for use after meals. From there the form moved into German student tradition, and then crossed the Atlantic.

An 1867 Yale song book combined "Good Night Ladies" (2) with "Merrily We Roll Along." Fuld[*] tied the first to a song written by Edwin Pearce Christy for his minstrel show in 1847. Henry Randall Waite[*] published the other in 1868 as a setting for Sarah Josepha Hale's[*] 1830 words for "Mary Had a Little Lamb" (2). Yale's association of the two into a single valedictory persisted. A ministerial-school graduate, Ferdinand Van Derveer Garretson (1839-1919), edited the college's song book.

Carol Domoney[§] collected a version of "Good Night, Comrades" (3) from a Boy Scout who had attended Rotary (Mich BSA) in the 1950s. Widjiwagan (Hawaii CFG) and Wampatuck (Mass P girls) know "Merrily We Go to Camp" (2).

In the 1950s, Kitanniwa sang "Now run along home and jump into bed" (9) to "Merrily" when Blue Birds were dismissed early. Leah Culp has sung "Green Trees" (56), "Taps" (73), and "Run Along" as a medley. At Warren (Mich P coed), Eleanor Crow says, they combined "Run Along" with "Playmates" (8). Aleta Huggett[§] was told, girls sang this "on a corner by our school" after their weekly Girl Scout meetings in the 1940s. Ann Beardsley says, it still is used primarily with Brownie meetings. Harbin[*] published the text in 1927.

Brooklyn Boy Scouts (NY BSA) parodied Hale's verse as the "Featherbed Song" (2), "I Wish that Girl Were Mine" (2), "Lamb Sandwich" (1), "Mary Had a Swarm of Bees" (1), and "Nancy Had a Little Dog" (1). Treasure Island (Penna BSA) and Brooklyn Scouts sang "Mary Had a William Goat" (2). More recently, Seth Clay included a verse about eating lamb sandwiches in "It Ain't Gonna Rain" (4). Fowke found "Goat" still was known in Newfoundland in 1960.[331] *Paradology* publicized it in 1927.[367]

The dining hall spirit of the student medley persists in the Boy Scout tradition of following "Bravo, Bravissimo" with "Han Skal Leve" (15). Mason published the first in a medley with "Johnny Can You Count Twentyfive" in an 1841 collection, *The Gentlemen's Glee Book*. In 1925, *Scouting** magazine published an expanded "Bravo," claiming it had been written for the 1924 jamboree in Ermelunden, Denmark. In 1928, the group* published it in the medley, "Danish Honor Chorus," as it had been learned at the international gathering. The editor said, it "has become very popular in camps all over the country."

Perhaps the most common medley in camps is "I've Been Working on the Railroad" with "Dinah Blow Your Horn" (28). Sigmund Spaeth* saw the latter as an "embellishment" of Christy's "Good Night Ladies." Fuld* traced the words for "Someone's in the kitchen with Dinah" to sheet music published in London in the 1840s.

One of the most popular combinations at Kitanniwa in the 1950s was "There's a Long, Long Trail" (22), followed by "Let the rest of the world go by" (5). They followed "Shine on Harvest Moon" (5) with "The bells are ringing for me and my gal" (4). The last was written in 1917 by George William Meyer, Edward Ray Goetz, and Edgar Leslie. Ernest Roland Ball and Joseph Keirn Brennan produced "Let the Rest" in 1919.

In the late 1950s, Kitanniwa converted "In the Evening by the Moonlight" (16) into a medley by adding a tag ending, "Rack 'em up / Stack 'em up," borrowed from pool-hall slang. Some camps follow the first verse of "Cannibal King" (32) with part of "Under the Bamboo Tree" (10), and then "If You'll Be M-i-n-e Mine" (4). Wakoma (Wash CFG) and Wolahi (Calif CFG) both attach the "Rack 'em up" ending.

Melodic Variation

Given the reliance on melody as a mnemonic device, surprisingly little textual variation exists in pretty songs. One reason may be campers who like them are older, and have larger vocabularies than younger children. They are less likely to mishear words. In addition, slower tempos facilitate listening.

When variations do occur, they usually are insignificant or obscure words. In "Woodchild" (6), Hitaga (Iowa CFG) sings "I hymie in the morning." June Rushing Leibfarth[S] collected "How high me in the morning" from Arnold (Tex GS) in 1962.

Although textual variation decreases in the pretty song portions of camps' repertoires, tunes become altered in tradition. Harmonies never become standardized. These musical changes transform songs with stable texts into folk or folklike music.

The simplest melodic variation is singing different notes. Such alterations were described in PEP for a tune that had become amorphous. He Bani Gani (Md CFG) goes down, rather than up, on the words "you'll never know dear" in "You Are My Sunshine" (10).

Adding melisma, or singing several notes to the same syllable, also is common. Young girls at Wyandot County's 4-H day camp (Ohio 4-H) added notes to the syllables "down," "day" and the "all" of "all day" in "All Night, All Day" (33) in 1974. Jolene Robinson Johnson (Wash CFG) uses additional melisma with "Dark Brown Is the River" (28). A friend of Ann Marie Filocco[S] knew an ornamented version of "Make New Friends" (68).

The tune June Rushing Leibfarth[S] collected for "They Call the Wind Mariah" (22) from Silver Springs (Tex GS) in 1964 used less melisma on the central syllable of "Mariah." Brush Ranch (NM coed) sings "Miriah," according to Mary Barnes. Melacoma (Wash CFG) has "Mirriah." Zanika Lache (Wash CFG) transcribed "Moriah." The song is from Alan Jay Lerner and Frederick Loewe's 1951 musical *Paint Your Wagon*.

Harmony

Many use the word harmony to describe any piece of melodic music in which at least two notes are sounded simultaneously. Musicologists, generally, limit the term to music written in the style introduced by Haydn and elaborated by Beethoven, which features a melody supported by three-tone chords.

Standardized choral forms use two male parts (tenor, bass) and two female, called descant and alto in the earliest books, and now termed soprano and alto. When an all-male group performs, the parts are high tenor, sometimes called falsetto by Southern groups, tenor, baritone, and base. When an all-female group sings, the parts are high soprano, lead soprano, low soprano (mezzo-soprano), and contralto.

Physics prescribes the permissible chords within a scale. Three generally are used: the tonic built on the first note of the scale, the dominant on the fifth, and the subdominant on the fourth. Guitar chords are indicated by the tablature or letters written near the notes. Piano music exploits more variations.

Parallel Harmony

The most common harmonic pattern exploited in camps has two groups sing the same, or essentially the same, melodic line with different notes. They are usually a third apart, like C and E. Parallel harmony can be improvised easily. Azalea Trails (Calif GS) uses this device with "The Silver Moon Is Shining" (17) and "White Buffalo" (5). Wintaka (Calif CFG) employs it with "Hey There" (10). Wyandot (Ohio CFG) uses parallel melodies with "Camp Fire Prayer" (38) and "Old Father Time" (18). Wasewagan (Calif CFG) uses such harmony with the last song, as well as with "White Wings" (36).

Convergent Harmony

A second form of harmony is convergent. With "Tell Me Why" (78), two groups begin a phrase an octave apart. With each syllable, they come closer together, ending in parallel thirds. Katie Hickey[§] collected a version from a friend who worked at Matollionequay (NJ YWCA). It used converging harmony for only the last three lines.

Divergent Harmony

Divergent is a third form. Two groups begin together and move in opposite directions. This usually is limited to the last line of a verse, like "Peace, I Ask of Thee O River" (88), or to the end of a line, like "Taps" (73). Azalea Trails (Calif GS) uses this terminal device with "Dark Brown Is the River" (28) and "Look Wider Still" (8). Final line harmony is used with "Louisiana Lullaby" (6) at Wasewagan (Calif CFG), and with the version of "Give me a Rose" (16) Kathleen Solsbury[§] collected from The Timbers (Mich GS) in 1970. The last sometimes is sung "bring." A third, middle part may be added to "Taps."

195

Elaborate Harmony

Another harmonic form features two or more parts composed with closely similar words. In "Swinging Along" (44), the second melody is a descant, a more elaborate line above the main one. Gladys Jacobs arranged the version known by most. Jan Smyth (Ohio P coed) remembers, at church camp, girls would sing one part, boys the other.

Descants commonly are sung with "Slumber My Pretty One" (9) and "Little Drop of Dew" (24). Wintaka (Calif CFG) sings "This Land Is Your Land" (64) with a second part. Yakewi (Ohio CFG) uses such harmony with "Little Ships" (12).

"Slumber" and "Dew" were spread by public-school music books. The first, by M. Louise Baum and Arthur B. Targett, was used for fourth and fifth grade classes in 1923 by Thaddeus Philander Giddings.[*] Frank Dempster Sherman's words for the second appeared in several primers between 1896 and 1931 with other melodies. The camp tune has some affinities with several, but is different from them all. The Columbia art professor's original poem had a second verse.

In some cases, like "Cloud Ships" (13), another melodic line, an alto, is sung below the main one. "As I Greet Wintaka" is sung with two parts at the California Camp Fire camp. Girl Scouts at the 1965 Senior Roundup in Farragut State Park, Idaho, recorded the Krone's arrangement of "Swing Low, Sweet Chariot" (31) with the "swing low chariot, swing low chariot" chant (4). Max Thomas Krone (1901-1970) and his wife, the former Beatrice Perham (1901-2000), founded Idyllwild Summer Arts camp (Calif coed) in 1950.

Jean Mayo MacLaughlin (Fla GS) and Madeline Gail Trichel (La GS) have sung two parts with "All Night, All Day" (33) in Southern Girl Scout camps. Kathleen Solsbury[§] collected two-part versions of "Joy Is Like the Rain" (15) and "Come and Go with Me to That Land" (16) from The Timbers (Mich GS) in 1970. Wintaka (Calif CFG) uses two parts with some echoes in "Been Riding" (8). Peter, Paul and Mary recorded "Come and Go."

Timbraic Harmony

The other kind of harmony in camps results from untrained voices singing outdoors. Technically, any note is an abstraction of many pure tones or harmonics vibrating simultaneously. In the same way, we learn, as children, to assemble jumbles of noises into texts, we learn to combine these minutely different aural vibrations into tones. Lowest is the fundamental. The others, each proportionally higher, are overtones. The combination of the fundamental and its overtones, together with the varying strength of each, produces the timbre of a voice.[501:96]

When one person sings, a single note, generally, is heard. When several people sing, the individual timbres may vary and a variety of minutely different tones may be heard. Trained musicians learn to minimize differences. In camps, vibrating partials can produce the illusion of harmonic singing, even when each person is singing the same note. As mentioned in KUMBAYA, this can stimulate individuals to improvise against one of the perceived tones.

A sense of timbraic harmony may develop among people who are not trained as children to western tonalities. Fletcher said, she "first detected this feeling for harmony" among the Omaha when she transcribed their songs and played them back on the piano.

> the song played as an unsupported solo did not satisfy my memory of their unison singing, and the music did not "sound natural" to them, but when I added a simple harmony my ear was content and the Indians were satisfied.[326:10]

As she listened more carefully, she realized men and women sang in parallel octaves, and that the "different qualities of male and female voice bring out harmonic effects." She noted, "one becomes aware of over tones."[326:11]

Harmony campers hear is more than the sounds produced by individual voices. Music heard in the outdoors differs from that heard inside. The best times for fun songs are dining hall meals. Hard, bare walls, like those in the "In Lodges" photograph of Kitanniwa, throw sounds back on themselves. This augments loudness and preserves higher pitched tones. The resulting feeling of group participation encourages involvement.

When groups move outdoors, normal interactions of sound waves with temperature and humidity are magnified. Sound's speed decreases with decreasing temperature. Its fullness decreases with humidity, which absorbs the higher-pitched sound waves. Since most outdoor singing is done around a camp fire in the early evening when temperatures are cooling and humidity is increasing, sound waves are moving slower and losing more of their upper overtones. Lower, more mellow tones become stronger.[265]

Robert Erickson suggested much of what I am calling timbraic harmony was the choric effect, which "common sense leads one to guess [. . .] is the result of small random variations in pitch, loudness, timbre and precision of attack." Other important factors are "the size of the sound space" and "its dispersion, especially on a horizontal plane."[321:51] Sounds would have been fuller in the bowl at the Friendly Acres evening camp fire pictured "In Town," than in the afternoon council fire shown in "Rituals."

Whether the sound is perceived to be bad unison singing, standard or naïf singing, or something more complex, timbraic harmony is the central quality of camp singing that separates it from "schooled music." The existence of this sound quality led Fredrica Beyerman Depew to write:

> I loved Miniwanca (Mich P sep) and I loved the sound
> of those songs from that many voices, especially with the
> harmony. There's nothing else like it. And when you no
> longer go to camp, there's no where else you can find it.

Folk Aspects

Harmony can be learned from scores, in which case it is not folk, or from exposure. The first occurs in arts camps like Lighthouse (Penna coed), where Susan Fromberg remembers they staged several musicals a year. At Interlochen (Mich coed), concerts are so professional, Interlochen Public Radio records them for later broadcast.

In some Eastern camps like Loyaltown (NY J boys), Steven Diner says they hold auditions for their talent shows. Productions are rehearsed for several weeks. Eleanor Crow remembers similar extravaganzas at Aloha Hive (Vt girls). They mounted one based on the 1954 Broadway version of *Peter Pan* when she was there in 1976.

Music in such programs generally cannot be considered folk. Much of the lore surrounding the preparations is similar to theater folklore anywhere. Yet, the memories, the anticipations, in short the emotions, very much are part of the experiences that set camps apart as folk communities.

Occasionally, a production song does enter a camp's repertoire. Joseph Carleton Borden remembers in the 1920s or early 1930s at Rotherwood (Me boys):

> One year a stage production in the camp theater included at least two songs which became part of the singing repertoire that season and carried over into the following years - "Daisy, Daisy, give me your promise true" (17) and "Hallelujah" (1).

Similarly, Nathaniel Bruce Lawrason[S] talked to someone in the 1940s who had been in a male quartet at camp. He was told, they "nearly wore out both versions and the original" of "Silver Threads among the Gold" (2) and its parodies.

An appreciation of timbraic harmony may be developed earlier by girls than by boys. When Petzold studied the ways elementary-school students responded to specific musical elements, the only area in which he found differences between the two was timbre. Girls, generally, were better able to recognize variations.[464:133-135]

This means girls' camps may be more likely to improvise against a sound, while boys may apply a formula like parallelism. At Blue Haven (NM P coed), Wesley Cox says, as a result of continued exposure, "people usually make-up harmonies on all songs as they go." At Celio (Calif CFG), Patricia Ann Hall says the whole sense of harmonic balance:

> stayed the same and your group would usually divide themselves without really formally dividing themselves. Some people would always just naturally take both parts when you'd be singing in a group . . . .
>
> It didn't matter. It's funny. It's something that was never worked out, but you just naturally knew, as with many camp songs that have those parts that just occur in the chorus. Everyone sorta felt, and if too many people were doing one part, somebody would strike out and do the other part. It was always pretty well balanced.

Case Study Repertoire

Six of the nineteen case-study songs can be considered pretty ones. "Kumbaya," the best known, entered camp tradition from the mass media or with people who had learned it elsewhere. Rohrbough's version used divergent parallel harmony. The initial "Kum ba's" were sung in unison, the rest in thirds. Since the spiritual usually is sung slowly, people improvise other harmonies or simply respond to timbraic effects they hear.

"Rose" is a round. Tobitt's first two measures use half notes, which are set against quarter notes in the second two. Measures five and six also employ quarter notes that are contrasted with the half and whole notes in the final two bars. Whether it is sung with two or four parts, half the group is always singing sustained tones while the other half is singing melodic phrases.

The first two bars use descending motifs, while the second two use ascending. When sung against each other, they create divergent harmonies. Measures five and six are higher than the rest creating a descant effect. The last two undulate around the melodic center of the first two.

Among indigenous pretty songs, "Witchcraft" has been the most widely published. Kitanniwa in the 1950s used divergent harmony followed by some parallel parts in the central section. The parallelism varied from session to session. Girls also used a divergent part on the concluding phrase.

"Flicker" was intended for instrumental accompaniment. Its rhythmic and melodic techniques make it difficult to improvise an independent harmonic line. In contrast, the slow tempo of "A Canoe May Be Drifting" invites parallel and timbraic improvisation.

"Ash Grove" is the other pretty song that may be known outside camps. In 1943, Benjamin Britten[†] arranged it as an art song with piano accompaniment for tenor Peter Pears. In camps, the melody often is sung with a descant composed by Tobitt, which we learned from *Music Makers.*[†]

Patricia Ann Hall[†] (Calif CFG) uses more staccato phrasing with both the melody and the descant than is usual. Lucille Parker Munk[†] (Mich CFG) has sung the two parts of Tobitt's arrangement so often, her tune merges them. Young women at Kitanniwa[†] and Yallani[†] (Calif CFG) added timbraic and parallel harmonies on selected passages. Harmonies at Kitanniwa varied from singing to singing in the 1950s.

Case Study: Ash Grove

"Ash Grove" (72) describes a stock subject of landscape painters in this country since Thomas Cole (1801-1848). A river flows through quiet land, often with a tree in the foreground. Its melody, "Llwyn Onn," predates the lyrics. Edward Jones (1752-1824) introduced it in London in 1802 in his *Bardic Museum*.

Henry Brinley Richards[†] (1817-1885) won a prize in 1832 at the Gwent-Morgannwg Eisteddfod (sing competition) for his piano arrangement. In 1873, he announced the publication of *The Songs of Wales*[†] with new words by John Oxenford. Oxenford (1812-1877) was an English playwright, who had translated Goethe's autobiography. His two-verse version (C-2:4) is published widely, but often with variations.

Thomas Oliphant's (1799-1873) two-verse poem is the more common text in camps. The Madrigal Society president worked with John Thomas[†] (1826-1913) to create new lyrics and translations for Welsh tunes. This one was included in the first volume of *Welsh Melodies* in 1862.

Tobitt introduced his words into the camp repertoire in the 1936 edition of *Sing Together*.[†] In some camps, verses from both poems have been combined to create local variants (version C). These medleys may function to extend the pleasure of singing this particular melody and its harmonies.

Explication

In Welsh, "onn" mean "ash" and "llwyn" means "grove." The tree was sacred to the Vikings, who harassed Ireland in the ninth century and attacked England in the tenth. In the *Younger Edda*, Snorri Sturluson (1179-1241) recorded man was created from an ash tree wrenched from the earth. Woman came from an elm.

As the symbol of creation, ash yule logs were burned in ceremonies celebrating the sun's return after the winter solstice. John Williamson[*] suggested, the associations with rebirth also existed in Brittany and the Lowlands around 1500. There the tree was combined with the cherry in *The Start of the Hunt*, one of the unicorn tapestries. Cherries were connected to the return of the sun, but in the farmer's spring, not the cattleman's winter. As such, they figured in the divination rhyme quoted in AN AUSTRIAN.

The ash is the tree in the tapestry that contains the initials "A. E." Historians believe the letters identify the patron as Anne of Brittany on the occasion of her 1499 marriage to Louis XII.[551] Several centuries before, Celtic Brittany had diplomatic ties with the Danes against the Franks.

Intertwined letters suggest a legend Benjamin Thorpe[*] reported from the island of Giske in 1851. According to a Norwegian ballad, "Axel Thorsen og Skiøn Falborg," two lovers, who had been separated by their parents, were buried in the same graveyard. As the ash trees planted over their graves matured, the branches entwined. With time, her tree died, but his survived.

Images of interlaced grave plants are more familiar to us from "Barbara Allen," although the motif is not recorded in any version of ballad 84 reprinted by Child.[*] Two camps know it as "Red Rose and the Briar" (2). Jean Mayo MacLaughlin (Fla GS) remembers singing a variant of "Barbara Allen" (1) in Florida.

Wales was less affected than Ireland or northern England by contact with the Norse. Edward Jones[†] said the melody's title had no hidden symbolic meaning. It was simply "The name of 'Mr. Jones's Mansion'" located in the agricultural northeast of Wales.

Trees would have overrun any land left fallow by a gentlemen farmer. Ashes routinely were cut to encourage new growth from stumps, which then could be harvested for firewood. The wood burns well, even when green. Its combustibility was the reason it was associated with lightening from the gods, and with yule logs.

One cannot write a paean to real estate or firewood and expect to be successful. Instead, Oxenford and Oliphant created songs of mourning. One wrote the musings of an older man looking back on his life, with phrases like "friends of my childhood" (C-3) and "dear ones" (C-2). Oliphant described feelings of a young man, who goes "wandering in search of my lover" with a soul laden with "deep sorrow" (C-5).

Each was less interested in ash trees as a copse, than in the generic grove of trees that had come to represent the ideal cemetery. In 1840, Congregationalists had opened Abney Park in London, with the expectation the burial ground would become a public arboretum. They borrowed their ideas from Mount Auburn, an 1831 real-estate development outside Boston. According to Stanley French, American developers of the first rural graveyard independent of a church hoped:

the plenitude and beauties of nature combined with art would convert the graveyard from a shunned place of horror into an enchanted place of succor and instructions. The world of nature would inculcate primarily the lessons of natural theology[334:78-79] [. . .] the thought automatically inculcated by the decent cemetery would assuage the suffering of the mourner; it would make the young and careless pensive, the wise wiser.[334:84]

In our less-sentimental times, campers have returned to Jones' positivism. They only sing the first verse of Oliphant, oblivious to any connotations of the phrase "pensively roam" (A-1).

Textual Variation

Many variations in the text of what Karen terHorst (Mich GS) knows as "The Oak Grove" can be attributed to folk digestion of alien poetic forms. Lines in both poems are longer than camp song lines. Some transcribe it in paragraph form, while others, like Watervliet (Version B-2), break lines in half. While the latter transcription fits the melodic repetition pattern, it obscures the original ABAB CDED pattern. As a result, end words, which were controlled by that rhyme scheme, have become open to change (*i.e.*, "rove" removed from "grove" becomes "roam").

Also altered are the more affected words like "streamlets," which has become "streams" at Kushtaka (Alaska CFG). June Rushing Leibfarth[§] heard "streambed" at Arnold (Tex GS).

Music

Ancient Wales had both instrumental and vocal traditions, often perpetuated by blind men who left no written records. John Playfield was the first to publish their tunes in the 1655 edition of *The English Dancing-Master.*[*] The first description of their singing style comes from Giraldus Cambrensis, who traveled with Baldwin, Archbishop of Canterbury, in 1188.

He observed part-singing was common, even among young children. He emphasized the uniqueness of Welsh tradition by adding the only other people who used harmony in England were those who lived north of the Humber. They were in the modern-day counties of York and Northumberland on the eastern coast, and Lancashire on the west. The northerners only used two parts, a hummed base and a melodic treble. He said, "when a choir gathers" in Wales:

> you will hear as many different parts and voices as there are performers, all joining together in the end to produce a single organic harmony and melody in the soft sweetness of B-flat.[349:242]

The term "B-flat" may be anachronistic. Even the language of Welsh medieval modes was not established when this was written. Giraldus, like Fletcher, was an individual educated in contemporary music theory who was trying to find ways to describe the harmony he heard with his culture's Norman vocabulary. His work survives in Latin copies made in the late 1300s. The translation is based on an authoritative version created in 1868 by James Francis Dimock, long after "B-flat" was accepted terminology.

Welsh bards, who celebrated military virtue, were suppressed by the English beginning in 1284. Henry Mills actively squashed what he could of the choral tradition when Calvinist-influenced Methodists began improving congregation singing in the 1780s.[300]

Following the American and French revolutions, Edward Williams (1747-1826) anticipated national music movements on the continent, discussed in KUMBAYA. He organized the first revived eisteddfod in London in 1792. Jones' collection appeared ten years later.

After reviewing the history of Welsh music, Kidson[390] dismissed claims "Llwyn Onn" was Cambrian. Instead, he suggested it was part of a tune cluster first documented in the third volume of Playfield's collection of 1726 as "Constant Billy." Sharp* later included it in an anthology for morris dancers. Playfield's reputation developed in the 1600s, before the introduction of lithography mentioned in AN AUSTRIAN, and carried over to later editions. Morris dancing had been suppressed by the Puritans, and revived in 1899.

Three years after the Playfield version, John Gay used the melody in *The Beggar's Opera* for "Cease Your Funning" in 1729. Gay was raised in Barnstaple, on the south side of Bristol Channel. Wales lies on the northern shore. His Berlin-born musical collaborator, Johann

Christoph Pepush, may have Germanized the melody. Ralph James used their variant in 1730 for *The Fashionable Lady*.

The tune did not surface again until 1802. Soon after, John Parry suggested it was the source for Gay's tune. When the song became popular, he claimed he was the composer. Chappell[†] was willing to let him take credit for his variant. He thought the song more likely was "the production of some grateful bard whom Mr. Jones entertained."

Popularity

"Ash Grove" (72) is one of the great favorites among women. More than 70% of those in girls' camps recognized it in 1976, while a third of the women in coed camps knew the song. Less than 20% of the men in coed and boys' camps sang it. This is an American cultural phenomenon. In England, choral director Sydney Hugo Nicholson[†] included an arrangement in his 1903 *British Songs for British Boys*. Scouts[†] published it there in 1925 and 1954. Roger Whittaker[†] recorded a version in 1977.

Canadian Scouts[†] included it in a 1932 song book. The editorial committee chairman, Lesslie Rielle Thomson (1886-1958), was a nuclear engineer. An astronomer, E. Russell Paterson, oversaw the editorial work. Notes on music were provided by organist John Joseph Weatherseed.

In this country, it was known on the Folk Revival circuit in the late 1950s, when Ed Pearl named his Los Angeles folk and blues club after the song. Harry Nilsson[†] used the elegy for a demo recording in California in 1962.

Joan Fulton,[§] who collected songs from Wasewagan (Calif CFG), noted in the 1940s and 1950s, the tune was "very popular all over southern California, although the words are never the same. Many camps and groups have made their songs to fit it, and there is one fairly well known version with words about the Pacific Ocean." Version B includes Watervliet's (Mich girls) local lyrics.

Mary Lang says, it always is used on serenades at Newaygo (Mich YWCA). In Wisconsin, Josephine Weber (Wisc CFG) recalls its use for council fires and serenades. Patricia Ann Hall remembers this as "the one song in particular that I really associated with the big kids" at Celio (Calif CFG).

Among Girl Scouts, Julie Sherwood[S] heard it was an evening campfire song at Molly Luman (Ohio GS). Carol Simon[S] was told, in some Ohio camps, it is "mainly for campfires, church services and Scouts Own." The last "is a Girl Scout meeting held in the troop, at camp, or by two or more troops together in which Girl Scouts reaffirm their ideals."[198:45]

Parody

With its moderate tempo, "Ash Grove" fell between the fun songs and pretty ones reserved for special occasions at Kitanniwa in the 1950s. It could be used anytime. In our first year in the senior unit, 1958, it was sung more often, even when we were washing dishes, because one girl could handle the descant. In fact, it was sung so often, it aggravated jealousies. Some girls created a parody, "Down yonder brown outhouse," by making the two-word substitution. They never felt the need to complete the song. The contextual parody was not repeated.

Version A is from someone who was there the year we sang it so often, but was not a recognized singer. Her recollections reflect a very important characteristic of folk groups: individuals are assigned specific roles. The girl with the good voice would be considered an active bearer of the group's traditions by von Sydow,[528:219] the one whose existence was critical for its manifestation. Eighteen years later, she remembered few songs she had sung. Polly McIntyre, on the other hand, was the custodian for the repertoire, the passive tradition bearer who participates and remembers. She was key to the persistence of tradition.

Version A

Text from Polly McIntyre, Camp Kitanniwa (Mich CFG), late 1950s; transcribed February 1975. Guitar chords from Ann Beardsley, Camp o' the Hills (Mich GS), 1964-1970; Camp Ken-Jockety (Ohio GS), 1976. Polly's photograph appears in "Coming of Age."

Down (D) yonder green valley, where stream (F) lets mean (G7) der,
When twi (C) light is fa (F) ding I pensively (G7) rove (C)
Or at the bright noontime in sol (F) itude wan (G7) der

Amid (D) the dark shades (F) of the lone (C) ly ash (G7) grove. (C)
Tis there where the black bird is (C) cheerfully singing
Each (C) warbler enchants with his note (G7) from a tree
Ah (C) then little think I of sad (F) ness or sor (G7) row
The ash (C) grove, the ash (F) grove, spells beau (C) ty for (G7) me (C)

Version B

Text from Camp Watervliet for Girls (Mich girls), 1970s; variations from A emphasized in shared verse. Guitar chords with verse 1 from a former Girl Scout camper; collected by Carol Shuster, Ohio State University, 1973. Guitar chords with verse 2 from Clarena Snyder, Great Trails Camp (Ohio GS), 1963, 1965, 1967-1968.

1. Down (C) yonder green valley
   Where streamlets (F) meander (G)
   While twilight (C) is fading (F)
   I pensive (C) ly (G) **roam** (C)
   Or (C) at the bright noon **tide**
   In sol (F) itude wander (G)
   Amid (C) the dark shades (F)
   Of the lonely (C) ash (G) grove (C)
   'Tis (C) there where **blackbird**
   Is cheer (G) fully singing
   Each warbler (C) enchants
   With his **notes** (G) from **the** (D) tree (G)
   Ah then (C) little think I
   Of sorrow (F) **or sadness** (G)
   The ash (C) grove, the ash grove (F)
   Spells beauty (C) for (G) me. (C)

2. Just (D) off of Lake Sherwood (A7)
   The bright sun is (Dm) shining (G7)
   The campers (C) are waking (F)
   To (C) have a good (G7) day (C)
   The (C) camp's name is Watervliet (Am)
   And we know it can't (Dm) be beat (G7)
   The peo (C) ple are (F) swell
   And we all are (C) good (G7) friends (C)

207

We adore all the scenery (Am)
The lakes trees and (Dm) greenery
The horses (C) and rabbits (Am) are
fun to (G7) care (D) for (G7)
And in (C) the late eve (Am) ning
When programs (Dm) are ending (G7)
And sha (C) dows are bending (F)
We all go (C) to (G7) sleep. (C)

Version C

Text from Ann Beardsley, Camp o' the Hills (Mich GS), 1963-1970; Camp Ken-Jockety (Ohio GS), 1976. Verses 1 and 5 from Thomas Oliphant, variations from Oliphant emphasized. Verses 2 and 3 from John Oxenford, verses 2 and 3 in reverse order, variations from Oxenford emphasized. Verse 4, a repeat of part of verse 2, is closer to the original Oxenford.

(Typed)
1. Down yonder green valley where streamlets meander
   Where twilight is fading, I pensively **roam**
   Or at the bright noontide in solitude wander
   Amid the dark shades of the lonely ash grove
   Tis there **where** the blackbird **is** cheerfully singing
   Each warbler enchants with his notes from the tree
   Ah then little think I of sorrow or sadness
   The ash grove entrancing spells beauty for me

2. **My laughter is over, my step loses lightness**
   Old countryside measures steal soft on my ear
   I only **remember** the past and its brightness
   The dear ones I mourn **for** again **gather** here
   From out of the shadows their loving looks greet me
   And wistfully searching the leafy **green** dome
   I find other **faces fond bending** to greet me
   The ash grove, the ash grove, alone is my home

3. The ash grove how graceful, how plainly tis speaking
   That harp through **its** playing has language for me
   When over its branches the sunlight is breaking
   A host of kind faces is gazing on me
   The friends of my childhood again are before me
   Each step wakes a mem'ry as freely I roam
   With soft whispers laden, its leaves rustle over me
   The ash grove, the ash grove that sheltered my home

4. From ev'ry dark noon they press forward to meet me
   I lift up my eyes to the broad leafy dome
   And others are there, looking downward to greet me
   The ash grove, the ash grove that sheltered my home

(Hand written)
5. Still **does** the bright sunshine o'er valley and mountain
   Still warbles the blackbird its note from the tree
   Still **twirbles** the **woodbeam o'er** streamlet and fountain
   But what are the beauties of nature to me?
   With sorrow, deep sorrow, my **soul** is laden
   All day I go **wandering** in search of my love
   Ye **echo**, o tell me, where is **my young maukine**
   "He sleeps 'neath the green turn down **yonder** ash grove"

SECTION III

Camp Philosophy
Influences on Repertoire

Camp Philosophy Influences
on Repertoire

Camping has been smelted from an American past when everyday life could descend into unimaginable hardship without warning. The mingling of Presbyterian evangelism, German Romanticism, British public school traditions, and social snobberies of the newly rich produced a general view of camp life and three subtypes I call the traditional, the progressive, and the recreation camp.

Camp Meetings

Before our Civil War, the most important social institution in the West was the camp meeting. It began when Barton Warren Stone preached for seven days at Cane Ridge, Kentucky, in August of 1801. More than ten thousand people came by wagon to the watershed between the Licking and Kentucky rivers. Sydney Ahlstrom said, "At night, when the forest's edge was limned by the flickering light of many campfires, the effect of apparent miracles would [have been] heightened."[237:433]

Presbyterians planned the gathering as a Holy Fair. The tradition had flourished in Scotland after the end of Puritan rule, when the Roman Catholic Charles II was installed on the throne in 1660. Groups congregated for days in late summer to celebrate communion with shared meals between sermons that reinforced their faith.[499]

Lowland Scots took their open-air services to Ulster, where the church was not protected. Elsewhere in Ireland, Roman Catholics held outdoor schools during slow periods in agricultural cycles. Civic gatherings and education on the island were limited to members of the Church of England.

Howell Harris began preaching outside in Wales in 1737. George Whitefield delivered his first outdoor sermon to miners near Bristol in 1739. Both were part of an Oxford group, derisively called the Methodists, who sought to reform the Anglian church.

Two others, John and Charles Wesley, were sent to Georgia in 1736 by James Oglethorpe to convert Natives. On the voyage out, they met a group of Moravian refugees who did not cower during a storm. They stayed on deck to sing and pray.

After the brothers returned to London, Whitefield went to the colonies to move the German-speaking group to Pennsylvania. Some 12,000 heard him speak in Philadelphia's town square, 20,000 in a New York field, and 15,000 on Boston Commons. While there, he came under the influence of New England Calvinists.

During the period they were separated, the Wesleys drew closer to Moravian theology and music. John even traveled to their main colony in Saxony in 1738. In 1741, the two split over man's ability to seek salvation. John Wesley's welcoming theology transformed the Holy Fairs. Whitfield's spread to Wales.

John Calvin believed entire congregations should sing psalms, not the selected few used in Roman Catholic services. When he went to Strasbourg in 1538, he heard Germans singing versions set by Martin Luther. He began producing his own psalter in 1539, the first of five editions. Charles Wesley expanded English practice by using lyrics to describe feelings of salvation that followed from his brother's theology. He made group singing part of camp meetings.

Baptists never accepted the Puritan practice of psalm singing. Many rejected Mason's attempts to modernize psalms with European vocal settings. William Walker produced an alternative song book in 1835, *Southern Harmony*. His parents had migrated from Leipzig when he was a child. The Saxons raised him near the Scots-Irish settlement of Spartanburg, South Carolina, where he became an Old Regular Baptist.

Benjamin Franklin White* and his brother-in-law, Elisha James King, published *Sacred Harp* in 1844. White was a South Carolina-born Missionary Baptist who wrote some of the tunes, and collected others from his neighbors. He converted Holy Fairs into Sacred Harp singing conventions in the South.

Just before Cane Ridge, Presbyterian and Congregational leaders had met in May to consider the best ways to expand into Ohio. The 1801 Plan of Union allowed the two to combine congregations in small settlements and use whichever clergymen were available. Their ecumenicalism introduced the idea of non-sectarian gatherings. Holy Fair communal meals persisted in the tradition of Dinner on the Grounds between breaks in Sunday services for many denominations.

Resorts

In the East, geography dictated early settlement locations. Ports, like Philadelphia and Charleston, sprouted where ships could anchor safely. The low lands were near swamps, which soon bred yellow fever, malaria, and cholera. From the earliest years, the prosperous ushered their families to healthier areas. After the Revolution, the very wealthiest Americans, the rice planters from South Carolina like James Hamilton's parents, gravitated to Newport, Rhode Island.[534:20-21] The nullification leader was mentioned in KUMBAYA.

Civil War

Early days of our Civil War were accompanied by the rhetoric of noble war. Young boys yearned to emulate the brave men marching by day and camping by night. Students at the Gunnery School for Boys in Connecticut "were sometimes permitted to march, roll up in their blankets and sleep outdoors."[432:29] In 1861, Frederick William Gunn (1816-1881) and his wife, the former Abigail Brinsmade (1820-1908), took them on a forty-mile hike to Milford.

Boys did the same everywhere. However, Viola Mitchell and Ida Barksdale Crawford believed the Gunns were the first to organize more formalized camping. Outings at Connecticut's Lake Waramaug featured "boating, sailing, tramping and fishing."[432:30]

Some realized war was less beneficial for the soul. George Williams organized the Young Men's Christian Association in London in 1844. In 1861, the group recruited volunteers in this country to take aid and religious comfort to the wounded. Despite brutalities of combat, every conflict since the 1860s, at least until Vietnam, has inflamed the imagination of young boys. The 1920 *Boy Scout Song Book*[*] included bugle calls.

Post-Civil War

After the war, cities grew where coal-burning factories polluted the air. Respiratory diseases, like tuberculosis, spread. Those with the wherewithal summered their families. First, resort hotels in places like Newport flourished. Then, people turned to Maine where Thomas Laighton had built a hotel on Appledore Island in the early 1850s.

Railroads were built to move coal and lumber from isolated areas. Track owners developed intermediate stations to increase traffic. A hotel opened in Saratoga Springs, New York, in 1802. The spa remained small, with some hotels catering to South Carolinians.[273:490] James Hamilton spent time at nearby Ballston Spa in early 1829 where other Southerners congregated.[534:105]

Then, in 1860, the Rensselaer and Saratoga railroad improved connections to Albany for invalids seeking mineral-water cures. In 1864, Warren Leland and his brothers bought what became the Grand Union Hotel. Just before they declared bankruptcy in 1871, they advertised the most exclusive cottages had "eight airy rooms with bath and closet."[274] The resort boasted an opera house, casino, and racecourse.

Alexander Turney Stewart bought the property. By 1877, it was advertising indoor plumbing "in every room of the hotel."[357] Just before he made his investment, the Delaware and Hudson began offering rail service to New York City. The resort's exclusiveness was publicized when the hotel refused to admit Joseph Seligman, a powerful railroad financier, because he was Jewish.

Charles Hallock started publishing *Forrest and Stream* in 1873. George Bird Grinnell took over a few years later. In 1887, a railroad controlled by the Delaware and Hudson reached Saranac Lake in New York. Just when the upper-middle classes could reach Saratoga, the remote Adirondacks opened to wealthier hunters.

The upper class was expanding. In 1880, the Episcopalian bishop of Albany, William Doane, and the president of Harvard, Charles Eliot, built rustic cabins on Mount Desert Island off the coast of Maine. People, who spent their winters surrounded by others as rich and powerful as themselves, soon discovered they could only spend so much time with a local guide. Doane persuaded friends to join him.

Laighton's daughter, Celia Thaxter, was a poet who turned the hotel into a salon for writers and artists, like John Greenleaf

Whittier and William Morris Hunt. Houghton, Mifflin published her description of life on the island in 1894. Childe Hassam provided color lithographs. *An Island Garden* became a model for genteel, artistic living in the wild.

In Connecticut, Charlotte Vetter Gulick remembered, for twenty years beginning sometime around 1890, she, her husband, and children "camped on the Thames River." They were in their mid-twenties when they embarked on their lonely errands into the wilderness. The Gulicks soon "invited friends and relatives to camp nearby. One summer there were seventy-five people about us in family groups." To fill time between meals, they fell back on habits acquired in camp meetings:

> Every morning we all met to sing. Sometimes we gathered around a fire, according to the weather; but unless it rained we met out under the sky, and sang sometimes for hours at a time. Our favorites were some of the immortal old hymns. If I could ask those who made that group what they now remember of those summers with the greatest pleasure, I believe that most would speak of the singing together.[146:14]

Camp meetings, under one name or another, continued in the rural South and Midwest. Retreats usually convened in mid to late summer between bouts of intense farm labor. When people read about hotels like the Grand Union, they hankered after its comforts, but without temptations to sin.

In 1884, Lewis Miller and John Vincent merged the upper-class resort with the camp meeting. They built a Methodist summer center on Lake Chautauqua in southwestern New York. Guests at the Athenaeum Hotel attended lectures by leading speakers.

Social Milieu

Resort hotels fomented new social interactions. Members of local elites, who had spent their lives among their peers in different metropolitan areas, shared dining rooms and sweeping porches with unknown men, who paid heed to their wives and daughters. Edward Digby Baltzell* noted, the first response was the development of social registers that functioned as field guides to the rich.

Next, ambitious individuals began refashioning themselves on strangers they met with greater status. In Philadelphia, people who had been Quakers became Episcopalians. Sons who had gone to the University of Pennsylvania aspired to Harvard, Yale, and Princeton. Adolescent boys attended preparatory schools that fed the newly desirable colleges. Groton, Saint Paul's, and Saint Mark's superseded local private academies that had been established before the Republic.

The emergence of a national social elite, who sent their children to exclusive boarding schools in winter, created a demand for similar summer institutions. A Dartmouth sophomore was first to respond. His father was a Newport Episcopalian clergyman, whose ancestor had been an itinerant Presbyterian preacher in North Carolina. Ernest Berkeley Balch[*] (1860-1938) later wrote:

> I first thought of the boys' camp as an institution in 1880. The miserable condition of boys belonging to well-to-do families in summer hotels, considered from the point of view of their right development, set me to looking for a substitute. That year and 1881 I had thought out the main lines of a boys' camp. That year, also, with two boys I made a short camping trip to Big Asquam. In 1881 I occupied and bought Chocorua Island.

Boys lived in rough cabins in central New Hampshire, south of the White Mountains. They were responsible for their own housekeeping, while they learned to sail, fish, and survive in the wild.

The emphasis on living without servants lasted until World War II. Then, groups like the Community Fund encouraged organizational camp programs to serve more children. They not only did not have servants, but also already were making their own beds and doing household chores. What was daring for one population group was routine for another. One song that vanished from the Kitanniwa repertoire in the early 1950s, "There Was a Girl Who Came to Camp" (7), ended:

> She wouldn't make her bed because it tired her so
> She wouldn't wash the dishes, sweep the cabin floor
> The Camp Fire Girls just picked her up and threw her out the door

Jean-Jacques Rousseau

Early preparatory schools were more than places for socialites to leave their children while they traveled to Europe, and more than incubators for the aspiring social elite. At Groton, Endicott Peabody molded his students into muscular Christians. In France, Phillipe Ariès believed, boarding schools rose from the "conviction of moral necessity for a more suitable setting for children"[244:281] derived from the ideas of Jean-Jacques Rousseau.

The Frenchman believed individuals were capable of good or evil, depending on the environment in which they were raised. His 1762 novel, *Émile*, argued education's goal was teaching individuals how to live.

During Napoléon's wars, in a Swiss community twice occupied by the French, Johann Heinrich Pestalozzi (1746-1827) tested Rousseau's ideas with local orphans. The pedagogue rejected rote learning in the schoolroom. He preferred keeping children close to nature, where he could work from concrete objects, like rocks, to abstractions. Pestalozzi argued the progression from one to the other was a natural function of the development of their minds as they matured.

When the ideas of Rousseau and Pestalozzi fused with those of the Romantic Movement inspired by Goethe in Europe, they led to a belief in the curative powers of nature. In 1854, Hermann Brehmer opened the first sanitarium in Silesia to treat tuberculosis with fresh air, exercise, and good diet.

Seventh Day Adventists established the most famous in this country in Battle Creek in 1866. Representatives from different parts of the country had organized the national church in the city in 1863. John Harvey Kellogg became the hospital's head in 1876. His brother, Will Keith Kellogg, manufactured flaked cereals for the Western Health Reform Institute.

Physicians were among the most widely read. Some founded their own camps to provide healthier environments where they could promote exercise programs and better diets. Joseph Trimble Rothrock* (1839-1922) organized North Mountain School of Physical Culture in 1876 near Wilkes-Barre, Pennsylvania, where he was practicing medicine.

In a commendation sent to *The Medical Times and Register*, he asked how many of his readers had "met with cases in which the power of being happy and contented in the wilderness would have aided greatly in the restoration of the patient." He then insinuated access to such remedies was best reserved for the elite. He added, "he who develops in his own son such power adds to the child's chances of success in life."

As men like Rothrock turned their camps into successful business operations, they often recruited children of their higher status friends and patients to fill empty bunks. Sandra Alice Wampler Sehman says, she went to Mount Tyrol (Penna coed) because her father's physician was a co-owner.

The premise a brief stay in the country could repair a person's health spread to clergymen. Willard Parsons (1842-1907) graduated from Union Theological Seminary in 1871, then spent three years at a Plymouth Church mission in Brooklyn, New York. His supervising pastor was Congregationalist Henry Ward Beecher, brother of Harriet Beecher Stowe.* She was sending royalties from one her books, *The Mayflower*, to support "the care of the poor in a destitute section of Brooklyn."

From there, Parsons was called to a small Congregational church near the New York-Pennsylvania border in the Pocono mountains. Differences in the two environments provoked him to ask his parishioners to provide summer homes for poor children living in city tenements in 1881. How many thought they were getting free farm labor is not known. A New York newspaper formalized The Tribune Fresh Air Fund Aid Society in 1888.

Progressive Camps

Fresh air camps were one response to problems caused by mass migrations to cities that had begun with the Irish and Germans in the late 1840s. Factories needed men, but Europe expelled families. Men died in mines and mills. Indigent women and children remained. Women worked in garment factories, scrubbed floors, and did other menial work. Children wandered the streets.

The Progressive Movement consolidated isolated reactions to rapid industrialization. The YMCA began English classes for Germans in Cincinnati, Ohio, in 1856. Churches like Beecher's opened mission centers with reading rooms and church clubs for women.

More formal resettlement centers followed. Jane Addams opened Hull House in Chicago in 1888. In 1894, a group of Jewish women in Cleveland, Ohio, started a center where they taught English, sewing, and other marketable skills. Two years later the group joined the National Council of Jewish Women, and organized the Council Educational Alliance to manage a settlement house.

The Educational Alliance in New York organized its first camp in Cold Springs in 1902. It evolved into Surprise Lake (NY J boys). In 1907, Helen Bauldauf suggested Cleveland's Alliance raise money for its own summer camp. Within a few years, Wise (Ohio J coed) was handling 200 children every two weeks, a thousand every summer.

Albert Brown* (1901-1994) remembered the only goal in the early years was providing healthy food and fun. Sidney Vincent* recalled the site was "more appropriate for a commercial resort than a kids' camp." David Warshawsky* remembered the staff provided medical examinations. Boys were left to amuse themselves. "There never was any difficulty in starting a ball game."

In San Francisco, James Edward Rogers* (1884-1959) took small groups on 150 to 250 mile hikes to Calaveras Big Trees, Yosemite Valley, and Monterey. When people suggested a more stable program, he tried a camp financed by the boys themselves. The first year, he took them to a fruit ranch near Vacaville, California. They worked during the day to pay for their use of land at night. While it provided fresh air, Rogers concluded, "a month of hard work could not be, in reality, a pleasant outing."

During the winter, he found sponsors for his Boys' Club venture. One, Joseph Perkins Chamberlain, was active in reforming the state's child labor laws. The other, Dr. O. N. Orlow,* was more shadowy. He probably was the Olaf N. Orlow who collected Japanese art in San Francisco. He may have been the O. N. Orlow who died in the Bronx in 1924. That man claimed to be "Johann Salvator, long mysteriously missing Arch Duke of Austria."

Evelyn Hopson Wood, mentioned in PEP, discovered homeless boys were jailed in Georgia, because the state had no other way to care for them. The Baptist organized Fledglings to help youngsters coming under control of the courts.

In Michigan, the troubled were sent to the Beulah Land Farm for Boys near Boyne City. One young man accused the director of "gross indecency." Floyd Starr (1913-1967) bought a farm near Albion,

Michigan, for fifty boys left homeless when Herman Swift* was jailed in 1913.

William Alexander Smith (1854-1914) organized the Boys' Brigade in Glasgow, Scotland, in 1883. He promoted "Christian manliness." In Wisconsin, John Edward Chapin* (1829-1911) asked boys in 1899 why they were out after curfew. They said they wanted an army, like the ones fighting in Cuba and the Philippines. The Presbyterian minister gave them a Boy's Brigade to organize drills.

Financial support and enthusiastic leadership obviously were not enough. When the number of children increased beyond a dozen, more structured programs were needed.

In England, youth leaders adopted Robert Baden-Powell's (1857-1941) military training manual, *Aids to Scouting.** Smith asked him to modify it for the Brigade. The Boer War veteran organized a camp on Brownsea Island, near the English Channel coast, to test his revisions. Groups began forming around his *Scouting for Boys** as soon as he released it in 1908. In 1910, reformers in this country, many associated with the YMCA, introduced his program as the Boy Scouts.

Frank Fellows Gray (1863-1935), a friend of Baden-Powell, organized military exercises at his New Jersey Boy Scout camp. They were cancelled when he became too ill to supervise. When the war games were revived in the late 1920s, Harold T. Cruikshank, Junior, (1917-2002) remembers, the older boys were divided into two groups. One team hunted the youngest campers, who had been wakened in the night and told to hide themselves in the woods. The other acted as their protectors.[129:62]

Camping was becoming profitable. Adirondack guides had organized in 1891 to set labor rates and general standards for hunting. An annual Sportsman's Show began in 1895 in New York's Madison Square Garden. Companies displayed improved boats and better weapons. States built booths to advertise the advantages of their particular patches of wilderness.

Taylor Statten* (1882-1956) left the YMCA to open a private camp in Ontario's Algonquin Park in 1921 to train "potential Canadian leaders." Frank Howbert Cheley (1889-1941) had established Eberhart for the South Bend, Indiana, YMCA in 1910, then worked for the organization in Saint Louis, Missouri. In 1921, he opened the private Bear Lake Trail School (Colo boys) in Rocky Mountain National Park to "help boys grow into manhood in the great outdoors."[285]

Directors organized the American Camping Association, now the American Camp Association, in 1924. A few years later, Cheley told them, he had "known many boys who have been seriously and perhaps permanently endangered from the character standpoint by camping experience."[211:15] The next year, 1929, the Y published Hedley Seldon Dimock* and Charles Eric Hendry's *Camping and Character*. It provided directors with suggestions for organizing their camps, and methods for measuring their successes. Their model was Statten's Ahmek (Ont boys).

Brown remembered, the ACA held its first training conference in 1925 at Bear Mountain, New York. The next year, Wise (Ohio J coed) introduced "nature lore and woodcraft." Older boys built an "Indian Council ring." Songs like "Follow the Trail" (10), "Inn of a Starry Sky" (3), and "Border Trail" (27) entered the repertoire.

Camp Communities

Rousseau did not simply argue a return to nature could restore individuals to some better physical or mental condition. Before the American Revolution, he suggested government began with a social contract entered by people living in a state of nature. An ideal community was one that replicated that process. Starr called his institution Starr Commonwealth because his boys were self-governing. Rogers called his camp the State of Columbia because the boys organized it themselves. Statten made Seton's council ring the center of group life.

The idea of a summer community for people with shared values expanded from Chautauqua. Methodist ministers had organized the Ocean Grove Camp Meeting Association earlier, in 1869. When the New York and Long Branch Railroad arrived in 1875, more people went to the New Jersey shore. In the 1880s, after Chautauqua, buildings replaced the tents.

Detroit Methodists organized a center at Bay View on Little Traverse Bay in 1875. Michigan Presbyterians followed with Wequetonsing in 1877. Bay View added a Chautauqua-like program. In 1918, Albion College took over its administration so students could receive credit for their summer studies.

Family resort communities flourished after Ford's Model T made automobiles and decent roads available. Masons in Fresno, California, established Paradise Park on land near Santa Cruz in 1924. White land developers from White Cloud, Michigan, and Chicago opened Idlewild in Lake County in 1912. They marketed their lots to Black professionals from Chicago and Detroit. Some from Battle Creek subscribed. One said, "just to own land."[540:48]

In New York City, United Workers Cooperative opened Camp Nitgedaigit (NY J coed) in 1922. Sholem Aleichem's Folk Institute established Camp Boiberik (NY J coed) the next year near Rhinebeck as a secular Yiddish-speaking community. The same year, a Workmen's Circle established Lakeland in Dutchess County for adults, and Camp Kinderland (NY J coed) for children.[431]

These groups were formed by the first wave of immigrants from the Russian Empire who fled the pogroms after Alexander II was assassinated in 1881. They often were aided by the successful descendants of earlier Jewish migrants from German-speaking areas. In New York, the Educational Alliance had developed when Jacob Schiff, a railroad financier, promised money to support smaller groups if they would merge. In 1893, Isador Straus became the first head. His father had migrated from the Palatinate in 1854 to Georgia. They moved to New York after the Civil War, where he and his brother bought Macy's in 1895. Schiff had left Frankfurt after the Prussians took control of the city in 1866.

In Cleveland, Samuel Daniel Wise (1875-1953) gave the Educational Alliance land for its first camp. His father, Daniel Weis, had left the southern Palatinate, probably in the 1860s.

Another surge of migrations occurred after a rebellion against another tsar failed in 1905. Many of these refugees had some emotional kinship with radicals who stayed behind. They were the ones who were more likely to be interested when Communists finally took control in 1917.[542]

Ronnie Gilbert* was born in 1926. Her father was part of the first group. He came to this country with his parents when he was a child from Ukraine. Her mother came directly from Warsaw in her teens. Some half-brothers paid her way after her parents died in epidemics. He was apolitical. She was active in trade unions and joined the Communist party.

Conflicts between generations were exacerbated when the party tried to coopt the Workmen's Circles. The older organization, which had begun as a mutual-aid society, vacated Kinderland to establish

Kinder Ring (NY J coed) in 1926. In 1924, party members abandoned their siege of Nitgedaigit to establish Camp Unity (NY coed), mentioned in KUMBAYA.

Political camps experimented with utopias. The Worker's Order developed Wo-Chi-Ca (NY agency coed) near a tributary of the Delaware river in New Jersey. Gilbert remembers, they "were indoctrinated in very socially conscious ideas" by a deliberately diverse staff. The camp expanded from serving Jewish children to include Blacks and Puerto Ricans while she went there.

Meantime, children of Russian immigrants were becoming rabbis. In the 1920s, they took power back from the laity to transform settlement houses into synagogue community centers. Instead of assimilation, they emphasized maintaining their religion within American society.[387] In 1911, Surprise Lake (NY J boys) became associated with the Young Men's Hebrew Association. In 1917, it was folded into the Federation of Jewish Philanthropies.

Warshawsky remembered, in the early years, Wise (Ohio J coed) was Orthodox, simply because parents of most of the campers were immigrants from Eastern Europe. Ida Schott did not start a campaign to make the kitchen kosher until 1924. The camp did not have a rabbi on staff until 1925. Its current site was purchased in 1965 on behalf of the Jewish Community Center.

Recreation Camps

One consequence of the national elite's migration to the Episcopalian church is choirs became more important in church services than the congregational singing that originally inspired singing schools. In 1890, Elliot White,* rector of Grace Church, Newark, rented facilities to train Episcopal choirboys, then bought land for Nejecho (NJ P boys) in 1910.

His camp attracted participants from Princeton. Boys translated their interest in music into stage revues based on the university's Triangle Club. They began performing in neighboring New Jersey towns. White was born in 1861, the son of Freeman Josiah Bumstead. He later served in Saint Mark's, Philadelphia, that city's mecca of upward mobility.[251]

Church camps were slower to develop. Baptist George Walter Hinckley (1853-1950) is credited with the first experiment with seven boys from his Rhode Island congregation in 1880. The idea of religious family resorts held more appeal to many than did sovereign holidays for children. Ahlstrom said, the YMCA faced "much puritanic criticism" for "fostering athletic recreation and defending the values of 'play'."[237:742]

Sumner Francis Dudley (1854-1897) was probably the first to establish a genuinely religious camp through the Y in 1885 on Lake Champlain in New York. Eventually, individual churches and church governing boards did create camps, often with rented facilities that functioned as summer Bible schools or choir camps or both.

Camps devoted to the arts were inspired by Mabel Dodge. After she moved to Taos, New Mexico, in 1919, she married a member of the Pueblo, Antonio Luhan. Like Vetter Gulick who invited Seton to Sebago-Wohelo (Me girls), Dodge entertained Pueblo folklorist Elsie Clews Parsons. Like Thaxter, she drew writers and painters to her estate. Her most famous guests were D. H. Lawrence and Marsden Hartley.

Interlochen (Mich coed) is the most important art camp for Kitanniwa, and much of the nation. Joseph Edgar Maddy (1891-1966) founded it in 1928. The Music Supervisors National Conference recycled a private girls' camp, also called Interlochen (Mich girls), near Traverse City, Michigan.

The idea of intense training in small groups since has spread to sports, with centers like Don Kerbis's Tennis Camps (Mich coed) near Watervliet, Michigan. Concordia College sponsors Language Villages (Minn coed) in Minnesota. Retreats for weight loss, computer training, and whatever else interests adolescents have followed.

While recreation camps are diverse in their sponsors, they share two ideas: an Arcadian setting enhances education and, even there, children need breaks. They differ from traditional and progressive camp directors, who see music as an extension of their programs to inculcate values. These individuals see it as a respite where anything, within reason, is acceptable so long as it refreshes, enthuses and, perhaps, inspires campers to apply themselves to their studies.

Relationship to Repertoire

Camping's history shows each philosophy can be associated with a particular social movement: recreation camps with camp meetings and subsequent experiments with religious training, traditional camps with the development of a national social elite, progressive camps with attempts to improve human character.

The three did not develop in isolation. Vetter Gulick, the woman who pioneered the Camp Fire Girls in a traditional camp, espoused progressive ideals. She said, she and her husband "agreed that in all things our first consideration should be for our children—where we should live, and how we should live"[146:13]

At the same time, she drew upon Congregational camp meetings for her program. Rogers said in 1915:

> After breakfast in the bungalow all went to the craft house, where every morning they met to sing. The girls sat Turk-fashion on the floor facing Hiiteni [Vetter Gulick] and Alaska [Kempthorne], who had taken her place at the piano. Two carefully selected hymns were sung, then everyone stood and repeated the Lord's prayer, after which they sang more hymns and camp songs to their heart's content. It was difficult to stop singing. Often Hiiteni allowed the singing hour to encroach upon craft-work time.[147:48]

While it is possible to make guesses about a camp's philosophy based on the organizing sponsor, it is difficult to identify the philosophy of any one camp without visiting. Director's beliefs may not match campers' experiences. Gilbert remembers, when she was eleven, her parents separated, and her mother abandoned assimilation. "And she wanted that for me, but it was a little late." When she went to Wo-Chi-Ca (NY agency coed), she was more interested in music, than politics. Paul Robeson became her model, not party ideologues.

If identifying a camp's philosophy is difficult, defining the contribution ideas make to a camp's corpus of songs is more elusive. There is nothing equivalent to the longitudinal and developmental psychology studies done by the Gesell team or Piaget. At best, social scientists design experiments to prove a set of core ideas exists. Historians look at past incidents when norms broke down and values were exposed.

Précis

To delineate Kitanniwa's aesthetic, I look at song forms found more often in other types of camps. Parodies like LOLLYPOP and open-ended songs like I WISH I WERE are more common in Boy Scout and recreation camps. Call-response songs like A BEAR are used in progressive ones.

I include ballads like SKYBALL PAINT as a control. They seem to be sung in all camps, and thus represent a form more influenced by camp diffusion networks than by camp philosophies. If they represent any intellectual bent, it is that of folklorists.

For each form, I discuss variations that exist in camps. Next I focus on Kitanniwa's repertoire to suggest reasons the form is less popular there than elsewhere. In each chapter, I describe a situation where camp discipline was relaxed or violated, and the camp's philosophy stood revealed.

The final chapter, WITCHCRAFT, defines the basic themes of the traditional camp philosophy, not as a function of organizational structure, but as a set of values. These mores, which arose from the many sources of camping, may be shared by many recreation and progressive camps. They help isolate what makes a camp, any camp, a world apart from everyday life in town.

Skyball Paint: Ballads

To many of us, a ballad is any "slow, romantic" song.[241] To folklorists, it tells a story. The link between the two perceptions was forged during World War I era reactions against new forms of commercial music, characterized by one displaced songwriter as "Turkey Trots, Ragtime and Lewed Doggerel."[549:15] Once narrative songs were juxtaposed to dance music, then any song not used for fast dancing became a member of the same musical category, a commercial-music ballad.

Child Ballads

Of all song genres, ballads as narrative have most captivated folklorists. Many collections, including this one, begin with a section of Child ballads, like Child 62, "Gypsy Rover" (21), placed in numeric, chronological order. Other ballads fall meekly behind, trailed by the rest of the collection. To standardize the organization of such books, George Malcolm Laws, Junior, indexed the available American collections. He selected what he believed were the other legitimate folk ballads sung in the United States.

Broadsides

In *American Balladry from British Broadsides*,* he looked at ones originally printed on large, single sheets of paper that had one or more songs on one side. The commercial music medium developed around 1500, about fifty years after Johannes Gutenberg developed a practical movable-type printing press. With changes in technology, like those mentioned in AN AUSTRIAN, the term expanded to include garlands, chapbooks, and songsters.

He grouped ballads by subject. Within these categories, identified by letters, ballads were numbered. Few of his British broadsides are sung in camps. Best known is "Stewball" (14), which he numbered Q22. It entered camps through the Folk Revival, principally recordings by the Weavers, Joan Baez, and Peter, Paul and Mary.

American Ballads

The most common songs from *Native American Balladry** in camps are those from Black tradition. "Blue Tailed Fly" (Laws I19) is sung "Jimmy Crack Corn" (8).

Laws I18, "Dem Bones" (37), was known as "De Creation and the Fall" at Surprise Lake (NY J Boys) in 1938. Newman Ivey White* discovered the original in a songster published in 1891 by Ike Simond.[509] The Black, banjo-playing comic performed for white audiences.[510] By the next year, the expression "dem bones gwine rise again" had entered common usage.[547]

Sandburg* gave the song wider exposure in 1923. It was included in the 1930 Boy Scouts* song book, then began to be published widely after World War II. At least three Richard Dorson students at Michigan State collected it. Yetta Kamelhar[S] heard it in Brooklyn and in the South. Rosalind Havens[S] learned it from a Black, Harvard student. Mary Robinson[S] was told the Student Christian Foundation on campus was teaching it.

More recently, some have banned the song. James Hirsch[S] was told, it had been taught at Ahwahnee (Calif BSA) in 1968 or 1969, then proscribed in 1971.

Laws included a list of ballads of doubtful currency. These songs clearly were ballads, but he was not convinced they truly were in tradition. Here he included several versions of the "Titanic," none related to the camp ballad.

He also included a list of ballad-like and folklike American songs that shared many characteristics with ballads, but which he could not accept as true narratives. These included "Down in the Valley" (33), "Erie Canal" (11), "Get along Little Dogies" (12), "On Top of Old Smoky" (18), "Shenandoah" (33), and "Tom Dooley" (12).

Short Narratives

Narratives range in length from epics, like *The Iliad*, to descriptions of single incidents. So long as scholars believed folklore reflected the era of King Arthur and Robin Hood, they disregarded shorter works as debased. Child documented the progression in narrative complexity when he included "The Mermaid" (23) as a continuation of "Sir Patrick Spens." The shorter ballads are important because they reinforce children's abilities to tell stories.

Laws did not recognize British broadsides that survived in truncated versions. "Frog Went a-Courting" (5) appeared in 1549 in *Complaynt of Scotland*. The anonymous tract opposed any union between England and Scotland that might result from a proposed marriage between Edward, son of Henry VIII, and Mary of Scotland.

The Opies said a London comedian, John Liston, revived "The Love-sick Frog" in 1809.[452] Some camps know a hip variant in which the frog fails to woo Molly, a hatcheck girl at the Coconut Grove (2). Wohelo (RI CFG) sings the "Frog in the Spring" variant.

"The Keeper" (33) is another British broadside not acknowledged by Laws. Joseph Martin published "The Huntsman's Delight" in the 1680s. He suggested the does were young women. A shorter version, "The Frolicksome Keeper," appeared around 1760 with the added "Jockey. Master" chorus. Sabine Baring-Gould* collected what he called a "very gross" text from Peter Sandry of Saint Ervan, Cornwall. He revised it for publication.

The melody, apparently, was more important than the lyrics. He collected it from two other people with "Green Broom." Ralph Vaughan Williams heard only two verses from Jim Austin of Cambridgeshire in 1906.[456] Sharp collected just the chorus from Jane Lovell Gulliver (1862-1910) of Combe Florey, Somerset, in 1908.[479] The camp text comes from another he learned from Robert Kinchin in Ilmington, Warwickshire, then expurgated.[506]

Itsy Bitsy Spider

"Itsy Bitsy Spider" (33) originated as "The Rambling Soldier." John Whiting published it in Birmingham, England, with the line, "I am a roving rambling solider." The protagonist of the 1817 broadside just had been discharged from service in Britain's war with Napoléon.[479] It appeared in this country in *Fred May's Comic Irish Songster* of 1862. Its ending had been changed to, "For I am the rambling son of poverty / And the son of Michael O'Feer."[277]

The next transformation was recorded in 1870. James Garland sold sheet music in New Brunswick, New Jersey, with the last line modified to, "I'm the son of a, son of a, son of a, son of a, son of a gambolier." L. M. claimed it had been written at a resort hotel on Washington Rock. Dartmouth published a variant in 1898 that changed the chorus to, "I'm a son of a, son of a, son of a, son of a gun for beer."

Helen Merriam[S] collected a parody, "son of a gun of a spider went up the water spout," in Battle Creek in 1952. Arthur Walbridge North had printed similar words in 1910. The Californian assumed they already were common place.[446:279-280] Anne Lutz says her father, Frank Eugene Lutz, an entomologist noted for his work with fruit flies, sang "There was a bloomin' spider went up a bloomin' spout" to her before 1920.

Boy Scouts[*] published "the blasted, bloomin' spider" in 1920, with a note it was a college song. Kappa Alpha Theta had a sorority version in 1925. Two years later, Harbin[*] published "The Spider and the Spout" in *Paradology*. In those years, it must have traveled to England. In 1959, the Opies said, "it has been known for half a century."[451]

The verse went through a baby talk phase when it was known as "inkie pinkie pider" at Red Wing (Penna girls) in 1931, according to Ethel Martin. In the late 1940s, Watanopa (Mont CFG) was singing "eeny weeny 'pider." Aleta Huggett[S] collected "inty-tinky spider" from Appleblossom (Mich GS) in 1949.

By then, it was settling into the more familiar "eensy weensy spider went up the water spout," reported by Suzanne Howe[S] from Kitanniwa around 1944. Those words began to be published in the 1940s.

Its melody was used for "Johnny Verbeck" (26) in 1876. The "I'm a Rambling Wreck from Georgia Tech" adaption was printed in the school's 1908 yearbook.[342] That fight song has been adapted at Burch (BSA), Irondale (Mo BSA), the Van Buren Youth Camp (Mich agency coed), and by Denver Boy Scouts (Colo BSA). Pittsburgh (Penna BSA) and Denver Scouts sang "I'm a Scouting Trooper" (2). Seth Clay used the melody for "Sunday School" (15). Tawakani (Ida CFG) sings "Spider" to "Puffer Billies" (33).

Camp Ballads

"Streets of Laredo" (9) is another camp ballad derived from an older British broadside, "The Unfortunate Rake" (Laws Q26). Laws made it the first of his songs of cowboys and pioneers, B1. In Washington, it has been used for "Paths of Niwana" (Wash CFG).

Other short narrative songs that would fit this category are "Corn" (13), "Ol' Texas" (31), and "Been Riding" (8), with its "joggin' along to nowhere" chorus. "Clementine" (23), "Patsy Orry Aye" (29), and "Blood on the Saddle" (6) are more humorous. Aloha Hive (Vt girls) and Hitaga (Iowa CFG) have local songs to "Old Chisholm Trail" (4).

Songs of crime and murder, Laws E, would include "Waltzing Matilda" (23), "Spider's Web" (21), and the Kingston Trio's "Banua Jail" (10). The last two are comparatively new in tradition. Andrew Barton Peterson wrote the first in 1895. His tune was derived from a Scots regimental march, "Thou Bonnie Wood o' Craigielea," as remembered by Christina Macpherson. Military groups spread the ballad in World War II. "The Fox" (7) describes an animal thief.

Laws' miscellaneous category, H, would encompass the many humorous songs dealing with animals, like "Little Gray Mouse" (15). The sometimes-banned "Little Skunk's Hole" (30) was collected by Fowke from Nancy Takerer. She learned it in Kingston, Ontario, in the 1940s.[332] "Bill Grogan's Goat" (19) details a death avoided.

"The Cat Came Back" (15) describes a series of violent incidents each followed by the chorus, "And the cat came back, the very next day." Henry S. Miller published the song in 1893 for the minstrel stage. By the 1920s, it had entered Southern fiddle tradition. John Carson of Georgia recorded it in 1924, Doc Roberts of Kentucky in 1925. Spaeth* believed it might have condensed from the older French "Le Chat de Mère Michel." A new last verse about a hydrogen bomb was added in the 1950s. Instead of repeating the usual chorus, Wakoma (Wash CFG) concludes with a simple "Meow."

Love Ballads

Native American Balladry's miscellaneous category would include the love and courtship stories. That this had no such class reflected the continued use of selected British songs here. *British Broadsides* had four categories.

A few camp ballads fall into category M, family opposition to lovers. June Andrews[§] collected the sometimes-banned "I Love Little Willie" (5) from Lyman Lodge (Minn GS) in 1938. The lyrics were well known when Frank Clyde Brown began collecting in North Carolina in the early 1920s.[277]

"The Big Blue Frog" (10) or "Phrog," recorded by Peter, Paul and Mary, deals with societal opposition to cross-cultural relationships. "Suitors" (25) reverses the usual conflict.

Ballads of faithful lovers, Laws O, would include "Fair Rosie" (11), "Mandy Was a Little Bahama Girl" (22), and "Walking at Night" (27). "A Joggin' Along" (14) and "A Boy and a Girl in a Little Canoe" (33) are more jocular. The Kingston Trio's version of "Three Jolly Coachmen" (6) was bawdier. "Frozen Logger" (3), recorded by the Weavers in 1951, described a woman faithful to her dead boyfriend. "For Baby (For Bobby)" (14) was recorded by both John Denver and Peter, Paul and Mary.

Ballads of unfaithful lovers, Laws category P, would include "House of the Rising Sun" (10), which came from Black tradition (Laws I). No songs of lover's disguises, category N, are sung in camps. Peter, Paul, and Mary's "Cruel War Is Raging" (30) is classed as O33.

"Three Fishermen" (51) would represent a song of sailors (Laws K). Verses describing the fight between "Abdul, the Bulbul Ameer" (10) and Ivan Skavinsky Skiver would fit Laws J, songs of wars. Percy French wrote it in 1877, while he was an engineering student at Trinity College, Dublin.

Camp Written Ballads

Most ballads sung in camps are from folk and commercial music sources. Few seem to have been written internally, except, of course, the ephemeral trip, color war, and other local songs that chronicle events in specific sessions. Instead, as mentioned in THE MERMAID, short songs may follow Krohn's[*] impulse to expansion and become ballads.

"Cannibal King" (32) exists in two versions. In one, fitting Laws O, the king and the dusky maid fall in love. In the other, fitting Laws P, she kills him when she learns he has been unfaithful. Manhattan's Troop 582 (NY BSA) had a Laws O variant in which the wife met the king with a rolling pin. Carol Simon[S] collected an alternative in which they raised a family. Other songs, which exist in ballad versions in camps, include "Desperado" (44) and "Bee-i-e-i-e" (14).

Narrative Patterns

Camp songs mentioned in this chapter as ballads have been so identified because their texts describe incidents or tell complete stories. Axel Olrik went further. The Danish folklorist believed they were part of a folk literature that "would include myths, songs, heroic sagas, and local legends. The common rules for the composition of all these Sage forms we can then call the epic laws of folk narrative."[450:131] Among these were the operation of the laws of opening, of the appearance of items in threes, of contrasts, and the unity of plot.

One element stressed by Olrik was the law of closing. For him, "the Sage ends by moving from excitement to calm."[450:132] In camp songs, this desire for closure may take the form of a moral. Unlike those found in traditional American ballads, fun song lessons often dissipate moods with comic effects.

"Clementine" (23) has one of the best known:

> Now ye Girl Scouts heed the warning to this tragic tale of mine
> Artificial respiration would have saved my Clementine

This version is from Ann Beardsley (Mich GS). Comic morals also exist for "Sippin' Cider" (35) and "She Sat in Her Hammock" (8).

Textual Tag Endings

A desire for closure has led to tag endings. These comic verses exist independently, and may be used whenever appropriate. "My um-pah's better than your pa-pah" is used with "Qui Qua Quonnie" (6) at Blue Haven (NM P coed). Eberhart (Ind YMCA coed) appends it to "I've Been Working on the Railroad - Dinah" (28).

"Way down yonder in the cornfield," often sung with "Bill Grogan's Goat" (19), is used with "Bee-i-e-i-e" (14) by Gary Flegal (Mich agency coed). Susan Dunn[S] collected a version of "Old Hogan's Goat" that ended, "gone to yi yi yi yi - poor goat."

Last Line Repetition

Another way to end a non-narrative song is repeat part of the last line three times. At Kitanniwa, Lucille Parker Munk learned "Mister Moon" (20) with:

> Oh, Mister Moon, moon, bright and shiny moon
> Won't you please shine down on
> Please shine down on
> Please shine down on me

June Rushing Leibfarth[S] collected a version from Arnold (Tex GS) in 1959 that ended, "And grandma too."

Last-line repetition has been used with "Mmm, and a Little Bit More" (11) at Kamaji (Minn girls), according to Judy Miller. Rimrock (Wash YWCA) has sung such an ending with "Crocodile" (51). N. Cunningham[S] collected a similar version of "Castle on the River Nile" (9) from Ak-O-Mak (Ont girls) in 1949.

Football Cheers

College football yells provided the formula for the ending to "Wienie Man" (13) learned from Texas Girl Scouts by Naomi Feldman[S] and Mary Rogers:

> Weenie man, weenie man
> Rah, rah, weenie man
> Yeah weenie man

Judy Miller (Minn girls) uses a similar ending with "Junior Birdsmen" (30). Valley Mill (Md coed) ends "Doodle Doo" (34) with "whoo." Matollionequay (NJ YWCA) ended "Swiss Navy" (16) with "whoo, whoo," according to Katie Hickey.[S] In 1974, Kitanniwa campers ended "I'm Wild about Horns" (9) with "ooga, ooga."

Extended Tags

Sometimes, tags become so long, they overshadow the text. William Daniel Doebler[S] collected a Holiday House (Mich P girls) version of "At the Boardinghouse" (10) with a conclusion that alternated tempos:

> Spareribs were too much for me (faster)
> Don't mean your mother (slower)
> Spareribs were too much for me
> Don't mean your sister
> Spareribs were too much for me
> Don't mean your brother
> Spareribs were too much for me
> Don't mean your grocer
> Spareribs were too much for me

Other songs with extended tag endings include "Everything's Going My Way" (8) at Wasewagan (Calif CFG), the "Titanic" (32) at Wyandot County's 4-H day camp (Ohio 4-H), and a local Goodwill/Pleasant (DC agency sep) song.

Two in a Scene

Another narrative pattern observed by Olrik was the law of two to a scene. This is found most clearly in dialogue ballads, called "answer back songs" by Fowke[331] and "question-and-answer songs" by Winn.[553] The oldest Child ballads, the ones with the lowest numbers, used this narrative form.

The most common dialogue in camps is between a young woman and a parent or lover who vainly tries to persuade her to work or marry. She refuses until she receives something she wants. This tale type is found in the "Deaf Woman's Courtship" (10). A tête-à-tête between lovers is found in "Soldier, Soldier" (5) and the racier "Barnacle Bill the Sailor" (3). In "Billy Boy" (11), the conversation is between a youth and his mother. In "Vrenalie" (30) and the "Riddle Song" (24), the exchange is between a lover and an unidentified third person.

Repetition

Olrik emphasized the use of repetition, especially repetition in threes. European folk tales and songs often showed the responses of three individuals to a situation, usually with the first two considered bad and the last good. Sometimes three similar responses were contrasted with a fourth, preferred one. As will be remembered in "The Mermaid" (23), nineteenth-century writers first juxtaposed the captain and first mate to the cabin boy, then later had the cook comment on all three. Native Americans and many Buddhists consider four the ideal number.

Ballads use repetition to pace narrative. Refrains slow a story, and thence build suspense. Contrary to vernacular use, folklorists reserve this term for lines or parts of lines repeated in every stanza. "Tra la la" was used as a refrain in the variant of "Coming down from Bangor" (4) collected by Donna Quist§ from Camp-in-the-Woods (NY YMCA) in the middle 1940s. Felicia Rosenthal§ collected a variant using "umpda."

Refrains can be used with a wide range of fun songs, including camp-specific and organizational ones. Judy Miller remembers a 1972 Kamaji (Minn girls) unit song that used "la di dah." In the late 1930s, a Kalamazoo Girl Reserves' (Mich YWCA) song repeated "there's a party here tonight" after every line.

Girls in a Minnesota Camp Fire camp in the 1940s used "heigh ho for Tanadoona" as a refrain. Their local song was set to Helen Taylor and Easthope Martin's "Come to the Fair" (2). She was a London poet and translator, he a composer from Worcestershire, England.

A burden is a stanza that is repeated after every verse of a song, using the same tune as the verse. The best example is "Kumbaya" (90). When the repeated stanza is set to a different tune than is used with the verses, it is a chorus. While both burdens and choruses may be used with ballads, they also occur in other sorts of fun and pretty songs. Choruses are the more common form of stanzaic repetition.

Mass Media Ballads

Ballads are one camp genre widely used by public-school music-book editors, who borrow from anthologies of folk songs. The widely published "Riddle Song" (24) and "On Top of Old Smoky" (18) owe their initial familiarity to the Folk Revival. Other ballads known in camps through the Revival are "Lemon Tree" (10), recorded by Peter, Paul and Mary, and "Scarborough Fair" (7), sung by Simon and Garfunkel. Country music contributed "Smokey the Bear" (6), recorded by Gene Autry in 1952, and "Scarlet Ribbons" (8), sung by the Browns in 1959. Harry Belafonte introduced the last in 1952.

Cante Fables

The Folk Revival promoted several cante fables, like version B of "Eskimo Hunt" (21). Katie Hickey[§] heard "Little Bunny Foo Foo" (22) at East Coast folk festivals. She also collected a variant of the "Rooster" (12) sung in this style from Matollionequay (NJ YWCA). Many versions of "Ragtime Cowboy Joe" (27) begin with a spoken verse followed by a sung chorus.

Kitanniwa Repertoire

Before the Folk Revival, many ballads sung in camps came from folk tradition, either directly or indirectly. The ones known at Kitanniwa in the 1950s can be divided by their sources into four groups.

One set came from CRS or CFG song books: "The Cuckoo" (33), "Vrenalie" (30), "Walking at Night" (27), and "A Joggin' Along" (14). Most had gestures and all dealt with courtship. The chorus for the last comes from "Jim along Josie." Edward Harper introduced it in a blackface farce in 1838, a few years before the Virginia Minstrels. Others copied him, and versions proliferated. Kitanniwa's verses came from *Sing High, Sing Low.* Sanders[*] identified it as a "New England Folk-song arranged by L. R. Ring."

A second group included the ballads that enjoyed the most enduring popularity: "Dem Bones" (37), "Itsy Bitsy Spider" (33), "The Mermaid" (23), "She Sat in Her Hammock" (8), and "She'll Be Coming 'round the Mountain" (41). All but "Hammock" had gestures and all but the one verse "Spider" had more than three verses. "Dem Bones" was sung only after evening meals. "She'll Be Coming" was used primarily at morning sing. Joyce Gregg Stoppenhagen remembers singing it, "'til we were blue in the face" in the late 1950s. The others were heard anytime, although "Hammock" fell from the repertoire in the late 1950s.

All these ballads have folk origins. They probably entered the camp repertoire through campers or staff who heard them in folk-group singing situations outside camp. Robert Winslow Gordon,[*]

who edited a song column for *Adventure Magazine* in the 1920s, received a version of "Hammock" learned from a group of Camp Fire Girls. They were in Front Royal, Virginia, at the northern end of the Shenandoah valley. His correspondent went on to say, he had "shared a room with the son of a Pennsylvania Dutch farmer who claimed it was an old Dutch song." The Opies reported "Under the Lilacs She Played Her Guitar" was a "community song," like "Polly Wolly Doodle" (11), in England.[453:445]

Repertoire Violation

Kitanniwa's third group of 1950s ballads encompassed those introduced by an outsider that somehow violated unwritten rules of the camp repertoire. Around 1956, a Girl Scout from Texas taught "Ol' Texas" (31), "Sippin' Cider" (35), the "Bear Hunt" (16), and the "Titanic" (32). The first two were longer than usual, and their length was emphasized by being sung with two-part echoes. The third was a group recitation. The counselor's photograph appears in "Coming of Age."

"Ol' Texas" was very popular, but suppressed by counselors the next summer because, they claimed, it had been oversung. The next two were done once or twice a session, during morning sing, but were not learned well by younger campers. They were not used at meals, so they could not be learned by older campers and staff.

The director immediately banned the "Titanic" for reasons no one quite understood. In defiance, some continued to sing it privately for several summers. Indeed, all seven people I contacted, who were in camp that session, remembered it. Joyce Gregg Stoppenhagen, who was on staff at the time, still does not accept the legitimacy of the decision. She knew it had been forbidden in a Girl Scout camp, but thought, if it were okay in her church camp, there should be no problem.

One possibility, which no one considered, was the director knew people who had been affected by the tragedy. Alternatively, she may have been concerned some parent might complain, or had in the past. Jayne Garrison (Mo CFG) said, that was the case at one camp she attended where "one of the Board members had a relative die in the *Titanic*." When such a personal reason exists, rumors usually follow, based on either private knowledge or conjecture. None did.

Instead, people thought she objected to the lighthearted treatment of tragedy. Perhaps it violated some rule of etiquette, that a well-bred young lady simply did not mention such things. Joann Brisler (Vt C girls) said her camp did not sing it because "people die in it." Loretta Krebs (Ohio GS) and Kathryn Thomas (Ohio GS) said it was "offensive (light of tragedy)."

Joyce pointed out, that made no sense. Little difference exists between its chorus,

> Group 1: To the bottom of the sea
> Group 2: Husbands and wives, little children lost their lives

and that of "The Mermaid":

> But, we poor sailors go skipping to the top
> And the land lubbers die down below, below, below

A third possibility was that, while "land lubbers" was almost a nonsense phrase, she feared mentioning deaths of "little children" would somehow bother the youngest. More likely, some would have experienced a frisson that alleviated any private apprehensions.

The chorus, with its short section of comic echoes,

> Group 1: It was sad
> Group 2: So sad
> Group 1: It was sad
> Group 2: So sad

followed by one group holding "sea" while the other sang the next line, was the reason it was sung by the ten- and eleven-year-old girls I observed elsewhere. Warren (Mich P coed) called it "Oh It Was Sad." In 1976, He Bani Gani CFG (Md CFG) sang a chorus, one verse, and a variant chorus. Girls at the Wyandot County 4-H Day Camp (Ohio 4-H) in 1974 repeated verses so they could sing the chorus again. The narrative held no interest for either group.

Another possibility for the ban was the ballad violated the implicit ritual isolation of camp. The difference between the "Titanic" and "The Mermaid" was everyone knew an ocean liner sank in 1912. No one believed the other because of the mermaid. Once the omen lost its supernatural significance and became simply some fantastic creature, it provided a fairytale cloak of invincibility to "sank to the bottom of the sea, kerplunk." It was no different than the fate of Little Red Riding Hood.

Whatever the reason, some unseen fault line existed between what the director considered appropriate for a traditional camp repertoire and what was accepted by the recreation-oriented church camps attended by many campers. In 1976, I asked if anyone knew of a time when this song had been banned. Eighteen women, most from Girl Scout or Camp Fire camps, said it had been banished. Edward Peter Dowdall (NY BSA) wrote back, "what is there to be banned about it? Version I know is clean."

Case Study: Skyball Paint

The fourth group of ballads sung at Kitanniwa comprised those that were part of the general camp repertoire, including the already mentioned "Titanic" (32). Many survive only in camp tradition. "Skyball Paint" (16) is the one most remembered from Kitanniwa in the 1950s. It was one of the few remembered from those years by Sheila Simrod Friedman. Joyce Gregg Stoppenhagen volunteered her recollections. Barbara Rosoff Nizny recalled it as "Skyblue Paint" from the early 1950s.

Robert Wylder[†] collected the ballad in Montana as a work song, but thought the "unusual, complicated internal rhyme" suggested a possible literary source. His contention is supported by the fact it was performed by Girls of the Golden West. Millie Good (1913-1993) and her sister Dolly (1915-1967) first were heard in 1933 on the *National Barn Dance*, broadcast by radio station WLS. Heather MacPhail[§] said, she heard George Gobel sing "Skyball" on television in the early 1950s. Gobel worked the *Barn Dance* from 1933 to 1942.

Explication

"Skyball Paint" deals with the relationship between a man and an untamable horse. The motif is common to other western narratives that fit Laws' category B, ballads of cowboys. Its narrative progresses through Olrik's three repetitions of the central incident: the horse triumphant in a calm description of the past, in an action-filled present, and in an anticipated comic future.

This narrative structure, characteristic of Child ballads, is called leaping and lingering. It omits unimportant details, even generalizing setting and characters, to focus on key events. Broadsides and American ballads feature detailed "and then, and then, and then" plots.

Each tableau features two characters: the horse and man, or the narrator and sheriff. It follows Olrik's Law of Twins, that when a weak or insignificant character confronted a strong protagonist, the weak was doubled. The first verse has "good men" opposing the horse. This use of the plural reinforces the thematic development that the narrator alone has found a way of salvaging his pride, bruised from conflict with the animal, by joining forces with the horse to better another person (the sheriff), whose strength comes from an association with the law.

The allusion to a "Confederate dollar" may hint at deeper misgivings about the legitimacy of law by Southerners who moved west after the Civil War. Skyball's language employs commonplaces like "fiery red" and "whoop and a holler." Circumlocutions exist in the last two lines of the first and second verses. The nonsense chorus uses cowboy work yells. These stylistic patterns suggest a cowboy or western poet.

"Skyball" is a nineteenth-century Scots and Northern Irish term for a rascal or a "lean or worn-out person or animal."[455] The sixteenth-century lowland Scots and northern English "skybald," learned by Cecily Raysor Hancock (Colo CFG), usually referred to a piebald horse. According to Charles Mackay,* "sky" was derived from a Gaelic word, "sgiath," which referred to a dark color. "Bald" came from the Gaelic "ball" for a spot. Use of "skyblue," instead, was a typical folk rationalization by someone who associated "skyblue" and "paint" with color, rather than with irregularly marked animals.

Music

Some affinities exist between this tune and that of "Oh! Susanna" (16). The version collected by Wylder used more compositional devices taken from European art music. We learned one with fewer variations in rhythm and less challenging intervals between notes in the melody. Kitanniwa's was remembered differently by two people who were in camp the same summer.

Popularity

At one time, folklorists were interested in discovering origins of folk songs. One technique developed by Krohn,[*] Antti Aarne[*] and others, the Finnish-geographic method, involved plotting textual variations on a map to reconstruct diffusion paths.

Using this technique, one would hypothesize "Skyball Paint" originated in the intermontane west and was forwarded to the Good sisters. Heather MacPhail[§] said she heard the song in 1944 at a camp in Coeur d'Alene, Idaho. Cecily Raysor Hancock was at Wilaha, a Camp Fire camp near Denver, Colorado, in 1943 and 1944. Wylder learned it from Bob Quebbman in Ashland, Montana, in 1947.

In Idaho, Janice Suzanne Jones[§] heard it from someone who went to Alice Pittenger, sponsored by the McCall, Idaho, Girl Scouts, between 1967 and 1969. Peggy Dawn Hansen, who was there in 1972, also knows the ballad. "Skyball" was included in Tawakani's (Ida CFG) 1960s song book and in Neewahlu's (Ida CFG) from 1970. The first is sponsored by the Twin Falls, Idaho, Camp Fire Girls, the other by Coeur d'Alene.

Nan Carol Brandenberger learned the ballad in the 1960s at Watanopa, the Missoula, Montana, Camp Fire camp. Kotomi, the Denver CFG camp, included it in its 1971 song book.

Several facts suggest the song began in the west. Not only is Wylder's tune more complex, but he collected it from a man. Every person who recognized the song in 1976 was female. That may be because the Good sisters were women raised in the Saint Louis, Missouri, area. It also may be aspects of the song, like the range of the melody and the wordiness of the lyrics, do not appeal to young boys.

A second reason is the geographic center of the *National Barn Dance* is Chicago. While the NBC radio network carried the program from 1933 to 1946, its appeal was probably greatest in the area between the Appalachians and the Rockies, and north of the audience for the rival *Grand Ole Opry* in Nashville, Tennessee. It is unlikely the ballad moved from Chicago to Idaho or Montana.

"Skyball" next is reported in the area just east and northeast of Chicago in the years, 1946-1952, when the smaller ABC radio network broadcast the *Barn Dance*. I learned it at Kitanniwa in the early 1950s. Tannadoonah (Ind CFG) included it on a song list in the late 1940s. Janice Knapp learned it in the 1960s, perhaps at Wathana (Mich CFG). While Connie Coutellier, the Wathana director in 1976, did not know the song, it was recognized in the 1970s by Marsha Lynn Barker and Janet Reed. They attended Michigan Girl Scout camps.

Janice was at Mawavi, the Washington, D.C., area Camp Fire camp, in the 1970s, where the song is known by Maude Katzenbach and Cheryl Robinson. Cheryl started going there in 1959. Others who know "Skyball Paint," who transferred from the immediate range of WLS to Washington, are Leah Culp and Karen terHorst. Leah attended camps in Ohio from 1948 to 1962. Karen alternated between Michigan and Virginia Girl Scout camps in the 1950s and again in the 1970s.

The ballad was known in Minnesota in the 1950s, where it probably also was introduced by a performer on WLS. Mary Westcott Walker, who went to Lake Hubert, a Minnesota girls' camp, said she learned it from her mother. Margaret Olson knows the song, and was associated with various Minnesota Camp Fire camps from 1970. A Minneapolis agency camp, Manakiki, included it in the song book they sent me in 1976. Carol Rau recognized the song in 1976 when she was at Trowbridge, the Fargo, North Dakota, Camp Fire camp located in Minnesota.

Others, who sing the ballad, attended camps that border one of the three repertoire centers. Linda Margaret Hanes went to Girl Scout camps in Oklahoma between 1965 and 1976. Jessie Adams, Inez Haggard, and Pat Sherman worked together on the questionnaire at Wohaleto (Tex CFG) in Texas in 1976. In Pennsylvania, "Skyball" is recognized by Sharon Richman, Mariana Palmer, and Adahi (Penna CFG).

The only ones who recognized "Skyball" from other areas were Marianne Culligan, Marjorie Orr, Becky Colwell Deatherage, and Elaine Sullivan. Marianne and Marjorie both attended Tyee (Ore CFG) in Oregon. Becky knows it from Comstock, a New York Girl Scout camp, and Elaine from San Juan Ranch, a riding camp in Ellington, Connecticut.

Girls of the Golden West[†] finally recorded the ballad in the 1960s, after folklorists and fans of early western and country music rediscovered them. By then, they were part of another tradition. The one they had fed in the 1940s had continued expanding in parallel, but discretely definable areas.

Version A

Text from Joyce Gregg Stoppenhagen, Camp Kitanniwa (Mich CFG), 1957 and 1959. Her photograph appears in "Kitanniwa Staff, 1950s."

1. Skyball Paint was a devil saint
   And his eyes were fiery red
   Good men have tried this horse to ride
   But all of them are dead

   Now I won't brag, but I rode that nag
   'til his blood began to boil
   Then I hit the ground and ate three pounds
   Of good old western soil

C. Sing hi hi, yippie i o
   Ride 'em high and down you go
   Sons of the western soil
   Sons of the western soil

2. I swore by heck I'd break his neck
   For the jolt he gave my pride
   So I slipped my noose on the old cayoose
   And once more took a ride

   I turned around, and soon I found
   His head where his tail should be
   So I says says I perhaps he's shy
   Or just don't care for me

Chorus

3. In town one day I chanced to stray
   Upon old sheriff Jim
   For a whoop and a holler and a counterfeit dollar
   I sold that nag to him

Now when Jim plants the seat of his pants
In Skyball's leather chair
I bet four bits when Skyball quits
That Jim will not be there

Chorus

Version B

Text from Heather MacPhail, a camp near Coeur d'Alene, Idaho, 1944; collected by Heather MacPhail, Indiana University; variations from A emphasized.

1. **Old** Skyball Paint was a **devil's** saint,
   His eyes were fiery red.
   He had a knot on the top o' his neck,
   That some might calla head.
   One day I tried that horse to ride,
   His blood began to boil.
   I hit the ground and ate three pounds
   Of good old Western soil!

C. **Singin'** hi-o, yippee **ki-o**
   Ride 'em high and down you go,
   Sons of the western soil!

   ———————————

2. I swore by heck I'd break his neck
   For the jolt he gave my pride.
   So I **swung** my noose on the old cayuse,
   And once more took a ride.
   He turned around and **I soon** found
   His head where his tail should be.
   So I sez, sez I, perhaps he's shy,
   Or just don't care for me.

Chorus

3. In town one day, I chanced to stray
   Upon old sheriff Jim;
   With a whoop an' a holler an' a counterfeit dollar,
   I sold that nag to him.
   When Sheriff plants the seat o' his pants
   In Skyball's leather chair,
   I'll bet four bits when Skyball **hits**,
   Old Jim will not be there!

Chorus

Lollypop: Parodies

Any song written to an existing tune may be termed a contrafactum. Such songs may or may not use the original lyrics as a model for their texts. When the original is paraphrased or alluded to in some way, the new song is a textual parody. While the term parody usually is taken to refer to humorous or satirical songs, texts may be either comic or serious.

"I've Been Working on the Railroad" (31) and "Drunken Sailor" (8) often are adapted for local songs that carry no burden of ridicule. "Railroad," used in at least seven camps, was published in an 1894 Princeton songster.[338] "Sailor," modified by six, began as a walk-away chantey. The second has obvious folk analogs, as may the first, but both have been standardized thoroughly.

The World War I era "It's a Long Way to Tipperary" (2) has been used at four camps, and for "It's a Good Time To Get Acquainted" (11). Jack Judge and Minnie Muir performed it in British music halls after Judge wrote the song in 1912.

Another World War I song, "Gee, But I Want To Go Home" (4), has been used at Melacoma (Calif CFG), Wolahi (Calif CFG), Parsons (Wash BSA), and Natsihi (Mich CFG), according to Carol Domoney.§ Nova Scotia-born Gitz Rice shaped the text. His 1917 Victor recording was adapted widely in World War II.

Closer to Kitanniwa, a Unitarian minister born in Comstock, about five miles from Kalamazoo, Michigan, composed "I've Got that Joy, Joy, Joy" (5). It has been modified for "I've got that Camp Fire spirit up in my head" (16). George Willis Cooke wrote a study of Ralph Waldo Emerson, and served congregations in Grand Haven, Michigan; Indianapolis, Indiana; Sheboygan, Wisconsin, and Massachusetts between 1872 and 1900.

Blue Bird Songs

"Playmates" (10) has been sung "Cubmates" (1) at Rokilio (Wisc BSA). Hidden Valley (Md CFG) and Wohelo (RI CFG) know "Blue Bird, come out and play with me" (2). Henry W. Petrie and Philip Wingate published the original in 1894. *Paradology*[367] printed the camp words in 1927. The Opies believed the version recorded by Saxie Dowell in 1940 influenced tradition in England.[453] He was born Horace Kirby Dowell in Raleigh, North Carolina. Petrie, who came from Bloomington, Illinois, died in Paw Paw, a town about twenty miles from Kalamazoo.

People writing for young campers often adopt what they believe are already familiar melodies. Seabow (Calif CFG) has a Blue Bird song to "Jesus Loves Me" (3), a nineteenth-century Sunday-school song by Anna Bartlett Warner and William Batchelder Bradbury. Yakewi (Ohio CFG) has a Blue Bird song to "Spoonful of Sugar" (2) from *Mary Poppins*. Vivian Sexton (Tex CFG) has sung "Campers, Whistle While You Work" to the dwarfs' tune in *Snow White*. Walt Disney's company released the last film in 1937. It issued *Poppins* in 1964.

Comic Parodies

Many comic parodies "originated in a space of time ranging from the Civil War to about 1900," according to Ira William Ford.* "My Grandfather's Clock" (10), sung "Grandfather's Sox" (1), was written in 1876 by Henry Clay Work. "My Wild Irish Rose" (5), burlesqued as "Irish Nose" (1), was composed in 1899 by Chauncey Olcott for *A Romance of Athlone*. "The Rosary," spoofed as "My Misery" (1), was written by Robert Cameron Rogers. Ethelbert Nevin created the setting in 1898. Manhattan's Troop 582 (NY BSA) reproduced the first, while the others were included in the Brooklyn Boy Scouts (NY BSA) song book in 1929.

Brooklyn Scouts also sang "Gum Chewing Girl" (1), the "Moss Covered Onion" (1), and the "Old Family Toothbrush" (1) to the "Old Oaken Bucket" (2). George Kiallmark's tune has been used with "My Vacation" (3). His 1822 melody was a setting for an 1817 poem by Samuel Woodworth. *Paradology*[367] publicized all the imitations in 1927.

Mixed Parodies

Some song texts have been employed as models for both comic and pretty parodies. "White Wings" (36) has been used for the comic socks mentioned in KOOKABURRA, and for local lyrics at Tawakani (Ida CFG). Jolene Robinson Johnson remembers a camp version from Kirby (Wash CFG). Linda Johnson knows one from Hitaga (Iowa CFG). The original was written in 1884 by Banks Winter, a tenor with Thatcher, Primrose and West's Minstrels.

"That's Peggy O'Neill" has been used for "Piggy O'Neill" (4) and a widely adapted local song, "That's a Camp Fire Girl" (8). The last has been sung "That's Teedy-Usk-Ung" by Sally Ann Brockley Parr (Penna girls), and "Who Is the Camp Fire Girl" by Vivian Sexton (Tex CFG). Harry Pease, Edward G. Nelson, and Gilbert Dodge produced it in 1921.

"My Bonnie" (15) has been sung "My Bonnie Has Tuberculosis" by Jean Mayo MacLaughlin (Fla GS). "Cowboy's Sweet Bye and Bye" (8) uses the melody of the verse, while the "Come Out" chant, sometimes done with "Cookie, Cookie" (30), uses the tune from the chorus. "My Mother's an Apple Pie Maker," with "My God, how the money rolls in" (5), employs both melodies. "Come Back to Tanadoona" (Minn CFG) has a verse that begins:

> Sometimes it's hard to be good
> And sometimes it's hard to be true
> But out at Camp Tanadoona
> They make an angel of you

Fuld[*] found the earliest known version in William Henry Hills' 1881 *Students' Songs*.

"There's a Long, Long Trail" (22) was written in 1913 by Yale University students, Alonzo Elliott and Stoddard King. Its comic parodies include "Long, Long Nail" (8) and the "Mummy Song" (3). Boy Scouts know "There's a Long, Long Trail to Camp" (6). Lyrics have been written to the melody at Burch (BSA), Hitaga (Iowa CFG), Tanadoona (Minn CFG), and in Ohio 4-H, according to Larry Ralston.

Decline of Parodies

While comic parodies seem to have stopped being produced in large numbers around World War I, they persisted in camp repertoires for another decade or so. Song books from Brooklyn Scout camps (NY BSA) and the Methodist Epworth League[367] are replete with such pieces.

Philip LaRonge[S] was told the nascent 1920s Mooseheart (Ill CFG) repertoire, mentioned in ASH GROVE, was mainly organizational songs by Neidlinger, current commercial tunes, and "a lot of parodies." At Wise (Ohio J coed), Albert Brown[*] remembered, before 1926, they sang "parodies of popular songs and songs from recent Broadway shows" along with "silly or absurd songs" and "Gilbert and Sullivan lyrics."

Reasons for the use, then the demise of burlesques, are numerous. Albert McLean[*] suggested vaudeville humor shifted, at the turn of the twentieth century, away from longer comic tales (analogous to extended parodies) and toward short, often one-line, jokes. He thought these transformations reflected the influx of Jewish and other immigrants from Eastern and Southern Europe.

When the audience for vaudeville changed, so did the performers, and so did the background of songwriters. The center of musical creativity moved from Chicago to New York. Men influenced by Vienna replaced those trained in Germany.

Egbert Van Alstyne, mentioned in ASH GROVE, represented the last of the older group. His father may have descended from Jan Martense, son of Marten Van Alstyne, who immigrated to New Amsterdam in 1643. "In the Shade of the Old Apple Tree" (1), which he wrote in 1905 with Harry Hiram Williams, is parodied as "Neath the Crust of the Old Apple Pie" (8). Joseph Carleton Borden sang the original at Rotherwood (Me boys) in the 1920s. Larry Ralston (Ohio 4-H) has heard "In the Shade of the Green Apple Tree" (1). Brooklyn Boy Scout camps (NY BSA) have their own comic version.

Harry von Tilzer represented the transition to the new. He was born in Detroit in 1872, his brother Albert in Indianapolis. Their father was a Polish Jew who changed his name from Gumbinsky to Grumm before settling in Goshen, Indiana. Harry left home at age fourteen to join a circus. When he entered show business, he took his mother Sarah's name and added the noble "von" to sound German.

He moved to New York in 1892 where he opened what became the first office in Tin Pan Alley.[388] His "Rufus Rastus Johnson Brown" (3) has been adopted as a tune, but not directly parodied.

Gus Edwards represented the next generation of immigrants who stayed East where they Americanized their names. Edwards was born Augustus Edwards Simon in 1879 to Jewish parents in Posnia, the area of Poland seized by Prussia in 1772. They settled in the heavily German Williamsburg section of Brooklyn, New York. He was haunting vaudeville houses when he was nine, writing songs when he was twenty. He produced his first Broadway musical in 1908.

Edwards' most famous melody, "School Days," has been sung "Camp Days" at three camps, and "Blue Bird, Blue Bird, happy friends" at five. Shawondasee (Tex CFG), Tanadoona (Minn CFG), and Wohelo (RI CFG) each has its own Blue Bird song. Will Cobb composed the lyrics in 1907. Vivian Sexton remembers the Shawondasee version.

A second possible explanation for parodies in the late nineteenth century is audiences may have needed a comic outlet for feelings stifled by stylized sentiments that were the only accepted public emotions of the period. World War I destroyed faith in the old virtues. Ernest Hemingway and F. Scott Fitzgerald changed the language.

Irving Berlin was born Israel Isidore Baline in a village in modern-day Belarus, where his father was a cantor. They escaped the pogrom of 1893 to settle on New York's lower east side, across the East river from Williamsburg. The teen-aged boy survived by singing in Bowery saloons. He was tutored to survive a darker world.

Copyrights

Another factor contributing to the decline of parodies was the copyright law. It went into effect between the songwriting apogees of Edwards and Berlin. By the end of the next world war, Oliver was telling YWCA leaders, "writing parodies is often illegal! It is against the law to write words to be sung to a copyrighted tune without permission of the copyright owner."[230:17]

She admitted the Y had been refused permission to publish organization lyrics written "for hit tunes like the *Oklahoma* songs, when the poetry or idea have had little value."[230:17]

A parody is not illegal. To make it so would violate the first amendment to the Constitution. Copyright laws prevent using music for profit without permission, often in the form of an agreement to make royalty payments. Following Holmes, the definition of profit was broad.

Girl Scouts, with their cookie sales, are the most vulnerable. Anything that enhances the group's prestige, at any level, may lead to revenue for councils and bakeries. They appear to be the most vigilant. When I sent my questionnaire in 1976, I invited individuals to send me copies of their camps' song books or song lists. I received material from 23 coed camps, seven all girls' camps, and four boys' camps. Only two Girl Scouts sent camp songsters. As a comparison, earlier I had received material from 45 Camp Fire staffs.

As mentioned in KUMBAYA, the solution in early song books had been to print the words of a parody and note the title of the familiar tune, much like hymnals still were doing. The reach of copyright law since has expanded. What has become important to surviving folk traditions are responses of camping and organization leaders who fear potential lawsuits and the subsequent alienation of sources for financial support.

Contemporary Parodies

For whatever reason, parodies are less common in contemporary camps in this country than in the past. Further, as the Knapps[*] observed of "On Top of Spaghetti" (8), they have become the domain of adults. Tom Glazer composed the paraphrase in 1963. The original, "On Top of Old Smoky" (18), has been used for a Les Chalets Francais (Me girls) song.

Other parodies of recent songs, which bear the mark of adult or professional composition, have not been sung much in camps either. Jolene Robinson Johnson (Wash CFG) has heard Bob Dylan's "Blowin' in the Wind" (57) as, "How many beans in a can of Hormel." Wilma Lawrence (Penna GS) mentioned "Ralph the Magic Seagull" (1). A Celtic-bluegrass band from Thunder Bay, Ontario, Flipper Flanagan's Flat Footed Four, performs the Peter, Paul and Mary take-off.

Variant Forms

Parodies may assume forms other than Kushtaka's (Alaska CFG) simple revision of "Home on the Range" (27) as "Home on the Tundra" (1). One is a narrative composed of snippets from other songs. Glen (Ohio CFG) has a version of "Old MacDonald" about cutting down the old pine tree. Tanadoona (Minn CFG) has one in which Peter Pumpkin Eater puts his wife in an old oaken bucket. Brooklyn Scout camps (NY BSA) had two medleys in the 1920s: one about "Henry Kelly" (1) who went to college, the other the "Insurance Song" (1).

A second variant form is the comic second verse, which may be sung alone. Gifford (Neb BSA) has sung "Katie Finnigan" as a second verse to "Michael Finnigan" (14). Saint Louis Boy Scouts (Mo BSA) have a second verse about "Mentholatum" to "Rheumatism" (11). Fowke collected a version of the last from Isabel Ricker Smaller. She learned it in Owen Sound, Ontario, around 1916.[331]

Clusters

The existence of multiple parodies to the same tune has led to some being grouped as verses of a single song. "Ham and Eggs" (6), done to "Tammany," is sung with a second verse, "Gasoline," at Gifford (Neb BSA) and the Brooklyn Scout camps (NY BSA). "I Had a Dog and His Name Was Fido" (5) has been combined with "Sal and I" (2) by Brooklyn Scouts. Seabow (Calif CFG) sings "Sis and I" as a separate song to "Reuben and Rachel" (4).

"Tammany" was written during a New York City election in 1905 by Gus Edwards and Vincent Bryan. "Reuben" was composed earlier, in 1871, by William Gooch and Harry Birch. Other songs that sometimes use the last are "Horse Named Napoleon" (2), "I Love Little Willie" (4), and "You're a Wonder" (5).

The existence of several parodies on the same theme has led to some mixed motifs. Brooklyn Scout camps (NY BSA) sang, "Sweet Rosie O'Grady was a seamstress by birth." Irondale (Mo BSA) has sung, "Sweet Rosie O'Grady was a blacksmith by birth." The last apparently was borrowed from "Poor little Annie Larinsky was a blacksmith by birth."

Maude Nugent wrote "Rosie," and introduced it in vaudeville in 1896. "Annie" appeared in the 1925 edition of *Stunt Songs for Social Sings*. Its editors, Annetta Byers Eldridge[*] (1899-1982) and Ruth Anderson Eldridge Richardson (1896-1976), were sisters raised in Franklin, Ohio, in the Miami River valley between Cincinnati and Dayton.

Both graduated from Denison University, founded by Ohio's Baptist Education Society. Annetta was active in the YWCA, and played tennis and field hockey while she was in school. Ruth was senior class poetess and on the tennis team. Their uncle, Harry Carleton Eldridge, was a playwright who ran the publishing business that issued their songster.

Topics

Topics of comic parodies fall into two general categories. One includes those written about the ugly, the obscene, the gross, the scatological, contamination, and other taboos in ways that address children's hidden obsessions. These were discussed in KOOKABURRA. The other group addresses subjects that hold special meaning.

In discussing patriotic parodies, like the Brooklyn Scout camps' (NY BSA) rendition of "America" (27) as "My chicken, 'tis of thee" (1), the Knapps suggested they served a distancing function. "By singing these parodies, a child is showing that the originals are important to him. However, he's also fending off the depersonalization that accompanies the insistent celebration of patriotism in some schools."[393:170]

The two categories are not exclusive. An important topic can be treated with crude images. This is clear in ephemeral parodies of camp songs that become so popular they may be oversung, and hence open to burlesque. Carol Shuster[§] collected a version of "Barges" (68) as "Trashtrucks." She also heard "Fish and Chips" (40) sung "Crackerjacks and Whiskey." Nancy Simmons (Colo GS) has sung "White Coral Bells" (77) as "White Ruffled Pants."

Advertisements

Advertisements have been included in parodies and comic songs for years. Many may have come from early promotional campaigns like the Model-T joke books distributed by Ford Motor Company. Corporate encouragement of brand recognition through humor may have stimulated at least some camp songs about cars like "Little Pile of Tin" (29). "John Brown's Flivver" (9) is sung "John Brown's Ford" at Watervliet (Mich girls), "John Brown's Chevy" by Vivian Sexton (Tex CFG), and "Old Mister Ford" at Patiya (Colo CFG).

Automobile verses have been added to "Itsy Bitsy Spider" (33) at Seabow (Calif CFG), to "Old MacDonald" (20) at Eberhart (Ind YMCA coed), and to "Grandfather's Whiskers" (8). Sally Briggs[S] collected an Ohio Boy Scout parody of "Let Me Call You Sweetheart" (6) that began, "Let me call you Lizzie / I'm in debt to you."

Other early advertising campaigns may be glimpsed in "The Billboard Song" (17) and in references to Listerine in the "Horses Run Around" (10). "The Billboard" changes so often, Ann Beardsley (Ohio GS) says one camp banned it, "probably because the counselors couldn't remember it." Homer and Jethro recorded a version in 1960.

Spoofs of advertisements may be like comic versions of patriotic material cited by the Knapps. They may provide ways for children to distance themselves from something to which they continually are exposed. Joyce Gregg Stoppenhagen (Mich P coed) remembers they had dining hall skits with radio station KORN at church camp in the 1950s, more than a decade before the *Hee Haw* television feature. Faux commercials are what she most remembers, especially a take-off on a Rice Krispies slogan. Kamaji (Minn girls) also mocks the dry cereal.

Commercial jingles for Nestlé's chocolate, Coke, and Pepsi have been used for unit or camp songs. Debra Janison remembers "G-I-B-O-N-S, Gibons is the very best" from Christopher (Ohio C coed). Judy Miller knows "Things go better at Kamaji" (Minn girls). Namanu (Ore CFG) sings, "We are ranchers riding high."

More recently, commercials have masqueraded as fun songs. "I'd Like To Teach the World to Sing" (11), recorded in 1971 by the New Seekers, originally was a Coca-Cola advertisement. "It's a Small World" (23), recorded by the Mike Curb Congregation in 1973, is associated with Disney World.

Nursery Rhymes

Nursery rhymes are another common source for parodies. The Opies suggested, when children become "seven or eight years old, they establish their independence by parodying the rhymes their parents taught them."[451:90]

"Old MacDonald" (20) has been localized to counselors and campers at Max Straus (Calif J boys), according to Tom Greiff. Betsy Wolverton (Ohio GS) has sung, "Ich Closclowski had a zoo." Carol Flack (Ala agency coed) sings "Old MacDonald" with nursery rhymes.

The last is like the Glen (Ohio CFG) medley that was so popular with the 13- and 14-year-old girls in 1974, they sang it in the dining hall despite the refusal of counselors to sanction it. Later, younger girls, who still were perfecting the text, sang it while waiting in line for the council fire to begin.

Fuld* found a list of animals with their sounds in Thomas D'Urfey's 1706 opera, *Wonders in the Sun*. James M. Sutherland* printed a minstrel show version in Bob Hart's *Plantation Songster* in 1862. He was a Methodist minister who turned to Broadway variety shows in 1859. He probably amassed then-current songs into the chapbook he issued to launch his own minstrel company.

A Yale song book from 1859 used our current melody for "Litoria! Litoria!" Nettleingham* printed the text and tune together in a London collection of World War I soldiers' songs in 1917. "Bingo" (50) shares the tune.

Contemporary camps prefer adapting nursery tunes for young campers' songs, rather than treating them with rough humor. "Twinkle, Twinkle Little Star" has been used for "Blue Bird candle burning bright" (1) and "Now our Blue Bird meeting ends" (8). Mawavi (DC CFG) has sung the first. *Camp Fire Magazine* published it in 1964. The "Closing Song" has been adapted as "Now our day of camping ends" at Seabow (Calif CFG). It spread from a record for Blue Bird leaders.

Its melody first was published in 1761 as "Ah! Vous Dirai-Je, Maman," and soon was known widely. Wolfgang Amadeus Mozart heard it in Paris in 1778. Jane Taylor published the verse in 1806 in *Rhymes for the Nursery*. William Edward Hickson introduced the combination in England in the 1838 edition of *The Singing Master*.[338] He owned *The Westminster* between 1840 and 1852, where he promoted education reform. His primer was marketed for day and Sunday schools.

Patiya (Colo CFG) has a Blue Bird song to "Here We Go 'round the Mulberry Bush." Adahi (Penna CFG) uses "Mary Had a Little

Lamb." Wohelo (RI CFG) has one to "Ten Little Indians." The last, written in 1868 by Septimus Winner, is used with "Bow Bow Belinda" (6), "Picking up Paw Paws" (6) and, sometimes, "Michael Finnigan" (14).

Sacred Songs

The greatest controversy concerning parodies centers on religious songs. In a 1955 guide for YMCA recreation leaders, Helen and Larry Eisenberg wrote:

> Some parodies are fun, a few are useful. But others cheapen the original, being completely unworthy of it, such as some "moron" songs like "Gee, Ain't It Great to be Crazy" (33) or "On a Hill Far Away Stood an Old Chevrolet." Certainly a jitterbug tune made from a dignified, reverent spiritual is in exceptionally bad taste.[214:49]

"Chevrolet" parodies "Old Rugged Cross" (6), which George Bennard wrote in 1913. The itinerant Methodist evangelist spent his time between crusades in Albion, Michigan.

"All Night, All Day" (33) is an example of an uptempo setting for a somber religious text. The original prayer, "Now I lay me down to sleep," was introduced in the 1727 edition of *The New England Primer*. Sanders* included it in *Sing High, Sing Low* in 1946. Perhaps because she described it as a "Negro spiritual," it is sung with added "Lordies" between lines of the chorus. Gary Flegal says, the Van Buren Youth Camp (Mich agency coed) treats it as serious evening closing song done with harmony.

Another example of a verse some find offensive is the grace, "Rub a dub / Thanks for grub / Yeah God." Two people mentioned it in 1976. James Hook set the "Dub a dub dub" rhyme to music in his *Second Volume of Christmas Box* in 1798.[452]

An aversion to ridiculing religion probably developed after World War II. Harbin* published "I'd Rather Have Fingers than Toes" (3) for the Methodist Epworth League in 1927. John Fawcett composed the original hymn, "Blest Be the Tie that Binds" (6), in 1772. The Baptist minister was documenting his decision to stay in West Yorkshire, rather than move to London, England. Mason recast it with music by Hans Georg Nägeli as "Dennis."

The distaste may be unique to this country. Laurel Ann Hall has sung "Uncle George and Auntie Mable fainted at the breakfast table" (1) to "Hark the Herald Angles Sing" in a Canadian coed camp. William Hayman Cummings reset Charles Wesley's carol to Felix Mendelssohn Batholdy's *Gutenberg Cantata* for male chorus, "Festgesang an die Künstler," in 1855.

Secular to Sacred Exchange

Such censure overlooks an old, and still vibrant, tradition. Among the earliest known contrafacta, in which "the original text is replaced by a new one, particularly a secular text by a sacred one, or vice versa," are ninth-century Gregorian chants.[242]

"God Save the King" moved between the two realms after it was published in 1744 for George II. When the Scots rebelled the next year, it was recast as "God save great George our king."[338] Charles Wesley used the tune for "Come Thou Almighty King" (6) in 1761. His anonymous text, subtitled "An Hymn to the Trinity," fell prey to continuing theological disagreements of English Methodists over predestination.[350]

A supporter of Whitefield, Selina Shirley Hastings, Countess of Huntington, had Felice Giardini alter Wesley's melody to something more respectful to the aristocracy. Mason revised Giardini's "Moscow" to fit the classic style of Haydn. His version appeared with his "Italian Hymn" in *The Handel and Haydn Society's Collection.* The original lyrics since have been altered to mute the martial rhetoric.

While Methodists were bickering, Prussia was dismembering the home of Bach and the Moravians. Saxony's elector had been king of Poland, when Prussia seized and divided it with Austria and Russia in the 1790s. Napoléon took Thüringen in 1806. When Prussia defeated him at Leipzig in 1813, it captured the man he had elevated to king, Friedrich August. The Saxon monarch was ransomed for more territory in the north in 1815.

Siegfried August Mahlmann wrote "Gott segne Sachsenland" to celebrate the king's return to non-Prussian Saxony to the tune for the Hanoverian's "God Save the King." When Mason was preparing *The Choir* for publication in 1831, he asked a Baptist seminary student to translate the hymn. Instead, Samuel Francis Smith wrote new words, which began "My country 'tis of thee" (27). Lutherans translate Mahlmann's poem as "God Bless Our Native Land."

Religious lyrics still are being set to familiar tunes. Foster (Iowa YMCA coed) sings "Be Present at Our Table Lord" (18) to the "Chevy Song." Some set the grace that begins "Thanks Be to God" (34) to "Windy," recorded by The Association in 1967. The "Doxology" (29) has been sung to "Hernando's Hideaway" at Trexler (NY P boys). Wanda Callahan remembers it with "Chim Chim Chimeree" (2) at Ithiel (Fla P coed).

"Be Present," promoted by the Methodist Women's Society as the "Wesley Grace," was written by John Cennick. He supported Whitefield.[383] The original tune for Thomas Ken's words, "Praise God from Whom all blessings flow," was introduced with Psalm 100 in the *Genevan Psalter*. Loys Bourgeois edited the 1551 edition for Calvin. Widjiwagan (Hawaii CFG) has Hawaiian lyrics, which begin "Hoonani i ka Makua mau."

"Hernando's Hideaway" is from *Pajama Game*, a 1954 musical choreographed by Bob Fosse. *Mary Poppins* introduced "Chim Chim Chimeree." Pennsylvania's Council of Churches* suggested the Disney tune in 1970. Ithiel is sponsored by Church of the Brethren, a descendant of German Anabaptists. Trexler is a Lutheran camp.

Seth Clay has altered "Peace, I Ask of Thee O River" (88) to "O Father" for Warren (Mich P coed). At Cherith (NY P girls), Carol Ann Engle sings "Boomdeada" (48) with the verse:

> I love the Father, I love his only Son,
> I love the Spirit, I love the three-in-one
> For He created me, redeemed and set me free,
> Praise Him, Praise Him, Praise Him, Praise Him

Sacred to Secular Exchange

In post-Civil War America, some songs made the reverse transition, from sacred to secular. George Pullen Jackson* traced "Aunt Rhody" (6) back to "Rousseau's Dream," from the 1840 edition of Walker's *Southern Harmony*. The title comes from an instrumental dance used in an opera by Jean-Jacques Rousseau, *Le Devin du Village*.

Mason used it with Samuel Pearce's "Sweet Affliction" in the *Handel and Haydn* collection.[521] Walker reproduced Mason.

"She'll Be Coming 'round the Mountain" (41) uses "When the Chariot Comes." William Eleazar Barton* published it twice in 1899 as a "recent Negro" melody. Henry Marvin Belden[277] and Arthur Palmer Hudson believed that, in turn, was "a parody or secularization" of "Old Ship of Zion." White[547] noted the common version first was mentioned in 1853 by Sarah Josepha Hale* as a camp meeting song. The motif was older. "Mountain" has been used for "She'll Be Comin' o'er the Tundra" at Kushtaka (Alaska CFG), and for three Hitaga (Iowa CFG) songs.

Boy Scouts have borrowed religious melodies from the more active evangelistic organizations. The Methodist-influenced Salvation Army promoted "Onward Christian Soldiers" (7). "Onward Boy Scouts" (5) used the original by Arthur Sullivan and Sabine Baring-Gold.

Man (NY BSA) has a local text to "Let the Lower Lights Keep Burning" (2). Philip Paul Bliss wrote the gospel song for *The Charm*. His Sunday-school collection was published in Cincinnati in 1871.

Brooklyn Scout camps (NY BSA) have sung their own lyrics to "Brighten the Corner" (3). Ina Duley Ogden's 1913 words were set to music by Charles Hutchinson Gabriel, and recorded by Homer Rodeheaver.

The chorus to "Jingle Bells" has been adapted at the Dixie Camps (Ga sep)[345] and at Hitaga (Iowa CFG). Vivian Sexton (Tex CFG) remembers two Camp Fire clones. James Pierpont published the original in 1857. A fragment of "Frosty the Snowman" can be detected in "I Wuv a Wabbit" (5). Gene Autry recorded the ballad in 1950.

Kitanniwa Repertoire

Kitanniwa's repertoire in the early years at the Sherman Lake, Saint Mary's Lake, and Clear Lake was much like those at Mooseheart (Ill CFG) and Wise (Ohio J coed). When I showed Lucille Parker Munk a Rohrbough collection, *Songs from the 20's*, she remembered fifteen, including two parodies, "John Brown's Flivver" (9) and "Bucolic Lyric" (1). The latter, which described a country boy and a Jersey cow, was sung to "Mighty Lak a Rose."

By the 1940s, interest in international and consensus American folk music had replaced such raucous fun songs as "Has Anybody

Seen My Kitty" (2). Still, contrafacta and parodies represented more than a third of the texts recognized by Lucille Parker Munk, Carol Parsons Sievert, and Kathleen Huggett Nye. These included "Swimming" (42), "Cookie" (30), "It Isn't Any Trouble Just To S-m-i-l-e" (25), "Perfect Posture" (22), and "Smile Awhile" (8).

Kitanniwa's repertoire in the middle 1950s bore the influence of people mentioned in AN AUSTRIAN who shunned parodies. Dickie's *Singing Pathways** was used to compile the 1940s song book. Zanzig's *Singing America** still was in the local CFG office in 1974.

The only camp-specific or organizational parodies and contrafacta sung at all camp events in the 1950s persisted from the 1940s. Newer ones were so disguised, they were not recognized as such. "Grand Old Duke of York" (24) and "Old King Cole" (14) were simply gesture songs.

Parodies were not even written much in special circumstances. One evening a camp session often was dedicated to skits mounted by each cabin. I only remember learning a song for one evening program, sometime around 1954. Our counselor used *Music Makers** to teach us a Tuscan tune. David Kilburn Stevens created the text for "Marianina" (11).

Even during the annual waterfront games, we only produced a team yell, not a spirit song. Instead of true parodies, comic words sometimes were substituted, like in "Down Yonder Brown Outhouse" mentioned in ASH GROVE.

Repertoire Violation

I remember only one person from Kitanniwa in the 1950s who liked parodies. The camp nurse was active in local civic theater productions. A photograph taken when she was dressed as a gypsy appears in "Kitanniwa Staff, 1950s."

Our first year in the senior unit, she and one of my tent mates staged a skit premised on *Romeo and Juliet* as a hillbilly feud. The next year, the two collaborated on a version of *Alice in Wonderland*, with the girl playing the Cheshire cat strapped to the rafters.

We had less time the first year we were CITs, but the nurse still managed to fabricate an occasion for us. While people were waiting for the flag-lowering ceremony on July Fourth, we stood on the main lodge steps to sing "You're a Grand Old Flag" (9) with a great show of unity. When we announced no state bragged, one girl took a pin to burst the balloon under the shirt of another who represented some state like Florida.

When I talked with former staff members who had been in camp in the late 1950s, I asked about the nurse. No one remembered her. I thought, at least someone close to the camp director would remember the potential dangers of young campers trying to imitate the vanishing cat.

I could not believe, no one remembered her. As with the woman who introduced the "Titanic" discussed in SKYBALL PAINT, I do not believe it was a case of animosity. The nurse was rehired, and I am told the Ship Titanic counselor was hired for another season after I left camp. The second time, she brought a guitar, but again left no musical legacy.

I have pondered many possible explanations for the nurse fading from memory. Certainly differences existed in age, responsibilities, and education between her and the counselors. But, such social distinctions do not usually lead to amnesia.

I only can conclude, once a camp develops a sense of itself, the dynamics of cultural perpetuation replicate our immune system. They build protective barriers to reject any person or idea that might force it to change too much. When shown viable alternatives, the culture ignores them.

One camp director, who has thought about this, wrote she had been to all girls' camps:

> where we sang much more than we do in this one (I've been here 9 years) [. . .] For a while I thought it was because it was co-ed and the boys are less inclined to sing than the girls. However, I have decided it is because they only have 2 week contact with each other per year and half of the 80 campers are new each year. It doesn't give us enough continuity. Staff is important, too. Most of my staff are home-grown CIT's. When I have a larger GS or BS staff we sing more.

She leaves unsaid that, even when she has been able to hire staff members who sing, they cannot alter a tradition that was there before she was hired and is perpetuated, in spite of her presence and best efforts to innovate, by "home-grown CIT's."

Kitanniwa in 1974 had survived the equivalent of a culture shock, signified by having had six directors in ten years. Its repertoire was more like the one remembered by Lucille Parker Munk, than any known in the decades between the opening and closing years. The 23 songs I heard, at three after meal sings during the experimental coed session, included three contrafacta, "A Bear" (32), "Cookie" (30), and "Climates" (8). Parodies included "We Are Crazy" (4) and "Junior Birdsmen" (30).

"Cookie" (30) uses Bob Carleton's "Ja Da" of 1918. Hickerson[*] says, "Birdsmen" adapted an Air Force song, William Clinches' "Spirit of the Air Corps."

Case Study: Lollypop

The parody with the most enduring popularity at Kitanniwa since the 1940s has been "Lollypop" (43), written to George Michael Cohan's "Harrigan." Joyce Gregg Stoppenhagen remembers in the late 1950s, "The kids *loved* it. And so did I, for the first two weeks in camp, and then you just don't want to hear it again, although I taught it to my Girl Scouts last year."

In the early 1970s, it still was being used as a touchstone. Kitty Smith described a song as "another one like 'Lollypop'."

Direct Parodies

"Harrigan," with its strutting machismo chorus, was a song begging to be lampooned when actor George Parsons introduced it in 1907. The University of Rochester song book from the next year included one with the line, "Rochester - that's here." A member of the class of 1909 wrote the version Gamma Phi Beta published in 1931. "Phi Kappa Psi Are We" was published in 1914.

Perhaps the earliest parody sung in camps was "Herpicide," about a shampoo introduced in 1899 by Dupont Morse Newbro.[*] He was born in Lansing, Michigan, then moved to Butte, Montana, where he owned a drug store. He returned to Detroit in 1901 to run The Herpicide Company.

Like the Ford Motor jokes, it could have been created by someone promoting the company, or by an amateur. The version published in 1925 in southern Ohio by the Eldridge sisters[†] followed the "Harrigan" chorus closely. It ended with a pun, "it's hair again on me."

"Lollypop" (A-1) was included with "Herpicide" in an undated song book edited by Albert Brown.[†] More than likely, it was issued in the mid to late 1920s. He worked at Wise (Ohio J coed) from 1921 through 1927 as a counselor, activities leader, and director. In 1928 and 1929, he directed Alliance (Ohio J coed), which shared the same sponsors and site near Painesville, Ohio.

Illustrations were by Edwin Kaufman (1906-1939), who graduated from the Cleveland School of Art in 1929. By 1930, he was doing etchings in New York City. The address for the printer, Junior Dramatics Pub. Co. of Cleveland, Ohio, belonged to Brown's widowed mother when she died in 1924.

The verse could not have been conceived before lollypops were mass produced, which was after "Harrigan" was written. George Smith claims he produced them in 1908. That same year, Racine Confectioner's Machinery Company marketed a machine in Wisconsin. In California, Samuel Born automated the manufacturing process in 1916.

"Lollypop" has been used in Britain since the late eighteenth century to refer to candy. Its usage is similar to our use of cotton candy as a metaphor for sticky sweetness.[455]

Second Generation Parodies

"Lollypop" was the more popular parody. Its burlesques can be identified by their form. They begin with a rhyming couplet, which identifies the object's inventor, and conclude with a couplet, which describes some distinguishing feature. Cavell's (Mich YWCA) version of "Herpicide" (C-3) has been modified to fit this form by dropping the pun found in the Eldridges' version.

"Castor Oil" is a direct copy that comments on the original, by suggesting a cure for overindulgence. Oil extracted from the castor bean was a common laxative at a time when the health conscious were concerned with cleansing their internal plumbing.

For years, girls at Kitanniwa were forced to drink a cup of water before breakfast. Carol Parsons Sievert remembers, they would take turns sitting near the screened side of their table, so they could dump it in the bushes.

Soon after I began going to camp, the director substituted a Wednesday serving of stewed prunes for breakfast. Lynn Russell Hickerson says, they always would sing the "Prune Song" (27) at Med-O-Lark (Me coed) in the late 1950s when confronted with this ounce of prevention.

"Davenport" (D-3) is an imitative parody that does not directly reference the original "Lollypop," but uses the same form. In the years when Grand Rapids, Michigan, was the leading producer of inexpensive wooden furniture, davenport became the generic term for any upholstered sofa copied from those manufactured by the more upscale A. H. Davenport Company of Boston.

The reference to "Oh Johnny" may date the verse to the song "Oh Johnny" (5), which was written in 1917. Emrich[†] collected the davenport verse from Diane Taub of Plainfield, New Jersey.

Joyce Gregg Stoppenhagen (Ohio GS) once knew a verse about watermelon. All she remembers are the rhymes, "fruit" and "beaut." Sheppard Mill (NJ GS) still was singing "Bubblegum" (D-2) in 1976, according to Dianna Masto.[§] That was probably the last of the parodies to enter tradition. Fleer introduced the gum in 1928 in Philadelphia after Walter Diemer, a 23-year-old accountant more interested in chemistry, cooked the first batch.

As Ford suggested, the interest in parodies had passed. Song writing was centered in New York. The "Prune Song" is late. Frank Crumit of Jackson, Ohio, and Harry Da Costa of New York City produced it in 1928. Abe Olman, the lyricist for "Oh, Johnny," was from Cincinnati, while the composer, Ed Rose, was from Chicago. Fowke collected "The Baby Prune" from Toronto, Ontario, third graders in 1960.[332]

Parody Medleys

When parodies no longer could be extended with new verses, people in camps began combining existing songs into medleys. "When You Come to the End of a Lollipop" (3) was inserted into "Lollypop" at Kitanniwa one summer around 1953. Its interlude, "You stop and chew the stick," was accompanied by biting the index finger. Brooklyn Boy Scouts (NY BSA) knew the verse in 1929.

Charlotte Duff remembers the song from girls' camps in the 1940s. It also was sung at Gifford (Neb BSA).

More recently, "I'd Rather Suck on a Lemon Drop" (10) has merged with the lollypop verse. When it is a separate song, as it was at Kitanniwa in 1974, there usually is a second stanza for the "refined" interlude. Tannadoonah (Ind CFG), sings the additional verse as:

> Oh, it makes me sick the way it smears
> It gets all in my hair and ears
> With a jellybean, I'm always clean
> But a lollypop, o ichy.

Jacqueline Orvis says, it was introduced into her Michigan Girl Scout camp from Illinois.

Contrafacta

Even though comic parodies no longer are being created in great quantities, songs still are being adapted for local purposes. Ethel Martin included a verse about Red Wing (Penna girls) in the camp song book in 1931 that had the spelling section and second couplet from "Lollypop." When Kappa Delta published "K-A-double-P-A" in 1936, the editors said, it already was an "old camp song." The camp verse for "Lollypop" was introduced to Kitanniwa by the late 1940s.

Inspirations for adaptations vary. The one from Cavell (Mich YWCA) may have been modeled on one known from another camp: "camp on a hill" (C-2) is close to Kitanniwa's "camp on a lake" (A-3). The unit song (version B) from Christopher (Ohio C coed), with the line "Barry Jon that's me," probably referred back to the original Cohan song. Seabow (Calif CFG) has two additions to "Lollypop," one a conventional verse about Hershey bars (E-3) and another about poison oak (E-2). The last is probably a mocking reference to a camp menace.

Situational Parodies

When songs become very familiar, they become subject to informal burlesques that never are elevated to independent versions. Some, like the pronoun substitution used with "Kookaburra" (85), may be reinvented, since they arise from unchanging developmental needs of children and adolescents. Seabow (Calif CFG) plays with them in version E.

Others are more spontaneous. One time in the 1950s, I remember hearing girls around age eleven shout "tramp" for "champ" in the Kitanniwa verse. The stanza almost always came to mind, sometimes even was sung by a few, when a water snake was seen in the swimming area. By then the song had become a means of communicating affection and dismay.

Music

Cohan (1878-1942) was born into a vaudeville family, whose immigrant ancestor, Michael Keohane, had been a tailor in County Cork in southeastern Ireland. By the time the grandson was eight, he was playing violin. At eleven, he was a solo buck-and-wing dancer. When he was twelve, he rejoined his sister, Josephine, and parents as The Four Cohans. A few years later, he began writing his own songs and skits, many of which owed their pacing to his experience as a dancer.[290]

In his early twenties, he produced *The Governor's Son* for Broadway in 1901. Over the next decades, he became one of the most prolific writers of commercial songs that entered camp tradition. These included "I'm a Yankee Doodle Dandy" (4) from 1904, "You're a Grand Old Flag" (9) from 1906, and "Over There" (5) from 1917.

He wrote "Harrigan" for *Fifty Miles from Boston*. A Maine newspaper described it as, "a mixture of melo-drama, comedy and farce with just enough music thrown in to give it variety."[291] *Munsey's Magazine* described Dave Harrigan as, "The most doggedly delightful villain that ever smoked a cigarette."[292]

Cohan's original tune is more complex than typical camp melodies. Modifications by oral tradition have not altered its identity. One change is in the next to the last line where he used an opening ascending phrase, followed by three descending sections. In camps, the upward phrase is repeated three times, followed by a new downward motif.

Another part of the original melody, which was alien to the camp aesthetic, was the use of long pauses to end the second and third lines. In most camps, these are filled by singing the last word twice. At

Wasewagan[†] (Calif CFG), girls hold the first note of the line, so the textual line ends on the rest.

William Daniel Doebler[§] collected a version from a former Runels (Mass GS) counselor in which the first syllable of the last word in the line was sustained. The last syllable then fell in the rest. It was accompanied by an ukulele.

At Kitanniwa[†] in the 1970s, campers clapped the rhythm and shouted, rather than sang. Clapping was not done in the 1950s, but shouting was. June Rushing Leibfarth[§] collected a version from Robinwood (Tex GS) in 1967 that filled another Cohan vaudeville pause with the sounds "plop" and "yech" in the last line before "for me." Dianna Masto[§] discovered a New Jersey Girl Scout version with spoken interludes (version D).

"End of a Lollypop" is an adaptation of "Perfect Day" (4), written in 1910 by Carrie Jacobs-Bond (1862-1946). She was born into a musical family in Janesville, Wisconsin. When her husband died in Iron River, Michigan, she began selling songs to support herself and her son. She moved to Chicago where she supplemented her income by running a boarding house for college students. "Perfect Day" has been used for "End of a Camping Day" (40) and for local songs at Blue Haven (NM P coed), Tanadoona (Minn CFG), Watanopa (Mont CFG), and Mayflower (Mass girls).[345]

Popularity

"Lollypop" is known everywhere in Camp Fire camps, but has spread more to girls' camps in the survey Midwest than in other parts of the country. Judy Miller says the camp verse did not arrive at Kamaji (Mich girls) until the 1960s. Girls in coed camps did not know the song, nor did many young men in 1976.

Version A

Text from Polly McIntyre, Camp Kitanniwa (Mich CFG), late 1950s; transcribed February 1975. Gestures from Camp Kitanniwa (Mich CFG), after lunch sing, 1974. Polly's photograph appears in "Coming of Age." Albert Brown's is in "Camping through Time."

Asterisks (*) indicate hand claps

1. L* O* dou* ble L* I* P* O* P* spells* lol* li pop*, lol* li pop*!
   That's* the on* ly de* cent kind* of can* dy*, can* dy*
   Man* who made* it must* have been* a dan* dy*, dan* dy.
   L* O* dou* ble L* I* P* O* P* you* see*
   It's* a lick* on* a stick*
   Guar* anteed* to make* you sick*!
   Lol* li pop* * for* * me*!

2. C-A-S-T-O-R-O-I-L spells castor oil, castor oil
   That's the only decent kind of medicine, medicine
   Man who made it must have been an Edison, an Edison.
   C-A-S-T-O-R-O-I-L you see
   It's a lick on spoon
   Guaranteed to cure you soon
   Castor oil for me!

3. K-I-T-A-N-N-I-W-A spells Kitanniwa, Kitanniwa
   That's the only decent kind of camp, camp
   Man who made it must have been a champ, champ.
   K-I-T-A-N-N-I-W-A you see
   It's a camp, on a lake
   Guaranteed to see a snake
   Kitanniwa for me!

Version B

Text from Camp Christopher (Ohio C coed), 1967-1968.

   B-A-double R-Y J-O-N spells Barry Jon
   Proud of all the spirit that's within us
   Devil the girls, that's the word agin us
   B-A-double R-Y J-O-N, you see?
   It's a name, that's a shame,
   We'll never get connected with,
   Barry Jon, that's me!

271

Version C

Text from Camp Cavell (Mich YWCA); collected by Joal Hess, Indiana University, 1949; variations from A emphasized.

1. L-o double l-**y**, -p-o-p spells lolly pop, lolly pop
   It's the only decent **kinda** candy, candy
   The man **that** made **'em certainly was a dandy**
   L-o double l-**y**, p-o-p-**u-c**,
   It's a lick on a stick
   Guaranteed to make you sick,
   Its lolly **pops**, for me.

2. C-a-m-p C-a-v-e-double l double-l
   That's the only camp you want to go to, go to
   That's the camp where everybody knows you, knows you
   C-a-m-p Ca-v-e-l_____
   It's a camp on a hill
   Where you really can't keep still
   It's Camp Cavell for me.

3. H-e-r-p-a-s-i-d spells herpasid, herpasid
   That's the only decent kinda hair goo, hair goo
   The man that made it was a scarecrow, scarecrow
   H-e-r-p-a-s-i-d **for me**
   First you rub, then you scrub
   Then you scrub, and you rub
   It's herpasid for me.

Version D

Text from Sheppard Mill Girl Scout Camp (NJ GS); collected by Dianna Masto, Douglass College, Rutgers, 1976; variations from A emphasized.

1. L-O- double L-I-P-O-P spells lollipop, lollipop
   That's the only decent kind of **candy**
   The man who made it must have been a **dandy**

L-O- double L-I-P-O-P you see
It's a lick on a stick
Guaranteed to make you sick
Lollipop for me!

And then there's (spoken)

2. B-U-B-B-L-E-G-U-M spells bubblegum, bubblegum
That's the only decent kind of chewing gum
That man who made it must have been a real chum
B-U-B-B-L-E-G-U-M you see
You chew it til it's stale
Then you throw it in the pail
Bubblegum for me!

And then there's (spoken)

3. D-A-V-E-N-P-O-R-T spells davenport, davenport
That's the only decent kind of love seat
The man who made it must have had a heartbeat
D-A-V-E-N-P-O-R-T you see
It's a hug and a squeeze
And an "Oh Johnny please!"
Davenport for me!

And then there's (spoken)

4. C-A-S-T-O-R-O-I-L spells castor oil, castor oil
That's the only decent kind of **medicine**
The man who made it must have been an **Edison**
C-A-S-T-O-R-O-I-L you see
It's a lick on a spoon
Guaranteed to **kill** you soon
Castor oil for me!

Version E

Text from Camp Seabow (Calif CFG), received 1974; variations from A emphasized.

1. L-O-Double L-I-P-O-P spells lollipop, lollipop.
   It's the only decent kind of **candy**.
   The man who made it must have been a **dandy**.
   L-O-double L-I-P-O-P, you see,
   It's a lick on a stick
   Guaranteed to make you sick,
   Lollipop for me --**not you**--
   Lollipop for me.

2. P-O-I-S-O-N O-A-K spells poison oak, poison oak.
   That's the only decent kind of rash,
   The man who made it must have been a smash.
   P-O-I-S-O-N O-A-K, you see,
   It's a leaf in ditch
   Guaranteed to make you itch,
   Poison oak for **you** --**not me**--
   Poison oak for you.

3. H-E-R-S-H-E-Y B-A-R spells Hershey bar Hershey bar.
   It's the only decent kind of candy,
   The man who made it must have been a dandy.
   H-E-R-S-H-E-Y B-A-R, you see,
   It's a snack in a pack,
   Guaranteed to make you fat,
   Hershey bar for me --**not you**--
   Hershey bar for me.

4. C-A-S-T-O-R O-I-L spells castor oil, castor oil.
   It's the only decent kind of **medicine**,
   The man who made it must have been an **Edison**.
   C-A-S-T-O-R O-I-L, you see,
   It's a lick on a spoon
   Guaranteed to **kill** you soon.
   Castor oil for you --**not me**--
   Castor oil for you.

Version F

Text from Camp Kirby (Wash CFG), received 1974; variations from A emphasized. Guitar chords from Shirley Ieraci (Ohio GS), 1970s.

1. L-O-double L-**Y**-P-O-P spells lollypop, lollypop,
   That's the only decent kind of candy, candy.
   The man who made it **surely was** a dandy, dandy.
   L-O-double L-**Y**-P-O-P you see.
   It's a lick on a stick guaranteed to make you sick.
   Lollypops for me!

2. Oh, I'd (A) rather suck on a lem (D7) on drop
   Than to trust (A) my luck to a lollypop,
   'Cause I always drop my lol (D7) lypop and it gets (A) all over icky.
   I've tried (D7) and tried (A) but nev (D7) er could find, (A)
   A lol (E) lypop half way refined (D7). (affected voice)
   So, I'd rather suck on a lemon drop
   Than to trust my luck to a lollypop,
   'Cause I always drop my lollypop and it gets all over icky.

3. When you come to the end of a lollypop,
   And you sit alone with a stick.
   When you come to the end of a lollypop
   And you have just one more lick.
   When you come to the end of a lollypop --- you stop!

I Wish I Were a Little ---:
Open Ended Songs

Improvisation became a valued skill in mid-twentieth century arts. Action painters like Jackson Pollock, beat poets like Allen Ginsburg, and, most of all, jazz emerged. Its familiar spirit hovered over popular music. Minstrel shows regularly had introduced new elements into their programs to lure audiences from their rivals. When Victor began recording Southern musicians in the 1920s, it captured the work of dance-band leaders and bluesmen who took known verses of songs, recombined them, and added new ones.

The "Crawdad Song" or "Honey Babe" (5), the Civil War soldiers' "Goober Peas" (5), and the Southern dance song, "Cindy" (9), are all open-ended lyrics shared by camp and American folk traditions.

You Can't Get to Heaven

"You Can't Get to Heaven" (34) moves from the known to the improvised. Many customary rhymes describe means of transportation like roller skates, rocking chairs, skis, and airplanes. A number mention automobiles. Impromptu verses, which often describe people, rarely are memorable. Robyn Arthur Kerr (Calif CFG) remembers singing, "You can't get to heaven on Susie's ear / Cause Susie's ear can't get too near." Viki Irene Cuqua (Ariz YWCA) recalls, "in Debbie's shoe, cause full of phew."

Other versions include "The Deacon Went Down" and "I Ain't Gonna Grieve my Lord." Dawn Hill says Vermont's Downer 4-H Camp treats the two as separate songs. The "Ain't Gonna Grieve" alternative has been common in Boy Scout tradition. At one time, Mendham, New Jersey, Scouts were singing "I Grieve My Lord."

Content

Several open-ended fun songs deal with place names, like states in "What Did Delaware" (16). Marvella Henry[S] was told, it was a favorite at a camp where "one table would sing a verse and another would answer." "In Chicago" (2) or the "Department Store," which may use city names, occasionally is banned, because its verses can be risqué. The tune for the first is "Our Boys Will Shine Tonight" (2).

In "Throw It out the Window" (15), campers sing familiar nursery rhymes, then replace the last lines with the chorus. "Jack and Jill went up the hill to fetch a pail of water" becomes:

> Jack fell down and broke his crown
> And threw it out the window
> The window, the second story window

At Tawingo (Ont coed), the song is a contest between boys and girls, according to Jack Pearse. Lisa Drumm[S] believed part of the appeal at Wyandot (Ohio CFG) was the juxtapositions "sometimes are a bit bawdy."

In "Did You Ever See a Horse Fly" (6), individuals or groups conjure new puns. Verses often are the same - a moth ball, a porch swing, a kitchen sink - but there always exists room for new ideas. Larry Ralston was dismayed when older boys in an Ohio 4-H camp he was directing began inventing ones like bottle neck.

Yetta Kamelhar[S] was told, they "went around and made up verses about the people at camp (counselors, cooks and etc)" to "Dinah Won't You Blow Your Horn" (3) at a New York camp. Loyaltown (NY J Boys) campers may make up additional verses to "Down at the Bingo Farm" (1). Names are altered in "Alice" (14) at Kotomi (Colo CFG), and in the "Quartermaster's Store" (11) at Ahwahnee (Calif BSA), according to James Hirsch.[S] Laurel Ann Hall says names and actions are substituted in "Little Tommy Tinker" (45) at Ak-O-Mak (Ont girls).

Calypso

Complete improvisation, instead of a fused recombination and invention, entered the Eastern camp repertoire with Harry Belafonte's calypso recordings in 1956. The genre originated in Trinidad as a contest between singers who extemporized rhymed verses on set topics, usually political or topical in nature. In the twentieth century, colonial subjects used it to make veiled comments on political affairs.

University Settlement House camp (NY agency coed) has a local, now stabilized, "Camp Calypso" sung to Belafonte's "Man Smart (Woman Smarter)." One verse dealing with age groups includes:

> The counselors are smarter in every way
> But I say, if you listen to me
> The campers are smarter at U. S. C.

A verse about units is:

> The Eagles are handsome, they try mighty hard,
> Go messin' with the Swans over in Renard,
> The Swans say the Eagles are not so neat,
> They go to a dance with two left feet

"Tangaleo" (5), the other frozen calypso song in camp tradition, is from Jamaica.

Formulaic Composition

Formulaic composition is the technique used to create new verses for improvised and open-ended songs. The first verse sets the rhyme scheme and rhythm, suggests a limited range of topics, and provides a model for developing an idea. Additional stanzas are created by applying the pattern. With "Hey Liddie" (10), the first line is, "there was a kid named ___." Its second line must end with a word that rhymes with the name and makes some comment on the person.

Ruth Crawford Seeger suggested, "the rhythmic vitality of the music lends ease to the process of improvisation. It gives a basis, a solid structure on which to build."[504:23] With "Hey Liddie Liddie," once the rhyme is selected, the rhythm suggests words that can be used to fill the line.

Woody Guthrie taped a version of "Hey Lolly" in 1944, which was not released until 1952. The Weavers performed "Hey Lilee" in the 1950s. It did not become widely known until the Limeliters recorded "Hey Li Lee" in 1961 at the Ash Grove in Los Angeles.

The original verses were readapted conventional ones. Substituting names came later, as did the distaste for fluid, open syllables noted in ESKIMO HUNT. Tim Bahr (Mo agency coed) knows "ludy ludy." Mikie Snell (Tex CFG) learned "hey lottie." Mariana Palmer (Penna YMCA girls) sings "hey laddy laddy."

New Verses

Seeger suggested, "the creative process involved in improvising on the patterns of such a song may not be far removed from that involved in making songs on their own."[5(4:22)] The apprentice phase may be adding verses to existing, fixed-length songs. Wampatuck (Mass P girls) has a second verse to "Gack Goon" (21) about a little green snake who goes "ssst." June Rushing Leibfarth[§] collected that verse, and another about a little white duck who goes "quack, quack" from Robinwood (Tex GS) in 1969.

Anne Beardsley (Mich GS) has a second verse to "Gray Squirrel" (14) "shake your bushy tail," which asks a turtle to "wiggle your head." Angela Lapham (Mich GS) sings brown squirrel. At Ka-esta (Ore CFG), a second verse to "Baby Bumble Bee" (19) describes bringing home a baby rattlesnake. Kotomi (Colo CFG) has verses about bringing home a baby dinosaur and a six-foot sailor boy.

"Oh, in the Moonlight" (12), apparently, began as a one-verse song about the beesies and bearsies. That is how Phyllis Southman[§] collected it in Michigan in 1948. Seth Clay (Mich P coed) knew that version in 1955. A second verse was added with sipsies and sapsies. More recently, Wolahi (Calif CFG) and Wakoma (Wash CFG) have a verse about campers. Wakoma also has one with girlsies. In the summer of 1974, Kitanniwa added a stanza about fishies who did dishies.

Wakoma (Wash CFG) has a third verse to "Skinnamarink" (28), which moves through "love you on the hillside," "on the level," "in my arms," and "like a devil." At Glen (Ohio CFG), the girls have a second verse for the round "To Ope Their Trunks" (15). It substitutes "brown" for "leaves of green" and "sap runs down" for "leaves them out." At Kotomi (Colo CFG), new verses have been written to "I know a wienie man" (13) about a popcorn man with his corny wife, and a peanut man with his nutty wife.

Long Beach, California, Camp Fire Girls have a second verse to "If All of the Raindrops" (23) about snowflakes and milk shakes. Hitaga (Iowa CFG) has one about snowflakes and chocolate cakes, and another about icicles and pop cycles. Kalamazoo Girl Reserves (Mich YWCA) included the original verse in their 1938 song book. More recently, it was published by Winn,[552] and recorded by Pete Seeger and Erik Darling (FC 7028).

Some songs are perceived more widely as open to additional verses than others. Both Kushtaka (Alaska CFG) and Janice Knapp (Mich CFG) have a second verse, "Do your ears hang high," to "Do Your Ears Hang Low" (61). Becky Colwell Deatherage (NY GS) sings "stand high." Seattle Scouts (Wash BSA) add a third verse, "Do your ears hang wide."

"Do your ears flip flop" is a second verse at Niwana (Wash CFG). "Yes, my ears hang low" is known at Kiloqua (Ohio CFG), Wampatuck (Mass P girls), and Teamsters' Health Camp (Mo agency coed). The Missouri camp, sponsored by Local 688, adds "I'm a Hayseed" (18) as a third verse.

Donkey Riding

Formulaic composition has been incorporated into "Donkey Riding" (35). Thomas Wood* reported the work song was used by men stowing deck cargo for the run from "Liverpool and Glasson Dock to Canada for timber" on "Lancashire ships and schooners." The original melody was the Scots "Highland Laddie." It has become so altered in tradition, Fowke now considers it a separate tune.[333]

As a capstan chantey, it was improvised. Most camps know the three verses Wood published in 1928. They were about Québec, off the horn, and Cardiff Bay. Seeger would describe it as, the kind of song that is "not finished, in the sense that a piece of fine-art ('classical') music, or even popular music, is finished. They are ready to grow."[504:23] Its inherent form has resurrected itself as new verses have been added to the Wood version.

One of the better known is:

> Were you ever in Widjiwagan Camp
> Where it's always nice and damp
> Up and down the hills we tramp
> Riding on a donkey.

At least five other people have mentioned the verse, beside the Hawaiian Camp Fire Girls. Julie Sherwood[S] collected a variant with stanzas about New York and Egypt from Molly Luman (Ohio GS). Sally Asher[S] heard a verse from Wilani (Ore CFG) about being in Tacoma. Jack Pearse (Ont coed) sings lines about Toronto, Montréal, and Ottawa in Ontario. Leah Jean Ramsey (Tex CFG) knows one about Bombay. Wilma Lawrence (Penna GS) has rhymes about the John and in the pool.

Work Songs

In folk tradition, songs like "Donkey Riding," which accompany labor, expand and contract to fit time available. In this country, once people migrated beyond the Appalachians in the late 1700s, wagon trains carried goods from Eastern suppliers in Lancaster, Pennsylvania, to the Ohio river port at Pittsburgh. Their pace was slow, perhaps fifteen miles a day. Howard Frey[*] noted, the men handling the teams of horses, mules, or oxen often sang to pass time while they were walking. He added, "They had a marked preference for the interminably long English ballads like 'Barbara Allen' (1) and 'Darby Ram'."

Since many driving Conestoga wagons had German ancestors, they also drew upon Deutsch traditions. One of the most common was "Liewer Heindrich," or "Dear Henry."[336] Camps know it as "There's a Hole in My Bucket" (13). According to Brendle[*] and Troxell, settlers imported the dialogue ballad in the 1700s. Then, it could feature two men or the more common bickering man and woman.

Ludwig Erk[*] and Franz Magnus Böhme included "Heinrich und Liese" in their authoritative collection of traditional music, *Deutscher Liederhort*. It since has been collected from nearly every German-speaking area from Bavaria to Pomerania and up into Estonia.[269]

In Scotland, women sang as they passed sections of fabric down the line to beat or mat fibers to fill interstices where threads crossed one another. Their waulking songs varied in tempo, often with repeated choruses of vocables like "tra la la."

The only tune from that tradition known in camps is "Road to the Isles." Carol Peterson used it for "Border Trail" (27). Marjorie Kennedy-Fraser published the melody in 1917 in *Songs of the Hebrides*. It has been so altered by passage through arrangements by classically trained musicians, including Patuffa Kennedy-Fraser and Kenneth Macleod, it bears little resemblance to the original. Patuffa was her daughter.

Although most occupational songs known in camps are treated as finite, three-verse texts, when analogous conditions arise, open-ended and very long songs may revert to their original purpose. Lisa Drumm[S] was told at Wyandot (Ohio CFG), "New River Train" (9) was used for hiking. Campers treated it like "a contest to see who can remember all of the words" and made up new verses.

At Butler (Ohio BSA), Richard Fazenbaker[S] was told "Green Grow the Rushes" (45) was not particularly "popular with campers, perhaps because of the length." But, because the staff liked it, the mix of Biblical and astronomical allusions was "sung on long hikes with small groups of people." Marsha Lynn Barker (Ill GS) also has said, it had been used as a hiking song. Carol Simon[S] was told, it was "sung after some strenuous activity like swimming or hiking" in an Ohio Girl Scout camp.

Commercial Songs

The accordion nature of the camp music aesthetic, which allows some songs to expand, means others shrink when necessary. In 1929, the Brooklyn Boy Scouts (NY BSA) song book contained a number of long songs, including "Bohunkus" (3), "I Had a Little Chicken Who Wouldn't Lay an Egg" (12), "The Tough Luck Song" (2), and "The Flea and the Junebug" (1). All but the last have been sung in other camps in shorter versions.

Most vaudeville songs underwent this editing process. In some cases, the form lingers, so once a camp version is established, new verses may be added. "Mountain Dew" (17) is in such an expansion phase. It stemmed from Irish tradition, and was introduced on

Broadway in the late 1870s by Edward Harrigan. *Pat Reilley's McGrogan the Cop Songster* disseminated his version.

Bascom Lamar Lunsford set the current, shortened form. The North Carolina-born lawyer and traditional performer worked with many who abetted the Folk Revival. Grandpa Jones recorded a version in 1947. *Sing Out!* published another in December, 1963.

New verses still are being added. Patricia McGreer (Wash CFG) knows one about "my Aunt Honey was a Playboy bunny." Watervliet (Mich girls) has a local verse about the nurse and the camp directors, which Carolyn Endsley remembers as:

> Velda came by with a tear in her eye
> Said that poor Henry had the flu
> Called in Lucille and she gave him a pill
> It was nothing but good old mountain dew

Contemporary camp versions of "Grandfather's Whiskers" (8) still are being abbreviated to three or four verses. Manhattan's Scout troop 582 (NY BSA) knew ten in 1950. Most camps today sing "Father's Whiskers," but Muskegon, Michigan's public schools' camp (Mich agency coed) uses "Grandpa's." The Brooklyn Scouts (NY BSA) song book for 1929 indicated their tune was "Hambone."

Traveling Verses

Many open-ended songs absorb material from familiar rhymes. Shirley Ieraci learned a version of "I'm a Little Acorn Brown" (18) from her grandfather. It included verses about a little piece of tin, I'm a TNT who wears ruffles on her pants, I'm a coconut (rather than acorn), and grandpa's beard. The last is the shredded wheat chorus from "Grandfather's Whiskers" (10). The first verse now is a separate song with an onomatopoeic chorus. At Tanadoona (Minn CFG), "Old Hunk of Tin" (29) is sung with a second verse beginning, "Got seat belts and a locking door." Fowke collected "I'm a Nut" from Nancy Takerer. She learned it in Saskatchewan in the 1950s.[332]

"On the Dummy Line" (10) has been sung at Loyaltown (NY J boys) with a verse about "Dirty Bill" who "lived on a garbage hill." That was collected as a rhyme by the Opies in England.[451] Saint

Vincent de Paul Ranch (Calif C boys) sings a "Hi Ho Silver" verse, which Emrich published separately.[319]

Brooklyn Scout camps (NY BSA) sang a verse about Doctor Beck hanging in the well as part of "My Vacation" (3). In 1940, Phyllis Southman[§] collected "Doctor Beck" from a Wisconsin camp in "Dummy Line." It also had verses about a gal in Mobile with a face like a lemon peel, and "Little Willie." He fell into an elevator shaft where his body was not found until "he was a spoiled child." Dummy lines were urban spurs whose small, steam engines were muffled to avoid startling horses.

Boom Boom

The most variable open-ended song currently in tradition is "Boom boom, ain't it great to be crazy" (33). Christopher (Ohio C coed) uses a "sugar and spice and everything nice" verse that most likely was formalized by poet Robert Southey.[*] Kotomi (Colo CFG) uses the "Pepsi Cola went to town" verse collected by the Knapps.[*] Joanmarie Schulz[§] heard the rhyme in Howell, New Jersey.

The Opies published the verse about a fight between two blind or dead boys as a separate item.[451] Fowke heard the stanza about the horse and flea shooting dice from Toronto third graders in 1962.[332] Manhattan's Troop 582 (NY BSA) had the dice players "sitting on a tombstone." Barnyard, curbstone, and corner also have been sung.

An elephant quatrain, which begins "Away down south where bananas grow" at Melacoma (Wash CFG), is sung cotton by Carolyn Endsley at Watervliet (Mich girls). Anna Mayberg learned palm trees at Wolochee (Wash CFG). It often is paired with a verse beginning "Way up north" about a penguin named Joe who wears pink socks or underwear. The two stanzas sometimes are sung with another, beginning "Away out west where the cactus grow." Fowke collected "South" from Toronto third graders in 1962.[332]

Troop 582's (NY BSA) version of "Boom, Boom" included variants of Dirty Bill, Doctor Beck, Farmer Jones who went bare, and a peanut sat on a railroad track. The first three are associated with "Dummy Line" (10). The last is from "It Ain't Gonna Rain No More" (4). Elizabeth Schuurmans[§] collected a version in 1943 from Lake Louise (Mich P coed) with "Little Willie" and "Doctor Peck" from "Dummy Line." Other camps sing verses about a lost combination to combination underwear, Eli who sells socks, and a woman from Mobile who slips on a lemon peel.

Church Camps

Open-ended and loosely structured songs seem to be particularly emblematic of camps that cater to first-time campers. They are learned quickly and often rely on familiar tunes. When improvisation does occur, children from the same church youth group, elementary school class, or Boy Scout troop can exploit esoteric knowledge to create rhymes for songs like "You Can't Get to Heaven" (34).

Historically, many church and 4-H camps used borrowed locations. They were run by ministers and extension agents with other responsibilities and skills. When the General Board of Education for the Southern Methodist Church in Nashville, Tennessee, published Harbin's *Paradology*[*] in 1927, it wished to provide a useful tool. More than 40% of its songs have been included in other camp songs books I have seen.

Short ones, like "John Jacob Guggenheimer Smith" (62), "Mother Leary's Cow" (31) and "Our Boarding House" (10), have been the most widely sung. Some rounds have been shared widely, including "Little Tommy Tinker" (45), "Sweetly Sings the Donkey" (30), and "Scotland's Burning" (13). Among his more accepted longer songs have been the ballad "My New Silk Hat" (39), the open-ended "We Are Table Number One" (7), and the collections of traveling verses found in "The Billboard" (17) and "Oyster Stew Song" (12).

Lake Louise (Mich P coed) was the most important United Methodist camp in southern Michigan. In 1943, Elizabeth Schuurmans[S] was told former campers there remembered "Cannibal King" (32) and traveling verses of "Boom Boom" (33). The next year, Alice Rhodes[S] was told they were singing "Do Your Ears Hang Low" (61) and "Nicky Nicky Nu" (23).

Aleta Huggett[S] knew people in 1949 who remembered the loosely constructed "New River Train" (9), "Ten in a Bed" (12) and the "Elephant Song" (17). They also told her about "John Jacob" (62) and "Pioneer" (9).

More recently, religious groups have provided central staffs to support ministers and offer better experiences for campers. Their focus remains inculcating values. In 1976, Trexler, a New York

Lutheran camp for boys, was singing contemporary religious songs, like "Jesus Is a Soul Man" (1) and "A Thing Called Love" (1). Its fun songs included "Rise and Shine" (67), along with the loosely formatted "There's a Hole in My Bucket" (33) and "Fish and Chips" (40). Jerry Reed wrote "Love" in 1968. Lawrence Reynolds composed "Soul Man" the next year.

Jewish Camps

Many Jewish camps followed a similar pattern of leavening religious material with fun songs. Surprise Lake Camp for boys in New York published a song book in 1938. It included the ceremonial "Call of the Fire" (49), the fun "Mistress Shady" (5), the commercial "Man on the Flying Trapeze" (4), and the camp-specific "Blue and White" (1).

A Jewish songster at the back contained Yiddish folk songs like "Geht a Goy" (get a guy), "Oif'N Pripitchik" (on the oven), and "Az der Rebbe Elimelech" (2, the Rabbi Elimelech). Its editor, Mordecai Kessler, worked for the Young Men's and Young Women's Hebrew Association in New York and, later, in Montréal.

His collection resembled Israel and Margaret K. Soifer's *The Camper's Song Pack*[*] of 1937. Their first part included "Abdul, the Bulbul Ameer" (10), "Billy Boy" (11), "McNamara's Band" (6), and "Ching-a-ling," better known as "The Chinaman" (4). "Water Boy" (4) had been promoted as a Southern convict song by Black concert tenor, Roland Hayes, in 1922.

Their second half, "Songs of Jewish Interest," was in Hebrew script, transliterated Hebrew, and English. It included "Rad Hay-yom," more commonly spelled "Rad Hayom" and translated "Day Is Done." "Dunday" (1) more commonly is spelled "Dundai." "Shabbat Hamalkah" (2) also is known as "The Sabbath Queen."

Israel was established in 1948. Revelations of Axis atrocities began seeping into our collective consciousness with the publication of Anne Frank's diary in English in 1952. Jewish cultural camps became more dedicated to preserving their heritage. At the Chicago Habonim camp located in Michigan, Hasea Swartzman Diner saved song sheets printed in Hebrew script with Hebrew transliterations. As the program developed during the summer, more ephemeral sheets were issued that, again primarily in Hebrew, included songs written during the summer, yells, and jokes.

Since those years, more details emerged about what became known in the 1960s as the Holocaust. Alain Resnais' documentary, *Nuit et Brouillard*, was shown in this country as *Night and Fog*. Maximilian Schell won an Oscar in 1961 for his role in *Judgment at Nuremberg*. After this was written, NBC broadcast a four-part series dramatizing the *Holocaust* in 1978.

The song book used in Oregon's B'nai Brith summer camp in 1976 is in Hebrew and Yiddish, with some English. Its contents vary from religious prayers, like "Avinu Malkeinu" recited between Rosh Hashanah and Yom Kippur, to love songs, like "Erev Shel Shoshanim" (evening of lilies or roses). It mixes old songs with some from the 1967 war ("Sharm el-Sheikh" by Ron Eliran) and the Zionist "Hatikvah" (6). It also contains dances ("Lech Lamidbar"), Yiddish rounds ("Lo Yiso Goy el Goy Cherev"), and songs with handclap rhythms ("Hafinjan"). When Susan Marcia Stearman (Md J coed) looked through the book, she noted the yells and district songs common in Maryland's B'nai Brith get togethers were missing.

What campers remember from self-identified Jewish camps as camp songs are not the specifically Jewish ones, but the fun songs, perhaps because the first exist outside. Sally Briggs[5] talked to a young woman who had gone to a New Jersey YM-YWHA camp, Cedar Lake. Her collection included camp mocking versions of "One Boy" (1) from *Bye Bye Birdie* (1960), and "Food, Glorious Food" (3) from *Oliver!* (1963); camp-specific songs like "E-S-T-H-E-R-S" and "CLC," and rowdy fun songs like "Underwear, Underwear" (1). She was told about one religious song, "Shabbat Shalom" (2), used during Friday night Sabbath services. Another drew on Jewish secular music idioms, "La Da Ti Da."

Roman Catholic Camps

Roman Catholic camps differ from those of Protestants who hope to indoctrinate, and from those of Jews who wish to perpetuate cultural values. Songs remembered from Catholic Youth Organization camps suggest their organizers want to build strong identifications with colleges run by religious orders.

Smith[5] collected CYO Michigan girls' camp songs in 1969, including "M-E-R-C-Y" from Mercy College of Detroit. Two were University of Detroit derived songs, "U. D. We Never Wanna, Wanna Leave You" and "D-E-T-R-O-I-T." Notre Dame's "Victory March" was the base for "Cheer, Cheer for Old CYO."

Debra Janison marked the songs in the Christopher (Ohio C coed) song book most popular with Akron, Ohio, CYO campers in 1976. These included "Boom Boom" (33) and the "Titanic" (32), as well as the slower "Have Fun Our Motto Is" (25) and the round "Make New Friends" (68). Favored lyrics with religious themes included "Rocka My Soul" (31) and "Dem Bones" (37). "All night, all day, angels watching over me" (33) and "Three Little Angels" (17) also held a special attraction. She said they had a chant they did "over and over and over":

> I was CYO born, and CYO bred
> And when I die, I'll be CYO dead!!
> Rah! rah! for our Camp,
> Rah! rah! for our Camp,
> Rah! rah! for our Christopher.

Boy Scout Camps

In the early years, Boy Scout councils published song books for use in camps and troop meetings. William Hillcourt saved ones produced in the 1920s by Treasure Island (Penna BSA), Irondale (Mo BSA), and Brooklyn Scouts (NY BSA). Among the songs included in all three were the comic ballads "Abdul the Bulbul Ameer" (10), "Belinda" (3), and "Bohunkus" (3). "Polly Wolly Doodle" (11) and "Wuzzy Wuzzy" (4) were collections of traveling verses, "Poor Ned" (3) of limericks, and "Kille Kille" (17) a string on nonsense syllables. "Last Baked Bean" (3) was sung to "Lena."

All included the organizational "Onward Boy Scouts" (5) and "Tramp Tramp Tramp the Scouts Are Marching" (3). They also published "Capital Ship" (9), "Sailing, Sailing" (3), and the "Sea Scout Chantey" (6). These reflected an interest in rowing and sailing.

Hillcourt (1900-1992) was born Vilhelm Hans Bjerregaard Jensen in Denmark. He taught Indian dance at the BSA camp at Bear Mountain, New York, in 1926, then wrote a manual for patrol leaders.[*]

For many years, he contributed articles to *Boy's Life* on camp craft using the name Green Bar Bill. His primary camp was near Mendham, New Jersey.

After World War II, Norman Hanner[§] collected songs like "John Jacob" (62) and "Patsy Orry Aye" (29) from a former No-be-bo-sco (NJ BSA) camper in 1946. In Michigan, Dean Wakefield[§] was told "Johnny Verbeck" (26) was being sung at Kiwanis (Mich BSA) in 1944. In 1950, Jean MacCready[§] heard "Aunt Rhody" (6), "Pick a Bale of Cotton" (17), and "Dis Ol' Hammer" (4) from someone who had attended Teetonkah (Mich BSA).

In the middle 1950s, Carol Domoney[§] collected the open-ended "New River Train" (9) and "On the Dummy Line" (10) from someone who had been to Rotary (Mich BSA). Her friend remembered the older "Damper Song" (16), "Kille Kille" (17), "My Vacation" (3), and the never-ending "Here we sit like birds in the wilderness" (14). Carol also heard the military-influenced "Quartermaster's Store" (11) and "Today Is Monday" (15).

Some twenty years later, Christine Sydoriak[§] collected lyrics in 1973 from a former Utica Lake (Calif BSA) camper who knew "Mountain Dew" (17) and songs from the Folk Revival. He preferred those with male principals, like "Tom Dooley" (12), or ones that dealt with the sea, like "Wreck of the Sloop John B." (12). David McFarlane[§] recorded more traditional songs from Wolfeboro (Calif BSA) in 1974. These included "Alice" (14), "Patsy Orry Aye" (29), "Sam, Sam the Lavatory Man" (1), "Ship Titanic" (32), and "Mountain Dew" (17).

James Hirsch[§] compiled a large collection from someone who had attended Ahwahnee (Calif BSA), Osceola (Calif YMCA), and Meriwether (Ore BSA). The ones he could confirm came only from Boy Scout camps were the loosely-organized "Catalina Madelina" (14), "Dem Bones" (37), "Quartermaster's Store" (11), and "Sippin Cider" (35). Among the religious songs was "It's me oh Lord, standing in the need of prayer" (9). Organizational verses included "Pink Pajamas" (20), sung as the "Region 12 Song," and "When the hand goes up the mouth goes shut" (1). He wrote his paper in 1973.

When I mailed my survey in 1976, I discovered little overlap between songs I listed and ones known in BSA camps. The ones young men in other types of camps remember from their days in Scouting were "Mountain Dew" (17) and "You Can't Get to Heaven" (34). "Dew" was checked by Tim Bahr (Mo BSA), Steve Bensinger

(BSA), Terry Wilbur Bolton (Wash BSA), and Gene Clough (Calif BSA). "Heaven" was known by Tim, Terry, Gene, and Tom Greiff (Calif BSA). In addition, Tom noted he had sung "Ship Titanic" (32) and "Birds in the Wilderness" (14) at Whitsett (Calif BSA).

Boy Scouts, like the Camp Fire Girls and Girl Scouts, have their share of organizational songs that either are learned dutifully or ignored. Gene Clough (Calif BSA) says, when he first enrolled, he learned the words to "Be Prepared" (2), because he was young and enthusiastic. He discovered, "it was never a song we sang with my troop or in camp or anywhere." In Ohio, Richard Fazenbaker[S] was told about a parody with verses like:

> Be prepared to hide your pack of cigarettes
> Don't make book if you can't cover bets
> And keep that pot well hidden
> Where you're sure it won't be found.
>
> And be careful not to turn on
> When the scoutmaster's around
> For he only will insist that it be shared
> Be prepared

Gene (Calif BSA) did say, "Trail the Eagle" (13) "was very popular with my old troop." In Ohio, Sally Briggs,[S] Charla Calderhead,[S] and Richard Fazenbaker[S] all said the region song (6) was chanted with "much vigor":

> Oh, we're the Scouts of Region Four
> You hear so much about
> The people stop and stare at us
> Whenever we go out

Richard added, the guys sometimes would substitute "swear" for "stare." Its tune is usually "My Name is Solomon Levi" (2). "Thunder, Thunderation" (3) has been used elsewhere.

Family Traditions

My questionnaire asked people if they could separate songs they currently were singing, from those they had known in the past. A number went further, and indicated when they first heard every song. A few remembered ones they had learned from their kin. Some students, who have submitted collections of camp songs to their universities' folklore archives, also noted some had passed through families.

These included ones parents typically teach young children, like "The Lady and the Crocodile" (51). Elizabeth Gottlin[S] collected it from a young woman, who had learned it from her mother. She heard it sometime around 1931 in the Bronx section of New York City. Heather MacPhail[S] talked to someone who had learned it from an aunt in Coeur d'Alene, Idaho, in 1941. Fowke collected the gesture song from Isabel Ricker Smaller, who had heard it in North Bay, Ontario, in 1924.[331]

Nan Carol Brandenberger learned "Wadaleache" (34) from her mother, who had gone to a girls' camp in Montana. Karin Lindquist[S] talked to someone who learned "Oyster Stew" (12) from her mother. She had learned it in Ann Arbor, Michigan. Phyllis Whitcomb learned "Birds in the Wilderness" (14) from her grandfather. Betsy Wolverton said her family had sung "Boom Boom" (33). Except for the first, these can all be open-ended songs or pastiches of traveling verses.

Several mentioned learning "Johnny Verbeck" (26). Cynthia Scheer[S] collected it from a woman, who had learned it from her mother, who learned it in camp. Heather MacPhail[S] collected a version from a woman, who had heard it from her father as "Doonagobeck."

Fuld[*] said, "Dunderbeck" was credited to Edward Harrington in the 1876 *Our Own Boys Songster*. This is the same Harrigan who introduced "Mountain Dew" (17), and the same man who was the model for the George M. Cohan song. He and his partner, Tony Hart, created musical revues in the 1870s that replaced blackface with recurring characters.

Two people mentioned learning "There's a Hole in My Bucket" (13) from their families. Mary Wescott Walker heard it from her mother, who learned it in a Minnesota girls' camp. Patricia McGreer sang it with her family in the Pacific Northwest. Others learned it in school, including 14-year-old Stephen Daniel Foulk and Marsha Lynn Barker.

Kitanniwa Repertoire

Meals, with people sitting in small groups that facilitate conversation (square dining tables or picnic tables), are the most common time for open-ended songs. At the Calhoun County 4-H Camp (Mich 4-H) in the early 1960s, six people at a table would huddle together to choose a verse to "Did You Ever See a Porch Swing" (6) and "This is Table Number One" (7). Kitanniwa's tables, which could seat five on a side, were too long for conferences. Conversation at a table was among smaller groups of friends who sat together. Collaborative, spontaneous, group songs were not possible.

If people at Kitanniwa knew open-ended or loosely structured songs, they probably learned them in church camps. However, not many were sung. People who had gone to church camps had no reason to sing them in the girls' camp, where the environment was less congenial. Besides, many grew as protective of those song traditions as they did the Kitanniwa one. Girls instinctively knew the dangers of mixing the two.

The sense of separation between two repertoires is not unique to Kitanniwa. Robin Kelley says the Lutheran church camp she attended in California for years was "much rowdier" than the Camp Fire camp where she was working in 1976. Eleanor Crow says she sang "Boom Boom" (33) at Warren, a Michigan Congregational camp, but it was "too corny" for Aloha Hive (Vt girls).

Marsha Lynn Barker (GS) has noted "There's a Hole in My Bucket" (13) is not "camp caliber" and "You Can't Get to Heaven" (34) is "a bus song." Terry Wilbur Bolton, who spent time in Boy Scout camps, suggested, "a number of songs I [have] known and are listed here I feel are sacrilegious and therefore I don't attempt to sing or teach them." He was working in Oregon at Big Lake Youth Camp sponsored by Seventh Day Adventists.

Repertoire wall permeability at Kitanniwa varied by song type. Pretty songs known in town, like "Home on the Range" (27), could be sung when a desire to continue singing temporarily lowered barriers. General fun songs only could be introduced in skits. By definition, comic dramatizations freed participants from direct association with content through a willing suspension of disbelief and other conventions of theater.

The two songs I learned at Kitanniwa from skits were "There's a Hole in My Bucket" (13) and "I Like Mountain Music" (3). The first was performed by another group. My cabin used the second in a burlesque of a local television show, Harry Smythe's *Buck Lake Ranch Jamboree*.

Repertoire Violation

When my peer group moved to the senior unit, we had the ideal venue for open-ended songs. The long walk to and from main camp was a journey through a transition land that was neither camp nor home base. No fun songs or pretty ones had the right tempo.

Unfortunately, we lacked any repertoire. One girl had been sent, every summer, to all seven sessions at this camp for as long as anyone could remember. Many others, including the girl with the good voice, were from a Camp Fire group that drew its members from a Roman Catholic school. This was the only camp they attended.

Since the girls who were recognized as leaders for activities or songs had no recreation camp experiences, we were left with what they knew from home. Many were songs from military tradition learned from fathers or brothers: "Catalina Matalina" (14), "My Gal's a Corker" (17), "I've Got Sixpence" (37), and "Left My Wife at Home in the Kitchen" (1).

Military Traditions

Kitanniwa was not a strongly patriotic camp, nor did it use many military regimens. We did not do morning calisthenics or other forms of vigorous exercise. Terms like inspection and K. P. were glosses for necessary household functions, like keeping the cabin and wash house clean, setting and clearing tables, bringing food and helping wash dishes. These terms were more egalitarian than those used by restaurants, like waiter and busboy.

Our most obvious military tradition was the use of a bugle to announce times of day. The camp owned an instrument. Every year, the director found some counselor who could play Reveille, calls for meals, Taps, and whatever was used for changes in activity. They served the same function as bells in school. Loud noisemakers like gongs have been used in other camps. Girls sometimes did sing "KP, KP come to the kitchen door" and "come and get it" to the lunch calls while they stood in line.

Like most camps, we sang Rukard Hurd's "Day is done" words to "Taps" (73). Daniel Butterfield, who commanded the Army of the Potomac in 1862, is credited with the original call. Hurd graduated from Chester's Pennsylvania Military College in 1878. The mining engineer was raised in Cincinnati, Ohio.

Lori Judith Weiss has sung "Taps" in Hebrew at Sabra (Mo J coed). Carol Shuster[§] collected gestures from Ohio Girl Scouts who raised their arms for the words "lakes," "hills" and "skies" before bringing them down into a friendship circle and humming it through one last time.

The only military song we commonly sang, "Old King Cole" (14), was so different, it would be considered a different version. The World War I words collected in Europe by Nettleingham[*] were a cumulative song that had the king calling for different ranks of men, instead of his "fiddlers three." It caricatured their responses in place of "fiddle, fiddle, fiddle went the fiddlers." Oscar Brand[*] said, it remained in troop repertoires in the second world war.

Our song began as a formulaic imitation of the first verse, substituting trombones and banjos. Then, like "An Austrian" (34), a different theme was added, in this case, a burlesque of ministers. Enjoyment came from anticipating the juxtaposition of elements in the final verse:

> Amen said the preachers
> (Hands in prayer position, sing slowly)
> Slap against the house went the painters
> (Slap hands loudly like cymbals, sing fast)
> In and out the shoe went the cobbler
> (Undulate hand like a snake)
> Plink, plink, plink went the banjos
> (Imitate playing a banjo)
> Oom-pah, oom-pah, oom-pah went the trombones
> (Imitate playing a trombone)
> Fiddle, fiddle, fiddle went the fiddlers
> (Imitate playing a fiddle)
> Happy men are we

Chappell* uncovered the nursery rhyme in the sixth volume of *Useful Transactions in Philosophy*, issued in 1709 by William King. That satire of current scientific publications was made by a man who had been secretary to Queen Anne, before she ascended the throne in 1702. King* was friends with John Gay, who used the verses we know in his ballad opera, *Achilles*.[364]

Covent Garden mounted the play in 1733 during the reign of the sometimes-absent George II. He still was a prince-elector to the Holy Roman Empire as duke of Braunschweig und Lüneburg. Political allusions to a king in the North or West of England between the time the Romans left and the Roman Catholic church established its power no longer are clear. References to ceòl as the Gaelic word for music are more obvious.[419] Gay was mentioned in ASH GROVE.

Other camps, whose current songsters have the musical version, rather than the military one, are Christopher (Ohio C coed), Eberhart (Ind YMCA coed), and Warren (Mich P coed). Seth Clay edited the last. He no doubt is the source for the Kitanniwa and South Bend, Indiana, Y camp versions, although the second substitutes jesters for preachers in the last verse. In the 1930s, Augusta (Calif CFG) had painters followed by cobblers before the parsons. Watanopa (Mont CFG) knew that version in the late 1940s.

Of the four songs introduced into the senior unit, "Left my wife" had the most obvious military use. It was a circular rhyme chanted to stay in step:

> Right from the country where I come from
> Hay foot, straw foot, skip by jingo,
> Left, left
> Left my wife at home in the kitchen
> The old gray mare and the peanut stand
> Did I do right? Right!

The words right and left were not prescriptive. I was told at the time, hay and straw once had been put on men's boots to help them tell left from right. Mark Lieberman* found references to the pejorative explanation as far back as the American Revolution, but no sign it ever had been actual practice.

It is surprising that, with the emphasis on hiking in so many camps, only two mentioned a similar chant. Ku Keema (Okla CFG) knows "Camp Fire Brush" as:

Hippo-hoppo bring out the moppo
Lefto righto lefto righto
Sound off: One Two
Sound off: Three Four

Its verses are about boy friends in various cities. Kotomi (Colo CFG) makes up ones like those associated with "Hey Liddy" (10).

Sexist Songs

Verbal cadences still were known when we were in camp. Perhaps their association with basic training made them less likely to be remembered by veterans than the risqué songs they passed on to their children. Deliberate or not, the songs we learned were the ones most designed to undermine our self-confidence, the ones that focused on ugliness and husbands glad of excuses to leave.

Summers during the adolescent years in an all-girls' camp were a reprieve from demands a girl's most important function was to be attractive. For one or two weeks, we were away from boys, from the style setters in town, and family members who continually reinforced images of femininity. We were free to test other roles symbolized by the jeans Joyce Gregg Stoppenhagen mentioned in KOOKABURRA. Perhaps these songs assuaged some amorphous anxieties, by allowing us, temporarily, to reject the limited female roles of the time by embracing obviously male songs.

Fewer songs exist about unattractive men. Only "Lavender Cowboy" (2) has been mentioned. Harold Brainerd Hersey, a Montana-born, eastern-bred, pulp-fiction publisher, wrote the words in 1923.

Case Study: I Wish I Were a Little ---

Kitanniwa's 1974 experimental coed session was closer to a church camp, than a traditional Camp Fire one. The presence of so many first-time campers forced the song leaders to seek common ground, and use methods borrowed from those camps. At Thursday lunch, counselors, sitting at tables spread in the open, started two loosely structured, open-ended songs: "Boom Boom" (22) and "I Wish I Were a Little ---" (17).

I Wish I Wuz a Little Rock

"I Wish" is one of those subterranean songs that persist without public notice. An eight-line verse expressing the basic idea found in the camp song, if one were an object one could do forbidden things, began spreading through publications of the cooperative movement. In 1913, Charles Bassett[†] of the U. S. Department of Agriculture used it in a speech to the National Nut Growers Association. He was extolling the merits of a pecan marketing exchange.

The same year, the poem was reprinted by *Co-operation*,[†] a general publication for co-ops in the country. It seems to have stayed current within communities in Texas that grew pecans, like Abilene,[†] Georgetown,[†] and Stephensville.[†] In two of those places it appeared in college yearbooks.

The Hotel and Restaurant Employes International Alliance[†] of Cincinnati published "I Wish I Was a Little Rock" in a 1916 issue of *The Mixer and Server*. The verse soon was picked up by other union or employee publications. Disston Saw Works[†] of Philadelphia published it in 1917. A few years later, young women at Bryn Mawr,[†] in suburban Philadelphia, titled their yearbook essay on their geology-class field trip, "I Wish I Were a Little Rock." In 1921, it appeared in a local Goodrich Tire ad placed in the Findlay, Ohio, high school annual, *The Blue and Gold*.

John Church Company of Cincinnati issued sheet music in 1917 with a tune credited to John Barnes Wells[†] (version D). Versions probably spread through the lecture and Chautauqua circuits. In January of 1920, Clay Smith[†] told readers of *The Lyceum Magazine* that Oliver Ditson had issued "another setting" for "I Wish I Were a Rock" as "The Weary Wisher" by Arthur Custance.[†] He added:

> This always was a surefire pianologue and while it has been used quite extensively still it should be in the repertoire of all those doing talking songs.

Custance used "wisht" and "wouldn't sleep," rather than the drink of the earlier version. Prohibition began January 20 of that year. Earlier, in 1919, The *American Organist*[‡] had called the arrangement, "an excellent encore."

Wells[*] probably was typical of the sort of man who would have spread such a piece, one with a good voice available for hire in refined situations. He was born near Wilkes-Barre, Pennsylvania, in anthracite-coal country in 1880. While he attended Syracuse between 1897 and 1901, he pledged Psi Upsilon.

In 1909, the tenor began recording for Victor. After his eclipse by celebrities like Al Jolson, he turned to coaching others in Princeton, and singing with the University Glee Club of New York. In his later years, he spent his summers in the Catskill mountains in Roxbury, New York, where he died in 1935.

The poem may have been distilled from something earlier. An Eugene, Oregon, newspaper from 1899 had a longer verse, "Jealous Jake" (version E). The editor was James Franklin Amis (1828-1912) who migrated west from Clay County, Kentucky. The Mexican War veteran was a founding member of the Grange in Lane County in 1873. Patrons of Husbandry pioneered the agricultural marketing co-op movement.

I With I Were a Little Fifth

In the late 1920s, a second song began appearing with a form (AA_1BA_1) close to that of the current camp song. While it still imagined the singer as an object, envy was directed toward individuals with handicaps. Its first two verses (fish and ship) indulged lisping. The third (simpleton) explored limits of being mentally deficient. Possible links between the two were implied in *Paradology*. Harbin[†] suggested both could be sung to "Believe Me, If All Those Endearing Young Charms" (4). He subtitled "Rock" the "Hobo Anthem."

Hillcourt found Harbin's "Lisping Song" on a song sheet published by Duluth, Minnesota, Cub Scouts some time before he retired from the organization in 1965 (version C). The group followed another Harbin suggestion and used the tune for "Auld Lang Syne" (9).

I With I Were a Wittle Thuger Bun

Isabel Ricker Smaller learned "I With I Wath a Fith" in the 1920s in Owen Sound, Ontario. The version she gave Fowke in 1962 had the three Harbin verses, plus two that expressed a fantasy like the current song. One about a "thafety pin" (safety pin) was included in the version published in 1938 by the Intercollegiate Outing Club Association[†] as "I With I Were a Wittle Thugar Bun." The other about "thome thlime" (some slime) had the same wish as "wittle bog of mud," added by the IOCA in its 1948[†] edition. Adahi (Penna CFG) is the only camp with verses like "slippery root" and "striped skunk" introduced in the 1948 collection. No one now uses a lisp.

Ellis B. Jump (1909-1989) of Dartmouth organized the IOCA in 1932 as a way for Eastern college hiking and camping clubs to exchange ideas. The likely editors in 1938 were John Willcox Brown (1915-2005) of Dartmouth and Gerald Martin Richmond (1914-2001) of Brown. In 1948, Richard Lundelius Best (1923-1994) of Cornell and Beth Arlene Ingraham Best (1925-2010) of Radcliffe became editors. She was later Beth Upton.

Richmond, a geologist, remained active with the Boy Scouts. Jump taught dentistry at the University of Oregon, and worked as a Quaker camp counselor in the 1960s. The Friend was raised in a Congregational home.

Isabel Ricker[*] (1910-1988), apparently, discovered music when she was six years old in Owen Sound. Her father was a teacher who moved from job to job, until he became head of the North Bay Normal School. Judging from songs she taught Fowke, her next important musical experiences occurred when she was a young teenager, perhaps through the Canadian Girls in Training, perhaps through what had been the Methodist church before a 1925 merger. She studied piano in high school.

Her son says she graduated from the local normal school and became a teacher. Her husband, John Smaller, was active in the Mine Mill and Smelter Workers. For a while the family lived in Sudbury, Ontario, where the union had a farm and summer camp. Ricker Smaller stayed alert to changes in music education, especially those associated with Carl Orff. Eventually, she set up music programs using his methods around Toronto, and coached the most promising musicians. One remembers:

> For several years, Isabel would collect my friend [name]
> and I from our homes on Sunday afternoons and drive
> us out to what seemed like the middle of nowhere for a
> couple of hours of consort playing [. . .] I have fond
> memories of many rides in her off-white coloured VW
> Beetle, the back seat of which was strewn with stray
> plastic recorder pieces, recorder cases, method books,
> photocopies of fingering charts, cleaning swabs, cork
> grease containers, pencils [. . .]

Her photograph appears in "Tradition Bearers."

Textual Variation

Unlike earlier forms of the song, which had fixed formats and
little variation, "I Wish" is free form. Its line repetition formula,
AABA, is simple. In the A line, one substitutes the name of some
object. In the B line, one needs to find two rhymed words to describe
the verse subject. The first is the end of a verb phrase. The second
ends the direct object phrase.

Some expectation exists the verse will be a bit daring, naughty, or
mildly scatological. Of the 31 I have seen, only three are merely pesky,
like the "bowl of Cheerios" in version B. Many stanzas rely on one
of the types of humor discussed in KOOKABURRA: two describe
messy aspects of food (A-1, A-4), two are slightly sadistic (B-4, B-6),
one is anal (B-1), and four are mildly voyeuristic (A-2, A-3, B-2, B-3).
They all express a desire to break some social convention.

The greatest variation between camps occurs with the use of
the grammatically correct "were" versus the defiantly wrong "was."
I suspect most use the verb that is most familiar, with older campers
reflexively producing the subjunctive. Younger ones probably use
"was" without any awareness it is a violation of strict form.

A number of familiar verses exist - version B is a composite,
in order of popularity - that may be sung in one of three styles. In
some camps, like the formal after-lunch sing in the dining hall at the
Wyandot County 4-H Day Camp[†] (Ohio 4-H), the verse order was
set and treated as a defined song. At Kitanniwa,[†] in the dining tent,
the verses were called out by various individuals. Elsewhere, different
people simply start a new verse.

Following the third pattern, girls at the Wyandot County[†] camp sang the usual verses on a cookout, then individuals tried to create new ones. At Shawondasee (Tex CFG), Patricia Ann Raine[†] was told it was:

> occasionally expanded by additional impromptu verses by [campers] indicating a desire to be counselors so that they could stay up late and enjoy other privileges reserved for counselors. The counselors might respond with a verse hinting envy of the campers and their lack of responsibility.

Its most variable verse, the one about a bottle of pop (A4), has been sung keg, can, or bottle of beer. Larry Ralston collected a song sheet somewhere in Ohio with a parody of "Puffer Billies" (33) that included the same rhyming key words as the second line:

> See the little soda jerk
> Jerk the little sodas
> Slurp slurp burp burp
> Down they go

A desire for closure has led to the development of a verse with a catch ending (B-7), a sudden cessation of singing that takes singers and listeners by surprise.

Music

The tune for "I Wish" is "I Was Born about Ten Thousand Years Ago" (4). That song, in which the narrator claims to have witnessed every major event since Adam and Eve, was known widely when Sandburg[*] included it in *The American Songbag* in 1923. Woody Guthrie performed it as "The Great Historical Bum." Presley recorded it in 1970 for *Elvis Now*, released in 1972. The melody also has been used for "How Do You Do" (11) and "If You're Happy and You Know It" (50).

It is a sped-up mutation of "Wondrous Love." Walker first published the hymn in *Southern Harmony* in 1835, with a recommendation to use the tune for "Captain Kidd."

"Kidd" was part of a larger song cycle that included "Sam Hall," mentioned in KOOKABURRA as "Sammy." Chappell associated them with "A Christmas Carol," which began "Remember O Thou Man," published in Thomas Ravenscroft's *Melismata* of 1611.[282:373-374] Anne Geddes Gilchrist* believed the last was a sacred paraphrase of "My Love Is Lyin' Sick, Send Him Joy." The Scots song was reported in the *Complaynt of Scotland* mentioned in SKYBALL PAINT.

Girls at the Wyandot County day camp used a much simpler tune than that published by the IOCA. At Kitanniwa, it was even more flattened, almost an undulating chant, perhaps because loudness was desired.

Popularity

In 1976, "I Wish" was better known in the survey Midwest than elsewhere. Forty to 50% of the people who answered my questionnaire in the five-state region recognized the song. Only 25% knew it in boys' or coed camps elsewhere in the country.

Nationally, it was known by more than 50% of the women in all girls' camps, especially those run by Girl Scouts. However, less than 38% of the women in CFG camps knew it and only 26% of the women in coed camps. Whatever its origins, today the humor appeals to the most independent group of girls, the Scouts.

Parodies

The naughty undercurrent has led to private verses like puff of pot or a Girl Scout who visits the Boy Scout camp after Taps. These generally are known by older campers and staff members.

Of the underlying "Ten Thousand Years Ago" (4), Lucille Parker Munk remembers at Kitanniwa, "This we used to sing. I never cared much for that song, but yet we used to sing it when we felt a little naughty."

Version A

Text from Camp Kitanniwa (Mich CFG), after lunch sing led by Jan Smyth, 1974. Her photograph appears in "Kitanniwa, 1974." Her previous camps were church camps, Pilgrim Hills (Ohio P coed) and Temple Hills (Ohio P coed).

1. Oh, I wish I was a little piece of orange, piece of orange
   Oh, I wish I was a little piece of orange, piece of orange
   I'd go squirty, squirty, squirty over everybody's shirty
   Oh, I wish I was a little piece of orange, piece of orange

2. Oh, I wish I was a little bar of soap, bar of soap
   Oh, I wish I was a little bar of soap, bar of soap
   I'd go slippy, slippy slidey over everybody's hidey
   Oh, I wish I was a little bar of soap, bar of soap

3. Oh, I wish I was a little mosquito, mosquito
   Oh, I wish I was a little mosquito, mosquito
   I'd go bitey, bitey, bitey under everybody's nightie
   Oh, I wish I was a little mosquito, mosquito

4. Oh, I wish I was a little bottle of pop, bottle of pop
   Oh, I wish I was a little bottle of pop, bottle of pop
   I'd go down with a slurp and up with a burp
   Oh, I wish I was a little bottle of pop, bottle of pop

Version B

Text a composite of the most popular verses; deviations in verse form from A emphasized. Verse 1 from Margaret Saunier, Camp O Tonka (Ky YWCA), 1961-1967, 1971-1975. Verse 2 from Camp Niwana (Wash CFG), 1970s. Verse 3 from Wyandot County 4-H Day Camp (Ohio 4-H), session for young girls held at Camp Trinity (Ohio P coed), sing after cookout, 1974. Verse 4 from Robin Kelley, Camp Yolijwa (Calif P coed), many years; Camp Metaka (Calif CFG), 1976; Camp Woodleaf (Calif P coed), 1976. Verse 5 from Widjiwagan Camp (Hawaii CFG), 1970s. Verse 6 from Ann Beardsley, Camp o' the Hills (Mich GS), 1963-1970; Camp Ken-Jockety (Ohio GS), 1976. Verse 7 from Monica Mahe Foster, Camp Shawondasee (Minn CFG), 1976.

1. I wish I was a little dirty birdy, dirty birdy
   I wish I was a little dirty birdy, dirty birdy
   I'd go up on the steeple and down on the people
   I wish I was a little dirty birdy, dirty birdy

2. **I** wish I **were** a fishy in the sea _____
   I wish I **were** a fishy in the sea _____
   I'd go swimming in the nudie without my bathing suity
   Oh, I wish I **were** a fishy in the sea _____

3. Oh, I wish I **were** a little vacuum cleaner, vacuum cleaner
   Oh, I wish I **were** a little vacuum cleaner, vacuum cleaner
   I'd go chuggy, chuggy, chuggy under everybody's ruggy
   Oh, I wish I **were** a little vacuum cleaner, vacuum cleaner

4. **I** wish I was a little piece of glass, piece of glass
   Oh, I wish I was a little piece of glass, piece of glass
   I'd go cutty, cutty, cutty and make everybody bloody
   Oh, I wish I was a little piece of glass, piece of glass

5. Oh, I wish I was a little cheerio _____
   Oh, I wish I was a little cheerio _____
   I **would rilley and I'd** rolley into everybody's bowly
   Oh, I wish I was a little cheerio _____

6. Oh, I wish I was a little foreign car, foreign car
   Oh, I wish I was a little foreign car, foreign car
   I'd go speedy, speedy, speedy over everybody's feety
   Oh, I wish I was a little foreign car, foreign car

7. Oh, I wish I **were** a little radio _____
   Oh, I wish I **were** a little radio _____
   I'd go click!

Version C

Text from Congdon Park Cub Scout Pack 243 (Minn BSA), undated song book; collected by William Hillcourt.

I with I were a little fifth,[1]
I with I were a fifth.
I'd thwim and thwim in the deep blue thea,[2]
I with I were a fith.

I with I were a little thip,[3]
I with I were a thip.
I'd thail and thail on the deep blue thea,[4]
I with I were a thip.

I with I wathn't thuth a thimp,[5]
I with I wathn't a thimp,
I'd thing a thong that had thom thenth,[6]
I with a I wathn't a thimp.

Translation
1. I wish I were a little fish
2. I'd swim and swim in the deep blue sea
3. I wish I were a little ship
4. I'd sail and sail on the deep blue sea
5. I wish I wasn't such a simpleton
6. I'd sing a song that had some sense

Version D

Text from John Barnes Wells, "A Little Rock," (Cincinnati, Ohio: John Church Company, 1917), sheet music.

I wish I was a little rock
A-settin' on a hill,
An' doin' nothin' all day long
But just a-settin' still.
I wouldn't eat, I wouldn't drink,
I wouldn't even wash!
But set and set a thousand years,
And rest myself, by gosh!

Version E

Text from "Jealous Jake," *Broad-Axe Tribune*, Eugene, Oregon, 24 November 1894, edited by James Franklin Amis; digital transcription of badly preserved newsprint with no posted notes indicating source or confirming date; editorial corrections made where digitizing errors obvious.

> Gee, I wisht I was a rock
> Yonder on the hill
> Doin' nothin' all day long
> Only settin' still:
> Jest soliloquizin' like
> For a century I
> On the ups and downs of life.
> Chumps these mortals be!
> Human Vein's work an' toil,
> Fuss an' fume an' fret
> Then they die, but that's your rock

The Other Day I Saw a Bear:
Part Songs

Slaves from sub-Saharan Africa introduced call-and-response songs into American music. The term can refer to the form of the verse and to the style in which it is sung. With the spiritual "Swing Low, Sweet Chariot" (31), the verse has a call-response form. Although camps rarely exploit the style, it is clear a leader could shout out lines and have the group answer "coming for to carry me home."

Style

Songs with a call-response form may be sung antiphonally or responsorially. Antiphony, or singing done by alternating choruses or groups, was used by He Bani Gani (Md CFG) with "Dem Bones" (37) in 1976. Kitanniwa treated the song responsorially in 1974. It alternated between a small group and a chorus.

A camp's preference for one technique or the other may be influenced by the presence of an individual who can lead. Gary Flegal remembers, at the Van Buren Youth Camp (Mich agency coed), "Tongo" (20):

> was new at our camp probably five years, five or six years ago. It came with this girl on our staff and she just had the most tremendous voice I ever saw. She'd just belt this song. God, she was really, you know, nice sounding voice and all of a sudden, whoom, here in the middle of the woods TONGO coming out of this this, I couldn't believe it. Nobody can do it the way [girl's name] used to do it.

June Rushing Leibfarth[S] was told "Dem Bones" (37) "takes a really fantastic song leader. All the campers do is just fall in on the chorus. So there are a lot of motions that go along with it. Mostly just adding personality to the song."

A camp's attitude toward solo singing is also important. When "Dem Bones" (37) was sung at Kitanniwa in the 1950s, anyone who knew the words was free to join the group singing the verses. Those who did not began learning by joining the chorus. Girls at Valley Mill (Md coed) and in He Bani Gani (Md CFG) tried singing responsorial songs when they were away from older people. Being able to sing such songs antiphonally was a private mark of achievement or inhabiting the camp tradition.

Echo Songs

The largest category of call-and-response lyrics is the antiphonal echo song. Each line is sung by one group, then repeated by the other, for the entire song. "I'm Going To Leave Ol' Texas" (31) is the best known. "Old Hogan's Goat" (19) was collected as an echo song from the Franklin Settlement House camp (Mich agency) by Susan Dunn.[S] Blue Haven (NM P coed) gives the same treatment to "My Harlan Goat."

Other echo songs, which have call-response lyrics and singing style, include "My Aunt Came Back" (15) at Tawanka (Mich CFG), and "London's Burning" (13) at Tanadoona (Minn CFG). "Sweet Adeline" (8) was sung as an echo song by Brooklyn Scout camps (NY BSA) in 1929. Jan Miller, Sandy Mulvaney, and Betty Zimmerman adapted it for an echo unit song at Hitaga (Iowa CFG) in 1959. The barbershop-quartet lyrics were published in 1903 by Richard Gerard Husch, who worked as Richard H. Gerard. Harry Armstrong wrote the melody in 1896 when he was eighteen.

Chants

Many echo songs, in reality, are chants. At Kitanniwa in the 1960s, Kitty Smith remembers they would shout "Tongo" (20) "back and forth." With "Flea" (39), she says, girls would yell from the beach, hoping to get an answer from the senior unit located on the hill across the lake. The second has been done as "Bee Say" by Cheryl Robinson

(DC CFG), and "Fi" by Roger Smith at Putnam (Mass agency coed). Kotomi (Colo CFG) knows "Chay Chay Koo Lay." "Ham and Eggs" (6) is another echo chant.

Echo-Unison Songs

Some songs use the echo form and singing style for only one section. In "You Can't Get to Heaven" (34), the verse is done antiphonally, and then repeated without lyric iterations by the combined groups. Ann Beardsley (Mich GS) sings "I'm on My Way to Freedom Land" (11) in this manner. However, groups only come together on the last line of each verse, the refrain.

Goodwill/Pleasant (DC agency sep) uses an echo for the first part of the verse and unison for the end of a local song. Kotomi (Colo CFG) treats "I Won't Grow Up" (5) that way. "Alouette" (29) is the best-known alternation between echo and unison. Its form and style have carried over to its parodies, "All You Etta" (5) and "Ravioli" (5). The song first saw print in Montréal in 1879 in a McGill College song book.[338]

Melacoma (Wash CFG) moves between groups echoing one another and groups singing together in "Land of Odin" (19). Both verses and choruses begin with echoes, then end in unison. Glen (Ohio CFG) uses a similar mixture with "Who Was in the Belly" (5). "Now let us sing 'til the power of the Lord" (12) has call-response verses combined with echo choruses.

In the 1950s, girls at Tanawida (Mich CFG) divided the "Jackie boy" dialogue in the "The Keeper" (33) between two groups. "Vrenalie" (30) was treated as a call-response by Kitanniwa in 1959. Girls divided with one group singing the "yo ho ho's" in the chorus and the other answering with the "tra la la's." In New York, Anne Lutz remembers:

> Two camps on opposite sides of Upper Cohasset Lake (in the Harriman section of Palisades Interstate Park - at Bear Mountain) used to sing "Little Sir Echo" (15) across the lake. One camp would start it and wait for the "echo" from across the way. This was slow, of course, because of the time required for the sound waves to travel over and back.

She adds, "Of course, more often two groups in the same camp sang with the echo effect."

Seth Clay (Mich P coed) sings "Give Me Oil for My Lamp" (10) partly in a call-and-response manner and partly in unison. Hidden Valley (Md girls) does "Harry Has a Head like a Ping Pong Ball" (6) that way. Some camps divide into parts for short passages in "Little Johnny England" (7). "Three Fishermen" (51) may be the best-known song with a divided chorus.

Variations

Formulas for echo parts can vary from camp to camp. With the "Quartermaster's Store" (11), Tayanita (Ohio CFG) sings a one verse chant about rats in grandfather's store in a strict two-group echo. Carol Domoney[5] collected a version in the middle 1950s from Rotary (Mich BSA) in which parts of each line were echoed. At Loyaltown (NY J boys) in the 1960s, one group inserted a few words into the other group's line thusly, "I have (hey) not (ho) brought my specs with me."

The formula can change in a camp as a song becomes familiar. At Glen (Ohio CFG), Rebecca Quinlan thinks they first sang "Follow the Drinking Gourd" (9) "as a complete song, but somehow . . . it just developed." Now it is sung with overlapping echoes, with the second part usually done by girls who have been in camp. When asked when the echoing part starts, she says, "It's just kinda like a feeling thing, you know, it's like 'A Plea for One World' (45)."

Functions

Campers' enjoyment in echo and other call-and-response songs may stem from one of two sources. Some places divide by gender, so songs channel bickering among groups in coed camps. Gesell and his staff found ten- and eleven-year-old children especially enjoyed these kinds of sexual rituals.[343:216, 344:99]

Echo Harmony

Call-response singing also is done for the harmony produced when one group sustains the last note while the other completes its part. Appreciation of this effect seems to come around the age of eleven.

When sixth-grade girls at Potomac Country Day Camp (Md coed) listened to my tape of their singing, their most favorable response was to their rendering of "Sippin' Cider" (35).

Sustained call and responses were one of the most common harmonic devices at Kitanniwa in the 1950s. With "Do Lord" (37), most would hold the "blue," while others would sing "blue horizon." Likewise, in "Above a Plain" (22), some would sustain the last syllable of "huyaya," while others sang the remainder of the line. A Tannadoonah (Ind CFG) songbook editor typed the first as "beyond the blues."

Kitanniwa's version of "Happy Wanderer" (48) came from a 1954 recording by the Obernkirchen Children's Choir. One group sang a high descant of "tra la la la," while the other held the final syllables of "val di ri" and "val di ra." Seabow (Calif CFG) uses "ho lu la." John Putnam (Wisc) remembers whistling the second part. Jan Smyth recalls, "All the campers and the girl counselors would sing one part, and the guy counselors would sing the other part" at an Ohio church camp.

Sustained calls and responses have remained part of Kitanniwa's aesthetic. In 1974, Jolene Robinson Johnson and Laura Clare Zahn sang "Say When" (12), alternating between unison and overlapping echo sections. The same convention has been used by the A-Ta-Ya Horizon Club (Mass CFG) with "Down in the Valley" (33) and by Glen (Ohio CFG) with "I Can Sing a Rainbow" (14).

Sustained calls are used for comic effects in "Ship Titanic" (32) and in a version of "Home, Sweet Home" (5) collected from Arnold (Tex GS) in 1960 by Jean Rushing Leibfarth.[§] Henry Rowley Bishop and John Howard Payne introduced the second in *Clari*. Their opera opened in London in 1823.

Origins

Origins of echo harmony, probably, lie in the singing schools. After our Civil War, editors began recommending the use of echoes in choruses for a few songs. In Bradbury's 1864 Sabbath-school collection, *The Golden Censer*, the chorus for "The Gathering" began with two parts, with words written under each staff:

These books included other songs that accommodated the mechanics of reproduction. When books were 12" wide, lyrics could be spaced properly. When pages shrank to 6", textual phrases were published above or below one another. Another song in *The Golden Censer*, which was intended to be sung by all groups, was printed:

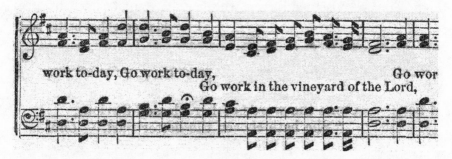

It seems possible that, after the singing master left, local groups misunderstood the new printing convention. They were pleased with the effects of songs like "The Gathering." When confronted with songs compressed to fit the page, they may have transferred the two-part harmony to songs like "The Lord's Vineyard."

Echo choruses became a stylistic technique associated with gospel quartets and country-music groups who recorded in the 1920s and 1930s. The style had been spread by revivalists, like Billy Sunday, before World War I. His music director, Homer Rodeheaver, used it for musical stunts to warm up audiences. From there, it was a short step to parodies.

Quodlibet

Haydn's harmony, which utilized a single melodic line set against a progression of chords based on a dominant note, was introduced into this country after the American constitution was ratified. Earlier part singing, termed counterpoint, relied upon multiple melodies. In quodlibets, two independent, existing works are sung simultaneously. Although it has antecedents in motets and liturgical music, the form, as we know it, developed in the late 1400s when folk tunes were used against each other. One of the earliest was found in the *Glogauer Liederbuch* from around 1480.[242]

People like Rodeheaver used them with groups in the early twentieth century. Posen* called them "partner songs." Virginia Musselman[216] labeled them "together songs." The Eisenbergs used the term "doublers."[214:60] James Franklin Leisy* preferred "contra song."

The one done at Kitanniwa since its earliest years is "The Patter" (10) combination of "Let Us Sing a Song to Kitanniwa" and "Let Us Get the Gang Together." In the 1950s, the staff sang it after the first meal of each camp session. The melody for "Let Us Sing" was "Up! Up! Up! in My Aeroplane," written by Gus Edwards and Matthew C. Woodward for the *Ziegfeld Follies* of 1909.

Quodlibets generally use well-known songs. Gary Flegal has sung the nineteenth-century army song, "The Girl I Left behind Me" (1), with Stephen Foster's "Ring, Ring the Banjo" (1) at the Van Buren Youth Camp (Mich agency coed). Posen* heard "When the Saints Go Marching In" (9) with "Good Night Ladies" (2) in a Canadian coed camp.

In some camps in the Palisades Interstate Park (NJ-NY), Anne Lutz has sung "There's a Long, Long Trail" (22) with "Keep the Home Fires Burning" (4). She also has done "Spanish Cavalier" (3) with "Solomon Levi" (2). The last combination was suggested in the 1923 edition of *The Golden Book of Favorite Songs*.[259] William D. Hendrickson composed "Cavalier" in 1881. "Solomon Levi" was in college tradition by the time it was published in an 1866 Harvard song book.

"Swing Low, Sweet Chariot" is a familiar contra song in contemporary camps. Margaret Olson (Minn CFG) and Patricia McGreer (Wash CFG) have sung it with "All Night, All Day" (33). Janice Engel has done it with "Kumbaya" (90) at Cherith (Minn P girls). Steve Bensinger has sung "Swing Low" with "Rocka My Soul" (3).

Nellie Mae Hastings has combined it with "Saints" (9) and "Dominique" (2) at Widjiwagan (Ill GS). Jacquelyn Orvis learned the triple combination in a recreation-music course at Central Michigan University. Jeanne Paule Deckers recorded the last, using the name Sœur Sourure. The Singing Nun began singing in the Girl Guides in Belgium.

Carol Flack (Ala agency coed) sings "Horsey, Horsey" (28) with "Merry Go Round" (26). "C-h-i-c-k-e-n" (11) is sung with "Rufus Rastus Johnson Brown" (3). Jack Pearse (Ont coed) sings "Rocka My Soul" with "Rock My Soul," a combination recorded by Peter, Paul and Mary. That pairing also exploits two rhythms, a simple form of polyrhythm.

Counterpoint

Other songs enjoyed for their contrapuntal effect have two sets of words and tunes formally associated with the one song. These differ from descants and altos, which use nearly the same words, and from quodlibets, which use existing songs.

At Kitanniwa in 1974, campers sang "Praise Ye the Lord" with "Alleluia" (18). Tannadoonah (Ind CFG) sings "Touba Ti Touba" with "Allay" (7). Other common two-part songs are "Horsey, Horsey" (28), "It's a Small World" (23), and "Tinga Singu" (7). Maude Katzenbach (DC CFG) has sung the chorus to Donovan's "Happiness Runs in a Circular Motion" (17) this way. "Zum Gali Gali" (14) has been sung with two and three parts.

Homophony

A seemingly related form of part singing has one group sing an onomatopoeic cadence, while the other sings a verse. Groups often combine on the chorus or refrain. Instead of counterpoint, this part singing utilizes homophony, the texture associated with nineteenth-century classical music. Some camps use a gender division with boys providing the rhythm.

Carol Parsons Sievert remembers doing "Grandfather's Clock" (10) in the 1930s at Kitanniwa with one group nodding their heads and making ticking sounds with their tongues hitting the roofs of their mouths. In the 1950s, half sang the verse to "Sarasponda" (59) and half the "boom da's." The two switched parts for the second repetition.

"I Love the mountains and the daffodils" (48) was treated similarly with a "boomdeada" part. Our ending was, "I love to live, I live to I love for / All these wonderful things." The Rohrboughs' version ends, "I love the fireside when all the lights are low." More verses since have been created. Some camps sing several, some only one.

"Zulu Warrior" (25) often is done with one group chanting "chief, chief." "We're from Nairobi" (14) has an "ungawa" part. "Sandy's Mill" (5) has an "oompah" part. Carol Simon[S] collected a church camp version in 1973 of "Wade in the Water" (8) in which girls sang the lyrics, while boys chanted "boom boom."

Mariana Palmer learned "Sweet Potatoes" (5) with one group singing "ru ru" at Lookout (Penna YMCA girls) in 1967. This originally appeared in Peter William Dykema's *Twice 55 Community Songs*[*] in 1947 as a "creole" song. The "counter melody" was by Hector Spaulding. Harvey Worthington Loomis did the translation. Pete Seeger recorded a version in 1960 (FC 7526).

Instrumental Imitations

Another group of homophonic songs includes those that imitate instrumental music. June Rushing Leibfarth[S] collected "McKinney Is Dead" (4) to the "Irish Washerwoman." One group at Robinwood (Tex GS) sang "whang whang" in 1967. She heard "Warsaw the Forty-Second" (5), with some girls holding their noses to make a droning sound. "Washerwoman" is a strathspey, first published in 1792.[338] "McKinney" more often is sung to "Scotland the Brave."

"Calliope" (12), as sung at Kitanniwa in 1974, had three groups imitating different rhythm parts of a German band. The fourth group sang the "Daisy, Daisy" chorus from "Bicycle Built for Two" (17). "More We Get Together" (32) more commonly is used for the melodic line.

"The Instruments" or "Orchestra" (17) is a multi-part homophonic song by Willi Geisler. Julius Herford, born Julius Goldstein, introduced the current arrangement after he fled Germany in 1939. An imitation of musical sounds also is found in regular monophonic fun songs like Kitanniwa's version of "Old King Cole" (14).

"Alexander's Ragtime Band" (3) and "McNamara's Band" (6) are monophonic commercial songs with this onomatopoetic appeal.

Irving Berlin composed the first in 1911. The second, by John J. Stamford and Shamus O'Connor, was published in 1917.

"Musikanter" (18), who comes from "German land," has been sung "Ich ben dur conductor" at Saint Vincent de Paul Ranch (Calif C boys), "Ich bin guten doctor" at Christopher (Ohio C coed), and "Eckum duckum doctor" at Niwana (Wash CFG). Translations include "I am the Concert Master" at Kotomi (Colo CFG), "I am the Great Musician" at Ohiyesa (Mich YMCA), and the more common "I Am a Music Maker." At Oweki, Pontiac, Michigan, Camp Fire Girls sing, "I am the music condor / I come from Slavic."

George Frederick Root published B. F. Bix's arrangement as "Johnny Schmoker" (4) in *The Silver Lute*. The 1862 singing book was intended for use in public schools and academies. Harbin's[*] version of "Johnny Schmoker" began "Ich kan spielen." British Scouts sing "Chonny Schmoker."[117] A similar range of English and German exists with "Nicky Nicky Nu" (23).

Part Songs

Call-response songs and singing style, echos, and quodlibets are part of a larger musical class that divides singers into separate vocal groups. Other such part music includes rounds and, in some camps, dialogue ballads. This seemingly diverse category exists because, once a group sings one such song, others come to mind through free association.

There also is a structural reason. At Kitanniwa, the pace of morning sing was rapid. One short song followed another, with only brief pauses for requests. The only variations occurred with different song types, or when time was spent teaching new material. Part songs interrupted the flow, because they required time to create groups, and needed constant supervision to keep groups going.

One alternative is to divide people at the beginning of a singing session. This increases the likelihood such songs will dominate. An alternative is creating permanent divisions. For Kitanniwa's after meal sings, the L-shaped dining hall made a natural division. Older campers and staff could keep parts going. The song leader did little more than indicate which wing would begin.

At Glen (Ohio CFG), when one table starts a round, people at the other tables sense when they should begin from their shared awareness of the spatial division in the rectangular area. Posen* visited a Canadian camp in which the division always was done along gender lines.

Kitanniwa Repertoire

A camp's preference for one type of part song over another may be determined by its predisposition toward egalitarian versus hierarchical social structures. The last chapter suggested recreation camps might sing more easily learned, open-ended songs than would traditional ones. Progressive camps are more likely to use song-leading techniques that allow every child to participate in his or her first sing with the answering group.

By incorporating the usual teaching method, lining out, into the text, call and response promises more efficient use of the limited time available for music. As a byproduct, boredom that accompanies rote learning is minimized. This method was used on records made by the Firesiders (FC 7510) at Killooleet (Vt coed), and by the Wagoners (FC 7030).

At the same time the goal of song leaders using responsorial devices often is democratic, song sessions themselves are hierarchical, with two roles, song leader and chorus. Winn calls songs, which employ such techniques, "follow the leader."[553] The Wagoners use the term "answer-back."

Kitanniwa in the 1950s preferred egalitarian part songs: those with harmonic effects, especially echo endings, descants and altos, along with songs that gave each group an equal part. When songs favored one side, like "Boomdeada" (48), groups traded so everyone sang every part every time. As mentioned in SKYBALL PAINT, when a pure call-response song like "Ol' Texas" (31) was introduced by someone from a more progressive camp tradition, it was suppressed by the staff.

Egalitarianism was not perfect. There still was a leader, although her role was muted in situations where campers could make requests. More important, by assuming children would learn by participation, such sessions ran the danger of becoming elitist, since only those who had been in camp knew every song. Although morning sing and various Blue Bird activities might initiate new campers, only part of the repertoire could be taught. After meal sings always mixed the known and unknown for first, and even second, year campers.

During the first night's camp fire at Sebago-Wohelo (Me girls), Rogers noticed, "Ce-ki-ca-ti [a counselor] led in some of the old-time camp songs, in which those who had been in camp before joined with hearty good will, while those to whom it was all new listened with something of sadness, but hummed the tunes, resolving to learn the words as soon as possible."[147:44] If local songs had not used familiar melodies, nothing would have helped new campers participate and overcome their feelings of isolation among reunited friends.

Repertoire Violation

After meal sings I observed at Kitanniwa in 1974 probably were atypical. Not only was it the end of a season made difficult by the loss of the main lodge in a spring fire, but it also was an experimental coed session. Many of the elementary- and middle-school-aged children had mild behavioral problems, and no particular desire to be there. Many probably were still at an age when they only wanted to repeat what they had mastered. With no returning campers, the shared repertoire was small, not large enough to support extended singing sessions that were routine earlier in the summer.

Thursday night's after meal sing began with three popular fun songs, "I'm Wild about Horns" (9), "Little Pile of Tin" (29), and "Junior Birdsmen" (30). To change the pace, the song leader began "A Bear" (32). The responsorial song required a dominant leader. A few staff members tried to transform it into an antiphonal echo, but campers did not follow. Some counselors then tried an impromptu dramatization. The song's structure and the skills of the leader kept children singing as they watched the antics.

"Ragtime Cowboy Joe" (27) followed. The 1950s fun song was known only by counselors in 1974. Next, they sang the traditional late-session cheer, "Cookie" (30), and another fun song, the nonsensical "Wadaleache" (34). Again, sensing flagging interest by the campers they had been observing for several days, some counselors formed a chorus line to sing the nonsense-laden "Catalina Matalina" (14). Since campers did not know the song, they watched.

After two more nonsense-language fun songs, "Skinnamarink, I Love You" (28) and "Eskimo Hunt" (21), the leader tried "Calliope" (12). It did not appeal. The religious-tinged "Them Bones" (37) may have breached the necessary ritual isolation between home and here for some. Again, the call-response song was not familiar. When some staff began to dramatize it, the group watched, but did not bother to join the chorus.

Counselors were not being rebellious or disruptive with their actions. If anything, they were trying to help. Many had grown up in camps: a few in Kitanniwa, some in other traditional girls' camps like Missaukee (Mich P girls) or Sealth (Wash CFG), and some in coed camps like Temple Hills (Ohio P coed) or Interlochen (Mich coed). Many had been together for two years and had fused their disparate backgrounds into a group tradition.

Some likely had welcomed the challenges of the final session, either from idealistic impulses or religious ones. Probably few had the formal training to deal with such situations. By week's end, many were fatigued by constant failures to elicit positive responses from their charges.

As long as the songs had been normal fun ones accepted by the young group, both campers and staff participated. When the songs were pure nonsense, those children, who, because of their behavior problems were under severe pressure to preserve an outward patina of rationality, became less willing to sing.

When the need arose to move beyond the familiar, to introduce new material, the staff divided on the best tactic. The song leader tried methods of progressive camps with call and response. When the campers were reluctant to join, staff members tried to amuse them into participation. Neither technique worked. A chasm between the staff and the campers was too large. The recreation tradition of "Junior Birdsmen" (30) could bridge the gap. Neither progressive singing techniques nor traditional girls' nonsense songs could.

Adding to the estrangement was the possibility that, if campers sensed any undercurrents of disagreement among staff members, they reacted as abused children often do. They withdrew and warily watched. The more the staff tried to engage them, the more they retreated.

Case Study: The Other Day I Saw a Bear

The responsorial call-response song, which precipitated the conflict in group-singing styles, was "The Other Day I Saw a Bear" (32). Its precursor may be the "Preacher and the Bear." The older minstrel song described a man who, when treed by an animal, hid on a branch. In the modern "Bear," a person runs from an animal and leaps for a tree branch.

In both, suspense is dissipated by a comic punch line. Brooklyn Scouts (NY BSA) in the 1920s were singing the first as, "Oh, Lord! If you can't help me, for goodness sake, don't you help dat bear!" In 1974, Kitanniwa was singing the second as:

> Now don't you fret
> And don't you frown
> 'Cause I caught that branch
> On my way down

The Preacher and the Bear

George Fairman (1881-1962) of Front Royal, Virginia, wrote "The Preacher and the Bear" in 1904. Arthur Collins made his first recording in 1905, then re-recorded it each time reproduction technology improved. According to Tim Gracyk,[*] one version still was being sold through Montgomery Ward in 1941 to what then was called the hillbilly music audience.

The lyrics were so popular, itinerant performers spread versions before radios or records were commonly available. Hubert Gibson Shearin[†] and Josiah Henry Combs collected it in Kentucky in 1911; White[†] in Auburn, Alabama, in 1916; Portia Smiley[†] in Virginia in 1919, and Brown[†] in North Carolina tobacco country in 1923.

Religious hypocrisy was ridiculed in the second line of version C, and implicitly punished in the chorus. Smiley's version, a tale rather than a song, identified the preacher as a Baptist. Blacks who recorded it later were gospel groups.

The preacher's race was communicated by dialect and the phrase, the "coon climbed out on a limb." This was emphasized in recordings made in the 1930s by artists like Honeyboy[†] and Sassafrass, and like the New Dixie Demons.[†] Ford[†] collected an Ozark version that described him as a "colored preacher."

Phil Harris[†] transmitted it outside the South. He was Jack Benny's bandleader in the late 1940s. Many learned the song from him or from family members who learned it from him.

Andy Griffith[†] released it in the 1950s on the album that featured "What It Was, Was Football." That monologue directed its humor against the rube, personified by Griffith, who was raised in the borderlands between the mountains and Piedmont in North Carolina.

Country artists continued recording the ballad in the 1950s. Jiles Perry Richardson, better known as The Big Bopper,[†] was from east Texas near the Louisiana border. Mac Wiseman[†] was raised in the Shenandoah valley of Virginia. Hylo Brown,[†] who was born in eastern Kentucky, recorded it in the 1960s. The New Christy Minstrels[†] performed a sanitized version for a larger white audience, beginning in 1962.

Jerry Reed[†] and Rufus Thomas[†] reintroduced it in 1970. Before then, someone had recast the scene with the individual trapped on the branch looking down at the bear. Pejorative comments on religion, Blacks, and even guns and hunting were removed by the use of the first person and the comic "don't you fret" verse.

In the same years, Jerry Clower[†] was telling a comic tale, "A Coon Huntin' Story," which focused only on the hunting, with a similar punch line. He honed his narrative skills as a fertilizer salesman in Yazoo, Mississippi.

Three Little Angels

The verse beginning "now down you fret" is shared with "Three Little Angels" (17), another song transformed in recent years. In the 1940s, it was a traveling verse, often associated with "On the Dummy Line" (10). Phyllis Southman[§] collected it in 1948 as:

> Little Willie all dressed in white
> Tried to get to heaven on the tail of a kite
> The kite string broke and Willie fell
> Stead of going to heaven he went to
>
> The dummy line

That verse now is repeated several times, each time with one less angel. The final iteration ends:

> But the kite string broke and down they fell
> They didn't get to heaven, they all went to . . .

> Now don't get excited, don't lose your head
> They didn't get to heaven
> They all went to bed

Carol Simon[S] collected an Ohio church camp version that decremented to zero, then started again with "Three little devils dressed in red / Tried to get to heaven on the end of a thread" before finishing with "now don't get excited, don't get upset." Kotomi (Colo CFG) says its tune is "Hush Little Baby" (8).

The verse was in Southern tradition before World War I. Eber Carle Perrow heard a version of "Shortening Bread" (7) in the Tennessee mountains in 1912 that strung together pejorative couplets about Blacks trying to get to heaven on a 'lectric car, a railroad track, the tail of a kite, and a peanut shell. Its final verse ended, "Tried to get to heaven, but they went to Hell."[463]

Earlier, William Oscar Scroggs[*] heard a version of the kite with "The Dummy Line" (10) that ended "Dey tried to go to Hebben, but they went to hell." Alabama Blacks passed their version to the economic historian in 1908. Donna Quist[S] heard a variant of that verse in 1943 at Camp-in-the-Woods (NY YMCA coed) that ended "landed in Cornell."

Key phrases were older. James Whitcomb Riley published "A Short'nin' Bread Song" (7) in *Home-Folks* in 1900. The version of that song known in camps may be derived from one recorded in 1927 by baritone Lawrence Tibbett or from one recorded by Nelson Eddy in 1937.

Textual Variation

Wording of "A Bear" varies from camp to camp. In verse A-5, all four lines rhyme, and have become interchangeable. Kotomi (Colo CFG) and Widjiwagan (Hawaii CFG) have another verse between A-3 and A-4 containing a line borrowed from movies. In Hawaii, it is sung, "I said to him, that's a great idea / So come on feet, lets up and fleet."

Music

"A Bear" takes its general form from its tune, "Sippin' Cider" (35), sung "sippin' soda" by Nancy Gail Maxwell (ND CFG). "Suckin'

Cider" or "Thucking Thider," as it also has been sung, was composed in 1919 by Carey Morgan and Lee David. Morgan was born in Brownsburg, Indiana, west of Indianapolis. David was from New York, where he was educated at City College, and Teacher's College, Columbia.

Its dedication to film comedian Fatty Arbuckle gave the song the glamour of Hollywood. Underneath, the lyrics must have drawn on the Kentucky culture that wept into Indiana. Morgan's grandfather, Daniel A. Madison Morgan, migrated from Pulaski on the Cumberland River near the Cumberland Gap.

Sandburg* received a version from H. Luke Stancil. He learned it from old men in Pickens County located near the southern tip of the Blue Ridge in northeast Georgia. Sandburg heard another variant from Jess Ricks, who heard it in Taylorsville, Illinois, near Springfield. He was probably Jesse Jay Ricks (1880-1944) who collected Illinois Civil War documents and was president of Union Carbide. Vernon Dahlhart recorded the courtship ballad in 1929.

Early versions progressed through a simple narrative to a comic climax that Carol Domoney§ collected as, "And now I have / A mother-in-law, / 'Cause I sipped cider through a straw." Every verse has a two-line couplet advancing the story and a variation on the line about cider.

It stayed in camp tradition where various comic devices were used to extend the ending. We sang it at Kitanniwa one year, maybe 1954 or 1955, when the narrator had seven kids and the final verse was:

Group 1: The moral of
Group 2: The moral of
Group 1: This little tale
Group 2: This little tale
Group 1: Is to sip your ci
Group 2: Is to sip your ci
Group 1: a-der through a pail
Group 2: a-der through a pail

All: The moral of this little tale
All: Is to sip your ci-a-der through a pail

The version Carol Domoney§ learned from Pilgrim Haven (Mich P coed) added sixteen kids and the moral, "don't you sip cider / you sip coke." Barbara Rust[S] collected a version from a Michigan State student who had seventeen kids with the end, "That's how I got my wood leg / Sippin' cider from a keg." Both were transcribed in 1955.

Another Michigan State student told Christine Nevans[S] in 1951 that, "sometimes while singing this song, the group splits up in two, some singing the part not in parenthesis [the original lyric] and the rest singing the part that is in parenthesis [an echo]."

Sandburg suggested the "ci" was drawn out, "as if to indicate a prolonged sip." At Kitanniwa, we had a catch in the middle of the word "ci-a-der." Perhaps it was meant to be a drunken hiccup, but it sounded more like a vocal trick used by Teresa Brewer.

Ann Marie Filocco[S] talked to a New Jersey Girl Scout who sang only one verse. She followed it with a parody about "the littlest worm" that was in the straw, got sucked in, and thereby drowned. Some camps have banned the original.

Popularity

The basic theme for the song, the unexpected meeting with a dangerous predator, is found in "Julianne" (4), a tragi-romantic ballad with a comic ending. It has been sung by Ann Beardsley (Mich GS), Janice Knapp (Mich CFG) and Lisa McCabe (Calif GS), as well as at Kowana (Tenn CFG).

In the antiphonal "Bear Hunt" (16) tale, each event is accompanied by gestures. At the end, they are done rapidly in reverse order to simulate a return journey by a person running in fear. Oweki (Mich CFG) does it responsorially. Others call it a lion or tiger hunt.

Joan Fulton[S] suggested Wasewagan (Calif CFG) knew another, unrelated song about a bear in 1953. Girls wrote their own version about an animal traveling with a circus, to fit two episodes in camp: one, when bear prints were found in the bottom of the pool; the other, when they formed a bucket brigade to fill the pool after plumbing had broken down.

"A Bear" is known best in the survey Midwest. In 1976, 64% of the people from that area knew the song, as compared with 37% elsewhere. Its diffusion, mainly, had been through girls' camps where it was known by 58% of the questionnaire respondents. Debra Nails says, she "learned this in Louisiana from a Michigan Girl Scout, then taught it in Texas, then in Tennessee."

Only 38% in coed or boys' camps claimed it. Given the two templates, the "Preacher and the Bear" and "Sippin' Cider," it probably was written by someone in the Southern-influenced part of the Midwest.

Reactions to the song vary by age. Joyce Quarto says, at the Muskegon, Michigan, public schools' coed camp, it was "used a lot." Carol Simon[S] collected a version from a Girl Scout in Ohio who told her it was "mostly sung at day camp by Brownies and Juniors. However, the seventh graders did the song if they had to only and didn't seem to like it." Marsha Lynn Barker (Mich GS) learned it at a camp staff reunion where she found it to be "obnoxious." No doubt for similar aesthetic reasons, Jan Smyth (Ohio P coed) remembers:

> two songs that we used to do that weren't in the books, but we'd very rarely do them after meals. It was more an informal thing. Like if your family group happened to be sitting around singing and they were the more silly type, like the "Cat Came Back" (15) and "Them Bones" (37) and the "Bear Song." But we rarely did them after meals.

Version A

Text from Camp Kitanniwa (Mich CFG), 1974; staff and campers at an evening meal, with a song leader and an impromptu dramatization of the lyrics by some counselors as the group sang.

All verses follow the repetition patterns of the first verse.

1. Leader: The other day
    Campers: The other day
    Leader: I saw a bear
    Campers: I saw a bear
    Leader: A great big bear
    Campers: A great big bear
    Leader: Away up there
    Campers: Away up there

    All: The other day I saw a bear
    All: A great big bear away up there

325

(One counselor, the bear, starts growling at another, chases her down the aisle between the tables.)

    2.   He looked at me
          I looked at him
          He sized me up
          I sized up him

    3.   He said to me
          Why don't you run
          I see you ain't
          Got any gun

    4.   And so I ran
          Away from there
          But right behind
          Came that bear

(The bear counselor's growling begins again.)

    5.   In front of me
          There was a tree
          A great big tree
          Oh glory be

(Leader has gotten onto a chair to be a tree. The bear continues growling at the other counselor.)

    6.   The nearest branch
          Was ten foot up
          I had to jump
          And trust my luck

(The trapped counselor jumps onto bench beside tree. The bear continues pawing and growling. This continues for the next two verses.)

    7.   And so I jumped
          Into the air

But I missed that branch
Away up there

8. Now don't you fret
   And don't you frown
   'Cause I caught that branch
   On my way down

9. That's all there is
   There ain't no more
   Unless I meet
   That bear once more

(Growling has ceased.)

10. Leader: The end, the end (soft)
    Campers: The end, the end (soft)
    Leader: The end, the end (softer)
    Campers: The end, the end (softer)
    Leader: The end, the end (softer)
    Campers: The end, the end (softer)
    Leader: The end, the end (softer)
    Campers: The end, the end (softer)

    All: The end, the end, the end, the end (loud)
    All: The end, the end, the end, the end

Version B

Text from Camp Tayanita (Ohio CFG), 1970s; variations from A emphasized. Gestures from Susan Meyer, Camp Eljabar (Penna YMCA), age 9; Camp Manitou-Wasting (Ont coed), ages 14-15.

All verses follow the repetition pattern of the first verse. Hand claps with the words they follow; all verses have same pattern as the second verse.

1. The other day   (All repeat)
   I met a bear   (All repeat)

Up in the woods   (All repeat)
Away up there   (All repeat)

(All:)
The other day I met a bear
Up in the woods, away up there.

2. He looked (clap) at me (clap)
    I looked (clap) at him; (clap)
    He sized (clap) me up, (clap)
    I sized (clap) **him up**; (clap)

3. **And then he says**
    Why don't you run
    I see you **don't**
    Have any gun

4. And so I ran
    Away from there
    But right behind
    Me was the bear;

5. **And then I see**
    In front of me,
    A great big tree
    O **Lordy me!**

6. _____

7. And **I** jumped
    Into the air
    And missed that branch
    Away up there;

8. Now don't you fret
    Now don't you frown
    I caught that branch
    On the way back down;

9. That's all there is
   There **is** no more
   Until I meet
   That bear once more
   (All: repeat the same)
   (All: THE END)

Version C

Text from Brooklyn Scout camps (NY BSA) song book, 1929; notes indicate it was sung in the "Key of E flat." The usual persimmon tree has been changed into cinnamon by boys in the north.

A preacher went out walking, 'twas on one Sunday morn,
Of course, it was agin his religion, but he took his gun along.
He shot for himself some mighty fine quail and one small measly hare,
And, on the road returning home, he met a great big, grizzly bear.
The bear walked out to the middle of the road, the coon he could
   hardly see,
And then he got so excited that he climbed up a cinnamon tree;
The bear sat down in the middle of the road, and the coon climbed
   out on a limb,
Then he raised his eyes to the Lord in the skies, and these words said
   to him:

Chorus
"Oh, Lord! didn't you deliver Daniel from the lion's den,
And so delivered Jonah from de belly ob de whale, and den
Three Hebrew chilluns from de fiery furnace? So de good book do
   declare.
Oh, Lord! if you can't help me, for goodness sake, don't you help dat
   bear!"

Witchcraft: Pretty Songs and Melody

An appreciation for pretty songs develops around age twelve, when individuals may begin responding to nature,[344:121] and "may experience the wonder, awesomeness and endlessness of space."[344:136] According to the Gesell Institute, this awareness coincides with a neoteric interest in religion[344:137] that prompts eleven- and twelve-year-olds to join the church choir.[344:103, 138]

These emotional responses have been channeled through the pantheism of Emerson, and the Romanticism associated with Goethe, into songs that celebrate the outdoors. Although medieval, German-speaking minnesingers explored the "varied beauties of nature,"[360:61] the themes found in camp repertoires owe more to a nineteenth-century glorification of folk life. George Mosse believed, Germans linked "the human soul with its natural surroundings, with the 'essence' of nature."[435:4]

An interest in the folk increased in Central Europe after Prussia defeated France in 1870. Otto von Bismark consolidated German-speaking feudal states into the first Reich the next year. Like the folk revivals mentioned in KUMBAYA, the völkische Bewegung was partly the response of individuals seeking to preserve heritages being lost to the industrializing forces of the nation state. Others were seeking remnants of a shared culture that might have existed before Frederick II granted princes territorial autonomy within the Holy Roman Empire in 1232.

Nature Hymns

These historical movements were reflected in the hymns sung in camps before the Folk Revival. The melody for "Fairest Lord

Jesus, Ruler of All Nature" (13) was published in 1843 in *Schlesische Volkslieder*. August Heinrich Hoffmann von Fallersleben and Ernst Friedrich Richter edited the collection of Silesian tunes.

Hoffman was a poet who had been banished from Braslau, now Warsaw, for offending Prussian officials in 1841. His travels invoked comparisons to followers of Jan Hus, who fled to Silesia after the Roman Catholic church burned the early Reformation leader for heresy in 1415. They later reorganized as the Moravians.

Richard Storrs Willis published the American version in 1850 in *Church Chorals and Choir Studies*. After the Bostonian graduated from Yale in 1841, he studied music in Saxony with Xavier Schnyder and Moritz Hauptmann. The latter was professor of music theory at Mendelssohn's music conservatory in Leipzig, where Richter was professor of harmony.

In his footnote to the "Crusader's Hymn," Willis introduced the idea the song preceded divisions within the Holy Roman Empire:

> This hymn, to which the harmony has been added, was lately discovered in Westphalia. According to the traditionary text by which it is accompanied, it was wont to be sung by the German knights on their way to Jerusalem.

The bishopric of Westphalia had been one of the most contentious in the German religious wars. While Münster was the Anabaptist center in the 1530s, the 1648 treaty ending the Thirty Years War decreed the area would be Roman Catholic.

The text has been traced to a hymn book published by Jesuits in Westphalia in 1677, the *Münster Gesangbuch*. References to the Crusades were part of the same yearning, mentioned in AN AUSTRIAN, that led Chateaubriand to assume "Malbrouck" dated back to Godfrey de Bouillon scaling the walls of Jerusalem in 1099.

Kitanniwa sang "For the Beauty of the Earth" (17) and "This Is My Father's World" (13) during religious services held on the steps to the lake during the two-week session. "Beauty" began as a poem by Folliott Sandford Pierpoint in an 1864 collection, *The Sacrifice of Praise*. Konrad Kocher composed the melody, "Dix," in 1838. The Stuttgart organist promoted four-part harmony in church music in Württemberg.

"Father's World" was inspired by Maltbie Davenport Babcock's walks along the Niagara escarpment in Lockport, New York. After his death, his widow, the former Kathleen Tallman, and Mary R. Sanford included the Presbyterian minister's text in *Thoughts for Every-Day Living*. A Presbyterian youth hymnal, *Alleluia*, published the melody, in 1915. Franklin Lawrence Sheppard says, "Terra Beata" was an English folk song he learned from his mother in Philadelphia.

"God Who Touches Earth with Beauty" (9) is the most important nature hymn written in camp. Its author, Mary Susanne Edgar (1889-1973), was trained by the YWCA. She later established a private girls' camp, Glen Bernard, in Ontario in 1922. The text has been set to various tunes.

Nature themes are found in contextual songs like the evening closing medley (25), "Green Trees around Us" (56), followed by the "Day Is Done" words for "Taps" (73). Nature and religion are joined in some patriotic songs, especially Irving Berlin's "God Bless America" (20) and Katherine Lee Bates' "America the Beautiful" (39).

Bates was a Wellesley literature professor who sent her poem to a Congregational magazine in 1895. In 1910, it was set to "Materna." Samuel Augustus Ward composed the melody in 1882 when he was an organist at Grace Episcopal in Newark, New Jersey.

Hiking

Interest in the volk led to the Wandervogel in 1901. The hiking groups mentioned in KUMBAYA sought a more systematic return to their purer, more natural selves. Joys of hiking are prominent in some international songs brought to this country, including "Tiritomba" (12) and "Morning Comes Early" (20).

Friedrich Wilhelm Möller composed "The Happy Wanderer" (48) for an orphans' choir organized in 1949 by his sister Edith. She and Florenz Siegesmund wrote the lyrics. Antonia Ridge made the best-known translation.

Franz Abt composed the "Foot Traveler" (7) in the volkstümliches lied tradition. The German art song was included in a school music-book, *School Bells*, being advertised in 1885. Osbourne McConathy added it to the 1922 revision of the third volume of the *Progressive Music Series*.

Some songs treat the hiking theme with more sedate melodies. In the 1930s, Zanzig found "Border Trail" (27) and "Follow the Trail" (10) were better known in all girls' camps than in boys' ones.[561:525] The "Hiking Song" (26) has the line "pack on my back." Neidlinger arranged his "Walking Song" (15) with two-part harmony.

"Hiking Girl" (7) used the melody from "When Irish Eyes Are Smiling" (4). Hitaga (Iowa CFG) also adapted the 1912 song by Ernest Roland Ball, Chauncey Olcott, and George Graff, Junior.

Gypsies

An interest in hiking and the allure of the mildly forbidden led to the use of gypsy imagery. In the 1940s, Kitanniwa was singing "Roam, Joyous Gypsies" (7) to "Glow Worm," and "Gypsy Loves the Open Road" (1) to "Baby's Boat" (20). Tannadoonah (Ind CFG) sings the first "Rove, Joyous Gypsies," according to Marilyn Dulmatch and June Walters.§

In the same years, Tanadoona (Minn CFG) wrote a trip song to "Gypsy Trail." Tod Buchannan Galloway of Columbus, Ohio, composed the melody in 1897 for a Rudyard Kipling poem.

Indigenous gypsy songs vary from those that perpetuate the allure of outdoor life,

> Gypsies the byways are beckoning
> Through the meadows that glisten with dew
>   . . .
> And evening will grant you contentment
> By the blaze of your Caravan fire

to ones that treat real adventures with mocking affection:

> Where have all the gypsies gone
> Four days ago
> We have reached our destiny
> Back to health and sanity

Watanopa (Mont CFG) sang the first to "Roses of Picardy." Girls at Hitaga (Iowa CFG) set the other to "Where Have All the Flowers Gone" (43) in 1963.

The suggestion out-of-camp trips were gypsies was publicized by the 1914 *Vacation Book of the Camp Fire Girls.* Hanoum advertised its program included a "'gypsy' through the White and Green mountains." Charles Hubert Farnsworth (1859-1947) and his wife, the former Charlotte Joy Allen (1868-1946), founded the Vermont girls' camp in 1909.

They may have been drawing on the fascination with Romany music affirmed by Dvořák's 1880 *Gypsy Songs*, based on poems by Adolf Heyduk. Viennese composers expanded the theme in operettas, like Johann Strauss II's *The Gypsy Baron* of 1885, and Franz Lehár's *Gypsy Love* of 1911. Sigmund Romberg introduced a gypsy band in his first American operetta, *Maytime*, of 1917.

Rudolf Friml studied with Dvořák in Prague, before immigrating in 1906. His "Song of the Vagabonds" from *The Vagabond King* of 1925 was used for Surprise Lake's (NY J boys) "Camping Song." "Camp Fire Girls Are Happy" (5) begins "Girls of every nation." The show also included "Some Day" (4). It has been used for a Hidden Valley (Md CFG) song and sung in the original in some camps. Ronnie Gilbert* says, her mother was a great Friml fan. His sheet music was stored in the piano bench.

From gypsies it was a short step to an interest in the exotic. "Pagan Love Song," written for a film set in Tahiti, has been used for "Sit with Me in the Firelight" (2), according to Vivian Sexton (Tex CFG). Surprise Lake (NY J boys) and Treasure Island (Penna BSA) had local songs to the 1929 melody. In the 1930s, Augusta (Calif CFG) used "Blue Hawaii," from *Waikiki Wedding*. Bing Crosby starred in 1937.

Sky

Some aspects of nature are mentioned more often than others. "Blue sky above me, the wind sweeping o'er me" (4) was written to "Marchéta." Another "Blue Sky" (5) begins, "When camp fires are burning low." The opening line of "Cowboy Night Song" (12) is "There's a blue sky way up yonder." The YWCA published the first in 1927.[227]

"Marchéta" was written in 1913 by Pennsylvania-German composer, Victor Schertzinger, as a "love song of old Mexico." Tallman H. Trask (1890-1974) used the tune for a "Scout Leader's Prayer" (10). He worked for the YMCA before he organized Boy

Scout troops in Los Angeles in 1919. A California Camp Fire camp, Augusta (Calif CFG), has local words to the melody.

Wind

Adahi (Penna CFG) has combined several wind songs into a medley. "Who Has Seen the Wind" (1) is followed by "Wind, Wind Heather Gypsy" (22), and ends with "Where Does the Wind Come From" (20). The first is based on a Christina Rosetti poem, the second on one by John Galsworthy. The last usually is sung "wind go."

Marie Gaudette (1894-1966), a nature advisor at Hoffman (RI GS), composed settings for the first two. After her death, Catherine Tilley Hammett (1902-1998) collected her work in *Marie Gaudette's Songs.* She was assisted by Constance Lavino Bell and Marion Roberts. Some of the musical transcriptions had been made earlier by Mary Alison Sanders. Gaudette's photograph appears in "Outdoors."

Sunrise

An interest in morning reveals itself in two of the more common graces, "Now the Day Commences" (36) and "God Has Created a New Day" (72). Jean Taylor wrote the first, Gaudette the second.

"I want to wake up in the morning where the morning glories grow" (19) is the most widely used commercial morning song. Judith Bittmann (Ohio GS) sings, "where the Miami waters flow." Marilyn Butler (NH girls) knows, "where the pine and the hemlock grow." Charline Carney (Mass girls) learned, "where the mountain laurels grow." Gene Clough says, he always assumed it was sung only at Yallani (Calif CFG).

More general nature themes are found in "Mountain Greenery" (1), by Richard Rodgers and Lorenz Hart. The 1926 melody is used for "Here at Miniwanca" (Mich P sep). Skyland (NC girls) sings the original words in North Carolina. Rodgers was the son of a German Jewish family in Queens, Hart the son of German Jewish immigrants in Harlem.

Hitaga (Iowa CFG) has a "Hymn to Camp" to Oscar Rasbach's 1922 setting of Joyce Kilmer's "Trees." Rasbach was born in Dayton, Ohio, and trained in Vienna. He settled in San Marino, California. Nelson Eddy made the most successful recording.

"The Silvery Sandy goes rippling by our Namanu home" was written in the Oregon Camp Fire camp in 1940 by Martha Berg, Dorothy Coe, Nancy Holbert, and Diane Powers. Orrin Tucker recorded its tune, "Apple Blossoms and Chapel Bells," in 1939. Soon after, he and Bonnie Baker recorded the song that made them famous, "Oh Johnny" (5).

"The World Is Waiting for the Sunrise" (2) has been used for Connetquot (NY BSA) and Kalamazoo Girl Reserve (Mich YWCA) songs. Scouts in Brooklyn (NY BSA) and Pittsburgh (Penna BSA) have sung the 1919 text by Gene Lockhart. Ernest Seitz composed the melody when he was a twelve-year-old student of Augustus Stephen Vogt, the son of 1848 German refugees to Canada. Seitz used the name Raymond Roberts to separate his more commercial work from his career as a Berlin-trained concert pianist in Toronto, Ontario.

Camp Fire

A camp fire is the central symbol in many songs. The YMCA's Boys' Work Secretary, Henry William Gibson (1867-1948), romanticized the routine evening program in the 1911 Boy Scout manual:

> Anyone who has witnessed a real camp fire and participated in its fun as well as seriousness will never forget it. The huge fire shooting up its tongue of flame into the darkness of the night, the perfect shower of golden rain, the company of happy boys, and the great dark background of piney woods, the weird light over all, the singing, the yells, the stories, the fun, and then the serious word at the close, is a happy experience long to be remembered.[126]

Seton is the one responsible for elevating the fire from a mere cooking, lighting, and heating necessity into the central, symbolic group experience. In a late edition of the *Birch Bark Roll*, he wrote, "The Sacred Fire. The rubbing stick fire has always been the sacred fire, the 'need fire' [. . .] with this we light the Great Central Fire of Council. It is the symbol of the One Great Spirit."[210:xxii]

Despite the implication this was a Native American practice, many of Seton's terms seem to have been borrowed from James George Frazier's 1890 survey of European mythology, *The Golden Bough*. The anthropologist associated sacred fires, lit in primitive, non-utilitarian ways, with Lithuanians, Swabians, Poles in East Prussia, Hungarians, Estonians, the yule log mentioned in ASH GROVE, and the Todus of South India. He did not mention them in his brief comments on American Indian beliefs.

Frazier mentioned the Need Fire as a practice of the Germanic Teutons of southern Scandinavia and of the Celts, including the Scots, Welsh, and Irish. He described Scots Druids lighting fires at Beltaine with boards and wimples like those used by girls at Sebago-Wohelo (Me girls). Rogers noted, Seton introduced the practice to the group.[147:66-69]

In *A Camp Fire Girl's First Council Fire*, Jane L. Stewart mentioned the Hand Sign of the Fire, and described lighting it "in the Indian fashion" with a block of wood and a drill stick.[145:241-242] Margaret Bradshaw McGee wrote "Mystic Fire" (6) the same year, 1914, to a southern California Indian melody.

Camp Fire Songs

Some campfire songs instruct the young and new in the meaning of rituals being performed while they are singing. Best known in Camp Fire camps are "Each Camp Fire Lights Anew" (84) and "Call of the Fire" (49), sometimes sung as a medley. Some have additional verses for the first, which is sung to "May Madrigal," according to a 1923 Girl Reserve* song book.

Susan Dunn§ collected a version of "Call" with "in a shadow," rather than "through the shadows." The 1940s Kitanniwa song book had "joy we're receiving," rather than "love." Its tune, "Wonderful One," is a 1923 adaption by Theodora Strandberg Morse, Paul Whitman, and Ferde Grofé of a melody by Hollywood's Marshall Neilan. Morse, born Alfreda Theodora Strandberg, married songwriter Theodore Morse. She used several pseudonyms.

Other self-referencing campfire songs include "Have You Ever Watched a Camp Fire" (8), "Rise up O Flame" (29), and "Sing around the Camp Fire" (8). Neidlinger wrote four-part harmony for "Burn, Fire Burn" (23). "Keep the Camp Fire Burning" (8) is sung to the

World War I "Home Fires" (4) by Ivor Novello, born David Ivor Davies, and Lena Gilbert Ford. "Let the Lower Lights Keep Burning" (2) is the melodic source for "Embers of Camp Fire" (5).

"By the Blazing Council Fire" (12), also sung "'Round the Blazing Camp Fire" (5), uses "'Til We Meet Again" (4). It is one of the few traditional camp songs that penetrated Wo-Chi-Ca (NJ agency coed).[409]

Its melody has been sung with the original words in some four camps, and for "Smile Awhile" (8). Tawakani (Ida CFG) has adopted the last as "Dream Awhile." Erne Mower used the tune for "Camp Sealth No Better Can Be Found" (2) in 1920. The Washington CFG song since has spread to Niwana (Wash CFG). Vivian Sexton (Tex CFG) remembers singing "Camp Fire Pledge" (1) to the tune.

Brooklyn Scout camps (NY BSA) have sung "Round the Camp Fire" to "Every Little Movement." Margaret Bradshaw McGee of Sebago-Wohelo (Me girls) used the 1910 tune, by Karl Hoschna and Otto Harbach, for the Camp Fire Girls' "Symbol Song" (11). Hoschna was born in Bohemia, studied in Vienna, and worked with Victor Herbert. Harbach was the son of Danish immigrants to Utah.

Twilight

The fact camp fires occur in the early evening has created an interest among camp bards in commercial songs dealing with twilight or starlight. Watanopa (Mont CFG) used "In the Starlight" for "In the Firelight." At Namanu (Ore CFG), Marjorie Jones used "Neapolitan Nights" in 1928 for:

> Above the rapids of Sandy River
> The forest rises in majesty,
> In mountain breezes the tall firs quiver
> To and fro with a low sweet melody

The camp's Kiwanis unit adopted "When It's Twilight on the Trail" (2) for "When It's Twilight on the Hill." "When It's Lamplighting Time in the Valley" was used for "When It's Firelighting Time at Hitaga" at the Iowa CFG camp in 1950.

Joseph Edward Carpenter and Stephen Glover wrote "Starlight" in 1878. "Neapolitan Nights" was composed in 1925 by John Stepan

Zamecnik and Harry David Kerr. Zamecnik studied with Dvořák in Prague and New York. In 1946, Gene Autry recorded "Trail," which had been introduced in the 1936 film, *The Trail of the Lonesome Pine*.

"Lamplighting Time" was written in 1933 by Harold Goodman and other members of The Vagabonds, a vocal trio who performed on the *Grand Ole Opry*. One member, Dean Upson was singing with his brother at Otterbein. The other member, Curtis Poulton, was in the glee club at the United Church of the Brethren in Christ college in Ohio.

"Love's Old Sweet Song" (5) is the best-known twilight song. Boy Scouts sing it as "Camp Fire Song" (2). Local lyrics exist at Blue Haven (NM P coed), Les Chalets Francais (Me girls), Dixie camps (Ga sep),[345] Hitaga (Iowa CFG), and Kitanniwa. James Lyman Molloy of County Kings, Ireland, and Graham Clifton Bingham of Bristol, England, based "Just a song of twilight" on an Irish folk song in 1888.

Some camps have sung "Abide with me, fast falls the eventide" (5). Scots-born Henry Francis Lyte introduced the hymn in his 1847 farewell sermon. William Henry Monk created a new setting, "Eventide," for *Hymns Ancient and Modern* in 1861. Both were high Anglicans.

Water

Water is treated as a symbol in "Across the Stillness of the Lake" (30), "A Canoe May Be Drifting" (10), "Dark Brown Is the River" (28), and "Peace, I Ask of Thee O River" (88). Manakiki (Minn agency coed) sings "peace on the river." Aloha Hive (Vt girls) has localized it to "Peace I Ask of Thee O Mountain." Hitaga has modified the first to "the stream" and "silv'ry echoes beam."

Tobitt said "Peace" was written in 1941 on the Kentucky River by Viola Wood and Glendora Gosling.[173] Eleanor Thomas* later added, it was during a Girl Scout staff training session on a river boat. Gosling (1908-1999) was from Cincinnati, Ohio, and graduated from the University of Michigan in 1933 where she was active in the Women's Athletic Association. She stayed involved with the alumni organization in Saint Clair, Michigan, after she married Frank George Miller.

A Montana Camp Fire camp adopted "Harbor Lights" for "We'll Sing to Watanopa." Hugh Williams and Jimmy Kennedy wrote the original. Williams was born Wilhelm Grosz. The Jew left Berlin in

1933 when Nazi's took power, then abandoned Vienna in 1934. Kennedy* was raised in County Tyrone in Northern Ireland.

Friendship

A promise of ideal friendships was intimated in Rogers's description of the opening night camp fire at Sebago-Wohelo (Me girls):

> And the songs, with the smoldering firelight and the lengthening shadows, whispered to those who understood of a time when the camp had been one at heart, and gave promise of happy days before them, when this should again be true, and the spirits of all gathered in this new circle should be blended into a complete union of comradeship and love.[147:44]

It is perpetuated in songs like "Make New Friends" (68) and "I want to be a friend of yours, mmm, and a little bit more" (11). Shawnee (Mo CFG) has a third verse to the Swedish "Who Can Sail" (14) that begins "Sorrow sings sadness all day."

Songs like "Let Us Sing Together" (34) become acts of reification when they describe friends singing at camp fires, preferably held at twilight at the water's edge, in hopes the act of singing will consummate the friendships. The theme is particularly interesting to organizations who hope to create loyalty to themselves. Camp Fire promotes "Sing Blue Birds Sing" (8). Girl Scouts have "Sing, Sing, Sing, Come My Friends" (7). Boy Scouts use "Sing Along, Oh Sing Along" (20).

Georgana Falb combined sunset, singing, and the camp fire in a 1945 Hitaga (Iowa CFG) song that began:

> Sun now has melted
> The camp is at rest
> We'll sing 'round our camp fire
> The songs we love the best

Return to Camp

While camps, as institutions, have incentives in instilling senses of place, campers independently choose to sing about leaving camp, camp friends, and the desire to return. Among the more familiar are "Mmm I Want To Linger" (47), "Remember" (64), "Aloha means we welcome you" (15), and "Picture Spot" (15), or "place of beauty rare."

Sealth* (Wash CFG) included several in its 1969 songbook published by CRS. The Rohrboughs first learned "Spot" from a 4-H camp. Haruko Yabusaki (1921-1991) provided their version of "Aloha." She majored in physical education at the University of Hawaii where she was active in the YWCA. She later worked for Honolulu's Parks and Recreation department.

"Aloha means" is not the same as "Aloha Oe" (6). That was written by Lili'uokalani, the last queen of the islands. Her Prussian-trained band director, Heinrich August Wilhelm Berger, created the orchestration. Boy Scouts* included Stephen Fay's English text in a 1920 collection. Jay Makoto Taniguchi sang it with harmony at Homelani (Hawaii P coed) in 1976. Kamaji (Minn girls) and Watanopa (Mont CFG) have local songs to the melody.

"Aloha means" was written at Aloha Hive, according to Eleanor Crow. Luther Halsey Gulick's brother, Edward Leeds Gulick (1862-1931) founded the Vermont girls' camp. Their parents and grandparents were Presbyterian missionaries in Hawaii, although Edward became a Congregational minister. Crow says, there still are "numerous grass skirts in the costume room."

Edward's wife, the former Harriet Marie Farnsworth (1864-1951), was the sister of the Farnsworth who founded Hanoum. The siblings were born in Turkey to Congregational missionaries. He collaborated with Sharp on the collection that introduced "The Keeper" (33) to America.[506] She graduated from Wellesley.

Anne Lutz has always considered "Old father time's a crafty man" (18) to be a Vassar song. Martha Alter (1904-1976) arranged the version in their college song book for "the glee club." She graduated in 1925, and became a classical composer. The "Year Song" (13), which begins "19-- no other year the same," is written to "Bobolink," according to Mildred Roe.[219]

Lullabies

After the last night's closing fire, many camps have serenades. Girls' camps often use lullabies like the Welsh "All through the Night" (20), the Appalachian "Hush Little Baby" (8), and the Mexican-American "At the Gate of Heaven" (14) and "Little Owlet" (23). Young women also sing "Louisiana Lullaby" (6), the "Lu-lu-lullaby" round (8), and "Slumber My Pretty One" (9).

Eleanor Farjeon wrote "Walk, Shepherdess Walk" (46) for *Nursery Rhymes of London Town* in 1916. She added music in 1919. Earlier, "Little papoose, my sunlight butterfly" (4) was sung. It had been composed in 1910 by Josephine Sherwood, a Radcliffe graduate. She adopted the name Josephine Hull when she began appearing in films where she won an Oscar in 1950.

Serenades have their origins in college singing traditions. Lantern Nights developed from ceremonies greeting new students. Bryn Mawr held its first in 1886. University of Michigan formalized the rite in 1915. These turned into formal sings, and then into serenades. *Songs of Lake Erie*, published in 1918, included the song used for the 1917 Senior Serenade. A 1923 Mount Holyoke song book implied serenades began there in 1920.

Fraternities at Michigan State in the 1960s still were staging candle-lit serenades outside dormitories or sorority houses of members' sweethearts who were newly pinned or engaged. When boys' camps incorporate the musical tradition, they are more likely to use songs associated with barbershop quartets.

Fairies

Lullabies reinforce an interest in fairies and other little people. Andrew Lang began publishing his color-titled collections of fairytale books in 1889, a year before Frazier. Rose Fyleman sent poems to *Punch* about fairy folk in the 1920s. Marie Gaudette (RI GS) set one, "Fairies Have Never a Penny To Spend" (3), to music.

Neidlinger's "Boating Song" (18), with "Ho! Good fairies, hearken to our call," was composed in three-part harmony. Adahi (Penna CFG) and Nancy Bryant (Ohio CFG) know a song that personifies fireflies as "lanterns of fairy folk." Joy Dunn described stars as "peeping through the fairies in the meadows" in a 1938 Namanu (Ore

CFG) song. A 1943 Hitaga (Iowa CFG) lyric had the line, "Friendship is gold, gold only fairies can build."

In the 1880s, Québec-born Palmer Cox began publishing his brownie stories, which drew upon Celtic mythology. When young girls in England refused to be called Rosebuds, Baden-Powell dubbed them Brownies in 1915.

The use of children's literature and folklore, ostensibly to amuse young people, may serve another function. It lets adolescents and young adults maintain ties with childhood pleasures through the guise of sharing them with those younger than themselves.

Moon

Songs containing anthropomorphic images of the night, especially the moon, are common on serenades. "Bed is too small for my tiredness" (30) ends with the line, "Lord, blow the moon out please." Although standardized for Girl Scouts by Thomas[*] in 1956, the Student Christian Foundation was teaching it at Michigan State in 1947, according to Mary Robinson.[S] Margaret Rinehart[S] collected it from a Missouri camp in 1951. Martha Jackson Stocker[S] heard it at Deer Trails (Mich GS) in 1952.

Mary Lang (Mich YWCA) sings "bed is too hard." Lisa McCabe (Calif GS) knows "too short." "Tiredness" is sung "tired head" at Mawavi (DC CFG) and Watervliet (Mich girls). The phrase, "a hill topped with trees," is sung "hillsides of trees" in the D.C. Camp Fire camp located in Virginia. The Michigan girls' camp knows "hilltop with trees." Hidden Valley (Md CFG) uses "hill soft with trees."

Other moon songs include "Baby's boat's a silver star" (19), "I See the Moon" (20), "Wee Baby Moon" (11), and "When the moon plays peek-a-boo" (6). Joan Fulton[S] collected a version of the second from Wasewagan (Calif CFG). She noted, it "had a somewhat different tune and most of the words were different" from one written by Meredith Willson in 1953 and recorded by the Mariners. "Mammy Moon" (9) was conceived as an harmonic arrangement by Neidlinger, but since has been dropped by most Camp Fire camps.

Among adapted commercial songs with this anthropomorphic theme are "Blue Moon" (3) at Skyland (NC girls), and "By the Light of the Silvery Moon" (2) at Tawakani (Ida CFG) and by Denver Scouts (Colo BSA). An Idaho Camp Fire camp uses "Moon over

Miami" for "Moon over Neewahlu, hearts beat as one / Gay days together underneath the sun."

"Blue Moon" was written in 1934 by Richard Rodgers and Lorenz Hart. Joe Burke and Edgar Leslie composed the second in 1935. Gus Edwards and Edward Madden published the last in 1909.

Dreams and Visions

Dreaming and wishing is another theme that embellishes serenades and other last night ceremonies. Vivian Sexton (Tex CFG) has sung "Camp of My Dreams" (3) to "Girl of My Dreams." Tawakani (Ida CFG) has sung "I'll Make a Wish Dear" to "I Had a Dream." Gene Austin introduced "Girl" in 1928. It became more famous when it was sung by Gene Autry in a 1939 film, *South of the Border*. The Mills Brothers introduced "You Tell Me Your Dream, I'll Tell You Mine" in 1931.

"Just a Dream of You" (2) has been used at Hitaga (Iowa CFG), and sung with the original words at Cohila (Calif CFG) and at Shawondasee (Tex CFG), according to Vivian Sexton. Charles F. McNamara first copyrighted it in 1910. The composer, Frank Henri Klickmann, was the son of a German immigrant in Chicago.

Nat Collins and Marty Hixson used "When You Grow Too Old To Dream" (2) for a Namanu (Ore CFG) song in 1959. The original, by Sigmund Romberg and Oscar Hammerstein II, was heard in the 1935 film, *The Night Is Young*. That, in turn, was based on Romberg's 1924 operetta, *The Student Prince*. Hammerstein was the New York-born grandson of a German Jewish immigrant. Romberg was a Hungarian Jew who studied in Vienna before migrating in 1909.

Love Songs

A focus on camp friendships and on children in lullabies does not lead to an interest in dating relationships. The only songs addressing real concerns of adolescents are comic verses that treat loneliness in courtship lightly. In "Oyster Stew" (12), a young girl goes to the junior prom "alone tee hee alone" where she sits next to the chaperone. She hopes someone will wink at her so, in Zanika Lache's (Wash CFG) version, "And then you'll see, that I'll not be / Alone, tee hee, all alone."

"I'm a Little Acorn Brown" (18) has a young woman call herself "just to hear my golden tone." She asks herself for a movie date where she gets "so fresh I slapped my face." Viki Irene Cuqua (Ariz YWCA) has sung the second as a verse to "Boom Boom" (33). Withers* published it as a separate rhyme. A young man could sing it as easily.

This scarcity does not mean love songs are not known. In the past, many were international ones describing joyous courtship, like the Ukrainian "Boat upon the Water" (2). Augusta (Calif CFG) and Watanopa (Mont CFG) knew it in the 1930s and 1940s. A few, like "Marianina" (11), fantasized a romance yet to begin. Still others dealt with separation or unrequited love, like "Silver Moon Is Shining" (17) and "Holla Hi" (14). Peter Kunkel translated the last.

Some sentimental commercial songs have been sung, including "I Want a Girl" (10), "I Know Where I'm Going" (5), and "Good Night Beloved" (5). Harry von Tilzer and William Dillon composed the first in 1911. The Weavers recorded the second. The last is from Vincent Písek's *22 Bohemian Folk Songs* of 1912. Anne Faulkner Oberndorfer included it in a music-training book, *What We Hear in Music*, she wrote for Victor Talking Machine Company in 1921.

More often, commercial songs' emotions are turned toward camps. "Pale Moon," a 1920 love song, is used for Watanopa's (Mont CFG) "Woodland Ways," and a Red Wing (Penna girls) song. Namanu (Ore CFG) has adapted "That Sweetheart of Mine" and "Dearie." Clare Beecher Kummer composed the last in 1905 for Sallie Fisher in *Sargent Blue*.

"Margie," introduced in 1921 by Eddie Cantor, has been used for a Tanadoona (Minn CFG) song, and for "Our Camp" (1), according to Vivian Sexton (Tex CFG). "Sweetheart of Sigma Chi" has been adopted at Tawakani (Ida CFG) and Shawondasee (Tex CFG). Byron Douglas Stokes and Frank Dudleigh Vernor wrote it in 1911 while they were students at the Methodist Albion College. They were referring to the fraternity, not to a woman.

"Tell Me Why" (78) and "Wisdom" (32) both contain the words "when God gave me you" that sound like traditional love songs. Like "Sigma Chi," both easily can refer to a camp or group. The first is taught to Brownies in Ohio, according to Carol Simon.§ Les Chalets Francais (Me girls) substitutes the camp name in their French version. It was recorded in 1951 by the Four Aces, one of the first Italian male quartets to emerge from South Philadelphia.

Carol Parsons Sievert associates "Wisdom" (32) with the Pi Beta Phi sorority. Jean Mayo McLaughlin (Fla GS) says, it "was *definitely* an 'organizational' song used in connection with GS promise and laws." Gary Flegal says, he learned it in school choir. Heather MacPhail[§] collected a version in 1952 from Hidden Lake (NY GS). Harmony has been used with it by Jayne Garrison (Mo CFG), Nellie Mae Hastings (Ill GS), and a friend of William Daniel Doebler.[§]

Some commercial tunes used for camp songs combine several themes. Love and place are found in James Frederick Hanley's "Just a Cottage Small" from 1925, and in Adam Geibel and Richard Henry Buck's "Kentucky Babe" (2) from 1896. "Sweet and Low" (4) uses nature, separated lovers, eventide, and a lullaby. Tanadoona (Minn CFG) has adapted all three. Bing Crosby recorded "Kentucky" with Fred Waring and his Glee Club in 1947. Alfred Tennyson wrote the words for the last in 1850, Joseph Barnby the music in 1863.

Case Study Repertoire

Melodies of the six pretty songs in the case studies share many characteristics with fun songs, but have some unique traits that may be age or gender related. Most of the nineteen use conventions of modern western music, including seven-note scales. "I Wish I Were," "Kookaburra," "Pep," "Rose," and "Skyball Paint" use six notes. "A Bear," "Boatmen," "Grand Old Duke of York," and "Eskimo Hunt" use five.

Many are written in the three simplest keys. Five have no sharps or flats ("Canoe," "Boatmen," "Flicker," "Rise," "Rose"). Four have one flat ("The Cuckoo," "Eskimo Hunt," "Kookaburra," "Pep"). Two have one sharp ("Ash Grove," "Lollypop").

"The Mermaid" has two flats. "A Bear" and "Kumbaya" have two sharps. "Duke" and "I Wish" are transcribed with three sharps. "Skyball Paint" has four. One, "Sailing," has no set sharps or flats, but introduces an accidental.

Accidentals, variations in the use of black keys from expectations set by a piano's key signature, are one element that separates pretty songs and commercial ones from the rest of the case-study repertoire. Three pretty songs use them, "Ash Grove," "Flicker," and "Witchcraft." "Canoe," "Kumbaya," and "Rose" do not.

All the songs written to commercial tunes from the past two centuries have retained their accidentals: "A Bear" to "Sippin' Cider," "Lollypop" to "Harrigan," "Swimming" to "Sailing, Sailing." Accidentals also are employed by the only newer commercial song, "Skyball Paint." "Boatmen," the other tune composed by a professional, is a fun song with no unpredicted sounds.

The reason the chromatic scale is restricted to pretty songs is children in the early elementary grades have difficulty with melodies utilizing half steps. This usually improves by the time they are ten, according to Orpha Kay Duell* and Richard Chase Anderson.

Regardless of the scale or key, the most common note found in eight songs is the orchestra's A. This is followed by G, one step down in the scale, used by four songs, and B, one step up, used by three. E, dominant in three songs, is one-and-a-half steps away from G. Upper C (used by two) is a half step apart from B. One song is centered on F.

While this sounds obscure, it simply means a child mostly sings one of six notes in the central to upper-central part of his or her vocal range. When boys or girls are speaking, their range is from A below middle C to middle C. When they sing unguardedly, their range is between middle C and upper C. To stimulate singing, rather than chanting, music educators suggest a song's first note should not be lower than F. Members of trained children's choirs can reach A below middle C, and F above upper C.[496]

Scientists test the ability of people to detect pitch by playing random pairs of pure tones and asking which is higher or lower. They find consistently correct identifications for tones below middle C, but the error rate rises dramatically between middle C and upper C, the range exploited by most songs.

The second most commonly found tone in eleven songs is below the first, including "Canoe," "Flicker," and "Witchcraft." In three songs ("I Wish," "Kookaburra," and "Kumbaya"), two tones are equally important. This would mean melodies of fourteen songs go into the safer, lower part of the tonal range.

Thomas Franklin Vance* detected a statistical variance in his tests showing women performed better when the second tone was higher than the first, but no pattern for men. He was not sure if the cause was biology, experience, training, or a better ability of men in 1914 to intuit the testing protocol and provide expected answers.

The only songs whose second most likely note is higher, and therefore slightly riskier, include a few pretty ones ("Ash Grove" and "Rose"), and the commercial song performed by Girls of the Golden West ("Skyball Paint"). Two fun songs, "Grand Old Duke of York" and "Rise and Shine," toy with the words "up" and "rise."

Some songs with downward contours begin a few phrases with the notes of a chord sung in ascending order. This is prominent in three pretty songs, "Ash Grove," "Canoe," and "Kumbaya." An opening arpeggio is used humorously in the introduction to the chorus of "The Cuckoo."

Even though individuals prefer using the central part of their vocal ranges and suspect dangers lurk in the upper part, more songs rise above upper C than go below middle C. This is probably because young children are more comfortable with their upper registers. Since their ability to detect pitch does not completely mature until they are around age twelve, the ease of getting close to a note is more important to them than accuracy.

General fun songs that employ notes in the upper range include "Duke" with a high D, and "The Boatmen" and "I Wish" with high E's. "Kookaburra" and "The Mermaid" have high F's. The others that venture above upper C are pretty songs or ones written to commercial tunes. "Lollypop" and "Witchcraft" use the high D. "Ash Grove," "Canoe," "Rose," and "Swimming" reach an high E.

The only fun song to use a low note is the opening part of the chorus of "The Cuckoo," which goes down to the lower A. "Skyball Paint" drops to a low B. "Witchcraft," reaches the low A.

Case Study: Witchcraft

"Witchcraft" (81) is one of the few camp-centered pretty songs noticed by folklorists. Linda Weaver included it in her 1974 *North Carolina Folklore* article, "Camp Songs: Reflections of Youth." Her version came from Betty Hastings. The North Carolina YWCA camp began allowing Black girls to attend in the early 1950s.

Margarett Snyder composed the song in 1935 for a girls' camp, probably the Y's Maria Olbrich (Wisc YWCA) on Lake Mendota near Madison, Wisconsin. The song entered sorority tradition early. Kappa Kappa Gamma[†] published a version in 1945, two years after the Y.[†]

Kalamazoo's Girl Reserves[†] (Mich YWCA) already had included it in their 1938 songbook. Boy Scouts[†] published it in 1939. Jean Hamilton[§] collected a version from a New York camp in 1944. Jan Goldsberry[§] heard it at Tannadoonah (Ind CFG) in 1948.

Snyder[*] graduated from the University of Wisconsin's conservatory in 1931, where she accompanied the glee club. In the middle 1930s, she led glee clubs for the Y, where she worked as director for the business, industrial and music group, and for the BPW. She also was active in those years as a piano accompanist and organ soloist.

She organized the Dane County Homemakers club chorus in 1949 for the state agricultural extension office, where she worked as a music supervisor in rural schools. Later, she helped run a Madison gourmet grocery, and gave private piano lessons.

In 1956, Snyder helped organize the Madison alumnae chapter of the Sigma Alpha Iota music honorary. She continued playing organ for the Plymouth Congregational Church until her death in 1961. Her estate went to the ΣAI loan fund for university music students, and is now a scholarship administered by The University of Wisconsin Foundation. Her photograph appears in "Composers."

Explication

The poem is constructed on binary oppositions. One is conflicting desires to leave camp for the wilderness (the trail) and to return (the camp fire). The second opposition is between witchcraft, the realm of gypsies and magic, and the everyday world of school and work. Within the "real world," there is a third opposition between one's normal time and the time one spends daydreaming. A fourth is implied: the specialness of camp and the predictability of town.

Textual Variation

"Witchcraft" is reprinted widely in Camp Fire and YWCA song books. The only variation is between singing "winding trail" or "winding road" in the second line. Some groups put their organization name in the last line, but most use the camp name.

Music

The tune and harmonies are typical of those created by individuals exposed to art song in camping's early years. Unlike many songs, it begins with a descent in the scale, using chromatic half steps. A minor feel is maintained, which makes it easy for singers to lose the melody. Virginia Lytle (Penna GS) says she can sing it, "if someone starts it for me." Susan Wells says, at Tawanka (Mich CFG), just the staff sings it at the wishing fire. Joann Brisler says, "only the nuns know it" at Marycrest (Vt C girls).

Aural learning has modified the tune. Certain sections, like "a winding" or "memories that linger," seem difficult, and vary from camp to camp. Other parts, like "road that beckons" or "constant and true," are more stable. They anchor variants to the original melody. Most camps sing "true" with melisma, rather than the single note that has been published.

Popularity

Snyder's song is known in all types of girls' camps in the survey Midwest, and in Camp Fire camps outside the five-state region. Few individuals in coed or all boys' camps in 1976 recognized it.

When Naomi Feldman[s] and Mary Rogers mentioned an old song list to their friends, which included "good stuff we don't sing any more," one immediately volunteered, "Like 'Witchcraft'." Another added, "'Witchcraft' I haven't heard 'Witchcraft' in years." Lavonne Shull said, it was a 4-H camp song in Elkart County, Indiana, in the 1940s. She was surprised to learn others knew it. At the time, she assumed they were copycats.

Version A

Text from Polly McIntyre, Camp Kitanniwa (Mich CFG), late 1950s; transcribed February 1975. Guitar chords from Carol Parsons Sievert, Camp Kitanniwa (Mich CFG), 1934-1942. Polly's photograph appears in "Coming of Age." Carol's is in "Kitanniwa, 1974."

If there were witch (D) craft, I'd made two wi (A7) shes;
A winding trail that beckons me to roam, (D)
And then I'd wish (D) for a blazing camp (A7) fire
To welcome me when I'm returning home.

But in this real (D) world (D) there is no witch (G) craft (G)
And golden wi (A) shes (A) do not grow on trees (D)
Our fondest day (D) dreams (D) must be the ma (G) gic (G)
To welcome back (A) those (A) happy memories.
Mem (G) ories that ling (D) er (D), con (A) stant (A) and true (D)
Bring (G) back sweet vi (D) sions, my Kitanniwa, (A) of you (D)

Version B

Text from Camp Manakiki (Minn agency coed), 1970s; variations from A emphasized. Guitar chords from Ann Beardsley, Camp o' the Hills (Mich GS), 1963-1970; Camp Ken-Jockety (Ohio GS), 1976.

If there were witch (C) craft, I'd made two wi (G7) shes
A winding **road** that beckons me to roam,
And then I'd wish for a (C) blazing campfire,
To (G7) welcome me when I'm returning home.

But (F) in this real (C) world there (G7) is no witch (C) craft,
And (F) golden (C) wishes do (G7) not grow on trees, (C)
Our fondest daydreams must be the magic,
To bring us back **these** happy memories.
Mem'ries that linger, constant and true,
Mem'ries we cherish, mem'ries of you

PHOTOGRAPHS

Coming of Age in Camp

Coming of Age in Camp

Right: 1953, age 9. I came by myself and took pictures of other girls, long forgotten. I am on the left. One of the cabins where we slept is in back.

Below: 1954, age 10. I came with a friend (right) who hated camp. The difference between town and camp was apparent in how we dressed the first day.

The next summer, I came with another friend who also did not like it.

After that, I came alone. The picture of He Bani Gani shows this transition period.

The following pages show the group that began coalescing in 1957.

Seven of the original 15 became CITs in 1960: Jean, Leslie, Marti, Pam, Pat, Sandra, and me. Lea also was accepted into the program, along with four new girls. I dropped out the next year and lost touch.

I know Leslie and Marti were counselors in 1962. Jean worked on the waterfront in 1962 and 1963.

Above: 1956, age 12. Overnight at High Banks Creek, Libby, Ship Titanic counselor, unknown, Judy, Jean, counselors. A counselor has no socks.

Below: 1957, age 13. Cabin group dressed for dinner in navy and white. Row 1: Leslie, Ann, Liz, Libby, Cathy. Row 2: Carol, Pat, Kathy.

1958 senior unit, age 14.

Left, clockwise from top: Jean, Pam, me, Marti, Sandra.

Below, Row 1: Leslie, Wanda, Cathy. Row 2: Polly McIntyre, Ann, Liz.

Sailor caps (across) were introduced by waterfront counselors, then spread to other counselors, then to us.

Polly provided versions for four case study songs.

Above: 1959 senior unit, session 1, age 15. Row 1: Leslie, Sandra, Ann, Liz, counselor. Row 2: Lea, Pat, Polly McIntyre, Pam.

Below: 1959 senior unit, session 2. Lakeview group, me, Lakeview group, Leslie, Sandi. The framed tents were screened with wooden floors.

1959 senior unit, session 2, ages 15 (us) and 14 (Lakeview group).

Above: Lakeview group, Ginger Hastings (Lakeview), Marti, Lakeview group; Pam at bottom. Ginger wrote the dedication poem.

Below: Rest of Lakeview, Michigan, group.

CITs

Counselors-in-training, or in some camps junior counselors, are the "I wanna be" for young campers. Everywhere, ties mark their status.

Above: Glen CITs, 1973. Hair is longer and clothing functional at the Ohio Camp Fire Girls camp.

Below: Glen staff reunion, 1995. Nancy Bryant, director in 1974, is behind the "MP." Rebecca Quinlan, CIT counselor in 1973, is behind the "LE." Ann is fourth from left above, and at the far left rear below. Deb is fourth from right above, and standing at the far right below.

Staff

Gary Flegal came of age in
Michigan's coed Van Buren Youth
Camp. He was a camper, junior
counselor, and counselor.

Charlotte Duff was a physical
education teacher who began
camping as a counselor, then
director at private girls' camps.
She worked at Wisconsin's Joy
Camps, Michigan's Chippewa
Trail, and Maine's Wabanaki.

He took classes from her at Albion
College, where she coached field
hockey. He is now a magician.

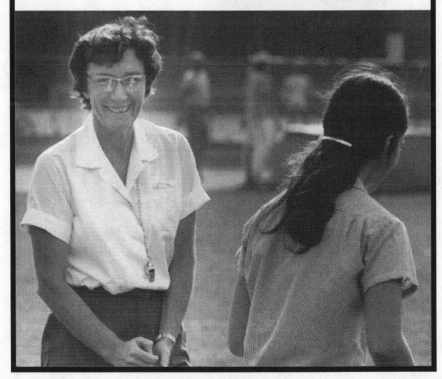

Singers

Patricia Ann Hall, above left, when she was going to Celio, 1960s. Ira Sheldon Posen at Interlochen, 1962. June Rushing Leibfarth, far left bottom, at the 1964 Girl Scout national encampment. Both Patty and Shelley are professional musicians.

SECTION IV

Gender Influences
on Repertoire

Gender Influences on Repertoire

Boys and girls generally share the same species imperatives for development in elementary and early middle schools. Their needs diverge with the onset of adolescence. Hormonal changes begin to differentiate them. Coed and single-sex camps have different coming-of-age experiences.

Variations in musical taste attributable to developmental changes in boys and girls have been mentioned, as I found evidence for their existence. The only challenge has been writers, like Piaget and Gesell, who use male pronouns to refer both to boys and to generic groups. Whenever authors do not make clear they are discussing males, one has to parse their texts carefully for intent.

Coed Camp Problems

Coed camp directors, especially in the years before oral contraceptives became available, had to ensure girls left camp in the same condition they arrived. This was no small task in the 4-H camp sessions I attended. However, problems were not unique to camps. Other events that brought older members into dormitory situations faced similar challenges. Sidney Vincent* remembered staff members at Wise (Ohio J coed) in the 1930s divided their time between young campers in the day and evening rendezvous on the cliffs.

Helen Hill Miller,* author of "Follow the Gleam" (14), admitted other problems could arise. She was surprised she was selected as a Bryn Mawr delegate to the 1920 YWCA conference at Silver Bay, New York, until she heard about the song-writing contest. She did not share the enthusiasms of many of her co-delegates, and "became more and more disgruntled at the sloppy sentiment that infected the meetings."

When "one of the main speakers took me for a walk by the lake and told me my eyes were like his wife's before she got fat, I announced my departure by the next morning's boat." During the night, the young women tasked with writing her college's entry in the song contest woke her for help.

> Suitably outraged, I said, "All right. I'll write you something that will just fit the prevalent mood.["] And between then and the time the boat left, I provided it. I went to NY, took the 20th Century [train] home.

She was not free. The song was so successful, she continually received letters from people who took the lyrics seriously, especially "some of the clergy who have written me over the years when in the course of preparing a collection of hymns." She finally wrote a letter for the file of her college alumnae association to shield herself.

Boys' Camp Problems

Attitudes toward sexual orientation in single-sex camps vary with the sponsoring organization. American Boy Scout leaders have made themselves infamous in the early twenty-first century for their censorious attitude toward homosexuals. As an organization, it has evinced the strongest need for obedience from its members.

Its founders were progressive reformers still enthralled by The Leatherstocking Tales, published by James Fenimore Cooper between 1823 and 1841. After Seton began publicizing his Woodcraft League of Indians in 1902, Daniel Carter Beard (1850-1941) and his sister, Mary Caroline, created Sons of Daniel Boone in 1905.

Seton stressed camping and nature studies. His parents had migrated to Ontario from Durham, in northeastern England, when he was six. He grew up in Toronto where his father, a failed ship owner, worked as an accountant. As a child, he explored the local woods to escape abuse at home. He did not discover frontier life until the 1880s when he moved to Manitoba.

After the first *Birch Bark Roll*,[*] he seriously began studying Northern Plains Native life. Before he published *The Book of Woodcraft and Indian Lore*[*] in 1912, he had the manuscript reviewed by Charles Eastman (1858-1939) and George Bird Grinnell. Eastman, better known as Ohiyesa, was a Santee Sioux physician and activist. The editor of *Forest and Stream* had been with the Pawnee on their last hunt in 1872. At the time he read Seton's work, Grinnell was preparing his own study of *The Fighting Cheyenes*.

Beard featured wood craft and wilderness survival. He was born in Cincinnati, Ohio, where his father, James Henry Beard, was a portrait painter. As a boy, he prowled the river banks. When he was at school in Covington, Kentucky, he absorbed tales of frontier life. In 1887, he and his older brother, James Carter Beard, bought land in Pennsylvania's Pocono mountains on Lake Teedyuskung for hunting and fishing. Erie Railroad had served the area since 1849.

Scout organizers hoped to meld the two men's programs into the one developed by Baden-Powell. In 1910, Beard was made National Scout Commissioner and Seton Chief Scout. Neither was interested in running the organization. The man hired in their places was not sympathetic to either. James Edward West (1876-1948) had lost his parents as a boy, then suffered from tuberculosis in the Washington, D.C., City Orphan Asylum where he was reared. As a lawyer, he spent his early career working for Theodore Roosevelt's War Department, the YMCA, and the Boys' Brigade.

West essentially thought like a businessman. Scouting was a product. His first challenge was establishing proprietary rights over anyone making private experiments, including the Girl Scouts. Juliette Gordon Low (1860-1927) had introduced the Girl Guides to Savannah, Georgia, in 1912 with support from Baden-Powell.

In 1916, West successfully lobbied congress for exclusive use of the symbols of Scouting. In return, he agreed one had to be an American citizen to be a member. He also enforced the military policy he had adopted the year before.

Seton was the first victim. He had written "there is no military meaning attached to the name Scouting" in the 1910 Boy Scout manual.[125:50] When pressed, he refused to renounce his Canadian citizenship. They excised his contributions from the next edition. He worked with Statten at Ahmek (Ont boys), then moved to the Sangre de Cristo foothills south of Santa Fé, New Mexico. He continued writing nature tales and illustrating them with his own drawings.

Beard, also a friend of Roosevelt, established a woodcraft department at Indiana's Culver Military Academy in 1911. In 1915, he left to open a private camp, the Dan Beard Outdoor School (Penna boys). He maintained an agreement with the local BSA council to recognize boys' achievements, but he kept control of the program and land. It became brother to Teedy-Usk-Ung (Penna girls), the camp Sally Ann Brockley Parr attended.

Forsaking these men and his original YMCA supporters, West sought new ways to expand the Scout program at minimal expense. In 1918, he began working with churches to transfer burdens of local troop organization to them. In exchange, he allowed congregations to use local standards for membership. Then, it meant condoning segregation. Now, it means placating conservative religious leaders.

Finally, he found the most cost effective way to provide wilderness experiences with the least responsibility for administrative liabilities. Beginning in 1926, he promoted troop camping. Councils provided safe sites. Troops themselves, each of those churches and other community groups, supplied the necessary manpower to work with campers. This eliminated all the distancing mechanisms and sinews of group continuity that enforce codes of acceptable behavior in traditional and progressive camps.

When one talks to former Scouts or reads student folklore collections, one often finds older campers who became disillusioned when they were brought closer to the bureaucracy. Their term may cover a great many offences. More occasional campers, the ones who go once or twice with their troop, very often are the ones who remember hazing behavior or dirty jokes.

Because former Scouts mentioned such incidents so often, I asked women if they had similar recollections. Generally, and this was in the middle 1970s, they recognized the drift of my questions. Several said they sometimes wondered, but never could recall anything concrete.

I should add, I only asked these questions in an extended interview when the person I was talking with had grown comfortable. Many were older than I, which meant they were in their forties or older. One was in her seventies.

The reason they wondered was not that they had noticed anything. In those years, women who supported same-sex organizations always were under suspicion of deviancy. They were intelligent enough to consider questions raised by others.

Cultural Perceptions

Erik Erikson recognized that, while the psychological development stages and terms defined by Freud were useful, they obscured differences between adolescents, young adults, and mature adults. He suggested each faced unique, age-related challenges. Acceptance by an in-group was very much a concern of adolescence.[322:262] A desire for intimacy concerned college-aged individuals.[322:263]

If one changes the lens from Freudian sexuality to Erikson gender, one can see many incidents described by male campers are actually group initiation rituals. Concerns with acceptance may have been as important to campers as demonstrating masculinity. We simply interpret them from a Freudian view, because that is the way our culture conditions us to think about men.

These platitudes reflect deep, often unexplored currents. When Gulick was addressing the first organizational meeting for the Camp Fire Girls, he said:

> This is my first point:—that there is a fundamental difference, and to copy the Boy Scout movement would be utterly and fundamentally evil, and would probably produce ultimately a moral and psychological involution which is the last thing in the world that we any of us want. We hate manly women and womanly men, but we all do love to have a woman who is thoroughly womanly, and then adds to that a splendid ability of service to the state.[141:22]

His solution was a compromise that allowed girls some independence within their traditional roles: camping centered on the hearth, "the domestic fire—not the wild fire."[141:22]

Camp Fire never had the drive for organizational hegemony found in the Boy Scouts and Girl Scouts. Individual members were freer to choose what mattered. In my home town in the 1950s, none of us had heard of Gulick. Most only gave a token nod to the organization. We passed the first three ranks to maintain our membership in friendship groups. We earned beads to make decorative designs on boleros, like those in the photograph of He Bani Gani. If anything, we probably found most of it slightly silly or a little embarrassing.

ICIA AVERILL

Even as a ten-year-old looking through the manual for the first time, I found it hard to believe anyone would have me sing:

> Wohelo for aye
> Wohelo for aye
> Wohelo, wohelo
> Wohelo for aye
>
> Wohelo for work
> Wohelo for health
> Wohelo, wohelo
> Wohelo for love

I took that song, remembered by 18 people or camps, as a sign of organizational ineptitude. An equally inane 4-H equivalent was easier to sing. At least they found a melody:

> I'm looking over a 4-H clover I overlooked before
> The first is for head, the second for heart
> Third is for hands that are doing their part
> No need explaining the one remaining
> It's health that we're striving for
> I'm looking over a 4-H clover I overlooked before

Its four-fold philosophy is an example of a YMCA idea that filtered through Seton. Y's usually organized four departments: educational, social, religious, and physical. Seton made it: the beauty way, the service way, the spirit way, and the body way. William Henry Danforth (1870-1955) made it mental, social, religious, and physical at Miniwanca (Mich P sep), a camp he established in southwestern Michigan in 1924. When the Gulicks adopted the ideas of Seton, they dropped the notion of intelligence for girls. That is why Camp Fire only has three keys to its motto.

One irony is the Scouts, who stress rugged individualism and prepare young boys for success in Darwinian corporations, were founded by a committee. Camp Fire Girls and Girl Scouts, who put young women into situations where they must subsume themselves into family-like groups, were founded by strong individuals, albeit ones with very different temperaments. In the early years, one called adult leaders Guardians, the other Commissioners and Officers.

Boys' Camp Rituals

Philadelphia organized the first formal Boy Scout camp, Treasure Island (Penna BSA), in 1913. Two years later, Edward Urner Goodman (1891-1980) and Carroll Andrew Edson (1891-1986) introduced Order of the Arrow. In its early years, the honor society was attacked as a secret organization. Some critics, including those recently released from the military, believed the only valid male peer group was one that arose when men faced danger or physical adversity. In one sense, the conflict was between men who had gone to elite schools with fraternities and boys from poorer families who had had to scrabble for opportunities.

Some responded by trying to convert the order into a middle-class service organization in the mode of groups, like Rotary and Kiwanis, that often served as sponsors. Others sought to turn the rituals into academic extensions of Seton's interest in life outdoors. High-school-aged members became so dedicated to performing Native dances and songs correctly, they attracted support from men like Ohiyesa.

Woody Crumbo (1912-1989) was a Potawatomi painter and musician who worked with Scouts in the Taos Pueblo of New Mexico and the Koshare Indian Dancers in La Junta, Colorado. The last are members of Troop 232.

When existing ceremonies of acceptance have been diverted to other ends, boys have responded with new rituals. Gene Clough says, Cherry Valley (Calif BSA) "has an 'honor society' for veteran campers called the 'Tribe of Torqua' and 'initiation' into the various degrees follows the Camp Fire the last night." Charla Calderhead[§] was told of a similar ritual in an Ohio Boy Scout camp where:

> Every year you had to accomplish certain things, and then on Friday night there was a ceremony, if you passed. On Friday's we'd go through an Indian ceremony. Go to a campfire and sit with 50-75 guys who all had passed. Then an Indian came dancing out to the fire. He told us a little story, and then went back into the dark. We're

just sitting there and then these braves (older guys in costumes) came running out of the woods with flares in their hands, and grabbed us all and we got into a single line and they ran us out to the ceremony ground, and they had witch doctors and medicine men and all kinds of stuff out there. We went through a ceremony and received our pipestone, and the braves took us back to camp. Each year we would go through a different ceremony through the fifth which is the highest. You'd go through the final ceremony and at the end, instead of having the Indians run you back to camp and throwing you into bed, they all took off their costumes and started talking to you and you'd have a real big party.

Beard created the most influential society, the Buckskin Men, at his Pennsylvania camp. The Old Guard of Glen Gray (NJ BSA) evolved into a self-perpetuating organization when Gray* fell ill in 1921. George Evans* described Akron, Ohio's Order of the Black Arrow for the *Scouting* magazine in 1930. He said he took his ideas from Dad Shuman's Buckskin Honor Society.

Girls' Camp Rituals

When I asked women what year had been their best in camp, they usually mentioned the early high-school years when they were fourteen or fifteen. They felt most at home with their friends and faced new challenges, like going on longer camping trips or earning Junior Lifesaving certificates.

Some camps have traditions that formalize the rite of passage. A friend told Julie Sherwood[§] at Molly Luman, an Ohio Girl Scout camp, a girl received a Bear Scare. It was:

a piece of leather thong with three knots in it. It is given at a friendship ceremony. One knot is tied in the leather and the person receiving it makes a wish for the world. When the second knot is tied, the person makes a personal wish. Then the leather is put on the wrist and the person receiving it and the person giving it help each other tie a square knot in it. It is worn for one year, then removed.

She continued:

> The name comes from a legend that the Indians used to place one on the wrist of their children to protect them against bears. Supposedly, it would attract his attention when he was attacking the child. He would try to see what it was by clawing it. As he did, the knots would catch his claws and prevent him from hurting the child.

She added, "It is not believed to be a true story."

At Sealth (Wash CFG), Magic Rings mark one's initiation. According to Pat Sanford:

> a magic ring is one of those special things that happens at camp which cannot be fully appreciated until you experience it. Anyone who wishes to have a magic ring comes together usually around a fire (but can be while walking alone, in a room, in the woods, in a boat, etc.). There is no "set" ceremony or procedure and that is what makes it magic. When someone wants to read a poem or start a song or share some feelings she (or he) just does so. This continues until the end. Usually people leave when they feel like it. Often times, people read a thoughtful poem and others want to copy it out. A collection of these is usually kept in a notebook which is also called a magic ring. My personal Magic Ring means a great deal to me as what is in there is *me*. (Many of my own thoughts and writings of my friends). I have several "volumes" - one for songs and one for poems and for a lot of miscellaneous [for] which I haven't found a home yet.

Ruth Archambault Brown (1896-1976), who organized Sealth (Wash CFG) in 1919, said the poetry sessions with their notebooks developed spontaneously. A young camper was responsible for the term.[345:400-401] When she left to found Four Winds (Wash girls) in 1927, she took the tradition with her. The University of Michigan graduate had published a collection of poems, *Magic Ring*, in 1926.

The term and tradition spread, especially after Gibson[*] mentioned them in his *Recreational Programs for Summer Camps* in 1938. Nancy Bryant knows a Glen (Ohio CFG) song written to "These Are a Few of My Favorite Things" (4) with the line, "cook outs and camp outs and magic rings." Kotomi (Colo CFG) and Patiya (Colo CFG) have a Blue Bird song to "Let Me Call You Sweetheart" (6) called the "Magic Ring Song."

Personal Song Books

Girls in the 1970s have been creating personal song books. Cathie Baugh, who came of age in Namanu (Ore CFG), calls hers Magic Rings. Patricia Ann Hall (Calif CFG), Janice Knapp (Mich CFG), and Janet White (Md P coed) call them Bandana Books. Most are 6" x 8" loose-leaf binders with songs typed, one to a page, and arranged alphabetically. Mariana Palmer (Penna GS) and Joyce Gregg Stoppenhagen (Ohio GS) use 3" x 5" cards. Clarena Snyder (Ohio GS) writes her songs longhand in 8 1/2" x 11" spiral notebooks. Bryna Selig (DC CFG) has two, one her "camper book - songs learned from 2-9th grades."

While the idea for such books may have come from an adult leader, badge requirements or commonplace, memory or scrap books, they have been accepted because they serve a function. They not only record repertoire, but their mere existence also confers status, much like beads and badges had earlier. Patricia Ann Hall (Calif CFG) says:

> The Bandana Book was THE status thing to have at Camp Celio (Calif CFG). Usually one didn't make one until one was in the High School Unit (Kalo), but the thicker the better.

Like any ritual object, the books have become circumscribed by taboos. She adds:

> One interesting thing was that the books seemed NOT to be used as a way of learning material, but more as a record of songs already learned. You usually didn't put a

song in your book till you had already learned it by rote; thereby making the book not a written transmission of material, but a record of orally taught and learned things.

She suggests the only time they were used during a sing was when someone needed to check guitar chords.

Another young woman from Ohio says:

Most of the songbooks I have seen have the songs arranged alphabetically, and concentrate on the slower, prettier songs. One reason is that these are more recently learned, or just beginning to be appreciated. It is also these which are more likely to be accompanied by guitars. The only people I have seen who consistently try to write down every song, both pretty and silly, are people like [name] who are camp directors. She sees her book as a resource for the camp staff, not as a personal book.

Patricia's book appears on the back cover. A photograph of her in camp appears in "Outdoors." Another is in "Singers."

Folk Groups

Kitanniwa in the 1950s was more informal. A sense of group just happened. When I was entering seventh grade, my 4-H photography project required I exhibit five portraits and five action shots at the county fair. One from an offsite overnight at High Banks appears on the second page of the preceding group of illustrations.

The next year someone suggested we take a cabin picture, the first I ever took in camp. Five of the nine were members of the same Camp Fire group in town. We already had self-selected by attending the only two-week session offered by the council.

When we were entering ninth grade we moved to the isolated primitive camping unit where we were responsible for cooking our breakfast and supper every day, rain or shine. Again, we took group pictures, this time by living unit. We were more self-conscious. We handed our cameras to someone, so we could be seen with the group.

For some reason beyond reach of memory, I only have pictures for two units and can recall only four of the people in the third tent.

Of the sixteen girls, six had been in the earlier photograph. I know at least three had been in the next cabin the previous year. Others may have been there and left no impression.

Girls' Camp Problems

The danger with the formation of adolescent, camp peer groups is they can amplify problems with cliques that can lead to scapegoating and even absolute usurpations of authority. When we were in the senior unit, two girls had some private rivalry they resolved by turning on a new girl while the rest of us were elsewhere.

Such incidents, though rare, are not unusual. At Kitanniwa and in one other case I have heard described, the victim was new to camping. We were told, the event that precipitated the Kitanniwa girl's ostracization occurred when she walked too close to someone chopping firewood. That person changed the arc of her hatchet and cut herself. In the other situation, the girl was from a family in which her brother committed suicide while she was in camp, suffering from an allergy to insects.

Conflicts usually are less dramatic. One woman remembered an obese girl who ran away when she was ridiculed, yet returned every summer through the CIT program. Another indicated her group turned against the new camp director, treating her as an evil stepmother. One woman told me, she never knew who would be the scapegoat, and always had a little fear she might return one summer to find herself the victim.

Each woman with whom I have discussed these incidents made similar comments. First, they felt a certain amount of guilt. Such things were not supposed to happen, especially in camp settings where friendship and harmony were stressed. At the same time, they had some awareness these events may have been important to creating the community that made their camp experiences so important to them.

Looking back, the most important factor at Kitanniwa was neither the existence of a folk group nor strong personalities. A traditional institution failed to anticipate an unusual situation. The girl, and some other scapegoats, may have benefitted from time in progressive camps where staff members were trained to deal with psychological problems, and campers had different expectations.

Kitanniwa's senior unit had a known limit of fifteen. The fact there were sixteen made it obvious some pressure had been exerted to accept the girl after the application deadline. The administration did not bother to rearrange tent assignments to put the new girl in one with five. Instead, it unwittingly singled her out by placing her in the one crowded by the extra cot.

Rather than dividing the six girls from the town group amongst the three tents, they made one tent for four of those girls, one for girls from various high schools, and one for girls from the town group mixed with others. Then they assigned the girl to the most, not the least, homogenous group.

Timing contributed to the problem. The first year in a primitive high school unit is often the most intense. After that, as girls move through senior units to become CITs, group life becomes routine. In our second year in the unit, our pre-sophomore summer, ten people were in the group photograph taken during a cookout. The other five were doing something else. We did not feel a strong need to find them.

The group was fragmented even more because we did not find someone to take pictures. Each of us is missing from our own photograph. Eight people in the group were ones who had returned, and two had joined without incident.

Some stayed an additional week. It no longer mattered we were the minority in a younger group's session. The last photographs of Kitanniwa in "Coming of Age" show the younger group used clothing to establish its sense of group. While we were testing the limits of dressing down, they emulated counselors who wore white shorts and tops.

Normally, CITs have the greatest cohesiveness. Many camps mark their status with ties. At Glen (Ohio CFG), the girls shown in the photograph have added an informal marker, knee socks. Rebecca Quinlan, their counselor at the time says they were not part of the camp uniform, and, in fact, she did not notice them. But, in their photograph, even those with bare legs have tan marks to signal their import.

My Kitanniwa group's sense of cohesiveness was gone by the time we were CITs. A major employer had closed its Battle Creek facility. Some girls had moved away. The administration excluded other members of our old group to make room for some legacy daughters and some girls from a cooperating council. No one thought to take a picture.

Both Girl Scouts and Boy Scouts have tried to counteract the tendency for adolescent campers to forge strong identities to camps, rather than to organizations, by offering different camps for different age groups. This means, each summer, strangers with similar interests are brought together.

Instead of building distinct adolescent song repertoires, Boy Scouts have developed a genre of greeting songs. These include "More We Get Together" (32), "We're All Together Again" (12), "Hail, Hail the Gang's All Here" (3), and "We're Glad To See You" (3). Some may be either greetings, recognitions of individual achievement, or expressions of fondness like "Ring out Three Cheers" (5) and "Tip up Your Glasses" (5).

Such songs appeared in many early Camp Fire and YWCA song books. One year we learned Neidlinger's "Our Guests" (6) to sing the night the board of directors made its annual visit. While many may never have been sung voluntarily in any camp, editors of Boy Scout song books have retained an affection for what they signify longer than others.

Coed Camp Rituals

Many recreation camps use public, rather than private, rituals to punish individuals who do not conform to group norms. Most occur during meals, the anchoring center of their communal life. They are the ones more likely to have groups chant,

> Mabel, Mabel get your elbows off the table
> This is not a horse's stable
> This is a first class dining table

or "Sing a song, x, sing a song" or "tell a joke, x, tell a joke" when someone breaks some rule of etiquette or is late. Some force the person to run around the dining table or hall, either on the inside or out. Counselors, junior counselors, and 4-H directors sometimes deliberately make mistakes to soften their authority, or develop a teasing atmosphere.

These group demonstrations of solidarity are not unique to coed camps. Gene Clough visited an all-girls' camp that sang "Bravo, Bravissimo" (15) whenever someone dropped or broke something.

However, girls' camps generally discourage such behavior. At Kitanniwa, "Mabel Mabel" (4) probably was introduced by girls who learned it at Clear Lake (Mich agency coed), the public-school camp we all attended. The verse is, after all, known widely. Both Fowke[332] and Roger David Abrahams* have published it as a jump-rope rhyme. At other camps, one woman said the "elbows on the table song" had been banned. Some have substituted tales about crushing fairy field mice as a way to promote better manners.

Lateness is the other act that prompts group condemnation. Diane Wyss remembers singing "Here we sit like skunks in the wilderness" (14) at the Girl Scout's Camp Pittenger in Ohio in the 1940s. Leah Jean Ramsey knows "We Are Hungry" (2) from Texas CFG camps.

Mary Greenman[§] was told in 1942, "Birds in the Wilderness" was sung when people were "waiting in line for lunch at camp." Rex Densmore[§] was told, in 1954, "girls would use [it] while waiting for their dinner at camp." At Kimball (Mich YMCA coed), Theora Trapp[§] was told, it "was sung after dinner was finished and we were waiting for our desert" in 1947.

Gene Clough (Calif BSA) remembers, when he was a camper, they sang "Birds" (14) the time he was late. He notes, in camps he has visited where these songs were common, campers sometimes deliberately came late. These sorts of bids for attention could become problems. Other late songs include "You Were Primping" (4), "You Were Late" (2), and "You're Always Behind" (5).

Kitanniwa did not sing such songs in the 1950s, for the simple reason camp sessions were not composed of people the same general age. The people who were late were usually the very youngest who became confused or lost. One did not ridicule Blue Birds.

Breaches of etiquette may have been treated more raucously in earlier years in girls' camps when the model for behavior was closer to the actual upper class. When camps expanded after World War II to include daughters of tradesmen who called at the back door and always had to be polite, girls had a more attenuated view of that group. In the 1930s, Carol Parsons Sievert remembers directing "Perfect Posture" (11) at slouchers. "Are You a Camel" (13) was used elsewhere. In 1976, Edward Peter Dowdall says "Vous Êtes en Retard" no longer was sung at Les Chalets Francais (Me girls).

When camps are forced to single out individuals to do routine chores, like taking food to and from the kitchen, they use standard procedures, not group formation rituals. At Kitanniwa in the 1950s, counselors simply posted task assignments. Gene Clough says at one camp he visited, a different unit supplied table hoppers each day, with the oldest unit assigned the first day.

Charla Calderhead[S] was told, in an Ohio 4-H camp, people were divided into tribes. Each day, one was given the chore of setting the tables. At the end of the meal, a can was passed containing Popsicle sticks with clean-up tasks written on them. One had the word "free."

Gene recalls, another camp he visited used an even more elaborate method:

> each table has a tree painted at one position, a sun at another, a flower at another, etc. - seven symbols in all, plus an eighth unlabeled position at each table for the staff member. There is a large spinner at the front of the room with symbols around it. It's spun twice at the start of each meal - once to select the hopper and once to select the dishwasher.

Gene's photograph appears in "Outdoors."

Divination rituals appeal to some invisible power for decisions or forecasts of the future, usually through an instrument that bears some "logical harmony" with the predicted event.[402:316] They may be used to reward individuals when selection cannot be made on merit or by applying the principle of equally shared responsibility. They were used at Kitanniwa to determine who ate the extra desert someone did not want, or who got the box of breakfast cereal when two people wanted the same variety.

Julie Sherwood[S] was told, Molly Luman (Ohio GS) used Horse 'n' Goggle. At Kitanniwa, Sally Heath recalls using the simpler counting-out rhyme, "Eenie meenie miney mo." I remember Rock, Paper, Scissors.

Counselor Life

The next major milestone in camp life is becoming a counselor. A passage away from fooling around with friends and toward accepting responsibilities can be difficult. At this time, new people enter, including some who wanted to attend private camps as youngsters, but whose parents could not afford them. They use their skills for upward mobility.

New groups are formed. The second year on staff is often the second high point in the camping lives for those who continue the progression. Charlotte Duff, whose photograph appears in "Staff," says she always spent two years in every camp. The first year, she learned all she could. The second, she contributed what she could. Viki Irene Cuqua says, "The same things I disliked about [the private camp] made me love and remember [it] my second year."

A final transformation awaits those who stay more than a few years, or begin changing camps. A new perspective develops that is shared among many members of the American Camp Association. One realizes there is no such thing as the best summer in camp. Instead, every summer is good, but in a different way. Irene adds:

> I have brought some of [that private camp's] traditions and songs to [my current camp], but it is so difficult. We are a "people" camp. We don't have a dream-like setting, lots of money or super equipment, but we have some of the most special people there are.

As peers change, counselors must adapt to new groups every year, much as they had done when they were Blue Birds or Brownies. They make the transition from the closed community of the early high-school days though their first counseling years, into professionals. They no longer can return to the folklike all-male or all-female cocoon that produces so much of a camp's folklore and music.

Repertoire

Effects of gender on repertoire vary by age. Naomi Feldman[§] and Mary Rogers were told, "When you're younger, after you've learned the first few, then you like to sing the ones you know." A singing session could last some time with very few songs. Carol Shuster[S] was told, girls in a young Girl Scout troop would extend a singing session, without pausing to learn new material, by simply singing "Five Little Angels" (17) instead of "Three."

When young people reached adolescence, the University of Texas students were told, girls became bored repeating the same activity, they "like the new ones the best." To extend an enjoyable singing session, they needed more songs. They had to be similar to each other, so as not to break the mood, but each had to be different.

Précis

The next three chapters discuss the many types of textual (RISE AND SHINE), stylistic (SWIMMING), and melodic (ROSE) repetition children have invented, with some comments on differences between boys and girls. A CANOE looks at the content of songs adolescents use to define themselves and their lives, especially in all girls' camps.

Rise and Shine: Textual Repetition

Formulaic techniques discussed in I WISH I WERE may be employed with a further expectation that replacements follow logic set by the opening verse. With "If you're happy and you know it clap your hands" (59), verb phrases advance an idea that enjoyment increases when happiness is reinforced by joyful actions. Random words like "sink or swim" are not used to create humor with non sequiturs. Winn called texts with thematic connections between verses "pattern" and "catalogue" songs.[553] Felix Johannes Oinas* suggested the term "frame repetition."

Frame Substitution

Many frame-substitution songs are religious with prototypes in camp meetings and revivals. "Let Us Break Bread Together" (8) is repeated "drink wine" and "praise God" at Trexler (NY P boys). "I'm gonna sing when the spirit says sing" (5) is repeated shout, cry, laugh, and love by Mariana Palmer (Penna YMCA girls). In "Oh, Sinner Man" (13), the Weavers repeated verses telling a sinner the rock, the sun, the moon, and the sea would not hide him.

"Down by the Riverside" (9), often called "Ain't Gonna Study War No More," lists actions one will try when one reaches heaven. Homer Rodeheaver published it in 1918 in *Plantation Melodies*. Edward Boatner* included a version in a songster he edited in 1927 for the Black National Baptist Convention, U. S. A. "You Can Dig My Grave with a Silver Spade" (11) has a similar progression.

Elements of nature are substituted into "Old Man Gray Chief" (5), or "great chief," who is master of the mountains, of lightening, and of white clouds. A 1940s Tanadoona (Minn CFG) song, "By the Light of the Moon" (2), was repeated "by the gleam of the stars" and "sigh of the pines." The universe is used in the Danish "Evening Star" (7), "Sun Is a Very Magical Fellow" (9), and "It's Going To Be a Long Winter" (14), spring, etc.

"Lær mig nattens stjerne" was written in 1861 by Christian Richardt and Carl Mortensen. Søren Damsgaard Rodholm produced the American translation. The head of the Danish Evangelical Lutheran Church began his career at the Fredsville church in Cedar Rapids, Iowa, the same city that sponsors Hitaga (Iowa CFG). Church headquarters are in Des Moines.

The substitution pattern for "Quartermaster's Store" (11) varies. At Loyaltown (NY J boys), it is beer that makes you queer, whisky that makes you frisky. Seattle Scouts (Wash BSA) have rats as big as alley cats and spiders in the cider. Adahi (Penna CFG) sings ants in yellow pants, frogs in yellow togs in the "Corner Master's Store."

Pete Seeger standardized a version from the 1930s Spanish civil war between Nationalists supported by Germany and Republicans sponsored by the Soviet Union (FW 05436). The quartiermeister function originated in Germany in the 1600s.

Count Downs

Number is the most common form of frame substitution. Some are count downs, which move backwards, like forty-nine or "Ninety-Nine Bottles of Beer on the Wall" (14) that one takes down and passes around. Fred Hannum Millis[§] collected "Forty-Nine Flies" from someone who had gone to a Traverse City, Michigan, area camp in 1940.

This is similar to one Kemp Plummer Lewis[*] collected from his grandfather in 1910 as "blue bottles were hanging on the wall." Kemp Plummer Battle, the former president of the University of North Carolina, was 78 years old. Belden and Hudson believed he referred to flies.[277]

June Rushing Leibfarth[§] heard "Ten Green Bottles" (14) sung with British pronunciation at the Sky-Wa-Mo (Tenn GS) National All-State Girl Scout Encampment in 1964. That version counts down bottles hanging on the wall that happen to fall. According to Nettleingham,[*] British soldiers sang "ninety-nine" with "hanging" in World War I.

Lewis said, it was sung "until the singer faints from exhaustion." Nettleingham directed men sing, "until tired." Girls' camps ban it. David Stanfield Sinclair says, even the Indianapolis Boys' Club camp discouraged it "after overuse."

"Ninety-Nine Bottles" is related closely to "Forty-Nine Miles from Home" (5) and "X More Days of Vacation" (2). Surprise Lake (NY J boys) sang the first as "Ten Miles" in 1938. Joann Brisler says, Marycrest (Vt C girls) does not allow the second until the last three or four days of the season.

Don LeMond (Mo BSA) learned "Ten in a bed and the little one said" (12) as "ten girls" and the "big one said." Jack Pearse (Ont coed) sings, "Seven men slept in a boardinghouse bed." Fowke collected "Roll Over" in Toronto, Ontario, in 1960 from Catherine Potts and Judy Crawford.[332]

"Junior Birdsmen" (30) pokes fun at count downs and advertising directed toward children. Watanopa (Mont CFG) sings the interlude as,

> It takes only five boxtops
> And four wrappers
> And three coupons
> And two bottle-bottoms
> And one thin dime

to order one's tin wings.

Counting Out

Among counting-out songs that move forward is "Ants Go Marching" (26). Tawakani (Ida CFG) knows "worms go marching." Sharp[*] introduced "One Man Went To Mow" (5) and "This Old Man" (30) in arrangements by Ralph Vaughan Williams and Sabine Baring-Gold, respectively. The bawdy "Roll Me Over" (8) is from World War II. Fowke collected "Ant" as a ball-bouncing rhyme from Toronto third graders in 1964.[332] One camp has banned the song.

"Tender Shepard" (7) includes a one, two, three count in each verse. Melacoma's (Wash CFG) chorus of "Cannibal King" (32) includes lines like, "years go by like one-two-three, a roo yow yow" and "four-five-six, a roo click click."

Patsy Orry Orry Aye

"Patsy Orry Aye" (29) relates the experiences of a railroad construction worker killed on the job, using dates to count out. "Paddy Works on the Railway" surfaced as a capstan chantey in the 1850s. Smith[*] found a description of "Pat's Apprenticeship" in an 1864 manuscript from the *Young Australia*. The Black Ball packet carried immigrants from London to Moreton Bay. It returned from the eastern coast of Australia with wool and other cargo. Paddy's verses then had four different lines (ABCD).

Lockwood Honoré[*] published a college-student version in 1891 with the first-line frame, two lines of narrative, and the "working on the railway" refrain. He used "For-o-my-or-o-my-or-o-my-ay" for a chorus. The Lomaxes publicized that version in 1934 when they included "Filimeooreireay" in *American Ballads and Folk Songs*. Beacon, New York's University Settlement Work Camp (NY agency coed) was singing their version in 1960.

Earlier, in 1930, Boy Scouts[*] published "Climbing up the Ladder" with the "Patsy oree, oree ay" chorus. It counted out the 1920s with verses like "A Boy Scout troop accepted me" and "My badge as a Tenderfoot I wore." Their verses had the same ABBC repetition form commonly sung in camps, in which one needs only learn line B.

Richard Runciman Terry[*] believed the melody came from another chantey, "The Shaver," which he learned from his great-uncle, James Runciman. John Short (1839-1933) provided his copy of "Poor Paddy." Short worked the coastal waters with his father when he was fourteen, then went to sea four years later. During our Civil War, he worked Yankee vessels, where his voice promoted him to shantyman, the man who called the work.

Variations

"Three Wooden Pigeons" (12) counts back to zero as the birds leave, then counts forward as they return. Nancy Simmons (Colo GS) knows "Three Chartreuse Buzzards." Tanadoona (Minn CFG) has "Three Blue Pigeons." Ann Beardsley (Mich GS) sings both "Five Blue Pigeons" and chartreuse buzzards. Most camps increment "One Elephant Went Out To Play" (17), but Melacoma (Wash CFG) increases the number to three, then decreases to the starting point.

"New River Train" (9) usually is counted out, but MeWaHi (Calif CFG) and Tall Oaks (Mich P girls) sing from ten to one. Joyce Lamb[S] collected a 1946 version with "La de ah, oh boy," followed by a whistle, between verses. Aleta Huggett[S] was told "Ka-di-a, oh boy" was used at Lake Louise (Mich P coed) in 1949. Carol Domoney[S] collected "Lotte dow, oh boy, hot stuff" and a wolf whistle from a former Rotary (Mich BSA) camper in 1955. The Teamsters' Health Camp (Mo agency coed) has "Midnight Train." Bill and Charlie Monroe recorded it in 1936.

"I've Got Sixpence" (37) is a monetary count down. Nancy Bryant (Ohio CFG) knows "counselors get their pay." Lisa Drumm[S] collected a version from Wyandot (Ohio CFG) where counselors sang "campers go away," while campers countered "counselors go away." *Gammer Gurton's Garland* published the rhyme in 1810 as "The Jolly Tester."

Harlan Elton Box, Desmond Cox, and Desmond Hall copyrighted the current version in 1941. Box, a former Canadian lumberjack, and Cox, a mining engineer, apparently teamed with others to copyright public domain songs like "Horsey, Horsey" (28) and "Quartermaster's Store" (11)[388:47-48] during the 1941 ASCAP strike mentioned in KUMBAYA.

"Bubblegum" (13) counts out verses like "My mommy gave me a penny to buy a henny," rather than the usual "see Jack Benny." That version was collected from Wyandot (Ohio CFG) in 1974 by Lisa Drumm.[S] The Intercollegiate Outing Club Association[*] published the penny/henny rhyme in 1938. Benny's radio program began in 1932.

Relations

Some frame-substitutions involve patterns of causality. "Rolling over the Billows" (15) traces links from cheese to love. Watervliet (Mich girls) has a final verse about the camp directors. Rebecca Kragh (Minn GS) knows "rolling over the meadows." Carol Rosensweig (Conn YMCA coed) sings "sailing over the ocean." A few camps have banned it as sexist.

Verses of "Say When" (12) go through most of the "Five W's and the H" of an ideal newspaper lead paragraph. Logical relations also are developed in "Peter and Paul" (5). The Opies labeled it an "infant amusement" in England.[452] Sutton-Smith[*] called it a "hand game" in New Zealand.

"Back of the Loaf" (59) uses a poem by Maltbie Davenport Babcock. *The Christian Work* included the text in a report of his funeral the week of 20 June 1901. It immediately was set to music, and continued to attract arrangers. Jane Blinn's version was in the 1927 YWCA song book.[220] Most camps have changed the grace to the more alliterative "back of the bread." Madeline Gail Trichel (Ohio GS) learned "behind the loaf." Mariana Palmer (Penna YMCA girls) sings, "back of the bread is the flower."

"Tall Girls, Short Girls" (9) had not developed its implicit logic when it was published in 1923 by the YWCA.* Then, one opposition was repeated twice:

> Big folks, small folks, short and tall,
> What you going to do when the resorts pall?

By the time Charlotte Duff learned it, someone had unfolded the logic to include all the likely combinations and improved the rhythm:

> Tall girls, short girls, fat and thin
> Whatcha gonna do when the heat sets in

"Six Little Ducks" (27) is "primarily directed to younger girls and considered silly by older girls" in Ohio Girl Scout camps, according to Debbie Saint Pierre.§ One reason may be it does not describe all the ducks ("fat one, thin one, there were two"). The verse structure leaves no room to explode the logic. The number of ducks is sometimes two or five. Neewahlu (Ida CFG) has four verses, rather than the usual one or two. It also has modified the one line to, "Fat ones, skinny ones, cute ones too!"

Extended-family members are used in the verses of, "It's not my brother, not my sister, but it's me, oh Lord / Standing in the need of prayer" (9). Papa, mama, and baby are repeated sections in the "Three Bears" (9). The nuclear unit also is exploited within the "Papa Moses shot a skunk" verse of "Boom boom, ain't it great to be crazy" (33).

"My Gal's a Corker" (7) uses parts of the body. John Stromberg composed it in 1895. John Alexander Stramberg, as he was born, left Milton, Prince Edwards Island, for New York where he wrote tunes for Joe Weber and Lew Fields' music hall. They were the main

Broadway producers between the revues of Harrington and Hart and the follies of Flo Ziegfield.

Another song using frame substitution is "Musikanter" (18) with musical instruments. "Hush Little Baby" (8) offers the infant an assortment of animals and objects.

Incremental Repetition

The most folklike form of frame repetition involves incremental variations that propel a ballad's narrative. In some cases, lines, verses, or verse groups are repeated exactly, with different situations, until the last iteration provides a climax. This final verse revelation, or punch line, exists in "She Waded in the Water" (8) and in most of the courtship dialog ballads mentioned in SKYBALL PAINT. It also is found in the "Three Bears" (9) hip group recitation, in skits like "Any Trains from the East?" and in many after Taps scare stories. Robert Southey crystallized an older folktale into the familiar "Bears" for the 1837 volume of *The Doctor*.

In the other form of incremental repetition, a narrative progresses through slight variations from verse to verse. A Kamaji (Minn girls) song, "I want to be a northwoods girl," has a second verse, "Now I am." Judy Miller remembers the song, written to "Ummm and a Little Bit More" (11), was popular in the 1950s. Camp aspirations through time are detailed in "There's a Long Long Trail to Camp" (6), apparently written at Treasure Island (Penna BSA).

Tawakani's (Ida CFG) version of "Mrs. O'Leary" (31) uses incremental changes in the line repeated between verses. The first repetition ends with "fire fire fire," the second with "water water water," followed by "jump lady jump" and a scream. Ann Beardsley sings the fire and water endings, then goes "ssss (roast beef)." Towanyak (Kans CFG) sings "Mother Hubbard." Melacoma (Wash CFG) has "Old Granny Leary." Wolahi (Calif CFG) knows "Old Mother Leary."

Theodore August Metz composed the original tune, "There'll Be a Hot Time in the Old Town Tonight," in 1886. The Hanover-trained musician moved to Chicago, where he worked for McIntyre and Heath Minstrels. A singer in the troupe, Joe Hayden, added lyrics that were current during the 1898 Spanish-American war.

Martha Jackson Stocker[S] collected a version of "Desperado" (44) from Deer Trails (Mich GS) in 1952 that utilized incremental repetition in the chorus. The first and second verses about the cowboy and cowgirl, respectively, ended with one "whoop." The third verse, in which they fall in love, ended with two "whoop's." The final verse, in which they have a child, ended with three "whoop's."

Other forms of incremental repetition are used in "Vrenalie" (30), "Little Green Valley" (5), and "I Gave My Love a Cherry" (24). The speeches in "The Mermaid" (23) build suspense.

Circular Ballads

Circular ballads are another form of narrative repetition. "Found a Peanut" (17) details events that follow from eating a rotten peanut, including dying and going to heaven (and, or hell, depending on the version) until the narrator finds another peanut. The defining characteristic is the first and last verses are the same, implying the whole song could be repeated indefinitely. The Opies called these "tales without end,"[451:31] and noted they were a stock joke. Fowke used the term "endless songs."[331] Some camps have banned it.

June Rushing Leibfarth[S] collected a narrative version of "Cannibal King" (32) at Silver Springs (Tex GS) in 1961. The first chorus ended "smack smack," the second "mama papa," the third "grandma grandpa," and the last "smack smack."

Nancy Twitchell Hunter[S] collected a variant of "There's a Hole in My Bucket" (13) from a camp near Springfield, Ohio, in 1936. When the dialogue began repeating itself with a second request for a straw, they sang:

But the straw is much too long, Lieber Heinrich, Lieber Heinrich.
Cut it short, Liebe Lissa, Liebe Lissa, (shouted) CUT IT SHORT!

Circular Songs

Circular repetition is not restricted to ballads. Short verses, like "Around the corner [. . .] a sergeant major once said to me" (7), may have a circular last line, but tell no story. In some cases, older songs have been truncated to accentuate their circularity. Sally Briggs[S] collected an Ohio Boy Scout version of "Michael Finnigan"

(14) in 1973 with four verses. Three ended, "Poor Old Michael Finnagen! Begin Again. (shout)." The last was, "Let's Quit. (shout)." Fowke collected a version from a Saskatchewan summer camp in the 1920s.[331] More recently, Abrahams* heard it used as a jump-rope rhyme.

Fowke collected an 1890s version of "Sandy's Mill" (5) in Toronto[331] with more narrative content than the one Tobitt introduced to camps in *The Ditty Bag*.[174] That song also has circular logic. In the early 1930s, Zanzig found 75% of those who liked the potentially circular "Bear Went over the Mountain" (8) were boys.[561]

A form of circular repetition, which has been used in recent years, is ending a song with an iteration of the first verse. This device is found with "Mandy" (22) and in Ann Beardsley's (Mich GS) version of "I'm on My Way to Freedom Land" (11), recorded by Peter, Paul and Mary. Her version of "Born Free" (16) uses frame substitution and illusory circular repetition.

Pete Seeger wrote "Where Have All the Flowers Gone" (43) in 1955. In 1960, campers at Woodland (NY coed) tinkered with the rhythm and added the circular repetition. Their counselor was Joe Hickerson.* "I'm gonna sing when the spirit says sing" (5), "The Sun Is a Very Magical Fellow" (9), and "Three Kids in a Sandbox" (14) use similar techniques.

Cumulative Songs

Another form of frame repetition is the cumulative song. In "An Austrian Went Yodeling" (34), the substituted parts of each verse are maintained in a recapitulating series repeated with each successive stanza. Winn suggested, "the last verse of a cumulative song is always a combination tongue twister and memory tester."[553] LaRue Thurston[215] called them "build-up songs." Many use gestures.

Like frame-substitution songs, of which they are a subset, the simplest is a counting or number lyric. In the East, Mike Cohen* believed "Green Grow the Rushes" (45) was "probably the most popular camp song" with participants in his Outdoor Travel Camps. "My Wealthy Aunt Brought Back" (15) is a musical analog to the memory game I Went on My Vacation and Took or I Went to the City and Bought.

Progressions in size, causality, or relationship require more attention to detail. "There's a Tree in the Wood" (5) describes a bird on the branch on a tree in a hole. "There's a Hole in the Bottom of the Sea" (16) adds details to a picture of a frog on a log in the sea. "There Was an Old Lady Who Swallowed a Fly" (12) describes the progressively larger animals she eats to catch the fly. These often are called "House that Jack Built" songs.

Animals

Catalogues of animals and their sounds exist in "Old MacDonald Had a Farm" (20) and "I had a rooster (cat) and my rooster pleased me" (9). The unexpected is found in Cohila's (Calif CFG) version of the second. They include a "birdy went meow --- (it was a very strange bird)," and end with "My little aardvark went 'how do you do, I am the first animal in the dictionary'."

Pete Seeger recorded "I fed my rooster on green berry tree" in 1955 (FC 7610). Tayanita (Ohio CFG) sings "under yonder tree." Cohila (Calif CFG) knows "sassafras tea." Niwana (Wash CFG) uses "Tenderleaf Tea."

Farm images also figure in "When I First Came to This Land" (20). A few girls' camps have revised it to remove sexist stereotypes.

"Alouette" (29) is another animal cumulative frame-song, only it employs parts of the body. Its verse order is unstable, since many who sing it do not know French: remembering any item suffices. According to a 1932 Canadian Boy Scout[*] song book, it lists body parts in the order in which a lark or skylark would be plucked. Interpretations given with American versions are more euphemistic.

Food

Foods are associated with days of the week in "Today Is Monday" (15). It may be an army song, perhaps dating from World War I. It once contained German references. In some camp versions, the rabbit stew called "hasenpfeffer" was served on Mondays. In the 1930s, Kalamazoo's Girl Reserves (Mich YWCA) and Treasure Island (Penna BSA) used "bread and butter." Brooklyn Scout camps (NY BSA) used "goulash" in the late 1920s. Their other foods differed.

Some camps, including Tawakani (Ida CFG), use Monday as washday, from "Here We Go 'round the Mulberry Bush." The remaining days still are devoted to diet. "All You Etta" (5) also uses food.

Decremental Repetition

Decremental songs repeat a verse, but each time omit another phrase or word. At the end, only gestures or gestures and a humorous set of isolated articles, prepositions, conjunctions, and other unimportant words remain. Winn called them "diminishing songs."[553] Sally Briggs[S] called them "omission songs." Lisa Drumm[S] labeled them "deletion songs." Forrest John Baird[*] classed them as "action deletion." "Elimination" and "subtraction" also have been used. Whitney French Bolton[*] suggested "decremental repetition."

Sources

The idea for decremental songs may have come from German tradition. One of the best known and oldest is "My Hat It Has Three Corners" (33). Kathleen Green (NY CFG) learned "Mein Hut" in New York in the 1960s. Marv Herzog of Frankenmuth, Michigan, recorded it in German in 1972 (7001).

"John Brown's baby has a cold upon his chest" (20) may be early, but Nettleingham[*] did not indicate decrementation was used in England with "John Brown's baby has a pimple" in 1917. Its tune, "John Brown's Body" (6), has been used with the vanishing "John Brown's Flivver" (9), "Oh, Sir Jasper" (2), and "Little Peter Rabbit" (19) has a fly or flea upon his nose or ear. Fowke called the last a "finger play."[332] She collected it from D. C. McCausland, who learned it in Grimsby, Ontario, near Niagara in the 1940s.

By 1927, Harbin[*] indicated "Around the Corner" (8), "Chester" (18), and the "Damper Song" (16) were in tradition. Joseph Carleton Borden remembers using motions and "silent words" with "There's a Long Long Trail" (20) at Rotherwood (Me boys) in the 1920s. "My Bonnie" (15) and "Three Blind Mice" (14) also have been decremented.

The only new frame decremental songs are "Deep and Wide" (9) and the German "Little Cottage in the Woods" (49). Lisa Drumm[S] collected the first from Wyandot (Ohio CFG). Some West Coast camps have a hip version of the second that begins, "In a pad in the forest green, boom boom boom boom" (2).

Variations

Word or phrase elimination usually comes from the beginning of a song. Those with silence that starts at the end, like "Oh, So Jasper" (2), often do not use gestures.

Some, like "Row Your Boat" (26), have been sung with forward or backward moving eliminations. Terminal decrementation has been used by Jonathan Amsbery at Shaver (NM YMCA coed), by Carol Ann Engle at Cherith (NY P girls), by Gary Flegal at the Van Buren Youth Camp (Mich agency coed), and by Beck Colwell Deatherage (NY GS). Madeline Gail Trichel (La GS) remembers with "Little Cottage" (49), they would "eliminate last words each time . . . like 'John Brown's Baby' (20)."

Decremental songs usually are sung without instrumental accompaniment. William Daniel Doebler[S] talked with a young woman who emphasized the chords on her ukulele just before the pauses in "John Brown's Baby" (20). Sometimes, humming is used in the wordless stretches with phrase omission songs to keep groups together. This was done with "Heads, Shoulders, Knees and Toes" (33) at Kitanniwa, and with "Swimming, Swimming" (36) by He Bani Gani (Md CFG). In "Bingo" (50), hand claps are substituted for the deleted letters, so it becomes "B-i-n-clap-clap."

Appeals

Repetitive songs may have several attractions. When seven- and eight-year-old children read aloud, their typical errors include the "omission of short familiar words."[343:396-297] William Daniel Doebler[S] found "John Brown's Baby" (20) to be reminiscent of "something you might sing at a fraternity drinking party."

Length, with its implicit violation of form, is another attraction. The delight many find is reflected in joking final verses. June Rushing Leibfarth[S] collected "Patsy Orry Aye" (29) with, "eighteen-hundred and fifty ten, if you like my song I'll sing it again." June King[S] collected an optional ending to "Found a Peanut" (17) that went "threw it away" and "learned my lesson."

In the early 1930s, Zanzig found 60% of those who liked the decremental "John Brown's Baby" (20) were girls. They represented only 40% of those who enjoyed the frame substitution "Today Is Monday" (15).[561] Song content, rather than form, may be responsible for those choices. Boys may not want to sing about babies. Girls may not like singing a song with military or German associations.

Many longer or more open-ended ones in military tradition may have arisen before the combustion engine, when only the cavalry rode horses. Nettleingham* noted a generation gap in World War I when:

> it was Tommy of the old Armies and the Reservists who sang and whistled the most. The Territorials who had had camp holidays ran him close, but the New Army boys will now march for hours and miles in a weary, hang-dog fashion without striking any one of the scores of marching dirges that exist.

Kitanniwa Repertoire

Kitanniwa in the 1950s did not sing many songs with textual repetition. "My Hat" (33) and "She'll Be Coming 'round the Mountain" (41) were used throughout the decade. "Old King Cole" (14) was sung through the middle 1950s. "Little Cabin in the Woods" (49) was introduced later. Other frame-repetition songs heard in camp, like "I've Got Sixpence" (37) and "Found a Peanut" (17), were known privately.

Instead, the camp had an endemic tradition that allowed girls sitting at dining tables to play games in the brief period after dishes had been cleared and before group singing began. When most at a table were young, the counselor started games one might play at club meetings in town, like Gossip or Electricity. With slightly older girls, the games might include memory posers like the cumulative I Brought Back from My Vacation, or pattern substitutions like Rhythm and Bizz Buzz. Sally Heath remembers Ala Baba, Ghost, and Simon Says.

Games increased in complexity with older girls. Who Stole the Cookies (2) was a circular chant that combined rhythm with memory. To begin, people were assigned sequential numbers. When a mistake was made, that person took the last number. Everyone between was reassigned. The trick was remembering one's number while chanting, clapping (ALL CAPS), and snapping one's fingers (lower case):

> Group: WHO stole the COOK ies from the COOK ie JAR
> It: Number TWO stole the COOK ies from the COOK ie JAR
> Two: Not ME
> Group: Yes YOU
> Two: Couldn't BE
> Group: Then WHO stole the COOK ies from the COOK ie JAR
> Two: Number FIVE stole the COOK ies from the COOK ie JAR

James Orchard Halliwell traced the game back to "the parson hath lost his fuddling cap."[366] It later was collected in Switzerland and Germany as "the Abbot of Saint Gall has lost his night-cap."[445] Both carry allusions to Protestants displacing Roman Catholics. The first emerged during the period when the Puritan Oliver Cromwell controlled England between 1653 and 1658. The second probably referred to the secularization of the Swiss Abbey in 1798 following the intrusion of Napoléon's troops. Joanmarie Schulz[§] collected it as a jump-rope rhyme in Howell, New Jersey, in 1976.

One Frog was a variation on counting-out songs. It required beating time, by slapping the table (ALL CAPS) and clapping hands (lower case), while taking turns incrementing the next part of the phrase:

> ONE frog, TWO eyes, FOUR legs, KERplop IN THE puddle
> TWO frogs, FOUR eyes, EIGHT legs, KERplop KERplop IN THE puddle IN THE puddle

Unlike college drinking games, from which some of these may have been derived, no penalty accrued at Kitanniwa for making a mistake, beyond laughter and chaos. In most cases, games simply were restarted. Girls were more intent on mastering them than winning. None went through many iterations before all the tables were cleared. Even so, a director in the late 1960s banned the games. They were not revived after she left.

Case Study: Rise and Shine

I heard no songs using textual repetition during my visit to Kitanniwa's coed session in 1974. A frame-substitution, counting-out song known in church camps in the 1950s had been converted into a ballad, "Rise and Shine" (67). It borrowed its chorus from a Black spiritual based on Isaiah 60:1, "Arise, shine; for thy light is come, and the glory of the LORD is risen upon thee."

One More River

"One More River" (4) was included in Henry Randall Waite's[†] *Carmina Collegensia* in 1868. The verses were reprinted in 1876 in a Columbia[†] song book, in 1879 in a University of Pennsylvania[†] songster, and in an 1885 Rutgers[†] book. Waite (1845-1909) was a senior at Hamilton College in Clinton, New York. He later worked as a journalist and attended Union Theological Seminary, then a Presbyterian school. His father was a Congregational minister.

White[547] believed the form, tune, and chorus were taken from an "old camp-meeting hymn 'There's One Wide River to Cross'." Thomas Wentworth Higginson[*] heard South Carolina slaves sing it during our Civil War, after they joined the Union army. The original probably was used for a military parody reprinted by the Illinois chapter of a Union officers' society, the Military Order of the Loyal Legion,[*] in 1894:

> We'll float together, we'll float together.
> There's one wide river to cross.

> Chorus. One wide river, there's one wide river to cross.

> Three of a kind they beat two pair.
> There's one wide river to cross. — Cho

The college version may have come from some still unidentified minstrel song or skit that emerged after Charles Darwin published *The Origin of the Species* in 1859. His work, and the concurrent discoveries in geology and archaeology, was raising uncomfortable questions for Christians. One response was songs, like "Sunday School" (15) and "I

Was Born about Ten Thousand Years Ago" (4), which explored how seemingly impossible events could have occurred.

The crisis in ideas became so severe humor alone could not distance people from their difficulties. Comic Biblical narratives were seen as Black creations. This allowed members of the audience to maintain their certitude about the universe, the need that initially gave rise to the dilemma, while easing the disquiet by watching people, not like themselves, suffer the logic of their personal quandaries.

Marc Connolly's *The Green Pastures*† was the most important dramatization. He based his 1930 Pulitzer Prize-winning play on a collection of Bible stories retold from a poor Black's view by Roark Bradford. *Ol' Man Adam and His Chillun'* was a best seller in 1928, three years after John Thomas Scopes was convicted for violating Tennessee's law against teaching evolution.

As Darwin's theory became understood better, interest shifted from general Biblical reviews to two critical events: the creation and the flood. "Dem Bones" (37), discussed in SKYBALL PAINT, is the best-known camp song dealing with Adam and Eve. The one describing the flood, "One More River," spread to every part of society.

The same year Rutgers published its version, 1885, James Jepson† was learning a variant in Mormon Snowflake, Arizona. In Cleveland, Ohio, a child, Benjamin Bourland, was hearing the version he would later teach James H. Hanford.† B. Coplan wrote down a version in 1915 or 1916 he heard whites singing in Birmingham, Alabama. J. C. Neal recorded the words he learned in western North Carolina in 1919. Lester Andrews Hubbard† collected the first. Mary Olive Eddy† published the second in 1939. White† discovered the last two manuscripts.

What these songs had in common, and what separated them from the Illinois Commandery parody, was they expanded Genesis 7:15, "And they went unto Noah into the ark two and two." The counting-out rhyme matched animal names with numbers. Different versions often shared the same pairs of words. Hubbard reported,

> The animals marched in two by two
> The polar bear and the kangaroo

while Eddy had,

> The animals went in two by two
> The elephant and the kangaroo

and White had two with:

> Animals came two by two
> The hippopotamous and the kangaroo

How the versions differed was they adapted different songs for their choruses or refrains. Jepson and Bourland used "Hurrah, hurrah!" from "When Johnny Comes Marching Home" (4). Neal used "There's one bright river to cross." Coplan used "Dem bones gona rise agin" (37). The three rhythms, all of which entered camp tradition, defined the number of syllables required in the name of the animal that joined the kangaroo. "One More River" with the elephant came to be the most common.

Fisk Jubilee Singers

In the same years minstrel performers were configuring the white man's view of Black music, the Fisk Jubilee Singers were performing genuine spirituals in concerts to raise money to run Fisk Normal School. The American Missionary Society and the Congregational Church had established the school in Nashville, Tennessee, in 1866 to educate students freed from cotton plantations. A collection[†] of their songs published in 1877 had one with a "rise and shine" chorus. It oscillated between two tones for the "rise and shine, and" phrase. Hall Johnson's Negro Choir used their version in *The Green Pastures*.

Fisk's group was so successful, imitators followed. Sharon Lytle[*] discovered some of her ancestors were described as "stars of the internationally famous, Delaware [Ohio]-based, Donovan's Tennessee Jubilee Singers." That group of nine freed men and women also used the name "The Original Tennesseeans" when they toured small cities in New York, Ohio, Indiana, and Iowa in the 1880s.

Their bass, Z. A. Coleman,[*] told one newspaper editor, he "was born a slave, but worked his way North, went to work in a hotel, and with his wages paid for schooling and music lessons." He apparently spent time in Cleveland before touring.

In 1883, he published a collection of "plantation melodies"[†] in Cincinnati that included a version of "Jacob's Ladder" (46) with the Fisk Jubilee Singers' "Rise and Shine" chorus. It used one note for the "Rise! Shine! and" section. That version, or the idea drawn from that version, entered camp tradition. Seth Clay (Mich P coed), Carol Flack (Ala agency coed), and Linda Margaret Hanes (Okla GS) all remember singing the current version of "Jacob's Ladder" (46) with a "rise and shine" verse.

Modern Song

The contemporary song that appends a "Rise and Shine" chorus to "One More River" emerged in the early or middle 1950s. June Rushing Leibfarth[§] collected "Noah's Ark" (Version B) from a day camp in Houston, Texas, in 1955. That same year, Pete Seeger[†] and Eric Darling recorded "Children of the Lord" for Folkways on *Camp Songs*. Instead of driving the animals crazy, they had the rain in verse four drive the counselors crazy, and dropped the final verse describing events after the storm.

On the surface, theirs was a typical camp localization. In fact, the differences in the two versions reflected changes in religious affiliation that had been occurring since the end of the second world war. Church membership increased dramatically between 1950 when 55% of those polled said they attended church and 1956 when the number had risen to 62%. The number peaked at 69% in 1960, then fell to 62.4% in 1970.[237:952]

Hidden behind the statistics was an internal shift from what were termed mainline churches, the Methodists, Presbyterians, Congregationalists and others who supported sleep-away camps. They were being replaced by more conservative, unaffiliated churches that grew in the wake of the first Billy Graham revivals, and television broadcasts by preachers like Robert Schuller in California, Oral Roberts in Oklahoma, and Rex Humbard in suburban Akron, Ohio. The center of gravity already may have moved by 1943. That year, the editor of a community song book, Harry Robert Wilson,[†] said "One More Ribber" had "been adopted by the students in most of our southern and western colleges."

The new evangelists preached more literal Biblical interpretations. Frame substitutions, which let singers create their own patterns and draw their own conclusions in the tradition of the Baptist belief in liberty of conscience, were replaced with unambiguous, homogenous narratives defining events. Little room remained for the types of disagreements that arose from variations. It no longer was enough to imagine, like Seeger, "how one would feel cooped up on the ark?" One now must accept the repopulation for the planet that occurs in the final verse as an explanation for the geologic record.

Explication

When an individual, or group of individuals, adapted "One More River" to use the "rise and shine" verse as a burden, other changes were made. "River's" verses were quatrains in which the second and fourth lines were duplicated (ABCB). The new song kept only the last line as a refrain and converted the second line into a repetition of the first (AABC).

That verse modification may have resulted from one of several impulses. If the person who created the song was sufficiently interested in Black music to find old spiritual collections, he or she may have been aware of three-line blues verses. They follow a single line, which is repeated, with a commenting one (AAB). Conversely, the change could have been motivated by a feeling the refrain was overused, making the song tedious to sing.

As already suggested, the current "Rise and Shine" refocused the narrative of "One More River" from the leaping and lingering reminiscent of Child ballads to a detailed broadside. Two verses from the older song (Version B, verses 2-3) were retained. Added were verses on God's instructions to Noah (verse 1), a description of the trip (verse 4), and a happy ending (verse 5). Commonly, the song varies from three to five of the verses collected by June. Extra verses are added to the end.

Its most enduring part has been the rhymes, especially those involving direct Biblical references, like "kangaroo" with "two." "Bark" draws upon "Make thee an ark of gopher wood" from Genesis 6:14. Hickory bark has been localized to birch in Michigan. On the West Coast, "Indian bark" is sung. Cedar is known in Texas and California camps.

The rhyme of "mud" and "flood" has been connected with an allied song cluster in folk tradition. Brown collected a version of "Gideon's Band" containing two Noah verses, one about the flood/mud, the other about an ark of "hickory sticks and poplar bark."[277:601-602] This apparently was a stage version of "One More River." Rimrock (Wash YWCA) sings only the two verses with those rhymes with the "Rise and Shine" burden.

Another song in the "River" cluster that came from the minstrel stage is "Who Built the Ark?" Ike Simond[†] included it in the same 1891 songster that contained "Dem Bones." This ballad, which emphasized the counting out, has been included in some public-school books, in this country and in England. "One More River" also reached England, where Nettleingham[†] reported a much-abbreviated version sung by British troops in 1917.

Music

"Rise and Shine's" tune was derived from "Jacob's Ladder" (46), which Leisy[†] noted it still resembled melodically and harmonically. The current tune is more syncopated than the spiritual known in camps, or the version recorded by Pete Seeger in 1980 (FW 36055).

The unusual rhythm has led to the introduction of hand claps. Most sing it with the verse-burden pattern borrowed from the Coleman original. A few, like Kirby (Wash CFG) and Melacoma (Calif CFG), use "rise" as the first and last verse (illusory circular repetition). Others follow June and treat "rise" as the final verse.

Sally Briggs[§] was told hand gestures were used with the verses at Angola on the Lake (NY YWCA). Mount Morris (Wisc P coed) has used a guitar accompaniment.

Jacob's Ladder

"Jacob's Ladder" was reported in Port Royal, South Carolina, where slaves flocked after Union forces captured the port in 1861. Higginson[*] published a version in 1867. Editors of *The Slave Songs of the United States*, issued the same year, believed it existed in "Methodist hymn-books."[240] No one has identified the Methodist hymn or camp meeting song they had in mind.

The variant melody probably came out of the Sacred Harp tradition of groups like David Parker Carter's family, who recorded it in Dallas in 1940. They called themselves the Chuck Wagon Gang to avoid confusion with the better-known Carters of southwestern Virginia. They were migratory farmers in west Texas. The Lewis Family, of Lincoln County, located just above the fall line on the Georgia Piedmont, recorded a version closer to the camp song in 1964, after "Rise and Shine" had crystallized. The one had been active since 1936, the other since 1951. Sacred Harp was mentioned in CAMP PHILOSOPHY.

Popularity

The burden is what excites campers. Larry Ralston says, at various Wyandot County, Ohio, 4-H camps, he has noticed:

> That thing has ten verses. And I watch. Now, a lot of times after they get going through it, the further they get along with the verses - and in that particular one, the verse and chorus is the same tune. And after they get going along, the thing gets confused and you'll have half the kids singing the chorus when they should be singing verse. And they'll just keep repeating the chorus.

Once its popularity was established, rituals ensued. Carol Simon[§] was told at Camp Christian (Ohio P coed):

> this song was only sung after breakfast at the church camp [her friend] attended for several summers. While singing the chorus, each person had to stand up, raise his hands above his head and clap his hands while moving from side to side. [Her friend] assured me that this song was guaranteed to make even the sleepiest of the campers more alert.

Among others who remember "Rise and Shine" as an after-breakfast song are Jan Smyth (Ohio P coed) and a friend of William Daniel Doebler.[§] This involves a pun on "rise and shine" as a term to get out of bed. Gary Martin[*] attributes the association with the U. S. military.

The earliest print occurrence he found was a 1916 Marine recruiters' bulletin.

In recent years, religious groups have been promoting the ballad. Mary Elisabeth Miller and Robin Kelley learned it from Young Life. David Stanfield Sinclair says InterVarsity Christian Fellowship recommended they use the song with the Indianapolis Boys' Club camp. The two organizations signed an agreement in 1971 with Campus Crusade for Christ and Navigators to cooperate in their evangelical campus programs.[355]

Their support has coincided with a decline in popularity in areas like Texas, where June collected the song. Dana Dawn Olmstead says, it was sung in the past, but not the present, at Ellowi (Tex CFG). At Friedenswald (Mich P coed), Diane Bauman (Mich P coed) calls it "old."

At the same time it is beginning to fade in some coed and boys' camps, where it is known by 90% of the people who answered my survey, it was recognized by almost everyone in a Camp Fire camp. Interestingly, it is better known in Camp Fire than in other traditional girls' camps, by five to four. It may be the mixed camping history of CFG staff and older campers makes their contemporary repertoire more porous to church influences than other traditional camps.

Alternatively, private camps may recruit children from a smaller section of society, one less influenced by evangelistic leaders. Camps in the East may be freer to let it revert to its folk origins. Joanne AvRutick (Md coed) remembers they sang verses about counselors made up by campers with the burden, "give them your story, story / children of the camp," in Maryland.

At Loyaltown (NY J boys), the older tradition of recasting Old Testament stories survived into the 1960s. Steven Diner says, "I can tell you, even from memory, what the most popular songs were. Every year it was 'Rise and Shine.' That was always in the top couple." At Kitanniwa in 1974, the new sixth verse brought back the counting-out rhyme and some naughtiness.

Version A

Text from Laura Clare Zahn, Camp Natsihi (Mich CFG) c. 1966; Camp Missaukee (Mich P girls) late 1960s through early 1970s; Camp-in-the-Woods (Mich YWCA) early 1970s; Camp Kitanniwa (Mich CFG) 1972, 1974. Gestures from Camp Rimrock (Wash YWCA), 1964; copy provided by Francine Walls. Laura's picture appears in "Kitanniwa, 1974."

C. So rise and shine and give God your glory, glory
Rise and shine and give God your glory, glory
Rise and shine and (clap) give God your glory, glory
Children of the Lord

1. The Lord said to Noah, "There's gonna be a floody, floody"
The Lord said to Noah, "There's gonna be a floody, floody
Get those children (clap) out of the muddy, muddy"
Children of the Lord

Chorus

2. The Lord said to Noah, "You better build an arkie, arkie"
The Lord said to Noah, "You better build an arkie, arkie
Build it out of (clap) birchy barky barky"
Children of the Lord

Chorus

3. The animals they came on, they came on in twosies, twosies
Animals they came on, they came on in twosies, twosies
Elephants and (clap) kangaroosies, roosies
Children of the Lord

Chorus

4. It rained and poured for forty daysies, daysies
Rained and poured for forty daysies, daysies
Nearly drove those (clap) animals crazy, crazy
Children of the Lord

Chorus

5. The sun came out and dried up the landie, landie
    Sun came out and dried up the landie, landie
    Everything was fine and (clap) dandy, dandy
    Children of the Lord

Chorus

6. The animals that came off, they came off in threesies, threesies
    Animals they came off, they came off in threesies, threesies
    Learned about the (clap) birds and beesies, beesies
    Children of the Lord

Chorus

7. Now this is the end of our story, story
    Now this is the end of our story, story
    Everything is (clap) hunky dory, dory
    Children of the Lord

Chorus

Version B

Text and gestures from a Houston, Texas, Girl Scout day camp, 1955; collected by June Rushing Leibfarth, Utah State University, 1971; variations from A emphasized. Guitar chords from Mount Morris (Wisc P coed), 1976. June's photograph appears in "Singers."

1. The Lord (A) said to Noah, "There's gon (D) na be a floody, floody,"
    Lord (A) said to Noah, "There's gon (D) na be a floody, floody,
    Get (A) those children out (D) of the muddy muddy
    Chil (A) dren of (E) the Lord." (A)

2. **So Noah he built him an arky** arky arky,
    Noah he built him an arky arky arky,
    Built it out of **hickory** barky barky,
    Children of the Lord.

3. The animals they came **in by twos, by** twosies twosies,
    Animals they came **in by twos, by** twosies, twosies
    Elephants and kangaroosies, roosies,
    Children of the Lord.

4. It rained and **rained** for forty daysies, daysies,
    Rained and **rained** for forty daysies daysies,
    Nearly drove those animals crazy, crazy,
    Children of the Lord.

5. The sun came out and dried up the landy landy,
    Sun came out and dried up the landy landy,
    Everything was fine and dandy dandy,
    Children of the Lord.

6. (Everyone stands)
    So rise and shine and give God **the** glory glory,
    Rise and shine and give God **the** glory glory,
    Rise and shine and give God **the** glory glory,
    Children of the Lord.

Version C

"Hallelujah to the Lamb," *Quietude* song book edited by Seth Clay, used at Junior High IV Camp, Pilgrim Haven (Mich P coed), c. 1956; repetition patterns assumed by editor, including incrementing number in first line of verses; similarities to A emphasized.

1. The animals came in one by one
    The cow came a-chewing on a caraway bun

C. Hallelu, Hallelu
    Hallelujah to the lamb
    Hallelu, Hallelu
    Hallelujah to the lamb

2. **The** rhinoceros **and the kangaroo**

3. The bear and the bug and the bumblebee

407

4. The old hippopotamus is stuck in the door

5. Thus the animals did arrive

6. The hyena laughed at the monkey's tricks

7. Says the ant to the elephant, "Who's you shovin'?"

8. Noah hollers, "Shut the gate."

Version D

"One More River," Ann Beardsley, Camp o' the Hills (Mich GS), 1963-1970; Camp Ken-Jockety (Ohio GS), 1976; repetition patterns assumed; similarities to A emphasized; rhyme and other similarities to C indicated below.

1. Old **Noah built** himself an **ark**
   There's one more river to cross
   And patched it up with **hickory bark**
   There's one more river to cross

C. One more river, and that's the river of Jordan
   One more river, there's one more river to cross.

2. He started in to lead his stock
   He anchored it with a great big rock

3. The animals entered one by one
   The elephant chewed a toasted bun[1]

4. The **animals** entered two by **two**
   The tiger and the **kangaroo**

5. The animals entered three by three
   The bear, the flea, the bumble bee[2]

6. The animals came in four by four
   The goat knocked down the galley door[3]

7. The animals entered five by five
    Said Noah bring 'em back alive

8. The animals entered six by six
    The monkey started playing trix[4]

9. The animals entered seven by seven
    The clock began to strike eleven

10. The animals entered eight by eight
    The lion growled it's getting late

11. The animals entered nine by nine
    Said Noah, we're all doin' fine

12. The animals entered ten by ten
    The thunder roared and the storm began

Similarities to Version C
1. C-1
2. C-3
3. C-4
4. C-6

Version E

"Noah's Ark," Brooklyn Scout camps (NY BSA) song book, 1929; repetition patterns assumed by songbook editor; similarities to A emphasized; rhyme and other similarities to C or D indicated below.

1. Old **Noah he built** himself an **ark,**[1]
        There's one wide river to cross;[2]
    He built it all of **hickory bark,**
        There's one wide river to cross.

C. There's one wide river,[2]
        And that's the river of Jordan.
    There's one wide river,
        There's one wide river to cross.

2. The animals went in one by one,
   There's one wide --
   And Japheth with a big bass drum,
   There's one wide --

3. **The animals** went **two by two,**
   The elephant and the kangaroo.

4. The animals went three by three,
   The hippopotamus and the bumble bee.[3]

5. The animals went in five by fives,
   Shem, Ham and Japheth and their wives.

6. The animals went in seven by seven,
   Said the ant to the elephant, "Who you shovin'?"[4]

7. And when he found he had no sail,
   He just ran up his old coat tail.

8. And as they talked on this and that,
   The ark it bumped on Ararat.

9. Then Old Noah went on a spree,
   And banished Ham to Afrikee.

10. Perhaps you think there's another verse.
    But there ain't!

Similarities to Versions C and D
1. D1
2. D refrain and chorus
3. C3 and D4
4. C7

Version F

"Rise! Shine! and Give God the Glory," from *The Jubilee Singers*, edited by Z. A. Coleman (Cincinnati, Ohio: John Church and Company, 1883).

1. Do you think I'll make a soldier, soldier?
    Do you think I'll make a soldier, soldier?
    Do you think I'll make a soldier, soldier
    The year of jubilee.

    (Yes, I think you'll make a soldier, soldier,
    Yes, I think you'll make a soldier, soldier
    Yes, I think you'll make a soldier, soldier
    The year of jubilee.)

C. Rise! Shine! an' give God de glory, glory,
    Rise! Shine! an' give God de glory, glory,
    Rise an' shine, an' give God de glory, glory
    The year of jubilee

2. Fighting for our Master Jesus, Jesus
    Fighting for our Master Jesus, Jesus
    In the battle He will lead us, lead us
    The year of jubilee

3. We are climbing Jacob's ladder, ladder
    We are climbing Jacob's ladder, ladder
    Ev'ry round we're climbing higher, higher
    The year of jubilee.

Version G

"Rise and Shine," from J. B. T. Marsh, *The Story of the Jubilee Singers with Their Songs*, 1877; repetition patterns assumed by editor.

C. Oh, brethren, rise and shine, and give God the glory, glory,
    Rise and shine, and give God the glory, glory.
    Rise and shine, and give God the glory for the year of Jubilee

1. Don't you want to be a soldier, soldier, soldier,
   Don't you want to be a soldier, soldier, soldier?
   Don't you want to be a soldier, soldier, soldier for the year of Jubilee?

2. Do you think I'll make a soldier,
   For the year of Jubilee?

3. Yes, I think you will make a soldier,
   For the year of Jubilee!

4. Then you must rise, etc.

Swimming, Swimming: Stylistic Repetition

Fun songs scrutinize singing style by repeating verses with systematic changes. The treatment of any one song may vary from camp to camp. It is the idea that is shared in tradition. The number of repetitions, when stipulated, is usually three.

Stylistic repetition is an anomaly, an exception to the patterns of Anglo-American folk singing. According to Charles Seeger, the prototype for a performance was set in the first verse for dynamics, timbre, pitch, tempo, duration, and stress. It then was repeated without conscious deviation until the song was finished. These patterns held for syllables (the smallest song unit), for stanzas (the largest unit), and for phrases.[503]

Appeal

Songs flouting conventions of traditional singing style may arise from the ways children use their vocal cords. Music educator Louise Kifer Myers described a child's speaking voice as "characterized by its softness, clearness, and high-pitched quality." To her, the singing voice "should be of the same type." The play voice, on the other hand, "is essentially strident, harsh and forced."[438:30-31]

Her recommendation, that the first two be encouraged at the expense of the play voice, was echoed by another music educator, Karl Wilson Gehrkens. He believed a "child must be taught always to think and to listen discriminatingly to the tones that he is producing." He added, when "children forget all about the sound of their voices [. . .] the effect of their singing is ugly rather than beautiful."[341:90]

Gehrkens went on to argue, "the typical child's voice has two divisions, commonly called 'registers'." The "tone quality of the chest register" generally is "poor" and the intonation "likely to be faulty." He reminded elementary-school teachers, "we discourage the use of this part of the voice."[341:91] The higher or head register was preferred.

The transition between the two is set in adult voices.

> In the child's voice the break occurs at different points in the scale at different times; higher up in the case of louder singing and lower in the case of softer singing. In other words, the child's voice has a "movable break," the point at which the voice goes from the lower register to the upper one depending upon the force with which he sings.[341:91]

Myers encouraged softer singing, because, should a child "become excited while singing, his singing voice will take on the undesirable qualities of his play voice."[438:31] At Yankee Trails (Conn GS), Deborah Southworth noted, they suppressed songs when the staff just got "tired of hearing kids yell them!"

Loudness

Younger campers, especially boys, like loud songs. At Loyaltown (NY J boys), Steven Diner says "Boris" (1) was requested, "because they got to yell 'hey!'" Serena Richardson has observed "John Jacob Jingleheimer Schmidt" (62) is a favorite of younger boys at Potomac Country Day Camp (Md coed) for the same reason. Gesell and Ilg observed children's voices become stronger and "generally loud" around age seven.[343:446]

Most songs that become louder with each repetition insert a chant between verses. In 1974, Tanadoona (Minn CFG) used,

> Same song
> Same verse
> A little bit louder
> And a whole lot worse

with "You Can't Ride in My Little Red Wagon" (8). This chant, which often includes verse numbers ("same song, second verse"), has been used with "I'm Henry the Eighth" (6) at Manakiki (Minn agency coed). Larry Ralston (Ohio 4-H) heard it with "We Sing Nothing" (6). Sally Briggs[S] collected it with "Michael Finnigan" (14).

Dynamic Contrasts

More common than progressively louder songs are ones that get softer each time, with one word or phrase sung louder. Campers conscientiously sing softer knowing the more they succeed, the greater their reward when they reach the shouted section. Seven-year-olds, who are learning to speak softly, have voices that suddenly get loud on them.[343:145, 466]

"John Jacob" (62) is the best-known illustration. Others include "Around the Corner" (7) at Valley Mill (Md coed), and "Old Lady Leary" (31) at Hidden Valley (Md CFG). Manakiki (Minn agency coed) sings the second louder each time. A loud-soft treatment was given to "My Name Is John Johnson" (12) at Kiroliex (Mich BSA), and to the more usual "Yon Yonson" at Tyrone (Mich YWCA). Ronald Turner[S] collected the first. Judy Hollin[S] heard the second. Fowke learned "Yon" from Lynn Fowke, who sang it in Saskatchewan in the 1950s.[332]

Manhattan's Scout Troop 582 (NY BSA) has begun "Our Paddle's Keen and Bright" (59) soft, gotten louder in repetitions, before getting soft again. A similar formula has been used with "Little Red Caboose" (18) by Seth Clay (Mich P coed). Storer Camps (Ohio YMCA coed) repeat "Ezekiel Saw a Wheel" (19) five times. All imitate sounds heard at different distances.

Softness

Repetition of a continually softer verse is less common, and done primarily by girls. Such treatment has been given to a variant of "Old Lady Murphy" (31) at Seabow (Calif CFG). Increasing softness was used with "Little Red Caboose" (18) at Augusta (Calif CFG) in the 1930s and Watanopa (Mont CFG) in the 1940s. Only an older group at Namanu (Ore CFG) sings the progressively quieter Balagan unit song written to the "Soldier's Chorus" from Charles Gounod's *Faust*.

Hums

A variation on the dynamic use of softness is humming a pretty song one final time. This often is done with "Each Camp Fire Lights Anew" (84) to make a third verse. Nancy Bryant hums a final iteration of "The Silver Moon Is Shining" (17) at Glen (Ohio CFG). Cecily Raysor Hancock did with "White Wings" (36) at Wilaha (Colo CFG) in 1944. Larry Ralston (Ohio 4-H) has heard it used with "As the Bright Flames Ascend to Heaven" (3). The last employs the 1770 tune for Ben Jonson's 1616 poem, "Drink to Me only with Thine Eyes."

Other camps hum the first part of the last verse, then repeat the final lines. This mixture of humming and text is used at Onahlee (Ore CFG) with "Wee Baby Moon" (11). Fleur de Lis (NH P girls) in 1955 and Zanika Lache (Wash CFG) hum part of the "Year Song" (13). Vivian Sexton (Tex CFG) has used beginning hums with "Each Camp Fire" (84), and Ka-esta (Ore CFG) with "White Wings" (36). An Idaho Camp Fire camp hums part of the last verse to "Moon over Neewahlu."

Timbre

Variations in timbre, or voice quality, are related to dynamics and tone, because seven-year-old voices are not simply louder, but "may reach a penetrating, piercing" sound.[343:153] Variability in vocal sounds is given full rein in the squeaky-voiced passages in "Boom boom, ain't it great to be crazy" (33) at Wasewagan (Calif CFG) and Kitanniwa.

Similar variations exist in most versions of the seed section of "The Prune Song" (27) and in "My High Silk Hat" (39). Tom Greiff knows "My Boy Scout Hat" from Whitsett (Calif BSA). Katie Hickey[§] collected a variant "Rooster Song" (12) from Matollionequay (NJ YWCA) that used a "high falsetto" on the last word of the last line of each verse, "Came into my ya-ha-ha-hard."

Boys' voices undergo another change when they are around thirteen, but few songs experiment with the voice's lower register. Blue Haven (NM P coed) sings the last verse of "Brain Boxer," also known as "Nicky Nicky Nu" (23), in a low, deep voice.

Contrasts between deep and squeaky voices were used in the dialogue parts of "The Three Bears" (9) group recitation at Glen

(Ohio CFG) in 1974. Debbie Saint Pierre[S] collected a dramatized version of "Deaf Woman's Courtship" (10) in Ohio.

Tempo

Tempo is another aspect of music children manipulate. Each repetition is faster of "Do Re Mi" (9) at Goodwill/Pleasant (DC agency sep), and "My Paddle's Keen and Bright" (59) at Wasewagan (Calif CFG). Nancy Bryant remembers increased speed with "Sarasponda" (59) at Glen (Ohio CFG). The Herald Tribune Fresh Air Camp (NY agency) repeated "Puffer Billies" (33), "each time with increased speed," in the early 1950s. June Rushing Leibfarth[S] heard "Doodledoo" (34) "repeated faster" at Robinwood (Tex GS) in 1966.

Many songs that accelerate subsequent repetitions also have gestures. Songs become tests of manual dexterity. This would happen with "Little Pile of Tin" (29) at Towanyak (Kans CFG) and "Skinnamarink" (28) at Kitanniwa. William Daniel Doebler[S] collected such a version of "Do Your Ears Hang Low" (61).

"Love Grows under the White Oak Tree" (29) is "repeated faster" by Nancy Bryant (Ohio CFG) and Jolene Robinson Johnson (Wash CFG). In the 1950s, Joan Fulton[S] was told the song was "sung again with the gestures, much faster" at Wasewagan (Calif CFG).

"Head, Shoulders, Knees and Toes" (33) has people standing and bending quickly in a version remembered by Nancy Bryant (Ohio CFG). Other songs, like "Slap Bang" (16) at Neewahlu (Ida CFG) and "Dum Dum Dad Da" (5) at Storer (Ohio YMCA coed), end in chaos. Peggy Hays[S] collected the last from a staff member.

Slowness

Deliberate slowness is rare. In elementary schools, Petzold found "all children experience significantly more difficulty in maintaining a steady beat at the slower tempo."[464:257] Debra Janison remembers singing a Christopher (Ohio C coed) song, written to the theme from the *Mickey Mouse Club*, "slowly and exaggerated -- almost as if we were drunk." Ten- and eleven-year-old girls requested a slow repetition of "My Hat" (33) at the Wyandot County 4-H Day Camp (Ohio 4-H) in 1974. It petered out.

Variations between fast and slow tempos within the same verse are tried, usually to emphasize some aspect of the text. Such alterations exist in the "Cat Came Back" (15) as done by Wintaka (Calif CFG) and Jolene Robinson Johnson (Wash CFG). Heather MacPhail[§] was told Keewano (Mich CFG) would begin "Walk Jim Along, Jim Along" (1) slow, then "sing faster and faster; last verse is slow, words dragged out." Gestures with the last parallel the verses in a frame-substitution that goes from "walk" to "step" through "run" to end, "let's sit down."

Seeger suggested steady tempos followed from the way traditional singers worked from "the sung syllable." When outsiders tried to sing folk songs, they were inhibited by their differing speech patterns. Trained singers overwhelmed spirituals with tones too considered. Commercial singers slowed tempos so lyric interpretations were clearer. Seeger noted a Folk Revival performer "can be identified almost without fail by his slowing down the cadences."

Choirs and glee clubs compound the problem. They must synchronize many voices, with differing enunciation habits, and so compromise on slower, artificial tempos everyone can produce. A good example is Pomona College's rendition of "Roundup Lullaby" (32). Ralph Haine Lyman's arrangement for the men's glee club was so strongly focused on harmony, the quarter notes became whole notes. Asymmetry in the rhythm disappeared.

His version apparently has entered tradition. Gene Clough heard a version at Wasewagan, the Pasadena, California, Camp Fire Girls camp, that was less chromatic than the original. June Rushing Leibfarth[§] heard a similar variant from Arnold (Tex GS) with a guitar accompaniment.

Oliver[*] told the YWCA in 1951, "After using this song for a long time, we find that it has been copyrighted! We see that the tune and words are slightly different and are glad to change our version to the correct one with the kind permission of the copyright owner." She graduated from Pomona after Lyman joined the faculty.

Wyandot (Ohio CFG) recorded "Wood smoke curlin' lazy from the pine log fire" with the tune in the 1970s. Carol Domoney[§] had collected a version in 1955.

Duration

Songs playing with duration, or what Seeger called the "prolongation of tones beyond the length of the tempo unit," are rare. They alter a melody in ways too difficult for children, who still are developing a concept of tonal pattern. Songs like "The Cuckoo" (33) hold a particular syllable longer than normal, but this occurs in every verse. At Kitanniwa, it was instigated by older campers and staff members.

At Runels (Mass GS), William Daniel Doebler[S] was told, girls would hold the last "long" in "It's Going To Be a Long Winter" (14). This was more an impromptu endurance test, than a conscious manipulation of duration.

Stress

Most songs that experiment with variations in stress or emphasis do so because they toy with syllabic emphasis in the lyrics. The best know is "Piccolomini" (15). Judy Miller remembers "piccoloMIni, picCOlomiNI / piccoLOmini, PIcCOlomiNI" at Kamaji (Minn girls).

Its title, no doubt, comes from Friedrich von Schiller's *Die Piccolomini* (1799), one of a dramatic trilogy dealing with the Thirty Years War (1618-1648). That conflict was the next episode in the religious wars that began with Martin Luther, and the subsequent Dutch rebellion against Spain. It overlapped with the English civil war that began in 1640.

Language Distortion

Linguistic variation may foster changes in tempo and duration when more syllables are squeezed into the same musical space. In one group of fun songs, the text is modified by applying a formula to distort familiar words. Christopher (Ohio C coed) has sung "Poor Old Slave" (28), "Pe-or old sle-ave," "piggety poor," and "piggety paggety poor." In the late 1950s, Kitanniwa used "pickety" for "piggety." Manhattan Scout Troop 582 (NY BSA) sang the first three, and added "poorsky," "poorovich," and "poor poor" in 1950.

George W. H. Griffin composed the original in 1851 for Ordway's Aeolian's. John Pond Ordway organized the minstrel troupe in Boston to promote his sheet-music business.

/P/ Labial

In many ways, iterations of language distortion songs resemble tongue twisters. Many rely on one of the first learned labials, /p/. Kirby (Wash CFG) repeats "Polar Regions" (3) as "these piggittolar reggityeagons." Glen (Ohio CFG) adds "picka picka picka picka picka picka bale of cotton" (17). The girls use hand gestures resembling pinching a clothes line from above.

Cecily Raysor Hancock (Colo CFG) labels her version of "piggidy polar riggidy regions" as "double talk." The Opies believed such language distortion formulae once were the exclusive idiom of adults who wished to speak privately in front of children.[451:321] By the 1950s, eight- and nine-year-olds were the ones interested in using codes like Pig Latin, according to Gesell and Ilg.[343:447]

Accents

Another form of linguistic variation, which can change tempo, duration and timbre, is the repetition of a verse in different accents. "Fried Ham" (15) is done at Tanadoona (Minn CFG) in southern, English, Chinese, baby, and opera voices. Ka-esta (Ore CFG) does some of those, plus a butler, a hillbilly, and a Martian. Members of a Long Beach, California, Horizon Club (Calif CFG) use the accents of a Blue Bird, a Boy Scout, a teacher, and a Camp Fire Girl.

Girls at Kamaji (Minn girls) announce the variant with, "same song, second verse, southern accent, whole lot worse." At least one California Girl Scout camp has rejected the song. The list of incompatible foods may mask remains of deep-seeded prejudices against ethnic groups.

"Tenement House" (11) is a language-distortion song that satirizes a Chinese immigrant advertising his laundry. It is not the same as the one Tannadoonah (Ind CFG) knows as "There was a poor old Chinaman / His name was Chink-a-cha-lou-cha-pan" (4), although both may be called the "Chinaman Song."

Bonnie Loomis (Ohio GS) learned "I livey iny tenamenty housey." Nancy Bryant (Ohio CFG) has sung "Me livee upee tenemenee housee." Katie Hickey[§] collected a Matollionequay (NJ YWCA) mocking song that began:

> We livee in a
> Teeney, weeney village
> We sleepee on a
> Pretty junkie bunkie
> We go to johnny
> Have a toughie timee
> Never any toilet paper
> Always on the floor

A nine-year-old girl learned "I livee ine teeny weeny house" in a Michigan camp in the 1950s, according to Judy Hollin.[§] The last two variants suggest the appeal for children perfecting the command of language transcends specific conditions that generated underlying negative stereotypes. Still, a number have banned it.

Jolene Robinson Johnson was told, they began singing "Wadaleache" (34) in an English accent after overhearing a young camper at Kirby (Wash CFG).

Intellectual Variation

Stylistic repetition songs enjoyed by the young are those that can be generated spontaneously. When campers become older, they still like the challenge of running permutations. While the young have no patience with considering how to produce the next variation, older campers like exercising their brains by repeating songs in a wordier manner.

The two most common do not change the music style, but introduce new parts into the tune. "Down by the Old Mill Stream" (17) often is repeated "down by the old, not the new, but the old." "In the Evening by the Moonlight" (16) is repeated in some camps with "rah-da-do-dah" after each phrase. Tell Taylor published the first in 1910. He was raised outside Findlay, Ohio, the sponsor for Glen (Ohio CFG). James Alan Bland composed the second in 1879. His father graduated from Ohio's Oberlin College in 1845, before the Civil War

Backwards Repetition

Repeating a song backwards has a strong appeal to campers who celebrate topsy-turvy days with their clothes on backwards, even inside out. Girls at Kitanniwa in the 1930s began the day with Taps, ended with morning swim, and began meals with dessert. One group of girls at the Wyandot County 4-H Day Camp (Ohio 4-H) sang "Men-A" on their skit night in 1974. Hitaga (Iowa CFG) has a senior unit, Agatih, which is the camp name spelled backwards. One camp attended by Linda Regan Knoblauch, Sinawak, was Kiwanis spelled backwards.

Sometimes a song is sung backwards by physically turning around, a variation on a common skit. Melacoma (Wash CFG) does the gestures in reverse order in the final verse of "If you're happy and you know it, do them backwards" (50). Backward repetition may be done by following "I had a little dog and his name was Fido" (5) with "Difo." "Row Your Boat" (26) has been collected as "Ore Your Boat" by Diane Davis[s] from Magruder (Ore P coed). Seattle Scouts (Wash BSA) repeat "Bingo" (50) as "Ognib."

At Kamaji (Minn girls) in the 1950s, Judy Miller says they sang one verse of "I'm a Hilisararious, a Rippimatanemy" (16) as,

> I'm a June bug
> I'm a beetle
> I buzzed and hit

then repeated it:

> I'm a bune jug
> I'm a teeball
> I uzzed and bit

These backwards repetitions are another form of code language the Opies termed "tangletalk."[451:24]

Simple Repetition

The importance of repetition, perhaps in deliberate defiance of demands for logic, is clear in songs that repeat a simple verse until people are tired or stopped by some superior. Seth Clay (Mich P coed) recommended singing "Little Red Caboose" (18) a second time, without variation. At the Brighton Fresh Air Camp (Mich J coed), Shirley Bidwell[S] was told the song, "may be continued indefinitely raising number each time."

Roberta Tupper Latvala[S] collected a version of "I Had a Dog as Skinny as a Rail" (2) in the 1940s that "was used constantly at the table . . . mostly to annoy the leaders . . . it lasted as long as the singers." Frank Wayne McIntosh[S] heard an Ohio version of "Spring Would Be a Dreary Season" (1) in 1940 that went "On and on and on, ad infinitum." Wampatuck (Mass P girls) sings "Day by Day" (6) "two or three times." Mariana Palmer remembers repeating "We Do Nothing, Nothing, Nothing" (6) at a Pennsylvania camp.

"Announcements" (18), usually followed by "What a terrible way to die," often is chanted at the ends of meals, especially in camps with flexible schedules. Gene Clough says at Wintaka (Calif CFG), "one had to make announcements with extreme care if this song was to be avoided." He remembers, "Some 'announcers' got it more often than others." Some camps have banned the song.

The fact repetition, itself, is what is valued is clear in the chorus to "Pioneer" (9) Martha Jackson Stocker[S] collected at Deer Trails (Mich GS) in 1952:

Ooh la la, ooh la la, ooh la la, repeat
Ooh la la, ooh la la, ooh la la, again;
Ooh la la, ooh la la, ooh la la, once more
Ooh la la, ooh la la, ooh la la, second verse

This not only acted as a bridge to repeating the main verse, but also contained internal repetition. The second singing usually concluded with "the end" in the last line.

Her verse began "If I had the wings of a pioneer-pioneer / Into the woods I would fly-would fly." It ended "There to remain till I die-I die." A variant, "Sing two ray ray, two rah rah, two rah la," is used with "If I Had the Wings of a Turtledove" (14) at Rimrock (Wash YWCA).

In the 1940s, Ronald Turner[S] collected a second verse from Kiroliex (Mich BSA), "straight into the woods I would chop" and "drop." Aleta Huggett[S] collected two more from Lake Louise (Mich P coed), stalk/balk and ride/hide. Massachusetts girls in 1955 sang "waterwings" and "back to Camp Fleur de Lis I'd float, I'd float." Ka-esta (Oregon CFG) knows "wings of a buzzard."

According to the Rohrboughs,[139] the tune is derived from "Botany Bay." Joseph Williams, Junior, wrote the original for the London stage in 1885 using the name Florian Pascal.

Kitanniwa Repertoire

Kitanniwa's repertoire of stylistic repetition songs in the 1950s was small. Only two allowed girls to shout: "John Jacob" (62) and "Pep" (39). "Do Your Ears Hang Low" (61), "Grand Old Duke of York" (24), and "Swimming" (36) allowed them to sing as fast as possible. The language distortion "Poor Old Slave" (28) was introduced late in the decade.

The limited repertoire does not mean such impulses were left in town. Simply, other activities provided girls with opportunities to exercise their vocal chords. Free swim in the afternoon, with its three buddy calls, allowed campers to make as much noise as they liked. No one shushed them when they shouted as they walked between the cabins where they slept and the main lodge where they ate, at least during the day.

Girls simply learned when and where they could do things that otherwise were not permissible. They probably did not yell as they passed the camp director. She might or might not have said anything, but one part of testing limits for acceptable behavior by children is they define their own rules that establish what can and cannot be done. This rule making is very much part of children's folklore, according to the Knapps.[393:31-44]

"Lemmi Sticks" (8) offered intellectual challenges for fourteen-year-olds in the senior unit in 1958. The game, an elaborate patty cake where sticks were used instead of hands, was derived from the Maori "Titi-Touretua." Elsdon Best* reported it in New Zealand in 1901, then published it there in 1925. Sutton-Smith* says he learned it in a teachers' training class in 1942 in Wellington, New Zealand, and knows it has been played by both Maori and white children there. Margery Lester* remembered, New Zealand Boy Scouts took it to Melbourne, Australia.

More than likely Mormon missionaries brought it to this country. Lynn Rohrbough learned his version from Leona Holbrook*

(1909-1980). Her parents were sent to New Zealand for three years when she was six-years-old in 1915. She later worked in summer camps in New York and New Hampshire, before joining the Physical Education faculty of Brigham Young University. Her photograph appears in "Outdoors."

From CRS or another source, the game spread rapidly. Gene Clough remembers a camp director from Minnesota introduced the game to Yallani (Calif CFG). Julie Sherwood[S] was told it had been taught in a Girl Scout leaders' training meeting in Ohio. Jacqueline Orvis learned it in a recreation music class at Central Michigan University. Gary Flegal saw it in a "kiddie PE" class at Albion College, but already had learned it at the Van Buren Youth Camp (Mich agency coed).

It did not take teenaged girls long to learn the eleven-syllable remnant of the original adolescents' song remembered by a missionary's child, or to master the basic gestures: pound the ground, clap the sticks, clap your partner's stick. Then, we reinvented the game exercising the same mental processes as Maori youth. We turned it into a circle game, which meant I could interact with the person on my left, then on my right. Next, we tried other ways to move the sticks. This quickly expanded from different cross patterns, to flips, tosses, and exchanges. Unlike the Maori, our attempts to work across the circle failed.

Case Study: Swimming, Swimming

"Swimming, Swimming" (36), a stylistic-repetition song that manipulated tempo, was sung in the Battle Creek Camp Fire camp from the 1940s through the 1960s. It probably diffused through regional CFG week-long leadership workshops held in camps by Kempthorne. Ruth Arnold (Mich CFG) penciled the words to the "swimming" verse on the cover of her 1942 workshop manual.

Textual Variation

Although the song never has been published, its words are remarkably similar from camp to camp. Perhaps it was stabilized by the repetition. The most common alteration is the modernization of swimming hole/cold to pool/cool. Watanopa (Mont CFG) has added a second verse about a red canoe, written through formulaic imitation (C-2).

At some time, probably in the 1940s, another verse was added to make a two- or three-verse song. "You're the Camp for Me" (10) may be sung independently. Nancy Gail Maxwell has used it in a medley with "Oh, come to where there's a lot of fun" at Trowbridge (ND CFG).

Music

"Sailing, Sailing," from 1880, provided the tune for "Swimming" and "You're the Camp." George W. Furniss introduced its verse and chorus in an 1887 Chicago songster, *Our College Boys' Songs*. Lockwood Honoré followed in 1891 in Cincinnati with *Popular College Songs*.

James Frederick Swift, its composer, was a pianist and bass-singer, whose education was limited to the Commercial School of Liverpool College. He worked as an organist for Methodist congregations, moving from church appointment to church sinecure, before dying in Wallasey, Cheshire, in 1931. When he composed secular pieces, he hid behind the name Godfrey Marks.

He may have been inspired by the success of Michael Maybrick,* a baritone born in Liverpool in 1844. He wrote "Nancy Lee" in 1878 using the name Stephen Adams. The art song in the form of a chantey had sold more than 100,000 copies by 1880. Augusta (Calif CFG) still knew it in the 1930s when it used the melody for "Camping Is the Life for Me."

Maybrick often returned to his home town where his concerts included this and other songs he wrote with naval themes. His lyrics were by Frederick Edward Weatherly (1848-1929), an Oxford-trained barrister with a knack for creating memorable texts.

How "Sailing" traveled from the pinched environs of an industrial English port to our elite universities is a mystery. Fuld* found early sheet music, which claimed it was sung by Egbert Roberts.* He was an unlikely source for its popularity. The bass was so unknown, he constantly was advertising his availability to sing oratorios. He did not perform at a Crystal Palace concert until 1883, three years after the song first was published. A reviewer said, Roberts "exhibited a fine voice, but he evidently has much to learn before he can use it to advantage." August Friedrich Manns initiated the concerts in 1855.

Swift's London publisher was Reid Brothers, who sold both sacred and secular sheet music for piano. Fuld indicated its New York agent was Williams and Son, a name lost in obscurity. Five years after the song was published, a company with the same name began manufacturing pianos in Chicago, using mail orders to sell to churches. It eventually offered Epworth models to Methodists.

"Sailing's" first American appearance was in a commercial collection exploiting the interest in college song books. Its editor was some kind of sales agent for the publisher, S. Brainard's Sons, which had relocated to Chicago from Cleveland in 1869. Furniss later worked for a larger publisher, Oliver Ditson, and lobbied for the copyright law.

Honoré[*] (1865-1917), the second American songbook editor, was the scion of a prominent Kentucky-Chicago family who earned his law degree from Harvard in 1891. As an undergraduate, he had been a member of the college glee club. He claimed his anthology contained, "the latest songs as sung at Harvard and other colleges."

The first actual college song books in which I found "Sailing" are from the University of Virginia in 1906 and Dickinson in 1910. Phi Kappa Psi was the first fraternity to publish it in 1914.

The verses, which rarely are printed, let along sung, eulogize the carefree attitude of seamen leaving port in a "gallant bark." Its chorus invokes dangers that dominated the earlier "Mermaid" (23):

Sailing, sailing, over the bounding main;
For many a stormy wind shall blow ere Jack comes home again

However, Swift implied the forebodings of disaster for sailing ships, which existed when the Child ballad was evolving, no longer were as potent for steamers. Explosions, not erratic winds, were the danger.

Oral tradition has simplified the melody in camps. The "swimming" verse is sung three times, each faster, at Neewahlu (Ida CFG), Wintaka[†] (Calif CFG), and Storer (Ohio YMCA coed), according to Peggy Hays.[§] Jean Hamilton[§] heard it sung three times, each softer. Seattle Scouts (Wash BSA) have sung it three times.

Most camps, including Kitanniwa, sing it twice, the second time faster than the first. Wintaka (Calif CFG) adds a catch ending, a final "but." Patricia Ann Hall says Celio (Calif CFG) has a local unit song, "Kalo, Kalo," written to "Sailing" and "Up We Go into the Wild Blue Yonder."

Gestures

Hand gestures burlesque daily swim classes. These motions are simple, and easily managed with faster iterations. Hidden Valley[†] replaces phrases by humming the melody until only gestures and humming remain. The Maryland Camp Fire camp has altered the durations in the tune by a slide, or glissando, between pairs of notes. This emphasizes the second of the two, when done with the nasal hum.

Popularity

"Swimming" was known by about half the women who answered my questionnaire in all-girls' camps. Slightly more knew it in the survey Midwest than elsewhere. Men in both coed and all boys' camps knew it better than women in coed camps.

Version A

Text and gestures from Patricia Averill, Camp Kitanniwa (Mich CFG), 1951-1960.

Asterisks (*) indicate the gesture associated with the starred word or phrase, earlier in the song, is repeated.

1. Swimming, swimming[1] in the swimming hole[2]
    When days are hot,[3] when days are cold,[4] in the swimming hole*
    Breast stroke,[5] side stroke,[6] fancy diving too[7]
    Oh, don't you wish you never had anything else to do
    But

2. (sung at a faster tempo)
    Swimming, swimming* in the swimming hole*
    When days are hot,* when days are cold,* in the swimming hole*
    Breast stroke,* side stroke,* fancy diving too*
    Oh, don't you wish you never had anything else to do
    But

3. (sung at original tempo)
   For Kitanniwa, you're the camp for me
   You're the camp that I love best, no other place I'd rather be
   Oh, Kitanniwa! Life's a merry whirl
   I sing to you a joyous song for I'm a Camp Fire Girl

Gestures
1. Dog paddle with hands
2. Form bowl-like circle with fingers of one hand touching fingers of the other hand
3. Wipe brow with hand
4. Cross hands across chest as if shivering
5. Do breast stroke with arms
6. Do side stroke with arms
7. Hold nose with one hand, put other up in air, as if jumping off dock

Version B

Text from Camp Wolahi (Calif CFG), 1970s; variations from A emphasized.

1. Swimming, swimming, in **our** swimming **pool**
   When days are hot, when days are **cool**,
   It's in **our** swimming **pool**
   Breast stroke, side stroke, fancy diving too
   Oh don't you wish you never had anything else to do.

   ————

2. Swimming, swimming, in **our** swimming **pool**
   When days are hot, when days are **cool**,
   It's in **our** swimming **pool**
   Breast stroke, side stroke, fancy diving too
   Oh don't you wish you never had anything else to do.

   ————

3. For Wolahi, **that's** the camp for me.
   No other place do I love best
   No other place **I'll** be
   For Wolahi**'s life is** a merry whirl.
   We'll sing **you** a joyous song.
   For **I am** a Camp Fire Girl.

Version C

Text from Camp Watanopa (Mont CFG), 1970; variations from A emphasized in first verse.

1. Swimming, swimming in **our** swimming hole
   When days are hot, when days are cold, in **our** swimming hole.
   Breast stroke, side stroke, fancy diving too
   Oh, don't you wish you never had anything else to do?

   ———

2. Boating, boating in our red canoe
   When days are hot, when days are cold, in our red canoe
   Bow stroke, jay stroke, fancy sculling too
   Oh, don't you wish you never had anything else to do?
   Hey!

Rose, Rose: Melodic Repetition

The most common melodic repetition in camp songs is the use of the same tune for every verse. Nearly all fun and pretty songs that follow this form may be called strophic. One could apply the term binary form for those with a verse and chorus, each with a separate melody. This would distinguish them from the few like "Kumbaya" (90) that use the same tune for both verse and burden. However, even songs with a verse and chorus treat the total unit with strophic redundancy.

Melodic Structure

Within verses, melodies are built from short phrases, which recur with minor variations. These variations usually appear at the ends of lines, rather than beginnings. Such repetitions make songs easier to learn. Children secure the first words, then fill the rest, both text and tune, later.

Melodies written by campers use few musical motifs, generally two. "A Canoe May Be Drifting" has an AA_1A_2B structure. "Flicker" is AA_1BA_1. Other songs with two phrases include those that developed from necessities of slave life, "Kumbaya" and "Rise and Shine." "I Wish I Were" uses a Southern singing-school tune.

Tunes borrowed from commercial music may have more variety, but the limit for fun songs seems to be four melodic units. Two of the case-study songs with three phrases are borrowed from other cultures, "Eskimo Hunt" and "Grand Old Duke of York." Three, the "Mermaid," "Lollypop" and "A Bear," use commercially disseminated airs. Professionally written or arranged tunes for "Swimming" and "Ash Grove" use four phrases.

Many songs with more melodic motifs are constructed from verses and choruses with fewer elements. Both verse and chorus of the four-phrase "The Cuckoo" utilize two units. "An Austrian" has lengthened its chorus with the accumulations. The professionally written "Boatmen" has a verse with three phrases and a chorus with two. "Skyball Paint's" verse and chorus each has three.

Only one song, "Witchcraft," has little repetition. A recent conservatory graduate composed seven different themes. "Pep" essentially is three short melodies merged into one. Tradition is reducing them to a few repeating phrases.

Rounds like "Kookaburra" and "Rose," because of their circular nature, use four independent phrases. This may make them harder to learn. The need to concentrate on one's own part makes them harder to sing.

Rounds

Rounds and canons introduce another form of melodic repetition into the camp repertoire. Technically, all rounds are a subcategory of the larger group, and may be termed canons, while not all canons are rounds. Both involve two or more vocal groups singing the same melody, but beginning at different times. The subsequent groups, the comes, repeat the melody already sung by the beginning group, the dux.

When a canon can be repeated, it is a round. Each section must be the same length. Each group must sing the same notes (imitated at the unison) or the same notes in octaves.

Canons do not need to be repeated and, thus, can embellish the melody with variations. Some have been incorporated into longer works. Johann Sebastian Bach published the *Goldberg Variations* in 1741. César Franck composed his *Sonata in A Major for Violin and Piano* in 1886.[242]

Distinctions between rounds and canons are not clear to most campers. They learn the word "round" first, then expand its meaning, usually correctly, to describe any song with two or more vocal parts that begin at staggered, regular intervals. In camps rounds, generally, are sung three times at the unison.

Early Rounds

Rounds sung in camps are among the oldest secular music still in active Western tradition. Jill Vlasto* found "Scotland It Burneth" (13) in Thomas Lant's 1580 manuscript. England now knows "London's Burning," perhaps, Vlasto suggested, because of the London fire of 1666. More recently, it has been sung "Fire's Burning" (10) or "Camp Fire's Burning."

Sally Briggs[S] collected a version from an Ohio Boy Scout who learned it in camp as "School's Burning." Some counselors at Hiwela (Wisc CFG) in 1963 substituted the name of a particularly unpleasant camper for Scotland in a private version, after the redhead got sunburned. Not only has the round been sung with a variety of texts, but Cecily Raysor Hancock also has heard it with both 3/4 and 4/4 meters.

Seventeenth-Century Rounds

Thomas Ravenscroft edited the first known collection of rounds, the three-volume *Musickes Miscellanie*. *Pammelia*, published in 1609, contained "Hey Ho, Nobody Home" (63). Its many variations include Leah Culp's (Md CFG) "hi ho, anybody home." Deborah Weissman learned a Hebrew version at Tel Yehudah (NY J coed). Elizabeth Mills Bachman has sung it in French in Oregon camps, and has heard it in German and Swedish. Dale Ulrich[S] was told, it was an Interlochen (Mich coed) tradition in 1953. A year earlier, in 1952, Heather MacPhail[S] heard a Chi Omega sorority version at Michigan State.

Deuteromelia, the second volume published by Ravenscroft in 1609, contained "Three Blind Mice" (14) and "Go to Jane Glover" (2). Halliwell[*] published the modern "Mice" words in 1842. Seattle Scouts (Wash BSA) use its tune with "Three Wooden Pigeons" (12). "Jane" is the model for "Go to the Blue Birds" (9).

John Hilton edited the next major round collection, *Catch that Catch Can*, in 1652. He wrote "Come Follow" (19), also sung "Follow, Follow."

Eighteenth-Century Rounds

Rounds were common in seventeenth- and eighteenth-century England, where they often had ribald lyrics. Catches gave the form a bad odor among the rising middle classes. As a result, fewer eighteenth-century rounds exist in camps, than ones from the seventeenth. The humorous "Sandy's Mill" (5) comes from the 1700s.

Young Children's Music

By the nineteenth century, rounds were seen as fitting only for children. Mason used "Glide Along, Our Bonny Boat" (2) in his first youth book, the *Juvenile Lyre* of 1836. "Scotland's Burning" (13) and "White Sand, Gray Sand" (6) were in *The Boston School Song Book* of 1841. Fowke reported the last was known in Saint John, New Brunswick, around 1920.[331]

In 1864, Mason applied Pestalozzi's suggestion that knowledge should be broken into elements that children could learn in progressively more complex exercises. *The Song-Garden* was the first U. S. set of music books conceived as a graded series. In the second volume, for the "more advanced grade," he used rounds to teach the "arrangement of scales" and instill "the habit of part singing."

Among the rounds he included was "Come to the Top of the Hill" (1), which Trelipe (Minn CFG) was singing as "Come to the Top of the Path" in 1970. "Glide Along" (2) became known as "Sail Along My Bonnie Boat" at the Storer Camps (Ohio YMCA coed), according to Peggy Hays.[§] He also included "Come, Follow" (19).

Bradbury, a Mason protégé, created music for use in Sunday schools. In 1844, he had used "O Give Thanks" (22) in *The Social Singing Book*. He reused it in later anthologies, including *The Mendelssohn Collection* of 1849 and *The Key-Note* of 1863. After *The Song-Garden* appeared, Charles Hubert Farnsworth published the round in his 1917 *Grammar School Songs*. Today, it is a grace. Bradbury cited Wilhem as his source. Farnsworth was mentioned in WITCHCRAFT.

Root, another Mason acolyte active in Sunday-school music, is known better today for his Civil War-era songs like "Tramp, Tramp, Tramp" (2). In 1869, he used "Johnny Well" (2) to teach rests in *The Triumph*. In *The Song Herald* of 1876, Horatio Richmond Palmer used a longer version to teach the repeat sign. Kushtaka (Alaska CFG) was singing the round in the 1960s.

Root included "To Ope Their Trunks" (15) in his *First Years in Song-Land* of 1879. The YWCA published the round in 1927.[220] Fowke reproduced a version Isabel Ricker Smaller heard in Owen Sound, Ontario, around 1916.[331] Ellen Merle Morgan (La CFG) knows the second line as "robes of green," rather than "leaves" in Louisiana.

Older Children's Music

Mason used fewer rounds in the third volume of *The Song-Garden*, which featured "exercises for the training of the voice." Unintentionally, he reinforced the perception rounds were not appropriate for older children or adults. Later school song books that assumed students could read music relied on more jocular fun rounds, mixed with a few from the contemporary stage.

Henry Romaine Pattengill* (1861-1939) published "Row, Row, Row Your Boat" (26) and "Scotland's Burning" (13) in songsters he edited for use in Michigan schools. Lucille Parker Munk remembers teachers using the 1905 *Pat's Pick*. She says many songs they sang during her first years at Kitanniwa in the 1920s were learned from his collections. His earlier, 1899, anthology was *School Song Knapsack*.

The Golden Book of Favorite Songs was the most innovative of the new community songsters. First published in 1915, it was revised in 1923 by eight music educators led by John Walter Beattie* (1885-1962). He was then Director of Public School Music in Grand Rapids, Michigan. My sixth-grade teacher, Mildred Towne Ford (1911-2010), used the paper-bound collection as a supplement in 1956. It included "Are You Sleeping" (20), "Good night to you all, and sweet be thy sleep" (12), and "Oh, How Lovely Is the Evening" (46). The book also had "Row Your Boat" (26), "Scotland's Burning" (13), and "Three Blind Mice" (14).

Stage Rounds

"Row Your Boat" (26) may have origins in the lands west of Lancaster, Pennsylvania, where German and Scots-Irish immigrants settled. George Kunkel, a bass singer, moved from there to Philadelphia where he organized Kunkels Nightingale Opera Troupe. He primarily toured the South, where he became famous for his impersonations of Uncle Tom. In 1852, he published "The Old Log Hut March" by Richard Sinclair. The lyrics were much like those composed by Oxenford for "Ash Grove," with a chorus ending:

All that's past is gone, you know.
The future's but a dream.[246]

Like any popular minstrel song, it was copied. George Christy and Wood Minstrels published its own version in 1854.[338]

After our Civil War, in 1881, the principal of the boys' high school in Lancaster introduced the current version in his *Franklin Square Song Collection*. The composer, Eliphalet Oram Lyte, taught at Millersville State Normal School, and edited *The Teachers' Institute Glee Book* for common schools in Lancaster in 1874. John Piersol McCaskey, who edited the *Franklin Square* anthology, prided himself on attending every meeting of the Lancaster County Teachers' Institute.

Camp parodies include "Glub Your Boat" (8), about a submarine, and "Chew Your Food" (2), known at Watanopa (Mont CFG) and by Vivian Sexton (Tex CFG). It has been used for local songs in Ohio 4-H, at Hitaga (Iowa CFG), and Les Chalets Francais (Me Girls).

The tune for "Are You Sleeping" (20), or "Frère Jacques" (10), first was published in 1811. A manuscript from around 1775-1785 suggests an earlier existence. Fuld[*] said, that miscellany contained songs from comédie en vaudeville, a French theatrical form featuring comedy and music. Charles Lebouc published the modern text and tune in an 1860 collection for young singers. Elizabeth M. Traquair introduced a translation in *Popular Nursery Rhymes* to London in the 1880s. Her version suggested Friar John overslept, and did not ring the bells announcing morning prayers.

It, too, has been parodied widely. A 1940s Kitanniwa song book included "Perfect Posture" (11) and "Shall We Tell You" (1). Other camps have sung "Scrape Your Dishes" (3), "We Are Crazy" (4), "We Are Hungry" (2), and "You Were Primping" (4). Carol Flack says Seale Harris (Ala agency coed) uses the melody for the grace, "God of Our Fathers."

Fun Rounds

Many rounds utilize onomatopoeia to produce constant drones as parts follow one another through the imitative passages. Animals are mimicked in the "Swan Sings" (5), "Hanky Tank" (22), and "Sweetly Sings the Donkey" (30). Skylark Ranch (Calif GS) knows "burro." Fowke collected "donkey" from Alice Kane, who learned it in Saint John, New Brunswick, around 1920.[331]

"Hear the Lively Song of the Frogs" (28) was included in Palmer's *The Song Herald*. It probably persists from "Frogs in the Pond" by

Charles Uttermoehlen. "Why Shouldn't My Goose" (23), sung duck by Anne Lutz (NJ-NY), and "Grasshoppers Three" (12) treat animals with the same spirit, but without noises.

Comic uses of onomatopoeia are found in "Poor Tom" (8) and "Puffer Billies" (33), sung "Puffa Dillies" by Vivian Sexton (Tex CFG). "Hello, Hello" (23) and "Laugh Ha Ha" (11) use the words that are the round's topic for the continuing sound.

"Little Tommy Tinker" (45) is sung "sat on a cinder" at Eberhart (Ind YMCA coed). Tawakani (Ind CFG) knows "Little Tom Tinker sat down on a clinker." "Little Tom" is used at Seabow (Calif CFG) and at Surprise Lake (NY J boys) where he was "burnt by a clinker" in 1938. That version was shared with Wise (Ohio J coed), a camp with the same historic sponsor.[275] Rimrock (Wash YWCA) knew "Little Johnny" who yelled the comic passage as "Ma Pa," rather than the usual "Ma Ma." Fowke collected it as a taunt from Isabel Ricker Smaller, who heard it in Owen Sound, Ontario, in the 1920s.[331]

Pretty Rounds

Some rounds replicate pitches of church bells. Best known is "French Cathedrals" (40), which begins "Orléans." "Little Bells of Westminster" (8), "Are You Sleeping" (20), and "Oh, How Lovely Is the Evening" (46) are less literal. Fowke heard the last two in summer camps in Saskatchewan in the 1930s.[331]

"We're on the Upward Trail" (25) is an older, pretty camp round that does not use onomatopoeia. Its source, the echo-unison chorus to "We're on the Homeward Trail" (1), was copyrighted by the Salvation Army in 1922. Cecily Raysor Hancock sang the original at Wilaha (Colo CFG) in 1944. "Buddies and Pals" (14), "Lu-la-la-la-by" (8), and "Man's Life a Vapor" (5) also have been sung as rounds.

Girl Scouts

Girl Scouts have been actively involved in introducing more melodious rounds into the general camp repertoire. Newell's* 1929 *Girl Scout Song Book* contained thirty, including "When E'er You Make a Promise" (13). The 1828 original by W. W. Shield[179] has been adopted for ceremonial uses. It also contained Newell's non-round grace, "Hark to the Chimes" (60).

The Scouts' interest in rounds may be attributed to their ties with the English parent organization. Newell published the version of "Chairs To Mend" (37), which Henry Walford Davies introduced to Britain's National Adult School Union in 1915 in *The Fellowship Song Book*. A longer version had been published in this country in *Bixby's Home Songs*. *Gammer Gurton's Garland* printed the first extant version in 1810.

Girl Guides

More important for the Girl Scouts of the U. S. A. was a 1934 song book edited for the Kent County Girl Guides by Gladys Crawter[*] and others. It included "Rise up O Flame" (29), the "Wayfarer's Grace" (26), and "Wind in the Willows" (11). Betty Askwith's translation of the "Hungarian Round" (11) began "Sweet the evening air."

They were the first to publish two songs written in this country, "God Has Created a New Day" (26) and "Peace, I Ask of Thee O River" (88). The first was treated as a round, although it normally is sung here as a monophonic grace.

Kent County Song Book was used by editors of camp-oriented songsters in this country, including the Soifers[*] in 1937. Carl Edward Zander[*] and Wes H. Klusmann used it for *Camp Songs* for the Boy Scouts in 1938, *Camp Songs 'n' Things* in 1939, and *Songs for Girl Reserves* in 1941.

Janet Tobitt

Janet Evelyn Tobitt (1898-1984) was an English woman who sold several collections through the American Scouts. She included the Slovak "Apple Cheeked Rider" (15) and "Kookaburra" (85) in *Yours for a Song*[*] in 1939. *The Ditty Bag*[*] of 1946 contained "Make New Friends" (68), "Whippoorwill" (16), and "White Coral Bells" (77).

Jean Mayo MacLaughlin (Fla GS) recalls "Friends" (68) is the "first song I ever learned in Girl Scouts." Gene Clough has found, in the Long Beach, California, area, "a lot of CFG people seem to regard it as primarily a Girl Scout song." The He Bani Gani (Md CFG) Camp Fire group sings it with ascending melisma on the word "keep."

White Coral Bells

"White coral bells upon a slender stalk" (77) has been sung "silver stock" in a version collected from Magruder (Ore P coed) by Diane Davis.§ "Deck my garden wall" was sung for "walk" by Jolene Robinson Johnson (Wash CFG) in 1974, and at Fleur de Lis (NH P girls) in 1955. Larry Ralston has a version with "dot my" from Conger (Ohio 4-H). Joan Graham§ collected a variant with "by my" in 1953 from Westminster, a Michigan Presbyterian camp.

The round was in tradition before Tobitt. Joy Camps (Wisc girls) adapted the tune for an indigenous song in 1936. In 1938, a Kalamazoo Girl Reserves (Mich YWCA) song book claimed it was Canadian. Gibson* publicized it that year in his *Recreational Programs for Summer Camps*.

A more recent local song has been written to the tune at another Michigan Presbyterian camp, according to Mike Olsen:

> White stately birch beside a sparkling lake
> Here we campers gather and new friendships make
> Presbytery Point is so like Heaven above
> Here we grow like Christ in joy, faith, hope and love

Coral or choral may be a metaphor, pun, or riddling description of lilies of the valley as church towers that contain series of bells. Otherwise, the first phrase refers to *Heuchera sanguinea*, a flower from northern Mexico, which rarely is white. Its common name comes from the color of coral found in reefs created by tiny sea animals. Both plants have spikes for floral heads, but seldom grow together. The woodland native prefers the shade, the highland one the sun.

Function

Tobitt told people, who bothered with the fine print at the end of *The Ditty Bag*, rounds "afford a painless even joyful introduction to part singing."[174:177] This was wisdom received from Mason. Similar remarks were made in a 1939 4-H camping manual prepared by Ella Gardner* and a 1945 YWCA music guide written by Oliver.*

For many years, such comments were repeated by organization leaders, with little effect on camp repertoires. Then, for reasons coinciding with the Folk Revival, the dictum migrated from ideology into everyday life in camps. Now, even campers and counselors make comments like those heard by Naomi Feldman[§] and Mary Rogers, "rounds are easy and sound good. They give the effect of harmony for children who are too young for real harmonizing."

More simply, Carolyn Regan listed rounds when asked which songs were sung with harmony at Nan-Ke-Rafe (Mass CFG) in 1976.

Decline of Music Education

The Folk Revival prompted individuals, especially those not already singing, to imitate music they heard on radio. Unlike live performances, recordings did not change. They also did not reproduce overtones. They either were not captured by recording equipment in environmentally controlled studios, or were removed later by engineers.

Performers learned, in live performances, their audiences wanted to hear what was already familiar from records. Inadvertently, the Revival introduced the concept of correctness. Not only could textual errors be emended, but unintended variations in tunes and harmony could be eliminated. One no longer improvised using folklike techniques, but reproduced known parts.

A secondary effect of the Revival, and the general social protests that coincided with it, was some churches and secondary schools began using contemporary music to attract enough students to justify budgets. Teachers spent less time rehearsing classical pieces in three- or four-part harmony, for single-sex or gender-mixed choirs, glee clubs, and choruses.

Singing-school books had included rudiments sections that went beyond teaching sight reading to introduce concepts of chords and western harmony. Their second halves were collections of religious music in all keys and accepted meters.

In the 1950s, many churches continued to teach the elements of harmony, the scales and their associated chords, but by example rather than by deliberation. Theory no longer was taught in junior or senior high schools, but choir and glee club members still read sheet music. My high school performed Händel's "Hallelujah" chorus every December.

My 1957 Camp Fire manual[*] assumed such vocal groups existed. I could earn an honor bead for participating "in a trio, quartet, glee club or organized chorus, or accompanying such a group for three months." Earlier, in 1934, the Mormon's Bee Hive Girls* rewarded learning "to harmonize your voice with others. Three times sing in a duet, trio or chorus."

After the crises of the late 1960s, fewer institutions exposed young people to the musical vocabulary used in camps. When children no longer grew up hearing harmony in camps, in schools or in churches, they could not develop emotional associations for it. When that experience was gone, the ability to improvise harmony was threatened. Cultural forms cannot survive once the mechanisms for their perpetuation are destroyed.

Part Songs

Once campers were less exposed to the vocabulary of German-influenced harmony, and once rounds began to be seen as harmony, boundaries between music categories disappeared. June Rushing Leibfarth⁵ was told an echo song, "Ol' Texas" (31), was a round. Ka-esta's (Ore CFG) songbook editor tells campers "Flea" (39) is a round, but they should "say first and last lines." Les Chalets Francais (Me girls) once thought "Little Sir Echo" (15) was a round.

A similar perception is transferred to songs with two parts, sung contra fashion, like "Sarasponda" (59) at Watervliet (Mich girls), "Warsaw the Forty-Second" (5) by friends of June Rushing Leibfarth,⁵ and "Horsey, Horsey" (28) by Josephine Weber (Wisc CFG). "Boomdeada" (48), sung to Hoagy Carmichael and Frank Loesser's "Heart and Soul" of 1938, has come to be treated as a round by some.

If contra-style songs could be considered rounds, it became logical to campers to treat songs with two harmonic parts, like Arthur Hamilton's "I Can Sing a Rainbow" (14), as circular canons. Kiwatani (Ohio CFG) believes both "Swing along the Open Road" (44) and "Tiny Drops of Dew" (24) are rounds.

Quodlibets

The increased interest in singing rounds as harmony has led to adapting them as quodlibets. "Are You Sleeping" and "Three Blind Mice" (combination, 3) often have been sung simultaneously, beginning together, contra style, or at intervals, canon style. Recently, people have been adding "Row Your Boat" (combination, 4) as a third part.

"Hey Ho, Nobody Home" (63) is sung with "Shalom Chaverim" (23) at Tayanita (Ohio CFG). Donna Gerardi (Calif CFG) has sung it with "Make New Friends" (68). Several Girl Scout camps sing the round with "Ah, Poor Bird" (11). At Christopher (Ohio C coed), Debra Janison has sung "Our Motto" (25) "in a round" with "Sons of God" (3).

"One Bottle of Pop" (40) is the counterpoint piece most treated as a round today. In some camps, each group sings each part in a prescribed order. At Tanadoona (Minn CFG), each has one part it repeats as new groups enter. It has not been published widely, and still exists in variants. Trexler (NY P boys) sings "fish sticks 'n' vinegar." Valley Mill (Md coed) knows "mayonnaise and Tootsie Rolls."

French Rounds

The displacement of songs sung with harmony left a void in the general repertoire that propelled a search for more rounds. International music was not a fertile resource. The round, primarily, has been an English form. The only French ones in American camps are "Frère Jacques" (10) and "Orléans Beaugency" (40). The second exists in a longer version in Europe.

German Rounds

Germans have been more likely to sing canons. Johann Gottfried Schmauk published *Deutsche Harmonie* in Philadelphia in 1847. The Lutheran singing-school book contained some canons with religious lyrics in its music fundamentals section. Following a few short pieces that could be sung as rounds, Schmauk instructed groups to combine in a group-harmony ending.

At Kitanniwa in the 1950s, two groups sang the grace "For Health and Strength" (87) once through, beginning at intervals. When the second part finished, the two joined to sing "For health" with diverging harmony. I have not seen this termination technique mentioned in English-language books.

Among the Deutsch rounds sung in camps is "Music Alone Shall Live" (45), which Patiya (Colo CFG) knows in German. The melody for "Oh How Lovely Is the Evening" (46) was written in 1826 by Christian Johann Philipp Schulz.

Several German composers named Schultze used the Latinized term for a local political leader, Praetorius, when they were writing in the late sixteenth century. Michael of Wolfenbüttel created "Jubilate Deo" (23). His uncle Christoph of Lüneburg produced "Rise up O Flame" (29). The Protestant duke of Braunschweig und Lüneburg controlled both cities.

International Rounds

Confronted by a dearth of international rounds, songbook editors and recreation leaders began adapting foreign songs to the form. Tobitt based the "Rally Song" (6), which began "Mil ha ba lou," on "a 'getting together' song from the Balkan peninsula."[172] "Let Us Sing Together" (34) was written to a Czech folk tune. Carol Parsons Sievert remembers singing it with "the Otonwi [senior unit] group that I belonged to that started back with little kids."

Another song adapted to the round form is the Dutch "From out the Battered Elm Tree" (23). Lucille Parker Munk, who taught it as a round at Tanawida (Mich CFG) in the 1950s, said, "That's one of my favorites." In 1974, Jolene Robinson Johnson (Mich CFG) and Carol Parsons Sievert (Mich CFG) sang it as a song with an echo chorus of cuckoos.

Bonnie Loomis (Ohio GS) knows it as a quodlibet with "I See the Moon" (20). Ann Beardsley (Mich GS) and Peach Creek (Tex GS) sing it as the first verse of a medley. "Twas on a summer's evening" is the second. "Mister Moon, You're out too Soon" (4) is the chorus. Several translations exist.

Before the Six-Day War of 1967, the romance surrounding Israel and its camp-like kibbutzim spread to Protestant camps. They discovered "Zum Gali Gali" (24). A Southern-born, New York-trained Episcopalian, Rue Ingram Moore (1927-2008), gave CRS its version of "Shalom Chaverim" (23).[134] "Hava Nashira" (17) often is known as "I Shall Arise" or "The Prodigal Son" in Camp Fire camps. Some have begun dancing the hora to "Hava Nagila" (20).

Other international songs now sung as rounds are the Danish "Rosen fra Fyn" (13) and the Moroccan "A Ram Sam Sam" (28). A visiting British Boy Scout introduced the first to Hiwela (Wisc CFG) in 1961. The group later published it as "Rosen Fra Fünn."[118] Filipino Scouts contributed "O Yepo" (20), usually transcribed as "Eppo."

Fun Songs

The increased interest in rounds heightened individuals' perceptions of the counterpoint potential in monophonic songs already in tradition. This renewal process, no doubt, added to the lives of songs like "More We Get Together" (32) at Manakiki (Minn agency coed). Kalamazoo's Girl Reserves (Mich YWCA) had converted "Pussy Willow" (8) in the late 1930s.

Patricia Ann Raine§ collected a round version of "Indians Are High Minded" (12) from Shawondasee (Tex CFG) in 1973. Several camps have banned it, rather than changing the noun, as had been done by those mentioned in PEP who sang "Camp Fire Girls are high minded."

Some songs treated as rounds have nonsense choruses, which may be converted into drones. Such adapted lyrics include "Ging Gang Goolie" (19), "Tzena, Tzena" (11), and "Above a Plain" (22), sung "above the fields" at Onahlee (Ore CFG).

Other older fun songs treated as rounds in several camps include "Animal Fair" (9), "Ezekiel Saw a Wheel" (19), "Gack Goon" (21), "Rocka My Soul" (31), and "Mrs. O'Leary" (31). Wanakiwin (Minn YWCA) sings "Old Mrs. Leary." Watervliet (Mich girls) treats "Dewey" (13) as a round. Its tune is "Puffer Billies" (33).

Pretty Songs

Pretty songs, like "A Plea for One World" (45) and "Happiness Runs in a Circular Motion" (17), have been sung as rounds in some camps. Others converted to part songs include "Who Can Sail" (14) at Kushtaka (Alaska CFG) and "Time To Be Happy Is Now" (5) at Wintaka (Calif CFG).

Similar versions of "In the Land of Olden" (19) exist at Shawnee (Mo CFG), of "Dee-ah-de-dum-dum" (5) at Molly Luman (Ohio GS), and of "Tender Shepherd" (7) at Robinwood (Tex GS). Jayne Garrison was at Shawnee, Aileen Yung at Molly Luman, and friends of June Rushing Leibfarth§ at Robinwood in 1966.

Namanu (Ore CFG) sings "Have Fun, Our Motto Is" (25) with two parts. High/Scope (Mich agency coed) sings four parts with the three verses of "I Gave My Love a Cherry" (24). "Happy Days to Those We Love" (9) evolved from an older song, "Leprechaun" (10).

Round Writing

Finally, the quest for new rounds has led to song writing. The idea is new, and its execution requires some musical skill. Angela Lapham knows the "Oak Hills Round" (1) from the Saginaw, Michigan, Girl Scout camp. A hundred miles away, Karen Johnson created a round setting for "It Is Such a Secret Place" (1) at High/Scope (Mich agency coed). She took her text from Antoine de Saint-Exupéry's *The Little Prince* of 1943.

In the early years of camping, more had the necessary training to produce rounds. Margaret Bradshaw McGee[*] (1889-1975), who wrote "My Paddle's Keen and Bright" (59) at Sebago-Wohelo (Me girls) in 1918, was educated at Oberlin. The Christian Scientist was born in Ann Arbor, Michigan, and worked for the YWCA before she became a field director for the Camp Fire Girls.

Anne Hopson Chapin[*] (1891-1979), who created "Whippoorwill" (16) in 1921, could write three-part harmony. After she returned from the Girl Scouts' national training school for officers at Plymouth Camp (Mass GS), she published a collection[*] of songs through Tremont Music in Boston. Of the twelve, six were rounds and "O Give Thanks" (22) was a canon.

She lived in Kent, Connecticut, where she played organ in the Congregational church, and occasionally directed the choir. One of her former students says, "She had a unique way of teaching piano, which none of us have ever forgotten, and some of us affectionately pretend not to have forgiven [. . .] She had little cardboard keyboards that she placed over the two real keyboards on her lovely grand pianos in the parlor. We had to learn to play many songs on them, without ever hearing our own sounds (and therefore, mistakes) for MONTHS before being allowed to play the real keys. It has forged a bond among us all, but we loved her dearly!"

McGee's photograph appears in "People Who Make It Possible." Chapin's at Plymouth (Mass GS) is in "Composers."

Instead of indigenous rounds, there are new quasi-organizational ones like "Poor and Carefree Stranger" (11) from the Swiss Girl Guides. June Rushing Leibfarth[§] collected "The Hills" (8) that "protect us by day and night" at the 1964 All-State Girl Scout Encampment accommodated by Sky-Wa-Mo (Tenn GS). Peach Creek Ranch (Tex GS) sings "surround us." Laurine Kelly[*] introduced "Kittens Have Whiskers" (6) and "Raspberries" (3) in *Gay Songs for Blue Birds* in 1951.

Literary Sources

Some new rounds, like favorites long in tradition, draw their inspiration from literary sources. "Promises" (8) comes from a 1922 Robert Frost poem, "Stopping by Woods on a Snowy Evening." "Make New Friends" (68) reworks a Joseph Parry poem, "New Friends and Old Friends." Parry[*] was the son of a Welsh ironworker who migrated to the iron-mill town of Danville, Pennsylvania, up the Susquehanna in 1853. His talents were recognized in the Welsh immigrant community. Friends helped him return to England to study composition.

The Bible has been used for "Every Man 'neath his Vine and Fig" (18), from Micah 4:13. "The Lord Is My Shepherd" (17) adapts the twenty-third Psalm. "Dona Nobis Pacem" (26) uses the Latin text from the Agnus Dei of the Roman Catholic mass.

Graces

The acceptance of rounds as beautiful music has resulted in greater openness to their use as graces. Even so, some are sung through once and treated like canons. Among the new or newly popular ones are "Allelujah, Amen" (22), "Ego Sum Pauper" (8), "Gelobet Sei" (14), "Jubilate Deo" (23), and "O Give Thanks" (22). Harry Robert Wilson adapted Mozart's "Alleluia, Alleluia" (33). Some use the Jewish "Hine Ma Tov" (10) as a round grace.

Thomas Ken wrote the words for the "Tallis Canon" (10), which began "Glory to Thee, my God this night," in 1695. Thomas Tallis had composed the melody in 1565, when English religious music under Elizabeth I was abandoning styles associated with the Roman Catholic church. It is used for "Morning Prayer" (8), which usually begins "Father we thank Thee for the night," and for "Father We Thank Thee for the Morning" (5).

Gender Aspects

In the 1930s, Zanzig found rounds were sung widely in girls' camps, but less so in boys'.[561:525-526] In the same years, Gibson found rounds to be the most popular music form at Chimney Corners, a Massachusetts YMCA girls' camp he directed.[345:164]

Kitanniwa Repertoire

A similar gender division existed at Kitanniwa in 1974, where the only circular canons sung in the experimental coed session were "Hanky Tank" (22) and "We Are Crazy" (4). When members of the staff were by themselves, they sang "Chairs To Mend" (37), "Hey Ho, Nobody Home" (63), "Oh How Lovely Is the Evening" (46), and "White Coral Bells" (77).

Kitanniwa in the 1950s did not sing rounds that exploited onomatopoeia like "Little Tommy Tinker" (45) and "Puffer Billies" (33). They were taught in 1956 at Clear Lake (Mich agency coed), the Battle Creek public school's camp. Neither did Kitanniwa sing the common ones known outside, like "Are You Sleeping" (20), "Row Your Boat" (26), and "Three Blind Mice" (14).

Instead, girls preferred those with sentimental topics, like "Oh How Lovely Is the Evening" (46), "Make New Friends" (68), and "Let Us Sing Together" (34). "White Coral Bells" (77) was more fanciful with its fairies. "Hey Ho, Nobody Home" (63) and "Chairs To Mend" (37) were introduced late in the decade. The most enduring were "Kookaburra" (85) and "My Paddle's Keen and Bright" (59).

Case Study: Rose, Rose

"Rose, Rose" (50) was one of the more popular in the early 1970s, according to Kitty Smith. It was included in collections made by Carol Parsons Sievert in 1973, and by Mary Tinsley Unrue in 1974.

Janet Tobitt introduced the quatrain in *Yours for a Song*[†] in 1939 with no annotation. The only other songs in the book with no attribution are another round, "At Summer Morn," and four graces. Since she was such an advocate for the form, one wonders if perhaps she did not craft this one.

Zanzig published the same words and tune in *Singing America*[†] in 1940, but in a different key. His headnote claimed it was English. The Rohrboughs reproduced Tobitt's version in the 1947 edition of *Joyful Singing*[†] for the Camp Fire Girls. It was not selected by the editors for *Music Makers*.[*]

"Rose" surfaced in tradition, probably in the 1960s, perhaps after Tobitt reissued *The Ditty Bag*.[†] Madeline Gail Trichel, who attended Girl Scout camps in Louisiana in the 1950s, says she did not learn it until the 1970s. Girls in her Scout troop taught it to her.

Explication

Joyce Gregg Stoppenhagen (Ohio GS) believes the original words (version B) dealt with themes from the Plantagenet War of the Roses (1455-1485). That dynastic battle ended with the marriage of Henry Tudor of Lancaster (the reds) to Elizabeth of York (a white, who became a red by marriage). "Wed" no doubt was substituted in tradition for "red," because it made more sense with the phrase about marriage to those with a limited knowledge of English history.

Textual Variation

Yallani (Calif CFG) has altered Tobitt's "that thou wilt" to "my will," in keeping with its attempts to eliminate traditional female stereotypes from the camp program. High/Scope (Mich agency coed) ends, "I'll marry that I may / If thou but stay." Ann Marie Filocco[§] collected a New Jersey Girl Scout version that ended, "I will never marry / Again----." Loyaltown (NY J boys) sings "Joan."

Music

Tobitt's original melody is very close to that of "Hey Ho, Nobody Home" (63). Their contours are nearly identical. "Rose's" tempo is much slower, and lacks the variations introduced by the use of melisma on "merry" and the rhythmic asymmetry of "**yet** will **I** be" of "Nobody." Azalea Trails[†] (Calif GS) recorded a much slower version, which emphasized the choral effects of "round harmony."

Linda Ann Barsness[†] and Judith Bischoff published a version in 1974 that was closer to the ones I heard sung than it was to Tobitt. They had added melisma to "thee" in the second line, and a low note for the added "sire" at the end of the third. The fourth was completely new. Wintaka[†] (Calif CFG) has added notes to the second "rose" in the first line.

Popularity

"Rose" is overwhelmingly a girls' song, although it was less known in the survey Midwestern Camp Fire camps than elsewhere. Josephine Weber remembers using it at council fires at Hiwela (Wisc CFG). June Rushing Leibfarth[§] heard, it was "one of the most often sung camp songs as a round" at Arnold (Texas GS). Peggy Hays[§] was told, it was "sung as a round" at the Storer Camps (Mich YMCA coed), "usually at campfires and on hikes. Especially pretty when sung on canoe hikes where the canoes are stretched over a half mile or more of river."

Jan Williky Boss used it to illustrate the inanity of the songs sung at a New Jersey girls' camp she disliked.

Parodies

"Rose's" popularity has led to camp-specific songs at Marycrest (Vt C girls) and Kamaji (Minn girls), as well as local parodies. "Roads," collected by Ann Marie Filocco,[§] has begun spreading in the Northeastern Girl Scout network. Becky Colwell Deatherage has sung "roam" at Comstock (NY GS).

Similar second lines in Ann Marie's "Road" (version E) and Ann Beardsley's (Mich GS) "Stroke" (version F), learned in Michigan, suggests the second parody was reconstructed or adapted by a Girl Scout counselor moving from one region to another.

Contrafacta

In recent years, the melody for "Rose" has been promoted for political and religious purposes. "America, America" (25), "Love, Love" (6), and "Peace, Peace" (3) have been sung separately, in medleys, and in quodlibets with each other and with "Rose."

Word of God included a variant of "Love" and "Jesus" in the first volume of its 1975 *Songs of Praise*.[†] It noted the origins were unknown. Its "Jesus," with its third line, "You have given me Your riches," was cloned from "America." The charismatic, evangelical, Roman Catholic group was founded in Ann Arbor in 1967.

Carol Ann Engle's (NY P girls) variant Version C, which begins "row, row," was written directly from "Rose." According to Judy Miller, Kamaji's local song, version D, was based on "Jesus" (version C). Some of the phrases are close to "America."

"America" was less likely to be sung in a Camp Fire camp than it was in other types of girls' camps in 1976. Within Camp Fire camps, it was more likely to be sung in other parts of the country than in the survey Midwest. The percentage of women in CFG camps in the five states who recognized the song was only marginally higher than the number of men anywhere in the country.

The same preference pattern existed with "Love." Women in girls' or coed camps in the survey Midwest were more familiar with the verse than were women outside the region. A greater percentage of men everywhere in the country knew the song than did women in CFG camps.

Glen[†] (Ohio CFG) sang "Rose" with "Love" as a round at lunch, at supper, and during the serenade the day I visited the camp in 1974. Their melody was closer to the one published by Word of God than it was to the one sung with "Rose."

Word of God's melody is the same as Barsness and Bischoff for the first two lines. Its last line is the same as the first line of "Rosen fra Fyn" (13). The third phrase descends the scale. This suggests the song entered the Ohio Camp Fire camp through religious channels rather than from Girl Scouts who were on staff.

Glen was unusual in combining "Rose" and "Love." Girls usually keep the songs separate, perhaps because they learn them in different situations. Jacqueline Orvis learned "Rose" at Camp o' Fair Winds (Mich GS), "Love" in a church group, and "America" from a friend in college. Kathleen Villiers-Fisher's[§] friend said she learned "Rose" and "America" at Sacajewa (NJ GS), "Ding Dong Wedding Bells" (1) at Chickagami (NJ GS), and "Love" from a friend.

When Ann Beardsley (Ohio GS) typed the songs for her personal song book, she put "Rose," "America," and "Love" on three separate pages. When she learned "Peace," she wrote it on another page, but she added "Ah Poor Bird" (11) and "Stroke" to her "Rose" page.

Quodlibets

"Rose" was published as a four-part round, but often is done with two. It has been sung canon or contra style in quodlibets with "Hey Ho, Nobody Home" (combination recognized by 15 who were asked) and with "Ah, Poor Bird" (recognized by 7). The three also have been sung together.

Mason published "Thou, Poor Bird" in 1866 in the third volume of *The Song-Garden*. It later was printed in a number of collections, including that made by Newell* in 1929.

Roger Smith used the melody with "Star Light, Star Bright" at Putnam (Mass agency coed). The wishing rhyme began appearing in this country in the late nineteenth century. Brown collected a variant in Garland, North Carolina, in 1921 from Elizabeth Janet Black.[276:182] She (1876-1939) was a teacher, poet, and historian raised on the coastal plain of Sampson County.

Jane Ann Matulich has sung "I Won't Be My Father's Jack" in combination with "Rose" and the other rounds at Skylark Ranch (Calif GS). The Opies tracked "Jack" to *Mother Goose's Melody*, which was published sometime around 1765.[452]

Jean Ritchie

Jean Ritchie has become associated with the round cluster. Her immigrant ancestor, James Ritchie, was born in Ayrshire in southwestern Scotland in 1757. He migrated to Virginia in 1768, as part of the Scots migration that began after the end of the French and Indian war in 1763 made the frontier safer. After serving in the Revolution, he shifted to Buncombe County in western North Carolina around 1791, then relocated to the Cumberland mountains of eastern Kentucky around 1813. Most family members joined the Old Regular Baptist Church.

Alan Lomax collected her family's music for the Archives of American Folksong in the 1930s. After graduating from a local college, she moved to New York City in 1946 to work for the Henry Street Settlement, where Mordecai Kessler was on the board of directors. There she met people involved in the emerging folk music revival, and began performing and publicizing her family's tradition.

She says the first round she learned as a child was "Hey Ho, Nobody Home."[485] In 1964, she used the tune for a new round, which began "What a goodly thing." It has been combined with "Ding Dong Wedding Bells" (1), "Ding Dong Funeral Bells," "Ah, Poor Bird" (11), "Shalom Chaverim" (23), "Hey Ho" (63), and "Rose." After she suffered a stroke in December of 2009, her fans began singing the "Peace Round" at midnight on New Year's Eve.

Version A

Text from Mary Tinsley Unrue, editor of Camp Kitanniwa (Mich CFG) song book, 1974; each line is a new vocal part. Her picture appears in "Kitanniwa, 1974." Tobitt's is in "Collectors."

> Rose, rose, rose, rose
> Will I ever see thee wed
> I will marry at thy will sire
> At thy will

Version B

Text from Camp Neewahlu (Ida CFG), 1970; variations from A emphasized. Guitar chords from Clarena Snyder, Great Trails Camp (Ohio GS), 1963, 1965, 1967-1968.

> Rose, (Am) rose, (Em) rose, (Am) rose-- (E)
> **Shall** (Am) I ev (D) er see (C) thee **red?** (D7)
> **Aye,** (G) mar (D) ry -- **that** (C) **thou wilt,** (D7)
> **If** (Am) **thou** (Em) **but stay!** (Am)

Version C

Text from Carol Ann Engle, Camp Cherith of Western New York (NY P girls), 1976.

> Row row row row
> Row your boat to Jesus side
> There forever to abide
> Lord, at Thy side

Version D

Text from Judy Miller, Camp Kamaji (Minn girls), 1970s.

> Kamaji, Kamaji
> You have meant so much to me.
> You have given us your spirit.
> We love you so.

Version E

Text from a New Jersey Girl Scout camper; collected by Ann Marie Filocco, Douglass College, Rutgers, 1975; three-part round.

> Roads, roads,
> Roads, roads
> Will I ever see thee end,
> I will never tarry
> Again ----.

Version F

Text from Ann Beardsley, Camp o' the Hills (Mich GS), 1963-1970; Camp Ken-Jockety (Ohio GS), 1976.

> Stroke, stroke, stroke, stroke
> Will I ever see the end
> Of the sandbars and the deadheads
> Stroke, stroke, stroke, stroke

Version G

Text from Camp Trelipe (Minn CFG), February 1970.

> America, America
> Shall we tell you how we feel
> You have given us your freedoms/riches
> We love you so.

Love, love, love, love
Love is the gospel of the world
Love thy neighbor as thyself
Love, love, love, love

Peace, Peace, Peace, Peace
Colors of the world live together
Wars will end as war will cease
Peace, Peace, Peace, Peace.

A Canoe May Be Drifting:
Indigenous Songs

Leave taking illuminates what is important about camp. Last night ceremonies rely upon indigenous songs to particularize emotions. "Now the Day Is Over" has been used for "Camp Is Nearly Over" (2) at Tanadoona (Minn CFG) and Tawakani (Ida CFG). Kitanniwa knew "Now Our Council Endeth" (1) in the 1940s. Some 29 camps have used it as a vespers or evening closing song.

Sabine Baring-Gould published the "Child's Evening Hymn" in *The Church Times* in 1867. At the time, he was betrothed, but not allowed to marry. Joseph Barnby composed the "Merrial" setting the next year.

Commercial farewell songs include "I'll Be Seeing You" from 1938, and "Leave Me with a Smile" from 1921. Hitaga (Iowa CFG) used the first in 1944. Vivian Sexton (Tex CFG) remembers the second with "Leave Camp with a Smile." Sammy Fain and Irving Kahal composed the first.

"Always" has been used for "Kitanniwa though We Stray" (4), in which camp names are substituted. Hantesa (Iowa CFG) adapted the melody for "Gypsy Heart." Tanadoona (Minn CFG) used it for "Camp Fire Maidens True" and "I'll Be Loving You." Irving Berlin composed the original.

Songs of Place

General pretty songs of place rarely are specific enough for last night rituals. Local ones have been written to commercial songs personifying states or locales. In 1956, an Iowa Camp Fire camp was singing:

> Is it true what they say 'bout Hitaga?
> Do the friendships you make really last?
> Do the stars tell their secrets to you?
> Do they shine? Do they grow?

"Is It True What They Say about Dixie," composed by Irving Caesar, Sammy Lerner and Gerard Marks in 1936, was recorded by both Al Jolson and Rudy Vallée.

TanKonKa Horizon Club (Ida CFG) wrote local words for "Carry Me Back to Old Virginny" (4) that began, "Carry me back to Tawakani / That's where the flowers, the trees and friendships grow." Tanadoona (Minn CFG) has different words to the song reworked in 1878 by James Alan Bland from older themes.

"Are You from Dixie" has been adopted for an Atali unit song at Kowana (Tenn CFG). "Swanee" was used for "Hail, Hail! Hiiteni" at the Luther Gulick Camps (Me girls). Hiiteni was the camp name for Vetter Gulick. George Linus Cobb and Jack Selig Yellen composed the first in 1915. The second, written in 1919 by George Gershwin and Irving Caesar, was associated with Jolson.

"O Tannenbaum" is the most useful place song. Fuld* discovered a German nationalist and youth leader, Rudolf Zacharias Becker, published the volkstümliches lied in *Mildheimischen Liederbuch* in 1799. Its melody is sung with "Softly Falls the Light of Day" (21), and camp-specific songs at Marycrest (Vt C girls), Treasure Island (Penna BSA), Wampatuck (Mass P girls), and by Denver Scouts (Colo BSA). Blue Haven (NM P coed) sings:

> Our fathers of old here roamed the trails
> Searching for gold within these vales
> But we have found wealth untold
> Blue Haven Camp! Blue Haven Camp!

August Zarnack created a tragic love song for the melody in his 1820 *Weisenbuch zu den Volksliedern für Volkschulen*. Ernst Anschütz recast it as a carol in 1824. Gifford (Neb BSA) sings "Oh Christmas Tree" with the humorous "Mule He Is a Funny Sight" (1).

Wampatuck (Mass P girls) chants "O Pumpkin Cards" (1) during its variation on other camps' Christmas in July celebrations. "Michigan, My Michigan" and "Maryland, My Maryland" (2) use the tune.

"Missouri Waltz" is used with "Underneath the silver beams of dear old mammy moon" (10). The song became associated with the presidential reelection campaign of Harry Truman in 1948. The next year Hitaga (Iowa CFG) created a local version with quotations from other Camp Fire songs. "Way Down at Namanu where the silvery Sandy flows / Pioneers are living as the days both come and go" was written by the Oregon CFG camp's Pioneers unit in 1941. Iowa's Frederic Knight Logan adapted the melody in 1914 from one created by John Valentine Eppel of Fort Dodge, Iowa. James Royce Shannon of Adrian, Michigan, added the lyrics.

"Here We Have Idaho" uses the melody associated with Helen Hill Miller's "Follow the Gleam" (14). Sallie Hume-Douglas composed the underlying "Garden of Paradise" in 1915. Her family migrated from Virginia to Columbia, Missouri, where she was born in 1867. Her sisters married men who settled ranch lands near Las Vegas, New Mexico. She followed, married, then taught in Hawaii. Baritone Keeaumoku Louis recorded her Hawaiian love song. In 1917, Alice Bessee and McKinley Helm adapted it for the University of Idaho's "Our Idaho." The state legislature did not make it the state's song until 1931.

In Ontario, Laurel Ann Hall has sung "Deep in the Heart of Ak-O-Mak" (Ont girls) to a 1941 Texas song by Don Swander and his wife, June Hershey. He was from Marshalltown, Iowa. She was born in Los Angeles.

In the East, the Philadelphia Boy Scout camp, Treasure Island (Penna BSA), used "Quaker down in Quakertown," written in 1916 by Alfred Solman and David Berg. "The Camp along the Delaware" was in both their 1920 and 1946 song books.

The Midwestern "I Want To Go Back to Michigan" has been used for "I Want To Go Back to Camp Again" (3). Doris Godsey used "Indiana" for Namanu's (Ore CFG):

> I'm dreaming now about the Sandy
> And it seems that I can see
> The rocky point and shore

James Frederick Hanley and Ballard MacDonald wrote the commercial song in 1917. They were born in Rensselaer, Indiana, and Portland, Oregon, respectively. Irving Berlin released "Michigan" in 1914.

Commercial songs of place often are adapted for indigenous camp songs when the words are perceived to fit, even if their histories might make them inappropriate. "Camp Warren Beckons" (Mich P coed) was sung to "Where the River Shannon Flows" in the 1950s. James Russell[*] introduced the original in 1911 in a vaudeville skit about Irish servant girls. United Irish Societies and Ancient Order of Hibernians protested his impersonations of young women.

"Roses of Picardy" was used with "Caravan Fire" at Watanopa (Mont CFG) in the 1940s. Dorothy Court performed it in London's music halls after the Battle of the Somme, one of the bloodiest of World War I. Her husband, Haydn Wood, orchestrated the poem by Frederick Edward Weatherly.

Sense of Place

A sense of place can become so strong, general songs may assume very personal meanings. Carol Shuster[S] was told, Great Trails (Ohio GS) "is bounded on one side by a river (stream)." Her friend used to think "Peace, I Ask of Thee O River" (88) "was written about that particular river." Debbie Saint Pierre[S] collected "Michael, Row the Boat Ashore" (66) from someone who said, "This was my favorite camp song at Girl Scout camp. It was sung in the evening down by the lake."

A belief in the significance of one's own camp creates a mechanism for absorbing strangers, if they can be accepted as representatives of a semi-mythic other who reinforce the importance of one's own world by blessing it by their appearance.

I simply fantasized the Ship Titanic counselor knew "Ol' Texas" (31) because she was from Texas. I was disillusioned when I discovered, years later, her four verses had been in the then current *Girl Scout Pocket Songbook.*[*]

Cynthia Scheer[S] was told by a former Girl Scout camper, "Dis Old Hammer" (4) "was brought to camp by a counselor from the mining regions of Pennsylvania, I believe, and so would appear to be an outgrowth of mining lore." Her friend then admitted some confusion, because "some of the phrases and speech mannerisms used suggest the Negro song." In fact, the frame-substitution lyric is related to the "John Henry" (2, Laws I1) cluster that spread in both Black and Appalachian traditions.

Upper Midwest

Indigenous camp songs often fuse personal experience with the environment. This merger of the self with something greater may explain the preference for lyrics like "Land of the Silver Birch" (30), which contain allusions to Native American life. The identification may be easier in a camp like Kitanniwa, which lies in the glaciated area that had been the domain of Northeastern Woodlands bands. They lived around lakes and invented the canoes campers learn to paddle. In the Southwest, Blue Haven (NM P coed) identifies more with the placer miners of 1883 than with urban-dwelling farmers of the Pueblos.

Tobitt heard "Silver Birch" was being sung at Ahmek (Ont boys) in 1940.[175] She suggested, it could be treated as an echo or two-part song. Only Marycrest (Vt C girls) and Kamaji (Minn girls) mentioned singing it as a round in the 1970s. Judy Miller says, the latter localized one line to "Where Kami Indian tribes."

Mary Satterfield Swanson remembers, she wrote "Canadian Wilderness" (12) in 1960 while she was on a Canadian canoe trip with Manito-Wish (Wisc YMCA coed):

> As we paddled through the lakes I had a keen sense of awareness of the past and the Indians who had originally inhabited the area. I wrote the song with an Indian rhythmic beat in mind, and tried to portray my feelings about the land that I loved so much.

Voyageurs were the only other people who used the canoe. The Frenchmen carried furs taken by the Ottawa and other groups to Montréal. They, too, come to mind on canoe treks in Michigan, Wisconsin, Minnesota, and Ontario. Mary originally called her song, "The Life of a Voyageur."

The West

The only equivalent conflation of camp activities with Native life might occur on Seton's plains, where Spanish horses were tamed. However, descriptions of the West usually borrow from movies. In 1927, Mabel Wayne and Louis Wolfe Gilbert wrote "Ramona" for a film of the same name. Helen Hunt Jackson's novel narrated the life of the daughter of a Cahuilla woman and a Scots man. Her heroine was raised by an old Mexican family just after the United States laid claim to California. Kunatah (NY BSA) and Surprise Lake (NY J boys) used the melody.

Mary Hale Woolsey wrote the lyrics for "When It's Springtime in the Rockies" with fellow Mormon Milton Taggart. Gene Autry introduced the song in a 1937 film of the same name. Other western singers recorded it, and it was adapted for "When It's Springtime in Alaska" (3). The composer, Robert Sauer, was born in Saxony and migrated to Utah after his conversion.

College Tunes

College alma maters are another source for malleable exogamous songs, because they are familiar, and carry pleasant private connotations. Best known is "Annie Lisle," written in 1857 by Henry S. Thompson. Archibald Croswell Weeks and Wilmot Moses Smith adapted it for Cornell's "Far above Cayuga's Waters" in the early 1870s.

Among Boy Scout camps who have used it are Rokilio (Wisc BSA), Treasure Island (Penna BSA), and Camp Dan Beard (Penna boys). The Brooklyn Scout's (NY BSA) version begins, "Once again are hills resounding." Urner Goodman wrote the Owaisippe (Ill BSA) localization.

Cornell's song has been used at Fleur de Lis (NH P girls) for "On the shores of old Lake Laurel / Far beneath the pines." Others who have adapted it include Presmont (Ohio P coed), according to Charla Calderhead,[§] and Surprise Lake (NY J boys).

"Halls of Ivy" was the theme for a radio and television program in the early 1950s. It primarily has been used in Camp Fire camps. Adahi (Penna CFG) and Mawavi (DC CFG) have "Oh, We Love Our Camp" (2). Hitaga (Iowa CFG), Neewahlu (Ida CFG), Niwana (Wash

CFG), Shawnee (Mo CFG), Wasewagan (Calif CFG), and Fleur de Lis (NH P girls) have other local songs. Most are simple substitutions like,

> How we love our dear Camp Shawnee
> That surrounds us here today

but some are more varied, like the Wi'li unit song:

> Oh we honor her we sing to her
> Our Camp Niwana dear
> At her feet Helena's waters
> At her head the boundless sky

Fred Waring recorded the original.

In the East, Luther Gulick Camps (Me girls) modified Princeton's "Orange and Black" for "On the shores of Lake Sebago / Where the sun's last red light glows." Surprise Lake (NY J boys) has its own version of New York University's "The Palisades." In the Midwest, Kalamazoo Girl Reserves (Mich YWCA) have sung "We're Loyal" (1) to "Illinois Loyalty." The YWCA* suggested the pairing in 1923.

Operettas

In the early years, local writers adapted tunes from light opera and operettas. Skyland (NC girls) and Tawakani (Ida CFG) have used "Toyland" from the 1903 *Babes in Toyland*. "Scout Hearted Men" (5) uses "Stouthearted Men" from *The New Moon* of 1928. Victor Herbert and Glen MacDonough composed the first. The other was by Sigmund Romberg and Oscar Hammerstein II. Herbert was born in Dublin, Ireland, but raised and educated in Stuttgart. His widowed mother had remarried and moved to the capital of Württemberg.

Classical Music

Familiar passages from classical music also have been redeployed. The Balagan unit at Namanu (Ore CFG) has a song to the second movement, the "Largo," of Dvořák's *From the New World*. Aloha Hive (Vt girls) and Fleur de Lis (NH P girls) have lyrics to "Country Gardens." Sharp* arranged the morris dance from a copy in Playfield's

The English Dancing-Master.[*] Percy Grainger refashioned Sharp's version in 1918.

Tanadoona (Minn CFG) has a "Lullaby," which begins "High above the rustling trees hangs the sky," to the "Élégie" of 1872 by Jules Massenet. The Minnesota Camp Fire camp also has an organizational song to "Consolation," the third part of Mendelssohn's *Songs without Words* of 1834.

Tawakani (Ida CFG) sings "Lullaby, then goodbye / Soon our camp days are ending" to Brahms' "Lullaby." Elsewhere, Mary Christine Ryan wrote "A 'Goodnight' Camp Song," better known as "Pearly Mists" (8), to the melody. A piano manufacturers' trade organization, the National Bureau for the Advancement of Music, copyrighted it in 1929, then published a version in an issue of *Camp Life*. Vivian Sexton says, she saw it in a Leila Fletcher piano instruction book. Johannes Brahms published the original in 1868 as "Wiegenlied: Guten Abend, Gute Nacht."

Among more general pretty songs, Edward Elgar's "Salut d'Amour," from 1888, is used for "Laughter Runs by on Silver Sandals Shining" (21). "Sun Is Up" (16) is sung to "Narcissus," from the 1891 *Water Scenes* by Ethelbert Nevin.

Poetic Settings

The interest in poetry that led to Magic Rings at Sealth (Wash CFG) inspired others to produce settings for favored verses. Marie Gaudette (RI GS) supplemented Sara Teasdale's "Barter" (4). *Singing Pathways*[304] used a Roumanian folk song with the 1917 poem.

"Four Leaf Clover" (7) was arranged by Leila Manuella Brownell (born 1870) a few years after Ella Higginson (1861-1940) published the poem in Portland, Oregon's *West Shore* magazine in 1890. Ella Rhoads' family moved west from Kansas when she was a child. The composer came from that layer of New York society where the deaths of her father and her husband (Peter Geddes) were noted by *The New York Times* in 1910 and 1918, but the paper only noticed her when she danced at the Nyack Country Club Cotillion in 1892. It probably entered camp repertoires through some sheet-music arrangement for piano, solo voice, or chorus.

Readapted Settings

Some poetry settings have been readapted. Brooklyn and Manhattan, New York, Boy Scouts sang "On the Road to Mandalay" (3). Its melody subsequently was used for the "Pilgrim Haven Song" (Mich P coed), "On the Way to Onway" (NH BSA), and Tanadoona's (Minn CFG) "The Road to High Adventure." Rudyard Kipling wrote the poem in 1890. Oley Speaks, born in the Virginia-influenced town of Winchester Canal, Ohio, composed the melody in 1907.

Agathe Deming's "Follow the Trail" (10) used William Luton Wood's setting for Robert Lewis Stevenson's "The Swing." Jessie W. White set Stevenson's "Where Go the Boats" to music as "Dark Brown Is the River" (28). Both were included in *A Child's Garden of Verses* in 1913, the year Deming graduated from Bryn Mawr. Two years later, she and her older sister, Eleanor, opened Miramichi (NY girls). The Woodcraft League camp was in New York's Adirondacks.

Organizational Songs

Closing night ceremonies in Camp Fire camps use indigenous organizational songs for council fires, especially the openings and closings. Abbie Gerrish-Jones (1864-1923) composed "Song of the Flame" (3), which began "Kindle, kindle little spark!" Helen Gerrish Hughes (born 1897) wrote the "Recessional" (42). Abbie was the sister of Helen's mother Elizabeth. Helen graduated from Berkeley, and taught in the San Joaquin valley of California.

Patiya (Colo CFG) remembers Mary Doctor composed "Now Our Council Fire Burns Low" (10). Kathryn Court wrote the "Camp Fire Good Night" (18), which begins "Now as the sun sinks slowly," to a Chippewa lullaby. The tune bears little resemblance to the one published in 1910 by Frances Densmore.[*] It may have passed through the hands of Seton, who was recommending the cradle song for closing in the *Birch Bark Roll*.[210]

Clara Hallard Fawcett (1887-1983) composed the "Closing Song" (12), which begins "Now our camp fire fadeth." She was Miss Penny, the marionette instructor at Kiwanis (Mass CFG), and later wrote books on doll collecting. "Wohelo, Spirit of Joy and Youth" (3) was written for the same camp in the 1920s by Helen Camp and Marion Ross.[149]

Among Girl Scouts, Gladys Cornwall Goff wrote "Girl Scouts Together" (13). Joseph Bovet composed the music for "Our Chalet" (8). The abbé and choral composer in Fribourg, Switzerland, wrote it in 1932 for the opening of the International Girl Guides' center. An activist for women's rights in Geneva, Emilie-Marguerite Droin-de Moorsier, supplied the original French lyrics. Betty Askwith, an English poet and novelist, made the translation.

Institutional Biases

Despite such spontaneous expressions of enthusiasm by members, national youth groups for girls, in the early years, bestowed their patronage upon male professionals. The Camp Fire Girls only official song book is by Neidlinger. His "Pretty Little Blue Bird" (6) was given national stature, even though it was published in the *Small Songster for Small Singers*[*] in 1896 before the Camp Fire Girls existed. His best-known song is the grace, "If We Have Earned the Right" (61).

John B. Archer[*] and George Newell[*] edited the first Girl Scout songsters. While Goff won an honorable mention in the 1941 national Girl Scout song writing contest, the winner was "Girl Scouts Are We" by John Rivenburg.[*] The judges were "Olin Downes music critic of the New York *Times*, Sigmund Spaeth radio's Tune Detective and Hugh Ross director of the Scola Cantorum of New York."

Men sponsored by the Camp Fire Girls and Girl Scouts shared the groups' progressive interests, and probably moved in the same social circles as the organizers. William Harold Neidlinger (1863-1924) was an organist and choral conductor who founded a school for retarded children in East Orange, New Jersey.

Newell described himself as "one of the American authorities on camp music" in an article he wrote for *The Outlook* in 1928. He compared the ideal, progressive camp for boys, whose mothers were spending their summers in resorts, with ones using military programs to earn a profit.[444]

Rivenburg was a young Eagle Scout in Creston, Iowa, where he died before the contest results were announced.

Impact of the Civil War

The use of Neidlinger and Newell can be explained as reasonable from a philosophical point of view. Nevertheless, it suggests national organizations were oblivious to traditions of female creativity that were feeding the groups' grass roots.

They had been developing since the Civil War. In less than five years, battles, diseases, and raids killed at least 10% of all marriageable men from the North, and 30% from the South, according to John Huddleston.* Any young woman born in the 1840s faced the possibility of life alone. Any woman born before could be bereaved. Maiden aunts and old maids became comic stage figures. They also were genuine challenges for families who did not have the material resources to support all their single women.

Widows no longer were condemned if they did not remarry. The husband of Rachel Welsh Knight, the grandfather of composer Frederick Knight Logan, died before the war, in 1859. She raised four children in wartime Washington, Pennsylvania, near Pittsburgh. When her daughter, Virginia (1850-1940), was left with a young son, she continued working as a coloratura before settling in Oskaloosa, Iowa, where she taught music. She had trained in Chicago, Boston, and New York.

Once girls like Virginia Knight Logan* lived in fatherless homes, they knew they could survive alone. Cultural roles, broadened by necessity of war, did not contract in the immediately ensuing decades. Carrie Jacobs-Bond, mentioned in LOLLYPOP, became a professional songwriter when she was widowed. So did Sallie Hume-Douglas.

Clara Edwards was born in 1887 in Minneapolis where she began her voice and piano training. She continued when she moved to Vienna with her husband. After he died, she began releasing her compositions. Gladys Seymour used her 1927 "By the Bend of the River" for "Beauty Stands at the Crossroads" (10), according to Hitaga (Iowa CFG).

None of the women performed or wrote for the stage. Eleanor Goldberg (1880-1928) was scandalous when she left Joliet, Illinois, for vaudeville when she was eighteen. As Nora Bayes, she wrote "Shine on Harvest Moon" (5) with her song-writing husband, Jack Norworth. "Just Like a Gypsy" (2), written with Seymour Simons, was used for local songs at Kitanniwa and Tanadoona (Minn CFG) in the late 1940s.

Logan was limited to performing with the Boston Ladies Symphony Orchestra and appearing in summer festivals run by Horatio Richmond Palmer, mentioned in ROSE. Mary Artemesia Lathbury (1841-1913) was born into a family of Methodist ministers. She wrote "Day Is Dying in the West" (13) for evening services at Chautauqua in 1877. In keeping with the common practice of naming tunes for places, William Fisk Sherwin's melody was called "Chautauqua."

The stereotype of the maiden aunt as willing babysitter or schoolteacher reinforced the view women naturally were suited for child care. Simultaneously, it created new, sometimes subversive, opportunities. Daniel Beard's sisters, Mary Caroline or Lina, born in 1852, and Adelia Belle, born in 1857, published adventure books for girls.

Jessie L. Gaylor and Alice Cushing Donaldson Riley published *Playtime Songs for the Schoolroom* in 1911, which included "Baby's Boat" (19). Laura Rountree Smith became a children's books author. Gaylor was born in 1863, during the war, Riley soon after in 1867. Smith was born in 1876, and composed "Little Sir Echo" (12) with John S. Fearis.

Impact of Modern Poetry

Aesthetic values began changing in the years coinciding with World War I. Cultural style setters applauded the Ash Can School of realistic painters. Sara Teasdale left Saint Louis, Missouri, where she was born in 1884, for New York. There she met poet Vachel Lindsay, who is remembered for "The Congo" with the line "Boomlay, boomlay, boomlay, Boom." She won the precursor of the Pulitzer Prize in 1918, Columbia's University Poetry Society Prize.

Hilda Doolittle was born in Bethlehem, Pennsylvania, in 1886, where she absorbed the expectations of her parents, a college professor, and a Moravian musician. She left Bryn Mawr after three semesters, then followed Ezra Pound to England in 1911. They produced Imagist poetry, a form of free verse that paralleled the Ash Can painters with everyday speech patterns to describe commonplaces. Amy Lowell, born into a prominent Massachusetts family in 1874, exploited the techniques to win the Pulitzer for poetry in 1926.

Poetry was elevated to a high art. Earlier writers, like Julia Ward Howe, Katharine Lee Bates and Ella Higginson, were denigrated as mere versifiers. Men like John Oxenford and his nephew, Edward Oxenford, no longer were asked to supply lyrics for melodies like "Ash Grove" (72) and "Funiculi" (7). Instead, women were asked to provide texts or translations for folk tunes. Anna G. Molloy created the English version of the Italian "Tiritomba" (12).

Katherine Davis set "Morning Comes Early" (2) to a Slovak tune. She was born in Saint Joseph, Missouri, in 1892, and educated at Wellesley. Later, she taught music at the Concord Academy, mentioned in KUMBAYA.

Eleanor B. Stock (1910-1994) wrote words for the Swedish "Spinning Song" (3). Violet Synge (1896-1971) translated the version of "Vrenalie" (3) published by Tobitt.[174] Dickie* included Stock's compositions in *Singing Pathways*. Synge later became Girl Guide commissioner in England.

Impact of the Phonograph

Beth Slater Whitson* (1879-1930) refused such constraints being imposed on young girls in the early twentieth century. While she had some poems accepted by *Appleton's* in 1906, she was determined to be a commercial songwriter, not a poetess. She used the family savings to visit Chicago, where she sat in the waiting room of the most important music publisher, until he noticed her.

Will Rossiter bought a few of her lyrics, referred her to another publisher who bought more, then sent her to a department store to listen to one of his demonstrators. Rossiter had pioneered promoting sheet music by hiring performers to sing or play his products in stores. While she was there, a local composer stopped by, read some of her work, and gave her his address.

She returned to Hickman County in central Tennessee. In 1910, she and Leo Friedman produced "Let Me Call You Sweetheart" (6). Rossiter apparently used his connections in New York to place the song with Victor's Peerless Quartet in 1911. Arthur Collins sang baritone on the session.

In the early years, recording companies needed to convince investors they were more than passing novelties. They used artists like John Barnes Wells, mentioned in I WISH I WERE, and the Peerless Quartet to lend their products the veneer of upper-class respectability. Once records were successful, artists like Harry Lauder and John

McCormack used them to promote personal appearances. Support for classical music faded as stage songs entered polite society.

Rosetta Duncan (1894-1959) and her sister, Vivian (1897-1986), introduced "Rememb'ring" in their vaudeville act, *Topsy and Eva*, in 1923. Barriers against genres of the masses were gone. It became "Remember" (64), paraphrased on the back cover. Augusta (Calif CFG) sang "Remember to just seek beauty" in the 1930s. The Duncans were born in Los Angeles and went on stage in New York in 1911 when they were in their teens.

Impact of Traditional Girls' Camps

The women mentioned above, whose songs have been used for camp closings, were born in the nineteenth century or were adolescents before World War I. Between them and the Folk Revival, few songs written by women were absorbed into the camp repertoire. That hiatus coincided with the shift in the geographic and cultural locus of commercial music mentioned in LOLLYPOP. Songwriters were concentrated in the New York of vaudeville, radio, and recording studios. It also paralleled changes in fun songs mentioned in AN AUSTRIAN.

The deprecation of female traditions implicit in the patronage choices made by national organizations for girls continued. The same sorts of women's institutions continued to mold the taste of upper-middle-class girls, but composers like Margaret Bradshaw McGee, Anne Hopson Chapin, Marie Gaudette, and Margarett Snyder no longer were accorded the same respect as Virginia Logan Knight. Every year, while their poems and songs were relearned in camps, their aesthetic became more estranged from the worlds of both popular and advanced literary arts. Sinclair Lewis lampooned it as Babbitry.

At the same time camps were perpetuating an older musical aesthetic, they were teaching girls independence, much as our Civil War had taught self-reliance to girls raised on *Godey's Lady's Book*. Social mores changed in the depression when Nancy Drew replaced the Camp Fire Girls of Jane L. Stewart. Short, tousled hair and skinny ties copied from Amelia Earhart, shown in photographs of Leona Holbrook[*] and Kitanniwa in the middle 1930s, replaced bloomers as signs of independence. Mothers who bought the clothes silently passed their attitudes to their daughters by sending them to camps.

In the 1950s, Mildred Wirt's Nancy Drew books, which had been commissioned for the name Carolyn Keene by the Edward Stratemeyer Syndicate, were rewritten with a less adventurous heroine. Programs like those at Kitanniwa were eviscerated. Older editions survived. Mothers, who wore large corsages for social occasions, sent their daughters to the woods armed with the knowledge of "Hi lo inny minny ki ki."

Evelyn Hopson Wood* published *Camp and Picnic Warbler* in 1929 just before she married William Sheffield Owen. She made sure her children all went to camp. Her daughter remembers, "our family gathered around the piano almost every night to sing folk songs, hymns, and all sorts of other types [. . .] camp songs were favorites of ours."

Ruth Anderson Eldridge* published *Stunt Songs for Social Singes* in 1925 after she had married Dorman Emmor Richardson. She worked for years as director of Detroit's YMCA. Photographs of her and her sister, Annetta Byers Eldridge, appear in "Collectors." Wood's is in "Tradition Bearers."

The garland of poetry and songs they were perpetuating, part Southern, part Midwestern, part Philadelphia, Boston and New York, no longer was mainstream. Men who defined upper-class taste ignored it. At the same time, it was not recognized as folk because it represented the distaff side of the social establishment. Each year that passed, it became more folklike without ever losing its halo of elitism.

Kitanniwa Repertoire

Indigenous pretty songs at Kitanniwa included those that could be sung anytime, and those reserved for closing ceremonies. The final evening program of a camp session in the 1950s was broken into phases. Before the council fire, girls returned from supper to the mustering area near the flag pole. They had added their Camp Fire ties and boleros or Blue Bird vests to their evening dress. While people were gathering, girls spent time looking at one another's jackets, and generally behaving like excited young girls.

A council fire did not differ in any significant way from those shown in "Rituals" that were celebrated in town. Seton had defined the format. The fire was a small teepee of kindling inside a log-cabin structure of logs. The ceremony's primary function was awarding beads to girls who had earned them. Every camp program was intended to include some honor-producing activities.

Songs included organizational ones, which would have been used in town, and slow songs that could be sung elsewhere in camp. In the later years, these included "Make New Friends" (68) and "Peace, I Ask of Thee O River" (88). "My Paddle's Keen and Bright" (59) also might have been sung.

The ones I remember were the ones reserved for the last night: "Across the Stillness of the Lake" (30), "A Canoe May Be Drifting" (10), and "Witchcraft" (81). Their message was reinforced by the lake front location, shown on the front cover, that embodied the oneness with nature as defined by the water, the sunset, and the fire.

Some weeks a wishing ceremony followed the council fire. A wishing boat is a candle stuck to a piece of cardboard that is set on water to float away. Problems with handing tiny fires to tired seven-year-olds in a crowd were managed by council-fire protocol. One entered and left by reverse seniority, with counselors followed by cabins with the youngest girls coming before the older ones. Blue Birds were the only ones on the beach with much of the camp staff in the area.

The consequence of age-group order was that, by the time older girls had their turn, they could see candle reflections in the water. This was heightened in the years after they moved the council ring and girls walked down a hill to the lake. Sometimes, counselors would paddle canoes to set boats floating toward shore. Sometimes Taps was played from one of the far hills. The one dramatized "A Canoe," the other "Across the Stillness."

For the susceptible, launching a boat and making a wish led to tears. As happens with many prolonged folk rituals, this one alternated emotional peaks with mundane activities. The council-fire mood was dissipated by sending campers to the communal bath house to brush their teeth.

Once girls settled in their cabins, and counselors could safely leave, the serenade began. They started with the youngest cabins, often singing lullabies like those mentioned in WITCHCRAFT. The older the girls, the longer the wait, and the greater the anticipation. As the serenaders approached nearby cabins, emotions increased, again with some breaking into tears. The greatest privilege was to be in a cabin where they sang "Remember" (64).

Origins

Closing camp ceremonies are not unique to traditional girls' camps. Most have some kind of closing ritual. As discussed in WITCHCRAFT, many devolved from Seton, sometimes directly, sometimes through diffusion. When the Ahmek (Ont boys) chief intoned Wakonda had "sent down the sacred fire from Heaven,"[212:74] it was because the camp owner knew Seton.

When Girl Scouts in Ohio in the 1970s sang "Rise up O Flame" (29), while "by magic, a ball of fire comes from the sky to light the fire," they were perpetuating something they knew only from tradition. Girl Scouts were not part of the progressive network that had included Seton, the Camp Fire Girls, Boy Scouts, and YMCA.

Julie Sherwood[S] was told Molly Luman's (Ohio GS) Fire from Heaven was:

> awe inspiring to watch. Someone climbs a tree near the fire circle, hanging a wire from the tree to the fire and threading a role of kerosene soaked toilet paper on the wire, and at the proper time lighting the toilet paper and sending it hurling down the wire into the fire. All this done without anyone noticing the person in the tree.

Janice Suzanne Jones[S] was told, the fire sometimes was built on a raft and lit by flaming arrows or by a hardy swimmer at Alice Pittenger in the late 1960s. Even when the fire was built on land, flaming arrows might have been used by the Idaho Girl Scouts.

The pacing, which leads to the heightened emotions in some camps, may have been borrowed, not from Seton, but from camp meetings and subsequent revival campaigns. Night after night, an evangelist exhorted people to join the mourners' bench. The final night altar call, when individuals were surrounded by neighbors who already had pledged, became more fevered than anything in summer camp. It is likely, in the early years when many camp traditions were being established, campers drew on their sacred experiences to create their secular rituals.

Not everyone is comfortable with these emotional climaxes. At Glen (Ohio CFG) in 1974, counselors snacked between the council fire and the serenade. Two formed a cancan line to reassert their identity by singing the "Girl Scout Pep Song" (7) and "Girl Scouts Together" (13). Carol Shuster[S] was told, girls had to learn the organizational songs, but always sang them ironically.

Shared Meals

A need to dissipate emotions is probably the reason many camps end the evening with a shared meal. At Hiwela (Wisc CFG) in 1963, counselors raided the kitchen, even if all they could eat was butter and raw onions on white bread. At Butler (Ohio BSA), Richard Fazenbaker[S] was told in the early 1970s:

> Red Charlies take place every Friday night after the camper ceremonies. The staff makes up a list of things they want from a quick service restaurant, and one of the older staff members goes out to get it.

His friend added:

> the term comes from a staff party which the staff had in 1969 at the waterfront where the food was brought from the Red Barn. Also, the person who brought the food had a walkie-talkie set up in his car, so the staff smuggling ring could sneak the food passed the ad building. The code name of the walkie talkie was Red Charlie.

Wishing Boats

Wishing boats may be the one ceremony found more often in girls' camps, at least those on water. Helen Hill Miller[*] was told, they were used at the YWCA Silver Bay conferences on Lake George, New York. Kathleen Huggett Nye remembers they were used only for the closing night of camp and maybe the Fourth of July at Kitanniwa. Hiwela (Wisc CFG) launched boats every week in 1963.

Ceremonial music at Kitanniwa varied from year to year. At Pittenger (Ohio GS) in the late 1940s, Diane Wyss remembers they took their boats to the Sandusky River and sang "Dark Brown Is the River" (28) as they watched them sail away. Tawakani (Ida CFG) has a song book with twelve "Dreamboat Songs" written to other tunes, including "Sweet Memories of Tawakani" to "Sweet Ad-o-line" (8), "Let Us Launch Our Dreamboat" to Whitson's "Let Me Call You Sweetheart" (6), and "I'll Make a Wish, Dear" to "I had a Dream, Dear." Counselors sing "The Wish We Will Make" to the "Sweetheart of Sigma Chi."

In Michigan, Tawanka (Mich CFG) always sings "Tell Me Why" (78) at the candle ceremony, and "Call of the Fire" (49) and "Witchcraft" (81) at the Wishing Fire. Katie Hickey[§] was told, in a New Jersey YWCA camp, "Tell Me Why" was sung "as a tribute to the camp (Matollionequay) during the Green Feather ceremony and another called the White Feather" with the camp name used in place of "you."

Case Study: A Canoe May Be Drifting

"A Canoe May Be Drifting" (10) has been sung at Kitanniwa at least since the early 1930s when Carol Parsons Sievert first went. It also is known in its magnet camps, Wathana (Mich CFG) and Merrie Woode (Mich GS), as well as at Fort Hill (Mich GS), a camp in Merrie Woode's sphere of influence. A counselor introduced it to Augusta (Calif CFG) in California in 1969. That camp's director does not know where the staff member learned the song.

Explication

"A Canoe" is a landscape poem in the Romantic tradition that can be traced back to seventeenth-century Italian painting. Salvator Rosa (1615-1673) often highlighted an abandoned object against a background of unfettered nature. The precision of the description in the first three lines echoes Imagist poetry.

The fourth introduces the presence of humans ("songs that will never grow old"). Its final four lines describe the emotions ("the love and the friendships") that follow from the location. With the wordiness of an essay, the text argues these feelings might not exist outside the special world of camp, because the landscape does not exist elsewhere.

For the lyric to succeed, "A Canoe" needs singers to be near a calm, sparsely inhabited lake area where something could be allowed to drift. In 1974, Carol Parsons Sievert remembered the effect on her as a young camper when they sang it while paddling the long, war canoe. She added, still anchoring her recollections with geography:

> I have vivid memories of singing it on junior hill - so I'd have been 10 or 11 and I'm now 50. I just don't remember a time not knowing it. It was such a favorite always. I can remember vividly hearing the counselors singing the harmony on top when I was living in cabin E because that was such a great year.

Lucille Parker Munk remembers, "we used to sing" it at Clear Lake and believes "there's just something about it, that's very peaceful."

Topographical associations are not unique to the three of us. Kitanniwa's 1974 director, Mary Tinsley Unrue, suggested when council fires were moved from Morris Lake to an area in the pines, the repertoire changed.

> All the songs that used to be canoe, water oriented have gotten into "Down Yonder Green Valley" ["Ash Grove" (72)], because we're out here in the trees. And, I don't think anybody does it consciously, but to sing about the waters and the ripples and everything when you're sitting in the middle of a forest [. . .]

Textual Variation

Pretty songs, as was mentioned in ASH GROVE, have fewer variations than others. Only minor differences exist between version A from Polly McIntyre, who was at Kitanniwa in the 1950s, and version B from Janice Knapp, who was at Wathana in the 1960s. Transposing "with" and "and" is the type that comes from oral transmission. The disparity in subject-verb agreement may be less a matter of grammar than musical flow.

Music

The tune's first and third lines, which are alike, are close to the opening phrase of "Red River Valley" (14). The major difference is, where the tune for "Canoe" rises on the second syllable of drifting, the tune for "Valley" drops. Slight differences also exist in the order of notes in the descending part of the phrase.

Suggesting a song bears some resemblance to an older one does not imply musical plagiarism. We hear many melodies as children that leave traces in our memories. We learn to like certain progressions of notes or certain rhythmic patterns. These personal repositories are tapped when we create a new melody, or a new text. When a composer does this, the repeated phrases become traits musicologists use to identify his or her style. When someone does this in camp, he or she is working within an inherited tradition.

"Canoe," like "Valley," relies on anapests (xxX), but otherwise treats the meter with more freedom. In his Imagist manifesto, Ezra Pound* wrote, "as regarding rhythm," he aimed "to compose in sequence of the musical phrase, not in sequence of the metronome." When I asked Carol Parsons Sievert to transcribe the melody for "A Canoe" as she remembered it, she wrote back:

> This is the toughest thing you ever asked me to do. As you know, camp songs simply sung around whenever you are schmalzed up and sung "as you feel them." I can put the notes down in two seconds, but to get the beat right, measure by measure, is a whole different thing. Further, when I did get it down and tried to replay it, it got so stuffy that didn't sound right [. . .] As you notice I've written the two verses to different measures beats as I noticed the difference.

Version A

Text from Polly McIntyre, Camp Kitanniwa (Mich CFG), late 1950s; transcribed February 1975. Her photograph appears in "Coming of Age."

> A canoe may be drifting at sunset,
> When the skies are all purple and gold
> And a camp fire down by the water
> With songs that will never grow old.

All these things may be found anywhere
And not bring any pleasure at all
It's the love and the friendship that dwell here
That makes this the best camp of all.

Version B

Text from Janice Knapp, Camp Wathana (Mich CFG), 1962-1972; transcribed 1977; variations from A emphasized.

A canoe may be drifting at sunset,
When the skies are all purple and gold,
With a camp fire down by the water,
And the songs that will never grow old.

All these things may be found anywhere,
And not bring any pleasure at all,
It's the love and the friendship that **dwells** here,
That makes this the best camp of all.

SECTION V

Midwestern Influences on Repertoire

Midwestern Influences on Repertoire

Each type of camp - the recreation, the traditional, and the progressive - inherited some customs from the same part of the Midwest: land west of the Appalachians and north of the Ohio River, the upper boundary of slavery.

A simple geographic condition, few routes moved past the mountains in the early nineteenth century, perpetuated cultural differences that had developed in isolated colonies in the 1700s. Families from New England edged west along the Great Lakes, some moving through Ontario. German, English, and Scots-Irish settlers from Pennsylvania made their way toward Pittsburgh, floated down the Ohio, and trudged up its tributaries. Men like Jean Ritchie's immigrant ancestor, who landed in Virginia, climbed through the Cumberland Gap into southeastern Kentucky and Tennessee, then wandered down the tributaries toward the Ohio.

DeWitt Clinton's Erie Canal gave priority to the northern route in 1825. Thomas Jefferson had authorized a pike west from Washington in 1806. The Cumberland Road, finally completed in the 1830s, reached the Ohio at Wheeling. From there, it spread overland on what was essentially the watershed between the Ohio and Great Lakes drainages through Columbus, Ohio, and Indianapolis, Indiana, to Vandalia, Illinois. Political opposition to internal improvements blocked regional roads in the South.

Northern Band

Battle Creek's immediate area was not opened officially until the Potawatomi treaty of 1821 with Pokagon. Then, men had to wait until the area was surveyed. Land offices opened in 1831. The first pioneers arrived from upstate New York.

Within its first decade, Battle Creek had formal associations of Methodists (1832), Quakers (1836), and united Congregationalists and Presbyterians (1836). By 1869, after our Civil War, it had added Baptists, Episcopalians, Seventh Day Adventists, a Society of Spiritualists who called themselves Progressive Friends, the Dutch-derived Reformed Church in America, and two freedmen's congregations. Their social clubs included Masons, Odd Fellows, Good Templars, and a German Workingmen's Benevolent Association.[495]

Twenty miles away, my home town only reported the more conventional Methodists, Presbyterians, Baptists, Episcopalians, Masons, and Odd Fellows in 1869.[495]

Central Band

Findlay, the sponsor of Glen (Ohio CFG) and seat of Hancock County in northwestern Ohio, is 28 miles from Upper Sandusky, the center of Wyandot County. In Upper, population growth can be deciphered from the founding dates for its local churches. Northerners came first. Presbyterians and Methodists organized in 1845.

Then came families from Pennsylvania, followed by those from German-speaking states. The English-speaking Evangelical Lutheran Church organized in 1849; the Church of God in 1851; Trinity Reformed Church of the Synod of the Reformed Church, which offered German and English Sabbath schools in 1852; the Roman Catholics, with a few Irish among the Germans in 1857; the United Brethren Church in 1858; Trinity Church of the Evangelical Association, with German and English Sunday schools in 1860; the German-speaking Evangelical Lutheran Church in 1868, and the Universalist Church in 1870.[405]

United Brethren were heirs to the Moravians who had contact with John Wesley and George Whitefield. Church of God was the formal name taken by followers of John Winebrenner, who broke with the German Reformed church in 1823. They had fled wars in the Palatinate in the 1730s.[237] One of his disciples, Jeremiah Tabler, led revivals in Upper in its early years.[405] The group founded its college in Findlay in 1882.

Soon after, Charles Oesterlin discovered natural gas. Findlay's population quadrupled. The Ohio Oil Company followed in 1887. At the time I visited Glen in 1974, Findlay was still corporate headquarters for Marathon Oil.

Southern Band

Water provided easier entrée into the Midwest than rutted roads. Cincinnati was founded on the Ohio river in 1788. Sometime before 1816, a group that included immigrants from German-speaking states began meeting at the home of Frederick Amelung. They included Philibert Ratel, a music and dance teacher from Philadelphia, and George Charters, a piano maker. In 1819, the Episcopal Singing Society was organized. The same year, English immigrants formed the Haydn Society.[354]

Napoléon precipitated the migration of educated Germans. When hereditary rulers failed to stop his troops from invading their lands, the middle classes demanded better security from a more centralized state. After the French leader was defeated at Waterloo in 1815, German princes reasserted their powers. Critics fled. Lowell Mason met Frederick Abel in Savannah. Stephen Foster met Henry Kleber in Pittsburgh. Amelung hosted the Appolonian in Cincinnati.

The failure of the Revolution of 1848 exiled thousands of educated German speakers. They joined famine-stricken German farmers and Irish refugees, who were streaming into the Old Northwest Territory in the late 1840s and early 1850s. Many bypassed the stony, worn soils of the Northeast, and the slave economy of the South.

By 1900, before the influx of immigrants from Southern and Eastern Europe, 54% of Cincinnati's population was German. Migrants sailing on the Hamburg America line debarked at Hoboken, New Jersey (58% German), and headed up the Hudson for the Erie Canal. At the transfer point to Lake Erie, Buffalo, New York, was 43% German. Detroit, on the narrows between Lakes Erie and Huron, was 41% German. Milwaukee, Wisconsin, on Lake Michigan was 70%. Along the Mississippi where the Rock Island railroad crossed the river, Davenport, Iowa, was 62% German. Saint Louis, Missouri, may have been slave country, but it sat on the Mississippi where the Missouri branched north to good farmlands in the interior. Its population was 45% German.[324:580]

Sängerfest

A constant influx of immigrants north of the Ohio meant interested individuals could remain cognizant of music developments in their German-speaking homelands. During the wars with Napoléon, Karl Friedrich Zelter organized liedertafel, modeled on the Knights of the Round Table. His male singing clubs limited their membership to the elite who shared nationalist ideas.

After the French emperor was exiled to Saint Helena in 1815, Nägeli expanded choral groups in the southern German states to include any man with a good voice. He was following Pestalozzi's suggestion that public singing nurtured the national spirit. Würzburg, in the kingdom of Bavaria, invited local singing groups to the first sängerfest in 1845. The next year, singing festivals were held in Philadelphia and Baltimore.

Barbara Lorenzkowski* remarked, such clubs did not survive the repression following the failure of the 1848 revolution. In Europe, group singing turned to folk music in sängerbunds (singing groups), which implicitly denied any support for a supra-state identity.

In this country in 1849, male choruses from Louisville, Kentucky, and Madison, Indiana, both located on the Ohio, joined in a Cincinnati sängerfest. Delegations arrived from Columbus, Saint Louis, and Milwaukee. People from Detroit attended the next one in 1851.[354:467] Upper organized its first sängerbund in 1858.[405] Buffalo sent both sängerbunds and liedertafels to Cincinnati in 1859.[480]

Its unaccompanied vocal music was a combination of familiar German composers, like Mozart, and then contemporary ones less known in this country, like Franz Abt (1819-1855) and Friedrich Silcher (1789-1860). The latter had provoked Wilhelm I of Württemberg in 1824, when he joined Tübingen University students singing "La Marseillaise" to commemorate storming the Bastille. Wilhelm's father, Friedrich II, had abrogated the duchy's constitution in 1806. He sent men to support Napoléon until his defeat in Moscow, then joined Klemens von Metternich's invasion of France in 1814. Ann Arbor, Michigan, began receiving refugees from Württemberg in the 1830s.

Abt settled in Protestant Zürich where both Pestalozzi and Nägeli had lived.

Central Band Traditions

Cincinnati hired Luther Whiting Mason for its public-school music program in 1856. The next year, Tulius Clinton O'Kane became principal of the city's fourteen district schools. He had graduated from Ohio Wesleyan in Delaware.[363]

O'Kane left in 1864 to work for Philip Phillips (1834-1905). Born in Chautauqua County, New York, Phillips had moved to Marion, about 25 miles north of Delaware, as a singing-school teacher for a music company. After fire destroyed his music-publishing company in Cincinnati in 1865,[363] Phillips became a concert singer. His tours in the immediate post-Civil War period included Detroit, Grand Rapids, Kalamazoo, and South Bend.[466] In the 1920s, those cities sponsored Kitanniwa's nexus of camps, Wathana (Mich CFG), Keewano (Mich CFG), Merrie Woode (Mich GS), and Tannadoonah (Ind CFG).

Singing-school organizations shifted west after the Civil War. In 1870, Root held a month-long convention in South Bend, Indiana, that ended with Haydn's *Creation*. Among the instructors was Thomas Martin Towne, who taught public and singing schools in Detroit.[363] One student was William Edward Chute,* who moved to Michigan near the Saint Clair river crossing. The son of a Nova Scotia Baptist deacon farmed in summers and taught singing schools in winters. D. C. McAllister* (born 1853), who grew up near Kalamazoo, began teaching singing schools in the area in 1871.

Delaware remained the cultural center for Methodists in central Ohio. O'Kane returned in 1867, where he became a teacher and choir leader in a local Methodist church. Phillips retired to the town in the middle 1880s.

Half a dozen years after O'Kane died, Lynn Rohrbough arrived from a community that frowned on dancing.[375:14] After he graduated in 1922, he went to Boston University. As mentioned in KUMBAYA, it was there he began publishing handy books of suitable activities for church youth groups. He borrowed his term for squat, 3 3/4" x 6 3/4", comb-toothed books from Daniel and Lina Beard. It was later he adopted the svelter, stapled format and customized contents pioneered for the Boy Scouts by Zander* and Klusmann.

While he was in Boston, the church lifted its restrictions on amusements, and permitted dancing on Ohio Wesleyan's campus. When Rohrbough returned to Delaware in 1929, his recreation open-houses provided a more godly alternative to secular activities available in town.[375:63]

Southern Band Traditions

Cincinnati's biennial singing festival was so successful, a group met in 1873 to organize a grander concert program to elevate "the standard of choral and instrumental music." They attracted 1,083 singers from thirty-six sängerbunds.

Judging from the music - Händel, Beethoven, Glück, Schumann, Mendelssohn, Liszt[354:468] - "improve" meant remove the most Germanic elements to bring it into conformity with Anglo-American preferences for vocal groups subordinated to orchestras like those demonstrated by Root. Charles Frederic Goss noted, rain moved the final day's open-air concert and picnic indoors:

> Thus Providence came in to take from the festival this vestige of the German custom which had done much to degenerate the Sängerfests from festivals of song to bacchanalian carouses.[354:468]

Eastern urban May Festivals imitated this experiment. Ann Arbor's began in 1893. The next year, Olivet College, twenty miles from Battle Creek, hired an immigrant from Konstanz, Baden, for its conservatory. In 1899, John Baptiste Martin (1866-1940) merged Battle Creek's German orchestra with his Olivet students into Michigan's first symphony.

German Universities

After the defeat of Napoléon, the more conservative German-speaking princes tightened controls on their universities. They asserted the institutions were instruments of their states. At the time, independent thinkers fled. After the failure of the 1848 revolution, the graduate schools developed into the most prestigious academic institutions in the western world.

In 1881, A. H. Baynes* said, for every American who went to an English school, a hundred went to Germany. Communities developed in every university town with members who ensured new arrivals were settled properly. He noted their membership books included the names of many famous individuals, but only mentioned Emerson.

American colony patriarchs were necessary because German student life was fragmented, no doubt from constant fear of informers. Students lived in solitary rented rooms, not the convivial colleges of Oxbridge. Sons of the nobility joined korps, whose primary purpose was staging fencing matches. The facial scars became the mark of their membership in the states' elites.

On Saturday nights, students flocked to taverns where great quantities of weak beer were drunk while young men sang. Baynes noted, unlike English students who prided themselves on their repertoires, on the number of songs they knew, Germans used song books. Commersbücher came with studs in their covers to keep them above beer spilled on the tables. They mixed student and folk songs.

If this Baynes were the Alfred Henry Baynes who was general secretary of the Baptist Missionary Society in London, and if students knew he planned to publish a report, they might not have sung the songs they knew from memory. The longer he stayed, the more reliant they might have become on their books.

American Colleges

The introduction of male choruses into universities in this country began before the Civil War. Harvard organized the first glee club in 1858, followed by the University of Michigan (1859), Yale (1861), and the University of Pennsylvania (1862). Like May Festivals, glee clubs soon absorbed the aesthetics and ambitions of paying performances, which diluted their German spirit.

Students found other places to sing. The first college songsters I have seen, published with music by commercial printers, were from Columbia (1876), Penn (1879), Princeton (1882), Rutgers (1885), and Yale (1889). They were followed by commercially produced fraternity song books. Delta Upsilon published one in 1884. Phi Delta Theta issued its third edition in 1886, Psi Upsilon in 1891, and Zeta Psi in 1897.

In these years, universities were writing their alma maters. Paul Nettl[*] noted, Yale and New York University used Karl Wilhelm's tune for "Die Wacht am Rhein." Dartmouth borrowed Friedrich Wilhelm Kücken's "Ach, wie ist's möglich dann." "Neath the Elm of Dear Old Yale" adapted Kücken's "Wer will unter die Soldaten."

These no longer were songs of liberal students, but those of men promoted by the state. Wilhelm (1815-1873) was named Royal Prussian music director in 1860, as a reward for his setting of Max Schneckenburger's 1840 poem, "Watch on the Rhine."

"Oh, how is it possible then" won Kücken (1810-1882) an appointment to the court of Paul Friedrich in 1839. The grand duke of Mecklenburg-Schwerin headed one of the most reactionary of the hereditary estates. "Who among the soldiers" was written in 1849 as the revolution was being crushed. Frederick Francis II revoked privileges he had granted in 1848. Augustus Zanzig's grandfather emigrated. Prussian authorities later recommended the song for young boys.

Northern Band Traditions

At the University of Michigan, fraternities fostered high-art and communal singing traditions. The Interfraternity Council Sing required choruses audition for the final performance. Music professionals judged the final ten. George Spasyk,[*] a 1949 graduate, remembers his Lambda Chi Alpha chapter prepared for weeks for the IFC Sing with:

> each voice part perfecting its part before all four were brought together in 4-part harmony. The beauty of it all was that very few of the brothers could read music - it was all done by memorizing the parts. Even those who couldn't carry a tune in a bucket wanted to be on stage to represent Lambda Chi Alpha. They were put in the back row and silently mouthed the words, but their very presence and enthusiasm inspired the singers, perhaps to a higher level of performance.

More important, he remembers gathering around the piano in the fraternity house and:

> before and after dinner running through their extensive repertoire of songs, which included just about all of the Lambda Chi and Michigan songs ever written, most sorority sweetheart songs, many other fraternity songs (or parodies thereof), all of the Big Ten and Notre Dame fight songs (and dirty parodies thereof), and a host of party songs, some appropriate in mixed company, most appropriate only for stag parties.

The difference between Spasyk's recollections and Baynes' observations is more than the smell of beer. For the one, music in a Midwestern university functioned as an escape from the messiness of everyday life, even with off-color songs. In the other, it was part and parcel. Lambda Chi's withdraw from the dining room to sing. Germans lay their song books on beer-sodden tables.

Camp Traditions

Traditions like the IFC sing may have been the conduit for transferring German harmonic theories from colleges to camps like Kitanniwa. After dinner sings may have been the model for the general repertoire in recreation camps. Germans themselves created the main singing context for fun songs: the after meal sing at the table where one has just completed eating, food spills have not yet been cleaned, and one could sit any old way.

Précis

In this section, THE BOATMEN examines the negative influence of Midwestern and German music on rhythm in camp fun songs. GRAND OLD DUKE OF YORK explores the positive influence in the creation of gesture songs. FLICKER looks at the persistence of German Romantic ideals in pretty songs after the upheavals of the late 1960s.

Oh, the Boatmen Dance: Rhythm

Rhythm is the music element most recently treated playfully by camp fun songs. A girl quoted in KOOKABURRA may have told Carol Shuster[§] she sang "Mandy" (22) for the harmony. A friend told Sally Briggs,[§] at Angola on the Lake (NY YWCA), "I liked this song particularly because of the rhythm."

The difference reflects changes in American music since the early years of camping. Then, ragtime and jazz were maturing from experiments by Blacks and Creoles living in New Orleans and other Mississippi and Missouri river cities.

Onomatopoeia

Using words, like Vachel Lindsay's "boomlay boom," to imitate drums represented the first attempts to incorporate early-twentieth-century ideas of rhythm into camp songs. Many with rhythmic onomatopoeia have been written locally. An Idaho Camp Fire camp sings, "I told my folks I was in love with Neewahlu, Boom boom boom boom." Betsy Alexander, Mary Rae Hyland, Margie Keane, and Evie Salz wrote "bogga bogga bogga, I don't want to leave Hitaga" (Iowa CFG) in 1948.

A New Hampshire camp sponsored by the American Youth Foundation has sung:

> We've got the hogan that leaks like a sieve
> Boom boom boom boom Merrowvista Merrowvista
> And when it rains we run to the biff [toilet]
> Boom boom boom boom Merrowvista Merrowvista

Boom boom lines have been added to the ends of songs like Kamaji's (Minn girls) "Underneath the Norway Pine." Judy Miller remembers "A-boom-boom, A-boom-boom / A-boom-boom-boom-boom-boom-boom!" In 1955, Fleur de Lis (NH P girls) used two booms to end each verse of "Poor Old Slave" (28). An Hitaga (Iowa CFG) unit song ends with eight.

Rhythmic Tag Endings

Boom endings are related to sung rhythmic tags like "down in the graveyard, slurping" (XxxXx XX), "jump in the breadbox, you crumb" (Xxx**X**x XX), and "confidentially, it stinks" (XxXxx XX). He Bani Gani (Md CFG) uses the first with "Plant a Watermelon upon My Grave" (24). Wolahi (Calif CFG) adds the second to the "Doughnut Song" (12). Conger (Ohio 4-H) has sung the last with "Little Skunk's Hole" (30). Fuld* found published versions of the "Shave and a Haircut" phrase dated 1899.

Some rhythmic endings may have come from college football traditions that go back to the turn of the twentieth century. Ti Ya Ni (Tenn CFG) ends a pep song with three rah's or three hand claps, and can be repeated, "as long as the girls wish to sing." In Missouri, a coed camp finishes a local song with the line, "And it all adds up to fun, at Teamster's Camp. (boom, Boom, BOOM)."

Syncopation

Syncopation was the specific element ragtime introduced into American music. According to Willi Apel, "emphasis on normally weak beats"[243] may be done in one of three ways.[242] Jamaica's "Caramy Achy" (24) holds a weak beat so a strong one is not heard. "Everybody loves Saturday Night" (7), from West Africa, has rests (no sound) on strong beats. "Harmony" (4) emphasizes the second and fourth beats of a 4/4 measure, rather than the usual first and third.

Ragtime

In these songs, syncopation gains its effect from being used sparingly. Ragtime piano repeated a variant of the last sort of syncopation in the melody played by the right hand. The left juxtaposed a steady, regular 4/4 rhythm.[262:7] This melodic pattern, which often took the form xXxXxXxX,[262:239] was used in "Ragtime Cowboy Joe" (27).

"Joe" blended three traditions that together transformed an Afro-American creation into a commercial-music genre. The 1912 lyricist, Grant Clarke, was born in Akron, Ohio, in the Midwest. One composer, Lewis F. Muir, began as a honky-tonk piano player named Louis Meuer in Saint Louis on the Mississippi. His partner, Maurice Abrahams, was a Russian-Jewish immigrant married to Belle Baker.* She was a vaudeville star who "combined the warmth and tender lament of the Yiddish folk song with the modern jazz lyric."

The song's appeal has been enduring. During World War I, British troops used it for "Tips," a comic description of life in France.[442] "Joe" spread to Germany. Ann Marie Filocco§ was told, it "was among the most popular songs at Lachenwald," a Girl Guide camp. Boy Scouts* published it in this country in 1930.

Commercial media continually reintroduce it. Alice Faye sang the lyrics in the 1943 film, *Hello, Frisco, Hello*. Jo Stafford recorded an arrangement in 1949. The University of Wyoming has adapted it. In 1974, girls in the Tent City unit at Glen (Ohio CFG) practiced its hand-jive gestures while standing in line for the council fire. Fowke[332] and Abrahams* both have collected it as a jump-rope rhyme.

Irregular Rests

Syncopation is more common in this country in Black than in white folk traditions. More often, traditional camp songs sung by whites use surrogate forms. Irregular rests give a syncopated feel to "A Bed is Too Small" (30), "I'm a Hynocereous" (16), "Sarah the Whale" (19), and "Did You Ever See a Fishie" (24).

Most of these are old or go back to college traditions, and now are enjoying renewed popularity. Evelyn Hopson Wood* published "Sarah" in the *Camp and Picnic Warbler* in 1929. "Hynocerous" appeared in a 1920 Rutgers' song book. Two borrowed minstrel show tunes.

"Fishie" is sung to "Old Zip Coon," which Bob Farrell introduced at the Bowery Theater in Manhattan in 1834. Several claimed they wrote it. Instead, Alan Jabbour* believed it was the offspring of an older instrumental, "The Rose Tree," transcribed in London in 1795. Dan Bryant gave it new life in the early years of our Civil War as "Turkey in the Straw" (2).

The melody is used for the "Doughnut Song" (12), "Little Skunk's Hole" (30), "I Had a Chicken Who Wouldn't Lay an Egg" (12), and "Do Your Ears Hang Low" (61). In 1944, Suzanne Howe[s] collected a version of the last from Waldenwoods (Mich coed) that used Leon Jessell's 1897 music for "Parade of the Wooden Soldiers." Mawavi (DC CFG) and Tanadoona (Minn CFG) have used "Parade" for local songs.

"Sarah" uses "Dixie" (14). Bryant's Minstrels introduced Daniel Emmett's song in 1859. Seabow (Calif CFG) uses it for "Little Skunk's Hole" (30). Denver Scouts (Colo BSA) sing "I'm Glad I'm a Scouter" (1) to the melody.

A Washington CFG camp localized the text about a leviathan in Frisco Bay who eats anything and everything to "at Melacoma there lives a whale." Niwana (Wash CFG) sings "Spirit Lake" about water north of Mount Saint Helens. Kotomi (Colo CFG) refers to one in Rocky Mountain National Park when it sings "Spirit Lake." Ute believed those who died during an 1832 Arapaho-Cheyenne raid haunt the headwaters of the Colorado river. Angela Lapham (Mich GS) calls her "Susie."

Other Techniques

Another technique, which alters the rhythmic pattern from the regular one/two/three/four, is the selective use of the dotted quarter and eight notes so XXXX becomes xXXX. Scottish snaps are used in "Warsaw the Forty-Second" (15), sung to "Scotland the Brave," and "Coming through the Rye" (2). "A Bed is Too Small" (30) and "My Paddle's Keen and Bright" (59) also employ them. "Rye's" original words were bawdier than those published by Robert Burns in 1800.

In the 1950s, Kitanniwa followed "We Welcome You to Kitanniwa" (22) with a hand clap that used Scottish snaps to end measures:

XXxX   xX   XXxX   xX   XXxX   XXxX   X

Albert Brown[*] believed the tune they used at Wise (Ohio J coed) was Ohio State University's "Across the Field," written in 1915 by a student, William Andrew Dougherty, Junior. Larry Ralston collected several versions of "We're Ohio's Sons and Daughters." The 1930s

4-H song was modeled on "Welcome," but probably used the OSU melody.

Leah Culp says the tune is really "Alabama Jubilee," written in 1915 by George Linus Cobb and Jack Selig Yellen. Gid Tanner (1885-1960) recorded it in 1926 with the Skillet Lickers, an influential fiddle-and-guitar string band from Georgia. Leah's photograph appears in "Singing" with He Bani Gani (Md CFG).

In 1940, buses arriving with new campers at Wo-Chi-Ca (NJ agency coed) in New Jersey were greeted with the same words used at Kitanniwa.[409:11] Emrich collected a parody from Denise Miness,[320] who learned it at Allen (NY coed). No one noted their tunes. The endings of the two are similar.

Singing School Traditions

Big bands, which emerged with Paul Whitman in the 1920s, smoothed the rough edges from early ragtime and jazz. Rhythm reverted to the few variations on a simple 4/4 that Leadbelly* once described as Baptist (common or long) and Methodist (short) meters. In the nineteenth century, Mason had made a point of introducing "many new rhythmic forms" in *The Psaltery* of 1845.

Men steeped in older traditions complained. A member of the Church of the Brethren wrote, "these multiplied varieties" of rhythm or meter found in some books "are not only unnecessary and useless, they are positively injurious, and only tend to involve the subject in difficulties." Jesse Bowman Aikin (1808-1900) then quoted Mason's 1842 comments from *Carmina Sacra*:

> "The most import requisite in all good performance," says the respected author quoted above, "is accuracy of time.—To acquire the habit of keeping good time requires much patience and perseverance; and it is in this that those who commence learning to sing are most likely to fail."

The shape-note innovator then offered his own pedagogic solution, use only one metric pattern:

To keep time, we must beat time, and when one mode of each measure only is used, correctness in keeping time is soon attained. The habit is soon formed of appropriating one beat to each half-note, or its equivalent, whether in equal or unequal measure.

. . .

This is the method used in this work. The music is so written that the measure and the counting, or beating, are always the same, whatever may be its character; and *the habit once formed is never to be changed.*[238:5] [emphasis added]

Men like Gid Tanner and other Appalachian musicians were beyond his influence. They supplemented rhythms their ancestors brought from Ireland, Scotland and England, with ones endemic to their instruments.

Modern Music Education

Early-twentieth-century education reformers discarded rote learning. At Teacher's College, Columbia, Satis Narona Coleman* had children make drums they used when they sang. Followers of Orff, like Isabel Ricker Smaller,* introduced recorders as inexpensive instruments for children to explore melody.

Both went beyond the commonplace view the arts, including music, literature, and painting, are allied, to demonstrate "speaking, singing and moving are integrally related." Patterns of speaking "lead to the evolution of rhythm patterns and these, in turn, lead to the development of melodic patterns."[448:36]

When Coleman's ideas were taken into public schools where rhythm bands were used in my first grade in the early 1950s, cognitive dissonance developed. In school, children were given an opportunity to explore. Outside their classrooms, they were exposed to pabulum by community and contemporary mass media.

I remember one Band Day at Michigan State University in the early 1960s where we first noticed drummers from big-city high schools. They twirled their sticks between beats on their bass drums with cadences that combined Afro-American and Scots regimental traditions. When our drummers tried to imitate, our director let it be known the instruments were school property and not to be abused.

He was defending a view of music that died before he was hired in 1958. Elvis Presley had made his television debut on *The Ed Sullivan Show* in September of 1956. ABC began televising Dick Clark's *American Bandstand* from Philadelphia in August of 1957.

The monotony of the early 1950s was gone. Children were hearing rhythm and blues, Southern white music that had absorbed blues techniques, and Northern urban ethnic traditions, especially those from South Philly. They wanted to imitate, even if their rhythmic impulses had atrophied. Old songs were revived and others rejuvinated, often with rhythmic gestures.

Hand Claps

Clapping on strong downbeats is the simplest way to introduce rhythm. In 1974, Kitanniwa used hand claps with verses to "Little Pile of Tin" (29). In Ohio, Glen (Ohio CFG) used them with "Pick a Bale of Cotton" (17) and one section of "Who Was in the Belly?" (15). Jan Smyth (Ohio P coed) has used hand claps with "Climates" (8). In the West, Wasewagan (Calif CFG) uses them with "Once I Went in Swimming" (7).

In Maryland, Hidden Valley (Md CFG) claps along to "She'll Be Coming 'round the Mountain" (41), and Valley Mill (Md coed) to "Wadaleache" (34). He Bani Gani (Md CFG) has clapped with "Hambone Am Sweet" (5), derived from "Watermelon Hangin' on the Vine." The song was in active tradition when it was recorded by fiddler Gid Tanner in 1926, and by banjo-playing Dave Macon in 1927. In 1936, mandolin-playing Bill Monroe recorded it with his guitar-playing brother, Charlie.

Regular hand claps often accompany religious songs and spirituals. This may follow from the perception it is common practice in some folk and some Black services. Debra Janison remembers clapping to "Do Lord" (37), "He's Got the Whole World in His Hands" (35), and "Rocka My Soul" (31) at Christopher (Ohio C coed) in the late 1960s. Kitanniwa was clapping with "Now let us sing 'til the power of the Lord" (12) in 1974.

Some local camp songs, like "We're from Camp Shawnee" (Mo CFG), use hand claps that probably draw on football yell traditions.

Hand Clap Variations

Alternating hand claps with some other hand or finger rhythmic gesture is a more complex way to play with one's ability to maintain rhythm. Marianne Culligan (Ore CFG) uses hand claps on the strong beats and finger snaps on the weak ones of "All Night, All Day" (33). Kitanniwa did the same in the 1950s. A similar alternation between hands and knees is used with "Flea" (39) by MeWaHi (Calif CFG), Jane Ann Matulich (Calif GS), and Tim Bahr (Mo agency coed).

Patty Cake Gestures

Patty cakes and associated patterns introduce more difficult rhythmic gestures. In the first, two individuals face one another. They clap their own thighs, clap their own hands, and clap the hands of their partners, often alternating between right, left, and both. Yakewi (Ohio CFG) uses such gestures with "Who Stole My Chickens" (6). Kitanniwa used them with "Vrenalie" (30) in 1959. Charlotte Duff knows it as "Maedele." Swiss Girl Guides* published "Meiteli" in 1957 without gestures.

A variant, in which partners sit beside each other in a line or circle, so individuals interact with two people, is used with "Ah Wooney Cooney" (27). Eleanor Thomas* told Girl Scouts "Kee-Chee" was a game from the Belgium Congo in 1956. We were told it was an Indian rain song. The Rohrboughs said, they received it from Ralph and Dorothy Fox.[134]

Patterned Gestures

With patterned gestures, individuals do routines, which may be more involved, by themselves. In the 1950s, Kitanniwa used such a sequence with the chorus of "A Jogging Along" (14). Girls would:

1. Slap thighs twice
2. Clap hands twice
3. Wave right hand over left, both palms facing down, parallel to the floor, twice
4. Wave left hand over right twice

5. Hit end of right fist on top of left fist, both held perpendicular to the floor, twice
6. Hit end of left fist on top of right fist twice
7. Point right forefinger upward while moving right shoulder forward
8. Point left forefinger upward while moving left shoulder forward
9. Nod head twice

The pattern lasted one beat more than the chorus, so when the chorus was repeated, gestures were associated with different words. It ended with step 7.

Patterned gestures are used with "Wadaleache" (24) and "Love Grows under the White Oak Tree" (29). Jolene Robinson Johnson (Wash CFG) introduced both to Kitanniwa in the 1970s from the West Coast.

"Wild oak" has been sung by Mikie Snell (Tex CFG), Josephine Weber (Wisc CFG), and Watervliet (Mich girls). "Wide oak" is known by Eileen Nelson (NY P coed), and was collected by Martha Jackson Stocker[s] in Bay City, Michigan. Carol Rosensweig (Conn YWCA) learned "under the old gum tree."

Wakoma (Wash CFG) uses patterned gestures with "Suitors" (25). Madeline Gail Trichel remembers "knee-slapping, hand-clapping, waving and finger snapping" to "Sandy's Mill" (5) at Wawbansee (La GS) in the early 1950s.

Rest Claps

Campers, who are unfamiliar with syncopation, sometimes use rhythmic hand claps to fill spaces or rests that alter the usual practice of singing every beat. Such claps have been used with "Caramy Achy" (24), "Did You Ever See a Fishie" (24), and "Rise and Shine" (67).

Hand claps may be added to the ends of one or more lines in songs like "We're from Nairobi" (14). This gives an illusion of the midline pause/clap pattern, but is not driven by rhythmic variation. Such end-line hand claps have been added to "There Was a Girl Who Came to Camp" (7) at Namanu (Ore CFG). Mariana Palmer (Penna YMCA girls) uses claps at the beginnings of the lines of "Baby Bumble Bee" (19).

A measure or half measure of hand claps is inserted into the middle of a line to give the same rhythmic feeling to "Mary Ann McCarthy" (5). Onahlee has two hand claps after some "tra la's" in "Foot Traveler" (7). In "Tzena, Tzena" (11), the Oregon Camp Fire camp inserts one clap after the second "Tzena" in the first and third lines of the chorus.

End and midline hand claps, used separately or in combination, are added to camp-specific songs like "Camp Kirby Is Our Kind of Place" (Wash CFG), "Welcome in, we're a jolly bunch from Kamaji" (Minn girls), and Christopher's (Ohio C coed) "Put Your Pack on Your Back." The last is sung to "The Caissons" (9). Sousa modified the 1908 composition by Cincinnati, Ohio's Edmund Louis Gruber. William Bryden and Robert Danford supplied the lyrics.

Literal Gesture Songs

Rhythmic hand claps and related hand and finger motions differ from other gesture songs in one important way. They are keyed only to the musical beat. Literal gestures are tied to text. In "The Cuckoo" (33), the finger snaps, hand claps, and leg slaps are coordinated with words in the chorus. The actions for "Little Pile of Tin" (29) include leg slaps, body shakes, hand claps, and nose touches cued to specific words in the chorus. At Hiwela (Wisc CFG) in 1963, other hand motions were used with the verse.

Ohiyesa (Mich YMCA coed) uses hand claps and body gestures with "Boom boom, ain't it great to be crazy" (33). William Daniel Doebler[S] collected a Holiday House (Mich P girls) version in which the elbow was hit on the table for the first "boom," and the palm slapped on the table for the second.

An elbow knock, table slap is used with "Slap Bang" (16) in many camps. Finger snaps done by a hand moving in an overhead arc are used with "Out in the Forest" (16). Heather MacPhail's[S] version of "Hark through the Forest" used finger snaps alone to end the chorus. Linda Margaret Hanes says "Slap, Bang" was banished from the dining hall at one camp she attended.

Using hand claps for the unknown part in "She Waded in the Water" (8) may be related to an euphemistic, bawdy-song tradition that substitutes onomatopoeic rhythm passages for explicit verbs.

Rhythmic-Literal Mixes

A few songs mix rhythmic and literal gestures. Sally Briggs[S] was told, in the first part of "A Ram Sam Sam" (28), people at Camp Hope (NJ agency coed) kept time by clapping. In the second part, they rolled their hands around each other.

Hand claps are used with "Dem Bones" (37) for the first part of the chorus and gestures for the last line, "whee them bones gonna rise again." In 1974, Kitanniwa was using patterned gestures (touch wrist, elbow, elbow, wrist) with the chorus of "Skinnamarink" (29) and literal hand and finger gestures with the verse.

Replacing words with hand claps in the decremental repetition of "Bingo" (5) is literal, but the claps themselves are rhythmic. Fowke saw it used as a handclap rhyme in Willowdale, Ontario, in 1963.[332]

June Rushing Leibfarth[S] collected a 1961 version of "Patsy Orry Aye" (29) from Silver Springs (Tex GS) with girls clapping once, then twirling their hands three times during the chorus. To campers, the changes were literal. Underneath, they may have been borrowed from those Scots tenor drummers who beat their drum on the first beat and twirled their sticks on the remaining three of a measure.

At the time June was a member of the Scottish Brigade drill team at Houston's Austin High School, mentioned in PEP. Traditions introduced by Beatrice Leola Lytle[*] apparently filtered into local Girl Scout camps. Both Silver Springs (Tex GS) and Robinwood (Tex GS), mentioned in A BEAR, where they imitated Scots pipers, are in the city's San Jacinto council.

The most challenging rhythmic-literal combination songs are ones that maintain the rhythm, but alter gestures on key words. In 1974, Yakewi (Ohio CFG) used literal hand claps and knee slaps in the first part of the chorus for "Toviska" (8), then alternated them in the last half.

At Glen (Ohio CFG), girls slap the table on every beat of the chorus to "Donkey Riding" (35), except the first syllable of "donkey," which is a hand clap. Julie Sherwood[S] collected a literal version from an Ohio Girl Scout. Leg slaps were used with "hey ho," hand claps with "away we go." A hand was waved like a cowboy on a bronco for "donkey riding."

Functions

Rhythmic gestures, sometimes, do more than provide amusement. At Glen (Ohio CFG), the staff claps as they sing "Onward We Go" (13) and "As We Trek along Together" (8) to temper the way girls enter the dining hall during the staff sing. They end the first by beating the table. Elsewhere, the rhythm for "Horsey, Horsey" (28) is beaten on the thighs to keep two vocal groups together.

Other traditions

In the years when cadences in commercial music were monotonous but young children were encouraged to explore rhythm, a genre of rhythmic, non-singing rhyme games developed on playgrounds. The hand claps, initially based on existing Mother Goose-type patty cakes, have been elaborated. Some have adopted a few of the traveling verses found in camp songs.

Fowke saw third graders treat "I Eat Worms" (7) as a clap game in a Toronto, Ontario, school in 1960.[332] Elizabeth Gottlin§ collected "Playmates" (10) as a handclap rhyme in New Jersey in 1976. Joanmarie Schulz§ found "Playmates" and "Three Little Angels" (17) in Howell, New Jersey, the same year. Joanmarie was told, "Playmates" was almost as common as "Oh Mary Mack Mack Mack" (2). Pairs of girls sometimes did the last in the lunch line at Kitanniwa in the 1950s.

Girls there sometimes would do the related ball-bouncing rhyme, "One Two Three O'Leary," on the cement volleyball court before the afternoon sports-and-games class. Fowke collected several variants in Canada, including "Alary" and "Bologny." The oldest came from Mrs. W. T. H. Baillie, who heard "A-Twirlsy" from her daughter in Toronto in the 1930s.[332] She may have been the former Edith May or Mary Edith Legat of Sandgate. Her husband, William Harold Trevorrow Baillie, was on the zoology faculty at the University of Toronto.

The idea for patterned-gesture songs may have a different origin, the movements used with schuhplatter. One still sees the "Bavarian dance in which the dancers slap their knees and soles with their hands"[242] at local polka and German-American festivals. While it does not include singing, the gestures are associated with music and may have been in the kinesic vocabulary of children with Southern German heritages.

Case Study Repertoire

Kitanniwa's 1940s song book included several songs with asymmetric rhythms: "Old Father Time" (18), "Border Trail" (27), and "There Was a Girl" (7). The last two used Celtic-influenced tunes. By the time I attained the age of memory at camp, the first two no longer were being sung. "Girl" was retreating.

Case-study songs from the 1950s indicate that, while counselors still sang "Ragtime Cowboy Joe" (27) and "Roundup Lullaby" (32), most songs known by campers were rhythmically simple. Except for "Ash Grove" and "The Cuckoo," written in 3/4 time and "Swimming" in 6/8, they used 2/4, 4/4, or 2/2 - variations on that simple meter advocated by Aikin. Among case-study songs, which entered the repertoire after 1960, only "Kumbaya" used 3/4 time.

A strong emphasis on the first and third beats is most obvious in "Grand Old Duke of York," which is supposed to sound like a march. "Lollypop" retains the rests and occasional dotted quarter notes followed by eighth notes from "Harrigan," but firmly maintains a strong dancer's rhythm.

Most songs with XxXx rhythms also use one of the two-beat poetic meters discussed in PEP, the iambic xX or the trochaic Xx. However, "Kumbaya" and "Swimming," written in waltz time, do not use three-beat anapests. "Flicker" and "Canoe May Be Drifting," written in common time, do use the xxX poetic foot.

Techniques that reconcile two metric patterns introduce variety. "Sailing, Sailing," the tune for "Swimming," uses dotted quarter notes followed by quarter notes to fill three musical beats with two poetic ones. "Canoe" uses dotted quarter notes followed by two eighth notes to fit three poetic beats into two musical ones.

In some songs, deviations from evenly accented whole, half and quarter notes are introduced to support lyrics. "The Mermaid" uses eighth notes for the asides ("and we were not far from shore"). It uses dotted quarters on the downbeats to emphasize the rhythm ("'twas FRIday MORN when").

"Skyball Paint" uses dotted quarter notes to emphasize key words that fall on the main beats. The associated eighth notes come before ("devil's SAINT") or after ("RIDE but") depending on the text.

"Kookaburra" uses whole and sustained whole notes in two phrases to keep the round parts together. This emphasizes the textual

"STOP kookaburra" and "save some there for ME." By the nature of its lyrics, "Pep" relies primarily on eighth notes, but they are spaced regularly and fall on the beat.

Other songs have altered the regular pattern of quarter notes for melodic interest. In "Ash Grove," each syllable gets one beat, but many get two eighth notes within their single beat. For instance, "down yon der" and "val ley" have one syllable for one beat for one note. "Green" has two notes for the beat for the syllable. These short glissandi occur in almost every phrase, but never on downbeats.

"Witchcraft," the other case-study song from the 1950s, begins many measures with a quarter note on the downbeat. The following dotted quarter bleeds into the third beat and often ends a textual phrase. This makes the second or offbeat the more important part. Among the places this is used are "witchCRAFT i'd," "wiSHES, a," and "real WORLD there." The slow tempo disguises its syncopated nature, but the irregularity remains obvious.

The introduction of songs like "Kumbaya" in the 1960s expanded Kitanniwa's rhythmic vocabulary. It stressed the last syllable of the key word ("kumbaYA"). Thus, almost every measure started with a dotted quarter note that emphasized the beat while giving a staccato feel to the word. Midwestern speech patterns for a three-syllable word would have accented the middle "ba." Southerners often emphasize the first ("KUMbaya").

"I Wish" uses a dotted quarter on the second beat. This places emphasis there, rather than on the primary beat in the measure. However, when one claps, it feels like "Eskimo Hunt" and "A Bear." "Eskimo's" chorus is rhythmically even, while the verse uses dotted quarter notes. "Sippin' Cider," adapted for "A Bear," uses long half notes on the first beats ("girl," "saw," "ci," "straw").

"Rise and Shine" is the most syncopated of the case-study songs. Most measures begin with a quarter note followed by a half note (oh RISE and SHINE). This places the stress just after the beat. "Flicker" begins each phrase and measure with eighth notes that build to a climax with a dotted quarter on the third beat and final word ("wind in the PINES").

"Rose," as published by Tobitt, was a round composed only of half and quarter notes. In tradition, some half notes have been broken into quarters by adding more words to the text. The two measures that end the two major parts have additional glissandi. In one case this falls on the second beat ("see THEE wed"), in the other on the third and fourth ("at MY will"). A canon imposes strict conventions, but, within these, people no longer have been willing to settle for the slow pace of the older song.

Case Study: Oh, the Boatmen Dance

"The Boatmen" (28), as it was published by the Rohrboughs and is sung in camps, uses evenly accented quarter and eighth notes for most of the melody. Exceptions include the transition into the last line of the verse, which uses a dotted quarter and an eighth note (SHORE he). A similar pattern is used in the first measure of the chorus (OH the). The gestures, stomping on the downbeat and clapping on the upbeat, emphasize a martial, rather than a syncopated rhythm.

History

Daniel Emmett wrote "De Boatmen's Dance" for the historic first performances by the Virginia Minstrels mentioned in AGE GROUP INFLUENCES. At least two companies[†] in Boston published sheet music in 1843 with an introduction, verse, chorus, and interlude. Within a year, minstrel dancer Thomas Rice[*] was performing an imitation that entered tradition as "Down the River - Down the Ohio" (9).

When Oliver Ditson[†] reprinted "De Boatman Dance" as "sung by the Ethiopian Serenaders," it used four of the shared verses and dropped the interlude. The 1882 collection of minstrel songs capitalized on the late-nineteenth-century revival of minstrel troupes.

Only the first verse is sung today with the chorus. A second verse, written in dialect, was added in the 1929 Girl Scout version.[†] The main textual variations in camps have arisen from people's unconscious response to dialect. Some use the plural of Emmett, some the singular of Newell.

None of Richard Dorson's Michigan State students reported the song in camps in the 1940s or early 1950s. By the middle 1950s, it apparently was entering tradition. Aaron Copland had reintroduced it in his *Old American Songs*. Benjamin Britten and Peter Pears, who performed the art song rendition of "Ash Grove" (72), premiered Copland's version in 1950. June Rushing Leibfarth[§] collected the first verse at Tejas (Tex GS) in 1957.

Kathleen Huggett Nye asked me:

> Do you remember "The Boatmen?" They brought back
> from Wathana (Mich CFG). [The director] hated it when
> girls stomp . . . that one's from Wathana, from a CIT trip;
> that was not a Kitanniwa song.

I barely remembered it, so she must have been referring to either
1958 or 1959 when I was in the senior unit. We no longer attended
morning sing or ate many meals in main camp. Joyce Gregg
Stoppenhagen, who was on staff in 1957 and 1959, is the source for
version A. She clearly remembered it as a Kitanniwa song. Four
others, who were in main camp from that time, remember the song.
Three, who were in the senior unit, do not.

Our exemption from camp routine blinded us to changes creeping
into the repertoire with girls who had grown up with Presley. Our
escape from rhythmic tedium still took the older form, games, like
"Lemmi Sticks" (8) and "Who Stole the Cookies" (2), which combined
rhythm with tests of mental agility.

Explication

The Virginia Minstrels advertised they were impersonating "the
negro boatmen on the Ohio River."[439:131] A few weeks later, they claimed
they were performing a "much admired song in imitation of the Ohio
Boatman." [420:42] The phrases delivered several meanings to the audience.

A body of tall-tale exaggerations extolling frontier virtues and
brawls had sprung up around Mike Fink and the flatboats that plied
the Ohio in the years just after the American Revolution. By the time
Mark Twain* was growing up in a Mississippi river town, memorats
had solidified into a view of:

> heavy drinkers, coarse frolickers in moral sties like
> the Natchez-under-the-hill of that day, heavy fighters,
> reckless fellows, every one, elephantinely jolly, foul-witted,
> profane; prodigal of their money, bankrupt at the end of
> the trip, fond of barbaric finery, prodigious braggarts; yet,
> in the main, honest, trustworthy, faithful to promises and
> duty, and often picturesquely magnanimous.

The wharves of Natchez-under-the-Hill were the termination for many early poled-boat trips. The frontier between British/American territory and French/Spanish claims lay at a bend where the nature of the Mississippi changed. Spain took control in 1779. Manuel Luis Gayoso de Lemos founded the city of Natchez in 1789, then attracted settlers from Kentucky with land grants. Thomas Pinckney's treaty of 1796 moved the Spanish and French to the other side of the Mississippi, then to the south.

During the Spanish years, a polyglot community of French, Spanish, Choctaw, Chickasaw, Africans, and frontiersmen developed that later nurtured men like Wallis Willis and his master, mentioned in KUMBAYA. Chateaubriand visited in 1791, then published *René*. His 1805 novel created the romantic image of the area here and for Europeans.

Emmett's original lyrics referred to common stereotypes it solidified: the boatman worked hard, ran through his money, danced "all night til broad daylight," and went home with the "gals in de morning." When the narrator visited a boat, he got slugged "in de callaboose" by a man who lived by stealing livestock along the banks. The camp song's verses refer to sedentary ne'er do wells who lived by the river and could not be bothered to maintain their shacks.

Daniel Decatur Emmett

Emmett not only used common images of the boatmen, but he also used the same musical idiom that existed before Mason introduced German aesthetics to this country. Carl Frederick Wittke believed the first important minstrel song, "Old Zip Coon," was derived from "a rough jig dance, 'Natchez under the Hill',"[556:16-17] in "The Rose Tree" cluster. Hans Nathan noted, while many who followed the Virginia Minstrels used four-part music, Emmett never did.[439:128]

Little is known about his musical influences. He was born in 1815 in Mount Vernon, Ohio, on the upper reaches of the Muskingum river. Emmet's father's father was a Methodist circuit rider. His father was a blacksmith, who moved west from Staunton in the Shenandoah valley of Virginia.

On the maternal side, Emmet's grandfather was born in Virginia, and moved to Maryland before relocating to Ohio. Either he or his wife Martha was part Native American. She and her daughter, Sarah, had some music training.[317]

Emmett told a friend, he had always been interested in music: "I hummed familiar tunes, arranged words to sing to them and made up tunes to suit words of my own."[315] When he was the same age as modern girls who become interested in music, he was working on what would become "Old Dan Tucker" (2).

When he was about fifteen-years-old, a touring show needed a replacement fiddler for a performance in Mount Vernon. Emmett auditioned with "Old Dan Tucker." His Methodist parents disdained his interest in theater. He left home when he was seventeen.[317]

Records show he joined the army in Cincinnati as a fife player and learned to drum. Thereafter, he worked in traveling circuses where he claimed he learned to read music. From there, he learned the banjo, which then was a slave instrument, and began working with people like Frank Brower, who was born in Baltimore.

Music

The sheet music suggests the original "Boatmen" was more complex than the camp song. Dotted quarter and eighth notes on the third and fourth beats were used more frequently in the melody. At several places in the verse and in the chorus, the two hands did not play chords simultaneously. Instead, the score had the left playing a chord on the downbeat and the right playing one of the offbeat. As shown below, these countered the vocal asymmetric figure.

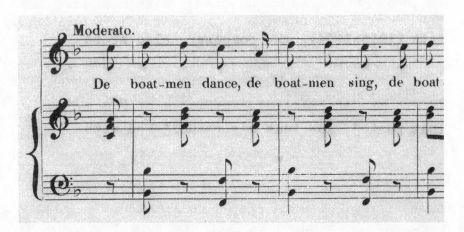

This melodic rhythmic pattern comes from the notes inégales (**X**x) that Henry Purcell introduced into England after the Restoration of 1660. The motif was filtering into popular music when Emmett's great-great-grandfather Abraham migrated to Virginia from England in 1671. The family had supported Cromwell in the civil war, and some members had followed him to Ireland.[316] In camps, the motif is used with "Roundup Lullaby" (32).

The piano part, rather than providing a harmonic accompaniment in the German tradition, simulated the percussive minstrel-show performance. It contained, depending on which hand was favored, a nucleus of syncopation.

"Boatmen" employs only five notes, with a leap to a series of high E's in the chorus. Nathan suggested the use of E came from the banjo. On a four-stringed instrument, like those used in the 1840s, the E string was the one strummed by the thumb. Later, in 1865, Frank Buchanan Converse[†] used a modified version of the tune in his instruction manual for the instrument.

Gestures

Nathan reprinted paintings and lithographs from pre-Civil War years that showed performers sitting askew with their limbs akimbo, as if they were in constant motion. In one of the Virginia Minstrels from 1843, all four men had at least one foot flexed, suggesting one or several were beating time.

The "Dance de boatmen dance" interlude could have been used for one person to stand and do a few steps while the others sang. Before the Virginia Minstrels, dances were the most important part of stage shows. Two members of the troupe, in fact, were dancers, Dick Pelham and Frank Brower. The other two had accompanied dancers. Billy Whitlock had played banjo for John Diamond. Emmett had played fiddle for Brower.

In part, they drew on Elizabethan court choreography. Jigs were characterized by the "lively stamping of the heels and rapid footwork with a quiet torso."[497:411] Galliards relied upon "leg thrusts and leaps."[497:359]

The next phase of court dance did not disseminate as widely. Small-stepped minuets were too complex for many at court. They did not percolate to the masses.[497] Elizabethan dances were the ones remembered by immigrants like Emmett's ancestor. They may even have contributed to the idiosyncratic dance style George M. Cohan and his sister Josephine perfected in their Irish-descended vaudeville family.

In the years immediately after the Virginia Minstrels' first performance, William Henry Lane revolutionized dance. The free Black, who was born in Providence, Rhode Island, performed as Juba. He apparently learned from Jim Lowe, a Black dancer in Manhattan's Five Points district, and from white minstrel dancers like Diamond, Pelham, and Brower.

Juba, or someone using his name, toured England with the Ethiopian Serenaders. He was performing with Pell's Serenaders in England in 1848 when another performer sang "Ohio Boatman."[386] Pell was Pelham and his brother.

Fancy footwork associated with clogging that developed in Lancashire textile mills, breakdowns and cakewalks were introduced later, after Black artists could perform more openly. The movements associated with the first shows still would have been large, unrestrained, and loose-limbed.

Camp gestures retain this spirit. Stomping the foot on the downbeat and clapping on the offbeat are simple. Raising the left hand while stomping on the syllable "hi" of "Ohio" is not. The mental processes that coordinate two patterns, a physical movement and a mental vocal one, must be interrupted. Concentrating on lyrics makes it hard to maintain rhythm. That difficulty, in turn, creates a challenge, which leads to further requests for the song.

Popularity

"Boatmen" has been used by public-school text publishers and others who want music to supplement American history lessons. Most use verses like those published by Ditson, and have had no effect on the popularity of the song, which seems restricted to girls' camps.

Version A

Text from Joyce Gregg Stoppenhagen, Camp Kitanniwa (Mich CFG), 1957, 1959. Gestures from Camp Kitanniwa (Mich CFG), after lunch sing, 1974. Joyce's photograph appears in "Kitanniwa Staff, 1950s."

Gestures

F   for a foot stomp with hands thrown wide apart

C   for a hand clap

H   for one hand raised over the head, while the other remains in open, foot stomp position

1. Oh (H) the (C) boat (F) men (C) dance (F) and (C) the boat (F)
        men (C) sing (F)
    And (C) the boat (F) men (C) do (F) most (C) an (F) y (C)
        thi (F) ng (C)
    When (F) the (C) boat (F) men (C) come (F) on (C) shore (F)
    They (C) spend (F) all (C) their mon (F) ey (C) and they work (F)
        for (C) more (F)

C. High (H/F) ho (C) the boat (F) men (C) go (FC)
    Up (H/F) and down (C) the ri (F) ver (C) on the old (F)
        ba (C) teau (FC)
    Hi (H/F) ho (C) the boat (F) men (C) go (FC)
    Up (H/F) and down (C) the ri (F) ver (C) on the O (F) hi (H) o (FC)

2. Have (F) you (C) ev (F) er (C) seen (F) where (C) the boat (F)
        man (C) live (F)
    In (C) a house (F) in (C) in a hol (F) low (C) with a roof (F)
        like (C) a sieve (F)
    The (C) boat (F) man (C) says (F) if (C) he had (F) one (C) wish (F)
    If (C) he gets (F) much (C) wet (F) ter, he's (C) a gon (F) na
        be (C) a fish (F)

Chorus

Version B

Text from Camp Wakoma (Wash CFG), 1970s; variations from A emphasized.

C. Hi ho the boatmen go
    Up and down the river on the **O-hi-o**
    Hi ho the boatmen go
    Up and down the river on the O-hi-o

1. **The** boatmen dance and the boatmen sing
   And the boatmen do most anything.
   When the boatmen come on shore
   They spend all their money
   And they work for more.

Chorus

2. **Ever see** where **a boatman lives**?
   In a house in a hollow **that leaks** like a sieve.
   Boatmen say if **it gets much worse**
   Or it gets much wetter
   He's gonna be a fish.

Chorus

Version C

Text from Daniel Emmet, Prentiss sheet music, 1843; first verse only, variations from A emphasized in shared sections.

1. **De Boatman** dance **de Boatman** sing,
   De Boatman up to eb'ry thing,
   When **de Boatman got** on shore,
   He spends his money and **works** for more.

I. Dance de Boatman dance,
   Dance de Boatman dance.
   Dance all night 'till broad day light,
   Go home wid de galls in de morning.

C. Hi **row de** boat**man row.**
   Floating down de riber O-hi-o.
   Hi **row de** boatman **row.**
   Floating down **de riber** Oh-hi-o.

Grand Old Duke of York: Gestures

Gestures, motions, or actions are one of the most characteristic aspects of camp songs. Indeed, many in the first American organizational song book, Neidlinger's 1912 *Songs of the Camp Fire Girls,*[*] used movements. Gestures also are one of the most traditional aspects. They rarely are written down. When they are noted, descriptions can be so vague one still needs to see them to reproduce them.

Most camp and commercial songsters simply use keywords or add, "has motions." Even then, those remarks cause confusion. Folklorists and songbook editors have no standard terms. I am grouping songs by parts of the body, indicating alternative phrases.

Hand Gestures

Hand gestures use fingers and hands, usually held at chest to waist level, with bent elbows. Kitanniwa used them with "The Mermaid" (23), "Swimming" (36) and "Eskimo Hunt" (21), as well as with many decremental and cumulative songs like "An Austrian" (34). They have been called dramatic, pantomime, mimic, and imitative motions.

The movements often rely on stereotypes. It is not uncommon to find the same motion in several songs. Donkey ears have been added to "Donkey Riding" (35) in New Jersey Girl Scout camps, according to Ann Marie Filocco,[§] and to "Sweetly Sang the Donkey" (3) by Treasure Island (Penna BSA) in the 1940s.

Animals are squished in "Baby Bumble Bee" (19) and in the version of "I Eat Worms" (7) collected by Peggy Hays.[§] Squishing is done by rubbing the palms together, much as is done in rolling coils of clay.

Stereotypic gestures stabilize a largely unwritten form. When an action is forgotten, a convention may be substituted. This, apparently, happened with the version of "The Crocodile" (51) collected by William Daniel Doebler.§ The crocodile is made by placing one hand, palm down, on top of the other. Normally, the positions of the two hands are switched for, "And the lady was inside." In William's version, the stomach was rubbed. Cub Scouts* recommended the same movements in 1969.

Gestures and Childhood Development

Hand and finger gestures may serve an important function for young campers. According to Gesell and Ilg, "most of the organization" of the neuromuscular system "takes place in the first ten years of life, and proceeds with an orderly sequence."[343:225] In the most observable progression,

> Batting requires a higher order of coordination on the part of the eyes, hands, fingers, body posture and feet [than does tossing a ball . . .] Batting form during the years from five to ten improves perceptibly, not merely because practice makes perfect, but because the total neuro-muscular system of the child undergoes progressive growth changes.[343:227]

Fine, or smaller, muscle skills mature concurrently. At seven, children prefer doodling to writing[343:228] and use both hands to play piano, but with unequal pressure.[343:236] A year later, "there is an increase of speed and smoothness in fine motor performance."[343:228] It is manifested in areas like writing (speed), piano playing (dexterity), and song gestures (dexterity speed tests).

Sources for improvement lay with an eight-year-old's ability to distinguish "between original and acquired" movement,[343:447] and a new ability to recognize right and left on another.[343:443] The first allows a child to isolate gestures for practice. The second makes imitation easier.

Generally, by age nine, children's neuromuscular development is dictated less by demands of species growth. Their "eyes and hands are now well differentiated. The fingers also show new differentiation." Hands generally can be used independently. Children like to write at top speed.[343:228] They are interested in correctly fingering the piano keys, and playing staccato, which gives "better control over the sounds" produced.[343:206]

A fourth-grade child "reveals his psychomotor makeup [. . .] in the gestures which he makes under tension or excitement."[343:230] Parents now report a child "to be either good or poor with his hands."[343:197-198]

Upper Age Limit

Neuromuscular changes create an upper limit for a growth phase in which movement can be enjoyed for itself. Gesture songs do not function as a safety zone for children to overcome frustrations arising from uncoordinated muscles. Instead, they present an arena where they may show competence. They feel sure they can perfect movement routines, if not today, then before the end of camp.

The fact such mastery occurs may explain why former campers are willing to describe their problems learning gestures in self-mocking memorats of triumph over adversity. Problems in other areas, if they existed, either are not mentioned or hold no interest to others.

Lower Age Limit

The lower level for this phase of developmental competence in hand motions seems to be about age eight. Even though there is "likely to be a gap between what he wants to do with his hands and what he can do,"[343:237] the third grader likes "to dramatize and express himself in a variety of postures and gestures."[343:168]

Children younger than eight seem to have difficulties doing many hand-gesture songs. One young woman told Julie Sherwood,[S] she learned "Donkey Riding" (35):

> at age four while attending day camp with her mother (a leader). Her earliest memories relating to the song were of not being able to remember the motions, and once learned, not being able to do them fast enough.

Carol Parsons Sievert says, she "can remember being so young that I couldn't snap my fingers and being frustrated at not being able to keep up" when "Out in the Forest" (16) was sung at Kitanniwa in the 1930s.

Young Camper Repertoire

Because differing motor skills exist, a group of songs with much simpler actions is reserved for young campers. At Kitanniwa, they were done when Blue Birds met in their own Valley Lodge, but rarely would have been sung in all camp sings in the main lodge.

Fowke labeled three, "Itsy Bitsy Spider" (33), "Six Little Ducks" (27) and "I'm a Little Teapot" (2), as "fingerplays." She collected the first two from Nancy Takerer, who learned them in Kingston, Ontario, in the 1940s. She heard "Teapot" from Lynn Fowke, who learned it in Saskatoon, Saskatchewan, in the 1950s.[332] I remember the first and third from my Blue Bird years at Kitanniwa.

Kathleen Huggett Nye recalls, she used to sing "I like to catch brass rings on the merry go round" (26) a "lot for Blue Birds" at Kitanniwa in the 1950s. Lisa Drumm[S] collected the song from two former Blue Birds. They said, their motions included standing and sitting to imitate riding horses, and miming words like "play croquet" and "crochet."

Lucille Parker Munk sang "Playmates" (10) with that age group at Tanawida (Mich CFG). Her gestures were simple mimic ones, not the ones used when the song is treated as a handclap rhyme on playgrounds.

Older Camper Repertoire

A need to exercise rapidly developing fine motor skills passes by age ten, when increased stamina and gross muscular growth turn children's interest to more demanding physical activities.[344:40] Even so, there always remains a challenge in songs with gestures that employ rhythm or abstraction or are difficult to learn.

This, especially, seems true with "Junior Birdsmen" (30). One makes upside-down flying goggles with one's thumb and forefinger joined in a circle. Next, one twists one's wrists to place them in front of one's eye by resting one's fingers on one's jawbones. One young man, remembering his years as a junior counselor in a Maryland coed camp, admitted, it "was kind of embarrassing; one of my campers had to show me how to do it." Marsha Lynn Barker (Mich GS) does not consider it a dining hall song.

Alternating between right thumb to left forefinger and left thumb to right forefinger is not as complicated. Still, it can be challenging. At Kitanniwa, Carol Parsons Sievert:

> can remember bursting at "Ensy Wensy Spider" (33) in the dining room. I can remember sitting there, getting hysterical, not at my own [. . .], but seeing the girl across from me, breaking up so we couldn't finish.

Looking back, she ascribed their adolescent pleasure to "a certain release that older people get when they get to act like a kid just for a while."

Usage

No expectation exists that hand gestures be employed for every word or phrase in a song, but only when appropriate. They are used for just the third line of "Puffer Billies" (33) in some camps. Further, no song must use finger and hand motions. Although some songs seem to be sung with them consistently, there always are camps that abstain.

Among the ones usually accompanied by literal hand gestures are "A Boy and a Girl in a Little Canoe" (33), "Dewey Was the Grass" (13), and "Little Bunny Foo Foo" (19). Also common are "My High Silk Hat" (39), "This Little Light of Mine" (24), and "You Must Pay the Rent" (6). Kitanniwa used actions with "Do Your Ears Hang Low" (61) and "We Are the Redmen" (32) in the 1950s, and with "Little Pile of Tin" (29) in 1974.

Other songs seem to have gestures only in particular camps or areas. Ohiyesa (Mich YMCA coed) mentions them with "I Am a Great Musician" (18) and "The Instruments" (17). Tayanita (Ohio CFG) uses hand gestures with "He's Got the Whole World in His Hands" (35). Jean Mayo McLaughlin (Fla GS) learned some with "Perfect Posture" (11).

Sally Briggs[§] collected hand gestures with "Old Mill Stream" (17) from a former Cedar Lake (NJ J coed) camper. "All Night, All Day"

(33) has literal hand motions in some New England camps. Phyllis Bonnie Newman learned them at Truda (Me girls). William Daniel Doebler[S] collected them from a former Runels (Mass GS) counselor.

Didactic Hand Gestures

Some hand motions reinforce other educational functions. Josephine Weber (Wisc CFG) has used deaf signing with "Jacob's Ladder" (46). The "Silent Grace" uses Indian sign language for "May the Great Spirit overhead" (8). "Kumbaya" (90), as mentioned earlier, has been sung with both.

Considering the minimum age in most camps, there is no tutorial value in making the letters "V is for the fun we all know." The contra part is sung with "Oh Give Out a Cheer for Camp Val Verde" in the Texas Camp Fire camp.

Using the fingers to count is pure amusement in "Three Blue Pigeons" (12) at Tanadoona (Minn CFG) and with "Ten in a Bed" (12) at Ohiyesa (Mich YMCA coed). The Y camp has people stand in a group and come or leave in its version of "Five Blue Pigeons."

Paddling motions, which Jane Ann Matulich (Calif GS) remembers using with "My Paddle's Keen and Bright" (59), are no more instructional than those used with "Swimming" (36). Vera Helgesson Hollenffer gave the Rohrboughs their first version of the first. She taught physical education in San Francisco's Lux School for Industrial Training for Girls in the 1930s. She used May Day dances in their spring pageants.

Arm Gestures

Sally Briggs[S] remembers a friend who used gesture songs, like "My Hat" (33), when she worked with mentally retarded children at Camp Hope (NJ agency coed). She used ones that exercised the whole arm more than the wrist and finger joints with nine- to eleven-year-old boys who could not speak. She hoped to reinforce hand-eye coordination.

"Rocka My Soul" (31), commonly, is sung by throwing the arms up over the head for "so high you can't get over it," dropping the arms in front of the body for "so low you can't get under it," and stretching the arms sideways for "so wide you can't get around it."

Similar gestures are used with "Deep and Wide" (9), "I'm Downright, Uptight" (5), and "Slap Bang" (16). Kitanniwa used them with "Oh in the Moonlight" (12) in 1974. The "Damper Song" (16) is older.

Seattle Scouts (Wash BSA) move their arms up and down in "Rheumatism" (11). At Lachenwald (Germany GS), Ann Marie Filocco[§] was told "To Ope Their Trunks" (45) was "sung around the campfire or at dinner."

> The campers made up an action which they did to this song. At the end of it, the kids would fling their arms out to the side one at a time, in an attempt to hit their neighbor in the face. They didn't mean to actually hit anyone, but would just joke around.

In some camps, people throw up their arms twice in the third line of "Little Tommy Tinker" (45). Carol Simon[§] was told, at Camp Christian (Ohio P coed), "Tommy" was "usually sung at the morning song fest after breakfast to wake people up." This, like "Rheumatism" and "To Ope," generally is treated as a round.

Body Gestures

Lyrics of many songs using body gestures, like many using arm motions, contain prescriptions for action like "One Finger, One Thumb" (30). Blue Haven (NM P coed) sings "keep growing," rather than "keep moving." Boys in another camp call it the "Spastic Song."

"Head, Shoulders, Knees and Toes" (33) was introduced on the waterfront at Kitanniwa in the late 1950s to warm people's bodies on cold mornings. Peggy Hays[§] was told, it was "used as a wake up song in the cabins, at morning camp fires, and before breakfast in the dining hall" at Storer (Ohio YMCA coed). Fowke collected it as a singing game from Lynn Fowke, who learned it in Saskatoon in the 1950s.[332]

Some other prescriptive body movement songs are "If You're Happy and You Know It" (50) and "I've got that Camp Fire spirit up in my head" (16). The substituted, cumulative items of "Nicky Nicky Nu" (23) exist separately as an infant or toddler's finger rhyme, "brow bender, eye winker."[452]

Ohiyesa (Mich YMCA coed) has campers touch relevant body parts for "I'm Being Eaten by a Boa Constrictor" (17). Kiloqua (Ohio

CFG) does the same with "This Old Man" (30). A 1958 film, *Inn of the Sixth Happiness*, revitalized it in camp tradition.

Some prescriptive songs refer to the body through a series of puns. The same basic idea is found in "Chester Have You Heard about Harry" (18), "Under the Spreading Chestnut Tree" (19), and Zanika Lache's (Wash CFG) version of "Tony Chestnut" (1).

Other body-movement songs use frame repetition to indicate new parts of the body. "My Ship from China," or "The Fan Song" (5), as sung by Nancy Bryant (Ohio CFG), has cumulative actions. Homelani (Hawaii P coed) uses frame substitution with "Father Abraham Had Seven Sons" (7). Ruth Crawford Seeger[*] published an alternative circle game. Ernst Wolff recorded it as a German children's song, "Adam Hatte Sieben Schne" (FC 7271), with gestures for lines like "With their feet they tap, tap, tap." Janice Engel says it had been banned at Cherith (Minn P girls), "cause the floor boards got bad."

Facial and Head Gestures

Facial and head gestures may be considered a subcategory of body motions when used in songs like the "Brownie Smile Song" (7), "It Isn't Any Trouble Just To S-m-i-l-e" (25), and "Smile Awhile and Give Your Face a Rest" (8). June Rushing Leibfarth[§] collected a version of "Glink Glonk" (21) from Arnold (Tex GS) in 1958 that used eye blinks. Jayne Garrison has stuck out her tongue at the end of "Sweetly Sings the Donkey" (30) at Shawnee (Mo CFG).

Standing Gestures

Many songs using body gestures require campers be on their feet. Standing itself can be a gesture, as when the 1974 Kitanniwa staff stood, chorus-line fashion, to sing "Catalina Matalina" (14). Leah Jean Ramsey (Tex CFG) remembers the group swaying with their arms on each other's shoulders to "Under the Bamboo" (10). Heather MacPhail[§] collected a version of "More We Get Together" (32) in 1943 in which girls from Sweyolakan (Ida CFG) sat and swayed. When they bent forward and backward, they tried to throw one another off balance.

In some standing songs, one begins by sitting or kneeling, then springs up, as in "Rise and Shine" (67). Girls in Madeline Gail

Trichel's Ohio Girl Scout troop stand to sing "Hear the lively song of the frogs in yonder pond" (28). They go down on "crick, crick" and jump on "baromp," "so that everyone [is] jumping in four sections." Other rounds sometimes given this same stand-sit treatment are "Why Shouldn't My Goose" (23) and "Little Tommy Tinker" (45). Roberta Tupper Latvala[S] was told the last:

> was always sung at meal times at conferences to impede the slow eaters. It was necessary to rise on the last line or be sent around the room at a steady jog. I heard this one more than ten years ago.

Janice Knapp (Mich CFG) has sung "My Bonnie" (15) with people standing or sitting on every "B." Richard Fazenbaker[S] was told, at Butler (Ohio BSA), the boys would sometimes divide into two groups with one standing while the other sat. They sometimes used "body" for "Bonnie." Some people stand for every "alleluia" in "Praise Ye the Lord, Alleluia" (18). Donald Eberhardt[S] collected a version of "More We Get Together" (32) in which campers stood or sat on the words "together" and "friends."

"Way up in the Sky" (40) is another song with a wake-up theme used in many camps at breakfast, often with stand-sit gestures. Marsha Lynn Barker (Mich GS) said it was not sung in the dining hall in one camp she attended.

Mobility Gestures

Music professionals often label songs done while standing as "singing games." Many in camps consider them gesture songs, because movements lack the competitive or testing qualities they associate with the word game. This, especially, is true of songs combining mobility with hand gestures.

"Fair Rosie" (11) is the most common such song in CFG camps. It follows a girl through the stages of Camp Fire to meet a prince charming. Patiya (Colo CFG) sings "Thornrosa." Marie Leske introduced it in Germany as "Dornröschen."[264:552-3] She was a Moravian Brethren orphan, raised in Switzerland and married in Saint Louis, Missouri, in 1858. She returned to Germany as a widow in 1859 where she edited books for girls.

"When the Papa and the Mama" (5) focuses on parent-child relationships, especially near the age of courtship. He Bani Gani (Md CFG) combines mobility with hand gestures for "Swiss Navy" (16). They use a chorus-line formation and body gestures with "Mrs. O'Leary" (31). A photograph of them doing a gesture song appears in "Singing."

Other mobile gesture songs involve body actions, like "Vive l'Amour" (30). Leah Culp (Md CFG) says, it "starts with two to six people who gradually gather up everybody - singing and holding hands in a crooked line."

"One Elephant Went Out To Play" (17) is better known. Louis Lambert* collected "La Ronde des Cocus" as a men's dance in 1906 in Languedoc, in the south of France. Tobitt* published it in 1938.

Josephine Weber (Wisc CFG) has done it standing in a line. She places her hands on the hips of the person in front of her. Holding hands between the legs is more common. Aleta Huggett§ was told, in 1949 at Lake Louise (Mich P coed), "someone would start the ditty while the kids were lying around on their bunks." Manakiki (Minn agency coed) has the elephant on a toadstool, rather than a spider's web.

Hokey Pokey

Campers generally consider "Hokey Pokey" (16) to be a dance, perhaps because it is done with a phonograph record. Folklorists collected it as a singing game, "Looby Lou," in England and Scotland in the nineteenth century. William Wells Newell* saw it in Boston in the 1820s where it was "danced deliberately and decorously." In Scotland, Robert Chambers* saw a slow circle dance sung to "Lullibullero" that featured grotesque movements. By the 1880s, Newell said it had been turned into a "romp."

The commercial version emerged during World War II at Murray's, a club in London's Mayfair district. It then was the center of Allied military planning. Jimmy Kennedy* says, one night in 1942, Canadian soldiers there were joking around with a children's game. He claims he took their song and turned it into "Cokey Cokey."

Alfred Taboriwsky, the bandleader at the time, remembered it differently. His Jewish parents had fled Vilna during the Russian pogroms in the early 1880s. During World War I, they sent him to

Boston, where he heard a "hokey pokey" rhyme. When Al Tabor*
returned to England, he became a society bandleader. He claims to
have created "Hokey Cokey" at Murray's during the blitz of 1940.

After the war, Roland Lawrence LaPrise* introduced "Hokey
Pokey" at Sun Valley, an Idaho ski resort. Larry, as he was called, had
served in France during the war as an army musician. He claimed he
based it on a French-Canadian song he heard as a child in Detroit. His
father, Joseph Alphonse LaPrise, had migrated from Canada in 1890.

In the same years, Robert Matthew Degen and Joseph Peter
Brier played a version at a summer resort near Delaware Water Gap
in the Pocono mountains of eastern Pennsylvania. Degen's father
was a farmer in the Scranton, Pennsylvania, area. Brier's paternal
grandparents had migrated there from Germany.

Ray Anthony released a commercial version with Jo Ann Greer in
1953. That same year, Harold Courlander recorded the original as a
Black ring game in Alabama (FS 7004). Val Verde, a Texas Camp Fire
camp, is the only one to report using the folk variant.

Other songs with mobility gestures that sometimes are treated as
dances in camps include "Three Blind Mice" (10) and "Salty Dog"
(10). "Miserlou" (5) and the Danish "Seven Jumps" (6) or "Syvspring"
are less common. Others, like "Patty Cake Polka" (5), the Virginia
Reel (24) and various forms of popular dance like jitterbugging, which
use records, are not considered songs.

Kitanniwa used "Hokey Pokey" (16), the Mexican Hat Dance,
the Virginia Reel (24), and Grand March for evening and rainy-day
programs. "Weevily Wheat" (2) was tried once.

Pretty Songs

Although some, like "Barges" (68) and "Kumbaya" (90), have
motions, many think them inappropriate for pretty songs. Becky
Colwell Deatherage (NY GS) has some gestures for "Wee Baby
Moon" (11), and Dolores Bossaller (Mo GS) to "A Bed Is Too Small"
(30). Elizabeth Mills Bachman (Ore coed) knows actions for "Swing
Low, Sweet Chariot" (31), and Viki Irene Cuqua (Ariz YWCA) to
"We're up at Los Cerros" (19).

The one gesture Kitanniwa's director discouraged in the 1950s
was swaying during "Green Trees" (56). We sang it as we stood,
holding hands with arms crossed in a friendship circle, to end evening

programs. This must have been considered appropriate in other camps, perhaps the church camps many also attended, because the swaying often began. She always stood rigid.

Carol Shuster[S] was told, one Ohio Girl Scout troop would "Stand in circle with arms crossed; gently sway during singing ['Taps'] and after it is sung, leader squeezes hands." The hand squeeze is repeated around the circle like the game Electricity. Usually the leader says "Good Night" when the signal returns to him or her.

Sources

Folklorists and commercial songbook editors may distinguish gesture songs from singing games because they suspect the two have separate origins. At one time, folklorists believed ballads, like those collected by Child, arose from communal dances. Newell (1839-1907) believed the "history of the game-rhyme is encapsulated in that of the ballad."[445:xvi]

He argued they had been part of pagan May games, which had celebrated fertility and the return of spring. His primary example was "As We Go Round the Mulberry Bush." He included a Massachusetts variant, "barberry bush," in 1883 in *Games and Songs of American Children.*

When Alice Bertha Gomme[*] (1853-1938) compiled her collection of British children's games in 1894, she still was hoping to detect traces of such composition. Benjamin Albert Botkin[*] says, she failed.

She did find "Mulberry Bush," which she believed descended from another circle game, "Merry-ma-tansa." She described the latter as a divination ritual for identifying the future husband of a girl in the circle. Only the one who stood in the center, in place of the sacred tree, knew the name.

Halliwell[*] reported the ring dance in 1849 as "The Bramble-Bush" in his *Popular Rhymes and Nursery Tales.* Asa Fitz published it in this country in *The First Exercise Book* of 1858.[338]

While such examples are tantalizing, Curt Sachs[*] suggested most circle dances go back to the period documented by Playfield's collection of country dances. *The English Dancing-Master[*]* was issued in 1650, during the last years of Cromwell. It stayed in print, in various forms, until 1728, just after the accession of the German-speaking George II. As such, it was part of the general period of metropolitan licentiousness that followed Puritan rule. Like hymnals of the time, the books contained only melodies, and directions for movement. Judging from written records and drawings, Sachs believed the dances were at least as old as the court of Elizabeth I.

Contredanses fell from favor with the English aristocracy when the Hanoverian court arrived, and dancing became more lugubrious. By then the figures had spread to France, where people grew bored waiting their turns in large circles and long lines. They broke into smaller groups.

These evolved into the four couples of the cotillion, then the quadrille, and later the square dance. Cotillions were developed fully by 1723, taken to Germany in 1741, and re-imported into England in 1770.[497:422] In nineteenth-century England, circle games were abandoned to children, primarily girls between the ages of nine and eleven.[453:27]

In this country, Botkin* (1901-1975) suggested necessity revived circle games on the frontier. Social events outnumbered fiddlers and dance callers. Sung verses could be varied to extend a dance, but usually included a familiar chorus from a circle dance and verses with embedded instructions from square dances.

In Oklahoma, and many other parts of the country, some religious leaders regarded dancing and the fiddle as enticements to sinful behavior. Play parties were accepted by many, though not all, preachers. They were games, not dances, sung, not accompanied. Botkin found his students usually could do dances, if they said they were exercises taught in their physical education classes.[267:22]

Ragtime and the accompanying fox trot, introduced in 1914 by Vernon and Irene Castle in Irving Berlin's Broadway show, *Watch Your Step*, revived latent concerns of religious spokesmen.

Twice 55 Games with Music, sponsored by the National Recreation Association, provided an alternative for church youth leaders. Peter William Dykema* (1873-1951), a Grand Rapids, Michigan, native, edited the 1924 anthology. Earlier, he had been music director for the Ethical Culture School in New York.

In the introduction, James Edward Rogers heralded it as, "the answer to the dance problem." He went on to say, "games move better with music; the music gives order, discipline, decorum, joy and control to the programs." He added:

Monotony, repetition and ill will fly before the team mates, Rhythm and Exercise, Movement and Joy. The combination of the two instincts of rhythm and play, especially in this jazzy, hectic age of commercialized amusements, is fraught with potential curative powers. I believe this movement is the therapy of our civilization.

Rogers was mentioned in CAMP PHILOSOPHY.

As the reasons for play parties changed - partly because they were less successful as alternatives to the 1920s' Charleston, Black Bottom, and Shimmy - circle dances were discarded by adolescents. They merged in children's repertoires with existing singing games and nursery rhymes that had hand clap or finger gestures. Some singing games have been introduced into camps much as other familiar forms of children's lore have been.

Judith Amidon[§] collected "Paper of Pins" (3) from a Girl Scout who had learned it in the South. Karen terHorst learned "Captain Jinks" (3) in a Girl Scout camp. The first is derived from an English courtship rhyme published by Halliwell[*] in 1844. Mercedes Steely[*] collected it as a play party in Wake County, North Carolina, near Raleigh, in the 1930s. Botkin[*] reported the second in Oklahoma.

Exercise Songs

Gesture songs evolved from other nineteenth-century American beliefs about proper behavior. Fitz (1810-1878) was one of the first to publish them. Movements in his 1846 *The Primary School Song Book* either were in the spirit of singing games ("This is the way we wash our face") or had literal pedagogic lyrics. One round began "horizontal, horizontal / perpendicular, perpendicular."

He represented a beginning point in the evolution of the genre, because the songs were perceived to be physical exercises, rather than games. As such, they probably were influenced by the gymnasium in Germany. Rousseau's *Émile* inspired the movement to integrate physical education into the humanities curriculum. Pestalozzi encouraged it. In 1856, Fitz published *The Exercise Song Book*, mentioned above as the source for "Here We Go 'round the Mulberry Bush." He elaborated in 1865 with the *Gymnastic Song Book*.

Within the dominant American culture represented by public-school texts, Fitz was an evolutionary tangent. Mason elaborated Pestalozzi's suggestion individuals should learn rudiments first, but he did not accept movement. Gesture songs did not appear in public-school collections for another half century. When they did, they were very much like those used by Fitz.

The only gesture song in *The Golden Book of Favorite Songs*,[259] "Smile Awhile" (8), was called "A Gymnastic Relief." The only gesture song in Pattengill's* 1899 and 1905 Michigan rural-school collections was a "Hand Exercise Song."

Singing Schools

Exercise songs did not die with Fitz, but continued evolving in a different environment. *The Forest Choir* of 1867 is the first song book I have seen that anticipates the modern genre. Many of the "exercise songs" Root included in his secular singing-school text used either rhythmic or arm motions. The directions for "The Launch," a frame substitution song, were:

1. Arms folded
2. Describe circles above head
3. Strike hands together
4. Hands moved as in swimming
5. Hands plunged downward
6. Beat time
7. Extended arms with waving motion or undulations

The idea of including gesture songs in singing-school books did not become widespread. Phoebe Palmer Knapp is the only person I have found who used gesture songs immediately after Root. The Methodist hymn-writer included one as an "infant class exercise" in *Notes of Joy*, published two years later in 1869.

The idea must have survived at the folk level in singing schools. Fully developed "motion songs" surfaced in William Howard Doane's *Sunny-side Songs* in 1893 and Edmund Simon Lorenz's *Temple Echoes* in 1896.

Doane (1832-1915) was raised a Congregationalist in Connecticut where his father ran a textile mill. He became a Baptist, then moved to Cincinnati, Ohio, in 1861. He managed a machine-tool manufacturing company, wrote hymns, and supervised the Mount Auburn Baptist church Sunday school.

Lorenz's (1854-1942) parents were Adventists who left the Volga community of Messer as part of the German exodus mentioned in AN AUSTRIAN. They settled in Dayton, Ohio, where he became a Brethren pastor, and religious music publisher.

Regional Contributions

Mason's selective use of Pestalozzi may signify a fundamental difference between Boston and Cincinnati. The one absorbed German ideas into an existing social structure dominated by schools like Harvard. The other absorbed Germans.

In the years when German and Scandinavian schools were experimenting with physical exercise for both boys and girls, elite private American boys' academies copied English models of college athletic competition (rowing, rugby). They transformed the gymnasium from an holistic educational institution into a place for physical exercise done for its own sake.

Rugged activity often was, and is, part of the camp regimen for boys. Singing gesture songs represented less a change in their daily schedule, than a diminution. Attitudes toward exercise for upper-class women have been more ambivalent in this country. Many, like Gulick, have seen young girls, first and foremost, as future mothers. Any activity that might jeopardize their fecundity has been discouraged.

Physical exercise often was disguised. In the same way Gulick* promoted Camp Fire as "service to the state" by "womanly women," a 1913 Girl Scout manual was sold as *How Girls Can Help Their Country*.[193] Baden-Powell and his sister, Agnes (1858-1945), wrote the section, "Games to Develop Strength." Among their recommendations were:

> Staff exercises, to music if possible. Maze and spiral; follow-my-leader, done at a jog-trot in the open air. A musical accompaniment when possible. If done indoors, all the windows in the room must be kept open top and bottom. Sing the tune
>
> . . .
>
> Morris dances (old English country dances) and the folk-songs.[193:74-75]

Morning exercise drills at Sebago-Wohelo (Me girls), shown in a 1915 photograph in "Routines," were subtended into an exhibition of folk dancing at the season's close.[147:234] At Waldemar (Tex girls) in the 1920s, Beatrice Leola Lytle* taught archery, canoeing, and Martha Graham-style dance.

Thus, while dance was accepted as exercise in conservative rural areas, the progressive elite only countenanced exercise for girls if it were introduced as dance. The camouflage of exercise with music in girls' camps often meant any freedom to move required acceptance of such music forms.

This may have helped keep gesture songs in the repertoire of older female campers. The repertoire retention, no doubt, was abetted by the association of the songs with young children. Exercises were not physically dangerous. As discussed in KOOKABURRA, they actually contributed to girls' training for motherhood by allowing them to practice sacrificing their own interests for those of children.

Town versus Township

Another important difference between the gesture song and the circle game or play party is the one developed among the upper-middle classes in towns and cities. At the time, the distinction between town and township carried as much significance as that between urban and suburban today. This cultural distinction was clear in the Camp Fire and 4-H camps I attended in Michigan and the ones I visited in Ohio.

Ohio had received more German immigrants than Michigan. However, by the time I was in 4-H in Michigan, land transfers meant farmers were as likely to have German or Danish surnames as they were English. Younger members who attended the Calhoun County, Michigan, 4-H camp wanted to do "Bingo" (50) and "Oh, Johnny" (5), two circle dances that recalled play parties. Young girls who attended the Wyandot County, Ohio, 4-H Day Camp replayed records of "Ally Cat" (1) and "Little Black Book" (1) to master routines with elaborate patterned gestures that used toes, feet, and knees.

William Swords introduced "Bingo" on the London stage in 1780. By the middle nineteenth century, it had been turned into a children's circle game. The person in the center pointed to people who needed to answer with the next letter of the spelled section or become It.[352]

526

Calhoun County's motions for "Bingo" were very close to a play party discovered in 1920 in Hillsdale County, to its immediate south and east. Gardner[*] collected her version from Ruth Barnes. They combined a circle dance with a grand right and left. "Oh Johnny" alternated a circle with a promenade.

The Victor Folk Dance Orchestra probably made the recording of "Bingo" (45-6172). Muskegon, Michigan's public school camp included it on a list of dances they gave their counselors, including Patricia Anne Prentice in the 1960s. Bent Fabric recorded "Alley Cat" in 1962. Jimmy Dean recorded "Little Black Book" the same year. Western square dance promoters disturbed instructions for both routines.

Glen (Ohio CFG) maintained some ties to its German and religious past despite being connected through Marathon Oil to the chain of social contacts that serviced the national social elite described by Baltzell.[*] It was an active consumer of gesture songs, rather than dances hidden within songs. In discussing the taffy-pulling motions used with "Ging Gang Gooey Gooey" (19) and her twelfth year at the camp, Rebecca Quinlan said:

> The funniest thing in the whole world is that the CITs brought that back . . . like the second summer I was down there at Camp Glen on staff, and it was like we were so tired of the song. It was the eighth session, Thursday night spaghetti supper, you know, and we're sitting there, and my co-counselor and I were sitting at opposite ends of the table. And so we were just joking around and we made up these motions, you know, and I mean it was like two, like three days left of the camp, the last session of 1970. Then, I came back two years, two summers later and this was an integral part. I mean, these were the motions to that song. And I just went, I just laughed so hard I can't tell you . . . I did it, and it was a joke, it was a joke . . . But we were so obviously making fun of the song and it caught on.

Rebecca's picture, when she was a young camper at Glen (Ohio CFG), appears in "Routines." She and Nancy Bryant are in the photograph of the Glen staff reproduced in "CITs."

Kitanniwa Repertoire

Battle Creek is not the county seat of Calhoun County. Consequently, Kitanniwa was isolated from the countryside where echoes of play parties survived. The Adventist sanitarium with the accompanying cereal companies, and a military base created a more diverse population than existed in Findlay, Ohio.

In the 1950s, it was a conservative user of gestures. Actions were done with perhaps a third of the common fun songs. Sporadically, girls around the age of ten or eleven added private motions to verses like "Kookaburra" (85). However, no attempt was made to find new gesture songs or to add them to existing ones, like Glen (Ohio CFG) did in the middle 1970s.

Three Kitanniwa songs began as singing games, but had been transmuted into gesture songs. "Jim along Josie," derived from the same minstrel song as "A Joggin' Along" (14), has been collected as a circle game in Oklahoma by Botkin[*] and in Arkansas by Randolph.[478] Katherine Ferris Rohrbough's version was from about 1870 in Green County, New York, located along the Hudson in the Catskill mountains.[491] Fowke collected it as a parallel line dance from Elizabeth Blair, who learned it in Saint Elmo, Ontario, around 1905.[332]

"The Mermaid" (23) final verse was used in a singing game, "Gala Ship," which Gomme[†] discovered embedded in a Scottish version of "Merry-ma-tansa." In the 1893 game, girls alternated "The Mermaid" verse with one asking the girl in the center to "choose your maidens one by one." "Down goes" was accompanied by a curtsey, a combination Botkin[*] found in play parties. The Opies[†] found reports of it as a sweetheart-naming ring game in Galloway, Ireland, in 1898, and as a forfeit circle game in Glasgow, Scotland, in 1912.

The dance has not been reported in this country, but Sandburg[*] did include the verse in his version of "The House Carpenter" (Child 243). Henry Shoemaker[†] collected only the one verse in 1918 from John Chatman of Clinton County, Pennsylvania, in the lumber country along the upper Susquehanna. He assumed it was a fragment. It may, instead, simply have been more evidence the verse has lead an existence independent from the ballad. Whether it was derived from the ballad or was an existing rhyme used by Charles Sloman to improve "The Mermaid" is unknown.

The Opies[†] since have found it transformed into a jump-rope rhyme in Swansea, Wales. It was especially popular in the 1950s.

"Grand Old Duke of York" (24) was treated as a circle game in the late nineteenth century. Sidney Oldall Addy sent a version from Sheffield in South Yorkshire to Gomme.[†] Children sitting in a circle slipped a ring on a string from hand to hand. The person in the center tried to detect who had it. Although she made no connection between the ring in this game and the grass ring in "Mulberry Bush," the symbolism, including the divination, may be the same. She said the game also was played "round a haycock in the hayfield."

Gomme was a founding member of England's Folk-Lore Society. She later advocated the then radical idea that play was an essential part of childhood. After publishing her groundbreaking collection, she produced singable anthologies of games that attracted the attention of fellow folklore activists, Sharp and Kidson. According to the Opies, writers like Eleanor Farjeon and Rose Fyleman began manufacturing new singing games.[453:22-25]

Sharp[†] suggested, since "Duke" often was sung with "A-Hunting We Will Go," it could be used as a second verse. Alternatively, it could be deployed with the same Virginia Reel-style long dance.[453] The version Kidson[†] published for the Board of Education in 1916 was the one used by the Rohrboughs in their 1940 *Handy Play Party Book*.[†] Kidson was also the source for the longways set used by Richard Thomas Chase.[†] The Appalachian folklorist hoped to reinvigorate the genre in the South with his 1938 collection of play parties.

Kidson published another version with a different first verse, which he suggested could be done as a military game with broomsticks. This probably was based on one collected by Gilchrist[†] from a servant. Lily Petch said, it was "a marching game at holiday time" in South Elmsall in West Yorkshire.[453:214] Earlier, Mary Dendy (1855-1933) had reported a "marching game" from Monton, Lancashire. Dykema[†] published Kidson's version in *Twice 55 Games*. Dendy worked to improve education for the "feeble minded."

Case Study: Grand Old Duke of York

At Kitanniwa in the 1950s and 1960s, "Grand Old Duke of York" (24) linked two verses with prescriptive gestures. The first part was transcribed as "The King of France with fourty thousand men" in a letter sent from Paris in 1620 by a glass merchant, James Howell.[†] Another reference to the verse occurred in a collection of anecdotes made by someone in Cambridge around 1627.[†]

In 1831, John Payne Collier[†] reprinted the first two lines from a 1642 tract. He said, they were called "Old Tarleton's Song." Richard Tarleton was jester to Elizabeth I. Since he died in 1588, at least a decade before events alluded to in the song, Kidson[389] believed the attribution was apocryphal.

Collier's more important comment was it had "since often received a different application." This signified it was in active oral tradition. Halliwell's[†] 1842 version had four lines.

William Henry Hills[†] (1859-1930) published the "Noble Duke" with the second verse that begins "when you're up" in his 1884 edition of *Students' Songs*. He was a journalist from Somerville, Massachusetts, who had published his first undergraduate song collection before he graduated from Harvard in 1880. He added new songs with his subsequent editions, which suggests he learned this version in the early years of the decade.

At the time, the combination probably was entering tradition in Britain. G. F. Northall[†] published the two verses from Warwickshire in 1892. Addy reported them from Sheffield before 1894.[352] Edward Williams Byron Nicholson[†] learned them from children in Golspie, a North Sea coast village in Sutherland, Scotland, in 1897.

The second verse is much like the "Gallant Ship." It suddenly was reported, known widely, and took on a separate existence. Brown[†] collected it as an autograph or friendship verse in 1923 from Mary Scarborough. She lived in Dare County, North Carolina, near the coast. Frank Brewster,[†] who was born in 1898, learned a variant,

> When you're up, you're up
> When you're down, you're down
> When you're up against [school name]
> You're upside down

as a football cheer in high school in Indiana. Harbin[†] published the yell for the Epworth League in 1920 in *Phunology*.

Explication

Kidson[389] traced the reference to the King of France to Henri III (1553-1610) of Navarre. The Huguenot convert had renounced his religion when he became Henri IV, first of the Bourbon kings. Catholic monarchs in Spain and the Holy Roman Empire, a generation after the Spanish attack on Flanders and the Netherlands memorialized by Goethe,* remained hostile. They believed he was raising an army against them when he was murdered in 1610.

The 1642 tract cited by Collier was *Pigges Corantoe, or Newes from the North.*† Charles Read Baskerville* noted, this satiric piece was published as a commentary during the early days of the English civil war. The Catholic king, Charles I, had been driven from London in January of that year and raised his army in Nottingham in August. The East Midlands were not the North as generally understood, but north of the Parliamentary center in London. His wife was Henrietta Maria, daughter of Maria de' Medici and the assassinated Henri IV. It could well have been an adaptation of the earlier verse to the then current situation, rendered deniable and doubly meaningful by the reference to the jester for the last Protestant monarch.

A reference to the "King of Spain and forty thousand men" appeared in Samuel Fisher's *The Rustic's Alarm to the Rabbies*† in 1660. His allusion suggested the two lines remained current as a conventional insult to be applied as needed, though they usually were connected to the turbulent years recorded in *Egmont*.[351] When Ferdinand evicted the Jews from Spain in 1492, many fled to Portugal. When Ferdinand took that throne, they escaped to Amsterdam. During the time of Elizabeth I, Philip II of Spain persecuted them in Holland. Fisher was a Quaker who spent the years of Puritan hegemony in Amsterdam trying to convert them.

The song's Duke of York was Frederick Augustus (1763-1827), second son of England's George III. He led an unsuccessful military campaign in Flanders against Napoléon in the 1790s. The jest in applying the verse to him was there were no hills in Flanders.

The Duke of York associated with this country was an earlier man, James II. When he was still a dangerous rival, his brother, Charles II, gave him former Dutch lands in 1664. After the Restoration of 1660, the sons of Henrietta Maria and Charles I were associated with the libertine London of the Playfield dances and bawdy rounds mentioned in ROSE.

Although the dukes responsible for New York and for the song were not the same, I can remember as a Blue Bird at Kitanniwa, connecting the song with this country's history. I imagined men marching in Manhattan. That association would be natural for children that age. According to Gesell and Ilg:

> Eight is interested in time far past, in ancient times. He likes to hear and to read about things that happened when his own country was new. But his chronology is rudimentary. He may not be able to say certainly whether or not George Washington is mentioned in the Bible.[343:187]

Grand versus Noble

"Grand" is the encomium used for the duke in oral tradition. "Noble" is the one published by Hills, Kidson, the Girl Scouts, and others. "Grand" carries the derisive connotations of a man "too big for his britches." "Noble" redeems him a bit from political satire of the day.

Camp Fire Girls and Boy Scouts were more likely to have said they learned "grand." Girl Scouts were more likely to have volunteered "noble" in 1976. While the terms were equally familiar in the Midwest and South, "grand" was more common in the West and Southwest. "Noble" was known better in the Northeast.

David Stanfield Sinclair (Ind agency boys) and Kiloqua (Ohio CFG) know "famous duke." Becky Colwell Deatherage (NY GS) sings "royal duke." Tayanita (Ohio CFG) has a "merry duke." Kent Burdair Hartung (Iowa YMCA boys) uses "grand old chief of Boone." Diane Erler (Me girls) learned "the man Napoléon." Les Chalet Francais (Me girls) has sung "Napoléon avait cinq cents soldats" as a round.

The main difference between versions A and B is the pronoun used to describe the soldiers. In the 1950s, it was customary to use "you" in place of "I," which was considered too assertive for a lady, and hence bad manners. It also was used as a generic, nonspecific term to encompass a group. It was easier to identify with the soldiers with the pronoun "you," which meant "me," when *you* were the one reenacting the soldier's drill than it was to refer to some third persons.

The number of soldiers varies a great deal in published versions, but seems to have no significance.

Music

Duke's melody may have descended from two branches of a single musical family spread through the popular stages and beer halls of England, France, the Austro-Hungarian Empire, and the German-speaking states.

The first tune associated with the "Duke" verse was "A-Hunting We Will Go." Thomas Arne composed it in 1777 for a production of *The Beggar's Opera*. Chase[†] collected the tune from eleven-year-old Harlan Rile of Morris Fork, Kentucky, some 25 miles upriver from Jean Ritchie's home in Viper. He lived one creek over, to the southeast, from where James Franklin Amis, mentioned in I WISH I WERE, was raised.

Brown[†] collected a similar melody from Jean Holeman (1884-1970) in Durham, North Carolina, in 1922. She was a teacher, folksong collector, and member of the local Presbyterian church.

The melody commonly associated with the second quatrain of "Duke" is a simplified version of "The Farmer in the Dell." Jan Philip Schinhan thought the version Maude Minnish Sutton (1890-1936) and Mary Wilder collected of "Farmer" was like the one they collected for "Looby Lou." He believed both were similar to "Was kommt dort von der Höh."[278] Hoffmann suggested the underlying tune of the German student song was "Bei Hall ist eine Mühl,"[371] first documented around 1780, a few years after Arne's success.

Sutton and Wilder were working in Buncombe and Rutherford counties near Asheville, North Carolina, in 1927. Arable valleys west of the Blue Ridge were settled by veterans of the American Revolution. Ancestors of Ritchie and Raleigh Britton Willis, mentioned in KUMBAYA, spent time in Buncombe County, which became a magnet for Baptists. While the Scots, Scots-Irish, English, and German-speaking settlers may not have mingled in the area, people interested in music, especially children, have ways of absorbing melodies.

Böhme published "Der Kirmesbauer," or "The Cherry Farm," in 1897. He noted it had been found in Saxony, Thüringen, and Brandenburg, the center of Prussia. The earliest version he located was from a choral society song book produced in 1826 by Chr. C. Kenser.[264:673-674] Imagery of the cherry tree, mentioned in AN AUSTRIAN and ASH GROVE, along with the subject of the ring game, the marriage of a farmer, suggests it too was derived from older courtship games of Europe.

Kidson[389] believed the tune used with the first verse of "Duke" was related to "Le Petit Tambour." In 1826, the same year as the first report of "The Farmer" in Germany, *Harmonicon* advertised the release of "With Helmet on His Brow," with words by G. W. Reeve. George William Reeve managed the lower-class Olympic Theatre between 1820 and 1821, where he adapted music from French and German stages for British audiences.

H. Arliss published Charles Dibdin's version as "A Soldier Must with Honor Live" in the third volume of *The Melodist*. He identified the 1829 tune as "Le petit tambour." Dibdin was likely the dramatist son of the more famous Charles Dibdin of the Theatre Royal who died in 1814.

John Oxenford, better known for "Ash Grove" (72), translated Louisa Stuart Costello's *The Book of French Songs* in 1872. A version of the "Brow" as "The Gallant Troubadour" included a note, it was "once to be found in every music-book."

In its February 8 issue for 1872, *Notes and Queries* published a letter from Edward Francis Rimbault describing "Brow" as a:

> French melody of no great antiquity, entitled "Le Petit Tambour." It was very popular in France about forty years ago, and perhaps originally belonged to some vaudeville.

"Petit Tambour" had been standardized by Josef Mayseder, concertmaster for the court opera in Vienna in 1810, and later solo violinist and composer.

"Farmer" first was identified in this country from the "New York streets" by Newell* in 1883. Subsequent reports came from Virginia in 1888, Saint Louis in 1895, and Toronto in 1893. Sharp noted it in England in 1912.[453] The inference is the game arrived with Germans fleeing Prussian dominance beginning in the 1870s, rather than by those who fled after 1848.

Hills' melody is the one used at Kitanniwa in the 1950s. He assumed four phrases and two verses. Both he and Northall[†] suggested it could be sung as a round. His tune may have come directly from Germany through someone who had studied there.

The "Farmer" melody has been used with "Forty Bottles of Beer on the Wall" at Patiya (Colo CFG), "Forty-Nine Miles from Home" (5), and "There Ain't No flies on Us" at Kiloqua (Ohio CFG) and Warren (Mich P coed). Surprise Lake (NY J boys) sang "Ten Miles" in 1938.

"We Want a Cook's Parade," the chant that follows "Cookie" (30), and the "terrible death to die" part of "Announcements" (18) use the tune. It also has been adopted for some Chicago Scout (Ill BSA) songs. "We're Glad To See You Here" (3) is known at Wohelo (RI CFG) and by Vivian Sexton (Tex CFG).

Gestures

The stand on the word "up" - squat on the word "down" actions are relatively new. As such, they may represent the adaption of the song as the age group singing it shifted from adults through students cheering football teams. They are simple enough for the youngest campers. The only challenge comes with the increased speed of position changes in the final line.

"Duke's" appeal must lie elsewhere. As mentioned in AGE GROUP INFLUENCES, the group that likes this song is in the transition phase between the egocentrism of the very young and the logic of adults, when individuals are evolving concepts of conservation of form. He or she "focuses on several aspects of a situation simultaneously, is sensitive to transformations, and can reverse the directions of his thinking."[468:168]

Riddling in the second quatrain (what is neither up nor down?) plays with these very mental abstractions: reversibility (up then down then up), the possibility of several simultaneous states (halfway up is halfway down; halfway is not up and not down), and the transformations between states (the last line).

In camps where different age groups sing together, the song can serve other functions. At Kitanniwa in the middle 1950s, it sometimes was used in morning sing when campers were growing restive. When the song was suggested, it usually brought groans from older campers and counselors. That response, in turn, meant younger campers might request the song simply to tease older people by forcing them to behave as active children rather than sedentary authority figures.

David Ginglend[†] and Winifred Stiles recommended a modified set of motions for retarded children. They substituted "finger play exercises and body and arm movements" for actions that manipulated knees. He directed day camps in New Jersey, and taught "able" or "trainable" children in Plainfield.

Popularity

"Duke" was included in several public-school music books in the 1950s, and more recently the game was used in commercial collections marketed for use with young children. Overexposure may explain why the song was not recognized by as many people as might have been expected in 1976. Seventeen-year-old Marilyn Butler (Tex GS) says, it was something she "knew a long time ago."

Even so, it is one of the few songs that clearly shows the influence of gender and region. More than half the people in camps in the survey Midwest recognized it. Elsewhere, less than half marked it. More men knew "Duke" than women, except in Camp Fire camps in the five-state region.

Version A

Text and gestures from Patricia Averill, Camp Kitanniwa (Mich CFG), 1951-1960.

> The grand old Duke of York[1]
> He had ten thousand men
> He marched them up the hill[2]
> And he marched them down again[1]
>
> And when you're up you're up[2]
> And when you're down you're down[1]
> But when you're only half way up[3]
> You're neither up[2] nor down[1]

Gestures
1. Kneel or sit
2. Stand
3. Squat midway between standing and kneeling

Version B

Text and gestures from Camp Kotomi (Colo CFG), 1971; variations from A emphasized.

> **Oh, the great Apache chief**[1]
> He had ten thousand men[2]
> He marched **up to the top of** the hill[3]
> And he marched them down again[4]
> And when **they were** up **they were** up[5]
> And when **they were** down, **they were** down[6]
> But when **they were** only half-way up[7]
> **They were** neither up **nor** down.[8]

Gestures
1. **Draw bow and arrow**
2. **March in place**
3. **March** as though "Up"
4. **March** as though "Going down"
5. Stand-up tall
6. Squat down
7. Half-squat position
8. Stand up, then squat down

Flicker: Recent Pretty Songs

The Folk Revival changed the camp pretty song repertoire, especially the subset used for everyday occasions. Patricia Ann Hall remembers at Celio (Calif CFG):

> That summer of 1962 one of my counselors had her accordion with her, and played "500 Miles" (51) and "Where Have All the Flowers Gone" (43) incessantly! I had never heard anything so beautiful, I thought. At night, she told stories about seeing this great new group of "beatnik folksingers" called Peter, Paul and Mary at the hungry i in San Francisco. It was all so glamorous. I already knew how to play the ukulele, so in emulation of her I went from camp, and learned those two songs on the uke . . . Over the next few years, those of us who played instruments and sang were treated with awe and respect, and it was, looking back on it, a privileged space we had all carved out for ourselves, those of us who were "folksingers" . . . The songs us "folksingers" would sing (I use the term QUITE loosely!!!) sometimes would become part of the repertoire, like "Four Strong Winds" (20), for instance of the whole camp, but more often they wouldn't.

Nature Themes

Many new pretty songs treat the same themes found in WITCHCRAFT, but with different images, and sometimes with different emphases. Nature remains important in "Little Green Valley" (5), "Mountains High" (5), and "Reach Up to the Sky" (26).

538

Shirley Ieraci (Ohio GS) knows a Girl Scout variant of "Winds Are Blowing" (18).

The same symbols - wind, skies, morning - occur in commercial songs sung in small groups by older campers and staff. "Four Strong Winds" (20) was introduced by Ian and Sylvia Tyson in 1963. Donovan recorded "Sun Is a Very Magical Fellow" (9).

Cat Stevens revitalized Eleanor Farjeon's "Morning Has Broken" (6). Mary MacDougal MacDonald (1789-1872) used the original tune, "Bunessan," for "Leanabh an Aigh." Lachlan Macbean translated the Baptist's text as "Child in the Manger" for his 1900 *Songs and Hymns of the Gael.* Percy Dearmer commissioned Farjeon's revision for the 1931 edition of *Songs of Praise.* MacDonald lived in a farming settlement on the island of Mull off western Scotland.

Some lyrics, like "Woodchild" (6), take an out-of-camp perspective that makes them more general than ones like "Tall Timbers" (7). "Hurry Sundown" (10), recorded by Peter, Paul and Mary, deals with troubles of agrarian life at twilight. "Island of My Desire" (9) mentions natural phenomena alien to camps outside Hawaii.

Religion permeates "I Know a Place" (38). No one knows why it is called Ruth or "Ruthie's Song." Sue Ann Thompson Kraus heard, "she was Girl Scout in Midwest. Kansas or Colo." Nancy Child Robinson wrote the first verse. A second was added in tradition. Some camps have a third.

"Joy Is Like the Rain" (15) has been used for unit songs at Hitaga (Iowa CFG). Its composer, Miriam Therese Winter (born 1938), is a Roman Catholic religious activist. Frankie Laine released "I believe for every drop of rain" (6) in 1953.

Nature and religion concur in some newer graces, like "Neath These Tall Trees" (26), Exner's "For Sun and Rain" (5), and "Thank You for Giving Me This Morning" (5). Walter Kent and James Kimball Gannon wrote the "Johnny Appleseed Grace" (70) for a 1948 Walt Disney film about John Chapman. Diane Bauman sings two verses at Friedenswald (Mich P coed). Leah Culp has taught four at Hidden Valley (Md CFG).

Hiking

Images of drifters and hoboes, taken from American folk tradition, have displaced the earlier hiking theme, borrowed from

Germany's Wandervogel, and Vienna's romance with gypsies. Among the rambling songs are "Been Riding" (8) and "I Am a Rover" (11). The New Christy Minstrels recorded "Green, Green" (11) in 1963. Tim Bahr says, they do not sing "Five Hundred Miles" (51) at the Teamster's Health Camp (Mo agency coed) until "toward the end of the session to prevent homesickness."

"King of the Road" (2) has been sung by Bryna Selig (DC CFG) and Wilma Jean Lawrence (Penna GS), and used for a 1965 Hitaga (Iowa CFG) skit song. "Walk Right In" has been used with "Life Is Good" at Trexler (NY P boys). "Ponder" (9) expresses the wish "that I may wander / This world until I die." Roger Miller recorded the first in 1965. Erik Darling and the Rooftop Singers introduced the second in 1962.

Childhood

Songs of childhood remain popular. However, A. A. Milne's *Winnie the Pooh* and James M. Barrie's *Peter Pan* have supplanted fairy tales as remembered childhood and adolescent literature.

Milne's heffalump has been incorporated into "Three Elephants Went Out To Play" (17) at Melacoma (Wash CFG), and into "If I Had the Wings of a Turtledove" (14) at Wasewagan (Calif CFG). Marilyn Butler (NH GS) and Wolahi (Calif CFG) sing Kenny Loggins and Jim Messina's "House at Pooh Corner" (2) from 1971. Loggins was in high school when he wrote it. The Englishman's characters have been owned and exploited by the Walt Disney Company since 1961.

"I Won't Grow Up" (5) and "Tender Shepard" (7) are from the Broadway adaption of Barrie's play. Eugene Field's "Wynken, Blynken and Nod" (4), from 1889, has been converted into a song by Donovan. Charles Schulz's *Peanuts* comic strip was used for a 1967 Off-Broadway musical, *You're a Good Man, Charlie Brown*. It introduced "Happiness Is Two Kinds of Ice Cream" (6).

Peter, Paul and Mary's "Puff, the Magic Dragon" (29) is the best-known Folk Revival song with childhood images. Wampatuck (Mass P girls) sings Tom Paxton's "The Marvelous Toy" (9) as "magical toy."

Quotations from nursery or game rhymes are found in "One for the Money, Two for the Show" (9). Jolene Robinson Johnson remembers "One for the Money, Sing for a Penny" (5) as a staff song at Kirby (Wash CFG). Both the Kingston Trio and Rod McKuen recorded "Ally Ally Oxen Free" (24).

Robin Wallace used *The Little Prince* in 1973 for a High/Scope (Mich agency coed) song that began, "To have a friend is something special." In 1965, Jane Miner wrote a ballad about the "Magician's Nephew" who "had lost all his power." He went to Hitaga (Iowa CFG) "where dreams come true." His strength returned because "There's magic in Hitaga's hills / And it's true for me and you."

Linda Johnson exploited J. R. R. Tolkien's work for "Song of the Hobbit." She spent most of her camping years at Hitaga, but was at Kitanniwa in 1974. Her photograph, with members of the Iowa CFG camp staff, appears in "Kitanniwa, 1974."

Some camps bestow vacation nicknames. At Sebago-Wohelo (Me girls), many assumed an Indian name for the summer. Then, George occasionally was used, perhaps taken from Nancy Drew's more adventurous friend. In 1976, one young woman who answered my questionnaire was called Pooh in camp.

Some songs reflect "a new sense of continuity and sameness" that Erikson said is characteristic of adolescence.[322:261] Earlier songs of maternal protection, like lullabies, have been replaced with overt comments on parenting and the importance of childhood. Their model often is Holden Caulfield from J. D. Salinger's *Catcher in the Rye* of 1951. "Teach Your Children Well" (3) and "Day Is Done" (23) are the most familiar. Crosby, Stills, Nash and Young recorded the first. Peter, Paul and Mary introduced the second.

Life Cycle

A concern with one's own continuity in the face of adolescent changes seems greater in more recent pretty songs, than it was in the past. "Turn Around and You're a Little Girl" (5) reveals an awareness of the ephemeral nature of childhood. "As Tears Go By" (8) and "Autumn to May" (8) are retrospective reflections. The first was composed by Malvina Reynolds, then altered by Alan Greene and Harry Belafonte in 1959. The Rolling Stones recorded the second in 1965. Peter, Paul and Mary introduced the last in 1962.

Death is acknowledged in songs like "Mandy" (22) and "Spider's Web" (21). June Rushing Leibfarth[§] heard "Walk Me Out in the Morning Dew" (1) at the Girl Scout Roundup in Farragut State Park,

541

Idaho. She was told, it "was supposed to be about a soldier who was dying, and he was talking to his wife, but I'm not sure whether there's any truth to that."

"Barges" (68) is the most common contemporary deathbed song. Gene Clough (Calif CFG) was told, someone was dying, and the barges were visible from a hospital room overlooking a river. Susan Conard (Calif CFG) heard the person was in San Francisco. I was led to believe she had leukemia. The song commonly is sung with two or three verses. Girl Guides published two in the 1968 edition of *Chansons de Notre Chalet*,* but only one of theirs is sung.

Local versions of the chorus begin "out of my tent flaps," and usually continue with "counselor's burning flashlights." Ann Beardsley (GS) knows "counselors I would like to live with you." Angela Lapham (GS) sings, "counselors I would like to go with you." Theresa Mary Rooney (NJ GS) learned, "I can see the counselors having a fight." Karen Williams (Minn GS) has a version about a black bear. Becky Colwell Deatherage (NY GS) knows one about Boy Scouts.

Place

The number of new, commercial place songs is small. "Moon River" (2), recorded by Andy Williams in 1961, has been sung in camp by Angela Lapham (Mich GS) and Clarena Snyder (Ohio GS). Hitaga (Iowa CFG) adopted it for "All Rivers Flow into the Sea." Orme Ranch (Ariz coed) sings "White Mountains Higher than a Mile," according to Kathryn Orme Jessup.§

A few sing Judy Collins' version of "The Lake Isle of Innisfree" (3). William Butler Yeats wrote the original poem in 1892.

Friendship

Girls may sing about friendship more than boys, who use greeting and other rituals to signify comradeship. Malvina Reynolds (1900-1978) wrote "Magic Penny" (10). The Jewish social-activist was known better for "Little Boxes" (6). "You've Got a Friend" (4) was written by Carole King, and recorded by her and by James Taylor. "Pack Up Your Sorrows" (4) is by Pauline Marden and Richard Fariña. He recorded it with his wife, Mimi. She and Marden are sisters of Joan Baez.

"Friendship Is a Shiny Thing" (10) is the best-known indigenous song. The subject lingers as a motif in "Flicker" (40) and "I Am a Rover" (11). "Bring Me a Rose" (16), "Have Fun, Our Motto" (25), and "There Are So Many Worlds To Explore" (8) contain several themes.

Love

Love, and being loved, is a far more important theme in recent pretty songs, than it was in the past. Lee Hays and Fran Moseley suggested gifts from nature were better signs of lasting affection than wealth in "Seven Daffodils" (8). When the Weavers' bass was thirteen and his sister was in her early twenties, their father died in an automobile accident. He was a Methodist minister in Arkansas. He christened his daughter Minnie Frank Hays. The Limeliters recorded the song in 1962.

Among the romantic lyrics used for camp-specific songs at Christopher (Ohio C coed) is "Song Is Love" (4), recorded by Peter, Paul and Mary in 1967. Smith[S] collected a different endogamous song from a Michigan CYO girls' camp in 1969.

At Hitaga (Iowa CFG), Carol Hill and Pat O'Brien used "First Time Ever I Saw Your Face" (4) for "First time ever I saw this camp / I saw the sun rise o'er the hill." Ewan MacColl wrote the original for his wife, Peggy Seeger, to sing in 1957. She is the daughter of Charles Seeger (1886-1979) and his second wife, the former Ruth Porter Crawford (1901-1953). Among her three stepbrothers were Pete (1919-2014) and John (1914-2010). Some of her three siblings also performed.

Many contemporary songs confront the possibility love is over, or, no matter how wonderful, will not endure. The theme suggests feelings of impermanence rooted in biological experiences are generalized to personal relations. In some, the song's narrator is a rover who knows he will leave the idyllic relationship he is describing. Harry Belafonte recorded "Jamaica Farewell" (14) in 1956. The New Christy Minstrels introduced "Today" (73) in 1964.

"The Seine" (6) treats a walk by the river as a pleasant, but unrepeatable romantic encounter. In "Green Fields" (6), a memory of walks in the wild turns bitter as the seasons change. "Lemon Tree" (10) scolds the unfaithful one by comparing her to a tree with unreliable fruit. The Kingston Trio recorded the first in 1959. Seattle, Washington's Brothers Four introduced the second in 1960.

"Plaisir d'Amour" (5) expresses deep despair underlined by its instrumental accompaniment. "Greensleeves" (12) takes a jocular attitude toward the unfaithful that contrasts with the beauty of its melody. Joan Baez recorded the one in 1965. The Weavers released the other in 1955.

Some commercial songs of lovers' separation have been modified to fit the older theme of leaving camp. Hitaga (Iowa CFG) has a 1965 song written by Connie Vreeland to "I Left My Heart in San Francisco." Christopher (Ohio C coed) has one to "Softly as I Leave You." Tony Bennett recorded the first in 1962. Frank Sinatra introduced the other in 1964.

Cultural Changes

Thematic continuities may have masked underlying cultural changes that were occurring in camps as younger siblings replaced their older ones. World War II deprivations and feelings of community lingered when those born in the middle 1940s were young. By the early 1950s, consumer goods, especially televisions, were more common. The war generation passed on values of self-reliance. Mass-media hysteria surrounding Joseph McCarthy reinforced expectations of conformity.

Contradictory values merged in the protests against the war in Vietnam and racial discrimination. Shock followed riots in Detroit in 1967, conflicts at the Democratic convention in Chicago in 1968, and the deaths of students shot by National Guardsmen at Kent State University in Ohio in 1970.

Some responded by narrowing their hopes for perfection to areas they could control. Camp Fire Girls rewrote the desires (poems) memorized by girls who wish to pass the four ranks. In the 1950s, Trail Seekers recited, "I desire to seek the way which shall become a delight to my feet."[152:87] Ten-year-olds now use "heart" for "feet."[154:9] Likewise, twelve-year-old Fire Makers used to say, "As fuel is brought to the fire, so I propose to bring my strength, my ambition, my heart's desire, my joy and my sorrow."[152:93] They now use "sensitivity" for "ambition."[154:11]

In both cases, active words consistent with the imagery of verses by Theodore Acland Harper and John Collier, respectively, have been replaced by more passive, emotional nouns. Sociologist David Riesman* wrote what he called other directedness was replacing inner directedness among young parents in 1950. A decade later, social psychologist David McClelland* identified the differences between achievement motivation of the one and affiliation motivation of the other. Tom Wolfe* dismissed the young as the "Me Generation" in 1976.

Riesman and McClelland, born in 1909 and 1917, represented the generation of older campers' parents in 1950. Wolfe, born in 1931, voiced the dismay of the next generation. Collier wrote his verse in 1912 when he was involved with immigration outreach at the People's Institute of New York. He did not discover the Pueblos or Native American problems until he visited Mabel Dodge in 1919. Harper was a New Zealand adventurer who knew Kempthorne. He became a storyteller at Namanu (Ore CFG) in 1925.

Religion

Some reacted to the late 1960s by redirecting their idealism toward more inward forms of faith. Religious music always was part of the Folk Revival. In 1963, Harry Belafonte recorded "Amen, See the Little Baby" (5). Peter, Paul and Mary rewrote "Go Tell It on the Mountain" (9). Judy Collins revived the Shakers' "Simple Gifts" (5).

During these same years, the Roman Catholic church was confronting the consequences of the Second Vatican Council. Before it ended in 1965, bishops accepted the use of vernacular languages in the mass. Ray Repp produced the first folk liturgy in 1964, *Mass for Young Americans*. It included "Clap Your Hands, All You People" (5), "Here We Are" (13), and James Thiem's "Sons of God" (3). His next mass, *Allelu* of 1966, included "Allelu, Allelu, Everybody Sing Allelu" (6). Both composers were born in 1942.

In the same spirit, Marycrest (Vt C girls) wrote a local camp song to "He's Got the Whole World in His Hands" (35). Camps like Saint Vincent de Paul Ranch (Calif C boys) began singing the Spanish-language grace, "Gracias Señor" (8), according to Frank Chavez.

As the Civil Rights and peace movements diverged, religious music began segregating itself. Judy Collins maintained the older, communal religious tradition in 1970 when she recorded the abolitionist hymn, "Amazing Grace" (13). A Canadian country singer, Gene MacLellan, wrote "Put Your Hand in the Hand of the Man" (8) in 1971 for Anne Murray. His song typified the newer, individualistic strain of gospel music.

By that time, the Folk Revival had displaced the older body of early-twentieth-century community and later international songs. When the coalition symbolized by Peter, Paul and Mary disintegrated, a vacuum opened in the general, pretty song repertoire.

Moral Re-Armament hoped to fill the gap with their entertainment troop, Up with People. Frank Buchman had organized MRA in 1938 in England. Its best-known songs were "Up, Up with People" (13), and "I Want To Be Strong" (5). Hitaga (Iowa CFG) included many more in its song book. Debra Nails remembers in Louisiana, "in the early 70s, there was an 'infiltration' of patriotic and religious songs, the result of so many older Scouts' participation in Up with People and Campus Crusade."

Kurt Kaiser and Ralph Carmichael produced the religious musical, *Tell It Like It Is*, in 1969. Campus Crusade for Christ began using one of its songs, "Pass It On "(24). At least one 1974 Kitanniwa staff member owned their *Pass It On* song book. The 1972 spiral-bound anthology contained "Seek and Ye Shall Find" (11) and "They'll Know We Are Christians by Our Love" (15). Linda Gerfin[s] was told, the second was "probably one of the songs best known to young Christians" in 1976. The two men represented the generation of Wolfe, the one before Repp: Kaiser was born in 1934, Carmichael in 1927.

Some songs continued to reflect the shared values, which had existed before the troubled summer of 1968. MRA promoted "What Color Is God's Skin" (6). Social Gospel leader, Washington Gladden, had published their "Oh Master Let me Walk with Thee" (5) in an 1879 issue of the *Sunday Afternoon* magazine. When others set his poem to music, he intervened and stipulated they use "Maryton." Henry Percy Smith's melody had appeared in an 1874 collection edited by Arthur Sullivan.

Following these successes, other more doctrinaire Christian groups began issuing song books or performing material from Folk Revival and other commercial music. A Presbyterian-derived youth-outreach group based in Colorado Springs, Colorado, produced *Sing with Young Life* in 1978. It featured the music of Peter, Paul and Mary, especially the later work of the born-again Stookey, along with John Denver, Cat Stevens, James Taylor, and Bob Dylan. This appeared just before the Jewish Dylan converted.

Methodists maintained a more ecumenical approach, signaled by their monthly newsletter, *Together.* It may have drawn its title from a 1969 public relations campaign by the National Conference of Christians and Jews. It featured The Youngbloods' recording of "Get Together" (9).

In 1973, Carlton Young (born 1926) edited *The Genesis Songbook*, which he described as "Songs for Getting it All Together." He included works by Simon and Garfunkel, Pete Seeger, and the Beatles. His publisher, Hope, had been founded in Chicago by a man who had attended the 1889 meeting that organized the Epworth League, Henry Sheperd Date (1858-1915). Young had overseen the 1966 revision of *The Methodist Hymnal.*

Peace, Brotherhood

A third response to the late 1960s was a genre of songs concerned with idealism, peace, and brotherhood that perpetuated the older spirit of community. Joanne AvRutick (Md coed) says, "I'll teach stuff like 'Let It Be' (4) by the Beatles, just because of a spiritual thing. Like, there are songs that bring people together, you know, and like, you know, that's important to me, 'cause singing's a good way to use all the energy to bring people together, instead of apart."

New songs of brotherhood include some commercial music, like "I'd Like To Teach the World to Sing" (11) and "It's a Small World" (23). Others refer to earlier statements. "No Man Is an Island" (43) borrowed from part 17 of John Donne's *Devotions on Emergent Occasions* of 1624. "One Little Candle" (17), recorded by Anita Bryant in 1967, alluded to the motto of The Christophers. A member of the Maryknoll brotherhood, James Keller, founded the Roman Catholic group in 1945.

Other contemporary pretty songs include "Everything is Beautiful" (7), "If I Had Wings" (8), "Let There Be Peace on Earth" (28), and "Joy to the World" (5). "I'm Proud To Be Me" (19) has been sung "I'm Glad" by Nancy Bryant at Glen (Ohio CFG) and at Tawanka (Mich CFG). Ray Stevens released the first in 1970. Peter, Paul and Mary recorded the second in 1967. Three Dog Night introduced "Joy" as "Jeremiah was a bullfrog" in 1970.

"Last Night I Had the Strangest Dream" (9) is enjoying new interest. Canadian Folk Revivalist Ed McCurdy composed the anti-war song in 1950. Other positive songs, like "We Shall Overcome" (16), have been replaced with more tentative ones, like "It's a Long Road to Freedom" (10). Miriam Therese Winter composed it for the Medical Mission Sisters in 1966.

These, in turn, have been supplanted by songs that only hope for peace, harmony, and brotherhood. "Liberty" (8) asks, "Won't someone help me, I wanna be free / Oh, where is liberty?" In "Land of Odin" (19), a bird flies every hundred years, but conditions remain unchanged.

The only current song to contain a potential program for action is "Corn" (13).

Plea for One World

Some group or groups have been trying to purge songs of brotherhood from camp repertoires. Seven Girl Scouts told me "Plea for One World" (45) has been banned. One said, it was communist. Several mentioned the unofficial title, the "United Nations" song. Girl Guides' introduced it in the 1962 edition of *Chansons** with no such attribution. They dropped it in 1968, and reincluded it in 1971.

Other songs banished for their political content include "No Man Is an Island" (38) at a camp attended by Suzanne Beaudet. Charles Smith says, "Where Have All the Flowers Gone" (48) was proscribed at Whitsett (Calif BSA) in 1971. One Girl Scout camp purged it for being sexist.

Marilyn Butler remembers another discouraged "Turn Back O Man" (1), although "not officially." Gustav Holst introduced the hymn as part of his *Three Festival Choruses* in 1917. He had initiated a collaboration between his London students and people in Thaxted, Essex, where he summered. Originally, he combined madrigals, morris dancing, and liturgical music in a Whitsun celebration. Clifford Bax supplied the text.

Marilyn associated the song with the 1971 musical, *Godspell*, where some believed it had an anti-war subtext. Holst worked for the YMCA in World War I. Oliver* included it in the YWCA song book that led to protests in the 1950s. Baptists may have disdained the original setting of psalm 154 in the 1551 edition of the *Genevan Psalter*.

"This Is My Country" (6) is the type song being used as a replacement. Al Jacobs and Don Ray wrote it in 1940. The copyright was assigned to what was then Fred Waring's Shawnee Press. More recently, it has been included in the *Pass It On* song book. A 1963 Hitaga unit song began, "This is our unit / Land of dreams come true."

Swiss Navy

Ironically, the one camp song with the most pacifist overtones has been sung for decades. The chorus to "Swiss Navy" (23) ends, "I don't want to fly over Germany / I just wanna be friendly." Ellen* told *Mudcat* readers in 2011, her grandfather had sung it during World War I flight training for what then were dangerous runs of untested equipment sans parachutes. She said they sang, "We are the kiwi-wis" or flightless birds.

The reference to flying sets a possible period of origin. Otherwise, the song reflects long-standing beliefs that, in time of war, the safest place to be is on a battleship. Of all battleships, those of the neutral, landlocked Swiss would be safest of all. No one ever wants to "march in the infantry" where men "shoot the artillery."

When Aleta Huggett§ reported the song in 1949, she noted her friend had learned it before World War II "had involved the United States," with a hint of apology. Some have made revisions. Tawakani (Ida CFG) sings, "I'm in the camp K. P." Terry Wilbur Bolton sings the "Lord's Navy" at Big Lake Youth Camp (Ore P coed). The Teamster's Health Camp (Mo agency coed) knows "I'm too young." Most sing it with what Aleta called "frantic motions of marching, riding and flying."

Harmony

The Folk Revival's impact on harmony, as discussed in ROSE, was gradual. In the early years, professional groups were more important in camps, than soloists. Almost everything from the 1962 album, *Peter, Paul and Mary*, remains in the repertoire, including "Bamboo" (19), "Cruel War" (30), "If I Had a Hammer" (27), and "This Train" (7).

Similarly, many Kingston Trio songs have stayed in tradition. These include "Tom Dooley" (12), "California Could Not Hold Me" (6), and "Greenback Dollar" (7). "Good News, Chariot's Coming" (8) was a favorite with Kitanniwa's second-year CITs in 1959.

Paul Simon and Art Garfunkel have remained important. The two released "Fifty Ninth Street Bridge Song" or "Feeling Groovy" (11), "Sounds of Silence" (10), and "I am a Rock" (6) in 1966. In 1970, the pair recorded "Bridge over Troubled Water" (6), "El Condor Pasa" (5), and "Song for the Asking" (5).

Solo artists have been less influential, partly because some have idiosyncratic vocal styles. Bob Dylan's "Blowin' in the Wind" (57) and "The Times They Are a-Changin'!" (7) are sung, as are Joni Mitchell's "Both Sides Now" (13) and "Circle Game" (9). Tom Paxton's "Bottle of Wine" (5) and "Going to the Zoo" (6) diffused through recordings by other artists, and publication in *Sing Out!*

John Denver has been the most successful performer in recent years. "Country Roads" (20), "Follow Me" (10), "Rhymes and Reasons" (5), "Rocky Mountain High" (5), and "Sunshine" (5) commonly are sung in camps. Although he was a soloist, his back-up singers, Bill Danoff and Taffy Nivert, provided guidance for part singing.

Harmony exists with some newer indigenous songs like "Barges" (68), "I Know a Place" (38), and "Mandy" (22). "I Am a Rover" (11), "May All of Your Dreams" (20), and "Spider's Web" (21) have been sung with harmony by Aileen Yung (Ohio GS), Maureen Therese Balsamo (Wash agency coed), and Wilma Jean Lawrence (Penna GS), respectively. Kathleen Solsbury[S] collected two-part versions of "It's a Long Road to Freedom" (10) and "Magic Melody" (5) or "Melodies" with guitar accompaniments at The Timbers (Mich GS) in 1970.

Instruments

The Folk Revival introduced instruments into environments where singing had been unaccompanied. Folklorist Jean Mayo MacLaughlin recalls in Florida Girl Scout camps:

Since we primarily engaged in primitive camping and had to lug equipment around, and because we really had no skilled instrumentalists anyway, we sang a capella almost always. Whenever I was with a group accompanied by instruments, I always noticed a sharp difference in repertory selected for singing, in attempts at and styles of harmonies, and in general group feeling of unity and leadership. An instrumentalist *always* took the spotlight, and generally narrowed the range of choices, since very few instrumentalists can really accompany anything and play in any key.

An instrument stabilizes notes by forcing people to listen to it, rather than to each other. Ruth Crawford Seeger said, the use of the piano with songs from American folk tradition "often gives to the tune a sharpness of line and to the song-experience a finality which is not fitting to this music."[504:26]

Fletcher noticed Omaha singers could not recognize their tunes when she played them on a piano. "Their ears were accustomed to the *portamento* [smooth transitions between tones] of the voice in song, which was broken up by the hammers of the instrument on the strings."[326:7]

Although a guitar purifies and simplifies tunes, especially chromatic ones, its impact has not been simply digestive. Instruments may make it easier to sing difficult or unusual patterns because they signal appropriate tones. Lori Judith Weiss says, at Sabra (Mo J coed), all the Jewish songs are accompanied, "especially in minor keys."

Guitar Repertoire

The songs most commonly accompanied today are those from the Folk Revival. Five or more people remember singing "Blowing' in the Wind" (57), "Five Hundred Miles" (51), "Kumbaya" (90), and "Today" (73) with a guitar in camp. "Where Have All the Flowers Gone" (43) has been sung with a guitar by three who answered my questionnaire in 1976. Two have sung "Donna, Donna" (51), "For Baby, For Bobby" (14), "Jet Plane" (29), and "Michael Row the Boat Ashore" (66) with an instrument.

Among the new indigenous songs sung with guitar accompaniment in several camps are "Barges" (68), "Blue Walking" (3), "Have Fun, Our Motto" (25), and "Spider's Web" (21). The last has been used for "Special Place" at Onahlee (Ore CFG).

"I Am a Rover" (11) has been sung with a guitar by Dana Dawn Olmstead (Tex CFG), "I Know a Place" (38) by Aileen Yung (Ohio GS), and "I'm Glad To Be Me" (19) at Tawanka (Mich CFG). Peggy Dawn Hansen (Wisc GS) remembers an instrumental accompaniment with "May All of Your Dreams Be like Daisies in the Field" (10). Wintaka (Calif CFG) uses one with "Winds Are Blowing" (10).

The only older pretty songs remembered with a guitar accompaniment are "Linger" (47), "Wisdom" (32), and "Witchcraft" (81). They were mentioned by Bonnie Loomis (Ohio GS), Jayne Garrison (Mo CFG), and Theresa Mary Rooney (NJ GS), respectively. Carol Parsons Sievert's chords, reprinted in WITCHCRAFT, suggest the difficulty in adapting older songs.

Rounds, generally, are sung without instrumental support. If a round is accompanied, each part must have the same pattern of chord changes. June Rushing Leibfarth[S] recorded a Texas Girl Scout using a guitar with "Vine and Fig Tree" (18).

Tempo

Guitars regularize tempos. Unaccompanied groups often drag as individuals listen to one another. The resulting variations, like those mentioned by Carol Parsons Sievert in A CANOE, are difficult for many accompanists to support. This is one reason singing-school leaders placed such emphasis on meter.

Strumming a guitar, or other stringed instrument, disciplines a player, in a way a keyboard, reed, or horn does not. The mechanical action makes syncopation easier. Kathleen Solsbury[S] collected an accented version of "Have Fun, Our Motto" (25) from The Timbers (Mich GS) in 1970.

A guitar's regular tempo provides a continuo that makes melismatic and other complicated melodies easier to sing. Once individuals grow comfortable with such stylistic techniques, they may transfer them to existing songs. Melisma is found in Wasewagan's (Calif CFG) version of Donovan's "Three Kids in a Sandbox" (14).

Yallani (Calif CFG) uses a guitar with some songs. The girls know a complicated melody with "Little Green Valley" (5). They sing "White Buffalo" (5) in unison with melisma and a minor phrase.

Pianos

Guitars are not the only instruments used in camps. Mary Tinsley Unrue took an accordion to Kitanniwa in 1974, where three staff members brought guitars. Deborah Weissman says an accordion was used in 1976 at Tel Yehudah (NY J coed). Debra Nails recalls twelve people played guitar or banjos at Marydale (La GS) that same year. Another Linda Johnson saw a guitar, banjo, and kazoos at Wanakiwin (Minn YWCA) in 1976.

In the 1920s and early 1930s, Joseph Carleton Borden remembers, at Rotherwood (Me boys), they would "sing once or twice a week, evenings around camp fire (a cornet would give the key) or inside the recreation hall (piano accompaniment)."

Madeline Gail Trichel remembers autoharps and guitars at Wawbansee (La GS). I remember a counselor at Hiwela (Wisc CFG) would occasionally use an accordion in 1963, but the instrument did not influence her song-leading techniques.

Kitanniwa did have a piano in the 1950s. It almost never was used during sings. Once songs learned aurally dominated the camp repertoire, a music counselor would have needed extraordinary skills to identify the beginning note of a requested song and to improvise chords.

The 1950s piano was not ignored. It stood in the open main lodge. Girls running through (and despite rules, girls did run through the empty space when they suspected they were not supposed to be there) would stop to pound out "Chop Sticks," "Peter, Peter Pumpkin Eater," "Heart and Soul," and the unnamed piece that begins:

F#G#A#	F#G#A#	F#G#A#	C#C#
BbAbGb	BbAbGb	BbAbGb	EbEb
F#G#A#	F#G#A#	F#G#A#	C#C#
F#GG#AA#A#			

"Chopsticks" has a respectable antecedent in Euphemia Allen's "The Celebrated Chop Stick Waltz" of 1877.[338] This was played by rolling a fist over the three black keys and picking out the last line with one finger. Madeline Gail Trichel (La GS) calls it "Tangerine," because a fruit would produce the same effect. Karen terHorst (Mich GS) calls it "Circus."

Trained musicians, no doubt, regarded such antics as barbaric. They did demonstrate, in the past, girls around age ten, the ones who usually were pounding keys, were familiar with pianos. That does not necessarily mean they could read music, but many probably were taking some type of lessons. It did mean they knew middle C on the keyboard. These girls, who would eventually grow into the camp's timbraic harmony, were not musical illiterates.

Borrowed Tunes

Folk Revival tunes do not seem to have been used often for color-war or other camp-specific texts. Hitaga (Iowa CFG) has the gypsy song quoted in WITCHCRAFT, which was composed to "Where Have All the Flowers Gone" (43). That, in turn, was inspired by a reference to a Cossack folk song in Mikhail Sholokov's 1934 novel, *And Quiet Flows the Don*.

Adahi (Penna CFG) has a local song to "Turn, Turn, Turn," which was based on Ecclesiastes 3. Boys at Loyaltown (NY J boys) wrote a trip song to the melody for "Donna" (51). Pete Seeger wrote "Turn" in 1959. "Donna" deals with the annihilation of Jews during World War II. Sholom Secunda and Aaron Zeitlin composed it for the Yiddish theater. Joan Baez recorded the translation by Arthur Kevess and Teddi Schwartz in 1960.

Since World War II, most local songs have used music from Broadway musicals. Only a few sing works like "Oh, What a Beautiful Morning" (9) and "Oklahoma" (3) from Richard Rodgers and Oscar Hammerstein II's *Oklahoma!* Most use airs for camp-specific purposes. The latter song from 1943 has been used at Hitaga (Iowa CFG), Interlochen (Mich coed), and Ahwahnee (Calif BSA), according to James Hirsch.[S] Kathryn Orme Jessup[S] heard "Surrey with the Tarp on Top" at Orme Ranch (Ariz coed).

In the years before the Folk Revival, most Broadway numbers in tradition were by Rodgers and Hammerstein. "I Love Miniwanca" (Mich P sep) employed "Hello, Young Lovers" from *The King and I* of 1951. In 1972, Kathryn Orme Jessup[S] collected a local fun song from

Orme Ranch (Ariz coed) that adapted "Honey Bunch" from the 1949 *South Pacific*.

Their most important musical was *Sound of Music*, which opened in 1959 and was filmed in 1965. "Eidelweiss" (27) is sung in the original, and used for Kamaji (Minn girls) and Neewahlu (Ida CFG) songs. Among graces using the melody are "Bless Our Friends" (2) at Tannadoonah (Ind CFG) and "Bless This Food" at Burton (Wash P coed), according to John Sinkevitch. Posen[*] heard "Thank You Lord on this Day" in a Canadian camp.

"Sound of Music" (4) is known in at least four camps, and has been used for "Newaygo Ideals" (Mich YWCA). Jolene Robinson Johnson uses the tune with "Sounds of Sealth" (Wash CFG). Hammerstein's lyrics are sung for "Favorite Things" (4), "Climb Ev'ry Mountain" (6), and "Do-Re-Mi" (9). Hitaga (Iowa CFG) has local versions of both "Things" and "Sounds."

Other musicals that have had several songs enter camp tradition also are from the middle 1950s. Lerner and Loewe's *My Fair Lady* opened in 1956. "I've Grown Accustomed to Her Face" was used at Miniwanca (Mich P sep) in 1971. "Wouldn't It Be Loverly" (2) has been adapted for a sailing unit song, according to Jolene Robinson Johnson (Wash CFG), and for an Hitaga (Iowa CFG) land-gypsy song. Miniwanca (Mich P sep) and Christopher (Ohio C coed) have had local songs to "If Ever I Would Leave You" from the team's *Camelot* of 1960.

Lerner and Loewe marked the end of the European immigrant tradition in Broadway musicals that owed so much to the Vienna of Sigmund Romberg. The Treaty of Saint-Germain-en-Laye dissolved the Austro-Hungarian Empire in 1919, ending World War I. Frederick Loewe was born in Berlin to Viennese parents who came to this country in 1924. His father, Edmond Löwe, sang lead in a Berlin production of Franz Lehár's *The Merry Widow*.

Alan Jay Lerner's[*] father's father Samuel emigrated from Ukraine. His mother's ancestors had come earlier from German-speaking lands. His father was successful enough in the retail trade to send him to Choate and Harvard. His summer camps, Androscoggin (Me J boys) and Greylock (Mass J boys), were traditional private camps for Jewish boys.

When Meredith Willson's *Music Man* opened in 1957, it was deemed unusual for drawing upon music traditions associated with his native Iowa, including quodlibets and barbershop quartets. "Lida Rose" has been used for "Miniwanca, Camp in the Sun" (Mich P sep). Steven Diner taught its most famous tune, a celebration of small-town brass-band music, at Loyaltown (NY J boys) in the early 1960s. Judy Miller says, Kamaji (Minn girls) adapted "Seventy-Six Trombones" for their "State Song."

Theater songs sung in camps with their original lyrics often have an inspirational theme, like "The Impossible Dream" (7) from *Man of La Mancha*. "Try To Remember" (10), from *The Fantastics*, voices the familiar desire to hold to the past with images drawn from nature. The first was by New Yorkers Mitch Leigh, born Irwin Michnick, and Joe Darion. Texans Harvey Lester Schmidt and Tom Jones composed the second. They opened Off Broadway in 1960. *La Mancha* is from 1965.

Few stage songs have been used for fun songs. "Hey, Look Me Over," from *Wildcat*, has been adapted at Christopher (Ohio C coed), Hitaga (Iowa CFG), Kamaji (Minn girls), and Kitanniwa. Judy Miller remembers a local Kamaji (Minn girls) song to "Step to the Rear" from *How Now Dow Jones*. The first was created in 1960 as a vehicle for Lucille Ball. Max Shulman wrote the story for the second in 1967, while his renown for creating Dobie Gillis still was strong enough to attract audiences.

Sweet Charity opened on Broadway in 1966. "If My Friends Could See Me Now" has been used at Cedar Lake (NJ J coed), according to Sally Briggs.[s] "Big Spender" has been adapted at Orme Ranch (Ariz coed), according to Kathryn Orme Jessup.[s] Nancy Gail Maxwell remembers a private staff bawdy routine. Jazz dancer Bob Fosse was the director.

Film Tunes

Film songs continue to include those sung for their lyrics, and those used for their tunes. "Born Free" (16), the theme from a 1966 movie, is an example of the first. "Georgy Girl" illustrates the second. Mrs. James Duncan wrote "Hey There Camp Fire Girl" for Hitaga (Iowa CFG) to the song from a 1966 film. Rebecca Quinlan remembers a color-war song at Lenore-Owaissa (Mass girls) written to "Thoroughly Modern Millie" from the 1967 movie. Les Chalets Francais (Me girls) adapted "Where Is Your Heart," the theme song from *Moulin Rouge* of 1952.

Continuing Interchange

The history of camp singing from the earliest years to the present suggests that, regardless of possible changes in the underlying American culture, the Folk Revival has been a normal phase in the supra-cultural process of oral tradition. According to Charles Seeger, the "gradual loss of the oldest songs in a repertoire, while new materials are being added, is a normal course of a vigorous tradition."[502]

From at least Word War II, traditions were not hearty in many camps. Too few new songs were being added. That stagnation often paralleled decay in other parts of camp programs. The resulting lack of innovation disposed people to sing commercial Folk Revival songs and try other ideas from the 1960s. This instigated a crisis. Seeger suggested such events occurred "where the loss in the older section [of the repertoire] is almost total and the new has little in the nature of oral tradition."[502]

Since the late 1960s, the camp repertoire has been retracing steps from the earliest years of camps. Then commercial music was used, while the songs that would become traditional were being created. This restoration of the traditional process has been obscured by the continued use of Folk Revival songs, which have taken the repertoire position once assigned community and older familiar tunes.

At the same time, Up with People and other fundamental, charismatic or born-again religious groups have been trying to influence camp programs. Girl Scouts and other progressive recreation specialists have responded with different goals for youth groups.

Debra Nails has observed the changes from the Folk Revival through Up with People to John Denver at Wawbansee (La GS). She said, "Recently, I visited (for two days) the camp which I attended, 1962-1965, and discovered - to my amazement - that a great number of the songs we sang years ago are still favorites with the campers there."

Repertoire may have changed. Debra's singing experiences, in both the 1960s and 1970s, are no different, folkloristically, than those of Madeline Gail Trichel at the same camp in the early 1950s. The elements that transform camp singing into a folk or folklike activity have survived the stagnation and revitalization phases of an ongoing tradition. That survival through cultural shifts may be the most folk aspect of camp singing. It indicates more than just some songs have survived in time and space, while undergoing changes.

Case Study: Flicker

Continuities in camp tradition are clearest in songs about camp fires. Only "Flicker" (40) is new. Others have been retained from the pre-Folk Revival years.

Judith Czerwinski[*] (1939-1999) composed the song in 1958 at Talooli (NY CFG). It spread through both Camp Fire and Girl Scout networks. Linda Ann Barsness[†] and Judith Bischoff published the words and music in 1974.

When Czerwinski graduated from high school in Baldwinsville, New York, in 1957, she knew she was no longer Judith Nancy, member of the school band and chorus. She was Judee. She was going to be somebody. She had the publicity photograph made that is reprinted in "People Who Make It Possible."

She spent her summers working in camps. After Talooli, she worked on the waterfront at Madeleine Mulford (NJ GS). At Lou Henry Hoover (NJ GS), she was called Dunc.

When the time came, she returned to Onondaga County to earn an associate's degree from Auburn Community College in 1963. When Mariam Marikar Luebs met her in 1984, she was a child care worker at a treatment center for emotionally disturbed children. Luebs said, "she always carried a backpack sewn with all kinds of decals and the children vied to earn the privilege to carry it. That's the kind of importance that she had in their lives!"

In 1992, the two published a children's book, *Vanilla and Chocolate*,[*] for Luebs' son. She was born in India in the southwestern coastal state of Kerala. The six-year-old was asking, "what it means for him to be an American." Czerwinski provided the illustrations.

Explication

"Flicker" uses synecdoches to evoke the emotions of camp. Shorthand references to nature - "wind in the pines," "moon in the heavens," "stars that shine" - are not intended to limn a mental image, as they do in "A Canoe May Be Drifting" (10). Instead, they capture sensations one feels sitting outdoors in the random way one notices them.

Technically, the poem represents a shift in emphasis from the older Imagist-influenced pretty songs to the newer, more subjective ones. "Canoe" created its wistful effects by using the conditional mood of "may be." "Flicker" exploits fragments without verbs.

Textual Variation

Czerwinski's original song (version C) was one verse, like the one Jolene Robinson Johnson introduced to Kitanniwa (version A). Little variation exists in texts from camp to camp, beyond the usual small ones that come from oral transmission: does the line begin "flicker" or "the flicker," is it "the camp fire" or "a camp fire?" Some reverse the words "moon" and "stars," but keep the rhymes. Shirley Ieraci (Ohio GS) sings "wind and the rain."

Most sing the verse, then repeat the burden twice. There usually is a "da da," "do do," or "o o" interlude between repetitions. A few camps have added their own second verse, so the burden is repeated once each time. At Shawnee (Mo CFG), the camp-specific stanza closely paraphrases the original:

The peacefulness of Shawnee, the silence of the night
The sun in the morning, all shiny and bright
A place where campers gather, make friends for all time
A place where city troubles are always left behind

At Namanu (Ore CFG), the added verse (version B) introduces more details about the local setting and friendship deepening into love.

Music

Czerwinski's melody has some affinities with "The Seine" (6) by Irving Burgie. He wrote calypso songs for Harry Belafonte and commercial ones for the Kingston Trio. "Flicker" is syncopated more strongly. That accented rhythm gives a minor feel to some passages. It has chromatic ascending phrases.

The tempo of Jolene Robinson Johnson's[†] (Wash CFG) guitar-accompanied version is quicker and more marked than

Wasewagan's[†] (Calif CFG) a capella one. Both use harmony in some sections. Wasewagan also sings it contra style with "I Know a Place" (38), as does Onahlee (Ore CFG) and Wintaka (Calif CFG).

Popularity

"Flicker" is a girls' camp song, known by about half the women who answered my questionnaire in 1976. It is not as well known in Camp Fire camps in the survey Midwest as elsewhere. Jacqueline Orvis, who was at Camp o' Fair Winds (Mich GS) in 1976, said it had been introduced by a Girl Scout counselor from Saint Paul, Minnesota.

In the manner of many new songs, Leah Culp says, at Hidden Valley (Md CFG), it is "sung by smaller groups rather than by everyone." In the more traditional pattern, Lisa Drumm[§] wrote, it is:

> a serious song that deals with the out of doors. However, it is often accompanied and speeded up to a hand-clapping rhythm for almost sacrilegious fun. The song reflects much of the philosophy of Camp Wyandot (Ohio CFG), in that it speaks of both nature and the friendship that can be found there.

Version A

Text from Jolene Robinson Johnson. She learned it at Camp Sealth (Wash CFG) in 1962 and taught it at Camp Kitanniwa (Mitch CFG) in 1973 and 1974. She later introduced it to Camp Tannadoonah (Ind CFG) in 1975 and 1976. Guitar chords from Camp Patiya (Colo CFG), 1971. Jolene's photograph appears in "Kitanniwa, 1974."

1. Flick (G) er of the camp (Em) fire, wind (C) in the pines (D7)
   A song (G) in the hea (Em) vens, the moon (C) that shines (D7)
   A place (G) where people ga (Em) ther makes friends (C) of all kinds (D7)
   A place (C or G) where all men's trou (Em) bles are al (C) ways left behind (D7)

C. Give (G) me the light of the camp (Em) fire, warm (C) and bright (D7)

And give (G) me some friends to sing (Em) with, I'll be (C) here
all night (D7)
Oh love (G) is for those who find (Em) it, I found (C) mine right
here (D7)
Just you (G) and I and the camp (Em) fire, and the songs (C) we
love (D7) to hear (G)

I. Da (Em) dum da da da le (C) Da de la (D7) DUM

C. Oh give me the light of the camp fire, warm and bright
And give me some friends to sing with, I'll be here all night
Oh love is for those who find it, I found mine right here
Just you and I and the camp fire and the songs we love to hear

Version B

Text from Camp Namanu (Ore CFG), 1970; variations from A
emphasized in shared sections.

1. Flicker of **a** campfire, wind in the **pine**,
   Stars in the heavens, **a** moon that shines,
   A place where people gather **meeting** friends of all **kind**,
   A place where **old man trouble is** always left behind,
   So give me the light of **a** campfire warm and bright,
   And give me some friends to sing with, I'll be here all night,
   For love is for those who find it, **I've** found mine right here,
   Just you and **me** and the campfire and the songs we love to hear.

2. So green are the valleys, sweet is the clover,
   Gone are the cold winds for ever more,
   The roses now are blooming, the oceans so blue
   The sun above is setting upon our love so new,
   For love is like a warm fire, soft and low,
   And when you're found your true love, your heart will always know,
   And as the leaves start falling and friends begin to part,
   These memories of the summer will stay in every heart.

Version C

Text by Judith Czerwinski, 1958; contributed by Gene Wichmann, 2013; variations from A or B emphasized. Judith's photograph appears in "People Who Make It Possible."

The flicker of a campfire, **the** wind in the pines,
the moon in the heavens, **the stars** that shine,
a place where people gather **to meet** friends of all kinds,
a place where old man trouble is always left behind . . .
So give me the light of a campfire warm and bright
and give me some friends to sing with I'll be here all night,
for love is for those who find it **and** I found mine right here,
just you and I and the campfire and the songs we love to hear.

PHOTOGRAPHS

People Who Make It Possible

People Who Make It Possible

The composers, collectors, and people who helped me with this project.

Right: Margaret Bradshaw McGee composed "My Paddle's Keen and Bright" at Sebago-Wohelo, Maine private girls' camp.

Below: Judith Czerwinski wrote "Flicker of a Camp Fire" at Talooli, New York Camp Fire Girls camp.

Above: Miss Dode, the director (left), Martha Jackson Stocker (next), 1956. Martha collected a version of "Kookaburra."

Below: Joyce Gregg Stoppenhagen (center) in dress whites, 1957. She provided versions of "Skyball Paint" and "Oh, the Boatmen Dance."

Kitanniwa Staff, 1950s

Right: Nurse telling fortunes on Spanish Night, 1960.

Below: Senior unit counselor Sally Heath (center) with Wanda, Liz, and Libby, 1958.

Front Cover: Kathleen Huggett Nye with CIT (in tie) and girls starting the teepee that goes inside a council fire, 1954.

Kitanniwa, 1974

Fire destroyed the main lodge in 1974, but left the stone foundation and chimney. Jan Smyth and Kitty Smith, below, in the replacement cook tent.

Right center: Jan Smyth, 2007.

Above top center: After Kitanniwa, Linda Johnson directed Hitaga; with Iowa Camp Fire Girls staff, early 1980s.

Opposite
Top: Jolene Robinson Johnson (left) 1969. Carol Parsons Sievert, 1945.

Bottom: Laura Clare Zahn (left) 2013. Mary Tinsley Unrue, 1969.

All provided versions of case study songs or information.

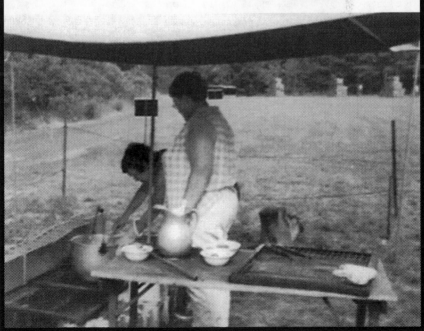

Collectors

Above right: Lynn Rohrbough, "Kumbaya," and Katherine Ferris Rohrbough, "The Cuckoo," 1925.

Above left: Ruth Anderson Eldridge, 1968, and right, Annetta Byers Eldridge, 1921, "Lollypop" as "Herpicide."

Bottom left: Max Vernon Exner, "Eskimo Hunt." Janet Tobitt, "Ash Grove" descant and "Rose." E. O. Harbin, "Pep" and "I Wish," 1955.

Composers

Above center right: Anne Hopson Chapin, "Whippoorwill," at Girl Scouts' Long Pond National Training Camp near Massachusetts shore, 1921. Bloomers have been abbreviated into knickers. Khaki has replaced navy. Middy ties are smaller. They still have long hair.

Bottom left: Margarett Snyder, "Witchcraft," 1956. Marion Sinclair, "Kookaburra," 1987, with book containing one of her poems.

Tradition Bearers

Above left: Isabel Ricker Smaller, early version of "I Wish," 1986. One of her former students says, "she was a very special role model for me!"

Evelyn Hopson Woods, early version of "Pep," 1926. Her Southern Baptist church remembers her as, "a patron saint, giving her blessing to all that was enriching and noble."

Below: Madeline Gail Trichel in Wawbansee primitive unit, Louisiana Girl Scout camp, 1950s. The Episcopal Peace Fellowship honored her work with prisoners with the Sayre Prize in 2006.

APPENDICES

A. Individual Participants

Information: individual's name, camping history, codes for information provided

Camping history: camp name and dates if at Kitanniwa, type, state
Church camp: any Protestant or Roman Catholic sponsored camp; most are recreation camps
Jewish are kept separate; many are progressive camps

Codes
A—Submitted a collection to a university archive
B—Song book
C—Conversation, interview, letter, or other communication
L—Song list
P—Photograph
Q—Returned questionnaire

Camp Kitanniwa

Arnold, Ruth. Kitanniwa, 1942-1943. B, L

Averill, Patricia. Kitanniwa, 1951-1960. CFG, 4-H, girls church camp, school camp. Mich, Wisc. B

Bennett, Beverly

Dulmatch, Marilyn. Kitanniwa, 6 years. CFG, YMCA. Ind, Ohio. L

Friedman, Sheila Natasha Simrod (1943-1993). Kitanniwa, 1952-1960. Jewish coed. Mich. L

Heath, Sally. Kitanniwa, 1957-1958, 1960-1963, 1965-1966. 4-H, private girls, church camp. Mich. P, Q

Hill, Denise. Kitanniwa, 1972-1973. GS. Calif, Conn, Mass, Mich, Ohio, Wisc. Q

Howe, Suzanne. A

Johnson, Linda. Kitanniwa, early 1970s. CFG. Iowa. B, C, P

Johnson, Jolene C. Robinson. Kitanniwa, c. 1973-1974. CFG. Ind, Wash. B, C, P

Joslin, Jane. Q

Kittinger, Sue Shafer. C

Leonardi, Claudia Lee McElhaney. Kitanniwa, 1955. CFG. Mich. Q

Marshall, Zuellen. Kitanniwa, 1974. C

McIntyre, Polly. Kitanniwa, middle 1950s through 1960. B, P

Munk, Claudia Lucille Parker (1902-1991). Kitanniwa, middle 1920s
through middle 1930s. CFG, GS. Mich, Ohio. C, P

Nizny, Barbara Rosoff. Kitanniwa, 1944-1951, 1954-1956. CFG, GS,
private girls. Ind, Mich. L, Q

Nye, Kathleen Huggett. Kitanniwa, 1954-1960. Church camp. Mich. C, P

Owen, Elizabeth

Quinlan, Rebecca. Kitanniwa, c. 1974. CFG, private girls. Mass,
Ohio. C, P

Randels, Katherine Alice Redner (1916-2008). Kitanniwa, 1926-1931.
Private girls. Mich. Q

Salo, Ann A. Orlik. Kitanniwa, 1955-1959. Q

Sievert, Mary Carol Parsons (1927-1992). Kitanniwa, 1934-1942,
1970s. YWCA. Mich. B, C, L, P

Smith, Kitty. Kitanniwa, late 1950s through early 1970s. C, P

Smyth, Jan. Kitanniwa, c. 1973-1974. Church camp. Ohio. C, P

Stocker, Martha Jackson. Kitanniwa, 1958. GS, agency. Mich, NY,
Wisc. A, P

Stoppenhagen, Joyce Gregg. Kitanniwa, 1957, 1959. GS, church
camp. Mich, Ohio. B, C, P

Taylor, Judy. Kitanniwa, 1974. C

Thompson, Roberta A. Kitanniwa, 1957-1975. Q

Tidball, Jean McLarty. Kitanniwa, 1952-1963. YWCA, church camp,
Jewish coed. Mich. Q

Unrue, Mary Tinsley. Kitanniwa, 1961, 1968-1974. School camp,
music camp. Mich. B, C, P

Zahn, Laura Clare. Kitanniwa, 1972, 1974. CFG, YWCA, church
camp. Mich. C, L, P

Women

Anonymous. Campbell Mountain. GS. Ky. Q

Anonymous. Cimarron. CFG. Okla. Q

Anonymous. Tayanita. CFG. Ohio. Q

Adams, Jessie. CFG. Texas. Q

Adler, Elizabeth Mosby. C

Alfred, Mary Jo. GS, special needs. Iowa, SD. Q

AvRutick, Joanne. Private, special needs. Md. C

Bachman, Elizabeth Mills. Private girls, private coed. Ore. Q

Balsamo, Maureen Therese. Special needs. Wash. L, Q

Barnes, Mary. Jewish girls, private coed, church camp. Ind, Md, NM. B, Q

Baugh, Cathie D. CFG. Ore, Wash. L

Bauman, Diane. Church camp. Mich. L, Q

Barker, Marsha Lynn. GS. Mich, Ill. L, Q

Beardsley, Ann M. GS. Mich, Ohio. B, Q

Beaudet, Suzanne M. GS. Mass, NY. Q

Beck, Laurie. GS, King's Daughters, YMCA girls, sports. Fla, Ill, Iowa. Q

Belk, Elaine Collins. CFG, church camp. Calif. Q

Bittmann, Judith J. GS, YWCA. Fla, Ga, Ohio. Q

Black, Ann. CFG. Ohio. C

Boss, Jan Williky. GS, Jewish girls, private coed. NJ, NY. C

Bossaller, Dolores A. GS. Mo. Q

Brandenberger, Nan Carol. CFG, private girls. Mont. Q

Briggs, Joan. GS. Iowa. Q

Briscoe, Virginia Wolf (c. 1942-1997). C

Brisler, Joann A. Girls church camp. Alaska, Vt. Q

Bryant, Nancy. CFG, church camp. Ohio. B, C, P

Butler, Marilyn. GS, private girls, church camp. NH, Texas. Q

Cahill, Sandra Bealieu. GS. Conn, NJ. Q

Callahan, Wanda. Church camp. Fla, Ind, Penna. Q

Carney, Charline A. Girls church camp, private girls. Mass. Q

Chernick, Deborah Ann. Private girls. Colo. Q

Christ, Susan H. CFG, private coed, private girls. Nev, NJ, NY, WV. Q

Clark, Connie M. CFG, YMCA, church camp. SD, Wisc. Q

Coco, Jo Ann. GS, private girls. Miss, NC, Texas, Wisc. Q

Coffin, Joanne. Q

Collins, Amy. CFG. Calif. C

Conard, Susan. CFG, private coed, riding camps. Calif. Q

Coutellier, Connie. CFG. Mich, Ohio. Q

Crow, Eleanor F. YWCA, private girls, church camp. Mich, Vt. Q

Culligan, Marianne. CFG. Ore. Q

Culp, J. Leah N. CFG, YMCA, Jewish camp. Md, Ohio. C, B, L, P, Q

Cuqua, Viki Irene. GS, YWCA, girls private, special needs. Ariz, Minn. Q

Darlington, Billie. C

Deatherage, Becky Colwell. GS. NY. Q

Depew, Fredrica Beyerman. Girls church camp. Mich, Wisc. C

Diner, Hasea Swartzman. Jewish camp. Mich. B

Duff, Charlotte A. (1926-2011). Private girls. Me, Mich, Wisc. B, C, P, Q

Endsley, Carolyn. Private girls. Mich. Q

Engel, Janice. Pioneer Girls. Minn. Q

Engle, Carol Ann. Pioneer Girls. NY. Q

Erler, Diane S. GS, YWCA, private girls. Iowa, Me, Minn, Wisc. Q

Findlay, Joan M. Church camp. Wisc. Q

Fisler, Ann M. CFG. Mich, Calif. Q

Flack, Carol. GS, special needs. Ala, Ohio, Penna, Va, WV. Q

Foster, Monica Mahe. CFG, church camp. Minn. Q

Fox, Margaret J. GS, adventure. Minn. Q

Fritz, Eloise Bawyer. C

Fromberg, Susan. Arts camp. Penna. C, Q

Garrett, Sharen Lou. Private girls, private coed, church camp. Ala, Ga, NC. Q

Garrison, Jayne. CFG, church camp. Kans, Mo, Texas. Q

Gerardi, Donna. Private coed, CFG. Calif. Q

Gorman, Janice Barto. CFG. Calif. Q

Green, Vickie. GS. Ga, SC. Q

Greene, Kathleen. CFG, church camp. Md, NY. Q

Gulick, Dorothy Merrill (1904-1990). Private girls. Me. Q

Haggard, Inez. CFG. Texas. Q

Hall, Laurel Ann. YMCA, private girls. Ill, Wisc, Ont. Q

Hall, Patricia Ann. CFG. Calif. C, L, P

Hancock, Cecily Raysor. GS, CFG, private girls, arts camp. Colo, Me, Mass, NM. B, Q

Hanes, Linda Margaret. GS, church camp. Okla. Q

Hansen, Peggy Dawn. GS, private girls. Ida, Wisc. Q

Hastings, Nellie Mae. CFG, GS, YWCA, church camp. Ill, Iowa. Q

Hermansdorfer, Katharine Lynn. CFG. WV. Q

Hickerson, Lynn Russell (1943-2011). Arts camp. Me. C

Hicks, Terri Lynn. CFG. Ohio. Q

Hill, Dawn L. 4-H. Vt. Q

Homer, Paula. GS. NM. Q

Hopen, Dianne Brown. Foreign language camp, other unspecified. Minn. Q

Horner, Nancy. CFG. Md. C, P

House, Karen. CFG. Q

Housenbold, Belinda. Coed. NJ. C

Hoyes, Mary S. GS. Ohio. Q

Humphrey, Leslie K. GS. NY. Q

Ieraci, Shirley. GS. Ohio. B

Jabbour, Jane. GS, music camp. Fla, NC. Q

Janison, Debra L. Church camp. Ohio. Q

Johnson, Carma Jean. Church camp. Mich. Q

Johnson, Linda A. YWCA. Minn. Q

Jones, Nancy Edmonston. Girls private. Minn. Q

Jones, Janice Suzanne. GS, church camp. Ida, Ore. A, Q

Karras, Ann. YWCA, 4-H, church camp, music camp. Iowa. Q

Katzenbach, Maude Applegate Thomas (1921-2013). CFG. DC. B, Q

Kelley, Robin. CFG, church camp. Calif. Q

Kennelly, Janet Sharon. GS, YMCA girls. NJ, NY. Q

Kerr, Robyn Arthur. CFG. Calif. Q

Klingmen, Jill. Settlement house. Minn. Q

Klonsky, Joanne. CFG. Calif. L

Knapp, Janice H. CFG. Mich, DC. B, Q

Kneeland, Mrs. Craig. GS. Conn, Mont. Q

Kneeland, Miss. GS. Vt. Q

Knoblauch, Linda Regan. GS, unidentified day camp. Conn, NJ. Q

Kragh, Rebecca. GS, foreign language camp. Minn. Q

Kramer, Katie. CFG. Mich. C

Kraus, Sue Ann Thompson. CFG, GS, church camp. Kans, Ohio, Va. Q

Krebs, Loretta. GS, church camp. Ohio. Q

Lang, Mary. GS, YWCA, agency. Mich. Q

Lapham, Angela. GS. Mich, Penna, Va. L, Q

Lawrence, Wilma Jean. GS. Penna. L, Q

Leibfarth, June Rushing. GS. Texas. A, P, Q

Leight, Joan. GS, church camp, arts camp. Penna. L

Leight, Miss. GS. Penna. L

Lemme, Susan Helen. YMCA. Vt. Q

Loomis, Bonnie. GS. Ohio. Q

Lutz, Anne (1906-1996). GS, private girls, private coed, nature
counselor. Conn, NJ, NY, Ohio. L, Q

Lux, Elizabeth Stavrum (1922-2010). CFG. Wisc. Q

Lytle, Virginia. GS. Penna. C

MacLaughlin, E. Jean Mayo. GS. Fla, Ida, NC. L, Q

Maisonneuve, Florence Louise. GS. Md. Q

Majerczak, Rosella Diehl Schweizer (1929-2012). Private coed, nature
   camp. Ohio, WV. Q

Matulich, Jane Ann P. GS. Calif. Q

Maurer, Rachel. Private coed. NM. Q

Maxwell, Nancy Gail. CFG, YMCA, church camp. Minn, ND. Q

Mayberg, Anna. CFG. Wash. Q

Mayo, C. Judith. CFG, church camp. La. Q

McCabe, Lisa. GS. Calif. L

McCallum, Diane. GS. Mich. L

McGreer, Patricia A. CFG. Ore, Wash. Q

McMullen, Jean Gentry. YWCA, private girls. Colo, Me, Mich. Q

McNeill, Reba. Agency for boys. DC. Q

Meyer, Susan. YMCA, arts camp. Penna, Ont. Q

Miller, Judy. Private girls. Minn. B

Miller, Mary Elisabeth. GS, agency. Md. Q

Mitlitzky, Sally. Jewish camps. C

Morgan, Ellen Merle. CFG, private girls. La, Texas, Vt. Q

Mullikin, Catherine L. CFG. Kans, Neb. L, Q

Mutia, Susan. Church camp. Ark. Q

Nails, Debra. GS. La, Tenn, Texas. Q

Negus, Susan Carol. CFG. Iowa. L, Q

Nelson, Eileen. GS, church camp. Penna, NY. Q

Nelson, Loretta Delaine. CFG. Kans, Okla. L, Q

Nelson, Marilyn. CFG. Calif. Q

Nelson, Nancy Marie. CFG, YWCA. Iowa. Q

Newman, Phyllis Bonnie. Private girls. Me. L, Q

Olmstead, Dana Dawn. CFG. Texas. Q

Olson, Margaret L. CFG. Minn. Q

Orr, Marjorie. CFG. Ore. Q

Orlowski, Susan. Church camp. Ind. L, Q

Orvis, Jacquelyn. GS, music camp. Mich. Q

Owens, Vicki L. CFG, GS, church camp. Wash. Q

Palmer, Mariana. GS, YMCA coed and girls. Md, Penna. B, Q

Parker, Janice. CFG. Penna. L

Parr, Sally Ann Brockley. Private girls. Penna. C, L

Poulter, Ruth Mack (1928-2006). YWCA, private coed, agency, church
   camp, music camp. Colo, Ill, Mich, Penna. Q

Prentice, Patricia Anne (1942-2013). CFG, YWCA, school camp.
   Mich, Wisc. Q

Prickett, Diana Jo. GS. Mich. Q

Quarto, Joyce. GS, 4-H, church camp, school camp. Mich. Q

Ramsey, Leah Jean. CFG, church camp. Texas. Q

Rau, Carol. CFG. ND. Q

Reed, Janet N. GS, school camp. Mich. Q

Regan, Carolyn. CFG, GS. Mass, NJ. L, Q

Richardson, Serena. Coed private. Md. C

Richman, Sharon. Coed, Jewish girls. Penna. Q

Rigoni, Frances Gay Withrow (1931-2010). CFG, music camp, school camp. Calif. Q

Robertson, Sharon Daniel. CFG. Texas. Q

Robinson, Cheryl. CFG. DC. L

Rooney, Theresa Mary. GS. NJ. L, Q

Rosensweig, Carol. YWCA. Conn. Q

Ross, Mary Ellen. GS, 4-H, special needs. NJ, Penna. Q

Sanford, Pat. CFG. Wash. C

Saunier, Margaret Ellen. YWCA, YMCA. Ky. Q

Scanley, Dorothy Anne. GS, church camp. Conn, NY. L, Q

Schindelholz, Jo Beth Marshall. CFG, GS, church camp. Wisc. Q

Schmatz, Ruth. Private boys, agency, school camp, church camp. Ill, NY, Wisc. Q

Schoenbach, Hannah. Arts camp. NJ. Q

Schuster, Joan T. Private girls, church camp. Wisc. L, Q

Sehman, Sandra Alice Wampler. GS, private coed, church camp. Md, Penna. Q

Selig, Bryna. CFG. DC. L

Sexton, Vivian Lee (1904-2003). CFG. Texas. L, Q

Sherman, Pat. CFG. Texas. Q

Shuldman, Ethel Helen. Jewish coed, school camp. Ore. Q

Shull, Lavonne. 4-H camp. Ind. C

Simmons, Nancy. GS. Colo, Conn. L

Snell, Mikie. CFG. Texas. L

Snyder, Clarena M. GS. Ohio. B

Southworth, Deborah. GS. Conn. Q

Stadler, Mary K. CFG, church camp. Calif. Q

Stearman, Susan Marcia. GS, Jewish coed. Md. C, Q

Sullivan, Elaine. Private girls, girls and coed church camps, riding camp. Conn, NH, NY. Q

Swan, Kirsten. YMCA girls. Mass. Q

Swires, Jo Ann. GS. Ill, Mich, Wisc. Q

Tabman, Rochelle. YMCA. C

terHorst, Karen. GS, church camp. Mich, Va. L, Q

Thomas, Kathryn L. GS. Ohio. Q

Torrey, Susan Ann. Rainbow Girls. Mass. Q

Trichel, Madeline Gail. GS, church choir camp. La, Ohio. C, L, P, Q

Tucker, Marguerite. GS. Ohio, WV. Q

Van Brug, Meribeth. Private girls, church camp. Mich, NC. Q

Walker, Mary Wescott. Private girls, private boys. Minn. Q

Walls, Francine. YWCA. Wash. B

Weber, Josephine (1909-1998). CFG, church camp. Iowa, Wisc. Q

Webster, Mary Satterfield (now Swanson). YMCA. Wisc. C

Weiss, Lori Judith. Jewish coed. Mo. Q

Weissman, Deborah. Jewish coed. NY. Q

Wells, Susan M. CFG, school camp. Mich. Q

Whitcomb, Phyllis M. GS, YMCA, church camp. Mich, Ind. Q

White, Janet. CFG, church camp. Md, Va. L

Whitehead, Margaret J. CFG. NY. Q

Wilfred, Marjorie Adele (1927-1990). CFG, GS, YWCA, church camp. Calif, Ill, La, Ohio, Okla, Wisc. Q

Wilkens, Mary Ann. CFG. Iowa. Q

Williams, Karen. GS, church camp, rec camp. Minn, NY, Wisc. Q

Wingrove, Patricia Louise. YMCA. Md. Q

Wiseman, Brooke M. GS, YWCA. Mich, Ill. Q

Wolf, Doris Rae. GS, church camp. Wisc. Q

Wolverton, Betsy. GS. Ohio. Q

Wray, Joanne. Church camp. Va. Q

Wyss, Diane. GS. Ohio. L

Yung, Aileen L. GS, YWCA. Mich, Ohio, Va, WV. Q

Zellers, Deb. CFG. Ohio. Q

Men

Anonymous. Lake Forest, Ill. Q

Adler, Thomas A. C

Amsbery, Jonathan H. YMCA. NM. Q

Bahr, Tim. Community coed. Mo. Q

Barraclough, Robert A. Q

Bensinger, Steve. BSA, YMCA. Q

Bertrand, Jim. Agency coed. Wisc. Q

Bolton, Terry Wilbur. BSA, church camp. Ida, Ore, Wash. L, Q

Bond, Earl H. YMCA, Boys Club. Calif, Ind. Q

Bonstrom, Dana. BSA. Ore, Wash. Q

Borden, Joseph Carleton (1909-1994). Private boys. Me, Penna. Q

Calvi, John. Private coed. Vt. Q

Chavez, Frank. Boys church camp. Calif. Q

Chitwood, Paul. Church camp. Texas. C

Church, Garet. Boys church camp. NY. Q

Clay, Seth Alton (1910-1994). Church camp. Mich. B, L

Clough, Gene. BSA, CFG, church camp. Calif. C, P, Q

Cox, Wesley B. Church camp. Texas. Q

Crowder, David Michael. Agency coed. Ohio. Q

Dickerson, James Spencer, Junior. BSA. Mo. Q

Diner, Steven. Jewish boys. NY. B

Dooker, Richard J., Junior. Private coed, church camp. Calif, Ohio, Ont. Q

Dowdall, Edward Peter, Junior. BSA, private girls, music camp. Me, NY. Q

Ephross, Paul H. YMCA, Jewish coed. Ill, Mass, NY. Q

Fennell, Bernard J. BSA. Minn. Q

Flegal, Gary Lee. Community coed, music camp. Mich. C, P, Q

Fort, John Richard. Private boys. Vt. Q

Foulk, Stephen Daniel. Private boys. Me. Q

Goodwin, James H., Junior. Agency. Mass. Q

Grant, Kenneth Lloyd. Private boys. Me. Q

Greiff, Tom. BSA, GS, YMCA, Jewish boys. Calif. Q

Grundke, Russell. Settlement house coed. Ohio. Q

Hartung, Kent Burdair. YMCA boys. Iowa. Q

Hoefner, Ferdinand. Church camp. NY. Q

Kneeland, Craig. YMCA. Conn, Vt. Q

Kowalski, Timothy J. Boys Club. Mich. Q

LeMond, Don. BSA. Mo. Q

Miller, George Mitchell. Church camp. NC. Q

Olsen, Mike (Chief Rising Sun). YMCA, church camp. Mich, Iowa. Q

Pearse, Jack (1926-2013). YMCA, private coed. Ont. Q

Pfaff, Carl. CFG. Calif, Ida. C

Posen, Ira Sheldon. Agency, Jewish coed, music camp. Mich, Newfoundland, Ont. A, C, P, Q

Putnam, John. Wisc

Ralston, Larry. 4-H. Ohio. B, C

Renney, Larry. YMCA boys. Mont. Q

Richards, Charles D. Church camp. Mich. Q

Rosenfeld, Arnold. Girls. Md. C

Scanley, Stephen Eliot. BSA. Conn. L, Q

Scott, Robert C. BSA. Wash. B, Q

Shipp, William H. GS, YMCA coed. Mich, NH. Q

Sinclair, David Stanfield. Boys Club, church camp. Ind. Q

Sinkevitch, John P. Church camp. Wash. Q

Smith, Charles D. BSA. Calif. Q

Smith, Larry R. BSA. Alaska, Mich, Wisc. Q

Smith, Roger. Agency coed. Mass. L, Q

Taniguchi, Jay Makoto. Church camp. Hawaii. Q

Weikant, David P. (1931-2003). YMCA, YWCA, private girls, agency, music camp. Mich, NY, Ohio. Q

Whiting, Paul M. BSA, YMCA, church camp, adventure. NY, Wisc, Ont. Q

Windsor, Douglas Crawford. Private boys, boys church, sports. NH, NY, Ont. Q

Other Sources

Anonymous. Battle Creek, Mich

Anonymous. Galilee. Church camp. Mo. Q

Anonymous. Jordan. YMCA. Me. Q

Anonymous. Nathan Hale. Church camp. Conn. Q

B. Archive Collections

Boy Scouts of America

New Brunswick, New Jersey. Archive. Headquarters since has moved to Irving, Texas.

Hillcourt, William (1900-1992). Collection of song books, song sheets and other papers related to music and the Boy Scouts, most between 1938 and 1950s

Douglass College

Rutgers University. New Brunswick, New Jersey. American Studies Department, Folklore Archives.

Filocco, Ann Marie. "Girl Scout Camp Songs" (1975). Lachenwald (Germany GS); unidentified New Jersey Girl Scout troop
Gerfin, Linda. "Songs of Inter-Varsity Christian Fellowship" (1976)
Gottlin, Elizabeth. Untitled paper (1976). Handclap rhymes, gross songs, parodies, animal songs, and jump-rope rhymes from Edgewater and Jersey City, New Jersey; Brooklyn, New York
Hickey, Katie. Untitled paper (c. 1975). Matollionequay (NJ YWCA)
Masto, Dianna. "'Lollipop': A Camp Song" (1977). Sheppard's Mill (NJ GS)
Schulz, Joanmarie. "Children's Rhymes" (1976). Howell, New Jersey
Villiers-Fisher, Kathleen. Untitled paper (1975). Chickagami (NJ GS), Sacajewa (NJ GS), Girl Scout National Center West (Wyo GS)

Indiana University

Bloomington, Indiana. Folklore Archives. I believe much of what I used was gathered by Richard Dorson (1916-1981) when he was teaching at Michigan State College/University between 1944 and 1957.

Allen, Ruby Anne. Girl Reserve conference

Amidon, Judith. Unidentified Girl Scout camps in South

Anderson, Marie. Unidentified camp

Anderson, Neola Rae. Black Hawk (Ill BSA); Emery (Mich agency)

Andrews, June. Lyman Lake (Minn GS)

Becker, Lawrence. Unidentified Illinois camp

Bezanson, Delores. Unidentified ranch

Bidwell, Shirley. Brighton Fresh Air Camp (Mich J coed)

Bygrave, Marilyn. East Lansing, Michigan

Clark, Frank. Tevya (NH J coed); unidentified Massachusetts day camp

Codd, Marjorie. Detroit, Michigan

Coleman, Audrey. Unidentified Girl Scout camp

Courtney, Pat. Unidentified Girl Scout camp

Cunningham, N. Ak-O-Mak (Ont girls); unidentified Girl Scout camp

Curtiss, Elizabeth. Talahi (Mich YWCA)

Densmore, Rex. Unidentified camp

Domoney, Carol. City and Country Camp (Mich); Missaukee (Mich P girls); Pilgrim Haven (Mich P coed); Rotary (Mich BSA); Wyandot (Ohio CFG)

Eberhardt, R. Don[ald]. Unidentified source

Findlay, Sandra. Westminster (Mich P coed)

Fulton, Joan. Wasewagan (Calif CFG); unidentified church camp

Gee, Betty Mae. Mimico, Ontario

Gelzer, Jacqueline Jay. O. C. Kimball (Mich YMCA coed)

Goldsberry, Jan. Kosciusko (Ind P coed); Tannadoonah (Ind CFG)

Graham, Joan L. Westminster (Mich P coed)

Greenman, Mary. Unidentified camp at School Lake, Brighton, Michigan

Grenard, Jack. Unidentified Boy Scout source

Guilbert, Marcia. Miniwanca (Mich P sep)

Hamilton, Jean. New York

Hanner, Norman F. No-be-bo-sco (NJ BSA)

Havens, Rosalind. Unidentified camp in Lake Geneva, Wisconsin

Henry, Marvella. Unidentified camp

Hess, Joal. Cavell (Mich YWCA)

Hollin, Judy. Camp o' Fair Winds (Mich GS); Tyrone (Mich YWCA)

Hope, Nancy. Unidentified Girl Scout mariner troop

Horr, Maribelle. Wellington, Ohio

Howe, Suzanne. Kitanniwa (Mich CFG); Waldenwoods (Mich coed)

Huggett, Aleta. Albion College Laboratory School (Mich); Appleblossom (Mich GS); Lake Louise (Mich P coed); Greenville and Gladwin County, Michigan

Hunter, Nancy T[witchell]. Unidentified camp near Springfield, Ohio

Jackson [Stocker], Martha. Bay City day camp (Mich GS); Birchrock (Wisc GS); Deer Trails (Mich GS); Edey (NY GS); Nayati (Mich agency)

Johnson, Sharon M. Deer Trails (Mich GS)

Kamelhar, Yetta. Unidentified Brooklyn, New York, camp

Katanick, Florence Ruth. Talahi (Mich YWCA)

King, June. Cadillac, Michigan

Kline, Patricia. Camp-in-the-Woods (NY YMCA coed)

Labb, Mary. Hill 'n Dale

Lamb, Joyce. Tall Oaks (Mich P girls)

Latvala, Roberta T[upper]. East Bay (Ill P coed)

Lawrason, N[athaniel] Bruce. Unidentified camp

Lazenby, Nancy. Detroit, Michigan

Lemanski, Thelma. Unidentified Girl Scout camp

Lickfeldt, Ardeth. Plymouth, Michigan, Girl Scout troop; unidentified 4-H camp

Lindquist, Karen. Unidentified camps in Rhinelander, Wisconsin, and elsewhere

MacCready, Joan. Teetonkah (Mich BSA)

MacMeekin, Ann. Saginaw, Michigan

MacPhail, Heather. Hidden Lake (NY GS); Keewano (Mich CFG); Sakakawea (Mich GS); Sweyolakan (Ida CFG)

McIntosh, Frank W[ayne]. Unidentified camp

McIntosh, Judy Lisse. Hillendale; Meadowbrook (NH girls)

Merriam, Helen. Battle Creek, Michigan

Millis, Fred H[annum]. Unidentified camp near Traverse City, Michigan

Minshull, Mary. Unidentified camp

Morrice, Marjorie. Unidentified camp on Long Lake, Michigan

Nevans, Christine. Unidentified camps

Oliver, Ellen. Clear Lake Camp (Mich agency coed)

Olsen, Kristine. Unidentified camp

Quist, Donna. Camp-in-the-Woods (NY YMCA coed)

Pearson, Barbara. Deer Trails (Mich GS)

Racklveft, Jack. Jack and Jill Ranch (Mich coed)

Reynolds, Jim. Unidentified camp

Rhodes, Alice. Lake Louise (Mich P coed); unidentified camp near Port Huron, Michigan

Rinehart, Margaret. Salem, Missouri

Robinson, Mary. Student Christian Foundation and American Youth for Democracy, both at Michigan State College

Rollins, Marilyn. Metamora (Mich GS)

Root, Carol Woodworth. Rotamer (Wisc agency coed)

Rosenthal, Felicia. Unidentified source

Rust, Barbara. Unidentified camp

Saperstone, Gloria. Unidentified New York camp

Scheer, Cynthia. Unidentified Girl Scout camp

Schoonover, Janet. Camp o' Fair Winds (Mich GS); Cavell (Mich YWCA); unidentified Girl Scout and YWCA camps

Schroeder, Betsy. Red Raider (Ohio coed)

Schumacher, Sally. Nashville, Tennessee

Schuurmans, Elizabeth. Lake Louise (Mich P coed)

Schwenn, Marilyn. Unidentified camp

Shaull, Keitha. Unidentified FHA camp

Sheldon, Ruth. Unidentified Battle Creek, Michigan, camp

Smith, Susan. Unidentified source

Snyder, Catherine. Unidentified camp

Southman, Phyllis. Unidentified camps, one in Wisconsin

Starrett, Elizabeth. Arden Shore (Ill P coed); unidentified Chicago, Illinois, YMCA camp

Stewart, Perianne. Fortune Lake (Mich P coed); unidentified camp

Tatar, Aurelia. Hayo-Went-Ha (Mich YMCA boys); unidentified camp

Thomson, Margaret. Unidentified source

Thompson, Kathryn. Unidentified camp

Toynton, Margaret. Unidentified camp

Trapp, Theora. O. C. Kimball (Mich YMCA coed); Boy Scout Jamboree in Irvine, California

Turner, Ronald. Kiroliex (Mich BSA)

Ulrich, Dale C. Interlochen (Mich coed)

Van Tiem, Lynn. Detroit, Michigan

Wakefield, Dean. Kiwanis (Mich BSA)

Walters, June. Metamora (Mich GS); Tannadoonah (Ind CFG)

Ward, Robert. Waterloo, Ontario

Weger, Ron, Junior. Unidentified camp

Westman, James. Cadillac, Michigan

Wilkie, Phyllis R. Rainbow Girl's camp at Crystal Lake, Michigan
Winfield, Claire. Unidentified Girl Scout sources
Wright, Nancy. Ryde Lake (Ont CGIT)
Wrzesinski, Janice E. Manistee, Michigan

Ohio State University

Columbus, Ohio. English Department, Folklore Archives.

Briggs, Sally. "Camp and Folk Songs" (1973). Angola on the Lake (NY YWCA); Cedar Lake Camp (NJ J coed); Hope (NJ agency coed); Shawnee (Penna coed); unidentified Boy Scout activities
Calderhead, Charla. "Camp Folklore" (1973). Beaver Creek (Ohio P coed); Muskingum Valley (Ohio BSA); Piedmont (Ohio 4-H); Presmont (Ohio P coed); Tuscazor (Ohio BSA); unidentified 4-H camp
Drumm, Lisa. "Songs of Camp Wyandot" (1974). Ohio CFG
Fazenbaker, Richard A. "Folklore of Camp Butler, Peninsula, Ohio" (1974). Ohio BSA
Hart, Chris. "A Collection of Folklore Miscellanea" (1973). Unidentified camp for retarded and physically handicapped
Hays, Peggy. "Summer Camp Folksongs, A Collection of 40" (1973). Storer (Ohio YMCA coed); unidentified Girl Scout camps
Saint Pierre, Debbie. "Children's Folk Songs" (1973). Storer (Ohio YMCA coed), Methodist Sunday school (Ohio); unidentified Girl Scout and church camps
Sherwood, Julie. "Camp Folklore" (1973). Molly Luman (Ohio GS)
Shuster, Carol. "Girl Scout Songs" (1973). Great Trails (Ohio GS); Columbus, Ohio, Girl Scout Troop
Simon, Carol. "Camp Songs" (1973). Camp Ohio (Ohio 4-H); Camp Christian (Ohio P coed); Myeerah (Ohio GS); unidentified Girl Scout camps

University of Oregon

Eugene, Oregon. The Randall Mills Folklore Archive.

Allen, Jennifer. "Recipes to Cook over the Campfire" (1974)
Asher, Sally A. "Camp Fire Girls' Lore" (1971). Wilani (Ore CFG)

Craig, Kathleen. "Camp Songs from Hamburg Cove" (1972). Claire (Conn P coed)

Davis, Diane. "Camp Songs" (1971). Magruder (Ore P coed)

Evans, Carol. "Camplore" (1972). Namanu (Ore CFG); Wakoma (Wash CFG)

Hirsch, James M. "Some Camp Songs" (1973). Ahwahnee (Calif BSA); Meriwether (Ore BSA); Osceola (Calif YMCA); Wi-Ne-Ma (Ore P coed); New York Girl Scout

Howden, Christine. "Religious Folksongs" (1971). Unidentified church camp

Jessup, Kathryn O[rme]. "Folksongs from the Orme Ranch Summer Camp" (1972). Ariz coed

Jones, Suzi [Janice Suzanne]. "Folklore from Girl Scout Camps in the Northwest" (1970). Alice Pittenger (Ida GS)

Keizur, Julia Dawson. "Family Folklore" (1971). Seabeck Conference Center, Seabeck, Washington [Presbyterians rent]

Kerr, Nat. "Folksongs of Methodist Camps" (1974). Loon Lake (Ore P coed); Suttle Lake (Ore P coed); Magruder (Ore P coed)

Knoper, Sharon. "Toast Song Tradition of Camp Onahlee" (1974). Ore CFG

Leck, Jean. "Collection of Childhood Folklore & Others" (1971). Unidentified camp

Loff, Sue. "Popular Camp Songs" (1975). Outward Bound; unidentified Boy Scout, Camp Fire, and church camps

McFarlane, David. "Lore of Camp Wolfeboro, Calif. & Berkley Boy Scout Songs" (1974). Calif BSA

Prentiss, Alexandra. "Folksongs from Camp Kilowan" (1971). Ore CFG

Stuart, Nan. "Mealtime Customs of the Multnomah County Outdoor School" (1973). Ore agency coed

Sydoriak, Christine. "Nor'wester and Utica AM Camp Songs" (1974). Nor'wester (Wash coed); Boy Scout camp site at Lake Utica, California

Tepfer, Gary. "Song of the Outdoor" (1970). Brooklyn, New York, Boy Scouts

Wilson, Theresa. "Northwest Camp Songs" (1975). Northwest Camps and Outdoor School; unidentified Camp Fire camp

Woolley, Betty Ann. "Camp & College Songs & Others" (1971). Colton (Ore P coed)

University of Texas

Austin, Texas. Center for Intercultural Studies in Folklore and Ethnomusicology.

Feldman, Naomi and Mary Rogers. "Make a Joyful Noise" (1970s). Arnold (Tex GS); Casa Mare (Tex GS); Crucis (Tex GS); Martha Foster Madeley (Tex GS); Peach Creek (Tex GS); Robinwood (Tex GS); Tanasi (Tenn GS); Waopecta

Kelsey, Mary Lou Sansone. "Brown Ledge - A Folk Community" (1972). Vt girls

Raine, Patricia Ann. "Camp Songs of Camp Shawondawssee" (1973). Texas CFG

Utah State University

Logan, Utah. Department of English, Folklore Archive.

Rushing [Leibfarth], June. "Camp Songs" (1971). Arnold (Tex GS); Robinwood (Tex GS); Silver Springs (Tex GS); Tejas (Tex GS); national Girl Scout roundups

Wayne State University

Detroit, Michigan. Department of English, Folklore Archive. Folklore program closed and archives were disbursed; these probably went to Michigan State University.

Doebler, William D[aniel]. Tape of camp songs (1965). Holiday House (Mich P girls); Runels (Mass GS); Sherwood (Mich GS); Tanglewood; unidentified Girl Scout day camp at Norton Lake, Michigan

Dunn, Susan. Tape of camp songs (1967). Franklin Settlement House camp (Mich agency)

Henry. Tape, (c. 1973). Unidentified Detroit, Michigan, Girl Scout troop

Hodor, Larry. Untitled paper (1973). Boy Scout Troop 1497 at Camp Rotary (Mich BSA)

LaRonge, Philip. Interview tapes (1977). Mooseheart (Ill CFG)

Smith. Tape of songs (1969). CYO Girls Camp (Mich C girls)

Solsbury, [Kathleen M.] Tape of songs (1969). Anna Behrens (Mich GS); Camp o' Fair Winds (Mich GS); Linden (Mich GS); Metamora (Mich GS); The Timbers (Mich GS)

_____. Tape of songs (1970). The Timbers (Mich GS)

Sternberg. Tape of songs (1972). Unidentified sources in Michigan and Ontario

C. Camps

Includes camps that are mentioned in the text or participated in one of the ways indicated below. Does not include every camp mentioned in personal camping histories.

Codes
A—Mentioned in a folklore collection in a university archive
C—Mentioned by a former camper, counselor, or visitor
L—Song list
Q—Returned questionnaire

Kitanniwa

Kitanniwa. Kitanniwa Council, Battle Creek, Michigan
1940s   *Camp Kitanniwa Song Book*, song book, late 1940s or early 1950s
1970s   *Mealtime Prayers*, song sheet, early 1970s
1973   *Camp Kitanniwa Sings "73,"* song book
1974   Visits include after meal sings led by Carol Parsons Sievert, by Jan Smyth, and by others; staff sing with Jolene Robinson Johnson (guitar), Carol Parsons Sievert (guitar), Jan Smyth (guitar), Kitty Smith, Judy Taylor, Sue Taylor (guitar), Mary Tinsley Unrue (accordion), Laura Clare Zahn; private interviews with several
1974   *I Believe in Music*, song book edited by Mary Tinsley Unrue
1974   Song book edited by Carol Parsons Sievert and Mary Tinsley Unrue
1974   Song sheets

Camp Fire Girls

A-Ta-Ya Horizon Club. South Shore Council, Mass. Record album, 1960
Adahi. Reading-Berks County Council, Reading, Penna. CRS song book cited by Holcomb;* camp song book, received 1974
Aloha. Buffalo and Erie County Council, Buffalo, NY. Q

Augusta. Piedmont Council, Piedmont, Calif. Song book, c. 1931; song book, received 1974

Caniya. Golden Gate Council, San Francisco, Calif. Q

Celio. Nevada City, Calif. C

Cheewin. Saint Paul Council, Saint Paul, Minn. Q

Cielo. Ventura County Council, Oxnard, Calif. Q

Cimarron. Oklahoma City Council, Oklahoma City, Okla. Q

Cohila. Burbank Council, Burbank, Calif. Song sheets, received 1974

DeKanawida. Salt Rock, WV. Q

El Deseo. Albuquerque Council, Albuquerque, NM. Song sheets, c. 1960

Ellowi. Council of Metro Dallas, Dallas, Texas. Q

Firefly. Greater Cincinnati Council, Cincinnati, Ohio. Q

Glen. No-We-Oh Council, Findlay, Ohio. Visit, lunch, supper, council fire, serenade, August 1974. Q

Hantesa. Heart of the Hawkeye Council, Des Moines, Iowa. *Every Girls*, 1922.* Q

Harriet Harding. Omaha Council, Omaha, Neb. L, Q

He Bani Gani. Camp Fire group, Pasadena, Md. Visit, June 1976; performances at Maryland Folklife Festival, 10-11 July 1976

Hidden Valley. Chesapeake Council, Baltimore, Md. Song book edited by J. Leah N. Culp; visit June 1976, include Blue Bird hay ride

Hitaga. Iowana Council, Cedar Rapids, Iowa. Song book, 1969. Q

Hiwela. Winnebagoland Council, Oshkosh, Wisc. Song sheets, 1963. Q

Horizon Club Choraliers. Maricopa Council, Phoenix, Ariz. Record albums

Ka-esta. Klamath Council, Klamath Falls, Ore. Song book, April 1975

Keewano, sometimes Keewano-Wohelo. West Michigan Council, Grand Rapids, Mich. A

Killoqua. Pilchuck Council, Everett, Wash. L

Kiloqua. Firelands Council, Sandusky, Ohio. Song sheets from various years, received 1974

Kilowan. Willamette Council, Salem, Ore. Song book index, received 1974. A

Kirby. Samish Council, Bellingham, Wash. Song book, received 1974

Ki-Tan-Da. Camp Fire group, Cedar Rapids, Iowa. Song included in Hitaga song book

Kiwanis. Greater Boston Council, Boston, Mass, now Camp Kiwanee. C

Kiwatani. Mahoning Valley Council, Youngstown, Ohio. Song book index, 1974

Ko-Ha-Me. Wichita Council, Wichita, Kans. C

Kotomi. Denver Area Council, Denver, Colo. Song book, 1971

Kowana. Clinch Valley Council, Oak Ridge, Tenn. Song list, 1967; song sheets, c. 1971-1972

Ku Keema Day Camp. Norman Council, Norman, Okla. Song book, 1975

Kushtaka. Chugach Council, Anchorage, Alaska. Song book, late 1960s

Las Vegas, Nev, camp. Q

Long Beach Council. Long Beach, Calif. District Two Workshop song book, 1972; Horizon club song list. C, L, Q

Mawavi. Potomac Area Council, Washington, D.C., located in Virginia. Song book, June 1972

McFadden. Ponca Area Council, Ponca City, Okla. Q

Melacoma. Cascade Council, Vancouver, Wash. Song book, summer 1974

Metaka. Rio Hondo Council, Calif. Q

MeWaHi. Yuba-Sutter Council, Marysville, Calif. Song book, March 1972

Minkalo. Central Valley Council, Stockton, Calif. Q

Monakiwa. Lubbock Council, Lubbock, Texas. Q

Mooseheart. Order of the Moose, Mooseheart, Ill. A

Namanu. Portland Area Council, Portland, Ore. Song book edited by Jean Bauer, Ann Burgess, Patti Shanks, and others, 1970 edition. A, L

Nan-Ke-Rafe. Brewster, Mass. Q

Natoma. Natoma Council, Paso Robles, Calif. Q

Natsihi. Saginaw Valley Council, Saginaw Mich. A, C

Neewahlu. Sacajewa Council, Lewiston, Ida. Song book, 1970

Niwana. Kitsap Council, Bremerton, Wash. Song book, received 1974

Onahlee. Mount Hood Council, Oregon City, Ore. Song sheets, received 1974. A

Otanya. Orange County Council, Orange, Texas. Q

Oweki Day Camp. Pontiac Council, Pontiac, Mich. Song book, received 1974

Patiya. Boulder Council, Boulder, Colo. Song book, c. 1968-1969; song sheets, c. 1971

Phi Gamma Chi. Horizon Club, Kenmore, NY. Record album, 1968

Ruth Lee. Baton Rouge, La. Q

Seabow. West Contra Council, Richmond, Calif. Song book, received 1974

Sealth. Seattle-King County Council, Seattle, Wash. CRS song book,* 1969. C

Shawano. Shawnee Council, Dayton, Ohio. Q

Shawnee. Shawnee Council, Kansas City, Mo. Two song books, received 1976

Shawondasee. Clay County Council, Minn. Q

Shawondasee. First Texas Council, Mineral Wells, Texas. A, C

Sweyolakan. Inland Northwest Council, Coeur d'Alene, Ida. A

Talooli. Onondaga Council, Syracuse, NY. C

Tanadoona. Minneapolis Council, Minneapolis, Minn. Song book, c. 1947; song sheets received 1974

Tannadoonah. Michiana Council, South Bend, Ind, located in Michigan. Song list, possibly 1940s; song book, 1971. A

Tawakani. Southwestern Council, Twin Falls, Ida. Song book, possibly 1960s

Tawanka. Monroe County Council, Monroe, Mich. Song books, 1968, 1971; song sheets received 1975. Q

Tanawida. Tanawida Council, Albion, Mich. C

Tayanita. Tayanita Council, Salem, Ohio. Song sheets, received 1976. Q

Ti Ya Ni. Clinch Valley Council, Oak Ridge, Tenn. Included with Kowana

Towanyak. Sunflower Council, Kansas City, Kans. Song sheets, received 1975

Trelipe. Minneapolis Council, Minneapolis, Minn. Song book, 1970

Trowbridge. Red River Valley Council, Fargo, ND, located in Minnesota. Q

Tyee. Umpqua Council, Roseburg, Ore. Q

Val Verde. Huaco Council, Waco, Texas. Song sheets, received 1975

Wa-May-Ka. Greater Fort Madison Council, Fort Madison, Iowa. Q

Wakoma. Tacoma Area Council, Tacoma, Wash. Song book, received 1974. A, Q

Waluta. Port Arthur Council, Port Arthur, Texas. L

Wasewagan. San Gabriel Valley Council, Pasadena, Calif. Tape made by Gene Clough, 1970s. A

Watanopa. Missoula Council, Missoula, Mont. Song book, late 1940s or early 1950s; song book, received 1975

Wathana. Detroit Area Council, Detroit, Mich. Q

Wi-Ta-Wentin. Sowela Area Council, Lake Charles, La. Q

Widjiwagan. Hawaii Council, Honolulu, Hawaii. Song sheets, 1971 and 1973

Wilaha. Denver Area Council, Denver, Colo. C

Wilani. Wilani Council, Veneta, Ore. A

Wintaka. Long Beach Area Council, Long Beach, Calif. Tape made by Gene Clough, 1970s. Q

Wohaleto. Telephone, Texas. Q

Wohelo. Narragansett Council, Providence, RI. Song list, March 1971; song book, March 1973

Wolochee. San Juan de Fuca Council, Port Angeles, Wash. Q

Wolahi. San Diego County Council, San Diego, Calif. Song book, received 1974. Q

Wyandot. Columbus Area Council, Columbus, Ohio. Record album; song sheet, August 1974. A

Yakewi. Cleveland Council, Cleveland, Ohio. Song sheets, October 1971; song sheet, Mach 1974; two other song sheets, received 1975

Yallani. Los Angeles Area Council, Los Angeles, Calif. Tape made by Gene Clough, 1970s

Yukita Day Camp. Buckeye Council, Fremont, Ohio. Song sheets, received 1975

Zanika Lache. North Central Washington Council, Wenatchee, Wash. Song book, 1 March 1976; song book, 1 June 1971; song sheets from early 1970s

Boy Scouts of America

Ahwahnee. San Bernardino Mountains, Calif. A

Belnap. Chicago Area Council, Chicago, Ill, segregated for Black scouts, located in Michigan. Songs included in Treasure Island song book

Black Hawk. Chicago Area Council, Chicago, Ill, located in Michigan. Songs included in Treasure Island song book. A

Brooklyn Council. New York, NY. Song book, 1929, collected by William Hillcourt. A

Burch. Rocky Mountain Council, Pueblo, Colo. Song book collected by William Hillcourt

Butler. Peninsula, Ohio. A

Cherry Valley. San Gabriel Valley Council, Pasadena, Calif. C

Chicaugau. Chicago Area Council, Chicago, Ill. Songs included in Treasure Island song book

Chief Seattle Council. Seattle, Wash. Song book edited by Bob Scott, 1976 revision

Connetquot. Brooklyn Council, New York, NY. Included with Brooklyn Council song book

Dan Beard. Chicago Area Council, Chicago, Ill, located in Michigan. Songs included in Treasure Island song book

Delmont. Boy Scouts, Montgomery County, Penna. Song sheet collected by William Hillcourt

Denver Council. Denver, Colo. Song sheets collected by William Hillcourt

Duluth Council. Duluth, Minn, Congdon Park Pack 243. Cub Scout song book; song sheets collected by William Hillcourt

Gifford. Omaha, Neb. Song book collected by William Hillcourt

Glen Gray. Oakland, NJ. Gray*

Hart Scout Reservation. Philadelphia Council, Philadelphia, Penna.

Ihpetonga. Brooklyn Council, New York, NY. Included with Brooklyn Council song book

Irondale. Saint Louis Council, Saint Louis, Mo. Song Book for Scouts

James E. West. Chicago Area Council, Chicago, Ill, located in Michigan. Songs included in Treasure Island song book

Kanohvet. Brooklyn Council, New York, NY. Included with Brooklyn Council song book

Kiroliex. Chief Okemos Council, Lansing, Mich. A

Kiwanis. Chief Okemos Council, Lansing, Mich. A

Kotohke. Brooklyn Council, New York, NY. Included with Brooklyn Council song book

Kunatah. Brooklyn Council, New York, NY. Included with Brooklyn Council song book

Lake Huron Council. Auburn, Mich. Q

Lake Utica. Camping site, Lake Utica, Calif. A

Man. Queens Council, Jamaica, NY. Song book, 1947, collected by William Hillcourt

Manhattan Council. New York, NY, Troop 582. Song book, possibly 1950s, collected by William Hillcourt

Many Point Scout Reservation. Viking Council, Minneapolis, Minn. Q

McDonald. Chicago Area Council, Chicago, Ill, located in Michigan. Songs included in Treasure Island song book

Mendham Council. Mendham, NJ, Troop One. Song sheets from 1940s collected by William Hillcourt

Meriwether. Oregon Cascade Pacific Council, Portland, Ore. A

Muskingum Valley. Muskingum Valley Council, Coshocton, Ohio. A

No-be-bo-sco. Bergen Council, Hardwick, NJ. A

Onway. North Essex Council, Raymond, NH. Song sheet, 2 October 1944, collected by William Hillcourt

Oseetah. Brooklyn Council, New York, NY. Included with Brooklyn Council song book

Owaisippe Scout Reservation. Chicago Area Council, Chicago, Ill, located in Michigan. Songs included in Treasure Island song book

Parsons. Chief Seattle Council, Seattle, Wash. Q

Pioneer Training Center. Cascade Area Council, Salem, Ore. Q

Pittsburgh. Allegheny Council, Pittsburgh, Penna. Song sheets from 1940s collected by William Hillcourt

Rokilio. Kettle Moraine Council, Sheboygan, Wisc. Song sheets collected by William Hillcourt

Rotary. Lake Huron Council, Clare, Mich. A

S Bar F Ranch. Saint Louis Area Council, Saint Louis, Mo. Q

Sacut. Brooklyn Council, New York, NY. Included with Brooklyn Council song book

Saint Louis Council. Saint Louis, Mo. Song book collected by William Hillcourt

Stehahe. Brooklyn Council, New York, NY. Included with Brooklyn Council song book

Teetonkah. Land-O-Lakes Council, Jackson, Mich. A

Tonawedan. Brooklyn Council, New York, NY. Included with Brooklyn Council song book

Treasure Island. Philadelphia Council, Philadelphia, Penna. Song book edited by Edward Urner Goodman and others, 1920; song book, 1946 edition, collected by William Hillcourt; song sheet, 1946, collected by William Hillcourt

Tuscazor. Buckeye Council, Canton, Ohio. A

Watchung Area Council. NJ. Song sheet collected by William Hillcourt

Whitsett. Great Western Council, Van Nuys, Calif. Q

Wolfeboro. Mount Diablo Silverado Council, Pleasant Hill, Calif. A

Boy's Clubs

Drusilla Farwell. Detroit, Mich. Q
Indianapolis Boys Club Camp. Indianapolis, Ind. Q
Oty-Okwa. Hocking Hills, Ohio. Q
State of Columbia. Columbia Park Boy's Club, San Francisco, Calif.
    Rogers*

Daughters of Rebekah

Tall Oaks Youth Camp. Baldwin, Mich. A

Four-H

Calhoun County. Marshall, Mich, held at Barry County 4-H camp. C
Conger. Wyandot County, Upper Sandusky, Ohio, rented facilities
    from Huron County, Ohio, Extension Office. Song sheets
    collected by Larry Ralston
Downer. Vermont Extension Service, Sharon, Vt. Q
Elkhart County. Goshen, Ind. C
Kelleys Island. Erie County, Ohio, Extension Office. Camp counselors
    camp song sheets, 1953, collected by Larry Ralston
Ohio. Utica, Ohio. A
Piedmont. Piedmont, Ohio. A
Pittenger. Wyandot County, Upper Sandusky, Ohio, rented facilities
    from Tiffin, Ohio, YMCA. Song sheet collected by Larry Ralston. C
Wyandot County. Upper Sandusky, Ohio, rented Trinity facilities from
    United Church of Christ, Upper Sandusky, Ohio. Visit include
    lunch and evening cook out, 12 July 1974; collection of song
    sheets dating back at least 30 years maintained by Larry Ralston

Future Farmers of America

FHA camp. A

Girl Scouts

Agnes Arnold. San Jacinto Council, Houston, Texas. A
Alice Pittenger. McCall, Ida. A

Anna Behrens. Michigan Trails Council, Grand Rapids, Mich. A

Appleblossom. Rent from Central Michigan University. A

Azalea Trails. San Gorgonio Council, Colton, Calif. CRS song book cited by Holcomb,[*] 1947; record album, 1966

Bay City, Mich, day camp. A

Beechwood. Sodus, NY. Q

Birchrock. Northwestern Great Lakes Council, Appleton, Wisc. A

Birdsall Edey. Penn Lakes Council, Meadville, Penna. Q

Camp o' Fair Winds. Fair Winds Council, Flint, Mich. A, Q

Camp o' the Hills. Irish Hills Council, Jackson, Mich. Q

Campbell Mountain. Licking Valley Council, Newport, Ky. Q

Casa Mare. San Jacinto Council, Houston, Texas. A

Cedarledge. Greater Saint Louis, Mo. A

Chickagami. Rock City and New Brunswick Council, NJ. A

Comstock. Seven Lakes Council, Geneva, NY. Q

Crucis. Timberlake Council, Azle, Texas. A

Deer Trails. Michigan Capital Council, Harrison, Mich. A, Q

Edey. Suffolk County, Bayport, NY. A

Ehawee. Riverland Council, Wisc. Q

Fort Hill. Singing Sands Council, Niles, Mich. C

Great Trails. Minerva, Ohio. A

Greenwood. Greater Minneapolis Council, Minneapolis, Minn. Q

Hidden Lake. Northeastern New York Council, Lake George, NY. A

Hilaka. Lake Erie Council, Cleveland, Ohio. Q

Hoffman. West Kingston, RI. C

Holly. Michigan Metro Council, Detroit, Mich. C

Julia Crowell. Lake Erie Council, Cleveland, Ohio. Q

Juniper Knoll. Chicago, Ill. Ella Jenkins recording (FC 7656)

Ken-Jockety. Seal of Ohio Council, Columbus, Ohio. Q

King's Lake Camp. Mid-Columbia Council, Wash. Q

Libbey. Maumee Valley Council, Cincinnati, Ohio. Q

Linden. Huron Valley Council, Linden, Mich. A

Little Cloud. Eastern Iowa and Western Illinois. Q

Lo-Co. Carolina Low Country Council, Charleston Heights, SC. Q

Lou Henry Hoover. Washington Rock Council, Westfield, NJ. C, Q

Lyman Lodge. Minnesota, probably rented from YWCA of Minneapolis, Minn. A

Madeleine Mulford. Montclair Council, Montclair, NJ, located in Pennsylvania. C

Martha Foster Madeley. Conroe, Texas. A

Mary White. Zia Council, Artesia, NM. Q

Marydale. Bains, La. Q

Merrie Woode. Glowing Embers Council, Kalamazoo, Mich. Q

Metamora. Pontiac, Mich. A

Molly Luman. Seal of Ohio Council, Columbus, Ohio. A, Q

Myeerah. Appleseed Ridge Council, Lima, Ohio. A

Oak Hills. Mitten Bay Council, Saginaw, Mich. C

Peach Creek Ranch. San Jacinto Council, Houston, Texas. Song sheets, received 1976. A, Q

Pittenger. McCutchenville, Ohio, rented facilities from Tiffin, Ohio, YMCA. C

Pottawotomie Hills. Kenosha Council, Kenosha, Wisc. Song sheets

Robinwood. San Jacinto Council, Houston, Texas. A

Ruby Lake. Greater Minneapolis Council, Minneapolis, Minn. Q

Runels. Eastern Massachusetts, Boston, Mass. A

Sacajewa. Central and Southern New Jersey, Cherry Hill, NJ. A

Sacajewa. Moingona Council, Des Moines, Iowa. Q

Sakakawea. Elk Rapids, Mich. A

Sheppard's Mill. Holly Shores Council, Bridgeton, NJ. A

Sherwood. Northern Oakland County Council, White Lake, Mich. A

Sherwood. Shawnee Council, Capon Bridge, WV. Q

Silver Springs. San Jacinto Council, Houston, Texas. A

Sky-Wa-Mo. Council of the Southern Appalachians, Elizabethton, Tenn. C

Skylark Ranch. Santa Clara County Council, San Jose, Calif. Song list, received 1976. Q

Spruce Ridge. Central New York Council, Syracuse, NY. C

Tanasi. Tanasi Council, Knoxville, Tenn. A

Te-Ata. Lenni-Lenape Council, Patterson, NJ, located in New York. Q

The Timbers. Fairwinds Council, Flint, Mich. A, Q

Tejas. San Jacinto Council, Houston, Texas. A

Texlake. Central Texas, Austin, Texas. A

Ticochee. Citrus Council, Winter Park, Fla. Q

Unalia. Lake to River Council, Niles, Ohio. Q

Virginia Anderson. Shemamo Council, Decatur, Ill. Q

Wabasso. Bay Path Colonial Council, Waltham, Mass. Q

Wah-Shah-She. Bluestem Council, Bartlesville, Okla. Q

Wakatomika. Heart of Ohio Council, Zanesville, Ohio. Q

Wawbansee. Pelican Council, Shreveport, La. C
Whip-Poor-Will Hills. Buckeye Trails Council, Dayton, Ohio. Q
Widjiwagan. Land of Lincoln Council, Springfield, Ill. Q
Yankee Trails. Connecticut Yankee Council, Farmington, Conn. Q

King's Daughters

Missaukee. Michigan branch. A, C
Wampatuck. Franklin, Mass. Song book edited by Cindy McGrath, 1974

Pioneer Girls

Cherith. Frazee, Minn. Q
Cherith. Buffalo, NY. Song sheets, received 1976. Q

Rainbow Girls

Rainbow Camp. Crystal Falls, Mich. A
Rainbow Camp. Hanson, Mass. Q

Young Men's Christian Association

Coed, unless noted otherwise
Billings. Ely, Vt. Q
Camp-in-the-Woods. Stockton, NY. A
Child. Helena, Mont, boys. Q
Dudley. Westport, NY, boys. C
Eberhart. South Bend, Ind, located in Michigan. Song book, received 1974
Eljabar. Dingman's Ferry, Penna. Q
Fitch. Youngstown, Ohio, located in Penna. Song book
Foster. Spencer, Iowa. Q
Greater Des Moines. Iowa, boys. Q
Hayo-Went-Ha. Central Lake, Mich, boys. A
Jack Hazzard. Stanislaus County, Modesto, Calif, boys. Q
Jordan. Bangor, Me, boys. Q
Manito-Wish. Milwaukee, Wisc. C
Mystic Lake. Lansing, Mich, boys. Q
O. C. Kimball. Hillsdale, Mich. A
Ohiyesa. Detroit, Mich. Song book, received 1976

Osceola. Anaheim, Calif. A
Rotary. Lynn, Mass. Q
Shaver. Albuquerque, NM, boys. Q
Storer Camps. Toledo, Ohio, located in Michigan. Song book, received
    1974. A
Tockwogh. Worton, Md. Q

Young Women's Christian Association/Girl Reserves

Includes YMCA camps for girls
Angola on the Lake. NY. A
Arbutus. Traverse City, Mich. C
Betty Hastings. Winston-Salem, NC. C
Cavell. Lexington, Mich. A
Camp-in-the-Woods. Mich. C
Chimney Corners. Becket, Mass, YMCA. Gibson[345]
Des Moines YWCA Camp. Iowa. Q
Kalamazoo Girl Reserves. Kalamazoo, Mich. Song book, 1938
Lookout. Philadelphia, Penna, YMCA for girls. C
Maria Olbrich. Madison, Wisc. C
Newaygo. Grand Rapids, Mich. Q
Matollionequay. Medford, NJ. A
Otonka. Lexington, Ky. Q
Rancho Los Cerros. Tucson, Ariz. Q
Rimrock. Yakima, Wash. Song book
Talahi. Detroit, Mich. A
Tyrone. Flint, Mich. A
Wanakiwin. Duluth, Minn. Song book, received 1976. Q
Wiyaka. Athol, Mass, located in New Hampshire, YMCA for girls. Q

Private Girls' Camps

Alford Lake. Union, Me. Q
Aloha Hive. Ely, Vt. Song book, 1966; two song books, received 1976. Q
Brown Ledge. Colchester, Vt. A
Chippewa Trail. Rapid City, Mich. C
Four Winds. Deer Harbor, Wash. C
Hanoum. Thetford, Vt. C
Interlochen. Interlochen, Mich. C

Joy Camps. Hazelhurst, Wisc. Song book, 1942. C
Kamaji. Cass Lake, Minn. Song book edited by Judy Miller, 1973. Q
Kehonka. Wolfeboro, NH. Q
Lake Hubert. Lake Hubert, Minn. C
Lenore-Owaissa. Hinsdale, Mass. C
Les Chalets Francais. Deer Isle, Me. Song sheets, received 1976. Q
Luther Gulick Camps. South Casco, Me, now Wohelo Camps. Song
    cards, possibly 1930s. Q
Mayflower. Orleans, Mass. Gibson[345]
Meadowbrook. Meredith, NH. A
Miramichi. Merrill, NY. C
Nicolet. Eagle River, Wisc. Q
Red Wing. Silver Lake, Penna. Song book edited by Ethel Martin, 1931
Runoia. Belgrade Lakes, Me. Q
San Juan Ranch. Ellington, Conn. Q
Sebago-Wohelo. South Casco, Me, now Wohelo Camps. Rogers*
Shining Mountain Ranch. Sula, Mont. Q
Skyland Camp. Clyde, NC. Song sheet, possibly 1976. Q
Teedy-Usk-Ung. Hawley, Penna. C
Truda. Oxford, Me. Q
Wabanaki. Hillside, Me. C
Waldemar. Hunt, Texas. C
Watervliet. Watervliet, Mich. Song book, received 1976. Q

Private Boys' Camps

Agawam. Raymond, Me. Q
Bear Lake Trail School. Estes Park, Colo. C
Chewonki. Wiscasset, Me. Q
Chocorua. Big Asquam Lake, NH. C
Dan Beard. Hawley, Penna. C
Gunnery School. Washington, Conn. C
Lincoln. Lake Hubert, Minn. Q
Mikquan. Nelsonville, Wisc. Q
North Mountain School of Physical Culture. Wilkes-Barre, Penna. C
Rotherwood. Alfred, Me. C
Sequoyah. Weaverville, NC. Song book, 1956
Wildwood. Brighton, Me. CRS song book cited by Holcomb*

Private Coed Camps

Allen. Oceanside, NY. Emrich[320]

Bear Pole Ranch. Steamboat Springs, Colo. Q

Brush Ranch. Tererro, NM. Song book compiled by Mary Barnes, 1976. Q

Dixie Camps. Clayton, Ga, brother and sister camps. Gibson[345]

Green Acres. Rockville, Md. C

Gwynn Valley. Brevard, NC. Q

Jack and Jill Ranch. Montague, Mich. A

Killooleet. Hancock, Vt. Firesiders recording (FC 7510). Q

Nor'wester. Lopez Island, Wash. A, Q

Orme Ranch. Mayer, Ariz. A

Outdoor Travel Camps. Cohen*

Pinnacle. Hendersonville, NC. Song book edited by Kathy Hansen and Chip Hansen, received 1974

Potomac Country Day Camp. Potomac, Md. Visit, 1976

Red Raider. Novelty, Ohio. A, Q

Shawnee. Waymart, Penna. A

Valley Mill. Germantown, Md. Visit, afternoon closing assembly, June 1976; performance at Maryland Folklife Festival, 9 July 1976

Waldenwoods. Hartland, Mich. A

Woodland. Phoenicia, NY. C

Jewish Girls' Camps

Council. Jewish Federation, Phoenixville, Penna. Q

Jewish Boys' Camps

Includes parallel private camps; private unless otherwise noted

Androscoggin. Wayne, Me. C

Greylock. Becket, Mass. C

Loyaltown. Hunter, NY. Song book edited by Steven Diner, c. 1963-1967; camp newspaper, 1963, 1965, 1967; undated song book; song list for exchange with Camp Poyntelle-Ray Hill, 1968

Max Straus. Jewish Big Brothers, Los Angeles County, Calif. Q

Surprise Lake Camp. Federation of Jewish Philanthropic Societies, New York, NY. Song book edited by Mordecai Kessler, 1938

Wigwam. Waterford, Me. Song book edited by Arnold M. Lehman and Abraham Mandelstam, 1921

Jewish Coed Camps

Includes parallel private camps

Alliance. Council Educational Alliance, Cleveland, Ohio. Brown[275]

B'nai Brith Summer Camp. Jewish Community Center, Portland, Ore. Song book, received 1976. Q

Boiberik. Sholem Aleichem's Folk Institute, Rhinebeck, NY. Mishler*

Brighton Fresh Air Camp. Jewish Welfare Federation, Detroit, Mich. A

Buck's Rock Work Camp. New Milford, Conn. Song book edited by Winnie Winston and Josh Rifkin, 1959

Cedar Lake Camp. New Jersey Federation of YMHA's and YWHA's. A, C

Habonim. Ichud Habonim Labor Zionist Youth, Chicago, Ill, located in Michigan. Song sheets

Kinder Ring. Workmen's Circle, Sylvan Lake, NY. Mishler*

Nitgedaigit. United Workers Cooperative, New York, NY. Mishler*

Poyntelle-Ray Hill. YMHA and YWHA, New York, NY, located in Pennsylvania. Song sheet, 1969

Sabra. Jewish Community Centers Association, Saint Louis, Mo. Q

Sidney Cohen. Children's Outing Association, Milwaukee, Wisc. Q

Tel Yehudah. Hadassah Zionist Youth Commission, Barryville, NY. Q

Tevya. Brookline, NH. A

Webatuck. Wingdale, NY. C

Wise. Council Educational Alliance, Cleveland, Ohio. Brown,* includes songs

Roman Catholic Girls' Camps

Includes parallel camps

CYO Girls Camp. Diocese of Detroit, Mich, Catholic Youth Organization. A

Marycrest. Sisters of Mercy, Grand Isle, Vt. Song book, possibly 1976. Q

San Benito. Benedictine Sisters of Chicago, Cañon City, Colo. Q

Teresita Pines. Catholic Daughters of America, Los Angeles, Calif. Q

Roman Catholic Boys' Camps

Saint Vincent de Paul Ranch. Saint Vincent de Paul Society, Los Angeles, Calif. Song book, possibly 1976. Q

Roman Catholic Coed Camps

Christopher. Catholic Youth Organization, Akron, Ohio. Song book edited by Uncle Ray, possibly 1974

Lawrence. Catholic Youth Organization, Gary, Ind. Q

Our Lady of the Hills Catholic Camp. Hendersonville, NC. Q

Protestant Girls' Camps

Fleur de Lis Camp. Episcopal Diocese of Boston, Mass, located in New Hampshire. Song book, c. 1955. Q

Holiday House. Girls' Friendly Society [Episcopal], Howard Park, Mich. A

Protestant Boys' Camps

Includes choir camps

Eagle's Nest. Episcopal Diocese of Newark, NJ. Q

Nejecho. Grace Church, [Episcopal] Newark, NJ. White*

Onaway. Boys' Brigade, Wisconsin Synod, Presbyterian Church, Neenah, Wisc. Chapin,* includes songs

Trexler. Lutheran Boys Camp Association, Merrick, NY. Two song books and set of song sheets, received 1976. Q

Protestant Coed Camps

Aldersgate. Kiwanis, United Methodist Church, and Title XX, Little Rock, Ark. Q

Arden Shore. Glencoe, Ill, Congregational Church camp for Chicago children. A

Beaver Creek. Presbyterian Church, Liverpool, Ohio. A

Big Lake Youth Camp. Seventh Day Adventist, Oregon Conference, Portland, Ore. Q

Blue Haven. Church of Christ, Lubbock, Texas, located in New Mexico. Song book, received 1976. Q

Burton. Baptist churches, Everett, Wash. Q

Caroline Furnace. Lutheran Church in America, Saint David's Church, Va. Q

Center Lake Bible Camp. Michigan Baptist General Conference, Tustin, Mich. Q

Christian. Disciples of Christ, Magnetic Springs, Ohio. A

Church camp. Described as Fundamentalist, probably in Oregon. A

Church camp. United Presbyterian use Seabeck Conference Center, Seabeck, Wash. A

Claire. First Congregational Church, Hamburg Cove, Conn. A

Colton. Lutheran, Colton, Ore. A

Covenant Cove Camp. Free Methodist Church, Prescott, Mich. Song sheet, possibly 1976. Q

Crystal Lake Camps. Christian Science, Hughesville, Penna. Song book edited by Richard Henry Lee, 1963 edition

East Bay Camp. Lake Bloomington, Ill, used by Presbyterians. A

Elko Lake Camps. Episcopal Mission Society, Parksville, NY. CRS song book cited by Holcomb[*]

Epworth. United Methodist Church, Lynbrook, NY. Q

Farthest Out. Congregational, Paynesville, Minn. Song books edited by Eva Shull and Russell Shull, 1960 and 1968

Fortune Lake. Northern Great Lakes Synod of the Evangelical Lutheran Church in America, Crystal Falls, Mich. A

Friedenswald. Central District, General Conference Mennonite Church, located in Michigan. Q

Galilee. United Methodist Church, Kansas City, Mo. Q

Highroad Program Center. United Methodist Church, Alexandria, Va. CRS song book cited by Holcomb[*]

Homelani. Salvation Army, Honolulu, Hawaii. Song sheets, possibly 1976

Ithiel. Church of the Brethren, Gotha, Fla. Q

Kosciusko. United Presbyterian Synod of Indiana, Winona Lake, Ind. A

Lake Louise. United Methodist Church, Holland, Mich. A, C

Loon Lake. Oregon Idaho Annual Conference, United Methodist Church, Portland, Ore. A

Magruder. United Methodist Church, Tillamook, Ore. A

Mar-Lu Ridge. Maryland Synod of the Lutheran Church, Jefferson, Md. CRS song book cited by Holcomb*

Merrowvista. American Youth Foundation, Saint Louis, Mo, located in New Hampshire. Song book, 1973; religious song book shared with Miniwanca, received 1974

Miniwanca. American Youth Foundation, Saint Louis, Mo, located in Michigan. Index to song book edited by Older Girls class of 1947; song sheets, 1974; other song sheets received 1974; religious song book shared with Merrowvista, received 1974. A, C

Mount Morris Lutheran Retreat. Wautoma, Wisc. Song sheet, received 1976

Nathan Hale. Salvation Army, Hartford, Conn. Q

Olmstead. Five Points Mission, United Methodist Church, Cornwell-on-Hudson, NY. Q

Pilgrim Camp. Wisconsin Conference of the United Church of Christ and Winnebago Presbytery. Q

Pilgrim Haven. Michigan Congregational Church, South Haven, Mich. A, C

Presbytery Point. Presbytery of Mackinac, Presbyterian Church, Mich. C

Presmont. Presbyterian Church, Piedmont, Ohio. A

Redbud Trail Retreat. First Presbyterian Church, South Bend, Ind, located in Michigan. Q

Redwood Camp. Mount Hermon Christian Camps, Mount Hermon, Calif. Q

Suttle Lake Camp. United Methodist Church, Suttle Lake, Ore. A

Tamarack. Wisconsin Baptist State Convention, Waupaca, Wisc. Q

Temple Hills. Evangelical and Reformed Church, Belleville, Ohio. C

Trinity. Trinity Evangelical and Reformed Church, Upper Sandusky, Ohio. C

Warren. Congregational, Mich. Song book, 1961, edited by Seth Clay; song list, 1955. C

Westminster. Westminster Presbyterian Church of Detroit, Mich. A

Wi-Ne-Ma. Christian Church (Disciples of Christ), Cloverdale, Ore. A

Woodleaf. Young Life, Challenge, Calif. C

School and Community

Clear Lake Camp. Battle Creek, Mich, public schools. A, C

Emery. Rotary Club, Muskegon, Mich. A

Multnomah County outdoor school. Multnomah County, Ore. A

Muskegon, Mich, public schools. Camp song book, received 1975

Nayati. Midland Kiwanis, Midland, Mich. A

Northwest Camps and Outdoor School. Northwest Regional Education Service District, Hillsboro, Ore, now Northwest Outdoor Science School. A

Palisades Interstate Park nature program, New Jersey and New York. C

Rotamer. Rotary Club, Janesville, Wisc. A

Teamsters' Health and Medical Camps. Teamsters Local 688, Pevely, Mo. Song book, received 1976

Van Buren Youth Camp. Van Buren County, Bloomingdale, Mich. C, Q

Settlement House, Fresh Air, etc.

Franklin. Franklin Settlement House, Detroit, Mich. A

Goodwill. Family and Child Services, Washington, D.C., located in Virginia, girls. Song book, 1969 or later, received 1976

Herald Tribune Fresh Air Camp. Fishkill, NY. Song book, edited by Dick Wagner, 1950s

High/Scope. Ypsilanti, Mich. Song book edited by Richard Lalli, 1974. Q

Hiram House. Settlement house, Chagrin Falls, Ohio. Q

Manakiki. Pillsbury-White Neighborhood Services, Minneapolis, Minn. Song book, received 1976. Q

Moss Hollow. Family and Child Services, Washington, D.C., located in Virginia. Same song book as Goodwill

Pleasant. Family and Child Services, Washington, D.C., located in Virginia, boys; founded as the segregated camp for Blacks. Same song book as Goodwill. Q

Putnam. Worcester Fresh Air Fund, New Braintree, Mass. Q

Unity. Communist Party, Wingdale, NY. Mishler*

University Settlement Work Camp. Beacon, NY. Song book, 1960

Wo-Chi-Ca. International Workers Order, New York, NY, located in New Jersey. Levine,* includes songs

Special Interests

Appel Farm, The. Elmer, NJ, private arts. Q

Concordia Language Villages. Concordia College, Moorhead, Minn (French). Q

Don Kerbis Tennis Camps. Watervliet, Mich. C
Idyllwild School of Music and the Arts. Idyllwild, Calif, private arts. C
Interlochen National Music Camp. Interlochen, Mich. Song book. A
Lighthouse Art and Music Camp. Settlement House, Schuylkill Haven, Penna. C
Med-O-Lark. Washington, Me, private arts. C
Seacamp. Miami, Fla. Q

Special Needs

Easter Seal. Pullman, Wash. List of songs in camp song book, received 1976. Q
Hope. New Jersey Association for Retarded Children, Hope, NJ. A
Indian Trails Camp. Grand Rapids, Mich, disabilities. CRS song book cited by Holcomb*
Merry Heart. Easter Seal Society of New Jersey, New Brunswick, NJ. Q
Seale Harris. American Diabetes Association, Mobile, Ala. Q

Adult and Family

Bay View. Methodist association. Little Traverse Bay, Mich. C
Chautauqua. Methodist association. Chautauqua County, NY. C
Idlewild. Near Baldwin, Mich, resort marketed to Blacks. Walker*
Kinderland. Workmen's Circle, then Communist Party. Sylvan Lake, NY. Mishler*
Lakeland. Workmen's Circle. Dutchess County, NY. Mishler*
Mount Tyrol. Newton Hamilton, Penna, hunting resort. C
Ocean Grove Camp Meeting Association. Methodist association. Ocean Grove, NJ. C
Outward Bound. A, C
Paradise Park. Fresno, California, Masons, located in Santa Cruz, Calif. C
Wequetonsing. Presbyterian association. Harbor Springs, Mich. C

National and International

Ahmek. Huntsville, Ont, private boys. C
Ak-O-Mak. Ahmic Harbour, Ont, private girls' sports. A, Q
Boy Scouts. International Jamboree, Ermelunden, Denmark, 1924. C
_____. National Jamboree, Washington, DC, 1937. C

_____. _____, Irvine Ranch, Calif, 1953. A

_____. Philmont Scout Ranch, Cimarron, NM. C

Girl Scouts. All State Encampment, Sky-Wa-Mo, Elizabethton, Tenn, 1964. A

_____. Edith Macy Conference Center, Briarcliff Manor, NY. C

_____. National Center West, Ten Sheep, Wyo. A

_____. National Training School, Plymouth Camp, Long Pond, Mass, 1921. Song book edited by Anne Hopson Chapin.* C

_____. Senior Roundup, Farragut State Park, Ida, 1965. Recording. A

Glen Bernard. Sundridge, Ont, private girls. C

Lachenwald. Girl Guides, Marburg, Germany. A

Manitouwabing Sports and Arts Centre. Parry Sound, Ont, private arts. Q

Ryde Lake. Canadian Girls in Training, Gravenhurst, Ont. A

Tawingo. Huntsville, Ont, private coed. Q

Young Women's Christian Association. Conferences use YMCA's Silver Bay Conference. C

Unidentified

City and Country Camp. Birmingham, Mich, existed in 1955. A

Flora Dale. Mich, possibly Silver Lake resort. Song book

Hill 'n Dale. Holly, Mich, existed in 1946. A

Hillendale. Existed in 1942. A

Long Lake. Mich, existed in 1950, may be only the location. A

Sinawak day camp. Probably in Connecticut, but could be New Jersey. C

Tanglewood. Girls camp of some kind. A

Waopecta. Probably Girl Scouts. A

D. Citations

Organizational Sources

Bee Hive Girls
(Mormon's Young Women's Mutual Improvement Association)

Other Sources
100   1934   Fox, Ruth May. *Handbook for the Bee-Hive Girls of the YWMIA*

Boy Scouts

Songs and Song Books
101   1920   Murray, William D., Frank Presbrey and Henry Van Dyke. *Boy Scout Song Book*
102   1925   Anonymous. "Bravo, Bravissimo," *Scouting*, 8 September
103   1928   Anonymous. "Bravo, Bravissimo," *Scouting*, 20 June
104   1930   Nichols, Alfred C., Junior. *Songs Scouts Sing*
105   1938   Zander, C. E. and Wes H. Klusmann. *Camp Songs*
106   1939   Zander, C. E. and Wes H. Klusmann. *Camp Songs 'n' Things*
107   1941   Nichols, Alfred C., Junior. *Songs Scouts Sing*
108   1963   Anonymous. *Boy Scout Songbook*
109   1969   Anonymous. *Cub Scout Songbook*
110   1970   Anonymous. *Scout Songbook*

Boy Scouts, England
111   1924   Anonymous. *Twenty Songs for Scouts*
112   1925   Anonymous. *The Hackney Scout Song Book*
113   1925   Anonymous. *Songs for Scouts*
114   1938   Anonymous. "Kookaburra," *Scout Leader*, November
115   1954   Anonymous. *The Scout Songbook*
116   n.d.   Anonymous. "Kookaburra," unidentified British Boy Scout publication
117   1962   Hazelwood, Rex and John Thurman. *The Second Gilwell Camp Fire Book*

118   1964   Thurman, John and Rex Hazelwood. *The Gilwell Camp Fire Book*

Boy Scouts, Canada
119   1932   Thomson, Lesslie R., *et alia. Songs for Canadian Boys*
120   1965   Anonymous. *Camp Fire Song Book*

Boy Scouts, France
121   n.d.   Anonymous, "Kookaburra," unidentified French Boy Scout publication

Boy Scouts, Italy
122   1947   Anonymous. *Canti di 1/2 Notte*

Other Sources
123   1899   Baden-Powell, Robert S. S. *Aids to Scouting*
124   1908   Baden-Powell, Robert S. S. *Scouting for Boys*
125   1910   Seton, Ernest Thompson and Robert S. S. Baden-Powell. *Boy Scouts of America*
126   1911   Gibson, H. W. "Hiking and Over-night Camps," in William D. Murray, George D. Pratt, and A. A. Jameson, *Handbook for Scout Masters*
127   1929   Hillcourt, William. *Handbook for Patrol Leaders*
128   1930   Evans, George. "Romance for the Older Boy," *Scouting*, April
129   1940   Gray, Frank Fellows. Luther Edmunds Price, *Thirty Years of Scout Camping, History of Glen Gray and Other Camps in Northern New Jersey, with Memoirs of Frank F. Gray*

Camp Fire Girls

Songs and Song Books
130   1896   Neidlinger, W. H. *Small Songster for Small Singers*
131   1912   Neidlinger, W. H. *Songs of the Camp Fire Girls*
132   1922   Anonymous. "We're Up at Hantesa," *Every Girls*, November
133   1947   Anonymous. *Joyful Singing*, CRS
134   1950[+]   Anonymous. *Music Makers*, CRS (middle 1950s)
135   1951   Kelly, Laurine. *Gay Songs for Blue Birds*
136   1961   Anonymous. *Music Makers*, CRS

137   1964   Anonymous.   "Blue Bird Candle," *Camp Fire Girl*, January-February
138   1965[+] Anonymous.   *Music Makers*, CRS (sometime between 1965 and 1972)
139   1969   Anonymous. *The Golden Year Song Book*, CRS for Sealth (Wash CFG)
140   1974   Anonymous. *Music Makers*, CRS (no date, received 1974)

Other Sources
141   1911   Gulick, Luther Halsey.   Speech, 22 March, at Horace Mann School, Teachers College, Columbia, quoted in Helen Buckler, Mary F. Fiedler, and Martha F. Allen, *Wohelo: The Story of Camp Fire Girls, 1910-1960* (1961)
142   1914   Anonymous. *Vacation Book of the Camp Fire Girls*
143   1914   Gulick, Luther Halsey.   "The Girl Who Goes Right," in National Conference on Race Betterment, *Official Proceedings*
144   1914   Stewart, Jane L. *The Camp Fire Girls at the Seashore*
145   1914   Stewart, Jane L. *The Camp Fire Girls First Council Fire*
146   1915   Gulick, Mrs. Luther Halsey. "Introduction," in CFG[147]
147   1915   Rogers, Ethel. *Sebago-Wohelo Camp Fire Girls*
148   1916   Anonymous. List of recommend music sources, *Wohelo*, July
149   1930   Fletcher, May. *The Book of the Ceremonials*
150   1934   Kempthorne, Edith M.   "Let's Sing," *The Guardian*, December
151   1952   Parks, Sue. "The History of Camp Fire in Battle Creek," Willard Library (estimated date)
152   1957   Anonymous. *The Book of the Camp Fire Girls*
153   1972   Anonymous. "Battle Creek Council History," Willard Library
154   1973   James, Laurie. *Adventure*
155   1975   McGee, Margaret Bradshaw.   Anonymous obituary, Oberlin, Ohio, *News-Tribune*, 27 March

Camp Fire Girls and Girl Scouts

Songs and Song Books
156   1946   Sanders, Mary Alison. *Sing High, Sing Low*

Four-H

Songs and Song Books

157 1950+ Anonymous. *Sing Along*, CRS for Michigan 4-H (sometime between 1950 and 1956 when I received my copy)

158 1957 Exner, Max V. *The Bridge of Song*, CRS for Iowa 4-H

159 1962 Anonymous. *For Happy Singing*, CRS for Ohio 4-H, received 1962

160 1966 Anonymous. *For Happy Singing*, CRS

161 1970+ Anonymous. *Sing Along*, CRS for Michigan 4-H (sometime between 1970 and 1974, when I received my copy)

162 1973 Graybeal, Jill. *Virginia 4-H Sings*, CRS

Other Sources

163 1939 Gardner, Ella. *Short Time Camps, A Manual for 4-H Leaders*

164 2004 Exner, Max V. Anonymous obituary, class of 1933, Columbia University website

Girl Scouts

Songs and Song Books

165 1921 Chapin, Anne Hopson. *Songs of the First National Training School for Girl Scout Officers*

166 1923 Anonymous. "Little Brown Tents," *The American Girl*, July

167 1925 Archer, John B. *Girl Scout Songs*

168 1929 Newell, George. *Girl Scout Song Book*

169 1930 Edgar, Marjorie. *Old Songs and Balladry for Girl Scouts*

170 1936 Tobitt, Janet E. *Sing Together*

171 1938 Tobitt, Janet E. *Singing Games for Recreation*, volume 3

172 1939 Tobitt, Janet E. *Yours for a Song*

173 1941 Tobitt, Janet E. *Sing Me Your Song O!*

174 1946 Tobitt, Janet E. *The Ditty Bag*; incorporated *Yours for a Song* and *Sing Me Your Song O!*

175 1949 Tobitt, Janet E. *Canciones De Nuestra Cabaña*

176 1949 Tobitt, Janet E. *Sing Together*

177 1955 Tobitt, Janet E. *The ABC's of Camp Music*

178 1956 Mitchell, Ray. *Dramatics and Ceremonies for Girl Scouts*

179 1956 Thomas, Eleanor L. *Girl Scouts Pocket Songbook*

180 1957 Anonymous. *Sing Together*

181   1958   Tobitt, Janet E. *Skip to My Lou*
182   1960   Tobitt, Janet E. *The Ditty Bag* (revised, combined edition)
183   1968   Gaudette, Marie. *Marie Gaudette's Songs*, compiled by Catherine
                 T. Hammett, edited by Marion Roberts, music
                 transcriptions by Mary Sanders and Constance Bell
184   1973   Bell, Constance. *Sing Together*

Girl Guides, England
185   1934   Crawter, Gladys, *et alia. Kent County Song Book*

Girl Guides, Australia
186   1970   Anonymous. *An Australian Campfire Song Book*

Girl Guides, New Zealand
187   1960   Anonymous. *Second Book of Songs*

Girl Guides, Switzerland
188   1957   Roberts, Marion A. *Chansons de Notre Chalet*, CRS, first edition
189   1959   Roberts, Marion A. *Chansons de Notre Chalet*, CRS, second
                 edition
190   1962   Anonymous. *Chansons de Notre Chalet*, CRS, third edition
191   1968   Anonymous. *Chansons de Notre Chalet*, CRS, fourth edition
192   1971   Anonymous. *Chansons de Notre Chalet*, CRS, fifth edition

Other Sources
193   1913   Baden-Powell, Robert S. S. and Agnes Baden-Powell.
                 "Games to Develop Strength," in W. J. Hoxie, *How
                 Girls Can Help Their Country*
194   1923   Boutelle, Grace Hodsdon. "Girl Scouts and Folk Songs
                 Find Each Other," *The American Girl*, July
195   1941   Rivenburg, John. Anonymous item in Renwick, Iowa,
                 Times, 17 July, announcing he had won the National
                 Song Writing Contest
196   1946   Anonymous. *Girl Scouts, Established Camps*
197   1951   Hill, Kathleen F. *Brief History of the Guide Movement in
                 South Africa*; cited by Tammy M. Proctor, *Scouting for
                 Girls: A Century of Girl Guides and Girl Scouts* (2009)
198   1953   Anonymous. *Girl Scout Handbook: Intermediate Program*
199   1977   Sinclair, Marion. Letter, 10 October

200   1979[+] Chapin, Anne Hopson.   Anonymous obituary, Harlem Valley, New York, *Times*, 12 April 1979; comments from Margaret Smith (2013)

201   1986   Sinclair, Marion. Poem and comments on "Kookaburra," in South Australia Council on the Ageing, *Late Picking*, edited by Stella Guthrie

202   2012   Sinclair, Marion. Biography by P. A. Howell, *Australian Dictionary of Biography*

Intercollegiate Outing Club Association

Songs and Song Books
203   1938   Brown, Will and Gerry Richmond. *IOCA Song-Fest*
204   1948   Best, Dick and Beth Best. *Song Fest*
205   1955   Best, Dick and Beth Best. *Song Fest*
206   1960   Best, Dick and Beth Best. *The New Song Fest*

International Youth Hostel

Songs and Song Books
207   1959   Graffam, William. *Songs, Lieder, Chansons*, CRS

Woodcraft League

Other Sources
208   1906   Seton, Ernest Thompson. *The Birch Bark Roll of the Woodcraft Indians*
209   1912   Seton, Ernest Thompson. *The Book of Woodcraft and Indian Lore*
210   1927   Seton, Ernest Thompson. *The Birch Bark Roll of the Woodcraft Indians*

Young Men's Christian Association

Other Sources
211   1928   Cheley, Frank. "Camping for Character," *Association Boys' Work Journal*, March, quoted by YMCA[212]
212   1929   Dimock, Hedley S. and Charles E. Hendry. *Camping and Character* (1939 edition)

213 1951 Hammett, Catherine T. and Virginia Musselman. *The Camp Program Book*

214 1955 Eisenberg, Helen and Larry Eisenberg. *How To Lead Group Singing*

215 1958 Thurston, La Rue A. *The Complete Book of Campfire Programs*

216 1963 Musselman, Virginia. *The Day Camp Program Book*

217 n.d. Exner, Max J. Janice A. Beran, "Max J. Exner: Naismith's Roommate - Later Coach, Teacher and Public Health Physician," LA84 Foundation website

Young Women's Christian Association

Songs and Song Books

218 1922 Botsford, Florence Hudson. *Botsford Collection of Folk-Songs*, two volumes, republished in three volumes in 1931

219 1923 Roe, Mildred. *Girl Reserve Song Book*

220 1927 Ireland, Imogene B. *The Song Book of the Y. W. C. A.*

221 1941 Zander, C. E. and Wes H. Klusmann. *Songs for Girl Reserves*

222 1943 Oliver, Marie. *Sing Along the Way*, CRS

223 1948 Oliver, Marie. *Sing Along the Way*, CRS, second, revised and augmented

224 1951 Oliver, Marie. *Sing Along the Way*, CRS, fifth printing

225 1957 Wheeler, Mary, Lura Mohrbacher, and Augustus Zanzig. *Sing Along*, CRS

226 1965 Wheeler, Mary B. *Sing Along! The YWCA Songbook*, CRS

Other Sources

227 1927 Anonymous. *An Adventure Book for Younger Girls*

228 1930[+] Snyder, Margarett. References from Madison, Wisconsin, newspapers, including the *Wisconsin State Journal*, 7 December 1930; the *Wisconsin State Journal*, 23 September 1952; *Capital Times*, 18 March 1961

229 1945 Oliver, Marie. *Let's Have Music*

230 1948 Oliver, Marie. *Let's Have Music*

231 n.d. Miller, Helen Hill. Letter to Mrs. Ward, Alumnae Association of Bryn Mawr College, on "Follow the Gleam"

232 2000 Oliver, Marie. Anonymous obituary, Monterey Peninsula, California, *Herald*, 29 January

233 2003 Oliver, Marie. Anonymous overview of the YWCA archives, Sophia Smith Collection, Smith College (estimated date)

References Cited in the Text

As much as possible, useful bibliographic information has been included in the text. The following could not be so incorporated. Biographical information appears with the subject, not the author. Genealogical information intended for private use on the internet is not included.

234   Aarne, Antti. *Verzeichnis der Märchentypen* (1910)

235   Abrahams, Roger D. *Jump-Rope Rhymes* (1969)

236   _____ and Alan Dundes. "Riddles," in Dorson[305]

237   Ahlstrom, Sydney E. *A Religious History of the American People* (1972)

238   Aikin, Jesse Bowman. *Christian Minstrel* (1847)

239   Allen, Jules Verne. "Singing Along," *New Mexico Magazine* (1935)

240   Allen, William Francis, Charles Pickard Ware, and Lucy McKim Garrison. *The Slave Songs of the United States* (1867)

241   American Heritage. *The American Heritage Dictionary of the English Language* (1973), edited by William Morris

242   Apel, Willi. *Harvard Dictionary of Music* (1972)

243   _____ and Ralph T. Daniel. *The Harvard Brief Dictionary of Music* (1961)

244   Ariès, Phillipe. *Centuries of Childhood* (1962)

245   Armitage, M. Theresa. *Singing School Series. Our Songs* (1939)

246   Baccus, Bob. "Old Log Hut," *Old Towne Brass* website

247   Baird, Forrest J. *Music Skills for Recreation Leaders* (1963)

248   Baker, Belle. Oliver B. Pollak, "Belle Baker, 1896-1957," *Jewish Women's Archive* website

249   Balakirev, Mily Alexeyevich. *Sbornik Russkikh Narodnikh Pesen* (1866)

250   Balch, Ernest Berkley. Letter to Porter Sargent, quoted in volume 5 of his *The Handbook of Private Schools*, reprinted on *Balchipedia* website

251   Baltzell, E. Digby. *Philadelphia Gentlemen* (1958)

252   Baring-Gould, Sabine, H. Fleetwood Sheppard, and F. W. Bussell. *Songs of the West* (1905)

253   Barnet, Sylvan, *et alia. A Dictionary of Literary Terms* (1960)

254 Barry, Phillips. Work summarized by D. K. Wilgus in *Anglo-American Folksong Scholarship since 1898* (1959)

255 Barton, William Eleazar. "Recent Negro Melodies," *New England Magazine*, February 1899

256 _____. *Old Plantation Hymns* (1899)

257 Baskerville, Charles Read. *The Elizabethan Jig, and Related Song Drama* (1929)

258 Baynes, A. H. "German Student Life," *Fraser's Magazine for Town and Country* 24:630-645:1881

259 Beattie, John W., *et alia. The Golden Book of Favorite Songs* (1923 edition)

260 Best, Elsdon. "The Diversions of the Whare Tapere: Some Account of the Various Games, Amusements, and Trials of Skill Practised by the Maori in Former Times," *Transactions and Proceedings of the Royal Society of New Zealand* 34:34-69:1901

261 _____. *Games and Pastimes of the Maori* (1925)

262 Blesh, Rudi and Harriet Janis. *They All Played Ragtime* (1971)

263 Boatner, Edward. *Spirituals Old and New* (1927)

264 Böhme, Franz Magnus. *Deutsches Kinderlied und Kinderspiel* (1897)

265 Bohn, Dennis A. "Environmental Effects on the Speed of Sound," *Journal of the Audio Engineering Society* 36:223-231:1988

266 Bolton, Whitney French. Conversations, 1977-1978

267 Botkin, Benjamin A. *The American Play-Party Song* (1937)

268 Brand, Oscar. "Old King Cole," *Sing Out!* (1962)

269 Brednich, Rolf Wilhelm. Letter, 20 December 1976

270 Brenan, Gerald. *South from Granada* (1957)

271 Brendle, Thomas R. and William S. Troxell. "Pennsylvania German Songs," in Korson[395]

272 Brewer, E. Cobham. *Dictionary of Phrase and Fable* (1898)

273 Britten, Evelyn Barrett. *Chronicles of Saratoga* (1959)

274 _____. "Writer Gathers Old Data on Grand Union Hotel," *Chronicles of Saratoga*, 26 September 1952, cited by Wikipedia, "Grand Union Hotel"[550]

275 Brown, Albert M. *The Camp Wise Story* (1989), edited by David B. Guralnik and Judah Rubinstein

276 Brown, Frank C. *The Frank C. Brown Collection of North Carolina Folklore*, volume 1, section of games and rhymes edited by Paul G. Brewster (1952)

277 _____. _____, volume 3, *Folk Songs from North Carolina*, edited by Henry M. Belden and Arthur Palmer Hudson (1952)

278 _____. _____, volume 5, *The Music of the Ballads*, edited by Jan Philip Schinhan (1952)

279 Brunvand, Jan Harold. *The Study of American Folklore* (1968)

280 Chambers, Robert. *Popular Rhymes of Scotland* (1842)

281 Chapin, John Edward. Anonymous, Neenah, Wisconsin, *The Boys' Brigade History and Songbook* (no date, through 1963)

282 Chappell, William. *The Ballad Literature and Popular Music of the Olden Time* (1859)

283 Chateaubriand, François-René de. *Itinéraire de Paris à Jérusalem* (1811)

284 Cheales, Alan B. *Proverbial Folk-Lore* (1876)

285 Cheley, Frank. Anonymous, "Cheley History," Cheley Colorado Camps website

286 Child, Francis James. *The English and Scottish Popular Ballads*, ten volumes (1882-1898)

287 _____. "Advertisement to Part I" (1882), in Child[286]

288 Chute, William Edward. *A Genealogy and History of the Chute Family in America* (1894)

289 Coffin, Tristram Potter. *The British Traditional Ballad in North America* (1950)

290 Cohan, George M. Anonymous obituary, *The New York Times*, 6 November 1942

291 _____. Anonymous review of *Fifty Miles from Boston* in *The Lewiston Daily*, Maine, 17 April 1908

292 _____. Anonymous review of *Fifty Miles from Boston* in *Munsey's Magazine* (1908)

293 Cohen, Mike. *101 Plus 5 Folk Songs for Camp* (1966)

294 Coleman, Satis N. *Creative Music for Children* (1922)

295 Coleman, Z. A. Sources include Warren, Indiana, *Weekly*, 29 September 1881; Winfield, Kansas, *Courier*, 19 January 1882; Waterloo, Iowa, *Courier*, 3 April 1889; Lynn Abbott and Doug Seroff, *Out of Sight* (2002)

296 Coles, Samuel B. *Preacher with a Plow* (1957)

297 Collins, Arthur. Jim Walsh, "Favorite Pioneer Recording Artists: Arthur Collins," *Hobbies*, November 1942, cited by Gracyk[356]

298 Czerwinski, Judith. Illustrations for *Vanilla and Chocolate*, available from the author, Mariam Luebs, at 236 Parsons Road, Camillus, New York, 13031. The price, including shipping, is $5.50

299 _____. Information from Linda Regan Knoblauch (1976); Susan Brooks, Deborah Hooker, Bonnie Kisselstein, Mariam Marikar Luebs, Gene Wichmann (2013)

300 Davies, John and Nigel Jenkins. *The Welsh Academy Encyclopaedia of Wales* (2008), cited by Wikipedia, "Music of Wales"[550]

301 Davison, Archibald T. "Hymn, English," revised by Leonard Ellinwood, in Apel[242]

302 Densmore, Frances. *Chippewa Music* (1910)

303 Dick, James C. *The Songs of Robert Burns and Notes on Scottish Songs by Robert Burns* (1903)

304 Dickie, Mary Stevens. *Singing Pathways* (1929)

305 Dorson, Richard M. *Folklore and Folklife* (1972)

306 Duell, Orpha K. and Richard C. Anderson. "Pitch Discrimination among Primary School Children," *Journal of Educational Psychology* 58:315-318:1967, cited by Marilyn Pflederer Zimmerman, *Musical Characteristics of Children* (1971)

307 Dundes, Alan. "The Henny-Penny Phenomenon: A Study of Folk Phonological Esthetics in American Folk Speech," *Southern Folklore Quarterly* 38:1-9:1974

308 _____. *The Study of Folklore* (1965)

309 Dykema, Peter, *et alia. Twice 55 Community Songs* (1947)

310 _____. *Twice 55 Games with Music* (1924)

311 Eisenberg, Larry. *It's Me, O Lord* (1992)

312 Eldridge, Annetta Byers and Ruth Anderson Eldridge Richardson. Biographical information from Heather Lyle (2013)

313 Ellen. Comments on "Swiss Navy," *Mudcat* website, 24 October 2011

314 Eltis, David, Philip Morgan, and David Richardson. "Agency and Diaspora in Atlantic History: Reassessing the African Contribution to Rice Cultivation in the Americas," *The American Historical Review* 112:1328-1358:2007

315 Emmett, Daniel Decatur. C. B. Galbreath, *Daniel Decatur Emmett, Author of "Dixie"* (1904)

316 _____. M. Mercedes Murray, "Maryland and Pennsylvania Emmetts and Some Descendants," Maryland Genealogical Society *Bulletin* 42:338-359:2001

317 _____. H. Ogden Wintermute, *Daniel Decatur Emmett* (1955)

318 Emrich, Duncan. *Folklore on the American Land* (1972)

319 _____. *The Nonsense Book* (1974)

320 _____. *The Whim-Wham Book* (1975)

321 Erickson, Robert. *Sound Structure in Music* (1975)

322 Erikson, Erik. "Eight Ages of Man," in *Childhood and Society* (1963)

323 Erk, Ludwig and Franz Magnus Böhme. *Deutscher Liederhort* (1893-1894)

324 Faust, Albert Bernhardt. *The German Element in the United States*, volume 1 (1909)

325 Fletcher, Alice C. *Indian Story and Song from North America* (1900)

326 _____. *A Study of Omaha Indian Music* (1893)

327 Flexner, Stuart Berg and Harold Wentworth. *Dictionary of American Slang* (1960)

328 Flickinger, Robert Elliott. *The Choctaw Freedmen* (1914)

329 Ford, Ira W. *Traditional Music of America* (1940)

330 Fowke, Edith. "'The Red River Valley' Re-Examined," *Western Folklore* 23:163-171:1964

331 _____. *Ring Around the Moon* (1977)

332 _____. *Sally Go Round the Sun* (1969)

333 _____ and Richard Johnston. *Folksongs of Canada* (1954)

334 French, Stanley. "The Cemetery as Cultural Institution: The Establishment of Mount Auburn and the 'Rural Cemetery' Movement," *The American Quarterly* 26:37-59:1974

335 Freud, Sigmund. *Wit and Its Relation to the Unconscious* (1916), in *The Basic Writings of Sigmund Freud*, edited and translated by A. A. Brill (1938)

336 Frey, Howard. "Conestoga Wagoners," in Korson[395]

337 Frey, Marvin and Helen Frey. *God's Shining Jewels* (2008)

338 Fuld, James J. *The Book of World-Famous Music* (2000 edition)

339 Gardner, Emelyn E. "Some Counting Out Rhymes in Michigan," *Journal of American Folklore* 31:521-536:1918

340 _____. "Some Play-Party Games in Michigan," *Journal of American Folklore* 33:91-133:1920

341 Gehrkens, Karl Wilson. *Music in the Grade Schools* (1934)

342 Georgia Institute of Technology. "Georgia Tech Songs Collection," school website

343 Gesell, Arnold and Frances L. Ilg. *The Child from Five to Ten* (1946)

344 _____, _____, and Louise Bates Ames. *Youth: The Years from Ten to Sixteen* (1956)

345 Gibson, H. W. *Recreational Programs for Summer Camps* (1938)

346 Giddings, Thaddeus P., *et alia*. *Music Education Series*. *Elementary Music* (1923)

347 Gilbert, Ronnie. Interview with Kate Weigand, Smith College archives, 10 March 2004

348 Gilchrist, Anne G. "Sacred Parodies of Secular Folk Songs," *Journal of the English Folk Dance and Song Society* 3:157-82:1938

349 Giraldus Cambrensis. *Descriptio Cambriæ* (1194), codified by James F. Dimock in *Giraldi Cambrensis Opera: Itinerarium Kambriae et Descriptio Kambriae* (1868), translated by Lewis Thorpe as *The Description of Wales* (1978)

350 Glover, Raymond F. *The Hymnal 1982 Companion* (1990)

351 Goethe, Johann Wolfgang von. *Egmont* (1788), translated by Michael Hamburger (1959)

352 Gomme, Alice Bertha. *The Traditional Games of England, Scotland, and Ireland* (1894)

353 Gordon, Robert W. Library of Congress, Archives of American Folksong

354 Goss, Charles Frederic. *Cincinnati, the Queen City, 1788-1912* (1912)

355 Govier, Gordon. "Campus Ministries Sign Agreement," InterVarsity Christian Fellowship news release, 14 February 2011

356 Gracyk, Tim. *Popular American Recording Pioneers, 1895-1925* (2000) with Frank Hoffmann

357 Grand Union Hotel, Saratoga Springs, New York. Advertisement, 15 April 1877, cited by Wikipedia, "Grand Union Hotel"[550]

358 Graves, Robert. *The White Goddess* (1948)

359 *Grove's Dictionary of Music and Musicians*, second edition edited by Fuller Maitland between 1904-1910. Comments on "Malbrouck" quoted in "Ancient Origin of a Famous Song," *Etude*, August 1910

360 _____. 1937 revision of 1927 edition edited by H. C. Colles. Anonymous, "Song: Germany"

361 Hale, Sarah Josepha. *Liberia* (1853)

362 _____. "Mary's Lamb," *Juvenile Miscellany*, September 1830

363 Hall, Jacob Henry. *Biography of Gospel Song and Hymn Writers* (1914)

364 Halliwell, James Orchard. *The Nursery Rhymes of England* (1842)

365 _____. _____ (1844 edition)

366 _____. *Popular Rhymes and Nursery Tales* (1849)

367 Harbin, E. O. *Paradology, Songs of Fun and Fellowship* (1927)

368 _____. Anonymous, "Introducing Our New Associates," *The Epworth Era*, volume 26 (1919)

369 Hickerson, Joe. Conversations, 1976

370 Higginson, Thomas Wentworth. "Negro Spirituals," *The Atlantic Monthly* 19:685-694:1867

371 Hoffmann von Fallersleben, August Heinrich and Karl Hermann Prahl. *Unsere Volkstümlichen Lieder* (1900)

372 Holbrook, Leona. CRS *Song Sampler #3*

373 _____. Anonymous, "Preliminary Register of the Leona Holbrook (1909-1980) Collection, 1927-1991," Brigham Young University

374 _____. Edward S. Henderson observed influence of Amelia Earhart (2013)

375 Holcomb, Larry Nial. *History of the Cooperative Recreation Service* (1972)

376 *Holy Bible*. King James translation (1611)

377 Honoré, Lockwood. *Popular College Songs* (1891)

378 _____. Obituary, *Harvard Alumni Bulletin*, 1917, signed by W. R.

379 Hood, Oliver. Theodore Pappas, "The 'Theft' of an American Classic," *Chronicles: A Magazine of American Culture*, November 1990

380 Huddleston, John. *Killing Ground: The Civil War and the Changing American Landscape* (2002), cited by Wikipedia, "American Civil War"[550]

381 Jabbour, Alan. Liner notes (1971), *American Fiddle Tunes* (AFS L62)

382 Jackson, George Pullen. *White Spirituals in the Southern Uplands* (1933)

383 Jacobs, Mary. "Wesley, Misquoted - Methodism's Founder Gets a Little Too Much Credit," *The United Methodist Register*, 16 September 2011

384 Jakobson, Roman. *Child Language Aphasia and Phonological Universals* (1968)

385 _____. "The Sound Laws of Child Language and Their Place in General Phonology," in *Studies in Child Language* (1971)

386 Juba. Playbill for Pell's Serenaders and Boz's Juba, 21 December 1848, reproduced by Wikipedia, "Master Juba"[550]

387 Kaufman, David. *Shul with a Pool* (1999)

388 Kennedy, Jimmy. J. J. Kennedy, *The Man Who Wrote the Teddy Bears' Picnic* (2011)

389   Kidson, Frank. *75 British Nursery Rhymes* (1904)

390   _____. "Welsh Music," in *Grove's Dictionary*[359]

391   King, William. G. A. Aitken, "Arbuthnot and Lesser Prose Writers," in *The Cambridge History of English and American Literature*, volume 9, edited by A. W. Ward and A. R. Waller (1912)

392   Kleber, Henry. Anonymous biographical note, *Pittsburgh Music History* website

393   Knapp, Mary and Herbert Knapp. *One Potato, Two Potato* (1976)

394   Koestler, Arthur. *The Act of Creation* (1964)

395   Korson, George. *Pennsylvania Songs and Legends* (1949)

396   Krohn, Kaarle. *Folklore Methodology*, translated by Roger L. Welsch (1971)

397   Lambert, Louis. *Chants et Chansons Populaires du Languedoc* (1906)

398   LaPrise, Larry. Anonymous biography, Rovi Corporation, *All Music* website

399   Laws, G. Malcolm, Junior. *American Balladry from British Broadsides* (1957)

400   _____. *Native American Balladry* (1954)

401   Leach, MacEdward. "Folk Etymology," in Leach[402]

402   Leach, Maria. *Funk and Wagnall's Dictionary of Folklore, Mythology and Legend* (1971)

403   Leadbelly [Huddie Ledbetter], John A. Lomax, and Alan Lomax. *Leadbelly: The Library of Congress Recordings* (Electra EKL 301/2)

404   Leckrone, Janet Grady. Conversations

405   Leggett, Conaway and Company. *The History of Wyandot County Ohio* (1884)

406   Leisy, James F. *Abingdon Song Kit* (1957)

407   Lerner, Alan Jay. Gene Lees, *The Musical Worlds of Lerner and Loewe* (2005)

408   Lester, Margery J. Letter quoted in CRS *Song Sampler #5* (1956)

409   Levine, June and Gene Gordon. *Tales of Wo-Chi-Ca* (2002)

410   Levy, Lester S. Personal communication to James J. Fuld, cited by Fuld[338]

411   Lewis, K. P. Collection, included in Brown[277]

412   Li, Fangfang, Jan Edwards, and Mary E. Beckman. "Contrast and Covert Contrast: The Phonetic Development of Voiceless Sibilant Fricatives in English and Japanese Toddlers," *Journal of Phonetics* 37:111-124:2009

413 Liberman, Mark. "Hay Foot Straw Foot," *Language Log* website, 29 June 2010

414 Logan, Virginia Knight. Edgar Rubey Harlan, *A Narrative History of the People of Iowa* (1931)

415 Lorenzkowski, Barbara. *Sounds of Ethnicity: Listening to German North America, 1850-1914* (2010)

416 Lytle, Beatrice. Doris L. Gass, "My Aunt Beatrice Lytle," Stillwater, Oklahoma, *NewsPress* 7 July 2007

417 Lytle, Sharon and Bijan C. Bayne. Exchange on Donovan's Jubilee Singers, *AfriGeneas Genealogy and History Forum* website, 13 February 2003

418 Mackay, Charles. *A Dictionary of Lowland Scotch* (1888)

419 Macleod, Norman and Daniel Dewar. *A Dictionary of the Gaelic Language* (1839 edition)

420 Mahar, William John. *Behind the Burnt Cork Mask* (1999)

421 Mann, Ralph. *After the Gold Rush* (1982)

422 Martin, Gary. "Rise and Shine," *Phrase Finder* website

423 Mason, Lowell. *The Handel and Haydn Society's Collection of Church Music* (1822)

424 Matusow, Harvey. *False Witness* (1955)

425 Maybrick, Michael. Anonymous obituaries in England's *The Liverpool Daily Post*, 27 August 1913; *The Liverpool Courier*, 27 August 1913

426 McAllister, D. C. William Smythe Babcock Mathews, *A Hundred Years of Music in America* (1889)

427 McClelland, David C. *The Achieving Society* (1961)

428 McLean, Albert. *American Vaudeville as Ritual* (1965)

429 Mechem, Kirke. "Home on the Range," *Kansas Historical Quarterly* 17:313-339:1949

430 Military Order of the Loyal Legion of the United States. *Songs of the Commandery of the State of Illinois* (1894)

431 Mishler, Paul C. *Raising Reds* (1999)

432 Mitchell, A. Viola, Ida B. Crawford, and Julia D. Robberson. *Camp Counseling* (1970 edition)

433 Moorhead, Gladys Evelyn and Donald Pond. *Music of Young Children: II General Observations* (1942)

434 Morton, Jelly Roll [Ferdinand Joseph LaMothe] and Alan Lomax. Library of Congress, Archives of American Folksong recordings, transcribed by Michael Hill

435   Mosse, George K. *The Crisis of German Ideology* (1964)

436   Motherwell, William. Work summarized by Child[286]

437   Murdoch, James. *Ethnological Results of the Point Barrow Expedition* (1894)

438   Myers, Louise Kifer. *Teaching Children Music in the Elementary School* (1956)

439   Nathan, Hans. *Dan Emmett and the Rise of Early Negro Minstrelsy* (1962)

440   Nettl, Bruno. *North American Indian Musical Styles* (1954)

441   Nettl, Paul. "German Melodies in American College Songs," *The American-German Review*, June-August 1947

442   Nettleingham, Frederick Thomas. *Tommy's Tunes* (1917)

443   Newbro, Dupont Morse. Albert Nelson Marquis, *The Book of Detroiters* (1914 edition)

444   Newell, George. "If You're Sending Your Boy to Camp," *The Outlook*, 9 May 1928

445   Newell, William Wells. *Games and Songs of American Children* (1883)

446   North, Arthur Walbridge. *Camp and Camino in Lower California* (1910)

447   Northall, G. F. *English Folk-Rhymes* (1893)

448   Nye, Robert E. *Music for Elementary School Children* (1963)

449   Oinas, Felix J. "Folk Epic," in Dorson[305]

450   Olrik, Axel. "Epic Laws of Folk Narrative" (1909), translated by Jeanne P. Steager, in Dundes[308]

451   Opie, Iona and Peter Opie. *The Lore and Language of School Children* (1959)

452   _____. *The Oxford Dictionary of Nursery Rhymes* (1952)

453   _____. *The Singing Game* (1985)

454   Orlow, O. N. Anonymous obituary, "Orlow, O. N. / Salvator, Johann," Olean, New York, *Evening Herald*, 3 April 1924, transcribed by M. Rodriguez

455   *Oxford English Dictionary, The.* (1933)

456   Palmer, Roy. *Folk Songs Collected by Ralph Vaughan Williams* (1983); republished as *Bushes and Briars* (1999)

457   Parkhurst, Melissa D. *To Win the Indian Heart* (2008)

458   Parry, Joseph. Lynn Reichen, "Welsh Ironman Wrote Songs We Still Remember," *Daily Item*, 23 August 2009

459   Pattengill, Henry R. *Pat's Pick* (1905)

460   _____. *School Song Knapsack* (1899)

461 Pennsylvania Council of Churches. *Celebrate: Resources for Camping Families* (1970)

462 Perrow, E. C. "Songs and Rhymes from the South," *Journal of American Folklore* 26:123-173:1913

463 _____. _____ 28:129-190:1915

464 Petzold, Robert G. *Auditory Perceptions of Musical Sounds by Children in the First Six Grades* (1966)

465 Pflederer, Marilyn Ruth. *The Responses of Children to Musical Tasks Embodying Piaget's Principle of Conservation* (1963)

466 Phillips, Philip. *Song Pilgrimage around the World* (1880)

467 Piaget, Jean. *The Language and Thought of the Child* (1926)

468 _____. Herbert Ginsburg and Sylvia Opper, *Piaget's Theory of Intellectual Development* (1969)

469 Pinckney, Josephine. Barbara L. Bellows, *A Talent for Living: Josephine Pinckney and the Charleston Literary Tradition* (2006)

470 Piper, Edwin Ford. Anonymous overview, "Edwin Ford Piper Folklore Collection," University of Iowa, Special Collections website

471 _____. Cited by Sandburg[498]

472 Pitts, William Savage. Isabella Power, "'The Little Brown Church in the Vale:' Its Author and Inspiration," *The Annals of Iowa* 12:101-116:1921

473 Playfield, John. *The English Dancing-Master*, editions published between 1650 and 1728

474 Posen, I. Sheldon. *Song and Singing Traditions at Children's Summer Camps* (1971 master's thesis for Memorial University of Newfoundland)

475 Pound, Ezra, Hilda Doolittle, and Richard Addington. "Imagism," *Poetry*, March 1913

476 Pound, Louise. *American Ballads and Songs* (1922)

477 Randolph, Vance. *Ozark Folksongs*, volume 2, *Songs of the South and West* (1948)

478 _____. _____, volume 3, *Humorous and Play-Party Songs* (1949)

479 Reeves, James. *The Everlasting Circle* (1960)

480 Reinecke and Zesch. *Geschichte der Deutschen in Buffalo und Erie County, NY* (1898), translated by Susan Kriegbaum-Hanks as *History of the Germans in Buffalo and Erie County, N. Y.*

481 Rexford, Eben Eugene. Anonymous, "A Famous Song," *Colonist*, 11 February 1904

482   Rice, Paul. Wayne W. Daniel, "The Rice Brothers," *Journal of the American Academy for the Preservation of Old-Time Country Music*, October 1996

483   Rice, Thomas D. *Jim Crow, American*, edited by W. T. Lhamon, Junior (2003)

484   Riesman, David. *The Lonely Crowd* (1950)

485   Ritchie, Jean. On "Hey Ho," *Musickit* website

486   Roberts, Egbert. Advertisements, *The Musical Times*, 1884

487   _____. Review of a Crystal Palace Concert by R. S., *The Musical Standard*, 28 April 1883

488   Rogers, James E. *State of Columbia* (1903)

489   Rohrbough, George Elmore (father). A. W. Bowen, *Progressive Men of Western Colorado* (1905)

490   Rohrbough, Lynn. Interview in Delaware, Ohio, 1974

491   _____. *Handy Play Party Book* (1940)

492   Rohrbough, Malcolm J. *Days of Gold* (1997)

493   Rothrock, Joseph Trimbel. Anonymous, "North Mountain School of Physical Culture," *The Medical Times and Register* 207-208:22 January 1876

494   Russell, James. Frank Cullen, *Vaudeville, Old and New* (2006)

495   Rust, E. G. *Calhoun County Business Directory for 1869-1870* (1869)

496   Rutkowski, Joanne. "The Nature of Children's Singing Voices," Texas Music Educators Conference, annual meeting, 2003

497   Sachs, Curt. *World History of the Dance* (1937)

498   Sandburg, Carl. *The American Songbag* (1923)

499   Schmidt, Leigh Eric. *Holy Fairs* (1989)

500   Scroggs, W. O. Published in Perrow[462]

501   Seashore, Carl E. *Psychology of Music* (1938)

502   Seeger, Charles. "Folk Music in the Schools of a Highly Industrialized Society," *Journal of the International Folk Music Council* 5:40-44:1953

503   _____. "Singing Style," *Western Folklore* 17:3-11:1958

504   Seeger, Ruth Crawford. *American Folk Songs for Children* (1948)

505   Sharp, Cecil J. and Sabine Baring-Gould. *English Folk-Songs for Schools* (1906)

506   _____ and Charles H. Farnsworth. *Folk-songs, Chanteys, and Singing Games* (1909)

507   _____ and Herbert C. MacIlwaine. *The Morris Book* (1907)

508 _____ and Ralph Vaughan Williams. *A Selection of Collected Folk-Songs* (1908)

509 Simond, Ike. *Old Slack's Reminiscence* (1891)

510 _____. William L. Van Deburg, *Slavery and Race in American Popular Culture* (1984)

511 Smaller, Isabel Ricker. Information from Alison Melville, Elizabeth Quinlan, and Harry Smaller (2013)

512 Smith, Cecily Fox. *A Book of Shanties* (1927)

513 Society for the Preservation of Spirituals. Anonymous, "Society for the Preservation of Negro Spirituals," Kenyon College website

514 Soifer, Israel and Margaret K. *The Camper's Song Pack* (1937)

515 Southey, Robert. Burton Stevenson, *Dictionary of Proverbs* (1820), cited by Opies[452]

516 Spaeth, Sigmund. *Read 'em and Weep* (1945 edition)

517 _____. Personal communication to James J. Fuld on "Someone's in the Kitchen with Dinah," cited by Fuld[338]

518 Spasyk, George. "Sigma Sings," on Lambda Chi Alpha, Sigma Zeta chapter website, 10 August 2012

519 Spencer, Robert F. "The Eskimo of Northern Alaska," in Robert F. Spencer and Jesse D. Jennings, *The Native Americans* (1965)

520 Statten, Taylor. Anne Warner, *To Grow in the Open Air* (2010 PhD dissertation for University of Western Ontario)

521 Steel, David Warren. *The Makers of the Sacred Harp* (2010)

522 Steely, Mercedes S. *The Folk-Songs of the Ebenezer Community* (1936 master's thesis for University of North Carolina), cited by Brown[277]

523 Stowe, Harriet Beecher. Letter to her publisher, 6 February 1876, The Gilder Lehrman Institute of American History website

524 Sutherland, James M. Biography, in Edward Le Roy Rice, *Monarchs of Minstrelsy, from "Daddy" Rice to Date* (1911)

525 Sutton-Smith, Brian. *The Folkgames of Children* (1972)

526 _____. Personal note on "Lemmi Sticks," American Folklore Society meeting, 1980

527 Swift, Herman L. Jack Hobey, *Lost Boys: The Beulah Home Tragedy* (2010)

528   Sydow, C. W. von. "Folktale Studies and Philology: Some Points of View," in Laurits Bødker, *Selected Papers on Folklore* (1948), in Dundes[308]

529   Tabor, Al. Alan Balfour, "The Hokey Cokey Man," *The Hokey Cokey Man* website

530   Taylor, Archer. *English Riddles from Oral Tradition* (1951)

531   Terry, Richard Runciman. *The Shanty Book, Part II* (1926)

532   Thomas, Isaiah. *The Worcester Collection of Sacred Harmony* (1786), cited by Wikipedia, "Stoughton Musical Society"[550]

533   Thorpe, Benjamin. *Northern Mythology*, volume 2 (1851)

534   Tinkler, Robert. *James Hamilton of South Carolina* (2004)

535   Twain, Mark. "Frescoes from the Past," chapter 3, *Life on the Mississippi* (1883)

536   Vance, Thomas Franklin. *Variation in Pitch Discrimination within the Tonal Range* (1914)

537   Vincent, Sidney Z. *Personal and Professional Memoirs of a Life in Community Service* (1982), excerpted in Brown[275] as "Mid-Years at Camp Wise"

538   Vlasto, Jill. "An Elizabethan Anthology of Rounds," *Musical Quarterly* 40:222-234:1954

539   Waite, Henry Randall. *Carmina Collegensia* (1868)

540   Walker, Lewis and Benjamin C. Wilson. *Black Eden: The Idlewild Community* (2002), quotation from Charles English

541   Warshawsky, David. Manuscript autobiography, excerpted by Florence Warshawsky, in Brown[275] as "Early Days at Camp Wise"

542   Wax, Dustin M. "'Brother, Friend, Comrade': The Workman's Circle and Jewish Culture, 1900-1930," Wax website

543   Wells, John Barnes. Anonymous obituary, *Catskill Mountain News*, 16 August 1935

544   Wheatley, Henry. *Dictionary of Reduplicated Words in the English Language* (1865), cited by Dundes[307]

545   White, Benjamin Franklin. William J. Reynolds, "B. F. White: The Sacred Harp Man," *Away Here in Texas*, March 1997

546   White, Elliot. Anonymous, "Camp Nejecho," New Jersey Anglican Diocese website

547   White, Newman I. *American Negro Folk-Songs* (1928)

548   Whitson, Beth Slater. "My Dreams Came True," *True Confessions*, February 1925

549   Wickes, E. M. "The Power of Ballads," *The Magazine Maker*, April 1913

550   Wikipedia. Used to verify names, dates, and other facts

551   Williamson, John. *The Oak King, the Holly King, and the Unicorn* (1986)

552   Winn, Marie. *The Fireside Book of Children's Songs* (1966)

553   _____. *The Fireside Book of Fun and Game Songs* (1974)

554   Wirsing, Dale R. *Builders, Brewers, and Burghers* (1977), cited by Karen Pearson and Elizabeth Holmes, "German Influence on the Northwest," University of Washington website

555   Withers, Carl. *A Rocket in My Pocket* (1948)

556   Wittke, Carl. *Tambo and Bones* (1930)

557   Wolfe, Tom. "The 'Me' Decade and the Third Great Awakening," *New York Magazine*, 23 August 1976

558   Wood, Evelyn Hopson. *Camp and Picnic Warbler* (1929)

559   _____. Information from Don Eggars (2008), Diane Owen Jordan, Sheff Owen (2013); Robert Eldon Bingham, *Wieuca: God's People on Mission* (1994)

560   Wood, Thomas. *The Oxford Song Book* (1928)

561   Zanzig, Augustus Delafield. *Music in American Life* (1932)

562   _____. *Singing America* (1940)

E. Publishing Histories
for Case Studies

The Mermaid

Earliest citation: *The Glasgow Lasses Garland*, the second piece, British Museum, 11621.c.3 (68), "Newcastle, 1765?"

-1849

Broadsides: Anonymous, "The Mermaid," De Marsan broadside; "The Mermaid," Deming broadside (1838)

   Britain: Anonymous, "The Mermaid," J. Arthur broadside; J. and H. Baird broadside; Birt broadside; Catnach broadside 53; Gilbert broadside 77; Pitts broadside; Ross broadside 77; H. Such broadside; "Sailor's Caution," Peterhead broadside (1815)

Commercial: Anonymous, *Forecastle Songster* (1849); *Forget-Me-Not Songster* (1835, 1842); *Pearl Songster* (1846); *Singer's Journal*, volume 1; *Uncle Sam's Naval and Patriotic Songster*

   Britain: Maria Callcott and William Hutchins, *The Child's Own Singing Book* (1843)

Folklore collections:

   Britain: William Motherwell, *Minstrelsy, Ancient and Modern* (1827)

1850-1899

Schools: Charles Livermore, *The Abridged Academy Song-Book* (1898)

Colleges: Case (1899), Columbia (1876), Delta Upsilon (1884), Princeton (1882), Psi Upsilon (1891), Rutgers (1885), Union (1895), University of Pennsylvania (1879), Yale (1889, 1893), Zeta Psi (1897)

Commercial: Anonymous, *Slam Bang Songster* (1870); *We Won't Go Home until Morning Songster* (1869); Samuel Chester Andrews, *The American College Songster* (1876); William Hill, *Student Songs* (1883); Lockwood Honoré, *Popular College Songs* (1891); Marsh, *Forecastle Songster*; *New Book of a Thousand Songs for the Million*; Emil Schwab, *The Best College*

Songs (1897); Laura Alexandrine Smith, *Music of the Waters* (1888); Henry Randall Waite, *Carmina Collegensia* (1868); *Student Life in Song* (1879)

> Britain: Anonymous, *Sailing Trade Garland*; H. Such broadside; John Ashton, *Real Sailor-Songs* (1891); Patrick Miller, *The Scottish Student's Song-book* (1891)

Folklore collections: Francis James Child, *The English and Scottish Popular Ballads* (1898); Edith Cutting, "A New York Songbag," *NYFQ* (1948); Harold W. Thompson, *A Pioneer Songster, 1841-1856* (1958)

> Britain: Sabine Baring-Gould, *English Minstrelsie*, volume 6 (1896); William Chappell, *The Ballad Literature and Popular Music of the Olden Time* (1859); *Old English Ditties*, volume 1 (189-); J. Woodfall Ebsworth, *The Roxburghe Ballads* (1896); William Henry Long, *A Dictionary of the Isle of Wight Dialect* (1886); Alfred Williams, *Street Ballads and Songs*
>
> Canada: Thomas Bayne, "Is Friday an Unlucky Day?" *NQ* (1883)

1900-1919

Colleges: Alfred (1902), Bowdoin (1906), Carleton (1919), Chi Psi (1915), Columbia (1904), Dickinson (1910), Grove City College (1913), Harvard (1913), Massachusetts Agricultural College (1912), New Hampshire College (1913), Ohio State (1900, 1916), Ohio University (1915), Pennsylvania State (1906), Rensselaer Polytechnic (1913), Sigma Kappa (1907), Simpson (1910), Tufts (1915), University of Minnesota (1911), University of Vermont (1913), University of Virginia (1906), Williams (1910), Zeta Psi (1903)

Commercial: Anonymous, *College Songs* (1907); *Heart Songs* (1910); *The Most Popular College Songs* (1906); Ralph L. Baldwin and E. W. Newton, *Standard College Songs* (1914); S. M. Bixby, et alia, *Bixby's Home Songs* (1909); David B. Chamberlain and Karl P. Harrington, *Songs of All the Colleges* (1906); Clifton Johnson, *Songs Every One Should Know* (1908); Luce, *Luce's Naval Songs* (1902); G. C. Noble, *The Most Popular Home Songs* (1913); Noble and Gilbert Clifford, *The Most Popular Songs for Every Occasion* (1912); George Rosey, *College Songs* (1909); Henry Randall Waite, *College Songs* (1906)

Britain: Anonymous, *Songs that Never Grow Old* (1913); Percy C. Buck, *The Oxford Song Book* (1916); H. Walford Davies, *The Fellowship Song Book* (1915); W. G. McNaught, *Sixteen National Songs*; Charles Villiers Stanford, *The National Song Book* (1906)

Folklore collections: Phillips Barry, "Folk-Music in America," *JAF* (1909); "Traditional Ballads in New England," *JAF* (1905); Henry M. Belden, "Five Old Country Ballads," *JAF* (1912); G. L. Kittredge, "Ballads and Songs," *JAF* (1917); "Various Ballads," *JAF* (1913); Josephine McGill, *Folk Songs of the Kentucky Mountains* (1917); Louise Pound, "Folk Songs of Nebraska and the Central West," *NASP* (1914); Henry W. Shoemaker, *North Pennsylvania Minstrelsy* (1919); Virginia Folklore Society *Bulletin* numbers 2-5

Britain: Edmondstone Duncan, *The Minstrelsy of England* (1905); H. E. D. Hammond, "The Mermaid," *JFSS* (1907); Alfred Edward Moffat and Frank Kidson, *The Minstrelsy of England* (1901); Christopher Stone, *Sea Songs and Ballads* (1906); E. T. Sweeting, "The Mermaid," *JFSS* (1907); E. T. Wedmore, "The Mermaid," *JFSS* (1907)

1920-1939

Organizations:

Boy Scouts: 105 (1938), 106 (1939)

Boys Scouts, England: 111 (1924), 112 (1925)

Girl Scouts: 168 (1929), 170 (1936)

Intercollegiate Outing Club Association: 203 (1938)

Religious groups:

Jewish: Israel Soifer and Margaret K. Soifer, *The Camper's Song Pack* (1937)

Schools: Randall J. Condon, Helen S. Leavitt and Elbridge W. Newton, *Assembly Songs and Choruses* (1929)

Colleges: Amherst (1926), College of Saint Elizabeth (1930), Columbia (1924), Marietta College (1926), Ohio State (1923), Princeton (1931), Rutgers (1920), Saint Lawrence (1921), Trinity College (1939), US Naval Academy (1926), Williams (1933)

Broadsides:

Britain: Anonymous, "The Mermaid," Harkness broadside 146

Commercial: Kenneth S. Clark, *The "Everybody Sing" Book* (1930, 1932); Nicholas De Vore, *Fifty Famous Favorites* (1930); Sigmund Spaeth,

Read 'em and Weep (1927); Katharine Stanley-Brown, *Song Book of the American Spirit* (1927); David Stevens and Peter William Dykema, *Sing!* (1937)

> Britain: Anonymous, *Francis and Day's Camp Fire and Fireside Song Book* (193-); Sydney Baynes, *Boosey's Community Song Book* (1927); H. Walford Davies, *The New Fellowship Songbook* (1931); Frederick J. Davis and Ferris Tozer, *Sailor's Songs or "Chanties"* (192-); Desmond MacMahon, *The New National and Folk Song Book* (1938); Ernest Newton, *The Ernest Newton Community Songbook,* (1927); Gerrard Williams and Gibson Young, *Community Singers Program #3* (1925); Thomas Wood, *The Oxford Song Book* (1928)

Folklore collections: Phillips Barry, Fannie H. Eckstrom and Mary W. Smith, *British Ballads from Maine* (1929); Lewis W. Chappell, *Folk Songs of Roanoke and the Albemarle* (1939); Josiah H. Combs, *Folk-Songs of the Southern United States* (1925); John Harrington Cox, *Folk-Songs of the South* (1925); Arthur K. Davis, *Traditional Ballads of Virginia* (1929); Mellinger Henry, *Folk Songs from the Southern Highlands* (1938); Arthur Palmer Hudson, *Folk Songs of Mississippi and Their Background* (1936); *Specimens of Mississippi Folklore* (1928); Mabel Major, "British Ballads in Texas," *TFSP* (1932); Louise Pound, *American Ballads and Songs* (1922); Dorothy Scarborough, *Songcatcher in the Southern Mountains* (1937); Cecil J. Sharp and Maud Karpeles, *English Folk Songs from the Southern Appalachians* (1932); Earl J. Stout, *Folklore from Iowa* (1936); *The Focus* volumes 3, 4; Virginia Folk Lore Society *Bulletin* numbers 8-10

> Britain: Gavin Greig and Alexander Keith, *Last Leaves of Traditional Ballads and Airs* (1925); John Ord, *The Bothy Songs and Ballads* (1930); Owen Alfred Williams, *Folk Songs of the Upper Thames* (1924)

> Canada: W. Roy MacKenzie, *Ballads and Folk Songs from Nova Scotia* (1928)

1940-1959

Organizations:

> Boy Scouts: 107 (1941)
> Girl Scouts: 176 (1949), 180 (1957)
> Intercollegiate Outing Club Association: 204 (1948), 205 (1955)
> Young Men's Christian Association: 213 (1951)

Religious groups:
  Methodist groups: James F. Leisy, *Let's All Sing* (1959)
Schools: *Birchard Music Series*, Kindergarten (1958); *Music for Living Series*, Grade One (1956)
  Canada: Ethel A. Kinley, *A Song Book* (1940)
Colleges: Hamilton College (1953), Princeton (1940), U. S. Naval Academy (1943, 1956), Zeta Psi (1958)
Commercial: Joe Mitchell Chapple, *Heart Songs Dear to the American People* (1950); Warren S. Freeman and Helen S. Leavitt, *Songs To Sing* (1943); George Goodwin, *Song Dex Treasury of Humorous and Nostalgic Songs* (1956); Alexander Milton Kramer, *Salty Sea Songs and Chanteys* (1943); John A. Lomax, *Our Singing Country* (1941); Edgar A. Palmer, *G. I. Songs* (1944); Sigmund Spaeth, *Read 'em and Weep* (1945); *Sigmund Spaeth's Song Session* (1958); U. S. Navy, *Navy Song Book* (1958)
    Britain: Felton Rapley, *Chappell's Community Song Book #2* (1955); Charles Villiers Stanford and Geoffrey Shaw, *The New National Song Book* (1958); Ralph Vaughan Williams and A. L. Lloyd, *The Penguin Book of English Folk Songs* (1959); Leslie Woodgate, *The Penguin Song Book* (1951)
  Canada: Albert Miller, *Folksongs for Young Folk* (1957)
Folklore collections: Tristram P. Coffin, *The British Traditional Ballad in North America* (1950); Henry M. Belden, *Ballads and Songs Collected by the Missouri Folk-Lore Society* (1940); Benjamin A. Botkin, *A Treasury of New England Folklore* (1947); Frank C. Brown, *Collection of North Carolina Folklore*, volume 2 (1952), volume 4 (1952); Alton C. Morris, *Folksongs of Florida* (1958); Ruth Ann Musick, "Ballads and Folksongs from West Virginia: Part II," *JAF* (1957); "Folklore in and near Kirksville, Missouri" (mss); "The Old Album of William A. Larkin," *JAF* (1947); Vance Randolph, *Ozark Folk Songs*, volume 1 (1950); Harold W. Thompson, *Body, Boots and Britches* (1940)
    Britain: Margaret Dean-Smith, *Guide to the English Folk Song Collections, 1822-1952* (1954)
    Canada: Helen Creighton and Doreen H. Senior, *Traditional Songs from Nova Scotia* (1950)

1960-1979
Organizations:
  Girl Scouts: 184 (1973)

Intercollegiate Outing Club Association: 206 (1960)

Schools: *Growing with Music Series*, Grade Two (1970), Grade Five (1970); *Music for Young America Series*, Grade Six (1966); *This Is Music for Today Series*, Grade Six (1971)

Colleges: Princeton (1968)

Commercial: Mike Cohen, *101 Plus 5 Folk Songs for Camp* (1966); Charles Hansen, *400 Super Song Fest #2* (1973); Ellen Jane Lorenz, *Men's Get Together Songs* (1962); Frank Lynn, *Songs for Swingin' Housemothers* (1961); John Jacob Niles, *The Ballad Book of John Jacob Niles* (1960-1961); Peggy Seeger, *Folk Songs of Peggy Seeger* (1964); Irwin Silber and Fred Silber, *Folksinger's Wordbook* (1973); Jerry Silverman, *Jerry Silverman's Folk Song Encyclopedia, Volume Two* (1975); David Stevens and Peter William Dykema, *Sing!* (1960); Wanda Wilson Whitman, *Songs that Changed the World* (1969); Marie Winn, *The Fireside Book of Fun and Game Songs* (1974)

Britain: Percy C. Buck, *The Oxford Nursery Song Book* (1961)

Folklore collections: Bertrand Harris Bronson, *The Traditional Tunes of the Child Ballads* (1972); Arthur Kyle Davis, Junior, *More Traditional Ballads from Virginia* (1960); Duncan Emrich, *American Folk Poetry* (1974); Helen Hartness Flanders, *Ancient Ballads Traditionally Sung in New England* (1965); Frederick Pease Harlow, *Chanteying aboard American Ships* (1962); Stan Hugill, *Shanties from the Seven Seas* (1961); Ethel Moore and Chauncey O. Moore, *Ballads and Folksongs of the Southwest* (1964); Charles A. Williams and Mabel Williams, "Tunes of Old Ballads and Folksongs" (mss, 1963)

Canada: Helen Creighton, *Maritime Folk Songs* (1961)

Recordings:

Commercial: Paul Clayton, *Whaling and Sailing Songs from the Days of Moby Dick* (1956); Hermes Nye, *Anglo-American Folk Songs*; Mitt Okun, *Every Inch a Sailor*; John Runge, *Concert of English Folk Songs*; Peggy Seeger, *Folksongs and Ballads*

Early country: Ernest V. Stoneman, "The Ragin Sea, How It Roars"

Archive collections:

Harvard University: Phillips Barry, George Kinloch, broadsides

Indiana University: Joan Fulton, Martha Jackson Stocker, Marjorie Morrice

United States Library of Congress, Archives of American Folksong:
Emma Dusenbury, A. J. Ford, Elizabeth Walker Ford, Robert W.
Gordon, Bascom Lamar Lunsford, Liza Place, Warren Roberts,
Ann Volkmann
University of Oregon: Kathleen Craig, Gary Tepfer
University of Virginia: Winston Wilkinson
Utah State University: June Rushing Leibfarth
Vanderbilt University: Mildred Haun, *Cooke County Ballads and Songs*
(1936)
Wayne State University: William Daniel Doebler
Britain:
Cambridge University, Clare College: Cecil J. Sharp
Kings College, Aberdeen: Gavin Greig
Plymouth Public Library: Sabine Baring-Gould
Cecil Sharp House: Duncan Edmondstone, "Folk-Song Airs of
the North East"
Society of Antiquities, Newcastle Upon Tyne: James Telfer, "Mr.
Telfer's Tunes"

Personal song books:
Patricia Averill, Nancy Bryant, Charlotte Duff

Camp song books:
Kitanniwa: 1974
CFG other: Kirby, Mawavi, Neewahlu, Zanika Lache 1971
Girls Midwest: Watervliet
Other: Brooklyn BSA camps 1929, Manhattan Troop 582 (BSA),
Mendham, NJ BSA, Surprise Lake, Treasure Island

Field recordings:
CFG Other: Hidden Valley

Single Verse as "Gallant Ship" Game

Earliest citation: Alice Bertha Gomme, *Traditional Games of England,
Scotland and Ireland* (1894-1898)

1900-1989

Schools: C. Ward Crampton and Mary Wollaston Wood, *Song Play Book* (1917, 1922, 1924); Dorothy La Salle, *Rhythms and Dances for Elementary Schools* (1951); Chester Geppert Marsh, *Singing Games and Drills* (1925)

Commercial: Nancy Langstaff and John Langstaff, *Jim along Josie* (1970)
Britain: Anonymous, *Kerrs' Guild of Play* (1912); Alice Bertha Gomme and Cecil J. Sharp, *Children's Singing Games* (1912); Lavina Edna Walter, *Old English Singing Games* (1926)

Folklore collections: Benjamin A. Botkin, *The American Play Party* (1937)
Britain: Annie G. Gilchrist and Lucie Broadwood, "Notes on Children's Game-Songs," *JFFS* (1915); Alice Gillington, *Old Hampshire Singing Games* (1910); Robert Craig Maclagan, *The Games and Diversions of Argyleshire* (1901); Iona Opie and Peter Opie, *The Singing Game* (1985)

References to "Sir Patrick Spens" Mentioned in Text

Folklore collections:
Britain: George Kinloch manuscript (Child 58P); William Motherwell manuscripts (Child 58C, E, F), William Motherwell notebook (Child 58L)

Reports from Individuals

Reports	Midwest	Other	Total	% MW	% Other	% Total
Kitanniwa	8		8	.50		.50
CFG	4	9	13	.33	.20	.22
Girls	14	19	33	.48	.30	.36
Coed Girls	1	2	3	.13	.07	.08
Boys	2	2	4	.14	.05	.08
Totals	30	38	68	.38	.22	.27

Total numbers of individuals who know "The Mermaid" and percent of those reports within entire sample. Sample numbers on last page of Publishing Histories.

Notes on Sources

Thomas Bayne was probably Thomas Wilson Bayne (1845-1931), headmaster of Larchfield Academy, Helensburgh, Dumbarton, Scotland.

Mrs. Notman may have been Miss Buchanan of Crofthead, a cotton mill settlement near Neilstoun, East Renfrewshire, Scotland.

Mrs. Charles A. Rich may have been Perley Pierce who married Charles Alonzo Rich in 1882. The New York architect retired to Charlottesville, Virginia.

The Long Lake camp may have been a YMCA camp, O. C. Kimball, located in Hillsdale County, Michigan.

Journal Codes

JAF: Journal of American Folklore
JFSS: Journal of the Folk-Song Society
NASP: Nebraska Academy of Society. Publications
NQ: Notes and Queries
NYFQ: New York Folklore Quarterly
TFSP: Texas Folklore Society. Publications

Kumbaya

Earliest citation: Society for the Preservation of Spirituals, *The Carolina Low Country* (1931), edited by Augustine T. Smythe, Herbert Ravenel Sass, Alfred Huger, Beatrice Ravenel, Thomas R. Waring, Archibald Rutledge, Josephine Pinckney, Caroline Pinckney Rutledge, DuBose Heyward, Katharine C. Hutson, and Robert W. Gordon

1930-1955

1955-1959
Organizations:
    Four-H: 158 (1957)
    Girl Guides, Switzerland: 188 (1957), 189 (1959)
    Young Women's Christian Association: 225 (1957)
Religious groups:
    Baptist groups: William J. Reynolds and Cecil McGee, *Songs for Fun and Fellowship* (1959)
    Christian Church, Disciples of Christ: Anonymous, *Christian Youth Chapbook* (1959)
    Lutheran groups: Anonymous, *A World of Song* (CRS 1958) for American Evangelical Lutheran Youth Fellowship
Commercial: Irwin Silber, *Sing Out!* (1958)

1960-1964
CRS song books include ones for Children's International Summer Villages of Cincinnati (1961), UNESCO (1960), United Methodist Church in the Philippines (1962)
Organizations:
    Boy Scouts: 108 (1963)
    Boy Scouts, England: 117 (1962)
    Four-H: 159 (1962)
    Girl Guides, Switzerland: 190 (1962)
Religious groups:
    Lutheran groups: Anonymous, *Campfire Songs* (1960)
    Methodist groups: Anonymous, *Adventures in Song* (CRS 1960) for

California, Nevada, Arizona

North American Ecumenical Youth Assembly: Anonymous, *Now Let Us Sing* (CRS 1961)

Protestant Episcopal Church: Anonymous, *EYC Song Book* (CRS 1961)

Roman Catholic groups: Anonymous, *Joyfully Sing* (CRS 1963) for Dominican Sisters, Sinsinawa, Wisconsin

Society of Friends (Quakers): Ellen Paullin, *Around the Friendly World* (CRS 1962) for Friends General Conference, Philadelphia, Pennsylvania

Schools: Marie Adler and Mabel Olive Miles, *Singing in Michigan* (CRS 1962); Carroll A. Rinehart, *Everybody's Singing* (CRS 1960) for Tucson, Arizona, public schools

Commercial: Joan Baez, *The Joan Baez Songbook* (1964); Guy Carawan and Candie Carawan, *We Shall Overcome* (1963); James F. Leisy, *Folk Song Fest* (1964); *Hootenanny Tonight* (1964); Irwin Silber, *Hootenanny Song Book* (1963); *Sing Out! Reprints* number 3 (1961); Weavers, *The Weavers Song Book* (1960); Augustus D. Zanzig, *Songs To Keep* (CRS 1962)

1965-1969

Organizations

Boy Scouts, Canada: 120 (1965)

Four-H: 160 (1966)

Girl Guides, Switzerland: 191 (1968)

Young Women's Christian Association: 226 (1965)

Religious groups:

Christian Church, Disciples of Christ: Anonymous, *Chapbook 2* (1966)

Methodist groups: Anonymous, *A Time To Sing* (1967) Hope Publishing Company; *Why?* (CRS 1968) for Southern New Jersey Conference, Methodist Youth Fellowship

United Presbyterian Church: Anonymous, *Let's Sing Together* (CRS 1965)

Schools: *Discovering Music Together Series*, Grade Three (1966), Grade Four (1966); *The Magic of Music Series*, Grade Four (1967); *Making Music Your Own Series*, Grade Six (1965)

Canada: *Basic Goals in Music Series: Sound Beginning* (1967); Colin E. Walley, et alia, *Fanfare Act I. A Course in Comprehensive Musicianship for the Junior High School* (1969)

Commercial: Otis Bainbridge, *Songs for All Occasions* (1968); Leon Dallin and Lynn Dallin, *Folk Songster* (1967); Harry Dexter, *The 101 Community Song Book* (196-); Albert Gamse, *The Best of Folk Music: Book One* (1968); James F. Leisy, *The Folk Song Abecedary* (1966); Norman Luboff and Win Stracke, *Songs of Man* (1965)

Britain: Donald J. Hughes, *A Second Youth Songbook* (1966)

1970-1979

Organizations:

Boy Scouts: 110 (1970)

Camp Fire Girls: 140 (1974)

Four-H: 162 (1973)

Girl Scouts: 184 (1973)

Girl Guides, Australia: 186 (1970)

Girl Guides, Switzerland: 192 (1971)

Religious groups:

Baptist groups: Charles F. Brown, *Sing 'n' Celebrate* (1971)

Campus Crusade for Christ: Bill Bright, *Pass It On* (1972)

Methodist groups: Charles Johnson, et alia, *Happiness Is a Song* (CRS) for North Indiana Conference; James F. Leisy, *The Good Times Songbook* (1974); Carlton Young, *The Genesis Songbook* (1973); *Songbook for Saints and Sinners* (1971)

New Now: Anonymous, *Folk Encounter* (1973); *Youth Folk Hymnal* (1971)

Young Life: Anonymous, *Sing with Young Life* (1978)

Schools: *Growing with Music Series*, Grade Six (1970); *This Is Music for Today Series*, Grade Three (1971); Frances M. Andrews, *Sing Together Children* (CRS, received 1974) for Pennsylvania State University Music Education Department

Commercial: Anonymous, *The New 1001 Jumbo Song Book* (1977); American Camping Association, *Sing!* (CRS); Linda Ann Barsness and Judith Bischoff, *Embers* (1974); Eleanor Chroman, *Songs that Children Sing* (1970); Christa K. Dixon, *Negro Spirituals from Bible to Folk Songs* (1976); Tom Glazer, *Songs of Peace, Freedom and Protest* (1970); Charles Hansen, *400 Super Song Fest #2* (1973); Alexander Shealy and Albert Gamse, *Golden Encyclopedia of Folk Music* (c. 1973); Irwin Silber and Fred Silber, *Folksinger's Wordbook* (1973); Jerry Silverman, *Folk Songs for Schools and Camps* (1970);

Jerry Silverman's Folk Song Encyclopedia. Volume Two (1975); William Simon, et alia, *Reader's Digest Family Songbook of Faith and Joy* (1975)

Recordings:

Commercial: Joan Baez, *Joan Baez in Concert* (1962); Robin Christenson, *You Can Sing It Yourself: Volume One* (1960); Folksmiths, *We've Got Some Singing To Do* (1957); Living Voices, *Impossible Dream* (1969); New Seekers, *Best of the New Seekers* (1973); Pete Seeger and Sonny Terry, *At Carnegie Hall with Sonny Terry* (1958); Seekers, *Introducing the Seekers* (1963); Weavers, *Travelling On* (1957-1958)

Religious audience: Jamall Badry, *Fill My Cup Lord* (1968); Cliff Barrows, *Cliff Barrows Now!* (1970); Bill Gaither Trio, *At Home in Indiana* (1972); Genesis Singers, *The Genesis Singalong* (1973); Re'generation, *H-a-p-p-i-n-e-s-s*

Organizational:

Camp Fire Girls: Phi Gamma Chi Horizon Club (1968)

Girl Scouts: National Round Up, Farragut State Park, Idaho (1965)

Archive collections:

Ohio State University: Sally Briggs, Charla Calderhead, Peggy Hays, Debbie Saint Pierre

University of Oregon: Sally Asher, Kathleen Craig, James Hirsch, Sue Loff

University of Texas: Patricia Anne Raine

Utah State University: June Rushing Leibfarth

Wayne State University: William Daniel Doebler

Personal song books:

Patricia Averill, Anne Beardsley, Nancy Bryant, Seth Clay, Shirley Ieraci, Jolene Robinson Johnson, Mariana Palmer, Larry Ralston, Carol Parsons Sievert, Clarena Snyder, Joyce Gregg Stoppenhagen

Camp song books:

Kitanniwa: 1974 song sheets

CFG Midwest: Oweki, Tannadoonah, Tayanita, Yakewi (two), Yukita

CFG other: Adahi, Cohila, El Deseo, Hidden Valley, Ka-esta, Killoqua, Kirby, Kotomi, Ku Keema, Kushtaka, Mawavi, Melacoma, Neewahlu, Niwana, Patiya, Seabow, Sealth, Shawnee,

Tanadoona, Tawakani, Towanyak, Trelipe, Val Verde, Wakoma, Watanopa, Widjiwagan (two), Wolahi, Zanika Lache (two)

Girls other: Aloha Hive (two), Rimrock, Wampatuck

Other Midwest: Christopher, Eberhart, High/Scope, Miniwanca, Muskegon, Onaway, Wyandot County 4-H Day Camp

Other: Brush Ranch, Farthest Out (1960, 1968), Loyaltown, Manakiki, Merrowvista, Mount Morris, Trexler, University Settlement Work Camp

Field recordings:

Kitanniwa: staff (1974)

CFG Midwest: Lucille Parker Munk (1974), Glen (1974)

CFG Other: He Bani Gani (1976), Yallani (Gene Clough, 1970s)

Other Midwest: Wyandot County 4-H Day Camp (1974)

Reports from Individuals

Reports	Midwest	Other	Total	% MW	% Other	% Total
Kitanniwa	10		10	.63		.63
CFG	9	39	48	.75	.85	.83
Girls	27	50	77	.94	.81	.85
Coed Girls	8	27	35	1.00	.93	.95
Boys	13	29	42	.93	.78	.82
Totals	67	145	212	.84	.83	.84

Total numbers of individuals who know "Kumbaya" and percent of those reports within entire sample. Sample numbers on last page of Publishing Histories.

Notes on Sources

Joe Hickerson, of the Archives of American Folksong, told me about the first collected version.

Anthony Saletan confirmed his role in a personal note dated 25 February 1977.

Kookaburra

Earliest citation: Marion Sinclair, "Kookaburra Sits in the Old Gum Tree," Australian copyright, 1934

-1949
Organizations:
   Boy Scouts, England: 114 (1938), 115 (1954)
   Camp Fire Girls: 133 (1947)
   Girl Scouts: 172 (1939), 174 (1946)
   Intercollegiate Outing Club Association: 204 (1948)
   Young Women's Christian Association: 222 (1943), 223 (1948)

1950-1959
Organizations:
   Boy Scouts, England: 116 (nd)
   Boy Scouts, France: 121 (nd)
   Camp Fire Girls: 134 (mid-1950s)
   Four-H: 157 (1950s)
   Girl Guides, Switzerland: 189 (1959)
   Intercollegiate Outing Club Association: 205 (1955)
   Young Women's Christian Association: 224 (1951), 225 (1957)
Religious groups:
   Baptist groups: William J. Reynolds and Cecil McGee, *Songs for Fun and Fellowship* (1959)
   Christian Church, Disciples of Christ: *Christian Youth Chapbook* (1959)
   Church of Jesus Christ of Latter Day Saints (Mormons): Carl Mesle and Franklin S. Weddle, *Camp and Fellowship Songbook* (CRS 1956) for Herald Publishing House, Independence, Missouri
   Lutheran groups: American Evangelical Youth Fellowship, *A World of Song* (1958)
   Methodist groups: Anonymous, *Sing It Again* (CRS 1958) for Nashville, Tennessee
   Protestant Episcopal Church: Rue Moore, *Sing Forth* (CRS 1955)

United Church of Christ: Anonymous, *Songs of Many Nations* (CRS 1958) for Church of Christ; Anonymous, *Songs of Many Nations* (CRS c1950-1960) for Congregational Church of Philadelphia, Pennsylvania

Canada: Canadian Council of Churches, *Lift Your Voices* (CRS 1955)

Schools: *American Singer Series*, Grade Six (1954); *Music for Living Series*, Grade Four (1956); *Music for Young Americans Series*, Grade Six (1959); *Our Singing World Series*, Grade Five (1950), Grade Six (1951); *Together We Sing Series*, Lower Grades (1952), Grade Six (1956)

Commercial: American Camping Association, *Joyful Singing* (CRS 1947); Beatrice Landeck, *More Songs To Grow On* (1954); Gloria Richman, *Ivy League Song Book* (1958)

Britain: Kenneth Simpson, *The First Round Book* (1959)

1960-1979

Organizations:

Boy Scouts, England: 118 (1964)

Camp Fire Girls: 136 (1961), 138 (1965-72), 140 (1974)

Four-H: 159 (1962), 160 (1966), 161 (1970s), 162 (1973)

Girl Scouts: 182 (1960)

Girl Guides, Australia: 186 (1970)

Girl Guides, New Zealand: 187 (1960)

Girl Guides, Switzerland: 190 (1962), 191 (1968), 192 (1971)

Intercollegiate Outing Club Association: 206 (1960)

Young Women's Christian Association: 226 (1965)

Religious groups:

Christian Church, Disciples of Christ: Anonymous, *Fellowship Songbook* (CRS 1962)

Congregational Christian Churches: *Songs of Many Nations* (CRS 1960-1974)

InterVarsity Christian Fellowship:

Canada: Paul Beckwith, *"Anywhere" Songs* (1960)

Methodist groups: Anonymous, *Adventures in Song* (CRS 1960) for California, Nevada, Arizona; Charles Johnson, *Happiness Is a Song* (CRS, received 1974) for North Indiana Conference; James F. Leisy, *The Good Times Songbook* (1974)

Roman Catholic groups: Anonymous, *Joyfully Sing* (CRS 1963) for Dominican Sisters of Sinsinawa, Wisconsin; Sister Marie Concetta, *Singing Fun* (CRS 1966)

Society of Friends (Quakers): Ellen Paullin, *Around the Friendly World* (CRS 1962) for Friends General Conference, Philadelphia, Pennsylvania

United Presbyterian Church: Anonymous, *Let's Sing Together* (CRS, received 1965)

Schools: *Concordia Music Education Series*, Grade Five (1967); *Growing with Music Series*, Grade Four (1970); *Making Music Your Own Series*, Grade Three (1964), Grade Four (1965); *The Spectrum of Music Series*, Grade Three (1974); *This Is Music for Today Series*, Grade Two (1971); Frances Andrews, et alia, *Sing Together Children!* (CRS, received 1974) for Pennsylvania State University, Music Education Department

Canada: *Basic Goals in Music Series*, Grade Two (1967), Grade Four (1965)

Commercial: Ruth Anderson, *Rounds from Many Countries* (1961); Evelyn Challis, *Songs for a New Generation* (1974); Eleanor Chroman, *Songs that Children Sing* (1970); Mike Cohen, *101 Plus 5 Folk Songs for Camp* (1966); Leon Dallin and Lynn Dallin, *Heritage Songster* (1966); Tom Glazer, *Treasury of Folk Songs* (1964); Frank Lynn, *Songs for Singin'* (1961); Donald Mitchell and Roderick Bliss, *The Gambit Book of Children's Songs* (1970); Elizabeth Poston, *The Children's Song Book* (1963); Irwin Silber and Fred Silber, *Folksinger's Wordbook* (1973); Jerry Silverman, *Jerry Silverman's Folk Song Encyclopedia, Volume Two* (1975); Marie Winn, *The Fireside Book of Children's Songs* (1966); Augustus D. Zanzig, *Songs To Keep* (CRS 1962, second edition, received 1974)

Folklore collections: Mary Knapp and Herbert Knapp, *One Potato, Two Potato* (1976)

Recordings:

Commercial: Disneyland Boys Choir, *It's a Small World* (1965); Peter Pan Chorus, *The Lion Sleeps Tonight*

Archive collections:

Indiana University: Marjorie Codd, Joal Hess, Judy Hollin, Martha Jackson Stocker, Helen Merriam, Phyllis Southman, June Walters, Claire Winfield

Ohio State University: Charla Calderhead, Debbie Saint Pierre, Carol
   Shuster
University of Oregon: Kathleen Craig, Sue Loff, Nan Stuart
University of Texas: Patricia Anne Raine
Wayne State University: Susan Dunn
Canada:
   Memorial University of Newfoundland: Ira Sheldon Posen

Personal song books:
   Patricia Averill, Nancy Bryant, Seth Clay, Charlotte Duff, Shirley
   Ieraci, Jolene Robinson Johnson, Larry Ralston, Joyce Gregg
   Stoppenhagen

Camp song books:
   CFG Midwest: Oweki, Tannadoonah, Tawanka, Yakewi (two)
   CFG other: Adahi, El Deseo, Hidden Valley, Ka-esta, Kotomi,
      Ku Keema, Melacoma, MeWaHi, Namanu, Neewahlu, Patiya,
      Seabow, Sealth, Tawakani (two), Wohelo, Wolahi
   Girls Midwest: Watervliet
   Girls other: Fleur de Lis, Wampatuck
   Other Midwest: Christopher, Muskegon Public Schools
   Other: Brush Ranch, Loyaltown, Manakiki, Merrowvista, Mount
      Morris, Seattle Boy Scouts

Field recordings:
   CFG Other: He Bani Gani (1976), Hidden Valley (1976), Wintaka
      (Gene Clough, 1970s)
   Other Midwest: Wyandot County 4-H Day Camp (1974)
   Other: Valley Mill (1976)

Reports from Individuals

Reports	Midwest	Other	Total	% MW	% Other	% Total
Kitanniwa	12		12	.75		.75
CFG	10	40	50	.83	.87	.86
Girls	25	51	76	.86	.82	.83
Coed Girls	5	19	24	.63	.66	.64
Boys	10	12	22	.71	.32	.43
Totals	62	122	184	.78	.70	.73

Total numbers of individuals who know "Kookaburra" and percent of those reports within entire sample. Sample numbers on last page of Publishing Histories.

Pep

Earliest citation: E. O. Harbin, *Paradology* (1927) quatrains 1-3, for Southern Methodist Church Epworth League

-1939
Commercial: Evelyn Hopson Wood, *Camp and Picnic Warbler* (1929) quatrains 2 and 3

1940-1959

1960-1979
Commercial: Linda Ann Barsness and Judith Bischoff, *Embers* (1974) quatrains 1-3, camper self-published

Recordings: None found

Archive collections:
University of Oregon: Nan Stuart
Wayne State University: Susan Dunn

Personal song books:
    Patricia Averill, Anne Beardsley, Nancy Bryant, Larry Ralston, Joyce Gregg Stoppenhagen

Camp song books:
    Kitanniwa: 1940s
    CFG Midwest: Oweki, Tannadoonah, Tawanka, Yakewi (three)
    CFG other: Adahi, El Deseo, Hitaga, Ka-esta, Kirby, Kotomi, Ku Keema, Namanu, Neewahlu, Patiya, Shawnee, Wakoma, Watanopa (1947, recent), Wolahi, Zanika Lache
    Girls other: Kamaji, Skyland

Field recordings:
  Kitanniwa: Jolene Robinson Johnson, Carol Parsons Sievert, Laura
    Clare Zahn (1974)
  Other Midwest: Wyandot County 4-H Day Camp (1974)

Reports from Individuals

Reports	Midwest	Other	Total	% MW	% Other	% Total
Kitanniwa	12		12	.75		.75
CFG	10	25	35	.83	.54	.60
Girls	14	17	31	.48	.27	.34
Coed Girls	1	6	7	.13	.21	.19
Boys	2	2	4	.14	.05	.08
Totals	39	50	89	.49	.29	.35

Total numbers of individuals who know "Pep" and percent of
those reports within entire sample. Sample numbers on last page of
Publishing Histories.

Eskimo Hunt

Earliest citation: Max V. Exner, *Tent and Trail Songs* (CRS 1962)

1960-1979
Organizations:
    Boy Scouts: 109 (1969)
Religious groups:
    Church of Jesus Christ of Latter Day Saints (Mormons): Anonymous, *MIA Let's Sing No 2* (CRS 1968) for Mutual Improvement Association
Schools: *Discovering Music Together Series*, Grade Three (1966)
Commercial: Linda Ann Barsness and Judith Bischoff, *Embers* (1974), Max V. Exner, *Tent and Trail Songs* (edition received 1974)

Recordings: None found

Archive collections:
Ohio State University: Peggy Hays

Personal song books:
    Anne Beardsley, Judith Bittmann, Terry Wilbur Bolton, John Calvi, Carol Ann Engle, Linda Regan Knoblauch, Debra Nails, Mary Ann Wilkens

Camp song books:
    CFG Midwest: Tannadoonah, Tawanka
    CFG other: Cimarron, Ka-esta, Kotomi, Long Beach Horizon Clubs, MeWaHi, Neewahlu, Niwana, Patiya, Sealth (CRS), Shawnee, Widjiwagan
    Girls other: Wampatuck
    Other: Manakiki

Field recordings:
    Kitanniwa: campers (1974)

Reports from Individuals

Reports	Midwest	Other	Total	% MW	% Other	% Total
Kitanniwa	1		1	.06		.06
CFG	8	16	24	.66	.35	.41
Girls	6	18	24	.21	.39	.26
Coed Girls	1	4	5	.13	.14	.14
Boys	1	6	7	.07	.16	.14
Totals	17	44	61	.22	.25	.24

Total numbers of individuals who know "Eskimo Hunt" and percent of those reports within entire sample. Sample numbers on last page of Publishing Histories.

An Austrian Went Yodeling

Earliest citation: Unknown

1960-1979
Religious groups:
  Church of Christ of Latter Day Saints (Mormons): Harold Neal, et alia, *Camp and Fellowship Songbook* (1970) Independence, Missouri
Commercial: Marie Winn, *The Fireside Book of Fun and Game Songs* (1974)

Recordings: None found

Archive collections:
Douglass College, Rutgers: Katie Hickey
Ohio State University: Peggy Hays, Julie Sherwood
University of Oregon: Kathleen Craig
Utah State University: June Rushing Leibfarth

Personal song books:
  Anne Beardsley, Nancy Bryant

Camp song books:
  CFG Midwest: Tawanka, Tayanita, Yukita
  CFG other: Adahi, Ka-esta, Kotomi, Long Beach, Melacoma, Niwana, Towanyak, Val Verde, Wolahi
  Girls Midwest: Watervliet
  Girls other: Wampatuck

Field recordings:
  Kitanniwa: Jolene Robinson Johnson (1974)
  CFG other: He Bani Gani (1976), Hidden Valley (1976)

The Cuckoo

Earliest citation: Walter Rein and Hans Lang, *Der Wundergarten* (1956), indicates the tune was a Tyrolese folk song published in 1887

-1939
German publications from Brednich:
   Germany: Hans Baumann, *Morgen marschieren wir, Liederbuch der deutschen Soldaten* (1939)

1940-1959
Organizations:
   Camp Fire Girls: 134 (mid-1950s)
   Four-H: 158 (1957)
   International Youth Hostel: 207 (1959)
   Young Women's Christian Association: 224 (1951), 225 (1957)
Religious groups:
   Baptists groups: William J. Reynolds and Cecil McGee, *Songs for Fun and Fellowship* (1959)
   Christian Church, Disciples of Christ: Anonymous, *Christian Youth Chapbook* (1959)
   Church of Jesus Christ of Latter Day Saints (Mormons): Carl Mesle and Franklyn S. Weddle, *Camp and Fellowship Songbook* (CRS 1956) Independence, Missouri
   Churches of Christ of the United States: Anonymous, *Songs Children Like* (1958)
   United Church of Christ: Anonymous, *Songs of Many Nations* (CRS 1958) for Church of Christ; Anonymous, *Songs of Many Nations* (CRS 1950-60) for Congregation Church, Philadelphia, Pennsylvania
Schools: *Birchard Music Series*, Grade Eight (1958); *Music for Living Series*, Grade Four (1956); *Together We Sing Series*, Grade Six (1956); Augustus D. Zanzig, *Vermont Sings* (CRS 1959)
German publications from Brednich:
   Germany: Anonymous, *Bruder Singer* (1951); *Jungscharlieder* (1956); Thilo Cornelissen, *Der Kreis* (1959); Katholischen Jugendwerk Österreichs, *Der Fährmann* (1959); Brandmeister Benno Ladwig, *Neues Feurwehrliederbuch* (1955); Leo Rinderer, *Singen macht groß Freud* (1957); Schleswig-Helsteinischen Heimatbund, *Liederbuch für Schleswig-Holstein* (1956); Heiner Wolf, *Unser fröhlicher Gesell* (1956)

1960-1979

Organizations:

Boy Scouts, England: 117 (1962)

Camp Fire Girls: 136 (1961), 138 (1965-72), 140 (1974)

Four-H: 159 (1962), 160 (1966)

Young Women's Christian Association: 226 (1965)

Religious groups:

Church of Jesus Christ of Latter Day Saints (Mormons): Anonymous, *MIA Let's Sing No 2* (CRS 1968) for Mutual Improvement Association; Harold Neal, *Camp and Fellowship Songbook* (1970) Independence, Missouri

Congregational Christian Churches: Anonymous, *Songs of Many Nations* (CRS 1960-74) for Ohio Conference

Methodist groups: Anonymous, *Adventures in Song* (CRS 1960) for California, Nevada, Arizona; Anonymous, *Why?* (CRS 1968) for Southern New Jersey Conference, Methodist Youth Fellowship

North American Ecumenical Youth Assembly: Anonymous, *Now Let Us Sing* (CRS 1961)

Protestant Episcopal Church: Anonymous, *EYC Song Book* (CRS 1961)

Roman Catholic groups: Anonymous, *Joyfully Sing* (CRS 1963) for Dominican Sisters of Sinsinawa, Wisconsin; Sister Marie Concetta, *Singing Fun* (CRS 1966)

Society of Friends (Quakers): Ellen Paullin, *Around the Friendly World* (CRS 1962) for Friends General Conference, Philadelphia, Pennsylvania

Schools: *Discovering Music Together Series*, Grade Six (1966); *Exploring Music Series*, Grade Four (1971); *The Spectrum of Music Series*, Grade Five (1974); *This Is Music for Today Series*, Grade Two (1971); Marie Adler and Mabel Olive Miles, *Singing in Michigan* (CRS 1962); Carroll A. Rinehart, *Everybody's Singing* (CRS 1960) for Tucson, Arizona, public schools

Commercial: American Camping Association, *Sing!* (CRS, received 1974); Leon Dallin and Lynn Dallin, *Heritage Songster* (1967); Robert E. Nye, et alia, *Singing with Children* (1962); Augustus D. Zanzig, *Songs To Keep* (CRS 1962)

New Zealand: Des Rainey and Juliet Rainey, *New Zealand Sings* (CRS 1962)

German publications from Brednich:

> Germany: Eifelverein, *Frisch auf! Rheinisches Liederbuch* (1960); Gustav Schulten, *Der große Kilometerstein* (1962)

Recordings:

Commercial: Disneyland Boys Choir, *It's a Small World* (1965)

Archive collections:

Wayne State University: Henry

Personal song books:

> Patricia Averill, Nancy Bryant, Seth Clay, Jolene Robinson Johnson, Polly McIntyre, Larry Ralston

Camp song books:

> CFG Midwest: Tannadoonah, Tawanka, Tayanita
> CFG other: El Deseo, Hidden Valley, Kotomi, MeWaHi, Neewahlu, Seabow, Sealth (CRS), Tawakani (two), Watanopa
> Girls other: Aloha Hive
> Other: Buck's Rock, Manakiki

Field recordings:

> Kitanniwa: Jolene Robinson Johnson, Carol Parsons Sievert, and Laura Clare Zahn (1974)
> CFG other: He Bani Gani (1976)

Reports from Individuals

Reports	Midwest	Other	Total	% MW	% Other	% Total
Kitanniwa	5		5	.31		.31
CFG	6	34	40	.50	.74	.69
Girls	20	39	59	.69	.63	.65
Coed Girls	3	10	13	.38	.34	.35
Boys	4	8	12	.29	.33	.24
Totals	38	91	129	.48	.52	.51

Total numbers of individuals who know "An Austrian Went Yodeling" and percent of those reports within entire sample.

Reports	Midwest	Other	Total	% MW	% Other	% Total
Kitanniwa	7		7	.44		.44
CFG	7	24	31	.58	.52	.53
Girls	9	14	23	.31	.23	.25
Coed Girls	4	6	10	.50	.21	.27
Boys	4	2	6	.29	.05	.12
Totals	31	46	77	.39	.26	.30

Total numbers of individuals who know "The Cuckoo" and percent of those reports within entire sample.

Of 70 people who know "The Cuckoo," 51 or .73 know "An Austrian." Of 124 people who know "An Austrian," 51 of .41 know "The Cuckoo." Sample numbers on last page of Publishing Histories.

Ash Grove

Earliest citation, melody: Edward Jones, *Bardic Museum* (1802)

Text: Thomas Oliphant, *Welsh Melodies* (1862), with music by John Thomas and Welsh words by John Jones

-1899

Folklore collections:

>   Britain: William Chappell, *The Ballad Literature and Popular Music of the Olden Time* (1859); Joseph Parry and David Rowlands, *Cambrian Minstrelsie*, volume 6 (1893)

Art song:

>   Britain: John Parry, "The Welsh Melody" in *Dramatic Recollections* (1833) other words; Henry Brinley Richards, "Llwyn Onn" (1832) no words; *The Songs of Wales* (1873) Oxenford

1900-1919

Commercial: Henry F. Gilbert, *One Hundred Folk-Songs* (1910)

>   Britain: Granville R. Bantock, *One Hundred Folksongs of All Nations* (1911); Percy C. Buck, *The Oxford Song Book* (1916); Sydney H. Nicholson, *British Songs for British Boys* (1903); Charles Villiers Stanford, *The National Song Book* (1906)

Art song:

>   Britain: Anonymous, *Contralto Songs, Volume One* (1900); *Mezzo-soprano Songs, Volume One* (190-); *Soprano Songs, Volume One* (190-)

1920-1939

Organizations:

>   Boy Scouts, England: 112 (1925)
>   Boy Scouts, Canada: 119 (1932)
>   Girl Scouts: 170 (1936)

Schools: *Concord Series*, Two (1931); Theresa Armitage, *Senior Laurel Songs* (1926); Randal J. Condon, Helen S. Leavitt and Elbridge W. Newton, *Assembly Songs and Choruses* (1929)

Commercial: Anonymous, *Songs for Every Purpose and Occasion* (1938); *Songs We Love To Sing* (1938); Harriet Garton Cartwright, *Song Treasury* (1927); Max E. Oberndorfer and Anne Oberndorfer, *A Century of Progress in American Songs* (1933); Peter William Dykema, et alia, *The New Green Book* (1930)

> Britain: Sydney Baynes, *Boosey's Community Song Book* (1927); Desmond MacMahon, *The New National and Folk Song Book*, part one (1938); Thomas Wood, *The Oxford Song Book* (1928)
> Canada: Ernest C. MacMillan, *A Book of Songs* (1929); *A Canadian Song Book* (1929)
> Germany: Heinrich Möller, *Das Lied der Völker*, volume 1 (1924)

1940-1959

Organizations:

> Boy Scouts, England: 115 (1954)
> Camp Fire Girls: 134 (mid-1950s)
> Four-H: 157 (1950s), 158 (1957)
> Girl Scouts: 176 (1949), 178 (1956), 180 (1957)
> International Youth Hostel: 207 (1959)
> Young Women's Christian Association: 225 (1957)

Religious groups:

> Christian Church, Disciples of Christ: Anonymous, *Christian Youth Chapbook* (1959)
> Church of Jesus Christ of Latter Day Saints (Mormons): Carl Mesle and Franklyn S. Weddle, *Camp and Fellowship Songbook* (1956)
> Lutheran groups: Anonymous, *A World of Song* (CRS 1958) for American Evangelical Lutheran Youth Fellowship
> Methodist groups: Anonymous, *Sing It Again* (CRS 1958)
> Protestant Episcopal Church: Rue Moore, *Sing Forth* (CRS 1955)
> United Church of Christ: Anonymous, *Songs of Many Nations* (CRS 1958) for Church of Christ; Anonymous, *Songs of Many Nations* (CRS 1950-1960) for Congregational Church of Philadelphia, Pennsylvania
> Canada: Canadian Council of Churches, *Lift Your Voices* (CRS 1955)

Schools: *Together We Sing Series*, Grade Six (1956); Theresa Armitage, *Junior Laurel Songs* (1943); Augustus D. Zanzig, *Vermont Sings* (CRS 1959)

Commercial: Irvin Cooper, *Tunetime for Teentime* (1942); Herbert Haufrecht, *Folk Sing* (1959); *109 Folk Songs and Ballads* (1958); Fowler Smith, et alia, *Songs We Sing* (1940-1941)

> Britain: Granville Bantock, *Songs of Wales* (1942); Felton Rapley, *Chappell's Community Song Book #2* (1955); Charles Villiers Stanford and Geoffrey Shaw, *The New National Song Book* (1958); Leslie Woodgate, *The Penguin Song Book* (1951)

> Canada: Ethel A. Kinley, *A Song Book* (1940)

> Norway: Olav Sollid, *S. F. U. Sangboka* (1951)

Art song:

> Britain: Benjamin Britten, *Folk-Song Arrangements, Volume One* (1943); Roger Quilter, *The Arnold Book of Old Songs* (1947)

1960-1979

Organizations:

> Camp Fire Girls: 136 (1961), 138 (1965-1972)

> Girl Scouts: 184 (1973)

> Young Women's Christian Association: 226 (1965)

Religious groups:

> Baptists groups: Cecil McGee and Bob Oldenburg, *Songs for Fun and Fellowship #3* (1969)

> Christian Church, Disciples of Christ: Anonymous, *Fellowship Songbook* (CRS, received 1962)

> Methodist groups: Anonymous, *Adventures in Song* (CRS 1960) for California, Nevada, Arizona

> Protestant Episcopal Church: Anonymous, *EYC Song Book* (CRS 1961)

> Roman Catholic groups: Anonymous, *Joyfully Sing* (CRS 1963) for Dominican Sisters of Sinsinawa, Wisconsin

> Society of Friends (Quakers): Ellen Paullin, *Around the Friendly World* (CRS 1962) for Friends General Conference, Philadelphia, Pennsylvania

> United Presbyterian Church: Anonymous, *Let's Sing Together* (CRS, received 1965)

Schools: *Birchard Music Series*, Grade Six (1962); *Discovering Music Together Series*, Grade Six (1966); *Growing with Music Series*, Grade Six (1970); *The Magic of Music Series*, Grade Five (1968); *Making Music Your Own Series*, Grade Six (1965); *The Spectrum of Music Series*, Grade Five (1974); *This Is Music for Today Series*, Grade Five (1971); Marie Adler and Mabel Olive Miles, *Singing in Michigan* (CRS 1962); Carroll A. Rinehart, *Everybody's Singing* (CRS 1960) for Tucson, Arizona, public schools

    Canada: *Basic Goals in Music Series*, Grade Six (1967)

Commercial: Anonymous, *357 Songs We Love To Sing* (1961); William Cole, *Folk Songs of England, Ireland, Scotland and Wales* (1969); Leon Dallin and Lynn Dallin, *Heritage Songster* (1966); Charles Hansen, *400 Super Song Fest #2* (1973); Herbert Haufrecht, *Folk Songs for Everyone* (1962); James F. Leisy, *The Folk Song Abecedary* (1966); Frank Lynn, *Songs for Singin'* (1961); Donald Mitchell and Roderick Bliss, *The Gambit Book of Children's Songs* (1970); Robert E. Nye, et alia, *Singing with Children* (1962); Anne Faulkner Oberndorfer and Max E. Oberndorfer, *The New American Songbook* (1961); Irwin Silber and Fred Silber, *Folksinger's Wordbook* (1973); Tomi Ungerer, at alia, *The Great Song Book* (1979); Augustus D. Zanzig, *Songs To Keep* (CRS, received 1974)

Recordings:

Commercial: Marty Brill, *The Roving Balladeer*; William Clauson, *Folk Songs* (1956); Tom Glazer, *I Like Holidays!* (1973); Will Holt, *Songs and Ballads*; Harry Nilsson, *Early Tymes* (1977); Victor Orchestra, "Ash Grove"; Roger Whittaker, *Folk Songs of Our Times* (1977)

Art song: Peter Pears (1944)

Organizational:

    Girl Scouts: Nanette Guilford, *Songs Girl Scouts Sing* (1956)

Archive collections:

Indiana University: Joan Fulton, Martha Jackson Stocker

Ohio State University: Julie Sherwood, Carol Shuster, Carol Simon

United States Library of Congress, Archives of American Folksong: Rae Korson, notes 19 December 1960

University of Texas: Naomi Feldman and Mary Rogers

Utah State University: June Rushing Leibfarth

Personal song books:

    Patricia Averill, Anne Beardsley, Seth Clay, Charlotte Duff, Cecily Raysor Hancock, Shirley Ieraci, Jolene Robinson Johnson, Polly McIntyre, Mariana Palmer, Larry Ralston, Carol Parsons Sievert, Clarena Snyder, Joyce Gregg Stoppenhagen

Camp song books:

Kitanniwa: 1974

CFG Midwest: Kiloqua, Kiwatani, Yakewi

CFG other: Adahi, Augusta, Hidden Valley, Hitaga, Kushtaka, Mawavi, Melacoma, Neewahlu, Niwana, Onahlee, Patiya, Seabow, Sealth (CRS), Shawnee, Watanopa, Wolahi

Girls Midwest: Watervliet

Girls other: Aloha Hive, Campbell Mountain, Manakiki, Peach Creek, Rimrock, Wampatuck

Field recordings:

Kitanniwa: staff (1974)

CFG Midwest: Lucille Parker Munk (1974)

CFG other: Patricia Ann Hall, Yallani (Gene Clough, 1970s)

Reports from Individuals

Reports	Midwest	Other	Total	% MW	% Other	% Total
Kitanniwa	14		14	.88		.88
CFG	9	28	37	.75	.61	.64
Girls	24	43	67	.83	.69	.74
Coed Girls	4	9	13	.50	.31	.35
Boys	5	4	9	.36	.11	.18
Totals	56	84	140	.71	.48	.55

Total numbers of individuals who know "Ash Grove" and percent of those reports within entire sample. Sample numbers on last page of Publishing Histories.

Skyball Paint

Earliest citation: Unknown

-1979
Folklore collections: Richard E. Lingenfelter, *Songs of the American West* (1968), contains Robert C. Wylder's version

Recordings:
Commercial: Girls of the Golden West, *Songs for You - Old and New* (BL-106)

Archive collections:
Indiana University: Heather MacPhail
Montana State University: Robert C. Wylder

Personal song books:
Patricia Averill, Cecily Raysor Hancock (1944), Joyce Gregg Stoppenhagen

Camp song books:
CFG Midwest: Tannadoonah
CFG other: Adahi, Kotomi, Neewahlu, Tawakani (old), Watanopa
Other: Manakiki

Field recordings:
Kitanniwa: Joyce Gregg Stoppenhagen (1974)

Reports from Individuals

Reports	Midwest	Other	Total	% MW	% Other	% Total
Kitanniwa	8		8	.50		.50
CFG	1	11	12	.08	.24	.21
Girls	4	8	12	.14	.13	.13
Coed Girls	0	1	1	.00	.03	.02
Boys	0	0	0	.00	.00	.00
Totals	13	20	33	.16	.48	.13

Total numbers of individuals who know "Skyball Paint" and percent of those reports within entire sample. Sample numbers on last page of Publishing Histories.

Lollypop

Earliest citation: Unknown

-1939
College: Kappa Delta (1936) local
Commercial: Albert M. Brown, *The Best One Hundred Songs for Camps and Clubs*, lollypop; Annetta Eldridge and Ruth E. Richardson, *Stunt Songs for Social Sings* (1925) herpicide

1940-1959

1960-1979
Commercial: Duncan Emrich, *The Whim-Wham Book* (1975) davenport; Charles Keller and Lady McCrady, *Glory, Glory How Peculiar* (1976) lollypop, davenport

Recordings: None found

Archive collections:
Douglass College, Rutgers: Dianna Masto (lollypop, bubblegum, davenport)
Indiana University: Carol Domoney (lollypop, davenport), Joal Hess (lollypop, local, herpasid), Kristine Olsen (lollypop)
Ohio State University: Lisa Drumm (bubblegum, lollypop, davenport, castor oil)
University of Oregon: Nan Stuart
Utah State University: June Rushing Leibfarth (lollypop, castor oil)
Wayne State University: William Daniel Doebler (lollypop), Henry, Sternberg

Personal song books:
Patricia Averill (lollypop, castor oil, local, end), Shirley Ieraci (lollypop, bubblegum, castor oil), Polly McIntyre (lollypop, castor oil, local), Larry Ralston (lollypop, castor oil, davenport)

Camp song books:
   CFG Midwest: Kiloqua (lollypop), Tannadoonah (lollypop, end),
      Yakewi (lollypop, bubblegum)
   CFG other: Ka-esta (lollypop, lemon drop), Kirby (lollypop, lemon
      drop, end), Kotomi (lollypop, end), Melacoma (lollypop, lemon
      drop), MeWaHi (lollypop, castor oil), Namanu (lollypop, lemon
      drop), Niwana (lollypop, lemon drop, castor oil), Seabow
      (lollypop, poison oak, Hershey bar, castor oil)
   Girls other: Red Wing (local), Kamaji (local), Wampatuck (lollypop,
      castor oil, davenport, local)
   Other Midwest: Christopher (local)
   Other: Blue Haven (lollypop, castor oil, end), Herald Tribune
      Fresh Air Camp (lollypop, castor oil)

Field recordings:
   Kitanniwa: campers (lollypop, 1974), campers (lemon drop, end,
      1974); Jolene Robinson Johnson, Carol Parsons Sievert and
      Laura Clare Zahn (lollypop, 1974)
   CFG other: Wasewagan (lollypop, Gene Clough, 1970s)

When You Come to the End of a Lollypop

Earliest citation: Unknown

-1979
Organizations:
   Boy Scouts: 109 (1969)

Commercial recordings: None found

Archive collections: None found

Personal songbooks:
   Charlotte Duff

Camp song books:
   Other: Brooklyn Boy Scouts, Gifford

Reports from Individuals

Reports	Midwest	Other	Total	% MW	% Other	% Total
Kitanniwa	13		13	.81		.81
CFG	6	25	31	.50	.54	.53
Girls	16	18	34	.55	.29	.37
Coed Girls	2	1	3	.25	.03	.08
Boys	1	6	7	.07	.16	.14
Totals	38	50	88	.48	.29	.34

Total numbers of individuals who know "Lollypop" and percent of those reports within entire sample. Sample numbers on last page of Publishing Histories.

I Wish I Were a Little ---

Earliest citation: Unknown

-1959
Organizations:
   Intercollegiate Outing Club Association: 203 (1938), 204 (1948), 205 (1955)
Religious groups:
   Methodist groups: E. O. Harbin, *Paradology* (1927)

1960-1979
Organizations:
   Boy Scouts, Canada: 120 (1965)
   Intercollegiate Outing Club Association: 206 (1960)
Commercial: Frank Lynn, *Songs for Singin'* (1961)
Folklore collections:
   Canada: Edith Fowke, *Sally Go round the Sun* (1969)

Recordings: None found

Archive collections:
University of Texas: Patricia Anne Raine
Wayne State University: Sternberg

Personal song books:
   Anne Beardsley, Monica Mahe Foster, Robin Kelley, Larry Ralston, Margaret Saunier, Joyce Gregg Stoppenhagen

Camp song books:
   CFG other: Adahi, Mawavi, Niwana, Widjiwagan
   Other: Duluth Boy Scouts

Field recordings:
> Kitanniwa: campers (1974)
> Other Midwest: Wyandot County 4-H Day Camp (1974)
> Other: Potomac Country Day Camp (1976)

I Wish I Wuz a Rock

Earliest citation: the verse was widely published. This mentions a few instances, classed by type.

Song
1917   Wells, John Barnes. "A Little Rock"
1919   Custance, Arthur. "The Weary Wisher"
1927   Harbin, E. O. *Paradology, Songs of Fun and Fellowship*, "The Hobo Anthem"
1940   Ford, Ira W. *Traditional Music of America*, "I Wish I Wuz a Little Rock"

Poem
1899   Eugene, Oregon. *The Broad-Axe Tribune*, 31 May, "Jealous Jake"
1913   Bassett, Charles E. "A Pecan Marketing Exchange: Why? How? When?" National Nut Growers Association, *Proceedings*
1913   Co-operative League of U. S. A. *Co-operation*, March
1915   *The American Blacksmith*, November, "A Wish"
1916   Hotel and Restaurant Employes International Alliance. *The Mixer and Server*, October, "The Human Drone"
1916   Southwestern University, Georgetown, Texas. *Sou'wester Yearbook*
1917   Buffalo, Rochester and Pittsburgh Railway Company. *Railway Life*, "Wishin'"
1917   Disston Saw Works. *The Disston Crucible*, February, "Amen!"
1918   Traveler's Protective Organization. *The T. P. A. Magazine*
1918   *The Western Architect*, from Root to Burnham
1919   *The Architect and Engineer of California and the Pacific Coast*, from Root to Burnham
1920   *Michigan Manufacturer and Financial Record*, 25 December, "Lazy, Thassal" by G. M.
1921   Salt Lake City, Utah. *Tribune*, 7 November

1921   Findlay, Ohio, High School. *The Blue and Gold*, yearbook, from Davis Johnson

1923   National Masonic Research Society, Cedar Rapids, Iowa. *The Builder Magazine*, February

1925   Hartford Steam Boiler Inspection and Insurance Company. *The Locomotive*, July, "As Vacation Approaches"

1926   Business and Professional Women's Club of Oakland, California. *Business Women's Herald*, 13 September

1927   Stephenville, Texas. *The J-TAC*, 11 February

1927   Simmons College, Abilene, Texas. *The Simmons Brand*, 19 February

1927   Danville, Virginia. *Bee*, 16 July

1928   Postcard from Asheville, North Carolina, Southeastern Louisiana University, Center for Southeast Louisiana Studies, Sullivan Collection

1930   Baltimore, Maryland. *The Afro American*, 17 May, "A Springtime Wish"

1931   Beach, North Dakota. *Golden Valley News*, 12 November

1948   Kokomo, Indiana. *Tribune*, 9 February

References to poem

1915   Ryder, Melvin. *Rambles Round the Campus*

1919   Bryn Mawr yearbook

1927   Ogden, Utah, *Standard Examiner*, 24 November

1930   Newsom, M. Eugene. "Rotary's Increasing Purpose," Rotary International convention speech

1930   Purucker, Gottfried de. "Have You Found Yourself?" Theosophy lecture, 6 July, in *Questions We All Ask*

1936   Wright, Isa L. *Aw Gee! I Wish I Wuz a Little Rock*, 29 June

1938   White, Emilie Margaret. "Maintaining Professional Interest," *The Modern Language Journal*

1975   El Paso, Texas, *Herald Post*, 22 February

Reviews

1919   Anonymous. "Arthur Custance," *American Organist*, July

1920   Smith, Clay. "Two new songs published by Oliver Ditson," *The Lyceum Magazine*, January

Reports from Individuals

Reports	Midwest	Other	Total	% MW	% Other	% Total
Kitanniwa	4		4	.25		.25
CFG	5	17	22	.42	.37	.38
Girls	17	30	47	.59	.48	.51
Coed Girls	5	7	12	.63	.24	.32
Boys	6	6	12	.43	.16	.24
Totals	37	60	97	.47	.34	.38

Total numbers of individuals who know "I Wish I Were" and percent of those reports within entire sample. Sample numbers on last page of Publishing Histories.

The Other Day I Saw a Bear

Publications: None found

Recordings: None found

Archive collections:
Ohio State University: Debbie Saint Pierre, Carol Shuster (two versions), Carol Simon
University of Oregon: Diane Davis, Nan Stuart
Wayne State University: Henry

Personal song books:
Nancy Bryant, Shirley Ieraci, Larry Ralston

Camp song books:
CFG Midwest: Tayanita, Yakewi (two), Yukita
CFG other: Kotomi, Niwana, Wakoma, Widjiwagan, Wolahi
Girls other: Wanakiwin
Other Midwest: Muskegon Public Schools
Other: Brush Ranch, Seattle Boy Scouts

Preacher and the Bear

Earliest citation: George Fairman using the name Joe Arizona, "The Preacher and the Bear" (Philadelphia: Morris Music, 1904)

-1919
Folklore collections: Herbert G. Shearin and Josiah Combs, *A Syllabus of Kentucky Folk-Songs* (1911); Portia Smiley, "Folk-Lore from Virginia, South Carolina, Georgia, Alabama, and Florida," *JAF* (1919)

Recordings:
General audience: Arthur Collins, "The Preacher and the Bear" (1905); Sousa's Band, "The Preacher and the Bear" (1906)

1920-1939

Folklore collections: Newman I. White, *American Negro Folk-Songs* (1928)

Recordings:

General audience: Honeyboy and Sassafrass, "The Preacher and the Bear" (1930); New Dixie Demons, "The Preacher and the Bear" (1936)

Country audience: John McGhee, "The Preacher and The Bear" (1927); Prairie Ramblers, "The Preacher and the Bear" (1936); Riley Puckett, "Story of the Preacher and the Bear" (1925)

Black audience: Golden Gate Quartet, "Preacher and the Bear" (1937)

Radio transcriptions: Claude Hopkins, "Preacher and the Bear" (1935) from Harlem; Roy Rogers, "Preacher and the Bear"; Sons of the Pioneers, "Preacher and the Bear"

1940-1959

Folklore collections: Frank C. Brown, *The Frank C. Brown Collection of North Carolina Folklore*, volume 3 (1952); Arthur Kyle Davis, Junior, *Folk-Songs of Virginia* (1949); Ira W. Ford, *Traditional Music of America* (1940)

Recordings:

General audience: Buffalo Bills, *1950 International Champions* (1950); Andy Griffith, *Shouts the Blues and Old Timey Songs* (1959); Phil Harris, "The Preacher and the Bear" (1947)

Country audience: Big Bopper, *Chantilly Lace* (1958), Mac Wiseman, *Great Folk Ballads* (1959)

Black audience: Jubalaires, "The Preacher and the Bear" (1947)

1960-1979

Recordings:

General audience: New Christy Minstrels, *In Person at The Troubadour* (1962); Eddie Smith, "The Preacher and the Bear" (1962)

Country audience: Hylo Brown, *Sings Folk Songs of Rural America* (1967); Jerry Reed, *Georgia Sunshine* (1970)

Black audience: Rufus Thomas, *Do the Funky Chicken* (1970)

Field recordings: Sam Chatmon (1978); Poplin Family of Sumter, South Carolina (1963)

Related commercial recordings: Jerry Clower, *Mississippi Talkin'* (1971)

Camp song books:
    Other: Brooklyn Boy Scouts

Reports from Individuals

Reports	Midwest	Other	Total	% MW	% Other	% Total
Kitanniwa	2		2	.13		.13
CFG	8	21	29	.67	.46	.50
Girls	24	33	57	.83	.53	.63
Coed Girls	3	8	11	.38	.28	.30
Boys	7	14	21	.50	.38	.41
Totals	44	76	120	.56	.44	.47

Total numbers of individuals who know "A Bear" and percent of those reports within entire sample. Sample numbers on last page of Publishing Histories.

Journal Codes

JAF: Journal of American Folklore

Witchcraft

Earliest citation: Margarett Snyder, "Witchcraft," manuscript copy received by United States copyright office 17 March 1937, unpublished piano arrangement with words

-1939
Organizations:
  Boy Scouts: 106 (1939)

1940-1959
Organizations:
  Camp Fire Girls: 134 (mid-1950s)
  Four-H: 157 (1950s)
  Intercollegiate Outing Club Association: 205 (1955)
  Young Women's Christian Association: 222 (1943), 223 (1948), 224 (1951), 225 (1957)
Religious groups:
  Church of Jesus Christ of Latter Day Saints (Mormons): Harold Neal, *Camp and Fellowship Songbook* (CRS 1956) for Independence, Missouri
  Protestant Episcopal Church: Rue Moore, *Sing Forth* (CRS 1955)
Colleges: Alpha Omicron Pi (1955), Kappa Kappa Gamma (1945)

1960-1979
Organizations:
  Camp Fire Girls: 136 (1961), 138 (1965-1972)
  Four-H: 159 (1962), 160 (1966)
  Intercollegiate Outing Club Association: 206 (1960)
  Young Women's Christian Association: 226 (1965)
Religious groups:
  Christian Church, Disciples of Christ: Anonymous, *Fellowship Songbook* (CRS, received 1962)
Schools: Marie Adler and Mabel Olive Miles, *Singing in Michigan* (CRS 1962)
Colleges: Alpha Xi Delta (1966)

Commercial: American Camping Association, *Sing!* (CRS, received 1974)
> Canada: Paul Beckwith, *"Anywhere" Songs* (1960)

Folklore collections: Linda Weaver, "Camp Songs: Reflections of Youth," *NCF* (1974)

Recordings:
Organizational:
> Camp Fire Girls: A-Ta-Ya Horizon Club (1960), Phi Gamma Chi Horizon Club (1968), Wyandot (1960s)

Archive collections:
Indiana University: Carol Domoney, Jan Goldsberry, Jean Hamilton, Judy Hollin, Martha Jackson Stocker, Sharon Johnson, Christine Nevans, Perianne Stewart
University of Texas: Patricia Anne Raine
Utah State University: June Rushing Leibfarth
Wayne State University: William Daniel Doebler
Canada:
> Memorial University of Newfoundland: Ira Sheldon Posen

Personal song books:
> Patricia Averill, Anne Beardsley, Nancy Bryant, Seth Clay, Charlotte Duff, Cecily Raysor Hancock, Polly McIntyre, Mariana Palmer, Larry Ralston, Carol Parsons Sievert, Joyce Gregg Stoppenhagen

Camp song books:
> Kitanniwa: 1940, 1974
> CFG Midwest: Kiloqua, Kiwatani, Oweki, Tannadoonah, Tawanka, Yakewi
> CFG other: Adahi, Augusta, Hidden Valley, Hitaga, Mawavi, Neewahlu, Patiya, Sealth (CRS), Shawnee, Tawakani, Towanyak, Widjiwagan, Wolahi, Zanika Lache (two)
> Girls Midwest: Kalamazoo Girl Reserves, Watervliet
> Girls other: Fleur de Lis, Peach Creek, Rimrock, Wampatuck
> Other Midwest: Miniwanca (three)
> Other: Blue Haven, Brush Ranch, Manakiki, Merrowvista

Field recordings:
    Kitanniwa: staff (1974)
    CFG Midwest: Glen (1974)
    CFG other: He Bani Gani (1976)

Reports from Individuals

Reports	Midwest	Other	Total	% MW	% Other	% Total
Kitanniwa	13		13	.81		.81
CFG	11	35	46	.92	.76	.79
Girls	22	36	58	.76	.58	.64
Coed Girls	3	6	9	.38	.38	.24
Boys	3	5	8	.21	.14	.16
Totals	52	82	134	.66	.47	.53

Total numbers of individuals who know "Witchcraft" and percent of those reports within entire sample. Sample numbers on last page of Publishing Histories.

Journal Codes

NCF: North Carolina Folklore

Rise and Shine

Phrase: Rise and Shine

The phrase "rise and shine" was used in a number of different religious songs after the Civil War. No attempt has been made to document them, but the following list gives an indication of the continuing interest in the phrase:

1876   Lathbury, Mary A. and P. P. Bliss. "Arise and Shine," described as "the Chautauqua song of 1876"

1888   Lowery, Robert. "Arise and Shine"

1923   Miller, Elizabeth B. and George B. Schuler. "Arise and Shine"

1962   Exner, Max V. "Rise and Shine," round in *Tent and Trail Songs* (CRS)

Chorus: Rise and Shine, Give God Your Glory

The combination of "rise and shine" with "give God your/the glory" is found in the following:

1877   Fisk Jubilee Singers. J. B. T. Marsh, *The Story of the Jubilee Singers with Their Songs*, "Rise and Shine"

1883   Coleman, Z. A. *The Jubilee Singers, a Collection of Plantation Melodies*, "Rise! Shine! and Give God the Glory"

1903   Fisk Jubilee Singers. J. B. T. Marsh, *The Story of the Jubilee Singers with Their Songs*, with supplement by F. J. Loudin, "Rise and Shine"

1930   Connolly, Marc. *The Green Pastures* play (1930), "Rise and Shine" by Hall Johnson

1936   Connolly, Marc. *The Green Pastures* film (1936), "Rise and Shine" by Hall Johnson Choir

Key Rhymes: Ark/Bark, Two/Kangaroo

The rhymes appear in folklore collections, often in just a few verses. The kangaroo always is coupled with another large animal, an elephant, rhinoceros or hippopotamus. The choice of animal may be dictated by tune that requires three, four, or five syllables. Among the instances reported by folklorists are:

1928　White, Newman I. *American Negro Folk-Songs*. "Yonder comes Noah stumbling in the dark" from Macon County, Georgia, has two/hippopotamus/kangaroo; "In come de animals two by two" from Auburn, Alabama, has counting out; contains a number of other versions and variants

1937　Scarborough, Dorothy. *Songcatcher in the Southern Mountains*

1939　Eddy, Mary O. *Ballads and Songs from Ohio*. "Old Uncle Noah" from Cleveland, Ohio, has ark/bark, two/elephant/kangaroo to "When Johnny Comes Marching Home"

1952　Brown, Frank C. *Frank C. Brown Collection of North Carolina Folklore*, volume 3. "Noah's Ark" has flood/mud and ark/bark with "Gideon's Band"

1961　Hubbard, Lester A. *Ballads and Songs from Utah*. "Noah's Ark" from Snowflake, Arizona, has ark/bark, two/kangaroo to "When Johnny Comes Marching Home"

When Robert Smith and Charles Leonhard reduced it for the youngest children in public schools, they used only two verses, those using ark/bark and two/hippopottamus/kangaroo in *Discovering Music Together Series, Early Childhood* (1958). They called it "Who Built the Ark"

Elaboration of Rhymes into a Counting Out Song

The song has been collected by folklorists, but not before it was published in a number of college song books. In the early years, it sometimes was called "Gideon." More recently, it occasionally has been called "Who Built the Ark" or some variation on "Noah's Ark." By 1900, the most common form was "One More River," sometimes done in dialect as "ribber" and sometimes as "one wide river."

-1899

Colleges: Columbia (1876) river; Princeton (1882) river; Rutgers (1885) "Old Noah"; Stevens (1871) Gideon; University of Pennsylvania (1879) river

Commercial: George W. Furniss, *Our College Boys Songs* (1887) river; Lockwood Honoré, *Popular College Songs* (1891) river; Emil Schwab, *The Best College Songs* (1897) river, Gideon; Ike Simond, *Old Slack's Reminiscence* (1891) who built; Henry Randall Waite, *Carmina Collegensia* (1868) Gideon; *Student Life in Song* (1879) Gideon

Folklore collections:

    Bahamas: Charles L. Edwards, *Bahama Songs and Stories* (1895) who built

1900-1919

Colleges: Bucknell (1913) river; Carlton College (1919) river; Dickinson (1910) river; Grove City College (1913) river; Juniata (1912) river; Lake Erie (1918) river; Ohio University (1915) river; Saint Lawrence (1905) river; Stanford (1905) river; Tufts (1915) river; University of Illinois (1918) river; University of Minnesota (1911) river; University of New Mexico (1905) river

Commercial: Anonymous, *Brewers Collection of Old College Songs* (1905) Gideon; *Most Popular College Songs* (1906) river; David B. Chamberlain and Karl P. Harrington, *Songs of All the Colleges* (1906) river; Gilbert Clifford, *The Most Popular Plantation Songs* (1911) river; Charles W. Johnson, *Songs of the Nation* (1912) river; G. C. Noble, *The Most Popular Home Songs* (1913) river; George Rosey, *College Songs* (1909) river; Henry Randall Waite, *College Songs* (1906) river; Albert Ernest Wier, *Book of a 1000 Songs* (1918) river

    Britain: H. Walford Davies, *Fellowship Songbook* (1915) river

Folklore collections:

    Britain: Frederick Thomas Nettleingham, *Tommy's Tunes* (1917) "One More River"

1920-1939

Organizations:

    Boy Scouts, England: 112 (1925); 113 (1925) second series, number 5, "One More Ribber"

    Boy Scouts, Canada: 119 (1932) "One More River"

    Girl Scouts: 168 (1929) river

Intercollegiate Outing Club Association: 203 (1938) "One More River To Cross"

Religious groups:

Jewish: Israel Soifer and Margaret K. Soifer, *The Camper's Song Pack* (1937) "Who Built the Ark? Noah, Noah"

Colleges: Columbia (1924) river; Knox (1923) river; New York State College for Teachers (1920) river; Rutgers (1920) river; Tau Delta Phi (1927) river; University of Pittsburgh (1929) river; University of Washington (1924) river; Washington State College (1922) river

Commercial: Anonymous, *Songs for All in the Song Hour* (1935) river; *Treasure Chest Community Songster* (1936); John W. Beattie, et alia, *The New Blue Book of Favorite Songs* (1928) river; Albert M. Brown, *The Best One Hundred Songs for Camps and Clubs*, "Noah's Ark" to Johnny; Peter William Dykema, *Twice 55 Games* (1924) Johnny; Hugo Frey, *America Sings Community Song Book* (1935) river; *Merrily We Sing* (1935) "Noah's Ark" with river; H. W. Gibson, *Recreation Programs for Summer Camps* (1938) "Noah and the Ark" with river; Ellen Jane Lorenz, *Get-Together Songs* (1935) river; *Men's Get-Together Songs* (1938) river; Max E. Oberndorfer and Ann Oberndorfer, *A Century of Progress in American Song* (1933) river; *The New American Songbook* (1933) river; Michel Whitehill, *Everybody's Favorite Community Songbook* (1935) river; Albert Ernest Wier, *Songs of the Sunny South* (1929) river

Britain: H. Walford Davies, *The New Fellowship Songbook* (1931) "One More Ribber"; Ernest Newton, *The Ernest Newton Community Songbook* (1927) "The Animals Went in Two by Two" with Johnny; Thomas Wood, *The Oxford Song Book, Volume Two* (1927) river; *The Oxford Song Book* (1928) "One More River"

Canada: Hugo Frey, *Canada Sings* (1938) river

1940-1959

Organizations:

Boy Scouts, England: 115 (1954) "One More River"

Intercollegiate Outing Club Association: 204 (1948) and 205 (1955) "One More River To Cross"

Religious groups:

Baptist groups: William J. Reynolds and Cecil McGee, *Songs for Fun and Fellowship* (1959) river

Winona Lake: Homer Rodeheaver, *62 Southern Spirituals* (1946) river

Commercial: Ruth Brampton, *Sing with Me* (1955) "One More River"; John W. Beattie, et alia, *The New Blue Book of Favorite Songs* (1941) river; *The Gray Book of Favorite Songs* (1951) "Noah's Ark" with river; Margaret Bradford Boni, *Fireside Book of Folk Songs* (1947) river; Hugo Frey, *Songs for America* (1941) river; Ruth Heller and Walter Goodell, *Singing Time* (1952) "One More River"; Margaret Johnson and Travis Johnson, *Early American Songs from the Repertoire of the "Song-Spinners"* (1943) river; Arthur Loesser, *Humor in American Song* (1942) river; Ellen Jane Lorenz, *Informal Get-Together Songs* (1955) river; *Women's Get-Together Songs* (1942) river; Ann Oberndorfer and Max E Oberndorfer, *The New American Songbook* (1941) "Noah's Ark" with river; Ruth Crawford Seeger, *American Folk Songs for Children* (1948) who built; Harry Robert Wilson, *Songs of the Hills and Plains* (1943) "One More Ribber"; Don Wright, *Youthful Voices, Book Three* (1954) "One More River"

Britain: Leslie Woodgate, *The Penguin Song Book* (1951) river

Canada: Alan Mills, *Folk Songs for Young Folk* (1957) river

Folklore collections: Vance Randolph, *Ozark Folk Songs* (1946) river

1960-1979

Organizations:

Boy Scouts, Canada: 120 (1965) river

Intercollegiate Outing Club Association: 206 (1960) "One More River To Cross"

Schools: *Discovering Music Together Series*, Grade Four (1970) "Noah's Ark" with river; *Making Music Your Own Series*, Grade Two (1964) "Who Built the Ark?"; *New Dimensions in Music Series. Expressing Music* (1970) "The Story of Noah" with credit to a 1929 version by John Jacob Niles

Britain: Gordon Reynolds, *The Oxford School Music Books*, Book Three (1961) "Who Built the Ark?"

Commercial: Anonymous, *357 Songs We Love To Sing* (1966) "Noah's Ark" with river; Oscar Brand, *Folksongs for Fun* (1961) river; Norman Cazden, *A Book of Nonsense Songs* (1961) river; Leon Dallin and Lynn Dallin, *Heritage Songster* (1966) river; George Goodwin, *30 Most Beloved Campfire and School Favorites* (1963) river; Charles Hansen, *400 Super Song Fest #2* (1973) with "one more river";

Ellen Jane Lorenz, *Informal Get-Together Songs* (1962) river; *Men's Get Together Songs* (1962) river; *Women's Get-Together Songs* (1962) river; Frank Lynn, *Songs for Swingin' Housemothers* (1961) "One More River"; Ann Oberndorfer and Max E Oberndorfer, *The New American Songbook* (1961) river; Marie Winn, *The Fireside Book of Fun and Game Songs* (1974) "One More River"

      Britain: Percy C. Buck, *The Oxford Nursery Song Book* (1961) river; Robert Noble, *Three Chords and Beyond* (1967) river

Folklore collections: Harold Courlander, *Negro Folk Music, U. S. A.* (1963) who built

Personal song books:

    Ann Beardsley ("One More River"), Seth Clay ("Hallelujah to the Lamb"), Larry Ralston ("One More River")

Camp song books:

    Other: Brooklyn Boy Scouts ("Mr. Noah," "Noah's Ark" with river); Herald Tribune Fresh Air Camp ("There's One More River"); Pittsburgh Boy Scouts (river)

Current Song

Current recombination of key rhymes with "rise, shine" chorus; no longer a counting out song. It usually is called "Rise and Shine" or "Noah."

-1979

Religious groups:

    Methodist groups: James F. Leisy, *The Good Times Songbook* (1974) "Rise and Shine"

Commercial: Jerry Silverman, *Jerry Silverman's Folk Song Encyclopedia, Volume One* (1975) "Rise and Shine"; *Folk Songs for Schools and Camps* (1970) "Give God the Glory"

Recordings:

Commercial: Pete Seeger, *Camp Songs* (1955) "Children of the Lord"

Archive collections:

Ohio State University: Sally Briggs, Peggy Hays, Carol Simon

Utah State University: June Rushing Leibfarth ("Rise and Shine")
University of Texas: Patricia Ann Raine
Wayne State University: William Daniel Doebler
Canada:
> Memorial University of Newfoundland: Ira Sheldon Posen ("Rise and Shine")

Personal song books:
> Joanne AvRutick, Anne Beardsley ("Noah's Ark"), Nancy Bryant, Seth Clay, Steven Diner ("Rise and Shine"), Mariana Palmer ("Noah's Ark"), Larry Ralston

Camp song books:
> CFG Midwest: Tawanka (no title), Tayanita ("Noah"), Yakewi ("Rise and Shine"), Yukita ("Rise and Shine")
> CFG other: El Deseo ("Noah's Ark"), Hidden Valley ("Rise and Shine"), Hitaga ("Lord Said to Noah"), Ka-esta ("Noah's Ark"), Kirby ("Rise and Shine"), Kotomi ("Noah"), Kushtaka ("Rise and Shine"), Long Beach ("Rise and Shine"), Mawavi ("Noah's Ark"), Melacoma ("Rise and Shine"), Patiya ("Noah's Ark"), Seabow ("Noah"), Shawnee ("Noah"), Tanadoona ("Rise and Shine"), Trelipe ("Noah's Ark"), Wakoma ("Rise and Shine"), Widjiwagan ("Noah"), Wolahi ("Rise and Shine")
> Girls other: Kamaji ("Noah"), Rimrock ("Rise and Shine")
> Other Midwest: Flora Dale ("Noah"), Mount Morris ("Rise and Shine")
> Other: Loyaltown ("Rise and Shine"), Manakiki ("Rise and Shine"), Teamsters ("Rise and Shine"), Trexler ("Rise and Shine")

Field recordings:
> Kitanniwa: campers (1974), Laura Clare Zahn (1974)
> CFG other: He Bani Gani (1976), Wintaka (Gene Clough, 1970s)

Reports from Individuals

Reports	Midwest	Other	Total	% MW	% Other	% Total
Kitanniwa	10		10	.63		.63
CFG	10	28	48	.79	.83	.83
Girls	27	52	79	.93	.84	.87
Coed, Boys	20	58	78	.93	.88	.53
Totals	67	138	215	.85	.79	.85

Percentages of individuals who know "Rise and Shine" within entire sample. Sample numbers on last page of Publishing Histories.

Notes on Sources

James H. Hanford may have been James Holly Hanford (1882-1969) of the English Department at Western Reserve University.

James Jepson was probably James Jepson, Junior (1854-1950), the son of a Mormon pioneer.

Swimming, Swimming

Earliest citation: Unknown

Publications: None found

Recordings: None found

Archive collections:
Indiana University: Jean Hamilton
Ohio State University: Peggy Hays
University of Oregon: Sharon Knoper

Personal song books:
   Ruth Arnold, Patricia Averill with camp, Larry Ralston, Joyce
   Gregg Stoppenhagen

Camp song books:
   Kitanniwa: 1940s
   CFG Midwest: Tannadoonah with camp, Tawanka with camp
   CFG other: Adahi with camp, Hitaga, Kirby with camp, Kotomi,
      Mawavi camp only, Melacoma with camp, Namanu, Neewahlu,
      Niwana, Shawnee, Watanopa, Wolahi with camp, Zanika Lache
   Girls Midwest: Watervliet
   Other: Saint Vincent de Paul Ranch, Seattle Boy Scouts

Field recordings:
   CFG other: He Bani Gani (1976), Hidden Valley (1976), Wintaka
      (Gene Clough, 1970s)

Reports from Individuals

Reports	Midwest	Other	Total	% MW	% Other	% Total
Kitanniwa	14		14	.88		.88
CFG	6	22	28	.50	.48	.48
Girls	18	25	43	.62	.40	.47
Coed Girls	0	9	9	.00	.31	.24
Boys	3	11	14	.21	.30	.27
Totals	41	67	108	.52	.39	.43

Total numbers of individuals who know "Swimming, Swimming" and percent of those reports within entire sample. Sample numbers on last page of Publishing Histories.

Rose, Rose

Earliest citation: Janet E. Tobitt, *Yours for a Song* (1939)[172]

-1959
Organizations:
Boy Scouts, England: 115 (1954)
Camp Fire Girls: 133 (1947)
Girl Scouts: 174 (1946)
Religious groups:
Protestant Episcopal Church: Rue Moore, *Sing Forth* (CRS 1955)
Commercial: American Camping Association, *Joyful Singing* (CRS 1947);
Allen L. Richardson, *Voices in Song* (1953); Augustus D. Zanzig,
Singing America (1940)
Britain: Kenneth Simpson, *The First Round Book* (1959)

1960-1979
Organizations:
Boy Scouts, England: 117 (1962)
Four-H: 160 (1966)
Girl Scouts: 182 (1960)
Commercial: Mike Cohen, *101 Plus 5 Folk Songs for Camp* (1966); Linda
Ann Barsness and Judith Bischoff, *Embers* (1974); Max V. Exner,
Tent and Trail Songs (CRS 1962 and edition received 1974); Jerry
Silverman, *Jerry Silverman's Folk Song Encyclopedia, Volume Two* (1975);
Mary Catherine Taylor and Carol Dyk, *The Book of Rounds* (1977)

Recordings:
Commercial: Bonnie Dobson, *Merry Go-Round of Children's Songs* (1963)
Organizational: Azalea Trails (Calif CFG)

Archive collections:
Douglass College, Rutgers: Ann Marie Filocco, Kathleen Villiers-Fisher
Ohio State University: Peggy Hays, Carol Shuster
University of Oregon: Diane Davis, Sue Loff
University of Texas: Naomi Feldman and Mary Rogers

694

Utah State University: June Rushing Leibfarth
Wayne State University: Susan Dunn

Personal song books:
> Ann Beardsley, Shirley Ieraci, Jolene Robinson Johnson, Jacqueline Orvis, Carol Parsons Sievert, Clarena Snyder

Camp song books:
> Kitanniwa: 1974
> CFG other: El Deseo, Kotomi, Kushtaka, Long Beach, Melacoma, Neewahlu, Onahlee, Sealth (CRS), Towanyak, Wakoma, Wolahi
> Girls Midwest: Watervliet
> Girls other: Peach Creek
> Other Midwest: High/Scope
> Other: Loyaltown

Field recordings:
> CFG Midwest: Glen (1974)
> CFG other: Wintaka (Gene Clough, 1970s), Yallani (Gene Clough, 1970s)
> Girls Midwest: Joyce Gregg Stoppenhagen (1974)
> Other: Valley Mill (1976)

Other Songs

Earliest citation: Unknown

1960-1979
Religious groups:
> Church of Jesus Christ of Latter Day Saints (Mormons): Harold Neal, *Camp and Fellowship Songbook* (CRS 1956) for Independence, Missouri, "Heavenly Father"
> Roman Catholic groups: Word of God, *Songs of Praise, Volume 1* (1975) "Love," "Jesus"
Commercial: Anonymous, *Spiritual Proofs* (CRS) "Peace"

Recordings: None found

Archive collections:

Boy Scouts of America: Bill Hillcourt ("Scouting, Scouting")

Douglass College, Rutgers: Ann Marie Filocco ("Roads,") Kathleen Villiers-Fisher ("America," "Love," "Ding Dong Wedding Bells") Ohio State University: Peggy Hays ("America")

University of Oregon: Sue Loff ("America")

Personal song books:

Ann Beardsley ("America," "Love," "Peace," "Stroke Stroke"), Becky Colwell Deatherage ("Roam"), Carol Ann Engle ("Row to Jesus Side"), Jane Ann Matulich ("I Won't Be My Father's Jack"), Jacqueline Orvis ("Love," "America"), Jolene Robinson Johnson ("America"), Larry Ralston ("America," "Love," "Peace"), Roger Smith ("Star Light, Star Bright")

Camp song books:

CFG Other: Adahi ("America"), Kotomi ("America"), Melacoma ("America"), Neewahlu ("America"), Patiya ("America"), Shawnee ("America"), Tanadoona ("America"), Trelipe ("America," "Love," "Peace"), Wakoma ("America"), Watanopa ("America"), Wolahi ("Love"), Zanika Lache ("America")

Girls Midwest: Watervliet ("America")

Girls Other: Kamaji (local), Marycrest (local)

Other: Saint Vincent de Paul Ranch ("Love"), Seattle Boys Scouts ("America")

Field recordings:

CFG Midwest: Glen (1974) "Love"

Reports from Individuals

Reports	Midwest	Other	Total	% MW	% Other	% Total
Kitanniwa	3		3	.19		.19
CFG	7	28	35	.59	.61	.60
Girls	24	36	60	.83	.58	.66
Coed Girls	3	8	11	.38	.28	.30
Boys	2	5	7	.14	.14	.14
Totals	39	77	116	.49	.44	.44

Total numbers of individuals who know "Rose, Rose" and percent of those reports within entire sample.

Reports	Midwest	Other	Total	% MW	% Other	% Total
Kitanniwa	0		0	.00		.00
CFG	3	18	21	.25	.39	.36
Girls	17	23	40	.59	.37	.44
Coed Girls	5	9	14	.63	.31	.38
Boys	4	11	15	.29	.30	.29
Totals	29	61	90	.37	.35	.36

Total numbers of individuals who know "America," "Love," or "Peace," with percent of those reports within entire sample. Sample numbers on last page of Publishing Histories.

A Canoe May Be Drifting

Earliest citation: Unknown

Publication history: None found

Recordings: None found

Archive collections: None found

Personal song books:
 Patricia Averill, Janice Knapp, Polly McIntyre, Carol Parsons Sievert, Joyce Gregg Stoppenhagen

Camp song books:
 Kitanniwa: 1940s, 1974
 CFG other: Augusta

Field recordings:
 Kitanniwa: staff (1974), Lucille Parker Munk (1974)

Reports from Individuals

Reports	Midwest	Other	Total	% MW	% Other	% Total
Kitanniwa	6		6	.38		.38
CFG	1	1	2	.08	.02	.03
Girls	2	0	2	.07	.00	.03
Coed Girls	0	0	0	.00	.00	.00
Boys	0	0	0	.00	.00	.00
Totals	9	1	10	.18	.11	.04

Percentages of individuals who know "A Canoe May Be Drifting" within entire sample. Sample numbers on last page of Publishing Histories.

Oh, the Boatmen Dance

Earliest citations: Daniel Emmett, "De Boatman Dance" (Boston: Prentiss, 1843) and "De Boatmen's Dance" (Boston: C. H. Keith, 1843)

-1899

Commercial: Frank B. Converse, *Frank B. Converse's Banjo Instructor* (1865); Oliver Ditson, *Minstrel Songs Old and New* (1882)

1900-1929

Organizations:

Girl Scouts: 168 (1929)

Commercial: Anonymous, *Heart Songs* (1910); Clifton Johnson, *Songs Every One Should Know* (1908); Dailey Paskman and Sigmund Spaeth, *Gentlemen Be Seated* (1926); Albert Ernest Wier, *Songs of the Sunny South* (1929)

1930-1949

Commercial: Carl Cramer, *America Sings, Songs and Stories of Our Country's Growing* (1942); *Songs of the Rivers of America* (1942); Margaret Johnson and Travis Johnson, *Early American Songs from the Repertoire of the "Song Spinners"* (1943); Frank Luther, *Americans and Their Songs* (1942); Fowler Smith, Harry R. Wilson, et alia, *Songs We Sing* (1940-41); Elie Siegmeister, *Work and Sing* (1944)

1950-1970

Religious groups:

Christian Church, Disciples of Christ: Anonymous, *Fellowship Songbook* (CRS 1962)

Schools: *Discovering Music Together Series*, Grade Five (1966); *Making Music Your Own Series*, Grade Six (1965); *Music for Living Series*, Grade Six (1956)

Canada: Colin Walley, et alia, *Fanfare Act I: A Course in Comprehensive Musicianship for the Junior High School* (1969)

Commercial: American Camping Association, *Sing!* (CRS 1974); Joe
  Mitchell Chapple, *Heart Songs Dear to the American People* (1950);
  Walter Ehret, *Let's Sing Together, Book One*; Herbert Haufrecht, *Folk
  Songs for Everyone* (1962); *'Round the World Folk Song* (1963); Stan
  Hugill, *Shanties from the Seven Seas* (1961); Jim Morse, *The Dell Book
  of Great American Folk Songs* (1963); Irwin Silber, *Sing Out!* (1959);
  Irwin Silber and Fred Silber, *Folksinger's Wordbook* (1973); Jerry
  Silverman, *Jerry Silverman's Folk Song Encyclopedia, Volume Two* (1975);
  Rufus Wheeler and Elie Siegmeister, *Tunes for Teens* (1954)
Art song: Aaron Copland, *Old American Songs* (1950)

Recordings:
Commercial: Ginni Clemmens, *"Sing a Rainbow" and Other Children Songs*
  (1965); Bob Gibson, *I Come for To Sing* (1957); Anne Grimes, *Ohio
  State Ballads* (1957); Ed McCurdy, *An Introduction to Folk Music and
  Folklore*; Shanty Boys, *Off-Beat Folk Songs* (1958)
Art song: William Warfield, *Old American Songs and Five Sea Chanties*
  (1952)

Archive collections:
United States Library of Congress, Archives of American Folk Song:
  Robert W. Gordon
Utah State University: June Rushing Leibfarth

Personal song books:
  Patricia Averill, Joyce Gregg Stoppenhagen

Camp song books:
  CFG other: Kotomi, Long Beach, Namanu, Neewahlu, Onahlee,
    Sealth (CRS), Shawnee, Wakoma, Wolahi
  Girls other: Rimrock

Field recordings:
  Kitanniwa: campers (1974)
  CFG other: Wasewagan (Gene Clough, 1970s), Wintaka (Gene
    Clough, 1970s)

Reports from Individuals

Reports	Midwest	Other	Total	% MW	% Other	% Total
Kitanniwa	7		7	.44		.44
CFG	3	17	20	.25	.37	.34
Girls	14	22	36	.48	.35	.40
Coed Girls	0	0	0	.00	.00	.00
Boys	3	0	3	.21	.00	.06
Totals	27	39	66	.34	.22	.26

Total numbers of individuals who know "Oh, the Boatmen Dance" and percent of those reports within entire sample. Sample numbers on last page of Publishing Histories.

Grand Old Duke of York

Verse Alone

Earliest citation: James Howell, letter from Paris, 1620, included in *Epistolae Ho-Elianae* (1645) [Kidson[389]]

-1799

1627   Sloan manuscript 1489, collection of jests and anecdotes by someone connected with Cambridge; France

1642   Anonymous. *Pigges Corantoe, or News from the North*, France

1649   Taylor, John. *Wandering To See the Wonders of the West*

1660   Fisher, Samuel. *The Rustick's Alarm to the Rabbies*, Spain

1800-1899

1831   Collier, John Payne. *History of English Dramatic Poetry*, vol 2, reprint *Pigges Corantoe*

1841   Wright, Thomas. *Political Ballads*, France, reprint *Pigges Corantoe*

1842   Halliwell, John Orchard. *The Nursery Rhymes of England*, edition 1, France

1843   Halliwell, John Orchard. *The Nursery Rhymes of England*, edition 2, France

1844   Halliwell, John Orchard. *The Nursery Rhymes of England*, edition 3, France, Spain

1846   Halliwell, John Orchard. *The Nursery Rhymes of England*, edition 4, France, Spain

1872   Elliott, James William. *National Nursery Rhymes*, France

1874   Elliott, James William. *Mother Goose and Nursery Songs*

1886   Halliwell, John Orchard. *The Nursery Rhymes of England*, edition 5, France, Spain

1900-1919

Commercial: L. E. Orth, *Sixty Songs from Mother Goose* (1906) France
    Britain: Frank Kidson, 75 British Nursery Rhymes (1904) France;
    Arthur Rackham, Mother Goose (1913) grand

1920-1939

Commercial: Katherine Elwes Thomas, *The Real Personages of Mother Goose* (1930) France

1940-1959

Religious groups:

> Church of Jesus Christ of Latter Day Saints (Mormons): Carl Mesle and Franklyn S. Weddle, *Camp and Fellowship Songbook* (CRS 1956) for Independence, Missouri, Napoléon as decremental

When You're Up - Verse Alone

Earliest citation: Unknown

1900-1979

Religious groups:

> Methodist groups: E. O. Harbin, *Phunology* (1920); *Paradology* (1927)

Folklore collection: Paul Brewster, *The Frank C. Brown Collection of North Carolina Folklore*, volume 1 (1952); list of sources includes Joan and Hallie Holeman

Two Part Rhyme

Earliest citation: Unknown

-1899

Commercial: William H. Hills, *Students' Songs* (1884) noble as round

Folklore collections:

> Britain: Edward Williams Byron Nicholson, *Golspie* (1897); G. F. Northall, *English Folk Rhymes* (1892) France, mighty as round

1900-1919

Colleges: Stevens Institute of Technology (1910) noble; Williams College (1910) grand

Folklore collections:

> Britain: Frederick Thomas Nettleingham, *Tommy's Tunes* (1917) brave

1920-1939

College: Williams (1933) grand

Folklore collections:

> Britain: Robert Graves, *Less Familiar Nursery Rhymes* (1927) duke of Cumberland

1940-1959

Schools: *Our Singing World*, Grade Four (1950) noble

Commercial:

> Britain: Sid G. Hedges, *The Youth Sing Book* (1953) grand, noble; Leslie Woodgate, *The Penguin Song Book* (1951) noble
>
> Sweden: Anonymous, *Singing Together* (1954) noble

Folklore collections: Frank C. Brown, *The Frank C. Brown Collection of North Carolina Folklore*, vol 3 (1952), noble, source identified as Misses Holeman; vol 5 (1952) noble, source identified as Jean Holeman

> > Britain: Iona Opie and Peter Opie, *The Lore and Language of School Children* (1959) Napoléon, France; *The Oxford Dictionary of Nursery Rhymes* (1952) France, brave

1960-1979

Organizations:

> Boy Scouts: 109 (1969) grand
>
> Boy Scouts, England: 118 (1964) noble
>
> Four-H: 162 (1973) noble

Religious groups:

> Baptist groups: Cecil McGee and Bob Oldenburg, *Songs for Fun and Fellowship #3* (1969) noble

Schools: Frances M. Andrews, *Sing Together Children* (CRS, received 1974) for Pennsylvania State University Music Education Department, noble

Commercial: William Baring-Gould and Cecil Baring-Gould, *The Annotated Mother Goose* (1962) brave old; Norman Cazden, *A Book of Nonsense Songs* (1961) noble; David R. Ginglend and Winifred E. Stiles, *Music Activities for Retarded Children* (1965) noble with gestures; Irwin Silber and Fred Silber, *Folksinger's Wordbook* (1973)

> > Denmark: Anonymous, *Lejrskole Sangbog* (1964) Napoléon
> >
> > Switzerland: Abbé A. Bessire, *Chantons* (1963) Napoléon

Folklore Collections: Duncan Emrich, *The Whim-Wham Book* (1975) grand

 Canada: Edith Fowke, *Sally Go round the Sun* (1969) grand

Singing Game

Earliest citation: Alice Bertha Gomme, *Traditional Games of England, Scotland, and Ireland* (1894) noble+up

1900-1919

Commercial: Carrie Bullard, *Most Popular Mother Goose Songs and Other Nursery Rhymes* (1910); Mari Ruef Hofer, *Children's Singing Games* (1914); Albert Ernest Wier, *Songs the Children Love To Sing* (1916) duke; *The Child's Own Music Book* (1918)

 Britain: Alice Bertha Gomme and Cecil J. Sharp, *Children's Singing Games* (1909) noble, several verses; Frank Kidson, *Eighty Singing Games* (1907) famous variant; *100 Singing Games* (1916) famous; Florence Hewitt Kirk, *Old English Games and Physical Exercises* (1914); Stanley V. Wilman, *Games for Playtime and Parties* (1914)

Folklore collections:

 Britain: Annie G. Gilchrist, notebook (1900)

1920-1939

Schools: *Music Education Series: Songs of Childhood* (1923); *Music Hour Series*, Kindergarten and First Grade (1929, 1932 Roman Catholic edition); *Singing School Series: Our Songs* (1939); *The Song Series*, Book Four (1923) France; C. Ward Crampton and Mary Wollaston Wood, *Song Play Book* (1917, 1922, 1924); Robert Foresman, *High Road of Song* (1931); Chester Geppert Marsh, *Singing Games and Drills* (1925)

Commercial: Richard Chase, *Old Songs and Singing Games* (1938) noble+hunting, long dance; Peter William Dykema, *Twice 55 Games with Music* (1924) famous+up as military burlesque; Elizabeth Gallagher and Carlo Peroni, *100 Favorite Songs for Children* (1930) France; Floy Adele Rossman, *Singing All the Way* (1931); Albert Ernest Wier, *Young America's Music, Volume One* (1939) France

 Britain: Owen Mase, *Ten Songs for Community Singing* (1926) noble with four verses; Ernest Newton, *The Community Song Book* (1928) noble with three verses; Edna Potter, *This Way and*

That (1930); Gerrard Williams and Gibson Young, *Community Singers Programme #5* (1925) noble with four verses

1940-1959

Organizations:

Girl Scouts: 181 (1958) noble+up as longways dance

Schools: *The American Singer Series*, Grade Three (1954) noble+up as dance

Commercial: Richard Chase, *Singing Games and Playparty Games*(1949) noble+hunting, longways dance; Beatrice Landeck, *More Songs To Grow On* (1954) noble+up+a-hunting as longways dance; Lynn Rohrbough, *Handy Play Party Book* (CRS 1940) noble as dance

1960-1979

Organizations:

Young Men's Christian Association: 216 (1963) noble as game

Commercial: Forrest J. Baird, *Music Skills for Recreation Leaders* (1963) noble+up; Beatrice Landeck and Elizabeth Crook, *Wake Up and Sing!* (1969); Nancy Langstaff and John Langstaff, *Jim Along Josie* (1970) noble

Singapore: Anonymous, *A Selection of Songs for Community Singing* (1969) noble with three verses

Folklore collections:

Britain: Iona Opie and Peter Opie, *The Singing Game* (1985) variants

New Zealand: Brian Sutton-Smith, *The Folkgames of Children* (1972) duke+up as longways dance

Recordings:

Commercial: Charity *Bailey, More Music Time* (noble); Robin Christensen, *You Can Sing It Yourself, Volume One* (noble); Ed McCurdy, *Children's Songs* (1958) noble: Nancy Raven, *Wee Songs for Wee People* (noble, a-hunting); Vivienne Stevenson, *101 Nursery Rhymes* (1970)

Archive Collections:

University of Oregon: Nan Stuart

Utah State University: June Rushing Leibfarth (grand)

Canada:

National Museum of Canada: Edith Fowke

Personal song books:
   Patricia Averill (grand), Nancy Bryant (noble), Larry Ralston (noble)

Camp song books:
   CFG Midwest: Kiloqua (mighty, grand), Yakewi (grand)
   CFG other: Kotomi (great Apache chief), Kushtaka (grand), Mawavi
        (grand), Patiya (Napoléon), Seabow (noble), Wolahi (noble)
   Other girls: Les Chalets Francais (Napoléon)
   Other: Homelani (grand), Manakiki (noble)

Reports from Individuals

Reports	Midwest	Other	Total	% MW	% Other	% Total
Kitanniwa	6		6	.38		.38
CFG	8	15	23	.67	.32	.40
Girls	14	22	36	.48	.35	.40
Coed Girls	4	9	13	.50	.31	.35
Boys	7	15	22	.50	.41	.43
Totals	39	61	100	.49	.35	.40

Total numbers of individuals who know "Grand Old Duke of York" and percent of those reports within entire sample. Sample numbers on last page of Publishing Histories.

Notes on Sources

Mary Dendy was identified as Miss Dendy by Gomme.

Flicker

Earliest citation: Judith Nancy Czerwinski, 1958, manuscript from Gene Wichmann

-1979
Commercial: Linda Ann Barsness and Judith Bischoff, *Embers* (1974)

Commercial recordings: None found

Archive collections:
Ohio State University: Lisa Drumm
University of Oregon: Sue Loff
Wayne State University: Kathleen Solsbury (1970)

Personal song books:
   Anne Beardsley, Shirley Ieraci, Jolene Robinson Johnson, Larry Ralston

Camp song books:
   Kitanniwa: 1974
   CFG other: Adahi, Augusta, Hitaga, Kilowan, Kirby, Kotomi, Long Beach, Melacoma, Namanu, Niwana, Onahlee, Patiya (two), Shawnee, Trelipe, Wakoma, Wolahi, Zanika Lache
   Girls other: Wampatuck

Field recordings:
   Kitanniwa: Jolene Robinson Johnson and Carol Parsons Sievert (1974)
   CFG other: Wasewagan (Gene Clough, 1970s)

Reports from Individuals

Reports	Midwest	Other	Total	% MW	% Other	% Total
Kitanniwa	2		2	.12		.12
CFG	2	28	30	.17	.61	.52
Girls	16	26	42	.55	.42	.46
Coed Girls	0	1	1	.00	.03	.03
Boys	2	2	4	.14	.50	.08
Totals	22	57	49	.28	.32	.19

Total numbers of individuals who know "Flicker" and percent of those reports within entire sample.

Sample Size

Reports	Midwest	Other	Total
Kitanniwa	16		16
CFG	12	46	58
Girls	29	62	91
Coed Girls	8	29	37
Boys	14	37	51
Totals	79	174	253

F. Credits and Permissions

Lyrics

"Kookaburra Sits in the Old Gum Tree," words and music by Marion Sinclair. Copyright 1934 (Renewed) Larrikin Music Pub. Pty. Ltd. All rights administered by Music Sales Corporation for the Western Hemisphere. International copyright secured. All rights reserved. Used by permission.

World Around Songs, 7036 State Hwy 80 South, Burnsville, North Carolina, granted permission to reprint "Ah Ta Ka Ta Nu Va" and "Cuckoo." Complete copies with music are available from them.

The rest, to the best of my knowledge, never were copyrighted, have become public domain, or meet standards of fair usage.

Photographs

Albion College's Stockwell-Mudd Library Archives and Special Collections provided the picture of Charlotte Duff. Used by permission.

Battle Creek, Michigan, Willard Library has copies of the Battle Creek Central *Paean*, the Lakeview *Log*, and early pictures of Kitanniwa. The first contains photographs of Mary Carol Parsons [Sievert] and Mary Tinsley Unrue; the second has several of Lucille Parker [Munk].

Battle Creek, Michigan, *Enquirer and News* first published the cover photograph of Kathleen Huggett [Nye] on 21 July 1954, and the poem by Ginger Hastings on its "Youth Today Page" in 1961 or 1962.

Bradbury, Wm. B. *Golden Censer* (New York: Biglow and Main, 1864) contains "The Gathering" (no attribution) and "The Lord's Vineyard" (no attribution).

Brigham Young University's Harold B. Lee Library, L. Tom Perry Special Collections in the University Archives, has the original photograph of Leona Holbrook. Used by courtesy.

Camp Hitaga (Iowa CFG) posted staff pictures on its web site, which included one with Linda Johnson.

Denison University provided photographs of Annetta Byers Eldridge and Ruth Anderson Eldridge Richardson. The second was taken in 1968; the other appeared in the 1921 edition of the yearbook, *Adytum*. Used by courtesy.

Emmett, Daniel. "De Boatman Dance" (Boston: C. H. Keith, 1843); original in Brown University, Harris Collection of American Poetry and Plays, "Series of Old American Songs," no 32.

Girl Scouts of the USA - National Historic Preservation Center provided the photographs of Marie Gaudette and Janet Tobitt. The first appeared in *Girl Scout Leader* in the summer of 1982. Used with permission from Girl Scouts of the USA.

Indiana University Northwest used the picture of Jan Smyth in *Northwest News*, July 2007.

Iowa State University Special Collections/University Archives provided the photograph of Max V. Exner. Used by permission.

Kent Historical Society of Kent, Connecticut, has Anne Hopson Chapin's papers. Photograph used by courtesy.

Maryland Folklife Festival took the picture of He Bani Gani in 1976.

Rainier Beach, Washington, High School, yearbook included the photograph of Jolene Robinson [Johnson] in the 1969 edition of *Valhalla*.

Rogers, Ethel. *Sebago-Wohelo Camp Fire Girls* (1915) published the photograph of folk dancing at the camp.

State Library of South Australia provided photograph SLSA:B70859/401 of Marion Sinclair, published 22 March 1987 by Messenger Press of Adelaide, Australia. Courtesy of the SLSA and Messenger Press.

United Methodist Church General Commission on Archives and History provided the photograph of E. O. Harbin. It appeared in the 1955 minutes of the Louisville Annual Conference of the Methodist Church journal. Used by courtesy.

Western Reserve Historical Society of Cleveland, Ohio, provided the photograph of "Jewish Orphan Home Campers with Boys' Leader Al Brown, 1924," PG 154; Bellfaire; Container 7; Folder 2. It appeared in Brown's *The Camp Wise Story 1907-1988* (1989).

Wisconsin Historical Society provided photograph WHS-92355. The picture of the Sigma Alpha Iota Music Sorority Alumnae with Margarett Snyder originally appeared in *The Wisconsin State Journal* in Madison on 7 June 1956. It was taken by Arthur M. Vinje and is in the Vinje collection.

Wohelo Camps provided the photograph of Embers (Margaret Bradshaw McGee) that appeared in *Wohelo: Down through the Years* by Charlotte Gulick Hewson (2000). Used by courtesy.

Other photographs were provided by individuals, their friends, or relatives named in the INTRODUCTION. The rest are in the author's possession. Complete names are given only for individuals mentioned in the text.

Note on the Book

Text is set in 12 point Garamond. Assistance from Xlibris provided by Jaysee Pingkian, Lorie Adams, and Mary Jervis. I owe the greatest debt to the people whose names I do not know, the ones who did the work transforming my photographs and manuscript into the book you are holding.

An index for the songs mentioned in the text may be found at http://www.campsongsfolksongs.com/. The author may be contacted at campsongs@cybermesa.com.